OECD ECONOMIC OUTLOOK

84

DECEMBER 2008

OECD

ORGANISATION FOR ECONOMIC CO-OPERATION AND DEVELOPMENT

The OECD is a unique forum where the governments of 30 democracies work together to address the economic, social and environmental challenges of globalisation. The OECD is also at the forefront of efforts to understand and to help governments respond to new developments and concerns, such as corporate governance, the information economy and the challenges of an ageing population. The Organisation provides a setting where governments can compare policy experiences, seek answers to common problems, identify good practice and work to co-ordinate domestic and international policies.

The OECD member countries are: Australia, Austria, Belgium, Canada, the Czech Republic, Denmark, Finland, France, Germany, Greece, Hungary, Iceland, Ireland, Italy, Japan, Korea, Luxembourg, Mexico, the Netherlands, New Zealand, Norway, Poland, Portugal, the Slovak Republic, Spain, Sweden, Switzerland, Turkey, the United Kingdom and the United States. The Commission of the European Communities takes part in the work of the OECD.

OECD Publishing disseminates widely the results of the Organisation's statistics gathering and research on economic, social and environmental issues, as well as the conventions, guidelines and standards agreed by its members.

The French version of the *OECD Economic Outlook* is entitled *Perspectives économiques de l'OCDE*.

The *OECD Economic Outlook* is published on the responsibility of the Secretary-General of the OECD. The assessments given of countries' prospects do not necessarily correspond to those of the national authorities concerned. The OECD is the source of statistical material contained in tables and figures, except where other sources are explicitly cited.

TABLE OF CONTENTS

This book has...

StatLinks

A service that delivers Excel® files from the printed page!

Look for the StatLinks at the bottom right-hand corner of the tables or graphs in this book. To download the matching Excel® spreadsheet, just type the link into your Internet browser, starting with the *http://dx.doi.org* prefix.
If you're reading the PDF e-book edition, and your PC is connected to the Internet, simply click on the link. You'll find StatLinks appearing in more OECD books.

Conventional signs

$	US dollar	.	Decimal point
¥	Japanese yen	I, II	Calendar half-years
£	Pound sterling	Q1, Q4	Calendar quarters
€	Euro	Billion	Thousand million
mb/d	Million barrels per day	Trillion	Thousand billion
..	Data not available	s.a.a.r.	Seasonally adjusted at annual rates
0	Nil or negligible	n.s.a.	Not seasonally adjusted
–	Irrelevant		

Summary of projections

	2008	2009	2010	2008		2009				2010				Q4 / Q4		
				Q3	Q4	Q1	Q2	Q3	Q4	Q1	Q2	Q3	Q4	2008	2009	2010
									Per cent							
Real GDP growth																
United States	1.4	-0.9	1.6	-0.3	-2.8	-2.0	-0.8	0.6	1.2	1.7	2.1	2.7	2.9	0.1	-0.3	2.3
Japan	0.5	-0.1	0.6	-0.4	-1.0	0.8	0.6	-0.3	0.2	0.7	0.9	1.0	1.0	-0.4	0.3	0.9
Euro area	1.0	-0.6	1.2	-0.9	-1.0	-0.8	-0.4	0.1	0.7	1.3	1.7	2.2	2.5	0.0	-0.1	1.9
Total OECD	1.4	-0.4	1.5	-0.2	-1.4	-0.8	-0.2	0.5	1.1	1.7	2.0	2.5	2.7	0.2	0.2	2.2
Inflation[1]									year-on-year							
United States	3.6	1.2	1.3	4.4	2.8	2.1	1.3	0.3	1.1	1.3	1.3	1.2	1.2			
Japan	1.4	0.3	-0.1	2.0	1.4	1.1	0.5	-0.3	-0.2	-0.1	-0.1	-0.1	-0.1			
Euro area	3.4	1.4	1.3	3.9	2.7	1.9	1.4	1.0	1.3	1.3	1.3	1.3	1.3			
Total OECD	3.3	1.7	1.5	3.8	2.9	2.3	1.7	1.1	1.5	1.5	1.5	1.4	1.4			
Unemployment rate[2]																
United States	5.7	7.3	7.5	6.0	6.5	6.9	7.2	7.4	7.5	7.6	7.6	7.5	7.4			
Japan	4.1	4.4	4.4	4.1	4.3	4.4	4.4	4.4	4.4	4.4	4.4	4.4	4.4			
Euro area	7.4	8.6	9.0	7.5	7.8	8.2	8.5	8.8	9.0	9.1	9.1	9.0	9.0			
Total OECD	5.9	6.9	7.2	6.0	6.3	6.6	6.9	7.1	7.2	7.3	7.3	7.2	7.2			
World trade growth	4.8	1.9	5.0	3.4	1.0	1.3	1.9	2.5	3.8	5.3	6.2	6.9	7.3	2.9	2.4	6.4
Current account balance[3]																
United States	-4.9	-3.9	-3.6													
Japan	3.8	4.3	3.9													
Euro area	-0.4	-0.1	0.0													
Total OECD	-1.5	-1.1	-1.1													
Fiscal balance[3]																
United States	-5.3	-6.7	-6.8													
Japan	-1.4	-3.3	-3.8													
Euro area	-1.4	-2.2	-2.5													
Total OECD	-2.5	-3.8	-4.1													
Short-term interest rate																
United States	3.3	1.7	2.0	3.2	3.6	1.8	1.4	1.7	2.0	1.8	1.8	2.0	2.5			
Japan	0.8	0.7	0.4	0.8	0.9	0.7	0.7	0.7	0.6	0.6	0.5	0.4	0.4			
Euro area	4.7	2.7	2.6	5.0	4.6	2.9	2.7	2.7	2.6	2.5	2.5	2.6	2.8			

Note: Real GDP growth, inflation (measured by the increase in the consumer price index or private consumption deflator for total OECD) and world trade growth (the arithmetic average of world merchandise import and export volumes) are seasonally and working-day (except inflation) adjusted annual rates. The "fourth quarter" columns are expressed in year-on-year growth rates where appropriate and in levels otherwise. Interest rates are for the United States: 3-month eurodollar deposit; Japan: 3-month certificate of deposits; euro area: 3-month interbank rate.

Assumptions underlying the projections include:
- no change in actual and announced fiscal policies;
- unchanged exchange rates as from 28 October 2008; in particular 1$ = 95.69 yen and 0.80 €;
- price of oil for a barrel of Brent crude is fixed at 60$;
- in the United States, the target federal funds rate is assumed to be eased to ½ percent early in 2009 and then, as the economic environment begins to improve, interest rates are raised towards the end of 2009 and in 2010 reaching 2½ per cent by December 2010;
- in the euro area, policy rates are assumed to be eased by 125 basis points by early 2009. They will then remain at 2% until mid-2010 before being gradually raised to around 2½ per cent by the end of 2010;
- in Japan, the policy interest rate is assumed to remain at 30 basis points in 2009 and 2010.

The cut-off date for other information used in the compilation of the projections is 14 November 2008.

1. USA; price index for personal consumption expenditure, Japan; consumer price index and the euro area; harmonised index of consumer prices.
2. Per cent of the labour force.
3. Per cent of GDP.
Source: OECD Economic Outlook 84 database.

StatLink 🔗 http://dx.doi.org/10.1787/501527526166

OECD ECONOMIC OUTLOOK 84 – ISBN 978-92-64-05469-1 – © OECD 2008

EDITORIAL
MANAGING THE GLOBAL FINANCIAL CRISIS AND ECONOMIC DOWNTURN

M any OECD economies are in or are on the verge of a protracted recession of a magnitude not experienced since the early 1980s. As a result, the number of unemployed in the OECD area could rise by 8 million over the next two years. At the same time, inflation will abate in all OECD countries and some even face a risk, albeit small, of deflation.

This *Economic Outlook* represents a substantial downward revision from just a few months ago: many of the downside risks previously identified have materialised. The financial turmoil that erupted in the United States around mid-2007 has broadened to include non-bank financial institutions and rapidly spread to the rest of the world. Following the collapse of Lehman Brothers in mid-September, a generalised loss of confidence between financial institutions triggered reactions akin to a "blackout" in global financial markets. Spreads in credit and bond markets surged to very high levels, paralysing credit and money markets. Prompt and massive policy action to restore confidence and provide liquidity appears to have successfully limited the period of panic, but the need for financial institutions to operate with less leverage and to repair their balance sheets remains. This process of adjustment will take time and impair the flow of credit, and is the key factor weighing on activity going forward.

I would like to emphasise upfront that the uncertainties associated with this *OECD Economic Outlook* are exceptionally large, especially those related to the assumptions regarding the speed at which the financial market crisis – the prime driver of the downturn – is overcome. Specifically, we assume that the extreme financial stress since mid-September will be short-lived, but will be followed by an extended period of financial headwinds through late 2009, with a gradual normalisation thereafter. On this basis, as well as our usual assumptions that exchange rates and the oil price are maintained at their recent levels, the main features of the economic outlook are the following:

- US output declines through the first half of next year, then gradually picks up as the effects of the credit squeeze abate, the housing downturn bottoms out and monetary policy stimulus takes hold. The recovery, however, is likely to be languid, as consumption is held back by the large losses in households' wealth. Inflation eases significantly, as the recent declines in commodity prices filter through the economy and as economic slack exerts downward pressure on prices.

- Euro area activity also falls over the next six months, as tighter financial conditions, subdued income growth and negative wealth effects from lower equity and house prices damp consumption and investment. Economic activity then gradually recovers as monetary easing gains traction and the effects of global financial market turbulence dissipate. Inflation will ease considerably, to reach a level by early next year that is consistent with the European Central Bank's inflation target.

- Japan has not been at the epicentre of the financial crisis, but after a brief growth spurt in early 2009 due to fiscal stimulus, output is set to stagnate over the second half of 2009, as the global economic downturn and the recent appreciation of the yen curtails external demand. With persistent economic slack and anaemic wage growth, deflation may return by mid-2009.

- Other OECD countries where the economic downturn will be severe include Hungary, Iceland, Ireland, Luxembourg, Spain, Turkey and the United Kingdom. These economies are most directly affected by the financial crisis, which in some cases has exposed other vulnerabilities, or by severe housing downturns.

- The major non-OECD countries are in many cases also slowing due to the combined effect of more difficult international credit conditions, earlier policy tightening, income losses due to lower commodity prices, and weaker demand from OECD countries. However the slowdown in growth is from high levels.

The financial crisis is not the only development shaping the projections. Other important drivers include ongoing adjustments in housing markets, which in many European economies, based on past housing cycles, still have a long way to go. Moreover, they come on top of negative wealth effects from the steep fall in equity prices. Partially offsetting these contractionary forces is the sizeable monetary stimulus, including non-traditional means, recently introduced and built into the projections, and the boost to real household incomes due to sharply lower commodity prices.

The projections carry both upside and downside risks, but they are skewed to the negative side for 2009. The dominant downside risks include a longer than assumed period before financial conditions normalise, further failures of financial institutions, and the possibility that emerging market economies will be hit harder by the downturn in global trade and foreign investor risk re-assessments. The upside risks are less significant, but adjustment in bank balance sheets may advance more quickly in response to the comprehensive and unprecedented policy measures introduced. Also governments may introduce policy stimulus over and above that factored into the projections. For 2010, widespread risks remain, but these are more equally distributed, reflecting the possibility of an earlier economic recovery.

Against the backdrop of a deep economic downturn, additional macroeconomic stimulus is needed. In normal times, monetary rather than fiscal policy would be the instrument of choice for macroeconomic stabilisation. But these are not normal times. Current conditions of extreme financial stress have weakened the monetary transmission mechanism. Moreover, in some countries the scope for further reductions in policy rates is limited. In this unusual situation, fiscal policy stimulus over and above the support provided through automatic stabilisers has an important role to play.

Fiscal stimulus packages, however, need to be evaluated on a case-by-case basis in those countries where room for budgetary manoeuvre exists. It is vital that any discretionary action be timely and temporary and designed to ensure maximum effectiveness. Infrastructure investment is often mentioned as a desirable instrument for stimulus. While it will boost both supply and demand, provided the investments are well chosen, infrastructure investment typically takes a long time to be brought on stream and, once begun, is difficult to wind down in line with a recovery in activity. Alternatives, such as tax cuts or transfer payments aimed at credit-constrained, poorer households, might prove more effective in boosting demand.

Once there are clear signs of a recovery taking hold, it will be necessary to begin promptly to unwind the macroeconomic stimulus in place to prevent inflationary pressures from gaining a foothold. At the same time, with high public debt in many OECD economies, it will be equally important that a credible fiscal framework is in place to ensure long-run public finance sustainability, especially in the face of spending pressures associated with population ageing.

Although the concerted efforts taken to stabilise financial markets appear to be working, governments must be prepared to modify them in light of evidence on their effectiveness. They must also be ready to expand them if the need arises. Such support should be limited to sectors or firms that are of systemic importance. Moreover, the now global scale of the financial crisis underscores more than before the necessity for international co-ordination to avoid measures that distort competition or effectively shift the problem to other countries. It is equally important that exceptional measures are designed and implemented in ways that allow their orderly removal as conditions in financial markets normalise. Individual countries may find it difficult, acting on their own, to unwind the exceptional measures that are currently needed, again pointing to the need for co-operation. At the same time, steps that encourage mortgage loan workout solutions merit consideration to reduce foreclosures which are costly to all parties involved and thereby lower the risk of further aggravating conditions in financial markets.

Reform of financial market supervision and regulation is clearly necessary to build a more resilient financial system. Here, our efforts need to focus on identifying the market imperfections that gave rise to the incentives for excess risk taking and high leverage, as well as the regulatory failures that together caused this unprecedented global financial crisis. This will involve, *inter alia*, strengthening and streamlining the prudential oversight of financial and capital markets, and plugging the gaps and inconsistencies in regulatory regimes. It also requires enhancing transparency of market instruments, transactions, and the governance rules that determine corporate incentives and decisions. The tendency for pro-cyclicality of financial markets and macroeconomic policies also has to be corrected and ideally reversed.

The recent G20 meeting initiated an action plan and a process for addressing many of these issues. I welcome, in particular, the commitment of the G20 to continue furthering multilateral co-ordination to overcome the immediate problems facing the global economy and to strengthen the international financial architecture over the medium term. For its part, the OECD will support the global concerted effort to re-launch the world economy. In this context, the OECD drawing on its structural analysis expertise will identify policy reforms that support the functioning and performance of financial markets and policies that promote higher growth.

The reform agenda is comprehensive and the many complex issues involved will take time to address. It will be important, therefore, to remain focussed on the objective of strengthening the global financial architecture. While substantial government intervention to support financial markets has proven necessary because of their systemic importance, back-pedalling on open and competitive markets would prove very costly, and pressures to move in this direction must therefore be resisted. Indeed, the experience of the past year has highlighted the importance of continuing with structural reforms that boost growth and strengthen the resilience of our economies to better withstand and absorb shocks. In this respect, a quick, successful completion of the Doha Round would contribute to supporting world growth, boost confidence, and demonstrate a commitment to competitive and open markets.

25 November 2008

Klaus Schmidt-Hebbel
Chief Economist

ISBN 978-92-64-05469-1
OECD Economic Outlook 84
© OECD 2008

Chapter 1

GENERAL ASSESSMENT OF THE MACROECONOMIC SITUATION

Overview

The financial crisis dominates the outlook

Massive government and central bank intervention to provide capital, liquidity and guarantees has averted the immediate risk of systemic failure of the financial system. Nevertheless, mistrust remains rife within the banking system and, together with ongoing de-leveraging to repair bank balance sheets, is impairing the flow of credit in many OECD countries. The financial crisis has spread to a wider range of institutions and markets, including emerging economies, which until quite recently seemed to have been relatively unscathed, and there have been huge falls in global financial wealth. The malfunctioning of financial markets will be the key factor weighing on activity going forward. Related to this to some extent, and further acting as a break on growth, will be the ongoing adjustment in housing markets, which is now a feature of almost all OECD countries. Weaker oil and other commodity prices will provide some relief by boosting real household incomes.

A severe downturn is in prospect

Activity is already declining in most major OECD economies and is expected to weaken further in the short-term, with area-wide OECD growth likely to be negative for a number of quarters and remain feeble for the remainder of 2009 (Table 1.1). For most OECD countries a recovery to at least the trend growth rate is not expected before the second half of 2010 implying that the downturn is likely to be the most severe since the early 1980s, leading to a sharp rise in unemployment. Widening slack

Table 1.1. **Growth is plunging**

OECD area, unless noted otherwise

	Average 1996-2005	2006	2007	2008	2009	2010	2008 q4	2009 q4	2010 q4
	Per cent								
Real GDP growth[1]	2.7	3.1	2.6	1.4	-0.4	1.5	0.2	0.2	2.2
United States	3.2	2.8	2.0	1.4	-0.9	1.6	0.1	-0.3	2.3
Euro area	2.1	3.0	2.6	1.0	-0.6	1.2	0.0	-0.1	1.9
Japan	1.1	2.4	2.1	0.5	-0.1	0.6	-0.4	0.3	0.9
Output gap[2]	-0.2	0.8	1.0	0.0	-2.6	-3.3			
Unemployment rate[3]	6.6	6.0	5.6	5.9	6.9	7.2	6.3	7.2	7.2
Inflation[4]	3.2	2.3	2.3	3.3	1.7	1.5	2.9	1.5	1.4
Fiscal balance[5]	-2.2	-1.3	-1.4	-2.5	-3.8	-4.1			

1. Year-on-year increase; last three columns show the increase over a year earlier.
2. Per cent of potential GDP.
3. Per cent of labour force.
4. Private consumption deflator. Year-on-year increase; last 3 columns show the increase over a year earlier.
5. Per cent of GDP.
Source: OECD Economic Outlook 84 database.

StatLink 🔗 *http://dx.doi.org/10.1787/501554181060*

and, more immediately, the effect of lower commodity prices will bring about a sharp reduction in inflation.

Uncertainty is exceptionally large and mostly to the downside

The major uncertainty concerning the depth and duration of weakness is the speed at which the financial market crisis is resolved. The current set of projections is based on the assumption that existing market panic will be fairly short-lived but will be followed by an extended period of severe financial headwinds, with a gradual normalisation of spreads and credit conditions starting late in 2009. Risks surrounding these projections are exceptionally large and skewed towards the downside over the coming year. Further setbacks in financial markets cannot be excluded, with failures of particular types of institution (for example hedge funds) or further weakness in particular asset classes (such as commercial property) carrying the risk of systemic implications which further delay the return to any degree of normalcy in bank lending. Of particular concern is the possibility of a negative feedback loop whereby additional real economy weakness exacerbates problems in already fragile financial markets which in turn lead to more de-leveraging, tighter credit and additional real economy distress, including the possibility of deflation. A further downside risk to activity is more serious contagion to non-OECD growth and so corresponding downside risks to world trade. Beyond 2009, risks surrounding growth are more balanced. Upside risks arise from the possibility that adjustment in financial markets may advance more quickly in response to the substantial and comprehensive policy measures introduced. Additional policy stimulus above that factored into the projections may also occur. On the other hand, previous experience of downturns in OECD countries associated with banking crises suggests that the recovery is typically more anaemic than usual.

Monetary policy can help

Conventional macroeconomic policy does have a major role to play. In early October 2008 there was an unprecedented co-ordinated cut in policy rates by the US Federal Reserve (the Fed), European Central Bank (ECB) and four other major OECD central banks, soon followed by rate cuts from central banks throughout Asia, including China. This was followed by a further round of policy rate cuts by all major OECD central banks in late October or early November. Despite these actions there is a need for an additional easing of monetary policy in the near term, even in the United States where it is already very accommodating. The authorities will be helped by the fact that inflation appears to have passed its peak and is falling, while inflation expectations have stayed well anchored.

There is a role for fiscal policy in some countries

Under normal conditions, monetary rather than fiscal policy is the stabilisation instrument of choice. However, these are not normal times. Current financial market conditions may have weakened the monetary transmission mechanism, in a few countries the scope for further monetary easing is limited and stimulus may be needed more quickly than can be delivered by monetary easing. In these circumstances, a number of countries have implemented or announced discretionary fiscal stimulus packages. Such policies need to be evaluated on a case-by-case basis. The scope for easing is constrained in countries that start from a weak fiscal position of high deficits or public debt, which may be aggravated by the short-term costs of stabilising their financial sectors. In some cases, fiscal easing could heighten perceptions of risk, provoking adverse financial market reactions. Strong political commitment to a credible medium-term framework for ensuring fiscal sustainability will increase the scope for and the effectiveness of any fiscal stimulus. If fiscal stimulus is undertaken, it should be timely and designed to have a large effect on aggregate spending. Temporary tax cuts or transfer payments aimed at credit-constrained households, for example, might boost consumption spending.

Solutions will have to be multi-faceted

Notwithstanding the significant actions taken to date, more actions may prove necessary to restore financial sector health. In this event, international co-operation is desirable to avoid measures that distort competition or which effectively shift the problem to other countries. It is equally important that measures are designed and implemented in ways that allow their orderly removal as conditions in financial markets normalise. Apart from dealing with current financial market distress, it will also be necessary to re-examine the features of the regulatory and supervisory framework that created incentives for excessive risk-taking and led financial institutions to increase leverage in non-transparent ways to levels that proved to be unsustainable. When addressing these issues, it will be important to focus on reforms to the global financial architecture, to balance growth and stability concerns, and at the same time resist pressures for a wider rollback of open markets which would prove costly.

Activity is declining

The US downturn is becoming more severe

Activity is now declining in all major OECD economies (Figure 1.1). Reflecting this, as well as falling commodity prices, high frequency measures of inflation are also showing a marked dip. Among the main OECD regions, activity is likely to contract most sharply towards the end of this year in the United States. Personal consumption has been falling, with a particularly sharp fall in spending on durables such as cars which are most sensitive to the availability of credit and heightened uncertainty. Declines in real disposable income and in household net worth foreshadow further weakness. House prices continue to fall, and there are few signs of an imminent end to the fall in residential construction. Business investment is also likely to continue to fall, amid low levels of confidence and sharply tightening financial conditions. Continuing to add an element of support are exports, although even this appears to be fading.

The euro area economy is contracting...

Euro area GDP declined in both the second and third quarters and is likely to fall also in the fourth. Private consumption has been weak, damped by subdued real income growth caused by high headline inflation. Investment is likely to have fallen sharply in the second half

Figure 1.1. **Activity is declining and inflation receding**
Annualised quarter-on-quarter percentage change

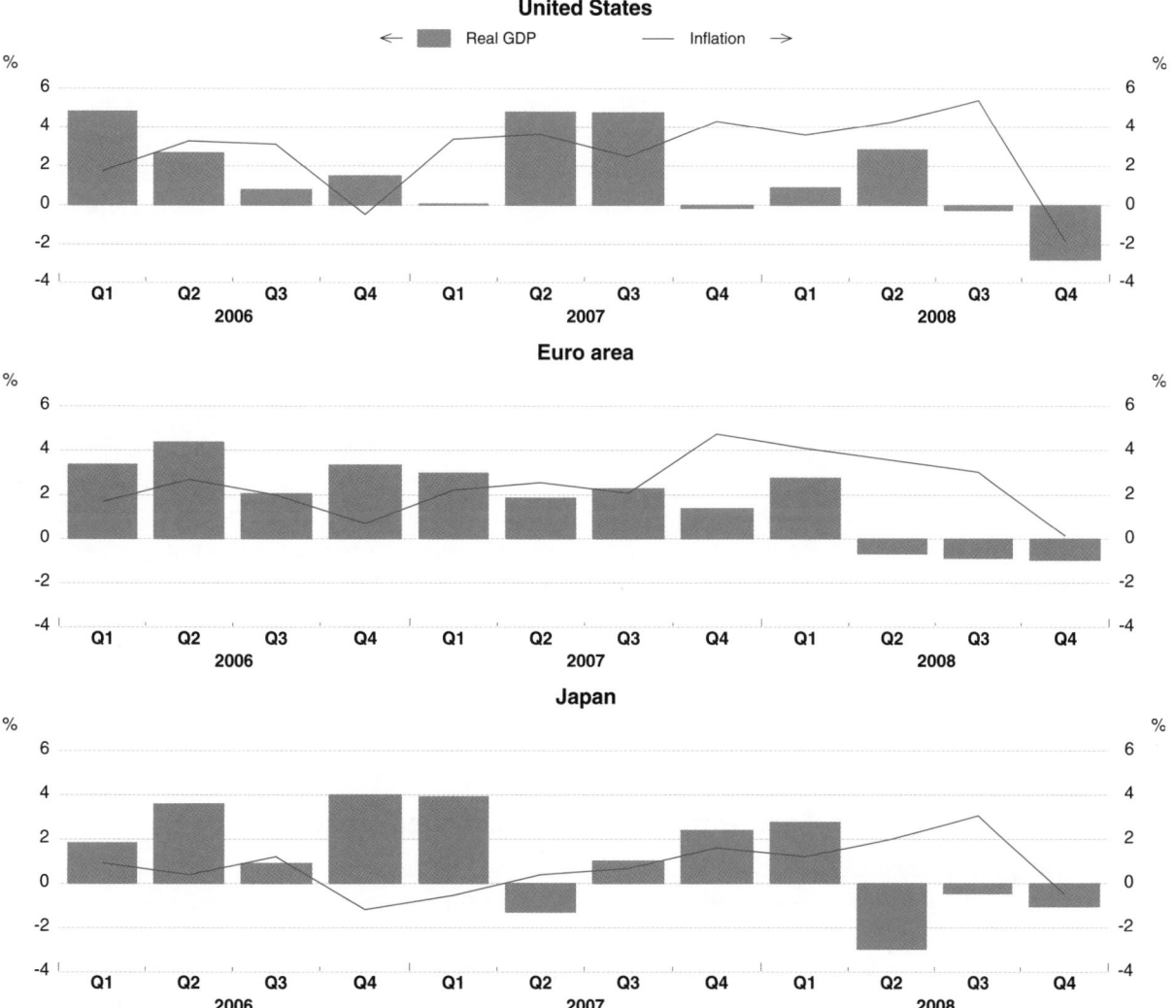

Note: The inflation measure is based on the personal consumption expenditure deflator for the United States, on the harmonised consumer price index for the euro area and on the consumer price index for Japan. Figures for the fourth quarter are projected.

Source: OECD Economic Outlook 84 database.

StatLink ⟨⟩ http://dx.doi.org/10.1787/488266367607

of 2008, reflecting tighter lending conditions and increased uncertainty. Over the same period, the contribution of net exports has also weakened, in response to the overall appreciation of the euro since 2006 and slower world trade growth.

… as is Japan's
After falling in the second quarter, Japanese activity is set to fall further to the end of the year. Exports, which have been an engine of growth over recent years, have decelerated markedly both in response to the appreciation of the yen and slowing external demand. Business investment, another important source of past growth, has also been declining, weighed down by stalling business confidence and reduced

export growth. Notwithstanding a temporary fall in the second quarter, residential investment continues to recover since the disruption caused by the regulatory change introduced in the middle of 2007.

Chinese growth has moderated...

Growth in the major emerging market economies has moderated but remains strong. In China, year-on-year growth fell to 9% in the third quarter of 2008, the first time it has not been a double-digit number in five years and continuing the slowdown that started over a year ago. While exports are slackening and capital formation has declined, there has been a rebalancing towards domestic consumption. Amid evidence that the economy is easing, the authorities have moved toward looser monetary policy. Moreover, the Chinese government has recently announced a stimulus package including a series of infrastructure projects over the next two years, although it is not entirely clear how much of this represents new spending. This fiscal stimulus, which was announced too late to be incorporated in the projections, is likely to boost growth significantly in 2009-10.

... as has that of other emerging economies

The slowdown in India, which began in the second half of 2007, became more pronounced in 2008, with growth now running at below 8%. The slackening in growth has been led by investment, with private consumption growth holding up. Russian activity is slowing sharply from strong growth in the first half of the year, as terms of trade gains have suffered a steep reverse and the international economy worsened. Brazilian activity is showing signs of easing due to past monetary tightening and slowing credit.

Labour markets have also weakened

Employment has declined sharply in the United States

With weakening activity, OECD area employment growth has also progressively turned down during 2008 (Table 1.2). The downturn took

Table 1.2. **Labour markets have begun to weaken**

	2005	2006	2007	2008 q1	2008 q2	2008 q3	2008 q4
	Percentage change from previous period, seasonally adjusted at annual rates						
Employment							
United States	1.8	1.9	1.1	-0.6	0.1	-1.6	-1.5
Japan	0.4	0.4	0.5	-0.6	-0.5	-1.0	-0.9
Euro area	1.1	1.6	1.8	1.5	0.6	-0.1	-0.8
Labour force							
United States	1.3	1.4	1.1	0.0	1.7	1.1	1.0
Japan	0.1	0.1	0.2	-0.6	0.1	-0.4	-0.5
Euro area	1.2	0.9	0.9	1.2	1.3	0.6	0.6
Unemployment rate			Per cent of labour force				
United States	5.1	4.6	4.6	4.9	5.3	6.0	6.5
Japan	4.4	4.1	3.9	3.8	4.0	4.1	4.3
Euro area	8.8	8.2	7.4	7.2	7.3	7.5	7.8

For 2008 q3 and q4 partly estimates and projections.
Source: OECD Economic Outlook 84 database.

StatLink http://dx.doi.org/10.1787/501580466076

effect earlier in the United States, where the unemployment rate has reached 6½ per cent and the rate of monthly job losses hit a five-year high. The weakening of the labour market is not yet clearly reflected in wages, although the acceleration in wage cost which was evident through much of 2008 appears to have come to an end (Table 1.3).

Table 1.3. **Wage developments remain moderate**

	2005	2006	2007	2008 q1	2008 q2	2008 q3	2008 q4
	Percentage change from previous year						
Labour productivity[1]							
United States	1.3	1.0	1.1	2.3	2.1	1.1	1.1
Japan	1.5	2.0	1.6	1.1	1.2	0.6	0.3
Euro area	0.7	1.4	0.8	0.3	0.1	-0.2	-0.3
Compensation per employee							
United States	3.6	3.9	4.1	3.0	3.8	3.9	3.7
Japan	0.1	0.1	-0.7	1.1	1.5	1.5	1.4
Euro area	1.8	2.3	2.4	2.9	3.2	3.4	3.1
Real compensation per employee[2]							
United States	0.3	0.6	1.4	0.9	1.8	1.2	1.4
Japan	1.4	1.1	0.1	2.7	3.1	3.5	0.4
Euro area	-0.2	0.4	0.1	0.8	0.9	0.7	0.3
Unit labour cost							
United States	2.3	2.9	3.1	1.0	1.9	2.9	2.8
Japan	-1.1	-0.8	-1.8	-0.1	0.7	1.2	1.5
Euro area	1.2	1.1	1.8	2.7	3.3	3.9	3.7

Note: For the total economy, year-on-year increase; last 4 columns show the increase over a year earlier.
    For 2008 q3 and q4 partly estimates and projections.
1. Productivity is measured on a per person basis.
2. Deflated by the GDP deflator.
Source: OECD Economic Outlook 84 database.

StatLink ⬛⬛⬛ *http://dx.doi.org/10.1787/501583281767*

Labour markets have softened in the euro area and Japan

In the euro area, unemployment is also rising, albeit less rapidly. There has been a modest pick-up in real wages. This, together with a dip in productivity growth, which may be unusually low for cyclical reasons, has contributed to acceleration in unit labour costs which are rising at an annualised rate of more than 3%. Employment is falling in Japan, with the unemployment rate edging up since the beginning of the year, albeit from low levels. Nominal wage growth has, however, picked up with positive growth in unit labour costs being achieved for the first time in more than a decade.

Forces shaping the outlook and associated risks

The outlook is dominated by the state of financial markets

The financial market crisis is the main force dominating the short-term outlook for activity, with a key question relating to its duration. Continuing housing market downturns in many OECD countries will be an additional drag. They will also interact with, and be an important determinant of, the duration of the financial crisis. On the other hand, the sharp fall in oil prices and the moderation of other commodity prices will provide some offset to these headwinds.

Financial markets and the projection

Financial markets were threatened with systemic failure...

The turmoil that hit financial markets in the summer of 2007 took a dramatic turn for the worse in mid-September 2008, spreading to encompass most of the world. Paralysis in credit markets started to spill over into lending, threatening the day-to-day functioning of the real economy. Ongoing suspicions about counterparty health and fear of severe downturns in some OECD countries and of a global recession led to near panic in financial markets, with equity prices falling worldwide. Risk premia in bond markets also picked up, as evidenced by OECD's synthetic indicators of such premia for corporate and emerging market bonds (Figure 1.2). The rise in these spreads is consistent with an increase in defaults beyond the historical highs of 2002, but likely also reflects an underlying increase in risk aversion and fear that a long-lasting downturn could reduce recovery rates in case of default.

Figure 1.2. **Risk premia have soared**

Deviation from average (in terms of standard deviations of synthetic indicator[1])

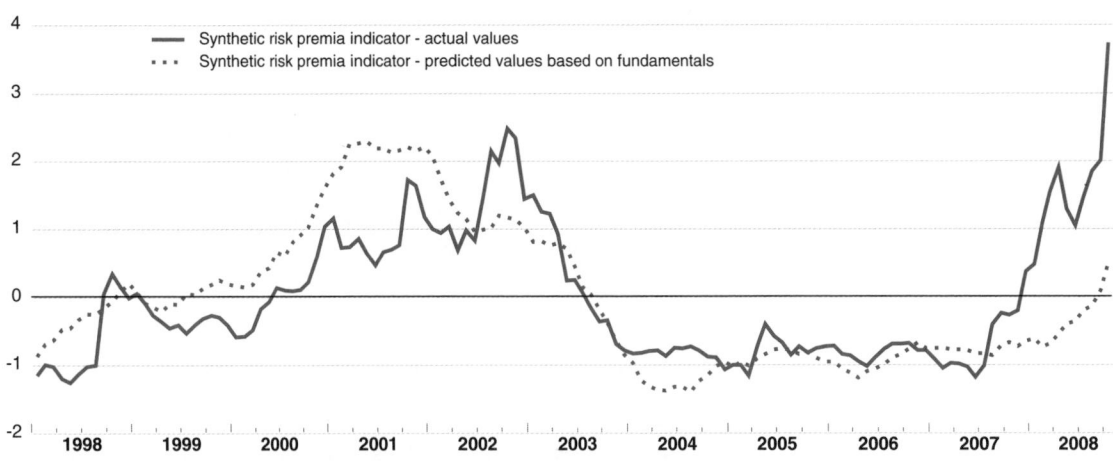

1. The synthetic measure is derived from risk proxies for corporate and emerging market bonds. In regression analysis, it seems to be well explained by a set of "fundamentals" including global short-term interest rates and liquidity, corporate default rates and the OECD's leading economic indicators, a proxy for expectations of the near-term outlook for the OECD cyclical position. The "predicted" values shown are the model predictions. See OECD (2006).

Source: Datastream; and OECD calculations.

StatLink ⚓ http://dx.doi.org/10.1787/488284535153

... and policy has responded promptly

In response, and complemented by policy action by authorities across the globe, the European and US authorities launched massive interventions in financial markets to confront head-on the crisis of distrust, illiquidity and insolvency that threatened financial markets with outright collapse. The central projections described in this *Outlook* are predicated on the assumption that, in the wake of this policy effort, financial stress quickly falls back to pre-September levels. Thereafter this lower-level financial stress is assumed to persist, before diminishing gradually starting in late 2009.

The evolving financial market crisis

Financial institution balance sheets are under extreme pressure,...

In the run-up to the crisis, financial institutions became increasingly over-leveraged. This was not always transparent as banks kept these assets off balance sheet (for example in Structured Investment Vehicles, SIVs) to avoid regulatory capital requirements and thereby increase profitability.[1] Subsequent large losses and write-downs on mortgage-linked assets, exposed this problem and left financial institutions even more over-leveraged.[2] To repair their balance sheets, banks have raised new capital but this has become increasingly difficult due to falling share prices (Figure 1.3) and losses suffered by investors who contributed to some of the

Figure 1.3. **Share prices have fallen sharply**

Share price indices, 1 January 2007 = 100

Source: Datastream.

StatLink ⟨⟩ http://dx.doi.org/10.1787/488380584281

1. Structured Investment Vehicles (SIVs) are typically funds that borrow short-term in commercial paper markets and purchase long-term asset-backed securities and are sponsored by a bank that provides back-up credit lines.
2. Bloomberg estimates suggest that total losses and write-downs related to mortgage-backed assets as at 29 September were $591 billion, of which $323 billion were in US banks and $230 billion in European banks. European losses were particularly concentrated in Swiss ($55 billion) and UK banks ($62 billion). Bank losses arose from direct holdings of mortgage-linked securities on balance sheet, but more importantly from losses connected with providing back-up credit lines to SIVs and bringing SIVs back on their balance sheets (Borio, 2008).

earlier capitalisations. Banks have also attempted to sell off mortgage linked assets, but a lack of liquidity in these markets and increased risk aversion since last summer have led prices to fall sharply to levels that, taken literally, would imply extremely high rates of default by historical standards. This in turn has required further write-downs of assets, exacerbating capital inadequacy and amplifying the deleveraging process.

... trust within the financial sector has eroded...

Ongoing weakness in financial institution balance sheets and increasing uncertainty about whether many are solvent came to a head in mid-September, in the wake of the bankruptcy filing by Lehman Brothers. The result was a sharp increase in the rates of interest that banks charge for lending to one another and a drying up of lending. The premia paid to insure against debt default by financial institutions soared, although they have since fallen back to pre-September levels (Figure 1.4). Bank-runs at the wholesale level, both actual and threatened, have forced the bankruptcy, effective nationalisation or merger of many large financial institutions in the United States and Europe. In the United States, the investment banking sector came under enormous pressure. Two of the five largest investment banks were merged with other banks under duress, one went bankrupt and the remaining two were forced to become more highly regulated bank holding companies but with permanent access to the Fed's lending facilities. Large commercial banks were also forced into mergers with other institutions and a large insurance company was rescued by the government. Some or all of the following features appear to be common characteristics of institutions in the United States and elsewhere that have come under pressure: a heavy reliance on wholesale funding, losses on US mortgage market linked assets, lending to high risk borrowers, high leverage prior to the crisis and exposure to declining housing markets.

Figure 1.4. **Bank credit default swaps have fallen from recent peaks**

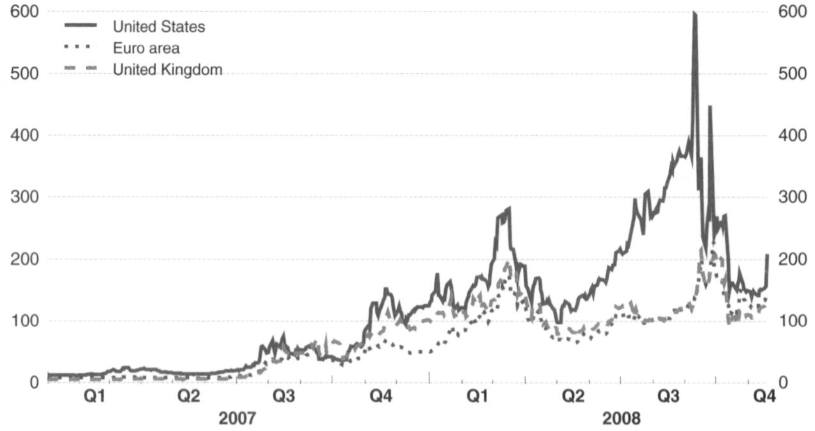

Note: Averages of 5-year credit default swap rates on senior bonds across the largest banks.
Source: Datastream.

StatLink 🔗 http://dx.doi.org/10.1787/488485751545

... and most countries are affected

The housing market downturn in the United Kingdom has exacerbated pressures on the mortgage market, resulting in the nationalisation of two major lenders, the takeovers of a further two under duress and government capital injections into a number of other large institutions. Deleveraging is gathering pace with lending growth to households and non-financial corporations falling sharply. Continental European banks have been less directly affected by the turmoil than their US counterparts. However, the crisis has spread quickly with numerous financial institutions requiring government rescues since the beginning of September: a major Benelux bank and a Franco-Belgian bank required capital injections and partial nationalisation; a large German real estate lender was recapitalised by a joint government/private sector consortium; the three largest banks in Iceland have been placed in receivership under direct government control; six minor Danish banks have been sold, merged or bailed out by the state; and Switzerland has injected capital into one of its largest banks. The Icelandic example illustrates the potential problems that could face small economies with out-sized banking sectors, even though that country provided an extreme case.[3]

Japan's financial system has not remained unscathed

Japan's banking sector and financial system initially appeared to be relatively unharmed by the crisis. However, indirect effects from the large falls in equity prices which have followed the global trend, as well as the appreciation of the yen resulting from the unwinding of the carry-trade, will slow the economy. This will increase bad loans and force large global Japanese banks to write down the value of their equity portfolios which remain relatively large.[4]

There is contagion to emerging markets

Emerging markets, although not directly hit by exposure to mortgage-linked asset losses, have been affected. Countries with large external financing needs, reliance on crisis-hit banks in Europe, dependence on commodity exports, high foreign currency loan exposure or high exposure to exchange rate risk via derivative contracts have been particularly hard hit. The provision of government lending and deposit guarantees in the advanced OECD economies has also contributed to capital flight away from emerging markets. Investors, increasingly concerned about economic prospects, have sold-off equities and currencies in emerging markets across the world. Indeed, as the financial crisis has worsened, the fall in emerging market equity prices has exceeded that in the advanced economies; the Morgan Stanley Capital International (MSCI) dollar index of emerging market equity prices fell

3. The ratio of total bank assets to GDP was 0.7 in the United States (commercial banks only), 2.1 in Australia, 3.5 in the euro area, 4.3 in Denmark, 4.7 in the United Kingdom, 6.8 in Switzerland, 9.5 in Ireland and close to 10 in Iceland (data on bank assets relates to mid-2008 and is obtained from the respective central banks).
4. In early November the government announced that it would exempt banks that operate only in Japan from marking their equity portfolios to market values until March 2012.

about 40% between the beginning of September and the first week of November, compared to a fall in the MSCI global dollar index of about 30%. Bond spreads for emerging market countries have also increased sharply since mid-2008 to their highest level since 2003. However, a return to historical highs is unlikely without a reversal of improved fundamentals (including lower inflation and debt), which has been an important reason for the reduction in emerging market bond spreads in recent years (Maier and Vasishtha, 2008).

Credit conditions have tightened considerably

In response to balance-sheet pressures and, increasingly, risk aversion, commercial banks in the United States and Europe have been tightening lending standards to both households and corporations (Figure 1.5) and the cost of capital has been elevated by high interest rate spreads (Figure 1.6). Even after the immediate financial crisis passes, lending standards are expected to remain tight and interest rate spreads wide until late in 2009.

Financial authorities have taken extensive action...

Faced with an intensifying financial crisis and negative feedback between the financial system and growth, European and US authorities, complemented by policy action elsewhere in the OECD, have responded with a multi-faceted strategy (Appendix 1.A1). Measures included steps to: address the illiquidity in key money and credit markets; reduce perceived short-selling pressures in equity markets through restrictions on this activity; organise rescues, including nationalisations to prevent the failure of troubled institutions; guarantee deposits and in some cases inter-bank lending to shore-up confidence and contain systemic risks; and carry out broad-based recapitalisation of banking sectors using public funds to deal with solvency concerns.

... expanding liquidity...

In a massive effort evident in the doubling of its balance sheet from mid September to early November, the Fed has deployed an increasingly wide range of unconventional tools to boost liquidity and substitute for faltering private sector credit activity in the United States. These tools include facilities to directly support lending to the corporate sector and large increases in the size of lending facilities and the range of collateral accepted. It has also acted to boost US dollar liquidity worldwide by expanding the number of central banks it will lend to *via* swap lines, which in some cases including the ECB have no limit. These actions have been complemented by central bank action throughout the OECD to boost liquidity including by accepting a very wide range of collateral.

... bank recapitalisation...

The authorities in continental Europe and the United States have moved to take equity stakes in a broad range of systemically important institutions, most commonly in return for non-voting preference shares. The authorities have also attached other conditions to capital injections to varying degrees in areas such as dividend policy, lending strategy and

Figure 1.5. **Banks are tightening lending standards**
Net percentage of banks tightening credit

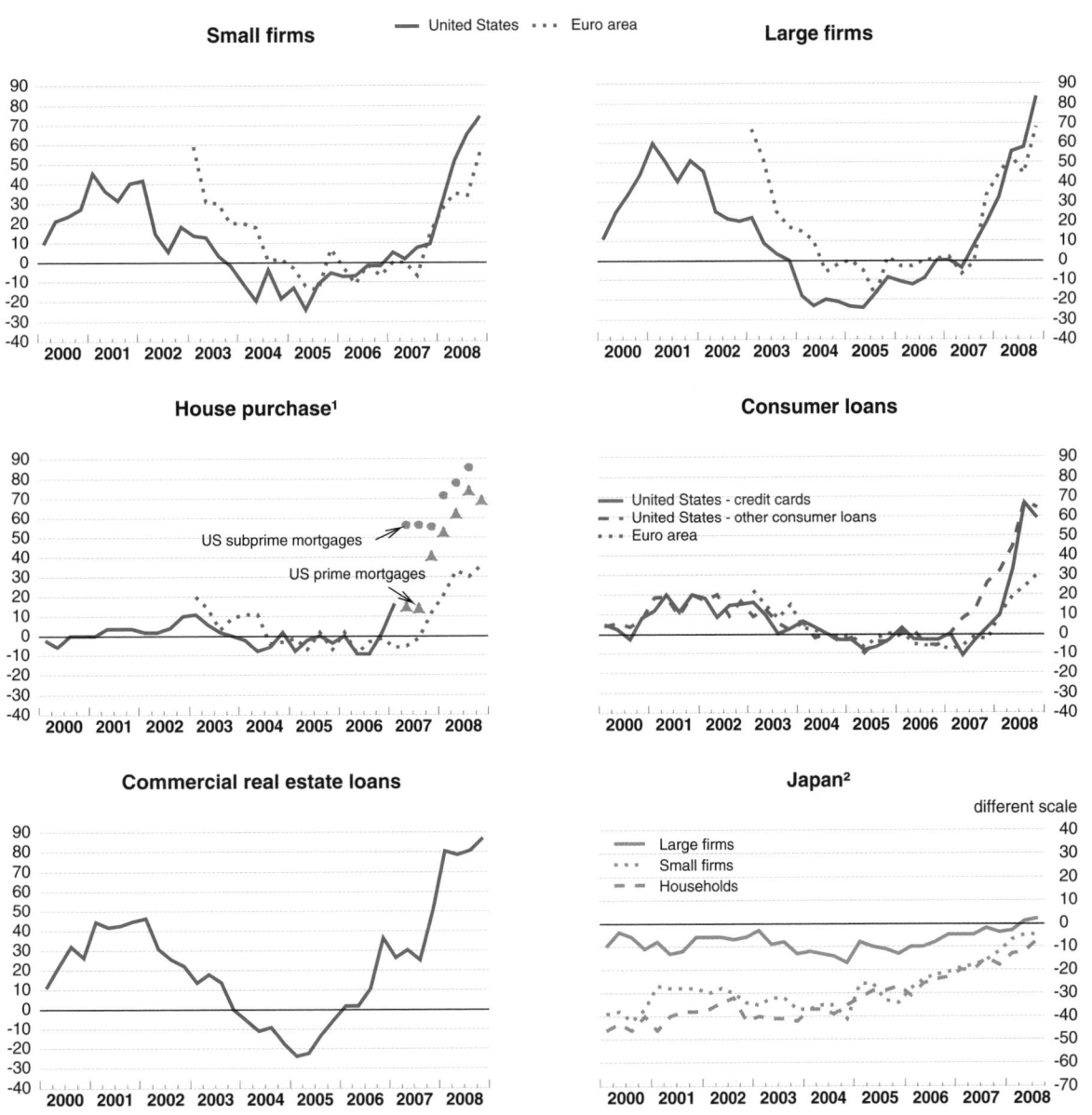

1. In the United States, starting in 2007q2 changes in standards for prime, non conventional (not displayed on this figure) and subprime mortgage loans are reported separately.
2. The Bank of Japan publishes a diffusion index of "accommodative" minus "severe". The data have then been transformed to show the net percentage of banks tightening credit, as for the United States and the euro area.

Source: US Federal Reserve, Senior Loan Officer Survey; ECB, The euro area bank lending survey; and Bank of Japan, Senior Loan Officer Opinion Survey.

StatLink http://dx.doi.org/10.1787/488514105262

executive compensation. This is designed to deal with the wide-spread bank under-capitalisation afflicting credit markets, and together with guarantees of bank lending, re-establish confidence in the financial sector and normal lending activity.

Figure 1.6. **Corporate bond yields have spiked**

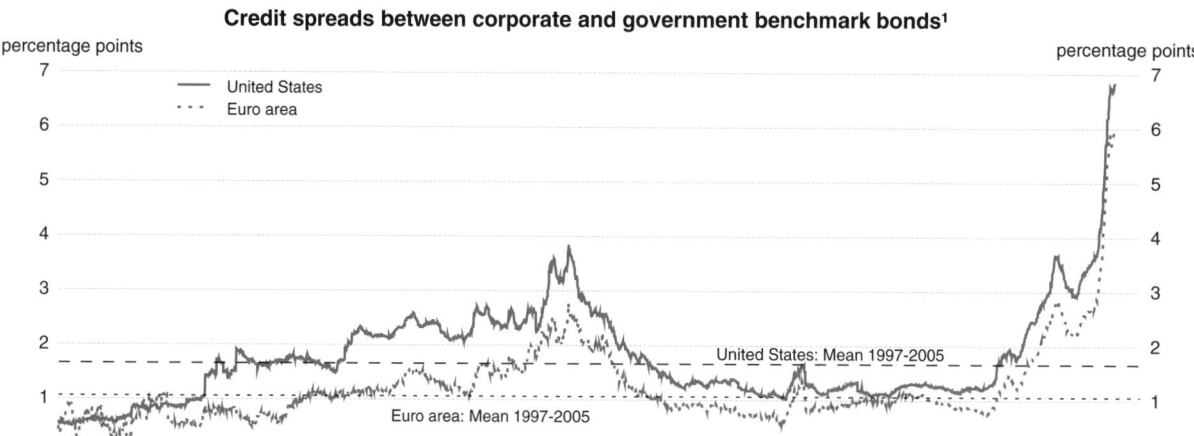

Credit spreads between corporate and government benchmark bonds[1]

High-yield bond spreads[2] and corporate default rates[3]

1. Merrill Lynch corporate BBB rated bonds. Spreads based on average yields for 5-7 years and for 7-10 years.
2. Spreads of high-yield bonds (Merrill Lynch indices) over government bond yields (10-year benchmark bonds).
3. Moody's: defaulting companies as a percentage of all rated companies; 12-month trailing average. Dotted line shows Moody's forecasts.

Source: Datastream; Moody's; and OECD calculations.

StatLink 🔗 http://dx.doi.org/10.1787/488526226147

... asset purchases...   Mortgage-linked securities markets are plagued by illiquidity – banks hold a huge amount and a wide variety of mortgage-linked assets of varying worth, but none can be sold except at fire-sale prices. To deal with this problem or help prevent it happening, several OECD governments have announced their willingness to directly purchase mortgage-linked securities from financial institutions. The United States originally proposed using the $700 billion Troubled Asset Relief Programme (TARP) to make purchases of illiquid mortgage-linked assets. However, as such purchases have proved difficult to organise and are not seen as particularly effective, the funds are now being used for a wider range of measures to combat the crisis including bank recapitalisation.

Switzerland has set up a fund to buy illiquid assets from one of its largest banks. Other OECD countries, including Australia, Canada, Denmark, Norway, Spain and Sweden, also intend to make purchases of mortgage-backed securities in order to help maintain liquidity in these markets.

... increasing deposit guarantees...

To shore up confidence in the banking system, governments across the OECD, including Australia, Austria, Denmark, Germany, Greece, Ireland, Portugal, Slovakia and Slovenia, have given explicit blanket guarantees of

Figure 1.7. **Bank loan growth is slowing**
Year-on-year growth rate

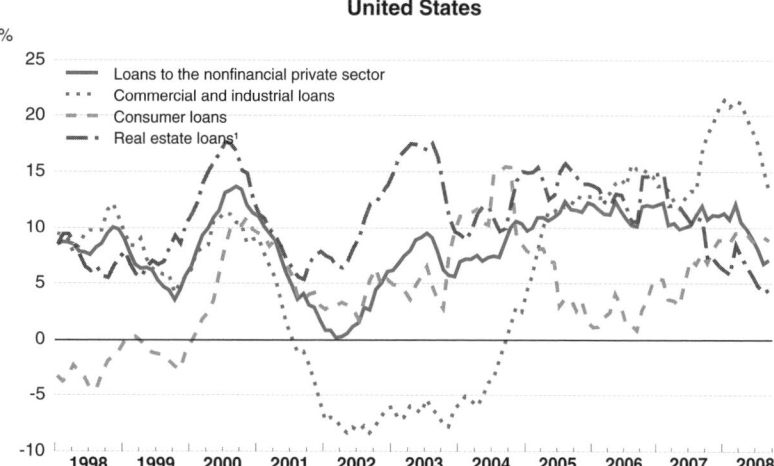

Note: Data refer to all commercial banks for the United States; to monetary financial institutions (MFIs) for the euro area. Year-on-year growth rates are calculated from end-of-period stocks. For the euro area, these are adjusted for reclassifications, exchange rates variations and any other changes which do not arise from transactions.

1. The definition of real estate loans for the United States is broader than housing loans as it includes also loans related to commercial real estate. Moreover, real estate loans can also include loans to the corporate sector.

Source: Datastream.

StatLink ㎜⬛ *http://dx.doi.org/10.1787/488580262401*

all banking system deposits.[5] The United States has increased its deposit insurance ceiling to $250 000 and all EU countries have agreed to raise their ceilings to at least € 50 000, and some countries, such as Belgium and the Netherlands, have gone further in raising the ceiling to € 100 000.

... and guaranteeing wholesale lending by banks

In order to unfreeze money markets and maintain bank access to wholesale funds, governments across the OECD have also announced they will guarantee wholesale lending by banks. The scale of intervention, the relative weight on the various approaches, as well as the details of their implementation are controversial, as is discussed in the Policy Requirements section below.

Private sector credit is slowing...

Despite all of these policy actions, credit growth is slowing across all major categories in the United States and the euro area (Figure 1.7). Some of the reduction in credit growth is likely to occur through reduced lending to private equity firms and hedge funds for leveraged buy-outs and other investments, where the direct negative implications for real activity are relatively minor. However, credit to households and non-financial corporations is also contracting with greater direct implications for the real economy.[6]

... and wealth has fallen sharply

The effect of the credit slowdown will be compounded by negative wealth effects from the sharp decline in equity prices through 2008 as well as past and ongoing falls in house prices. These will represent a substantial drag on consumption growth over the next couple of years, although there will be differences in the magnitude of these effects across countries. For the United States "back-of-the envelope" estimates suggest that wealth effects will build up, eventually subtracting as much as 1½ to 2% from annualised consumption growth towards the end of 2009 and early in 2010, dissipating only gradually thereafter. Estimates for the euro area suggest a similar timing, but a smaller subtraction to annual consumption growth of between ½ and ¾ per cent.[7] The smaller

5. For Ireland this only applies to the six largest banks, otherwise the limit is € 100 000.
6. Considerable empirical evidence, mostly relating to the United States where time series data is most readily available, suggests that over and above any effect from an increase in the cost of capital, tighter bank lending standards reduce growth (Bayoumi and Melander, 2008; Estrella, 2004; Guichard and Turner, 2008; Lown and Morgan, 2004; Swinston, 2008).
7. These calculations assume a marginal propensity to consume out of both housing and equity wealth of 0.0375 for the United States, which appears to be the estimate used by the Federal Reserve (OECD, 2008a). The same value of 0.0375 has also been taken for the marginal propensity to consume out of financial wealth for the euro area, which is the value found by recent OECD empirical work (OECD, 2008b). This empirical work does not find any robust evidence of an effect from housing wealth on consumption in the euro area. It is further assumed, for both the United States and euro area, that consumption adjusts gradually over the eight quarters following a shock to wealth. Extrapolations of financial wealth are made to the end of 2008 using equity prices and past historical relationships between equity prices and financial wealth. Beyond 2008 financial wealth is assumed to remain a stable share of personal income. US housing wealth is assumed to decline in line with the projection of house prices.

estimates for the euro area result from two differences: first, there is little evidence of an effect from housing wealth on consumption in the euro area (or most individual euro area countries);[8] second, financial and equity wealth are a much smaller multiple of personal income in the euro area compared with the United States. Financial wealth and debt, as a share of income, varies widely across OECD countries and has typically risen markedly over the past decade. Countries where household debt, particularly mortgages, has increased most are typically also those where consumption is most vulnerable to recent corrections in asset prices, notably house prices, and therefore likely to be weaker as households attempt to repair their balance sheets.

Car sales are an early indicator of pressures on consumption

Car sales, which have been falling since mid-2008 in the United States and Europe and more recently in Japan, are often an early indicator of pressures on consumption. There was an exceptionally sharp fall in US car sales in October, which were down nearly 30% on a year earlier, following the intensification of the financial crisis. Falling car sales partly reflect difficulties that car finance companies face in raising capital which in turn has led to credit being restricted to consumers as well as sharp falls in consumer confidence leading to the postponement of major outlays.

The total effect of tighter US financial conditions is very large

Recent OECD work that quantifies and combines the effects of various financial variables on US GDP into a financial conditions index (FCI) suggests that there has been a substantial deterioration in overall financial conditions since the beginning of the turmoil with the index reaching unprecedented levels in the final quarter of 2008 (Figure 1.8). Relative to mid-2007, the tightening of lending standards (which in September reached an all-time high), widening interest rate spreads and a plunging stock market have had an effect on activity which is estimated to be equivalent to a tightening in real long-term interest rates of about 10 percentage points, only about one-quarter of which has been offset by lower official interest rates.[9] The depreciation of the dollar over the year to mid-2008, which had been an important offset to tighter financial conditions, has since been largely reversed. The net overall tightening in financial conditions is estimated to reduce GDP by nearly 5% after a lag of four to six quarters.[10] These adverse effects on activity are likely to be particularly felt through weaker housing and business investment (Bayoumi and Melander, 2008 and Carlson *et al.*, 2008) as well as consumer spending on durables.

8. A possible explanation for the absence of any finding of a housing wealth effect in many continental European countries may be because of the difficulty of using housing as collateral to facilitate mortgage equity withdrawal (as discussed further below).

9. See Guichard and Turner (2008) for further details behind the construction of the FCI. Certain component variables have been projected to derive a value for the FCI in the fourth quarter (see notes to Figure 1.8 for details).

10. With the index registering levels outside the range of previous historical experience greater caution is warranted in interpreting these findings. For example, beyond a certain point the widening in bond spreads may cease to be a reliable linear indicator of future activity if the volume of trade in corporate bonds becomes thin.

Figure 1.8. **US financial conditions continue to worsen**

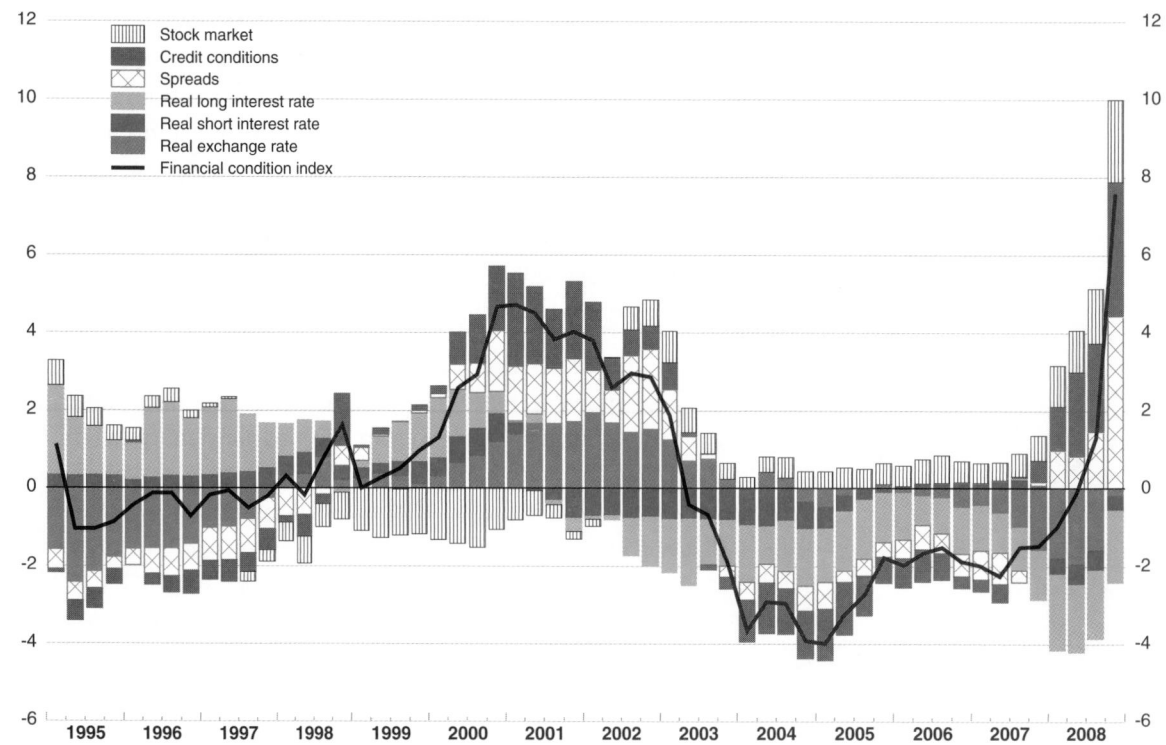

Note: A unit increase in the index corresponds to an effect on GDP equivalent to an increase in real long-term interest rates of 1 percentage point. Some components of the index have been projected for the fourth quarter of 2008, taking values which are consistent with the main projections where possible or, in the case of bond spreads and stock market capitalisation, taking an average of daily values from the beginning of October until the first week of November. For details of the methodology used to construct the index see Guichard and Turner (2008).

Source: OECD Economic Outlook 84 database; Datastream; and OECD calculations.

StatLink ⫘⫘⫘ *http://dx.doi.org/10.1787/488634152358*

Downturns are more severe following a banking crisis

Among OECD countries, downturns following major banking crises tend to be more severe than other downturns (Table 1.4); the total loss in output as measured by the cumulative output gap has on average been about double the output loss of a "normal" downturn for the same country.[11, 12] In nearly all cases the size of the output loss was greater

11. These calculations will understate (perhaps greatly) the true output losses if the banking crisis also adversely affects potential output growth (the calculations in Table 1.4 implicitly assume this is not the case). Other studies suggest that this might be the case given the finding that a full recovery of output to the projected trend level of GDP extended prior to the crisis is rare (Cerra and Saxena, 2008). However, as the authors acknowledge, such estimates tend to overestimate the loss if there has been a boom prior to the crisis. On the other hand, OECD estimates suggest that of the episodes distinguished in Table 1.4 the only country for which potential growth is clearly lower following the banking crisis is Japan (and much of this decline is explained by lower population growth).
12. The results in Table 1.4 are broadly consistent with recent analysis by the IMF (2008a), which suggest that: output losses are roughly twice as severe for a slowdown preceded by financial stress; output losses are about four times as severe for a recession preceded by financial stress compared with a recession without financial stress; and downturns are longer when accompanied by financial stress.

Table 1.4. **Downturns and recoveries following a banking crisis**

	Year of banking crisis	Cumulative output gap (% pts of GDP)			Maximum fall in business investment (% pts of GDP)			Maximum fall in housing investment (% pts of GDP)		
		In downturn following banking crisis	Average of other downturns	Ratio	In downturn following banking crisis	Average of other downturns	Ratio	In downturn following banking crisis	Average of other downturns	Ratio
United States	1988	-11.4	-6.2	1.8	-2.0	-1.3	1.5	-2.5	-1.1	2.3
Japan	1997	-12.3	-7.3	1.7	-5.5	-4.3	1.3	-5.4	-1.0	5.2
Spain	1977	-10.1	-6.0	1.7	-5.0	-3.2	1.6	-1.8	-0.2	7.3
Finland	1991	-40.6	-5.2	7.9	-9.1	-4.8	1.9	-4.0	-1.1	3.7
Norway	1991	-34.8	-6.5	5.4	-5.6	-6.5	0.9	-3.2	-1.3	2.4
Sweden	1991	-16.7	-4.3	3.9	-5.7	-2.4	2.4	-4.3	-1.3	3.3
Average		-21.0	-5.9	3.7	-5.5	-3.8	1.6	-3.5	-1.0	4.0

	Year of banking crisis	Recovery half life (quarters)			Change in the gap first six quarters from trough (% pts of GDP)			Average rate of change in the gap trough to zero (% pts of GDP, per annum)		
		In downturn following banking crisis	Average of other downturns	Ratio	In downturn following banking crisis	Average of other downturns	Ratio	In downturn following banking crisis	Average of other downturns	Ratio
United States	1988	5.0	2.5	2.0	0.3	0.6	0.6	0.3	0.6	0.5
Japan	1997	3.0	4.0	0.8	0.3	0.5	0.6	0.3	0.5	0.5
Spain	1977	2.0	4.2	0.5	0.6	0.6	1.0	0.9	0.6	1.7
Finland	1991	14.0	5.3	2.6	0.4	0.3	1.1	0.5	0.4	1.2
Norway	1991	1.0	1.0	1.0	0.8	0.9	0.9	0.4	0.9	0.4
Sweden	1991	7.0	3.0	2.3	0.5	0.5	0.9	0.3	0.9	0.3
Average		5.3	3.3	1.5	0.5	0.6	0.8	0.4	0.6	0.8

Note: The banking crises are taken to be "the big five" bank-centred financial crises identified by Reinhart and Rogoff (2008) plus the 1984 Savings and
    Loan crisis in the United States, which they refer to as being "just a notch below".
    A downturn is defined as a period of at least two years when the cumulative output gap is at least 2% of GDP and output falls at least 1% below
    potential output in at least one year.
    The maximum fall in business (housing) investment is defined as the largest fall in the business (housing) investment share of GDP over the
    preceding 4 or 5 years during the downturn (whichever gives the largest fall in investment).
    Output gap measures are taken from the OECD Economic Outlook 84 database except for Spain where the output gap is derived by taking a
    Hodrick-Prescott filter of the GDP because the historical data for the standard output gap measure is too short for Spain.
    The recovery half life is the number of quarters following the trough before the trough output gap is halved.
Source: OECD calculations.

StatLink http://dx.doi.org/10.1787/501614223525

than usually experienced both because the duration of the downturn was longer and its depth more severe. In addition the share of business investment and particularly housing investment in GDP tends to be hit hard in a downturn associated with a banking crisis; on average the fall in the business investment share of GDP is about one and a half times greater and the housing investment share four times greater than a downturn normally experienced by the same country. The recovery is also typically more muted following a banking crisis.

The situation is extremely fragile implying a major downside risk

After more than a year of chronic and more recently extreme stress in financial markets and the failure of numerous institutions across several OECD countries, confidence in financial market institutions is very low. Further strains could result from a number of sources: an intensification of housing downturns and mortgage defaults; further falls in commercial property prices and a widening of loan delinquencies in commercial property and other loan categories arising from weaker growth across the OECD; the collapse of highly-leveraged hedge funds;[13] pressure on pension funds;[14] and further failures of large financial institutions. If such occurrences were to prolong the period of financial stress then the downturn in activity would be both more severe and more protracted than the central projections discussed here.

The housing downturn is becoming more widespread

Housing investment is contracting in most OECD countries...

Tighter credit conditions, clearly apparent in mortgage markets in many OECD countries,[15] are reinforcing the synchronised housing downswing that was already underway. Over the past year, housing investment has decelerated in virtually all OECD countries, falling in a majority, and by more than 10% in seven countries (Figure 1.9). Large falls

Figure 1.9. **Real housing investment is falling in most countries**
Year-on-year growth rate

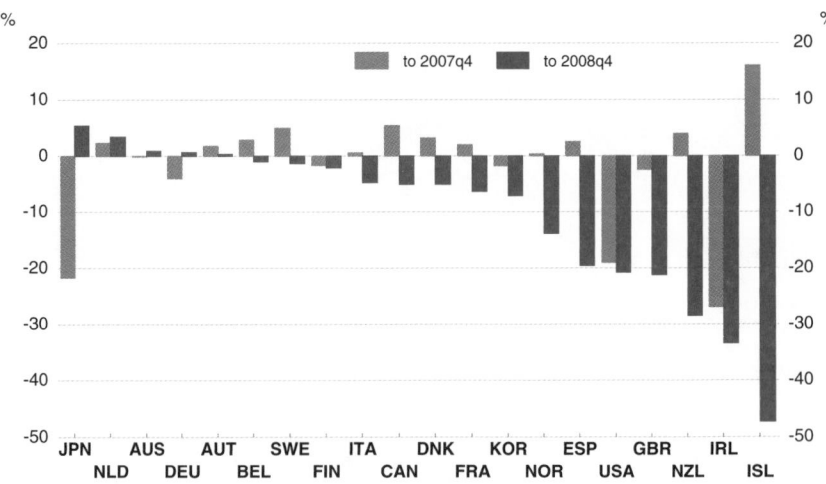

Source: OECD Economic Outlook 84 database.

StatLink http://dx.doi.org/10.1787/488670473784

13. Hedge funds have already suffered significant funding withdrawals since mid-2008. Hedge funds are a potential source of systemic risk because of their high leverage and because they often hold significant positions relative to market size. Hedge fund leverage is estimated as lying between 2 and 6 depending on the hedging strategy (McGuire and Tsatsaronis, 2008) and they manage a total of around $2 trillion in funds. Thus, if they default or their funding is withdrawn and they are forced to liquidate positions at fire-sale prices, then this can cause large losses to their creditors as well as putting strains on the balance sheets of non-related institutions with similar assets (Bernanke, 2006).
14. Sharp falls in equity prices have potentially severe implications for pension funds with private sector defined benefit schemes that have high exposure to equity markets being particularly vulnerable. Alternatively, employees close to retirement in defined contribution schemes could suffer substantial losses on their retirement pension.
15. The proportion of banks tightening lending standards for house purchase is at very high levels in the United States, the euro area and the United Kingdom.

Figure 1.10. **Residential permits are falling sharply**

Latest data, year-on-year growth rate[1]

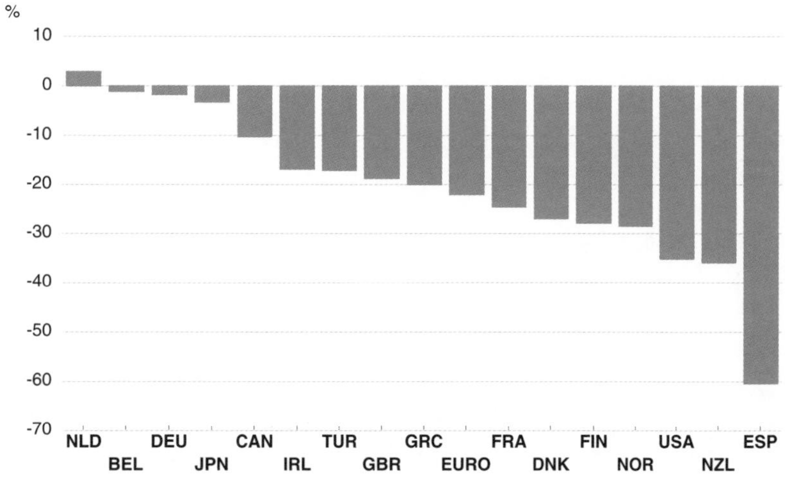

1. Monthly data mostly ending between March 2008 and July 2008; three-month average over the last year three-month average, seasonally adjusted.

Source: Eurostat; and OECD, Main Economic Indicators database.

StatLink ⟨⟩ *http://dx.doi.org/10.1787/488674548174*

in housing permits suggest that housing investment is likely to decline further in many countries over the near term (Figure 1.10).[16]

... and this contraction is likely to continue...

The scope for further adjustment in housing investment can be crudely assessed by relating the current position both to the most recent peak and to previous troughs in housing investment as a share of GDP (Figure 1.11). On this basis, most countries may be only in the early stages of the adjustment process. The share of housing investment in GDP could fall by a further 1 to 2 percentage points in many, and by more in a few countries, including Ireland, Spain and Denmark.[17] In the United States, the share of housing investment in GDP is now approaching the lows experienced in the past three housing cycles; however, there is no sign yet in the monthly rate of decline in housing starts or permits to suggest that the fall in housing investment will moderate in coming quarters.

... but with some important exceptions

There are, however, some important exceptions to the general tendency for housing investment to act as a drag on future growth. In Japan, following corrections of procedures and regulations,[18] housing

16. In most countries housing permits are a useful leading indicator for housing investment, although their significance needs to be interpreted with care. In particular, a given percentage change in housing permits usually translates to a smaller percentage change in housing investment, see Box 1.2 in OECD (2008c).

17. However, judging where the trough in housing investment will be based on previous cycles is particularly difficult for some countries, and especially Ireland and Spain. This is because the share of housing investment in GDP in both of these countries has, until the recent peak, been trending up since the mid-1990s, partly reflecting rapid population growth as well as a catch-up effect as the number of dwellings *per capita* is relatively low in comparison with other European countries.

18. In Japan, the poorly prepared introduction of stricter building regulations led to a sharp fall in housing investment during 2007.

Figure 1.11. **Housing investment may fall much further**

Housing investment as a share of GDP

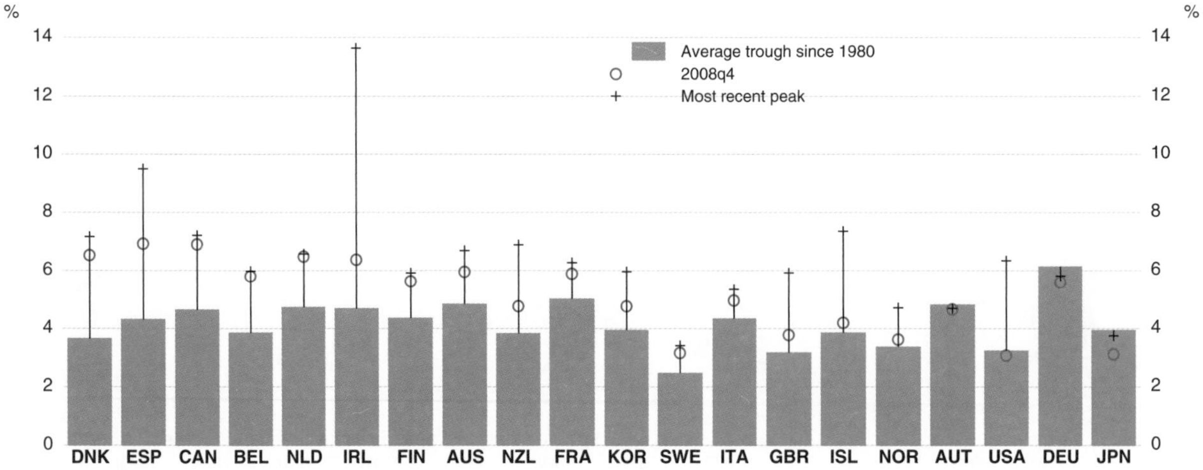

Note: Countries are ranked according to the difference between their position in 2008Q4 and the average of previous troughs.
Source: OECD Economic Outlook 84 database.

StatLink 🔗 http://dx.doi.org/10.1787/488705473036

investment is likely to recover, while in Germany, which did not experience a housing upturn earlier in this decade, housing investment is historically low in relation to GDP and is unlikely to fall significantly in the near future.

Real house prices are falling in many countries

Softening house prices confirm the picture of a widespread housing downturn; for all but a few of the OECD countries for which data are readily available, real house prices (deflated by the consumer price index) are clearly decelerating, and real house prices are falling year-on-year in about two-thirds (Table 1.5).

There are signs that the US housing downturn may be moderating...

The extent of any further fall in US house prices is of particular importance given their central role in the financial turmoil. House prices have already declined 19% from their peak according to the 20-city Case-Shiller index and 6% according to the Federal Housing Finance Agency (FHFA) purchase-only house price index. In relation to *per capita* incomes both house price indices are approaching their long-run averages.[19] Although the stock of unsold properties is falling and home sales may have stabilised (Figure 1.12), tighter credit conditions and forced sales associated with rising foreclosures suggest that house prices will continue to decline into 2009. The current projections incorporate a drop in

19. The house price indices produced by the Federal Housing Finance Agency (FHFA), formerly the Office for Federal Housing Enterprise Oversight (OFHEO), are more representative of house prices in different regions of the country, whereas the Case-Shiller house price index is more representative of houses purchased under different types of mortgage (including non-conventional ones) but less representative of houses purchased in rural areas. The Case-Shiller indices show both a more pronounced run-up in house prices during the boom as well as a more pronounced fall than the FHFA indices.

Table 1.5. **Real house prices are falling in most countries**

	Per cent annual rate of change				Level relative to long-term average [1]		
	2000-2005	2006	2007 [2]	Latest quarter [3]	Price-to-rent ratio	Price-to-income ratio	Lastest available quarter
United States	5.6	4.5	-0.3	-5.7	123	102	Q2 2008
Japan	-4.6	-3.3	-1.1	-1.6	69	66	Q1 2008
Germany	-3.1	-1.8	-2.2	-3.0	71	64	Q4 2007
France	9.4	10.0	4.9	-0.8	159	138	Q2 2008
Italy	6.5	4.1	3.1	1.0	127	114	Q1 2008
United Kingdom	9.8	3.8	8.4	-8.1	151	141	Q3 2008
Canada	6.2	9.1	8.4	-0.2	182	127	Q2 2008
Australia	7.8	4.1	8.8	-2.1	168	143	Q3 2008
Denmark	5.7	19.4	2.9	-5.0	162	143	Q1 2008
Finland	4.0	8.4	5.5	-4.0	146	105	Q3 2008
Ireland	7.9	10.5	-1.8	-10.9	167	133	Q2 2008
Netherlands	2.9	2.9	2.6	-0.1	156	158	Q3 2008
Norway	4.5	10.7	11.5	-6.8	158	121	Q3 2008
New Zealand	9.7	6.9	8.3	-8.2	150	146	Q2 2008
Spain	12.2	6.3	2.6	-5.0	187	147	Q3 2008
Sweden	6.0	10.6	8.6	0.8	160	120	Q2 2008
Switzerland	1.7	1.4	1.3	0.8	86	75	Q3 2008
Euro area[4,5]	4.6	4.0	1.7	-1.8	127	111	
Total of above countries[5]	4.2	3.6	1.5	-3.8	122	104	

Note: House prices deflated by the Consumer Price Index.
1. Long-term average = 100, latest quarter available.
2. Average of available quarters where full year is not yet complete.
3. Increase over a year earlier to the latest available quarter.
4. Germany, France, Italy, Spain. Finland, Ireland and the Netherlands.
5. Using 2000 GDP weights.
Source: Girouard *et al.* (2006).

StatLink 🔗 http://dx.doi.org/10.1787/501634025654

nominal house prices (based on the FHFA sales-only index) of 6½ per cent in the year to the end of 2008 and a further drop of 4% to the end of 2009.

... although there are downside risks

While the current projections imply a somewhat more severe and prolonged housing correction compared with previous US housing cycles,[20] there is still a downside risk given the financial crisis and the fact that typical business cycle effects have yet to kick in. Foreclosures are rising on all categories of mortgages (Figure 1.13), but appear so far to have been mainly driven by falling house prices rather than more general weakness in the real economy.[21] There is a risk going forward that the

20. Case (2008) presents evidence that "the macro indicators are at exactly the levels where the bottom has been reached in the last three housing cycles, and the state level relationship between house prices and income are not far off their traditional bottoms".
21. For evidence of the link between falling house prices and foreclosures see Case (2008), Demyanyk and van Hemert (2008), Gerardi *et al.* (2007), Greenlaw *et al.* (2008).

Figure 1.12. **The stock of unsold US houses is falling**

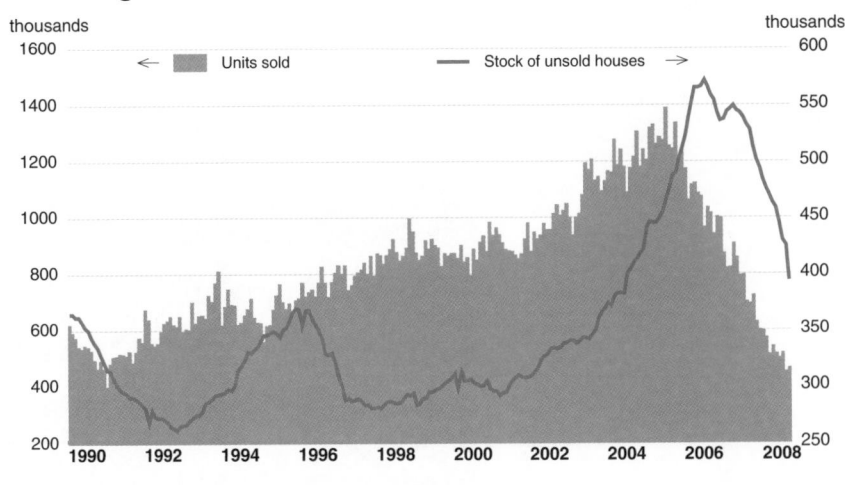

Source: Datastream.

StatLink http://dx.doi.org/10.1787/488715868881

Figure 1.13. **US foreclosure and delinquency rates are rising**

Share of loans

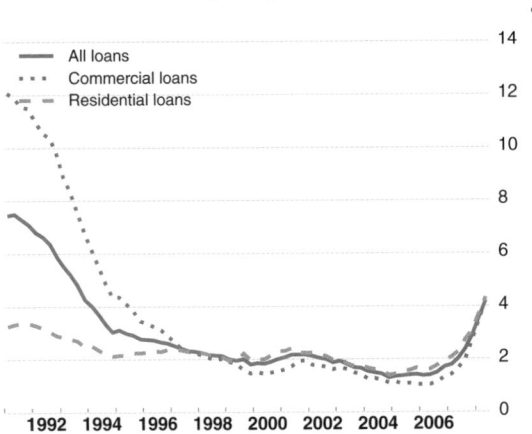

Source: Datastream.

StatLink http://dx.doi.org/10.1787/488770541300

deterioration in the labour market combines with worsening conditions in financial and housing markets to produce a spiral of foreclosures, falling house prices, tighter credit conditions and further weakness in the real economy, which would cause house prices to substantially undershoot any level consistent with fundamentals.[22]

22. Hatzius (2008) estimates that an additional 10% home price decline from mid-2008 levels would be consistent with total eventual residential mortgage credit losses of $636 billion, with the associated reduction in credit supply lowering real GDP growth in 2008 and 2009 by 1.8 percentage points *per annum*. If house prices were instead to fall by 20% from mid-2008 levels, losses would rise to $868 billion, with a correspondingly larger hit to GDP.

*Other countries
are also vulnerable
to falling house prices*

Many other countries also appear vulnerable to a fall in house prices, which in relation to either *per capita* incomes or rents are still well above long-run averages, and even previous cyclical peaks (Table 1.5 above).[23] A number of factors have driven up the fundamental level of house prices, particularly low nominal and real interest rates and the liberalisation of mortgage finance. In addition, rapidly growing house prices, by fostering expectations of continuing capital gains, may have led to some over-shooting of fundamentals. In previous housing cycles, the phase of contracting house prices typically lasted around five years with an average fall in real house prices of the order of 25%.[24]

*Falling house prices have
been driving US
foreclosures so far*

The linkage between falling house prices and foreclosures may be stronger in the United States than in other countries, given that the easing in US lending standards over the period 2004-06 meant that an unusually large fraction of homeowners ended up with little or negative equity in their properties once house prices started falling. The "no recourse" nature of some US mortgage loans may encourage borrowers to default once they have negative equity in their properties, although the situation differs across states and between different types of mortgages (OECD, 2008a). However, even where recourse is the statutory norm, loans may be *de facto* non-recourse because most states have a non-judicial foreclosure process, which is usually cheaper and quicker than systems where court action is required.

*House price effects depend
on mortgage markets*

The macroeconomic effects of any house price correction are likely to be larger among those countries where mortgage markets are more complete, which in turn facilitates equity withdrawal.[25] In addition to the United States, such countries include the United Kingdom, Canada, Australia and Netherlands and some in the Nordic area. These also tend to be the countries where consumption is most strongly correlated with house prices (Catte *et al.*, 2004). However, among the group of countries with more complete mortgage markets, falling house prices are only expected in the United States, United Kingdom and to a much lesser extent in Australia and Denmark. In both the

23. Indeed, it is noteworthy that, relative to these benchmarks, the rise in house prices in the United States does not appear at all exceptional in international comparison.

24. The main characteristics of real house price cycles from 1970 to the mid-90s can be summarized as follows: the average cycle lasted about ten years; during the expansion phase of about six years, real house prices increased on average by close to 40%; and in the subsequent contraction phase, which lasted around five years, the average fall in prices has been on the order of 25% (Girouard *et al.*, 2006).

25. Muellbauer (2007 and 2008) emphasises the transmission of housing wealth effects *via* changes in collateral for both the United States and United Kingdom and argues more generally that the link between housing wealth and consumption is likely to be dependent on the institutional set up of mortgage markets. He finds that for both Italy and Japan, two countries with relatively illiberal mortgage markets, that higher house prices reduce consumption as the young are forced to save more to be able to afford a house.

United States and United Kingdom weaker house prices and tightening lending standards have already led to substantial falls in housing equity withdrawal, which is likely to contribute to weaker consumption going forward (as "back-of-the-envelope" calculations referred to earlier illustrate for the United States).[26]

A commercial property slump could exacerbate financial stress

Falling property prices could further exacerbate financial stress to the extent that they lead to a downturn in the commercial property sector particularly given that commercial property market booms and busts have often been associated with banking crises. In the United States, commercial property prices have already fallen sharply[27] and the (30-day plus) delinquency rate on commercial loans has almost caught up with that on residential loans. This raises the spectre of a commercial property slump similar to that in the early 1990s, when delinquency rates eventually far exceeded those on residential property, leading to further serious financial problems for many banks. Moreover, the exposure of banks to commercial real estate lending (as a share of bank assets) appears as large as in the early 1990s and could be exacerbated if problems in securitised residential mortgages spill over into securitised commercial mortgages (Garner, 2008).

Commodity prices have fallen

Oil prices have been falling...

Oil prices have followed a rollercoaster path. In July 2008, the crude oil price peaked at $144 a barrel (Brent), having risen some 60% in less than six months, to reach an historic high in both nominal and real terms. Since then, it has fallen to around $50 a barrel, some $20 below the 2007 average (Figure 1.14, upper panel).[28] A major factor behind the recent oil price declines has been falling oil demand, as current and prospective global economic activity weakens. However, given that fundamental macroeconomic factors, which can account for much of the oil price rise from 1999 to 2007 (Box 1.1), have more difficulty explaining the levels attained in mid-2008, recent price falls may also represent a correction following earlier overshooting.

26. In the United States, estimates of the "active" component of housing equity withdrawal (which is composed of cash-out re-financing and home equity borrowing that are discretionary actions to extract home equity and so are more likely to be causally-related to spending) have fallen from an average of 5¼ per cent of personal income over the period 2003-06 to only 1% in the second quarter of 2008. For the United Kingdom, Bank of England estimates suggest that housing equity withdrawal has fallen from an average of 6% of post-tax income over the period 2003-06 to –1% in the second quarter of 2008.
27. US commercial property prices were down 9% in the year to third quarter of 2008 according to an index produced by the MIT Centre for Real Estate which includes the prices of industrial, retail, office and large apartment buildings.
28. The swing in the price of oil has been less extreme measured in euros (and many other currencies) as the dollar has tended to depreciate while oil prices were rising and has appreciated as they fell.

OECD ECONOMIC OUTLOOK 84 – ISBN 978-92-64-05469-1 – © OECD 2008

Figure 1.14. **Oil prices have been falling recently**

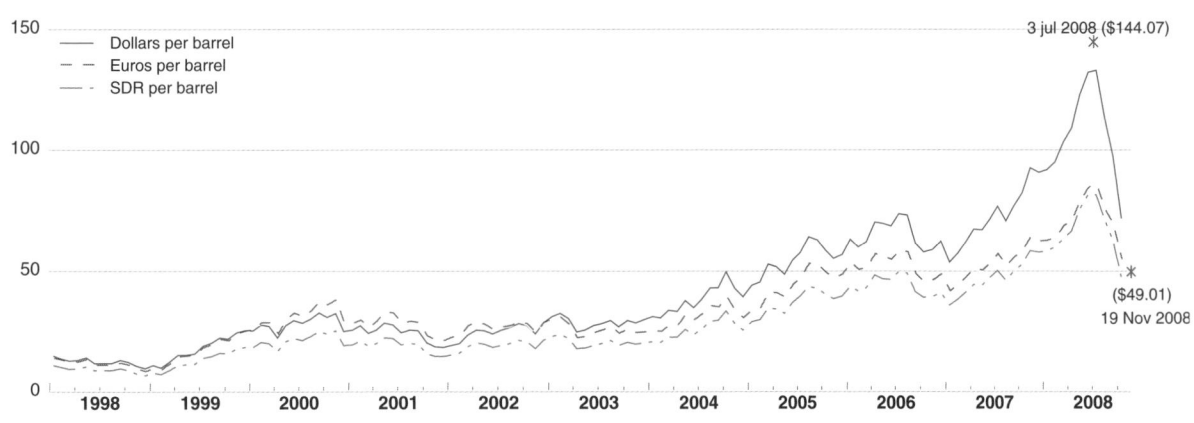

Oil prices
Brent crude, monthly averages

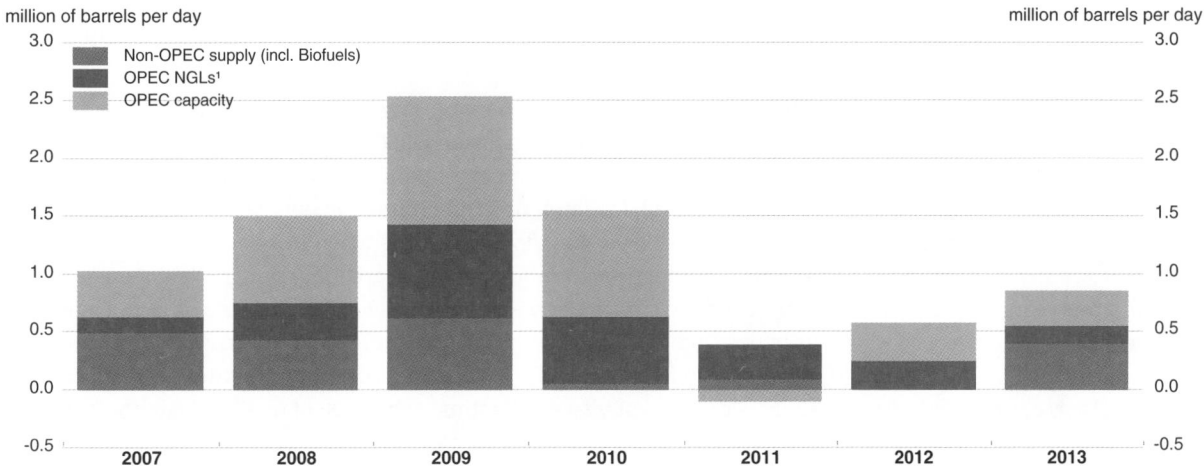

World oil supply capacity growth

1. NGLs refers to natural gas liquids.

Source: Datastream; IMF, Exchange Rates data; and IEA.

StatLink http://dx.doi.org/10.1787/488775237701

Box 1.1. **The rise in oil prices: how much can be explained?**

This box looks at how much of the dramatic rise in oil prices seen over the past decade can be explained by recourse to a straightforward and basic model of supply and demand for oil, calibrated with reasonable values for price and income elasticities. Such an approach, while admittedly simplistic, has the advantage of being able to analyse developments in both supply and demand.

Two versions of the basic model, described in Appendix 1.A2, were calibrated, one in which the price elasticity of demand rises from its short-term to its long-term value over ten years and another in which this process takes 15 years. In each case, the income elasticity of demand was held constant at its long-run value while the price elasticity of supply was held at its short run value, plausibly reflecting the time frame it takes for new production to come on-stream. Applying these latter two assumptions improved the fit of each version.

Box 1.1. **The rise in oil prices: how much can be explained?** (cont.)

Price projections are subject to large uncertainties due to difficulties in estimating price and income elasticities, shifts in economic structures and a lack of information about relevant variables such as capacity utilisation. Nevertheless both model versions seem to broadly capture the run-up in oil prices observed in this decade. For example, from 1999 until 2007, they can account for about 70 to 90% of the observed run-up in prices, depending on the speed of adjustment of demand to its long-run price elasticity (figure, upper left panel). However, including 2008 or looking at year-to-year changes more generally, the performance is less impressive. Indeed, price increases are substantially under-predicted for the past few years and over-predicted through the first years of the decade by the models.

To better understand what occurred over the past few years, demand and supply were predicted separately, treating actual prices as given.[1] This analysis suggests that the extent of the run-up in oil prices since 2003 was due to both much stronger than expected oil demand growth and, from 2005 onward, a weaker than anticipated oil supply response to rising prices (figure, upper right panel). Concentrating on these developments separately:

● The acceleration of world oil demand in the face of high prices was largely driven by buoyant oil consumption in emerging markets, coming in particular from China and the Middle East (figure, lower left panel). In these economies, demand was reinforced by the relatively high energy intensity of manufacturing production and construction, strong economic growth and subsidised fuel consumption. Oil demand in OECD economies drifted up more modestly.

● While oil supply might have been expected to rise with the very large increase in price, it has been relatively flat after 2004, on account of modest contributions from OPEC sources along with the secular decline of crude oil production in the OECD area (figure, lower right panel). OPEC supply restraint reflects agreed-upon production cuts. Outside the cartel, investment in oil production, which had been relatively subdued when oil prices were low during the 1990s, was slow to resume when prices rose. The time lags between investment decisions and new production coming on stream are long, ranging between seven and ten years or even more and project delays have been evident (IEA, 2006). Estimates of mature field decline-rates have recently been revised upward, implying that large additions to new production are needed each year just to hold world supply steady.[2] At the same time, costs of oil production and field development have increased steeply over the past years, reflecting a shortage of qualified labour as well as drilling and engineering capacity, coupled with high costs for raw materials.

● There were as well a number of special events that disrupted supply over this period ranging from climatic factors (hurricanes in the Gulf of Mexico) to geopolitical developments (disruptions to oil fields in Iraq, Nigeria and Venezuela). In addition, the depreciation of the dollar as well as a long period of low interest rates may have also weakened the supply response (Akram, 2008).

Going forward, the model (using the ten-year time frame for the adjustment of demand price elasticities) would predict only a small price increase between 2008 and 2010 from the 2008 predicted value of around $60. With economic growth as projected in this *Economic Outlook*, the oil price would increase to about $65 by 2010. Under an alternative scenario with growth 3 percentage points lower outside the OECD area in 2009 and 2010, the oil price would be roughly $60 in 2010.

1. The ten-year lag version of the model, which is more plausible in terms of response times.
2. According to IEA estimates, 3.5 million barrels per day of new production per year are needed to hold world oil supply constant (IEA, 2008). By comparison, over the past two years net annual additions to oil supply totalled 0.5 mb/d on average.

Box 1.1. **The rise in oil prices: how much can be explained?** *(cont.)*

Explaining oil price changes

Oil price: actual and simulated

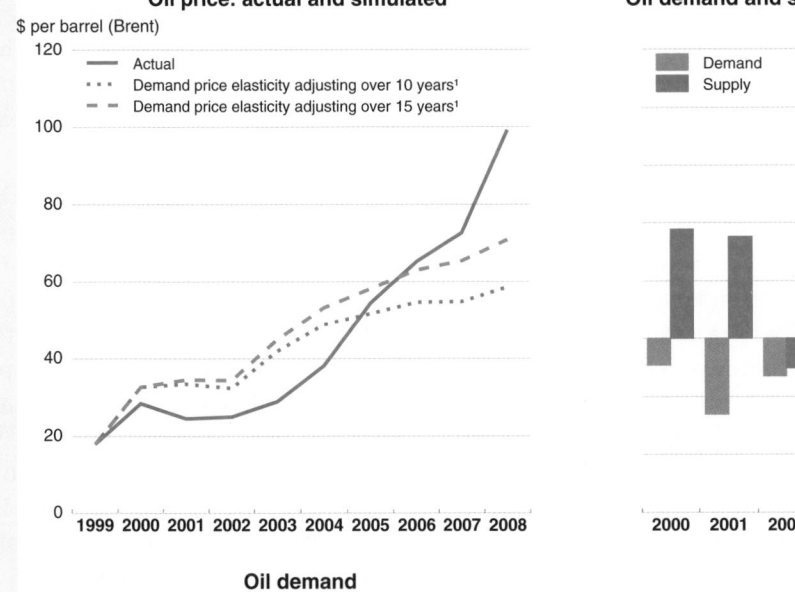

Oil demand and supply: actual minus simulated[2]

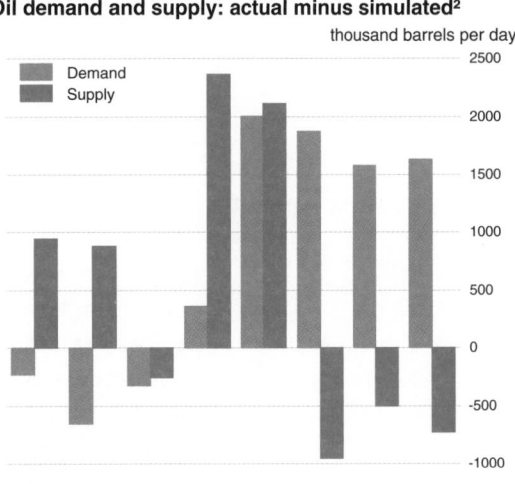

Oil demand

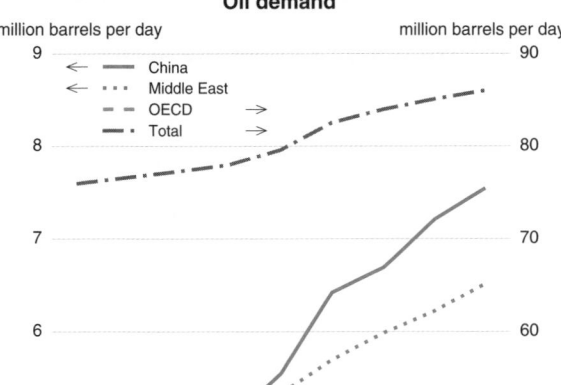

Oil supply[3]

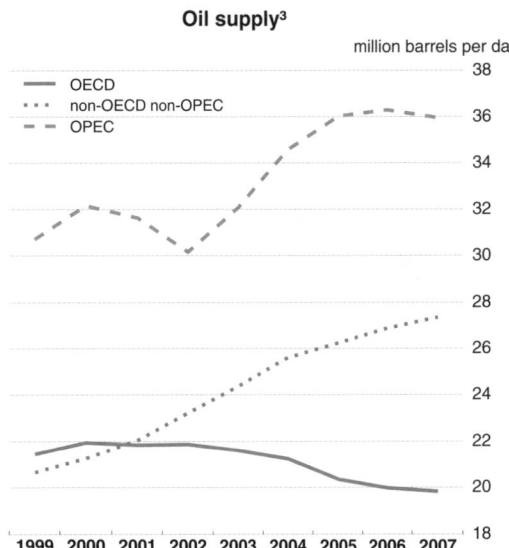

1. Adjustment from short-term to long-term.
2. Actual minus simulated change in demand and supply, respectively. Predictions of demand and supply are generated by using the model's demand and supply equations, respectively, treating prices and income as given.
3. OPEC including Ecuador and Angola; non-OECD non-OPEC excluding Ecuador and Angola; without processing gains and biofuels from sources outside Brazil and the United States.

Source: IEA; and OECD calculations.

StatLink 🔗 http://dx.doi.org/10.1787/500056317788

... and may remain around their current level...

The projections presented here are based on the technical assumption that the Brent price stays close to $60 per barrel.[29] With high oil-price volatility and considerable uncertainty about supply and demand, actual oil price developments are subject to a large degree of uncertainty. Over the coming quarters, weaker world economic growth will restrain oil demand, and world supply is likely to benefit from new projects going forward (Figure 1.14, lower panel). However, working in the opposite direction, OPEC announced its intention to tighten crude supplies in October and there is also evidence that delays in investment projects will continue to restrain oil supply.[30]

... as may other commodity prices...

Non-oil commodity prices have also declined from their recent peaks (Figure 1.15). Expectations of a record world wheat crop, continuing improvements in yield prospects for major coarse grains, and the recent downtrend in energy prices all contributed to the drop in food prices. Food prices are assumed to decline modestly over the next couple of years, bottoming out at a still-high level in 2010.[31] An increasing share of crops used for bio-fuel production as well as robust demand from emerging markets is likely to keep food prices relatively high in the medium term.[32] Softening demand for base metals reflects weakness in construction (damping in particular demand for aluminium, copper and zinc) and in manufacturing sectors, notably automobile production. Prices for metals and ores are assumed to stabilise around current reduced levels.

Figure 1.15. **Non-oil commodity prices are declining**

Index Jan 2000=100

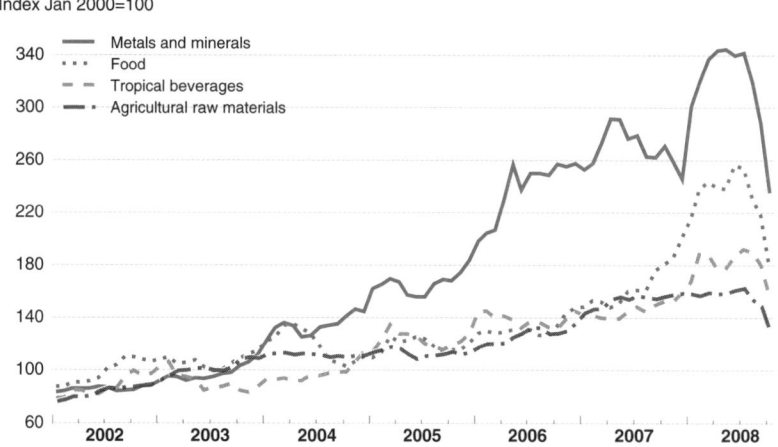

Source: OECD, Main Economic Indicators database.

StatLink http://dx.doi.org/10.1787/488827164288

... reducing inflationary pressures

The decline of commodity prices since the previous *Economic Outlook* is lowering inflation and hence improving real income growth among

29. Alquist and Kilian (2008) present arguments as to why a constant oil price assumption may provide better forecasts than using forward prices.
30. Slippage has been estimated at up to 12 months on average for the large projects surveyed by the IEA (2008).
31. This is in line with the food price projections presented in OECD (2008d).
32. See OECD (2008d and e).

consumers. Compared with the second quarter of 2008, international oil and food prices in dollars have fallen by around 40 and 30% respectively. For the United States, the corresponding impact on consumer prices is a fall by around 1¼ per cent. The effect on the euro area will only be about ¾ per cent, due to the recent depreciation of the euro against the dollar. In addition there are likely to be second round effects as other prices rise less due to lower transportation and other costs.[33] Though the exact timing of these effects is uncertain, the real income effects of recent commodity price developments will mitigate some of the effects of the financial turmoil.

Exchange rates have also been affected by the crisis

The dollar has risen   The worsening of the financial crisis in recent months, and with it heightened risk aversion, has spilled over into currency markets, in several cases reversing exchange rate trends that had been apparent since the onset of financial difficulties in mid-2007 (Figure 1.16). The dollar, which had been depreciating in effective terms up until early summer has since changed direction, posting gains against virtually all currencies. Its recent strength reflects in part its status as a reserve currency and in part the attractiveness of the liquid US Treasury bond market at a time of widespread uncertainty about counterparties.[34]

Figure 1.16. **Exchange rates have been affected by the turmoil**
Cumulative changes in nominal effective exchange rate

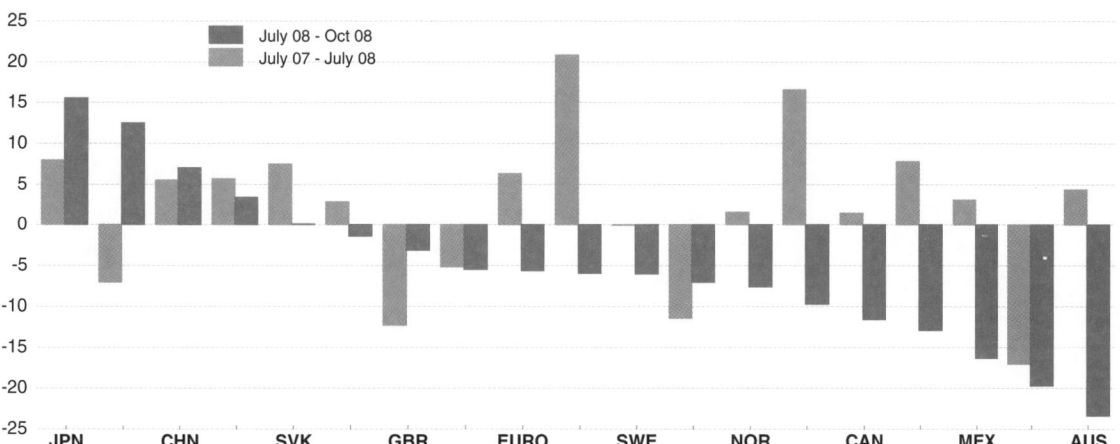

Source: OECD Economic Outlook 84 database.

StatLink http://dx.doi.org/10.1787/488876807828

33. These calculations are based on food and energy making up around 15 and 10% of the US consumption basket, respectively, and evidence that the long run pass through of international commodity price developments to domestic prices is around 0.05 for food and 0.25 for fuel for advanced economies (IMF, 2008a). IMF (2008a) also estimates that food prices have substantial effects on other prices. Other evidence suggests that just the recent movements in energy prices alone will reduce overall consumer prices by 1¼ per cent, though this estimate may overstate the effect (Fisher and Marshall, 2006).

34. An important implication is that the sizeable US current account deficit – which has been declining steadily since 2007 and is projected to continue to do so – is being financed smoothly.

*... as have the yen and
Swiss franc*

The recent rise in the yen against virtually all currencies reflects the unwinding of the carry trade in an environment of increased risk aversion and where interest rate differentials relative to Japan have narrowed and are likely to narrow further. While the Swiss franc has depreciated *vis-à-vis* the dollar, it has tended to rise against the currencies of Switzerland's more important trading partners, likely also reflecting some unwinding of carry trades.

*Many other currencies have
depreciated*

At the same time, most other OECD currencies have been depreciating in effective terms. Driving the extent of particular changes over this period seems to be perceptions of weakening relative economic prospects (the euro area and the United Kingdom), terms of trade declines (Australia, Canada, Mexico and Norway) and exposure to severe banking problems (the United Kingdom). For the most part, these currency changes have gone in the direction of helping economies to adjust to financial and demand shocks.

*Hungary and Iceland
experienced painful
disruptions*

For a number of smaller economies with specific vulnerabilities (notably large current account deficits, significant un-hedged foreign currency loans and/or rigid exchange rates), changes in investor sentiment could potentially have adverse effects. Such problems are dramatically illustrated by recent events in Hungary and especially Iceland. In Hungary sentiment towards forint-denominated assets deteriorated in October amid investor concerns about the large amount of un-hedged foreign currency loans of households. With the exchange rate coming under pressure, policy rates have been increased sharply to attract foreign financing. There has, however, been some improvement in the situation since the International Monetary Fund, World Bank and European Central Bank jointly offered Hungary € 25 billion ($32 billion) in loans. As noted above, Iceland suffered severe financial market dislocation beginning in early October as foreign investors withdrew funding from the country's three large banks.[35] In the wake of this crisis, the Icelandic króna depreciated massively *vis-à-vis* the euro and the dollar in a matter of days, and short-term money market rates rose to dramatic heights. The negative fallout for the economy is expected to be large, worsening an already deteriorated economic situation. A large financing package, involving various international bodies, is in the process of being negotiated, with the aim of restoring investor confidence.

Non-OECD growth is likely to provide less support to OECD activity

*Non-OECD economies have
been slowing...*

Over the past half decade, non-OECD economies as a group have grown rapidly, accounting for roughly half of the growth in world trade, and more recently have been an important source of demand for the aggregate OECD

35. Iceland's three main banks, which had combined assets of close to ten times the country's GDP, relied heavily on foreign sources for funding. Because of the size of their balance sheets, investors had serious concerns the central bank might be unable to act as a lender of last resort. In response, the authorities had increased foreign exchange reserves and arranged currency swap agreements with other Nordic central banks. These efforts were unsuccessful and the government has been forced to nationalise the banks.

economy as growth weakened. In the projections presented here, growth in major non-OECD economies is expected to slow in 2009, in most cases by over 1½ percentage points compared with the previous *Economic Outlook*, to below its trend rate, and then to recover in 2010 (see the following section for a fuller description of the non-OECD projections). At the same time, there are downside risks to these growth projections, each of which would affect countries differently. These include: core inflation pressures which have been evident in some of these economies; a further backing up of the cost of borrowing; and additional falls in commodity prices.

... and a significant further slowdown would have a large impact

To indicate the sensitivity of the current projections of OECD growth to a major slowdown in non-OECD activity, the OECD's Global Model has been simulated under the assumption that non-OECD domestic demand growth slows by 3 percentage points (Table 1.6).[36] While such a shock is

Table 1.6. **The effects of a slowdown in non-OECD domestic demand would have significant repercussions**

	Weaker non-OECD demand (3% ex post)		
	2009	2010	2011
United States			
GDP growth	-0.17	-0.34	-0.30
Inflation (consumer price deflator)	-0.03	-0.10	-0.37
Current balance (% of GDP)	-0.03	-0.19	-0.39
Euro area			
GDP growth	-0.21	-0.38	-0.51
Inflation (consumer price deflator)	-0.05	-0.18	-0.43
Current balance (% of GDP)	-0.01	-0.07	-0.23
Japan			
GDP growth	-0.36	-0.57	-0.63
Inflation (consumer price deflator)	-0.19	-0.29	-0.68
Current balance (% of GDP)	-0.30	-0.64	-0.92
Total OECD			
GDP growth	-0.24	-0.42	-0.47
Inflation (consumer price deflator)	-0.07	-0.19	-0.49
Current balance (% of GDP)	-0.08	-0.26	-0.47
Non-OECD			
GDP growth	-2.32	-2.45	-2.31
Current balance (% of GDP)	0.23	0.58	1.09

Note: In the simulations, nominal bilateral exchange rates are held unchanged. The monetary authorities are assumed to follow a Taylor rule and set short-term interest rates taking into account the deviation of output from potential as well as the difference between actual inflation and what is known about central bank inflation objectives. Regarding fiscal policy, the authorities are assumed to target a fixed debt-to-GDP ratio over the medium term.

Source: OECD Economic Outlook 84 database.

StatLink http://dx.doi.org/10.1787/501634486530

36. The model takes account of important international trade and financial linkages among the major economies and their accompanying feedback mechanisms. While highly aggregated, it does explicitly identify China and treats the other non-OECD economies as a group. For a description of the model and its properties, see Hervé *et al.* (2007) as well as Appendix 1.A1 in OECD (2008c).

large, it is not unprecedented.[37] In the event, all the major regions identified by the model would see a reduction in growth, with activity being hit by more in Japan, where linkages to non-OECD Asia are important. Absent in these simulations are any feedback effects onto financial market risk premia, which could have potentially large negative effects. There would also be a moderation in inflation,[38] which would provide some scope for more accommodative monetary policy. However, in countries where interest rates are already expected to be close to the zero bound the room for manoeuvre would be limited, and there would therefore be a heightened risk of deflation.

Growth prospects

Area wide growth is continuing to weaken

The assumptions underlying these projections are laid out in Box 1.2. Activity in the OECD area is projected to continue to decline over the first half of 2009 (Table 1.7). Indeed, in each of the first three quarters of 2009, OECD-wide GDP is expected to continue to be lower than a year earlier; the last time there was a fall in OECD GDP over the previous four quarters was in the early 1980s. Both consumption and particularly investment are expected to fall over the first half of 2009, while export volumes remain stagnant. Growth is then projected to firm gradually, only reaching potential rates by mid-2010 with growth in export volumes approaching trend growth rates about the same time. The OECD unemployment rate is expected to rise from a low of 5½ per cent at the beginning of 2008 to 7¼ per cent in 2010, its highest level since the mid-1990s.

Activity will decelerate across both the OECD and non-OECD

Notwithstanding the greater uncertainty attached to trend measures of output for emerging market economies, the OECD is more severely affected than the non-OECD insofar as growth during 2009 is likely to fall more below trend (Figure 1.17). World trade growth is expected to slump to less than 2% in 2009 (Table 1.8), its slowest annual rate of growth since 2001, and less than a quarter of its average over the previous five years.

Most countries will endure severe and prolonged downturns

For the OECD as a whole the depth of the coming downturn, as measured by the output gap, will be more severe than average,[39] and will be the most severe since the downturn experienced in the early 1980s. Those countries where activity is most affected, judged by the degree to which output is projected to fall below estimates of potential output (Figure 1.18), include: those most directly affected by financial turmoil,

37. In the case of China it represents about a one standard deviation change in growth, while for the other non-OECD economies (which are treated as a group in the model) the shock would be equivalent to just less than a two standard deviation change.
38. Some further, although modest, help would come from lower oil prices although this has not been incorporated in the simulation. Based on the oil demand income elasticities, discussed in Box 1.1, the weakening in global demand would lower the price of oil by 7% by 2010.
39. This considers all downturns since 1970, where a downturn is taken to be defined as in Table 1.4.

Box 1.2. **Policy and other assumptions underlying the projections**

Fiscal policy assumptions are based as closely as possible on legislated tax and spending provisions (current policies or "current services"). Where policy changes have been announced but not legislated, they are incorporated if it is deemed clear that they will be implemented in a shape close to that announced. The fiscal costs of the measures to support financial institutions could be large but for the most part they are not fully reflected in current projections for two main reasons. First, guarantees are contingent liabilities and thus are off balance sheet as long as they are not called. Second, several recapitalisation plans are still conditional. Nonetheless, an increase of 5% of GDP or more in both government financial assets and liabilities is factored in for Belgium, Iceland, Luxembourg, the Netherlands, the United Kingdom and the United States over the period 2008-09 (see Box 1.4). For the present projections, the implications are as follows:

● For the United States it is assumed that no additional fiscal stimulus package will be enacted next year and that the temporarily extended unemployment compensation programme will not be renewed after its expiration at the end of 2008.

● In Japan, the scheduled hike in the pension contribution rate will increase government revenue by about 0.2% of GDP per year through 2010. The projections incorporate the two supplementary budgets' expenditures (including ¥ 2 trillion, 0.4% of GDP, in lump-sum payments to households) in addition to spending cuts in line with the Fiscal Year (FY) 2008 budget and the medium-term fiscal reform plan.

● For Germany, the 2008 corporate tax reform as well as a net decrease in social security contribution rates are built into the projections, equivalent to around 0.4% of GDP. In 2009, the planned further decrease of the unemployment insurance contribution rate is expected to be compensated by higher contribution rates for health insurance. In France and Italy, the respective 2009 budgets involve ambitious plans for consolidation over the next few years, based on tight spending limits including cuts in public employment. The projections partially incorporate these plans but assume some slippage on the expenditure targets, as well as lower tax revenues due to weak activity.

Policy-controlled interest rates are set in line with the stated objectives of the relevant monetary authorities, conditional upon the OECD projections of activity and inflation, which may differ from those of the monetary authorities. The interest-rate profile is not to be interpreted as a projection of central bank intentions or market expectations thereof.

● In the United States, the target federal funds rate is assumed to be eased to ½ per cent early in 2009 and then, as the economic environment begins to improve, interest rates are raised towards the end of 2009 and in 2010 reaching 2½ per cent by December 2010. It is also assumed that much of the quantitative easing will be withdrawn over the course of 2009 and 2010 as financial market conditions normalise.

● In the euro area, policy rates are assumed to be eased by 125 basis points by early 2009, as inflation declines and activity contracts. They will then remain at 2% until mid-2010 before being gradually raised to around 2½ per cent by the end of 2010.

● In Japan, the policy interest rate is assumed to remain at 30 basis points in 2009 and 2010 amid little change in consumer prices.

The projections assume generally unchanged exchange rates from those prevailing on 28 October 2008, with $1 equal to ¥ 95.69 and € 0.80 (or equivalently, € 1 equals $1.25).

Over the projection period the price for a barrel of Brent crude is assumed to be fixed at $60. Food prices are assumed to decline somewhat over the next couple of years, with the decline levelling off in 2010, while prices for metals and ores are assumed to stabilise around current reduced levels.

The cut-off date for information used in the projections is 14 November 2008. Details of assumptions for individual countries are provided in Chapter 2, "Developments in individual OECD countries" and Chapter 3, "Developments in selected non-member economies".

Table 1.7. **Slower domestic demand, partially offset by net exports**

Contributions to GDP growth, per cent of GDP in previous period[1]

	2006	2007	2008	2009	2010
United States					
Final domestic demand	2.8	1.8	0.2	-1.7	1.3
of which: Business investment	0.8	0.6	0.3	-0.9	0.2
Residential investment	-0.4	-0.9	-0.8	-0.5	0.0
Private consumption	2.2	2.0	0.3	-0.8	0.9
Stockbuilding	0.0	-0.4	-0.3	0.0	0.0
Net exports	0.0	0.6	1.4	0.8	0.2
GDP	2.8	2.0	1.4	-0.9	1.6
Japan					
Final domestic demand	1.4	0.8	-0.1	0.6	1.0
of which: Business investment	0.7	0.3	-0.1	-0.2	0.4
Residential investment	0.0	-0.3	-0.3	0.1	0.1
Private consumption	1.1	0.8	0.4	0.4	0.4
Stockbuilding	0.2	0.1	-0.2	0.0	0.0
Net exports	0.8	1.1	0.8	-0.7	-0.4
GDP	2.4	2.1	0.5	-0.1	0.6
Euro area					
Final domestic demand	2.7	2.3	0.7	-0.6	1.1
of which: Business investment	0.8	0.7	0.2	-0.6	0.2
Residential investment	0.4	0.1	-0.2	-0.4	0.0
Private consumption	1.2	0.9	0.2	0.1	0.7
Stockbuilding	0.1	0.0	0.2	0.1	0.0
Net exports	0.1	0.3	0.2	0.0	0.1
GDP	3.0	2.6	1.0	-0.6	1.2
OECD					
Final domestic demand	3.0	2.4	0.9	-0.6	1.4
of which: Business investment	0.8	0.7	0.2	-0.7	0.2
Residential investment	0.0	-0.3	-0.5	-0.4	0.0
Private consumption	1.8	1.6	0.6	-0.2	0.8
Stockbuilding	0.1	-0.1	-0.1	0.0	0.0
Net exports	0.1	0.3	0.6	0.2	0.1
GDP	3.1	2.6	1.4	-0.4	1.5

1. Chain-linked calculation for stockbuilding and net exports in USA and Japan.
Source: OECD Economic Outlook 84 database.

StatLink ᵐˢ⌐ http://dx.doi.org/10.1787/501655624278

notably the United States, United Kingdom, Luxembourg and Iceland; countries where the financial turmoil has exposed other vulnerabilities, for example Hungary and Turkey; and those where housing downturns are most pronounced, especially Ireland and Spain and again the United States and United Kingdom. For the euro area the depth of the trough, with output falling more than 3% below potential, is greater than previous downturns, although there are clearly some major within-area differences: in Germany output falls 1½ per cent below potential; for France and Italy the depth of the downturn is larger and slightly greater than average historical experience; whereas, as previously mentioned, Ireland and Spain, by any standard, experience very severe downturns. Output in Canada and Mexico falls more than 3% below potential, mainly because of weakness in their main trading partner, but such a downturn is not exceptional by their own historical standards. Japan is among a small group of countries where output falls less than 1½ per cent below potential over the projection, though estimates of potential are

Figure 1.17. **Global growth is slowing**

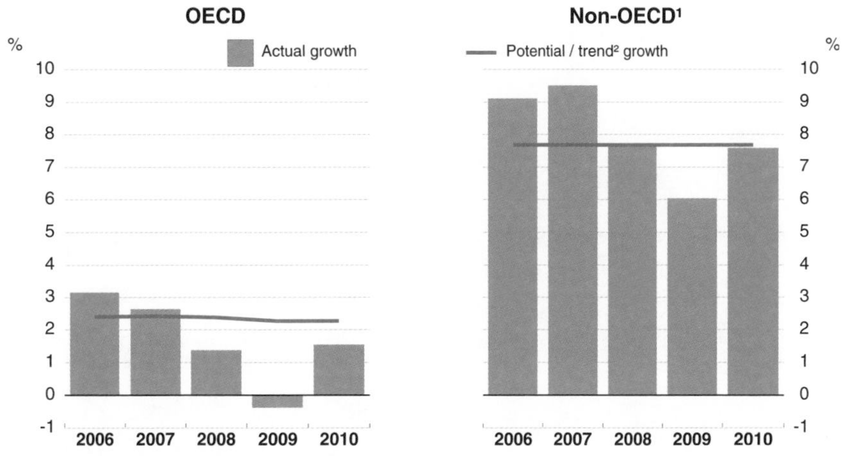

1. The non-OECD region is here taken to be a weighted average, using 2000 GDP weights and PPP's, of Brazil, China, Russian Federation and India which together accounted for about half of non-OECD output in 2000.
2. Trend growth for the non-OECD is the average over the period 2000-07.

Source: OECD Economic Outlook 84 database.

StatLink ᘓᘍ *http://dx.doi.org/10.1787/488886154735*

particularly uncertain in the case of Japan. For most countries the trough in the output gap is not reached until the first half of 2010 and it is only in the second half of 2010 that growth exceeds potential rates, so leaving large output gaps at the end of the projection.

US activity will fall until mid-2009 and recover only slowly...

The US economy will contract over the first half of 2009, with all categories of private sector final domestic demand falling. Consumer spending is projected to decline over the next few quarters reflecting weaker labour market conditions, lower wealth and tighter credit. Business investment is likely to keep on falling well into 2009 as expectations of weak output are reinforced by tight credit conditions. Exports will continue to boost economic growth, though more modestly due to weaker conditions in the rest of the world and the recent appreciation of the dollar. As financial stress begins to ease and the housing downturn finally bottoms out, around the third quarter of 2009, growth should resume. However, the recovery is likely to be weak, with the pace of activity only reaching trend rates by the second half of 2010. In particular, consumer spending will continue to be held back by negative wealth effects and reduced consumer confidence. The implied widening in the output gap, together with weaker oil and commodity prices, should bring inflation down to well below 2%.

... as will activity in the euro area

Economic activity in the euro area is also projected to decline further until the middle of 2009. Tighter financial conditions, subdued income growth, negative wealth effects, rising unemployment and enhanced uncertainty about the economic outlook will damp consumption and business investment. The drag on activity will be accentuated by further

Table 1.8. **World trade slows while external imbalances decline**

	2006	2007	2008	2009	2010
Goods and services trade volume	Percentage change from previous period				
World trade[1]	9.4	7.0	4.8	1.9	5.0
of which: OECD	8.3	5.4	3.2	0.4	3.3
NAFTA	7.0	4.7	2.2	-0.4	2.3
OECD Asia-Pacific	8.2	7.9	5.5	1.2	5.2
OECD Europe	9.0	5.1	3.1	0.6	3.3
Non-OECD Asia	13.0	10.3	7.0	5.2	8.8
Other non-OECD	9.5	10.5	9.3	3.7	6.3
OECD exports	8.8	6.2	4.5	0.8	3.6
OECD imports	7.8	4.6	1.9	0.1	3.1
Trade prices[2]					
OECD exports	3.6	7.7	8.0	-9.8	1.1
OECD imports	4.7	7.5	10.2	-10.4	1.0
Non-OECD exports	8.2	8.6	12.3	-8.0	1.2
Non-OECD imports	4.7	7.0	10.1	-4.8	1.3
Current account balances	Per cent of GDP				
United States	-6.0	-5.3	-4.9	-3.9	-3.6
Japan	3.9	4.8	3.8	4.3	3.9
Euro area	0.4	0.3	-0.4	-0.1	0.0
OECD	-1.6	-1.4	-1.5	-1.1	-1.1
	$ billion				
United States	-788	-731	-696	-562	-537
Japan	172	212	187	231	211
Euro area	43	39	-55	-8	-4
OECD	-591	-557	-650	-447	-444
China	250	372	399	437	472
Dynamic Asia[3]	129	175	182	292	340
Other Asia	-17	-34	-40	14	2
Latin America	50	27	-3	-38	-49
Africa and Middle East	289	336	438	-13	-59
Central and Eastern Europe	63	18	33	-28	-35
Non-OECD	763	894	1009	663	670
World	173	336	360	216	226

Note: Regional aggregates include intra-regional trade.
1. Growth rates of the arithmetic average of import volumes and export volumes.
2. Average unit values in dollars.
3. Dynamic Asia includes Chinese Taipei; Hong Kong, China; Indonesia; Malaysia; Philippines; Singapore and Thailand.
Source: OECD Economic Outlook 84 database.

StatLink ⬛📊 http://dx.doi.org/10.1787/501707801370

declines in residential investment, both as a result of very large falls in Spain and Ireland as well as significant declines in other countries, including France and Italy. Export growth will also be damped for some time as global demand growth slows. Improved financial market conditions, the effects of monetary policy easing and the fallback of headline inflation through 2009 will all help to support an eventual expansion. By the second half of 2010, activity is projected to rise more rapidly than potential, beginning to close the sizable negative output gap.

Japanese activity will stagnate in the second half of 2009

In Japan, output growth will be boosted by the fiscal stimulus over the first half of 2009 but is then projected to stagnate over the second half of the year. The recent appreciation of the yen together with slowing world

Figure 1.18. **The projected trough in the current cycle**
Output gap as a percentage of potential GDP

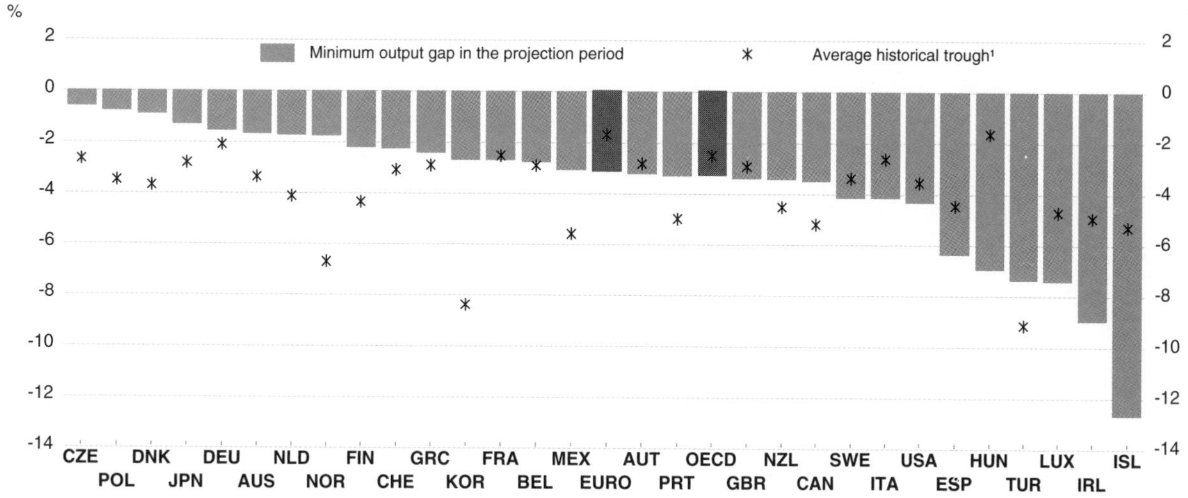

Note: Countries are ranked according to the size of the trough in the forecast period.
1. The trough is defined as the minimum output gap in a downturn, where a downturn is defined as in Table 1.4.
Source: OECD Economic Outlook 84 database.

StatLink ⚙ http://dx.doi.org/10.1787/500003327327

trade suggest that exports will fall during 2009 and make only a minimal contribution to growth in 2010. Instead, stronger domestic demand is projected to lead a modest recovery in GDP growth rising to around 1% (just below the potential rate) by the second half of 2010. Consumption spending will be underpinned by faster gains in real household income on account of slower falls in employment, modest increases in real wages and terms of trade gains. Stronger consumption growth will help to reverse the falls in business investment. The housing markets should continue to normalise, contributing to growth in both 2009 and 2010. The combined effect of past yen appreciation, lower commodity prices and a persistent modest output gap, suggest that headline and core inflation are likely to turn slightly negative during 2009.

UK and Canadian growth will not recover to trend until mid-2010

Activity in the United Kingdom will continue to shrink into the second half of 2009. Ongoing financial stress and housing market adjustment will lead to falling consumption and investment throughout most of 2009. The recovery during 2010 is likely to be muted with output growth only reaching trend rates during the second half of the year. Compared with other major OECD countries, Canada's banking system has been less directly affected by financial turmoil, and the correction in the housing sector is likely to be modest. However, activity will be held back by declining exports resulting from the downturn of its main trading partner and weak world trade growth, with the output gap not beginning to close until world trade growth gains momentum in 2010.

Activity in emerging markets will decelerate

The major emerging market economies will see some further deceleration in activity, reflecting weak demand in the OECD area, a re-pricing of financial risks and the lagged effects of earlier policy reactions to address inflationary pressures. Chinese growth is likely to moderate further in 2009, with over-supply in the housing market and global developments restraining investment and exports, before improving in tandem with the world economy in 2010. The current projections do not, however, incorporate effects from the recently-announced fiscal package. Indian growth is expected to decline further next year, as rising real interest rates weigh on domestic demand, before also recovering in 2010. In Russia, with a sharp reversal in the long upward trend in oil and metal prices, an end to the pattern of terms of trade gains fuelling rapid growth in domestic demand is firmly in prospect. The Brazilian economy should grow robustly, supported by solid domestic demand, although this will be moderated by ongoing policy tightening.

Macroeconomic policy requirements

The crisis requires a co-ordinated and multi-pronged approach

To relieve extreme stress in financial markets and eventually restore normal credit market functioning, policy must deal with three problems that are plaguing financial markets: a break-down of trust, under-capitalisation and illiquidity. A multi-pronged approach is called for and, as discussed above, is under implementation. It is important that announced plans are fully and rapidly implemented, and that international co-operation is stepped up to prevent distortion to competition, increase capacity to deal with cross-border bank failure and minimise negative fallout from policy interventions such as cross-border capital flight to guaranteed regions. Indeed, unilateral action within the euro area to guarantee deposits and other bank liabilities forced other countries to do likewise. Conventional macroeconomic policy instruments have an important role as well. The recent weakening in activity across practically all OECD countries, as well as intensifying financial stress and the fall in commodity prices, has led to a clear shift in concern away from combating inflation and toward limiting the extent of the coming downturn.

Immediate actions to relieve the crisis

There are signs the immediate crisis is being brought under control

Guaranteeing deposits and bank lending and providing equity injections have contributed to directly tackling the crisis of confidence that reached panic proportions in early October 2008 when the complete breakdown of credit markets was threatened with potentially dire consequences for the real economy. Indicators of financial stress within the banking system suggest that policy announcements have recently led to some improvements. Bank credit default swap (CDS) rates in the United States and United Kingdom have fallen back to the levels observed before the financial crisis intensified in September. Nevertheless, spreads between three-month inter-bank and expected policy rates remain unusually high, with least improvement seen in the euro area (Table 1.9). These policy actions are also important complements to the massive push by central banks worldwide to maintain money market liquidity and,

Table 1.9. **Indicators of financial market stress**

	Routine: before August 2007		Turmoil: Aug 2007 to 12 Sep 2008		Crisis: 15 Sep to 14 Oct 2008		Latest observation: 11 Nov 2008
	Average	Standard deviation	Average	Standard deviation	Average	Standard deviation	
Bank credit default swap rates[1]							
United States	21	6	158	97	271	60	**157**
Euro Area	13	4	79	33	170	24	**140**
United Kingdom	10	3	97	33	177	33	**128**
Three-month Treasury euro dollar spread	39	22	125	38	321	81	**210**
Three-month EURIBOR-EONIA swap index spread	6	1	62	16	118	41	**166**

1. An average of 5-year credit default swap rates on bank's senior debt.
Source: OECD calculations.

StatLink ᵃᵢₛₚ *http://dx.doi.org/10.1787/501721024338*

where necessary, directly substitute for private sector credit markets. Such liquidity efforts will need to be maintained in the short term and if necessary extended further. These combined actions have provided governments with a temporary window to implement long-term solutions.

Policy should address recapitalising the banking sector...

Increasing insufficient bank capital should be the first policy priority. Concerns about bank insolvency have severely undermined confidence, destroyed trust in the financial sector and virtually brought normal credit intermediation to a halt. The Japanese financial crisis experience in the 1990s suggests that government purchases of impaired assets from banks cannot resolve a crisis if banks remain under-capitalised (Hoshi and Kashyap, 2008).[40] Conversely, the presence of assets likely to undergo (further) write-downs or write-offs on bank balance sheets may also inhibit seemingly well-capitalised institutions from performing their normal functions. At any rate, international experience shows that a rapid recapitalisation of the banking sector is an important ingredient of a successful and fast resolution of a financial crisis (Ergungor, 2007 and IMF, 2008b).[41] Under-capitalised but viable institutions should be recapitalised quickly and insolvent banks should be managed in an orderly fashion with a view to winding them down.

40. Direct capital injection is also a much more cost-effective way to reduce leverage and increase bank capital than purchasing impaired assets. If leverage (total assets divided by equity) is equal to 10 and the authorities purchase 10% of the balance sheet, and this is used to retire debt, leverage will be reduced by 10% but if the same sum was used to inject capital leverage would fall by 50%.
41. If a broad range of institutions, including the healthiest, takes part in the programmes, this will reduce the stigma associated with participating and thereby increase the effectiveness of the injections.

... while ensuring private sector participation...

Governments faced with banks having extreme difficulty raising private capital quickly and the need to deal with imminent bank failures have resorted in many cases to public capital injections without private sector involvement. Building on the immediate stabilising effects of public capital injections, governments should move to encourage private-sector capital injections and where possible consider applying an implicit market test, for example making further public injections of capital only when they match contributions raised from the private-sector. Other measures to increase private sector capital contributions could include a broad compulsory rights issue. Conditions, such as those imposed by the UK recapitalisation plan, that require participating banks to maintain lending availability at certain levels to homeowners, may seem attractive but could lead to a further misallocation of capital and also delay needed adjustment of the housing market. Governments have also in some cases required the restriction or temporary suspension of dividend payments for banks participating in recapitalisation programmes since they deplete capital. They have also taken preference shares in return for capital injections. This helps to protect taxpayer interest by ensuring a priority claim on bank returns. However, it is important to strike a balance between protecting the tax-payer interest and ensuring that banks take up recapitalisation offers in sufficient numbers to mitigate systematic risk. Banks may be inhibited from participating in public recapitalisation by both the stigma of taking up government assistance and operational restriction conditions that attach to such assistance. It is therefore important that the authorities limit their involvement in the lending decisions of banks.

... and restoring liquidity to securitised credit markets

Restoring and maintaining liquidity in securitised credit markets is a secondary, complementary measure to recapitalisation. The provision of consumer and mortgage finance relies on securitisation of the debt repayments particularly in the United States and this has become increasingly important also elsewhere in the OECD. Restoring liquidity to private securities markets will help to lift credit flows, allow the private sector to avail itself again of the liquidity and credit risk management benefits of securitisation, permit better valuation of assets on balance sheets of financial institutions and reduce reliance on government lending substitutes. The US Treasury is proposing to fund a lending facility using the TARP to provide finance to the purchasers of consumer credit backed securities. This would be a further significant extension of effective direct government lending to the private sector already in place for mortgage lending through the government guaranteed GSEs and the Fed's commercial paper lending facilities. Policy efforts should focus on kick-starting the liquidity of private securitisation markets again but avoid measures that would influence the sectoral allocation of credit or seek to directly support particular industries of a non-systemic nature.

Transparent and complete markets must be maintained

Part of the policy response to the crisis has been the relaxation of mark-to-market rules for asset prices and also the imposition of short selling restrictions. Such changes risk increasing uncertainty and slowing the resolution of the crisis, in particular by allowing problems of under-capitalisation to fester. Relaxing mark-to-market rules may further exacerbate the opaqueness of bank balance sheets that has undermined trust in the financial system. While short selling restrictions can mitigate market panic (by reducing the skewness of negative returns and the frequency of extreme negative returns), they increase overall market volatility (Bris *et al.*, 2003) and induce behaviour counter to the policy goal of stemming price falls, such as investors selling off long positions that they can no longer hedge because they cannot take a short position elsewhere. More generally, they interfere with the price discovery process, by preventing incorporation of all relevant information into prices (Lamba and Ariff, 2006) and in the process reduce market liquidity (Daouk *et al.*, 2006).

Ensuring a return to healthy financial markets

Some policy initiatives have been unconventional

To relieve extreme financial stress and avoid the complete breakdown of credit markets, unconventional policy action was required on a massive scale. Circumstances have forced governments to increase their intervention in the financial sector to a level that is inconsistent with a well functioning private sector market for credit in the long term. In some cases, such as unsecured corporate lending in the United States, the authorities have intervened to directly substitute for the private sector, and across the OECD the seizing up of private sector money markets has required the authorities to substitute for them with a set of bilateral relations between the central bank and individual financial institutions. Governments have increased their exposure to the financial sector through direct equity holdings and the danger of lending being dictated by political considerations has increased. Central banks have accepted a far wider range of collateral against their lending than the government securities they would usually require, including mortgage-linked securities and shares. This has potentially exposed them to greater credit risk. In the near term, financial market conditions may require still further unorthodox policy interventions.

Governments will need a clear and co-ordinated exit strategy

Governments need a clear strategy to exit this situation. As conditions in financial markets normalise, governments should progressively remove these policy interventions, beginning with those that are the most detrimental to the normal operation of private sector credit intermediation. The exit strategy should be internationally co-ordinated and signalled in advance to avoid sudden movements in capital. Failing to co-ordinate risks prolong the adjustment period as countries wait for others to move first in removing various forms of guarantee so as to avoid disadvantaging their own banks.

Conventional monetary policy

Concern has shifted from inflation to downside risks to activity

Following the intensification of the financial crisis in mid-September, policy rates have been cut by virtually all OECD central banks, usually more than once and usually in large steps (Figure 1.19). These cuts took place against a background of extreme financial stress, actual and prospective activity weakness and moderating oil and commodity prices which have increasingly shifted the balance of concerns away from inflationary pressures towards downside risks to activity. Headline inflation, while still high, is declining. Moreover, inflation expectations appear to have remained reasonably well anchored (Box 1.3). Their level before the financial crisis was not unusual in light of the past pick-up in headline inflation and they have since fallen to levels in line with, or below, central bank objectives. Indeed, although not part of the central

Figure 1.19. **Policy rates have been cut**

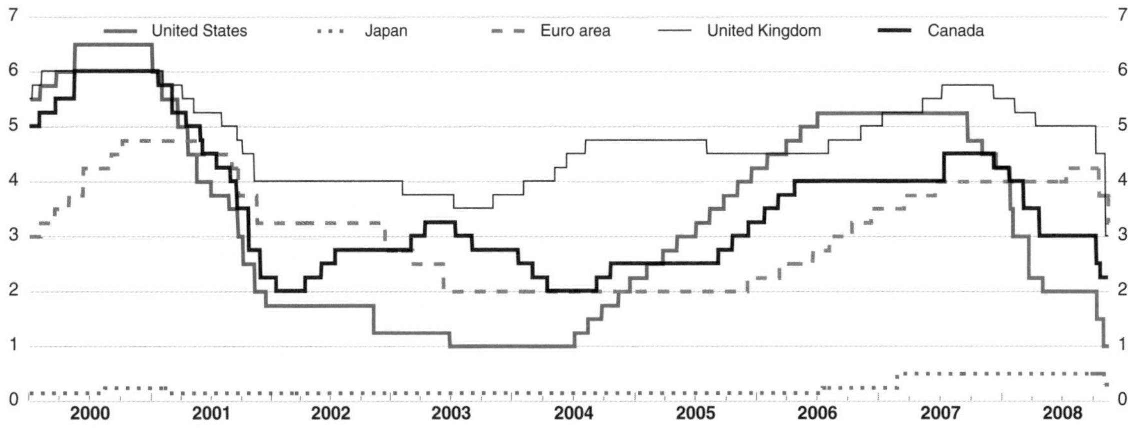

Source: US Federal Reserve; Bank of Japan; European Central Bank; Bank of England; and Bank of Canada.

StatLink http://dx.doi.org/10.1787/500015366064

Box 1.3. **Implications of inflation outcomes for expectations**

With most major OECD countries experiencing noticeable spikes in inflation rates, the anchoring of expectations has become a question of more than theoretical interest. Ideally, credible monetary policy should imply that households, firms and market participants look through recent fluctuations and focus on the central bank target (be it implicit or explicit) when they form their expectations of long-term inflation. A model has been estimated to provide a quantitative description of the strength and speed of the link between inflation outcomes and expectations. Expectations are measured as the yield differential between nominal and real long-term government bonds.[1]

In a first step, Granger causality tests on current inflation and expectations for the average inflation rate over the next ten years indicate that each series helps to forecast the other one. Such a link is to be expected even if monetary policy is fully anchored. The reason is that current inflation is a better predictor of inflation one-to-two years ahead than the central bank target because monetary policy does not aim at instantaneous achievement of the target. Quantitative estimates of the strength of the link are therefore needed to evaluate the stability of expectations in the face of shocks to current inflation.

Box 1.3. **Implications of inflation outcomes for expectations** (cont.)

In a second step, the model simply relates inflation expectations to actual inflation and a constant term. From an economic point of view, this model directly tests the degree of anchoring of inflation expectations, that is to say the extent to which they remain close to a constant value rather than being influenced by outcomes. From a statistical point of view, the model provides accurate coefficients because, even though inflation outcomes and expectations are non-stationary variables, they are co-integrated.[2] The criterion of statistical validity, however, restricts the coverage of G7 economies as inflation outcomes do not co-integrate with bond-implied expectations in Japan. To avoid monetary regime changes that would generate structural breaks, the model is estimated over the past ten years (or less where the necessary data are available only for a shorter period).

The equation is estimated on monthly data from January 1998 in the United States and the United Kingdom and March 2003 in the euro area through August 2008.[3]

Estimated link between inflation outcomes and expectations
Bond market expectations[1]

	United States	Euro area	United Kingdom	Canada
Constant term	1.2	1.7	1.8	1.9
Standard error	*0.1*	*0.1*	*0.1*	*0.1*
Inflation[2]	0.3	0.2	0.4	0.2
Standard error	*0.04*	*0.03*	*0.03*	*0.04*

1. Calendar month average of the differential between yields on nominal and real bonds.
2. Year-on-year rate of change in the price index (PCE in the United States, HICP excluding tobacco in the euro area, RPI in the United Kingdom and CPI in Canada) for the previous month.
Source: OECD calculations.

StatLink ⟐⟐⟐ http://dx.doi.org/10.1787/501802076650

The size of the coefficients on inflation in the above table confirms the presence of a link between outcomes and expectations. Because ten-year expectations include inflation over the next two years, over which current monetary policy has limited impact, a coefficient up to 0.2 can be deemed consistent with a strong nominal anchor. On this measure, expectations appear to be well anchored in the euro area.[4] In contrast, the size of the US and UK coefficients, which are greater (and significantly so from a statistical point of view), are consistent with either inflation expectations not being perfectly well anchored or with expectations that the US and UK monetary authorities aim to achieve price stability only over a relatively long horizon.

1. The data are taken from Datastream, the Federal Reserve Bank of Cleveland, the Bank of England and the French Treasury Agency. A cautionary note is that, in addition to capturing expected inflation, the yield differential is also influenced by other factors including the inflation risk premium and differences in liquidity between nominal and real bonds.
2. The short time horizon and the low power of co-integration tests mean that rejecting the null of no co-integration is statistically difficult. Against this background, co-integration is defined as detected when at least one of the following five tests reject the null of no co-integration at the 90% confidence level: the co-integration regression Durbin Watson, the CR Dickey Fuller, the single-step error-correction coefficient Student statistic using Ericsson and MacKinnon (2002) critical values, and Johansen's trace and maximum Eigen value.
3. Inflation is measured on the same price index as the one used for the adjustment of real bonds (implying the use of the retail price index [RPI] in the United Kingdom) except for the United States where Treasury inflation-protected securities (TIPS) compensate consumer price (CPI) inflation but where personal consumption expenditure (PCE) inflation enters the equation. The reason is that CPI inflation does not fulfil the statistical criteria for the model to be valid (it does not co-integrate with bond-implied expectations) while PCE inflation does.
4. However, the fact that (as elsewhere) euro area inflation expectations are integrated suggests that, while strong, their anchoring is not perfect.

projection, deflation would now appear to be a greater risk than an alternative where inflation expectations become unanchored, although neither eventuality has a very high probability.

Policy rates should be cut further in the United States...

The US Federal Reserve already has a very accommodative policy stance, having cut the Federal Funds target rate by 425 basis points since mid-2007 to only 1%, which is well below the level suggested by a simple Taylor rule. However, this accommodative stance is justified by the weakening outlook for activity and the tightening of credit standards and increased interest rate risk spreads triggered by financial market stress. Consumer price inflation (as measured by the personal consumer expenditure deflator) appears to have peaked, although it still remains high, while core inflation (excluding food and energy) is still above 2% (Figure 1.20). Moderating commodity prices and especially lower oil prices should bring about a fall in headline inflation below the core rate in coming quarters and the core rate itself should fall as lower oil and commodity prices feed through the economy. Moreover, the widening output gap should further help to bring down core inflation gradually to below 2%. Falling inflation and confirmation of the adverse impact of financial stress on activity would justify additional cuts in the Federal funds rate by around 50 basis points, to bring it to ½ per cent by early 2009. Once there are clear signs that financial stress is abating, which may not occur until towards the end of 2009, the Federal funds rate should be raised, first as a re-calibration to better financial conditions and then later in response to accelerating activity to ensure inflation expectations remain anchored.

... and in the euro area

The ECB has implemented two cuts of 50 basis points in policy rates since early October. In addition it has also recently introduced operational changes, switching from variable-rate to fixed-rate auctions of liquidity which, in the currently strained financial conditions, effectively amounted to a cut in rates by a further 75 basis points.[42] Headline inflation, as measured by the harmonised index of consumer prices, has passed its peak and fell to 3.2% in October, albeit still well above the ECB's target of 2% or less. As for the United States, weakening activity and falling oil and commodity prices should reduce both headline and core inflation, with the former falling faster. This together with a rise in labour

42. The ECB previously conducted variable rate auctions, whereby each week it announced the total amount of liquidity it was going to provide to the banking system. To obtain a share of this liquidity, banks entered bids in an auction specifying the interest rate they were prepared to pay, where the minimum bid rate was the official rate. This meant that the actual rates at which banks borrowed were generally higher than the ECB's official rate, but in normal conditions the difference was only of the order of 6-7 basis points. However, in the recent conditions of financial stress, the increased demand for money from banks meant that this difference became as high as 74 basis points. The operational change introduced by the ECB was to switch to fixed-rate auctions so that the ECB is prepared to provide however as much liquidity as banks want at exactly the minimum bid rate. In a separate operational change, the ECB narrowed the spread for lending overnight (outside the auction process) from 100 to 50 basis points.

Figure 1.20. **Inflation appears to have peaked**
12-month percentage change

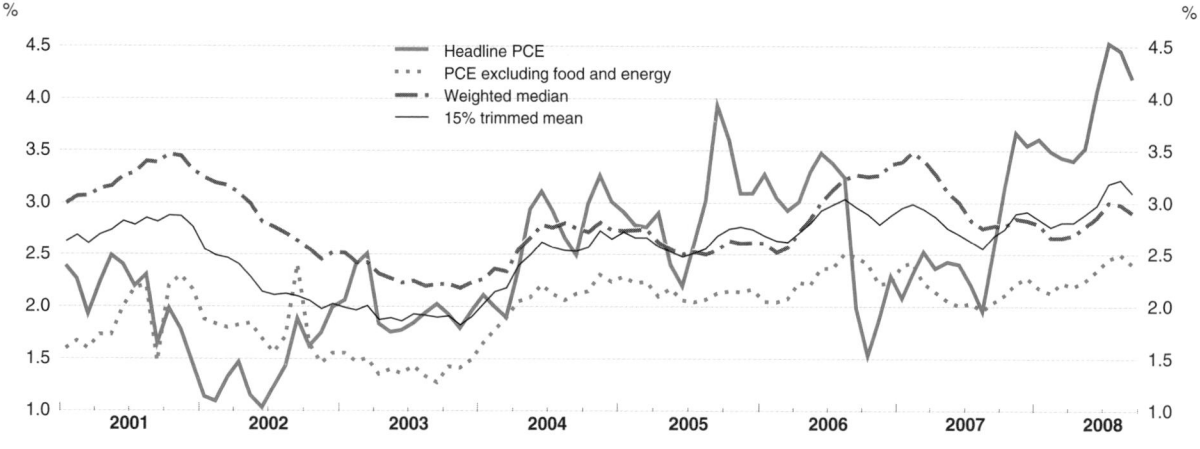

United States (PCE deflator)

Legend:
- Headline PCE
- PCE excluding food and energy
- Weighted median
- 15% trimmed mean

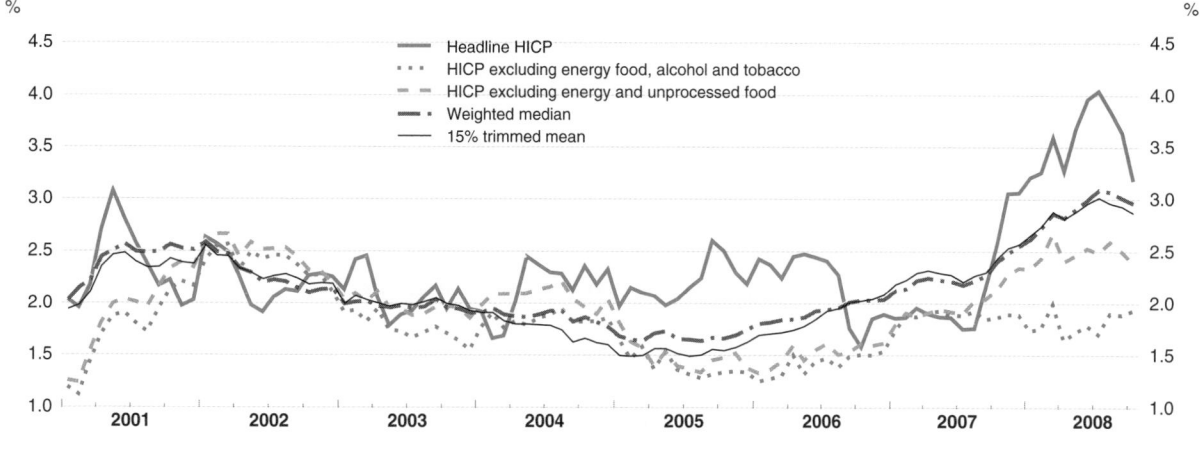

Euro area

Legend:
- Headline HICP
- HICP excluding energy food, alcohol and tobacco
- HICP excluding energy and unprocessed food
- Weighted median
- 15% trimmed mean

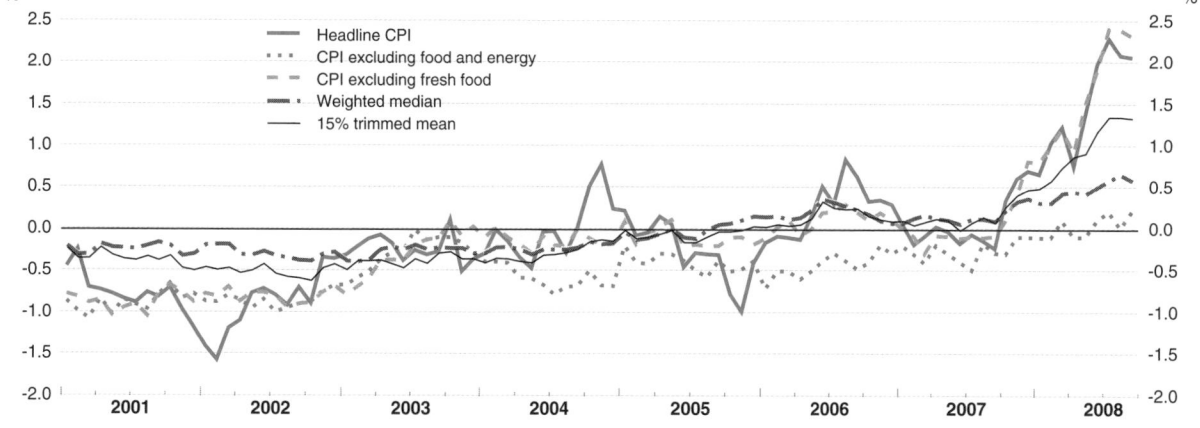

Japan

Legend:
- Headline CPI
- CPI excluding food and energy
- CPI excluding fresh food
- Weighted median
- 15% trimmed mean

Note: PCE refers to personal consumption expenditures, HICP to harmonised index of consumer prices and CPI to consumer price index.
Source: OECD, Main Economic Indicators database; and OECD calculations.

StatLink 📊 *http://dx.doi.org/10.1787/500023687221*

market slack will contain wage pressures and reverse the recent acceleration of unit labour costs. The recent rapid deterioration in the outlook for activity, evidence of falling inflation and stronger credit constraints warrant additional cuts in policy rates totalling around 125 basis points to bring the euro refinancing rate to 2% by early 2009.

Policy rates should remain highly accommodative in Japan

In Japan, the policy rate was cut from 0.5 to 0.3% at the end of October, amid growing concerns about weakening activity particularly stemming from the marked appreciation of the yen and further falls in stock market wealth. Headline inflation is falling from peaks in mid-2008 reflecting both weaker commodity prices and a stronger yen, while core inflation (excluding food and energy) has remained around zero. The risks to activity stemming from the global financial crisis and the appreciation of the yen, as well as the need to let inflation rise to create some buffer against the risk of deflation, argue for maintaining the current degree of monetary accommodation, possibly even beyond 2010.

Further cuts in UK and Canadian policy rates are warranted

In response to the rapidly deteriorating economic outlook, policy rates have been slashed in the United Kingdom. Nevertheless, because the economy appears particularly vulnerable to the combined effect of the financial turmoil and a severe housing downturn, further cuts in policy rates of around 100 basis points may be needed, bringing the repo rate to 2%. The Bank of Canada has also reduced policy rates, by 75 basis points since the beginning of October. Even though the economy appears less vulnerable to the immediate impact of financial turmoil or a housing downturn, the deceleration in demand from its largest trading partner is likely to justify further cuts of the order of 100 basis points which would imply an overnight rate of 1¼ per cent by early 2009.

The Swiss approach to setting monetary policy merits attention

The operational approach of the Swiss National Bank (SNB) is of interest because it seeks to directly target a market rate of interest, namely the three-month inter-bank rate (LIBOR) for the franc, which may have advantages during a period of acute financial stress. The franc LIBOR was chosen because it is a key determinant of the interest rate charged to firms and households for borrowing. The SNB influences this rate by changing liquidity in the market using repurchase agreements (repos) at various maturities.[43] A feature of the framework is a high level of flexibility in the frequency (usually daily), allotment (fixed rate tender) and maturity of these repurchase agreements. During the current crisis, directly targeting the three-month rate has allowed the SNB to keep better control of this key lending rate than other central banks that target shorter-term interest rates such as the overnight rate. To achieve this, the SNB has had to allow the overnight repo rate to fall to very low levels. This experience suggests that, especially under stressed

---

43. A repurchase agreement (repo) is a security that a commercial bank sells to the central bank in exchange for cash and agrees to purchase it back after a set term for a set price. The difference between the price paid by the central bank and that paid by the commercial bank to repurchase the security, expressed as a percentage, is the repo interest rate.

market conditions, it may be easier to stabilise market interest rates that directly influence private sector credit costs by targeting somewhat longer-term rates than most central banks normally would.

Fiscal Policy

Fiscal positions are set to deteriorate

The fiscal policy assumptions underlying the projections are based as closely as possible on legislated tax and spending provisions (Box 1.2 above). On this basis, the OECD area-wide deficit is expected to widen from just under 1½ to 2½ per cent of GDP between 2007 and 2008 (Table 1.10), mostly accounted for by a widening in the US deficit. The area-wide deficit is expected to further worsen by more than 1½ per cent of GDP to 2010, although this is almost entirely explained by cyclical factors rather than discretionary fiscal stimulus.

Table 1.10. **Fiscal positions are worsening**
Per cent of GDP / Potential GDP

	2006	2007	2008	2009	2010
United States					
Actual balance	-2.2	-2.9	-5.3	-6.7	-6.8
Underlying balance[2]	-2.7	-3.0	-5.2	-5.5	-5.2
Underlying primary balance[2]	-0.7	-1.0	-3.1	-3.3	-3.0
Gross financial liabilities	61.7	62.9	73.2	78.1	82.5
Japan					
Actual balance	-1.4	-2.4	-1.4	-3.3	-3.8
Underlying balance[2]	-3.7	-3.1	-2.7	-3.1	-2.7
Underlying primary balance[2]	-3.0	-2.4	-1.9	-2.1	-1.4
Gross financial liabilities	171.9	170.6	173.0	174.1	177.0
Euro area					
Actual balance	-1.3	-0.6	-1.4	-2.2	-2.5
Underlying balance[2]	-1.2	-0.9	-1.2	-1.0	-1.0
Underlying primary balance[2]	1.2	1.6	1.3	1.5	1.6
Gross financial liabilities	74.7	71.4	70.7	73.2	74.7
OECD[1]					
Actual balance	-1.3	-1.4	-2.5	-3.8	-4.1
Underlying balance[2]	-2.1	-2.0	-2.9	-3.1	-3.0
Underlying primary balance[2]	-0.3	-0.2	-1.2	-1.3	-1.1
Gross financial liabilities	76.0	75.0	79.7	82.8	85.8

Note: Actual balances and liabilities are in per cent of nominal GDP. Underlying balances are in per cent of potential GDP. The underlying primary balance is the underlying balance excluding the impact of the net debt interest payments.
1. Total OECD excludes Mexico and Turkey.
2. Fiscal balances adjusted for the cycle and for one-offs.
Sources: OECD Economic Outlook 84 database, see Annex 1 for further details.

StatLink http://dx.doi.org/10.1787/501742674880

The US deficit may remain large beyond 2008

The underlying US fiscal deficit has increased from 2¾ to 5¼ per cent of GDP between 2007 and 2008,[44] partly reflecting the implementation of the one-off tax rebates in early 2008. With the implementation of

44. The underlying fiscal balance is constructed so as to eliminate both the impact of one-off operations and cyclical developments. For details, see Joumard *et al.* (2008).

additional fiscal stimulus measures, appended to the *Emergency Economic Stabilisation Act*, the underlying deficit remains above 5% of GDP in 2009-10. However, the extent of the deterioration in the underlying fiscal balance does not just reflect discretionary fiscal measures (which account for around ¾ per cent of GDP), but also the disappearance of exceptional revenue buoyancy, which was driven by a prolonged period of high and rising asset prices and profitability. The long-term fiscal outlook appears very unfavourable; medium-term projections suggest that, in relation to GDP, within a decade the United States will be among the most heavily indebted of OECD countries,[45] and longer-term projections to the middle of the century highlight budgetary pressures, particularly relating to ballooning public expenditures on health.[46]

The rise in the euro area deficit is mostly cyclical

The euro area government deficit is projected to increase from under 1½ per cent of GDP in 2008 to over 2½ per cent in 2010, which is more than explained by cyclical factors, as the underlying balance improves slightly. This improvement in the underlying balance is a feature of the three largest euro area countries (particularly France and Italy), although the projection does not incorporate the effects of the recently-announced fiscal stimulus package in Germany. The extent to which cyclical factors can drive the deterioration in the headline deficit is most striking for Ireland, where the fiscal balance is expected to deteriorate from rough balance in 2007 to a deficit of 7% of GDP in 2010, and Spain, where the headline surplus of 2% of GDP in 2007 is expected to become a deficit of nearly twice that size.

The UK deficit widens

The underlying deficit for the United Kingdom is expected to deteriorate to nearly 5% of GDP by 2010 (corresponding to a headline deficit of 6½ per cent). This mainly reflects the loss of exceptional revenues (especially corporate tax and housing-related revenues) rather than discretionary fiscal actions. It also appears that the UK's fiscal rules will be re-formulated soon.

The primary deficit will widen in Japan

In Japan, a fiscal stimulus introduced in autumn 2008 will increase public spending by nearly 1% of GDP and implies that the underlying primary deficit widens slightly to over 2% of GDP. This suggests that meeting the objective of a primary surplus for the combined central and local governments by fiscal year (FY) 2011 could be difficult. Nevertheless, this objective should remain a high priority for macroeconomic policy, even if this is delayed beyond FY 2011, in order to begin to reduce the very high gross debt ratio (which is currently the highest ever recorded in the OECD).

45. The United States was projected to be among the most heavily indebted of OECD countries within a decade even before considering the additional costs of recent bail-outs (OECD, 2008c).
46. The Congressional Budget Office has projected that, in the absence of changes in federal laws, federal spending on Medicare and Medicaid health expenditure alone would rise from 4% of GDP in 2007 to 12% in 2050 (CBO, 2007). OECD projections suggest an increase in total public health spending under a "cost pressure scenario" from 7¼ per cent of GDP in 2005 to 12½ per cent in 2050 (OECD, 2006).

In current circumstances there is a case for an active fiscal policy

The weakening outlook for activity raises the case for counter-cyclical fiscal stimulus beyond that currently incorporated in the central projections. Indeed, a number of countries (including United States, Germany, United Kingdom and China as well as a number of small OECD countries) have announced their intention to undertake, or are at least contemplating, a substantial discretionary fiscal stimulus, but because the measures had not been legislated at the time the projections were finalised, they have not been incorporated in the projections. The presumption would normally be that monetary policy is preferred to fiscal policy as an instrument for economic stabilisation, but impaired monetary transmission mechanisms and, in some countries, little scope to cut policy rates further mean that the case for using fiscal policy should be considered. A further potential advantage of using fiscal policy in the current conjuncture – where many countries will face falling activity over the first half of 2009 – is that if carefully designed it can deliver more immediate stimulus. This would allow countries to take out some "insurance" against the possibility that financial conditions, or the downturn in the real economy, are even worse than expected. However, the case for using fiscal policy needs to be considered on a country-by-country basis.

Automatic fiscal stabilisers are larger in Europe

First, automatic stabilisers operate more powerfully in some economies, mitigating the downturn and leaving less need for discretionary measures. For example, more generous welfare systems in Europe as well as balanced budget rules for US states imply that the boost to demand from the automatic fiscal stabilisers during a downturn is much larger in Europe than for the United States.

The initial fiscal positions differ among countries

Moreover, scope for fiscal manoeuvre differs between countries. Those with high deficits and public debt could see their already weak fiscal positions undermined. In addition, in some countries the interventions taken to stabilise the financial system are adding to the contingent liabilities on the government balance sheet, which by their nature are highly uncertain (Box 1.4). Although in most cases there are corresponding assets of a similar value, previous experiences of banking crises among OECD countries suggest that the eventual fiscal costs can be large, although there is great variation (Box 1.5). Countries with exceptionally high debt levels and a poor fiscal track record may face an adverse response from international financial markets. This is particularly the case because in the wake of the financial crisis there has been a much greater discrimination of risk between countries. A striking illustration of this is that within the euro area, spreads on ten-year government bonds relative to those of Germany have risen, particularly for the most heavily indebted countries; in the cases of Italy and Greece, spreads have widened from around 25 basis points prior to the turmoil to about 95 and 130 basis points, respectively, in mid-November.

Box 1.4. **How are financial rescue plans reflected in fiscal positions?**

Many OECD governments have announced measures to support the financial sector, the extent and nature of the interventions varying across countries. The general principles to record these interventions in the current set of projections are described here.

General principles from the national accounts manuals

Four main forms of government interventions could in principle be used to support the financial sector: the granting of loan and deposit guarantees; the acquisition of equities as well as loans and bonds issued by the corporate sector; unrequited payments from the government which do not receive a financial asset in return; and debt assumption or cancellation.[1] So far, most of the announced rescue plans focus on the first two of these pillars.

Guarantees

Guarantees, such as those given to depositors or to interbank lending, are contingent liabilities for the general government. They are off-balance sheet as long as they are not called. They are not reflected in government net lending and debt data. In some guarantee schemes (including Sweden, the United Kingdom and the United States), financial institutions have to pay to the general government a fee on guaranteed issues. The associated revenue streams could thus contribute to improving the general government fiscal balance.

Acquisition of equities, bonds and loans issued by financial corporations

A financial transaction takes place when the government receives a financial asset in exchange for a capital injection. It is recorded in the balance sheet of the government as an increase in both financial assets and gross debt, by the same amount, to the extent that it is not financed by the selling of other general government financial assets. Such an operation has no impact on government net debt and net lending.

Unrequited payments from the government

If the government supports financial institutions with an unrequited payment (*e.g.* to cover exceptional losses) and does not receive financial assets of an equal value in return, the operation should be recorded as a capital transfer. It will be reflected in government net lending, and thus net debt.

Debt assumption and debt cancellation

When the government assumes a debt of a corporation, the counterpart transaction of the financial flows recorded in the financial account is a capital transfer. It is reflected in the government net lending, and thus in its gross and net debt.

Technical assumptions adopted for the fiscal projections

Three complications arise in implementing the general guidelines, making it necessary to apply technical assumptions so as to ensure consistency of treatment across OECD countries:

- When a financial transaction is involved and assets are bought at a price above what could be considered as a "fair price", it may be argued that a subsidy element is involved – the subsidy element would be the amount which is paid above the "fair price". This should appear "above the line", *i.e.* in government net lending. Defining the "fair price" is, however, far from easy. In the OECD fiscal projections, it was decided to record all financial transactions below the line (*i.e.* with an impact on gross debt and assets, but with no impact on net lending and net debt), unless statistical agencies have already decided otherwise.

- Plans to recapitalise financial institutions and/or buy troubled assets often specify a maximum amount which could be used, but this amount may not be fully used, if used at all. There are also uncertainties as far as timing is concerned. The amount of financial transactions included in the projections thus reflects both information and judgement as to the extent to which plans announced up to late October 2008 will be used over the projection period.

Box 1.4. **How are financial rescue plans reflected in fiscal positions?** (cont.)

- The value of government financial assets and liabilities may have fluctuated significantly in line with recent financial market developments. However, fiscal projections do not incorporate price effects on government financial assets and liabilities.

Actual implications of financial rescue plans, as recognised in the OECD projections

Government financial assets and liabilities are projected to increase by 5% of GDP or more over the period 2008-09 for Belgium, Iceland, Luxembourg, the Netherlands, the United Kingdom and the United States as a direct consequence of financial rescue plans (table). Government net lending is unaffected so far for most OECD countries.

Impact of financial rescue packages on government assets and gross debt
As a share of GDP

	Gross debt		Financial assets		Operations
	2008	2009	2008	2009	
Austria	1.0	0.0	1.0	0.0	Recapitalisation of Erste Group Bank
Belgium	6.2	0.0	6.2	0.0	Recapitalisation of Dexia, Ethias, Fortis and KBC
France	1.0	0.0	1.0	0.0	Recapitalisation of six banks (€10.5bn) and another 10bn (out of the €40bn) assumed to follow
Germany	0.8	0.8	0.8	0.8	Creation of a €80bn fund to recapitalise banks and asset purchases. 50% of this fund is projected to be used between 2008 and 2009
Iceland	4.2	95.6	4.2	95.6	Borrowing to support to the banking system, including an IMF loan plan and further loans from various countries
Luxembourg	7.6	0.0	7.6	0.0	Recapitalisation of Dexia and Fortis
Netherlands	5.0	0.0	5.0	0.0	Recapitalisation of Aegon, Fortis and ING
Spain	0.7	2.0	0.7	2.0	Creation of a €30bn fund to buy bank assets
Sweden	1.3	-1.3	1.3	-1.3	Investment in mortgage bonds
Switzerland	1.1	0.0	1.1	0.0	Purchase of convertible debt securities from UBS (CHF6bn)
United Kingdom	9.7	0.0	9.7	0.0	Borrowing to fund the nationalisation of two banks and recapitalisation of several others
United States	7.9	-1.6	7.9	-1.6	Troubled Asset Relief program (TARP); loans from the Treasury to the Fed; GSE mortgage backed securities[1]

1. In the United States, the TARP is projected to be activated partly in 2008 ($350 billion) and in 2009 ($350 billion). For GSEs, the projections include the purchase of mortgage backed securities ($100 billion between 2008 and 2009 to be paid back in 2009 and 2010). The $200 billion preferred stock agreement for GSEs is not projected to be activated. Fiscal projections also include loans ($700 billion) from the Treasury to the US Federal Reserve Bank in 2008, to be paid back in 2009 and 2010.
Source: OECD calculations.

StatLink 🔗 http://dx.doi.org/10.1787/501807274587

1. Based on material in OECD (2008b).

Box 1.5. **The fiscal costs of past OECD banking crisis**[1]

One important effect of banking crises is on governments' fiscal positions. Past episodes indicate that direct fiscal costs can be substantial but vary widely (table). Direct estimate of the costs would include the immediate costs of defaults on loans from the central bank, capital injections to insolvent or weak banks, the capitalised value of lending to insolvent banks or borrowers, and the cost of payouts to depositors and other creditors. In OECD countries, most of the costs have been related to recapitalisations. The Honohan and Klingebiel (2003) measure may overstate the direct costs in the medium run, as it gives the net present value of current supports assuming that they are continued; however, governments may be able to recover some of their outlays by selling interests they acquired in troubled institutions when the banks and markets recover. The direct costs depend, in part, on how the authorities chose to respond to the crisis. In terms of this narrow measure of budgetary costs, less government support is preferable to a more accommodative approach as it is both less costly in the short run and less likely to lead to future claims, as moral hazard is likely to be lower, But, these considerations need to be weighed against the overall costs to the public finances and the economic impact of stress on financial institutions.

The table also shows estimates of the fiscal costs associated with lost output. Again the cost estimates vary widely. However the costs can be very large, as they were for Finland and Norway.

Past experience shows that the overall budgetary costs of government intervention in banking crises can be very large among OECD countries with well-developed financial markets. However the cost is highly variable. The overall fiscal cost of a banking crisis is likely to depend on a number of factors, including the nature and size of the shock causing the crisis and how the crisis is managed. For example, the Finnish crisis was exacerbated by the collapse of exports to Russia, a major trading partner, and sharply lower world prices of forest products, while the protracted nature of banking sector problems in Japan contributed to costs there.

Fiscal costs of past banking crises as a share of GDP

	Episode	Direct fiscal cost	Fiscal cost of lost output[1]	Total
Finland	1991–1994	11.0	11.1	22.1
Japan	1992–[2]	9.1	9.1	18.2
Korea	1997–[2]	26.5	3.6	30.1
Norway	1987-1993	8.0	10.4	18.4
Sweden	1991–1994	4.0	3.6	7.6
United States	1981–1991	3.2	1.8	5.0
Unweighted average		10.3	6.6	16.9

1. Based on estimated output growth losses from Table 7 of Honohan and Klingebiel (2003) and elasticities of budget balance to GDP from Table 9 of Girouard and André (2005). Only reporting OECD country crises with a direct fiscal cost of at least 2% of GDP.
2. Episodes on-going at the time of the original analysis and may therefore not accurately reflect the ultimate costs of the episode. For the Japanese direct fiscal cost, an estimate calculated by Japanese authorities after the crisis, which does not adjust for recoveries, is used.

Source: Girouard and André (2005), Honohan and Klingebiel (2003) and national authorities.

StatLink ⬛🇸🇱 *http://dx.doi.org/10.1787/501824533673*

1. Central banks are not included in the general government sector.

Medium term fiscal objectives need to be strengthened

The need to minimise adverse financial market reaction and so enhance the effectiveness of any discretionary fiscal action underlines the importance of a credible medium-term framework, backed by political commitment, to ensure fiscal sustainability.[47] In the case of the United States, fiscal credibility would be strengthened by setting of explicit medium-term objectives for the fiscal deficit and indebtedness. For euro area countries the criteria for the setting of medium-term objectives for fiscal balances should differentiate more sharply between differing country circumstances and in particular be widened to include the initial and prospective level of indebtedness. For Japan a credible path to achieve the existing objective of a primary surplus needs to be re-established. For the United Kingdom, the existing fiscal rules, which are being re-formulated, need to provide clearer guidelines about the medium-term path to fiscal sustainability. Where political commitments are made to ensure medium-term sustainability, their credibility is obviously enhanced if they enjoy support from a wide political spectrum.

Not all fiscal actions are carefully designed

Where a discretionary fiscal stimulus is undertaken it is important that measures be designed to ensure that they are effective. Recent experience demonstrates the difficulties in designing and implementing a successful fiscal stimulus package. While the US tax rebate package was swiftly implemented to temporarily boost consumption in mid-2008, its stimulus faded just as the financial stress intensified. The fiscal measures appended to the TARP legislation appear to be an *ad hoc* mix of spending and (mainly) tax cut measures, mostly permanent in duration, where the incidence of the latter appears to fall mainly on middle- and high-income earners, with the likelihood that a high proportion will be saved rather than spent.

Fiscal measures need to be timely and effective

Fiscal measures need to be timely to ensure that they have their maximum impact when activity is weakest. This consideration generally argues against increased infrastructure spending given its long implementation lags and in favour of measures such as changes in taxes and transfers which can be implemented quickly. Empirical evidence suggests that fiscal multipliers are not high,[48] which underlines the need for measures to be designed to maximise their effectiveness on aggregate spending. For example, in the case of tax cuts or higher transfer

---

47. In this regard, evidence suggests that fiscal rules with embedded expenditure targets tend to be associated with larger and longer consolidations. This could in principle reflect that well designed fiscal rules are effective or that governments committed to consolidation are more likely to institute rules (Guichard *et al.*, 2007).

48. Regression analysis reported by the IMF suggests fiscal multipliers for advanced economies are only of the order of 0.1 in the impact year rising to about 0.5 after three years (IMF, 2008a). Macroeconomic model simulations are typically more encouraging; the OECD global model suggests that for the main OECD economies the government spending multiplier is about 0.8 in the first year. Micro-based evidence from the 2001 US tax rebate suggests that about 40% of rebates is spent within the first nine months.

payments, focussing on those on lower incomes might be particularly effective currently when more households are credit constrained.

Policy requirements for a stronger financial sector

The crisis highlights a strong need for financial regulatory reform...

The financial crisis has highlighted a large number of regulatory failures and brought into focus the weaknesses of current regulatory systems. But it has also created the political opportunity to introduce reforms to reduce the probability of future crises and better deal with them if they do arise. In particular, work is ongoing at the Financial Stability Forum (FSF)[49] to promote regulatory changes that will enhance financial stability (FSF, 2008). The many important issues which will need to be addressed include: how to ensure a better assessment and management of risks associated with off-balance sheet exposures; reviewing the use of ratings by both investors and regulators, including reforms to improve the quality of these ratings; minimising moral hazard in the securitisation process especially for loan originators; reducing systemic risk by moving the trading of assets such as Credit Default Swaps (CDSs) on to an exchange; reducing liquidity risk (difficulties in selling assets, meeting cash flow needs) and improving its management; and aligning the financial industry compensation models with long-term, firm-wide profitability. On a more narrow basis, the current crisis has highlighted particular systemic weaknesses in the United States and raised concerns relating to co-ordinated policy responses in Europe, which are discussed in turn below.[50]

... which in the United States should include abandoning functional regulation...

The current regulatory structure of US financial markets is based on the principle of "functional" regulation, which maintains separate regulatory agencies across segregated functional lines of financial services, such as banking, insurance, securities and futures. This system is no longer well suited to supervise financial institutions that increasingly operate across the traditional sectoral boundaries. No single regulator has all of the information to monitor systemic risk or the authority to take co-ordinated action throughout the financial system. A more "unified" cross-sectoral framework along the lines recently advanced by the US Treasury should be used as a basis for overhauling the current system (Treasury, 2008).

... and dealing with systemic risks of unregulated institutions...

Currently unregulated institutions, such as hedge funds and private equity firms, potentially pose systemic risks due to highly-leveraged positions and large overall positions in particular asset markets, even if this has not yet been a feature of the current crisis. Consideration needs to be

49. The FSF brings together national authorities responsible for financial stability in major international financial centres, international financial institutions and committees of central bank experts to promote international financial stability through information exchange and co-operation in financial market supervision.
50. This discussion draws heavily on the *OECD Economic Surveys* of the United States and euro area, OECD (2008a and b).

given to how to minimise investor moral hazard and the risk posed to the government from systemic events arising from the failure of these types of institutions, while at the same time maintaining an innovative financial sector, which is important for long-term growth. At a minimum, the market stability regulator should foster counterparty-risk management that discourages regulated institutions from becoming excessively exposed to highly-levered institutions outside of the regulatory framework.

... including the Government Sponsored Enterprises

Given the systemic importance of the GSEs and the almost complete freezing of the private label Residential Mortgage Backed Security (RMBS) market, policymakers had little choice but to bail-out the two GSEs to ensure that mortgage lending markets continued to operate. However, the longer-term advantages of these GSEs are doubtful. Since they can borrow at low rates, owing to their government guarantee, they provide a small subsidy to home ownership. But this subsidy is badly targeted and, as is now clear, the current set-up implies huge, asymmetric financial risks for the taxpayers and unfair competition for the private sector. In a longer-term perspective, the securitisation of mortgages should be turned over to the private sector, as in most other countries, in order to foster competition and reduce moral hazard risks. This gradual process should first require that the GSEs do not have access to preferential lending facilities with Treasury or the Federal Reserve to clearly signal that they no longer enjoy the backing of the federal government and then that they be divided into smaller companies that are not too big to fail. More generally, the need for recent policy interventions in individual institutions and the consolidation that has taken place over the past year highlight that the "too big to fail problem" is wide-spread in the United States. Future regulatory changes will need to tackle this issue.

The European framework for dealing with banking crises needs to be strengthened...

During the extreme financial turmoil in September, European governments co-operated swiftly to ensure the rescue of some major international banking groups. Furthermore, EU countries have quickly agreed on a broad set of policy guidelines to resolve the crisis. Nevertheless, the regulatory framework for preventing, managing and resolving financial crises in Europe needs to be strengthened, especially to deal with the reality that banking and finance involves major cross-border operations and that the financial sector is likely to become increasingly global in the future. The current *ad hoc* approach to financial institution failures has the disadvantage that *ex post* negotiations on burden sharing most likely lead to an under-provision of recapitalisation, because countries have an incentive to understate their share of the problem to incur a smaller share of the costs.

... by more efficient supervision...

Currently, information about the European Union's financial system is collected locally, using different methodologies. A centralised store of prudential information would improve supervisory capacity. It is also important to align responsibility and accountability for financial stability and avoid stalemates in decision-making.

... more uniform safety nets...

A financial safety net is important for preventing financial crises, limiting their cost once they occur and helping to resolve them quickly and efficiently. Safety nets usually involve deposit insurance and Emergency Liquidity Assistance (ELAs) as well as other regulatory procedures. The ECB has played an important role during the turmoil in providing liquidity to the market as a whole, but ELA to individual banks is the responsibility of national central banks. The absence of an explicit burden sharing arrangement for dealing with banking crises with cross-border dimensions could lead to potentially damaging delays. Deposit insurance schemes are an important element in containing any financial crisis. Even though a minimum deposit insurance floor is agreed at the EU level, terms and scale vary widely across the euro zone suggesting there may be a case for greater uniformity, especially given the potential for differences to generate destabilising cross-border flows in a crisis. Blanket 100% deposit guarantees without premium requirements should be avoided. In line with general insurance principles, deposit insurance schemes should require premium payments from the insured who benefit and involve at least some level of risk sharing.

... and specialised insolvency procedures for banks

Efficient resolution of bank crises would involve speed, specialist expertise, and a focused view on the interest of depositors and the general public. Having insolvency procedures specifically adapted to banks might facilitate this. In some European countries, banking supervisors have the right to petition for bankruptcy. However, in many others bank failures are covered by general bankruptcy proceedings (Eisenbeis and Kaufman, 2007) which can be slow and vary widely between member states.

Strengthening counter-cyclicality of macro policies

Low interest rates may have contributed to imbalances...

The current financial crisis highlights a long-standing debate about the conduct of monetary policy during credit and asset price booms. The current bout of financial turmoil itself was preceded by a run-up in asset prices. Opinion remains divided as to how far this may have been caused by the accommodative stance of monetary policy over the first half of the decade, and how far low interest rates at both the short and long ends of the maturity spectrum were the inevitable consequence of, respectively, a favourable supply shock as low-cost non-OECD manufacturers penetrated OECD markets and of a "global savings glut" (Bernanke, 2005). Nevertheless, over this period, there is a cross-country correlation between various indicators of housing market buoyancy and the deviation between actual interest rates and those suggested by Taylor rules (Ahrend *et al.*, 2008). This, however, reflects an *ex post* assessment with concerns about corporate balance sheets and the asymmetric risks associated with deflation driving the *ex ante* selling of interest rates.

... but using monetary policy to combat potential bubbles may be difficult

The issue of whether and how central banks should react to possible asset price misalignments also remains controversial, particularly because it is difficult to identify *ex ante* the presence and scale of any asset price bubble. On the other hand, even if asset price misalignments cannot be identified precisely, they may represent an additional consideration to be factored into monetary policy decisions so that they "lean against" any cycle in asset prices, without explicitly targeting them. In this context, high growth in credit aggregates may be helpful in identifying unsustainable asset price increases (Borio and Lowe, 2004).[51] However, monetary policy action is likely to be more useful in the earlier stages of a bubble, because tightening shortly before a bubble bursts can worsen the ensuing economic decline, but it is in the early stages that a bubble is particularly difficult to detect. In the case of large currency areas, responding to localised bubbles presents difficult choices for the authorities.

There is greater scope for using macro-prudential instruments

An alternative approach to tackling the build-up of a financial bubble, as well as providing a better buffer against its subsequent bursting, might involve "macro-prudential" instruments (Borio and White, 2004). This could include making capital adequacy, loss provisioning[52] or reserve requirements dependent on measures of credit growth or risks of overvaluation of assets. A potential drawback of this approach is that this may single out the banking sector and so result in a shift of activity to unregulated non-banking financial institutions. Such measures may entail some efficiency costs, but especially, though not exclusively, for areas in monetary unions, such costs should be set against the risk of being exposed to financial shocks with no ability to respond through monetary policy.

51. Recent Australian experience has been cited as a successful example of preventing an asset price boom from getting out of hand (Gruen *et al.*, 2005).
52. An option to make banks behaviour less pro-cyclical is to enforce a dynamic provisioning framework by which banks make provisions based on the losses expected when loans are originated rather than on actual losses. In such a framework, provisions rise during credit booms before losses materialise helping to protect banks when actual losses increase (Mann and Michael, 2002). Such a framework has operated in Spain since 1999 (Bank of Spain, 2002 and 2007).

APPENDIX 1.A1

A chronology of policy responses to the financial market crisis

The range of policy measures to the crisis has expanded

In response to the broadening of financial stress to a larger number of institutions outside the banking sector, the authorities in the United States and elsewhere have continued to expand the range of policy measures.[53] Policy action has been taken to tackle liquidity shortages and possible failure of systematically important financial institutions, and to deal with underlying sources of the crisis, the illiquidity of asset backed securities on financial institution balance sheets and the undercapitalisation and insolvency of financial institutions. Action has also been taken to restore household confidence in the banking sector and trust between financial institutions themselves. Figure 1.21 shows a measure of US and euro area money market stress from prior to the start of the crisis to the present. The dates when important initiatives to deal with the crisis were introduced are noted with square bracketed numbers that are referenced in the text.

Figure 1.21. **Money market stress**

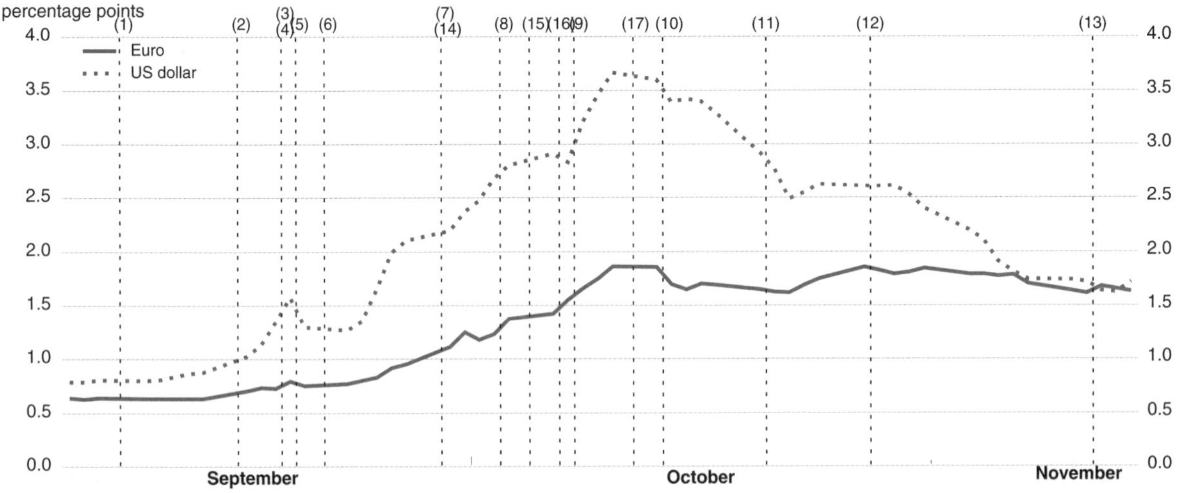

Note: Spread between three-month EURIBOR and EONIA three-month swap index for euro area; spread between three-month LIBOR and three-month overnight index swap for the United States.

Source: Datastream; and Bloomberg.

StatLink ⟡⟡⟡ http://dx.doi.org/10.1787/500024242700

53. See Box 1.1 in OECD (2008c) for a discussion of policy initiatives taken to deal with the crisis up to the summer of 2008.

Government sponsored enterprises were put into conservatorship

In early September of 2008, Freddie Mac and Fannie Mae, the government sponsored enterprises (GSEs) owning around half of total US mortgage assets, were under pressure with widening spreads on their debt, a sell-off of GSE issued securities and plunging share prices. The systemic risk posed by their failure prompted the US Treasury to put both into conservatorship, taking effective control of the companies, agreeing to inject up to $100 billion into each of them and to buy GSE securities on the open market [1].

US money markets froze and the Fed boosted liquidity

The 15 September bankruptcy of Lehman Brothers, a large investment bank with assets and liabilities of over $600 billion, had systemic consequences when it led to significant losses by a large money market fund [2]. Confidence in this latter asset type, regarded as equivalent in risk to a bank deposit in normal times, began to evaporate and investors started withdrawing cash from these funds. In turn, money market funds, a critical part of the short-term funding of the financial system, stopped rolling over their lending to banks and the commercial paper market. The resulting squeeze on liquidity sent interbank rates soaring and came close to shutting down money markets and the inter-bank payment system. In the midst of this near-panic, American International Group (AIG), a giant and systemically important insurance company, unable to raise sufficient capital to continue operations owing to suspicions about its financial health, was granted an $85 billion loan by the US Federal Reserve (Fed) in return for 80% of its share capital. In response to the severe malfunctioning of money markets, on 18 September the Fed, in order to lift dollar liquidity worldwide, increased the amount it would lend to other central banks *via* swap lines by $180 billion to $250 billion [3]. This was complemented by a temporary government guarantee of the entire $3.4 trillion in money market funds in the United States [4].

Purchasing toxic assets was proposed and the Fed increased its lending

On 19 September, in an attempt to tackle an underlying source of the crisis and calm markets, the US Treasury proposed establishing a fund (the Troubled Asset Relief Programme, TARP) with a cap of $700 billion for directly purchasing trouble assets held by financial institutions [5]. The price paid for these assets will be critical not only for the eventual fiscal costs, but also because it will determine ultimate bank losses and the capital adequacy of the banks, which in turn determines their lending capacity. The Fed also added a further facility to boost liquidity (allowing banks to loan funds for purchasing high-quality asset-backed commercial paper from money market funds, the ALMF). The provision of this and other facilities, such as the Primary Dealer Credit Facility (PDCF) already instituted to boost liquidity, have had a large effect on the Fed's balance sheet (Figure 1.22). Treasury securities have fallen from 87 to 40% of total assets between June 2007 and the end of September 2008. In order to shore up the Fed's balance sheet, the Treasury announced on 17 September, that it would sell additional securities and deposit the cash with the Fed. The expansion of liquidity facilities is increasingly substituting for the seized-up money market, which is deteriorating towards a set of parallel, bi-lateral relations between the Fed

Figure 1.22. **Assets of the United States Federal Reserve**

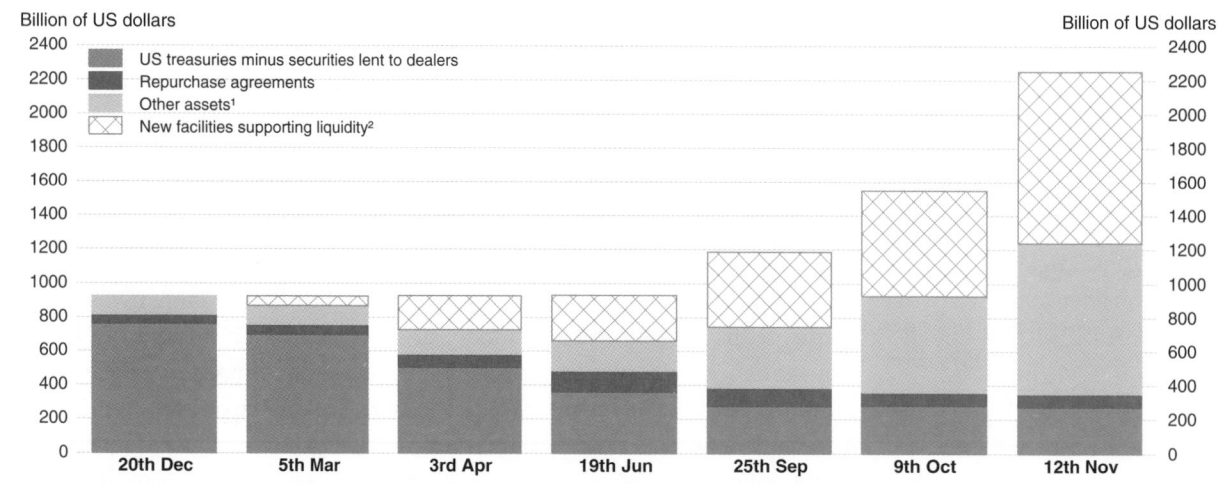

Note: Includes the Term Secured Lending Facility which is an off-balance sheet item.

1. Other Assets includes claims on Bear Sterns and American International Group (AIG), Treasuries Lent Overnight to dealers and swap lines with other central banks supporting US dollar liquidity.

2. New Facilities includes the Term Auction Facility (TAF), Primary Dealer Credit Facility (PDCF), Term Secured Lending Facility (TSLF), the Asset-Backed Commercial Paper Money Market Mutual Fund Liquidity Facility (ALMF) and the Commercial Paper Funding Facility (CPFF).

Source: US Federal Reserve.

StatLink 🖼 http://dx.doi.org/10.1787/500035236161

and individual banks. The Fed has in effect been forced to "nationalise" wholesale money markets in the United States.

Purchasing assets was rejected and market stress increased

In the wake of sharply falling share prices, on 19 September, the US authorities temporarily halted short-selling of financial shares. On 21 September, the two remaining large independent investment banks, Goldman Sachs and Morgan Stanley, became bank holding companies, with permanent access to the Fed's lending facilities but subject to closer supervision by the Fed and the stricter regulation applied to commercial banks [6]. On 24 September, the Fed extended its currency swap line arrangements to include the central banks of Australia, Denmark, Norway and Sweden. On 29 September, the United States House of Representatives rejected the TARP leading to heightened distress in credit markets. The Fed responded on the same day by more than doubling the dollars it will lend to other central banks worldwide to $620 billion and also doubling the size of domestic credit auctions to $300 billion [7]. The government also provided guarantees to Citigroup in return for a capital stake to assist Citigroup's takeover of Wachovia, the sixth largest bank in the United States. This deal was subsequently superseded by a takeover of Wachovia by Wells Fargo.

Central banks worldwide instituted a co-ordinated rate cut

On 3 October, the US House of Representatives followed the Senate and approved an amended TARP, including allowing equity injections under the programme [8]. In subsequent days, market concerns about the prospects for the world economy led to sharp falls in equity markets worldwide and money market spreads remained at extreme levels On

6 October, the Fed announced it would increase the TAF facility from $300 billion to $900 billion. The central bank of Australia also cut interest rates by 1%. In a bid to restore confidence and boost the economy, on 8 October, a co-ordinated policy rate cut was made by central banks around the world, including the Fed, the ECB, the Bank of England and the central banks of Canada, Sweden, Switzerland and China [9]. To relieve pressures particularly in the longer-dated commercial paper market, the Fed also created a further commercial paper funding facility (CPFF) to provide funds to purchase three-month unsecured and asset-backed commercial paper.

The Fed started paying interest on reserves

On 9 October, the Fed further augmented its liquidity boosting tools by starting to pay interest on reserves. By providing a floor on the Fed Funds rate, paying interest on reserves allows it to expand liquidity without having to prevent a change in the Fed Funds rate by selling its diminishing stock of Treasuries.[54] The ECB and central banks of Australia, Canada, England and New Zealand all pay interest on reserves. The Fed will maintain the incentive for the inter-bank lending market to operate by paying a rate of interest on reserve deposits below its reserves lending rate as other central banks do.[55] The Fed as well extended a further $38 billion loan to AIG. Also on 9 October, the temporary US ban on short-selling expired, and US equity prices plunged leading to sharp falls worldwide.

The US announced it will recapitalise banks

On 13 October, the Fed announced that an unlimited amount of US dollars was available *via* existing swap lines to the ECB, the Bank of England the central banks of Japan and Switzerland to support US dollar liquidity worldwide. On 14 October, the US authorities moved to directly tackle market concerns that banks were under-capitalised or insolvent by announcing a voluntary bank recapitalisation programme using $250 billion of funds allocated to the TARP and that nine major institutions had already agreed to participate and issue at total of $125 billion in preferred shares to the government. In addition to existing deposit insurance, they also provided a temporary guarantee of all senior debt of Federal Deposit Insurance Corporation (FDIC) insured institutions as well as deposits in non-interest bearing accounts [10].

The Fed expanded its support to money market mutual funds...

In response to money market fund difficulties in selling commercial paper assets to satisfy redemption requests, the Fed on 21 October announced the creation of the Money Market Investor Funding Facility (MMIFF) [11]. The MMIFF provides funding for the purchase of financial institution commercial paper from money market mutual funds thereby

54. If the Fed injects liquidity and does not sell Treasuries to sterilise the liquidity injection, excess reserves will be lent out by the banks in the inter-bank market, driving down the Fed Funds rate. This will also happen when interest is paid on reserves but the deposit rate paid on reserves puts a floor on how far it will fall.
55. See Keister *et al.* (2008) for a discussion of implementing monetary policy with and without interest payments on reserve balances.

making it easier for these funds to meet redemption requests and increasing their willingness to invest in commercial paper type assets. Together with the AMLF and CPFF, the MMIFF aims to improve short-term debt market liquidity and thereby availability of credit to the private sector.

... and widened its support of US dollar liquidity worldwide

To make it easier for banks outside the United States to obtain US dollar funding, on 28 and 29 October the Fed announced that it would extend its temporary currency swap lines to the central banks of New Zealand (up to $15 billion), Brazil, Korea and Mexico ($30 billion) and the Monetary Authority of Singapore ($30 billion) [12]. The US Treasury announced on 12 November that it would not purchase illiquid assets. It said it would instead use the TARP funds for recapitalisation, supporting the asset-backed securities market for consumer credit and mitigating mortgage foreclosures [13].

Europe rescued banks and guaranteed deposits

Outside the United States, the UK authorities banned short-selling in financial stocks on 19 September. They also encouraged the takeover of HBOS, a large UK mortgage lender under increasing funding pressure, by Lloyds TSB and moved to ensure that there would be competition approval. On 29 and 30 September, UK and European governments bailed out several major financial institutions including Bradford and Bingley (United Kingdom), Fortis Bank (Benelux), Dexia (Franco-Belgian), Hypo Real Estate (Germany), Glitnir (Iceland) and the Irish Government guaranteed the deposits of six major banks [14].[56] In response to ongoing extreme stress in financial markets and to avert outright panic, European authorities took extensive policy action over the period from 5-9 October. On 7 October, EU finance ministers agreed to lift deposit insurance ceilings from a minimum of € 20 000 to € 100 000 within a year and € 50 000 in the intervening period. Actual deposit insurance limits were or will be raised to varying amounts for varying periods: € 100 000 (Belgium, Greece, Ireland, Italy, Luxembourg, Netherlands, Portugal, Spain); € 50 000 (Estonia, Finland, Hungary, Sweden, Poland); £ 50 000 (United Kingdom). France and Italy kept their deposit insurance limits at the relatively high levels of € 70 000 and € 100 000 respectively. In addition several European countries have also provided additional guarantees of all deposits.

- Austria: On 8 October, the government announced it would guarantee all bank retail deposits. introduce guarantees for bank borrowing and provide new capital for the banking sector where needed,

- Denmark: On 7 October, the Danish government extended a guarantee to all deposits and also to inter-bank lending. Participating banks will have to pay an insurance premium and are collectively responsible for the first 2% of GDP in losses.

---

56. The Icelandic government announced a bailout of Glitnir but the bank was then subsequently put into receivership.

- Germany: On 5 October, the bailout of Hypo Real Estate was extended and the German government extended a guarantee to all non-corporate bank deposits [15].

- Iceland: On 5 October the government announced that it would guarantee the domestic deposits of the domestic banking system and on the following day passed legislation giving the Financial System Supervisor greater power to intervene in Icelandic banks. By 9 October, all three of the country's largest banks had been placed in receivership under direct control of the Financial System Supervisor.

- United Kingdom: On 7 October, festering doubts about the health of the financial sector continued to put severe pressure on bank shares, including those of the Royal Bank of Scotland. On 8 October, the UK government announced it would provide at least £ 50 billion in capital to UK banks in return for equity stakes [16]. Eight major institutions signed up to this facility and more were invited to do so. The UK authorities also agreed to provide a guarantee of the lending of institutions participating in the programme and they expected this to be taken up to a total of around £ 250 billion. In addition the Bank of England extended the special liquidity scheme, under which it lends against an extended range of collateral, to £ 200 billion.

- Slovenia: On 8 October, the authorities introduced a temporary guarantee of all deposits.

Markets panicked and Europe agreed on a crisis resolution strategy

On 10 October, a medium-sized Japanese life insurance company failed. Following a worldwide trend, the Japanese stock market fell 10%. The Bank of Japan injected ¥ 4 500 billion ($45 billion) into money markets to boost liquidity. In response to market panic and plummeting equity prices, European leaders met in an emergency session on 12 October and announced a major, far reaching initiative to steady markets and restore the financial system to normal operation. Policy intervention guidelines for action in two broad areas aimed at reducing credit market illiquidity and recapitalising the banking sector were announced [17]. Also on 12 October, Australia guaranteed all retail deposits and that a fee would apply for deposits greater than AUD 1 million, wholesale offshore lending by Australian banks and doubled its pledge to buy mortgage backed securities to AUD 8 billion. New Zealand announced a deposit insurance scheme covering all retail deposit taking institutions for deposits up to NZD 1 million in return for a fee and subsequently a wholesale funding guarantee facility for qualifying institutions. On 13 October, European governments announced the specific actions they would take including making guarantees of bank lending (Germany, France, Portugal and Spain), recapitalising banks (Germany, France and Italy) and purchasing mortgage backed securities (Spain).[57] Also on 13 October, Iceland requested formal assistance from the IMF. On 14 October, the Slovak

57. Belgium and Luxembourg have also offered bank lending guarantees.

Republic announced that it would increase its deposit guarantee to cover all deposits.

Government interventions continued to expand

Authorities across the OECD continued to introduce measures to combat the fallout from the financial crisis from mid-October. A broad range of policy measures are now in place in many OECD countries (Table 1.11).

Table 1.11. **Overview of main measures in OECD countries**

| | Traditional monetary instruments | | Crisis resolution instruments | | | | | | |
	Liquidity injections	Interest rate changes	Increased guarantee of private deposits	Guarantees for bank loans or debt	Fund to purchase commercial papers	Purchase mortgage bonds	Ban or restrict short-selling	Capital injections[1]	Option to purchase toxic assets
United States	x	cut	x	x	x	x	x	x	
Japan	x	cut	x				x		
Euro area	x	cut	x						
Germany			x	x			x	x	x
France			Already high	x			x	x	
Italy			x				x	x	
United Kingdom	x	cut	x	x		x	x	x	
Canada	x	cut	x			x	x		
Australia		cut	x	x		x	x		
Austria			x	x			x	x	
Belgium			x	x			x	x	
Czech Republic		cut							
Denmark	x	Increase /cut	x	x		x	x		
Finland			x	x			x		
Greece			x	x				x	
Hungary	x	Increase	x	x				x	
Iceland		Increase	x				..	x	
Ireland			x	x					
Korea	x	cut	x						
Luxembourg			x	x					
Netherlands			x	x			x	x	
New Zealand	x	cut	x	x					
Norway	x	cut	Already high	x					
Slovak Republic		cut	x						
Poland	x		x						
Portugal			x	x				x	
Sweden	x	cut	x	x		x		x	
Spain			x	x		x	x		
Mexico	x		x						
Switzerland	x	cut	x		x			(x)	x
Turkey	x	cut							

1. Capital has already injected in banks or money has been allocated for future capital injections.
Source: OECD.

APPENDIX 1.A2

A stylised model for oil prices

Oil demand is determined by price and income

This stylised model is similar to the approach adopted in the baseline scenario of Brook *et al.* (2004). Oil demand of region *c* for the ten-year adjustment model is calculated using:

$$D_{c,t} = D_{c,1999}\left(1 + e_{Y,c}\left(\frac{Y_{c,t}}{Y_{c,1999}} - 1\right)\right)\left(1 + e_{ST,c}\left(\frac{P_{c,t}}{P_{c,1999}} - 1\right) + \frac{1}{9}(e_{LT,c} - e_{ST,c})\left(\sum_{s=t-1}^{t-9}\left(\frac{P_{c,s}}{P_{c,1999}} - 1\right)\right)\right)\frac{N_{c,t}}{N_{c,1999}}$$

where *c* and *t* are region and year identifiers; Y is a regional measure of real income *per capita*; P is the real price deflated by the US private consumption deflator; N is the population, e_Y is the income elasticity; e_{ST} in the short-term price elasticity; and e_{LT} is the long term price elasticity (and $P_{c,s}$ is assumed equal to $P_{c,1999}$ for s before 1999). IEA (2006) estimates of the short-term and long-term price and long-term income *per capita* demand elasticities are used (Table 1.12). Data and forecasts for population and non-OECD GDP are based on IMF (2008a and c), assuming the population grows at the same rate over 2008 to 2010 as in 2007. Total oil demand is computed by aggregating over nine regions covering the world.

Table 1.12. **Demand elasticities of oil demand *per capita* by region**

	Price elasticity		Income elasticity
	Short term	Long term	
OECD North America	-0.02	-0.12	0.22
OECD Europe	-0.03	-0.11	0.49
OECD Pacific	-0.05	-0.25	0.39
Developing Asia	-0.03	-0.21	0.73
Middle East	-0.01	-0.07	0.67
Latin America	-0.03	-0.28	0.94
Africa	-0.01	-0.01	0.33

Note: The Developing Asia elasticities are used for both China and the rest of Asia and the OECD Europe elasticities are used for both OECD Europe and non-OECD Europe.
Source: IEA 2006.

StatLink ⬛ᴵˢᴾ http://dx.doi.org/10.1787/501762602465

Supply responds to prices   On the supply side, it is assumed that the uniform supply real price elasticity is 0.04 (the short-term elasticity applied in Brook *et al.*, 2004). Supply is given by $S_t = S_{1999} (1 + e_{S,p}(P_t/P_{1999} - 1))$. The oil price is set such that each year world demand plus changes in stocks (which are assumed to be exogenous) equal supply. While actual changes in stocks data are used to 2007, for the assessment over 2008 to 2010 it is assumed that changes of stocks will become successively less negative, equaling zero in 2010. Given that before 2000 the oil price fluctuated for a decade or more around a reasonably steady mean, demand and supply might be considered as having reached a stationary state at the beginning of the episode considered in Box 1.1 of the main text.

Bibliography

Ahrend, R., B. Cournède and R. Price (2008), "Monetary Policy, Market Excesses and Financial Turmoil", *OECD Economics Department Working Papers*, No. 597.

Akram, Q.F. (2008) "Commodity prices, interest rates and the dollar", *Norges Bank Research Department Working Paper*, ANO 2008/12.

Alquist, R. and L. Kilian (2008) "What Do We Learn from the Price of Crude Oil Future?" mimeo available at www-personal.umich.edu

Bank of Spain (2002), "Asset Price Bubbles: Implications for Monetary, Regulatory and International Policies", Speech Given by the Governor at the Federal Reserve Bank of Chicago.

Bank of Spain (2007), *Informe de estabilidad financiera*, No. 11/2007.

Bayoumi, T. and O. Melander (2008), "Credit Matters: Emprical Evidence on US Macro-Financial Linkages", *IMF Working Paper*, No. 08/169.

Bernanke, B. (2005) "The Global Saving Glut and the US Current Account Deficit", Sandridge Lecture, Virginia Association of Economics, Richmond, Virginia, March.

Bernanke, B. (2006), "Hedge Funds and Systemic Risk", Speech given at the Federal Reserve Bank of Atlanta's 2006 Financial Markets Conference.

Borio, C. and P. Lowe (2004), "Securing Sustainable Price Stability: Should Credit Come Back from the Wilderness?", *BIS Working Paper*, No. 157.

Borio, C. and W. White (2004), "Whither Monetary and Financial Stability? The Implications of Evolving Policy Regimes", *BIS Working Paper*, No. 147.

Borio, C. (2008), "The financial turmoil of 2007-?: a preliminary assessment and some policy considerations", *BIS Working Paper*, No. 251.

Bris. A., W.N. Goetzmann and N. Zhu (2003), "Efficiency and the Bear: Short Sales and Markets around the World", *NBER Working Paper*, No. 9466.

Brook, A., R. Price, D. Sutherland, N. Westerlund and C. André, 2004. "Oil Price Developments: Drivers, Economic Consequences and Policy Responses", *OECD Economics Department Working Papers*, No. 412.

Carlson, M, T. King and K. Lewis (2008), "Distress in the Financial Sector and Economic Activity", *Federal Reserve Board Finance and Economics Discussion Series*, No. 43.

Case, K. (2008), "*The Central Role of House Prices in the Financial Crisis: How Will the Market Clear?*", Conference Draft, Brookings Papers on Economic Activity.

Catte, P., N. Girouard, R. Price and C. André, 2004. "Housing Markets, Wealth and the Business Cycle", *OECD Economics Department Working Papers*, No. 394.

Cerra, V. and S.C. Saxena (2008), "Growth Dynamics:The Myth of Economic Recovery", *American Economic Review*, No. 98.

Congressional Budget Office (CBO) (2007), *The Long-term Outlook for Health Care Spending*, Washington DC.

Daouk, H., C. Lee and D. Ng (2006), "Capital Market Governance: How do security laws affect corporate performance?", *Journal of Corporate Finance*, No. 12.

Demyanyk, Y. and O. van Hemert (2008), "Understanding the Subprime Mortgage Crisis", February.

Eisenbeis, R.A. and G.G. Kaufman (2007), "Cross-border Banking: Challenges for Deposit Insurance and Financial Stability in the European Union", *Federal Reserve Bank of Atlanta Working Paper Series*, No. 2006-15a.

Ergungor, O.E. (2007) "On the Resolution of Financial Crises: The Swedish Experience", *Federal Reserve Bank of Cleveland Policy Discussion Papers*, No. 21.

Ericsson, N.R. and J.G. MacKinnon (2002), "Distributions of Error Correction Tests for Cointegration", *Econometrics Journal*, Vol. 5.

Estrella, A. (2004), "Banks and monetary transmission in the current US environment", Paper presented at the 25th SUERF Colloquium on "Competition and Profitability in European Financial Services: Strategic, Systematic and Policy Issues", Madrid, October.

Financial Stability Forum (FSF) (2008), "Report of the Financial Stability Forum on Enhancing Market and Institutional Resilience", April.

Fisher, E.O'N., and K.G. Marshall (2006) "The Anatomy of an Oil Price Shock" *Federal Reserve Bank of Cleveland Economic Commentary*, November.

Garner, A. (2008), "Is Commercial Real Estate Reliving the 1980s and early 1990s?", *Economic Review*, Federal Reserve Bank of Kansas City, Third Quarter.

Gerardi, K, A.H. Shapiro and P. Willen (2007), "Subprime Outcomes: Risky Mortgages, Homeownership Experiences, and Foreclosures", *Federal Reserve Bank of Boston Working Paper*, No. 07-15.

Girouard, N. and C. André (2005), "Measuring Cyclically-adjusted Budget Balances for OECD Countries", *OECD Economics Department Working Papers*, No. 434.

Girouard, N., M. Kennedy, P. van den Noord and C. André (2006), "Recent House Price Developments: The Role of Fundamentals", *OECD Economics Department Working Papers*, No. 475.

Guichard, S., M. Kennedy, E. Wurzel and C. André (2007), "What promotes fiscal consolidation: OECD country experiences", *OECD Economics Department Working Papers*, No. 553.

Guichard, S. and D. Turner (2008), "Quantifying the Effect of Financial Conditions on US Activity", *OECD Economics Department Working papers*, No. 635.

Greenlaw, D., J. Hatzius, A. Kashyap and H. Song Shin (2008), "Leveraged Losses: Lessons from the Mortgage Market Meltdown", US Monetary Policy Forum Conference Draft.

Gruen, D., M. Plumb, and A. Stone (2005). "How Should Monetary Policy Respond to Asset Price Bubbles?", *International Journal of Central Banking*, Vol. 1.

Hatzius, J. (2008), *Beyond Leveraged Losses: The Balance Sheet Effect of the Home Price Downturn*, Conference Draft, Brookings Papers on Economic Activity.

Hervé, K., I. Koske, N. Pain and F. Sédillot (2007), "Globalisation and the Macroeconomic Policy Environment", *OECD Economics Department Working papers*, No. 552.

Honohan, P. and D. Klingebiel (2003), "The Fiscal Cost Implications of an Accommodating Approach to Banking Crises", *Journal of Banking and Finance*, No. 27.

Hoshi, T. and A.K. Kashyap (2008), "Will the TARP Succeed? Lessons from Japan", *NBER Working Paper*, No. 14401.

International Energy Agency (IEA) (2006), *World Energy Outlook 2006*, Paris.

International Energy Agency (IEA) (2008), *Medium-term Oil Market Report*, Paris.

International Monetary Fund (IMF) (2008a), *World Economic Outlook*, October.

International Monetary Fund (IMF) (2008b), *Global Financial Stability Report*, April.

International Monetary Fund (IMF) (2008c), *International Financial Statistics*, accessed electronically in October.

Joumard, I., M. Minegishi, C. André, C. Nicq and R. Price (2008), *Accounting for one-off operations when assessing underlying fiscal positions*, OECD Economics Department Working papers, No. 642.

Keister, T, A. Martin and J. McAndrews (2008), "Divorcing Money from Monetary Policy", *Federal Reserve Bank of New York Economic Policy Review*, September.

Lamba, A.S. and M. Ariff (2006), "Short Selling Restrictions and Market Completeness: The Malaysian Experience", *Applied Financial Economics*, Vol. 16.

Lown, C. and D. Morgan (2004), "The Credit Cycle and the Business Cycle: New Findings Using the Loan Officer Opinion Survey", *Research Report from Stockholm Institute for Financial Research*, No. 27, September.

Maier, P. and G. Vasishtha (2008), "Good Policies or Good Fortune: What Drives the Compression in Emerging Market Spreads", *Bank of Canada Working Paper*, No. 2008/25.

Mann, F. and I. Michael (2002), "Dynamic provisioning: issues and application", Bank of England, Financial Stability Review, December.

McGuire, P. and K. Tsatsaronis (2008), "Estimating Hedge Fund Leverage", *BIS Working Paper*, No. 260.

Muellbauer, J. (2007), "Housing, Credit and Consumer Expenditure", paper presented at FRB/Kansas City Symposium on Housing, Housing Finance and Monetary Policy, Jackson Hole, WY, September.

Muellbauer, J. (2008), "Housing wealth and consumer spending", mimeo, available at http://www.voxeu.org.

OECD (2006), "Projecting OECD Health and Long-term Care Expenditures: What Are the Main Drivers", *OECD Working Papers, No. 477.*

OECD (2008a), *Economic Survey of United States*, forthcoming, OECD, Paris.

OECD (2008b), *Economic Survey of the Euro Area*, OECD, Paris.

OECD (2008c), *OECD Economic Outlook*, No. 83, OECD, Paris.

OECD (2008d), *OECD-FAO Agricultural Outlook*, OECD, Paris.

OECD (2008e), *Biofuel Support Policies*, OECD, Paris.

Reinhart, C. and K. Rogoff (2008), "Is the 2007 US Sub-Prime Financial Crisis So Different? An International Historical Comparison", *NBER Working Paper*, No. W13761.

Swinston, A. (2008), "A US Financial Conditions Index: Putting Credit Where Credit is Due", *IMF Working Paper*, No. 08/161.

Treasury (2008), "The Department of the Treasury Blueprint for a Modernized Financial Regulatory System", The Department of the Treasury, Washington, DC, March.

ISBN 978-92-64-05469-1
OECD Economic Outlook 84
© OECD 2008

Chapter 2

DEVELOPMENTS IN INDIVIDUAL OECD COUNTRIES

UNITED STATES

The US economy is facing extremely difficult conditions. The financial crisis has intensified at a time when growth had already been weakened by the prolonged housing downturn. A credit crunch is likely to result in a pronounced contraction in activity over the near term and a further deterioration of the labour market. Once financial conditions normalise, GDP growth should resume but at a slower pace than in past recoveries, in part because of negative wealth effects. In response to lower commodity prices and the opening of a large output gap, inflation should recede significantly to around 1½ per cent in 2010.

An additional fiscal stimulus package might become desirable in the near term if financial conditions do not quickly improve. Once the crisis has passed, the focus should shift to restoring fiscal sustainability by reducing the budget deficit and tackling the challenge of rising entitlement spending. The unfolding events since mid-2007 have highlighted the need for a major overhaul of financial regulation and supervision, a process which should be started soon also to boost investor confidence and thus help to revive the economy.

Economic weakness has become more pervasive...

The US economy was confronting substantial challenges even before the recent deepening of the financial crisis. Over the course of 2008, the housing market has remained a major drag on GDP growth. While home sales seem to have stabilised, foreclosures have continued to rise and construction activity and home prices have declined further. There is also mounting evidence that the rest of the economy weakened substantially during the second half of the year. Most noticeably, the pace of decline in payroll employment has stepped up since August, especially in manufacturing. The unemployment rate has climbed to well above its estimated structural rate. The declines in employment, together with earlier increases in food and energy prices, have diminished the purchasing power of households. These factors, in combination with the phasing out of the stimulus coming from the rebate cheques, have depressed real consumer spending in the second half of 2008.

United States

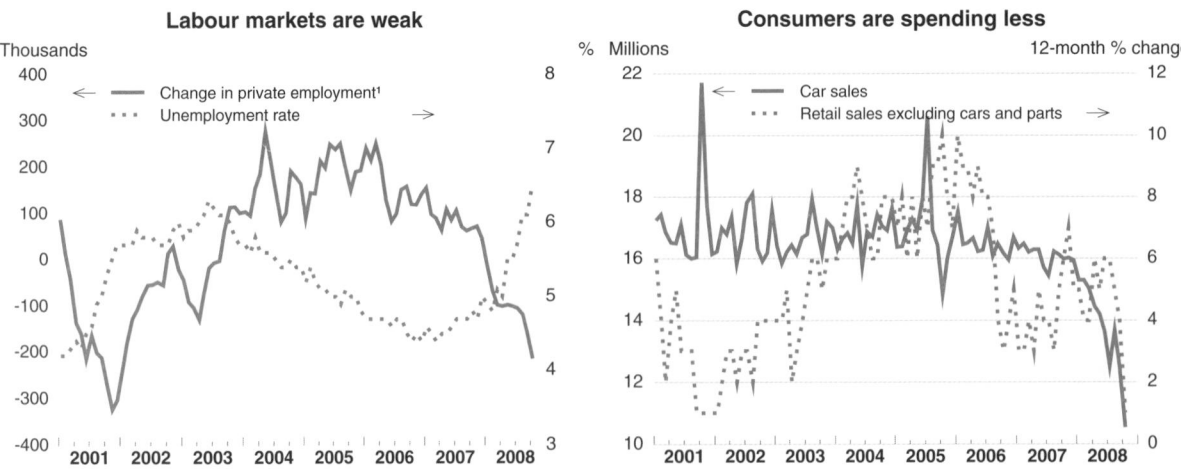

1. Three-month moving average of one-month actual change of total private employment.
Source: Bureau of Labor Statistics, OECD Economic Outlook 84 database, Datastream.

StatLink *http://dx.doi.org/10.1787/500142354006*

United States: **Employment, income and inflation**
Percentage changes

	2006	2007	2008	2009	2010
Employment[1]	1.8	0.9	-0.3	-1.0	0.5
Unemployment rate[2]	4.6	4.6	5.7	7.3	7.5
Employment cost index	2.9	3.1	2.9	2.2	1.6
Compensation per employee[3]	3.9	4.0	3.5	3.0	2.2
Labour productivity[3]	1.1	1.2	1.8	0.1	1.1
Unit labour cost[3]	2.9	3.1	2.2	3.4	1.4
GDP deflator	3.2	2.7	2.2	1.8	1.5
Consumer price index	3.2	2.9	4.3	1.6	1.5
Core PCE deflator[4]	2.2	2.2	2.3	2.0	1.4
Private consumption deflator	2.8	2.6	3.6	1.2	1.3
Real household disposable income	3.5	2.8	1.3	0.0	1.2

1. Whole economy, for further details see *OECD Economic Outlook* Sources and Methods,
   (http://www.oecd.org/eco/sources-and-methods).
2. As a percentage of labour force.
3. In the private sector.
4. Price index for personal consumption expenditure excluding food and energy.
Source: OECD Economic Outlook 84 database.

StatLink ⟜⟅⟆⟱ *http://dx.doi.org/10.1787/501862681123*

... hitting all sectors of activity

In the business sector, declining sales prospects and a heightened sense of uncertainty have begun to weigh on outlays. Industrial production – a good coincident indicator of equipment and software investment – has declined since the second quarter, and incoming data on factory orders and shipments foreshadow further weakness. Even investment in non-residential structures, which held up well until the third quarter of 2008, seems to have turned down. While exports have been the main engine of growth in recent quarters, the slowdown in

United States

The external sector remains dynamic

The Federal Reserve is expanding its balance sheet

1. Contribution to GDP growth. 2001-07: Q4/Q4, 2008: Q/Q at annual rate.
2. Total factors absorbing reserve funds.
3. As of 12 November 2008.
Source: OECD Economic Outlook 84 database, Federal Reserve.

StatLink ⟜⟅⟆⟱ *http://dx.doi.org/10.1787/500155610312*

United States: **Financial indicators**

	2006	2007	2008	2009	2010
Household saving ratio[1]	0.7	0.6	1.6	2.8	2.5
General government financial balance[2]	-2.2	-2.9	-5.3	-6.7	-6.8
Current account balance[2]	-6.0	-5.3	-4.9	-3.9	-3.6
Short-term interest rate[3]	5.2	5.3	3.3	1.7	2.0
Long-term interest rate[4]	4.8	4.6	3.8	4.1	4.8

1. As a percentage of disposable income.
2. As a percentage of GDP.
3. 3-month euro-dollar.
4. 10-year government bonds.
Source: OECD Economic Outlook 84 database.

StatLink ᵐˢ🖳 http://dx.doi.org/10.1787/502014065266

global activity and the recent appreciation of the dollar prefigure some softening here as well. Following moderate growth in the first half of 2008, there is likely to be a broad-based contraction of output in coming quarters. The only positive note is the recent drop in energy prices, which has reduced inflationary pressures and will attenuate the decline in real incomes.

The financial system is under extraordinary stress...

The financial crisis, not only in the United States but also in much of the rest of the world, has intensified. Falling home prices and the consequent deterioration of mortgages have led to substantial losses across the financial sector. Financial institutions' efforts to repair their balance sheets have constrained their lending. Furthermore, mounting

United States: **Demand and output**

	2005	2006	2007	2008	2009	2010
	Current prices $ billion	Percentage changes, volume (2000 prices)				
Private consumption	8 694.1	3.0	2.8	0.4	-1.2	1.2
Government consumption	1 957.5	1.6	1.9	2.8	2.3	1.4
Gross fixed investment	2 440.6	2.0	-2.0	-3.1	-7.3	1.4
Public	397.8	2.1	3.0	3.6	2.6	1.2
Residential	769.7	-7.1	-17.9	-21.3	-16.8	0.7
Non-residential	1 273.1	7.5	4.9	2.4	-7.6	1.7
Final domestic demand	13 092.2	2.6	1.8	0.2	-1.6	1.3
Stockbuilding[1]	43.3	0.0	-0.4	-0.3	0.0	0.0
Total domestic demand	13 135.5	2.6	1.4	-0.1	-1.6	1.3
Exports of goods and services	1 311.5	9.1	8.4	8.5	2.8	3.8
Imports of goods and services	2 025.1	6.0	2.2	-2.3	-2.1	1.6
Net exports[1]	- 713.6	0.0	0.6	1.4	0.8	0.2
GDP at market prices	12 421.9	2.8	2.0	1.4	-0.9	1.6

Note: National accounts are based on official chain-linked data. This introduces a discrepancy in the identity between real demand components and GDP. For further details see OECD Economic Outlook Sources and Methods (http://www.oecd.org/eco/sources-and-methods).
1. Contributions to changes in real GDP (percentage of real GDP in previous year), actual amount in the first column.
Source: OECD Economic Outlook 84 database.

StatLink ᵐˢ🖳 http://dx.doi.org/10.1787/502026073326

United States: **External indicators**

	2006	2007	2008	2009	2010
	\$ billion				
Goods and services exports	1 480.8	1 662.4	1 924.0	1 996	2 101
Goods and services imports	2 238.1	2 370.2	2 606.9	2 523	2 581
Foreign balance	- 757.3	- 707.9	- 683.0	- 527	- 480
Invisibles, net	- 30.8	- 23.4	- 13.4	- 36	- 57
Current account balance	- 788.1	- 731.2	- 696.4	- 562	- 537
	Percentage changes				
Goods and services export volumes	9.1	8.4	8.5	2.8	3.8
Goods and services import volumes	6.0	2.2	- 2.3	- 2.1	1.6
Export performance[1]	0.0	1.2	2.8	0.9	- 0.6
Terms of trade	- 0.8	- 0.1	- 5.2	2.1	0.8

1. Ratio between export volume and export market of total goods and services.
Source: OECD Economic Outlook 84 database.

StatLink http://dx.doi.org/10.1787/502040655643

uncertainty about the values of excessively complex and opaque mortgage-linked securities has progressively led investors to become more reluctant to bear credit risk. This has generated further declines in financial asset prices and a drying-up of liquidity. As a result, many securitisation markets, such as that for private-label mortgage-backed securities, have stopped working. In September, credit and money markets came to a near halt, with interest rates in these markets skyrocketing.

... which is spilling over to the real economy

The aggravation of the financial crisis is likely to affect economic activity through several channels, most notably by restricting the availability of credit. Banks are reducing credit card limits, and denial rates on automobile loan applications are reportedly rising. Even households with good credit histories face difficulties obtaining mortgages or home equity lines of credit. Businesses, too, are impaired by diminished access to credit. For instance, tighter bank lending standards – as evidenced by October's Senior Loan Officer Opinion Survey – and disruptions in the commercial paper market have made it harder for firms to obtain the working capital they need to meet routine expenses such as payrolls and inventories.

Household wealth is declining

The strains in financial markets have also led to a sharp drop in equity prices, which have fallen to a five-year low. Capital losses on corporate equities, combined with further losses in real estate due to continued falls in home prices, have put a considerable dent in household net worth, which will restrain consumer spending as households boost savings to rebuild their wealth.

Aggressive actions to contain the crisis have been taken

In response to developments in the housing and financial sectors, the US authorities have taken a series of aggressive steps to restore stability in financial markets and support real activity. They have intervened to support distressed financial institutions, most notably Fannie Mae, Freddie Mac and the American International Group (one of the world's largest insurance companies). Most importantly, the authorities have enacted a $700 billion rescue plan which has partly been used to recapitalize banks, and have also more than doubled deposit insurance to reduce the risk of bank runs. The success of these efforts in improving financial conditions will be the key determinant for the evolution of the US economy over the projection period.

Fiscal and monetary policies are very accommodative

The stances of fiscal and the monetary policy are extremely accommodative. The Federal Reserve has not only reduced its policy rate to very low levels but has also implemented innovative steps to address strains in financial markets and provide liquidity by creating new lending mechanisms, aggressively changing the size and composition of its balance sheet and extending credit also to non-financial corporations. Once the crisis has passed, this quantitative easing should be pulled back and the federal funds rate should be raised, first as a recalibration to better financial conditions and then in response to accelerating activity, to keep inflation expectations well anchored.

The economy will contract in the near term...

Despite the aggressive policy response, the US economy is likely to have already entered a recession and the near-term prospect is for further weakness. Consumer spending is projected to decline or remain sluggish over the near term, as labour market conditions continue to deteriorate and credit remains tight. Business investment is likely to continue to fall well into 2009 *via* the traditional accelerator effect, reinforced by the credit squeeze. International trade, in contrast, should remain a source of growth, although much less so than in the recent past.

... and growth will remain weak until 2010

As financial conditions normalise and the housing downturn bottoms out, the economy is projected to begin to grow again in the third quarter of 2009, albeit at a moderate pace since consumer spending is likely to be restrained by reduced confidence and loss of wealth. In 2010, economic activity, still supported by substantial monetary policy stimulus, is expected to gradually accelerate. Inflation should fall considerably from the elevated levels posted until the third quarter of 2008, in response to the drop in commodity prices and the opening of a substantial output gap.

Risks are on the downside

Even though a stronger-than-projected recovery is possible, risks for growth are skewed to the downside. If financial conditions fail to move back to the pre-September level in the near term, the implications for the broader economy would be quite adverse. A protracted credit crunch would hold back spending, production and job creation even further. In addition, the disruption in financial markets may have lowered GDP potential much more than estimated, further diminishing the prospects of a rapid recovery.

JAPAN

External shocks from the run-up in commodity prices and then international financial turbulence have brought Japan's expansion to an end. Equity prices have plummeted and the yen has appreciated substantially. With falling exports, activity is projected to remain weak through 2009, pushing up unemployment and reducing headline inflation to near zero. A recovery in domestic demand is projected to lift output growth to around 1% during 2010, still short of the growth of potential.

The cut in the policy interest rate by the Bank of Japan should be accompanied by measures to support activity by providing sufficient liquidity to the market to limit the impact of financial stress and mitigate deflationary pressures. While the fiscal stimulus announced in late October will cushion the downturn in 2009, it will be important to focus again on fiscal consolidation as the economy stabilises, given the very high public debt ratio and the costs of ageing. Structural reforms to boost productivity, particularly in the service sector, remain a priority to improve living standards in the face of a shrinking working-age population.

The negative impact of the terms-of-trade shock...

The expansion – the longest in Japan's post-war history – came to an end around mid-2008 with a sharp contraction in exports, reflecting the slowdown in world trade and marked yen appreciation. Weak exports are, in turn, reducing business investment, the second major driver of the expansion. The commodity price shock also lowered profitability as firms have had difficulty in fully passing on their higher costs. The rise in headline consumer price inflation, to a peak of 2.2% (year-on-year) in the third quarter of 2008, reduced household real income, thus damping private consumption. Household income was also negatively affected by deteriorating labour market conditions, as employment growth slowed, the job-offer-to-applicant ratio fell well below parity and wage growth stalled.

Japan

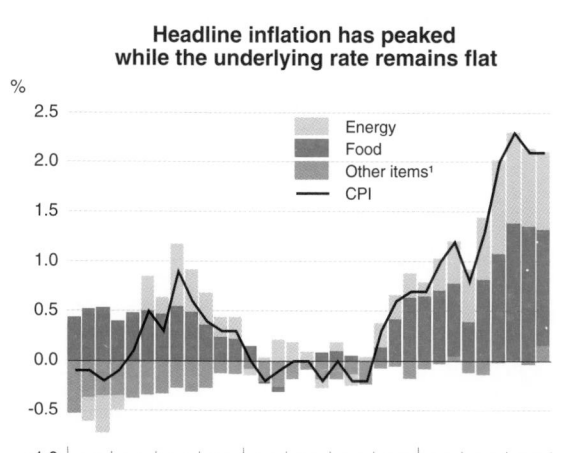

Headline inflation has peaked while the underlying rate remains flat

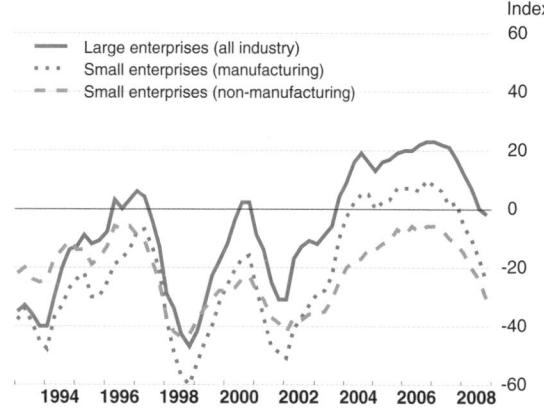

Business confidence has weakened[2]

1. Corresponds to the OECD measure of core inflation.
2. Diffusion index of "favourable" minus "unfavourable" business conditions in the Tankan Survey. There is a discontinuity between the third and fourth quarters of 2003 due to data revisions.
Source: Ministry of Internal Affairs and Communications; Bank of Japan.

StatLink ᔕᔕᓯ *http://dx.doi.org/10.1787/500166434416*

Japan: **Employment, income and inflation**
Percentage changes

	2006	2007	2008	2009	2010
Employment	0.4	0.5	-0.3	-0.7	-0.2
Unemployment rate[1]	4.1	3.9	4.1	4.4	4.4
Compensation of employees	1.6	0.3	1.3	-0.1	0.1
Unit labour cost	-0.8	-1.8	0.8	0.0	-0.5
Household disposable income	1.0	1.0	1.4	0.6	0.2
GDP deflator	-1.0	-0.8	-1.0	1.3	-0.3
Consumer price index[2]	0.2	0.1	1.4	0.3	-0.1
Core consumer price index[3]	-0.4	-0.2	0.0	-0.1	-0.2
Private consumption deflator	-0.3	-0.5	0.4	-0.2	-0.3

1. As a percentage of labour force.
2. Calculated as the sum of the seasonally adjusted quarterly indices for each year. In the Japanese official statistics, annual growth rates are based on the non-seasonally adjusted series, giving -0.3% in 2005 and 0.3% in 2006.
3. Consumer price index excluding food and energy.
Source: OECD Economic Outlook 84 database.

StatLink 🔗 *http://dx.doi.org/10.1787/502043681502*

... was aggravated by the global financial crisis

The global financial market crisis is further worsening economic conditions. Business confidence dropped to its lowest level in five years in September 2008, especially among small manufacturing companies, and firms have revised down their investment plans. The appreciation of the yen, by 16% in trade-weighted terms since July 2008, further dims the outlook for exports. Equity prices have dropped steeply – by 24% in October alone – leading to tighter financial conditions and reducing household wealth. The collapse of a real estate investment trust and a life insurance company in October 2008 raises concerns that Japan's financial

Japan

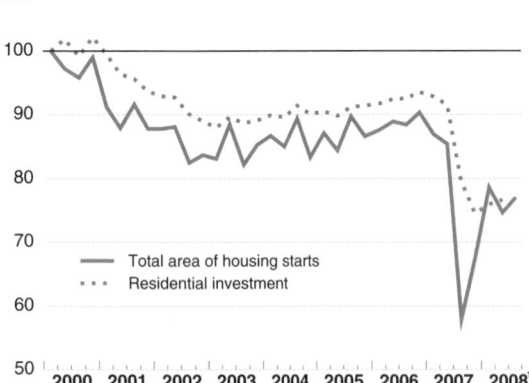

Housing investment has started to rebound
2000Q1=100

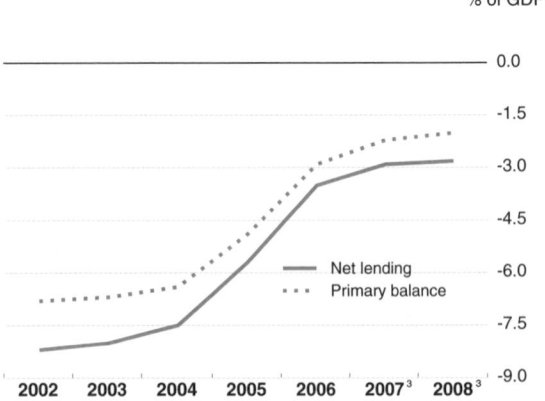

The fiscal deficit has stabilised[2]

1. The latest historical data is the third quarter of 2008.
2. Excluding one-off factors.
3. Estimated.
Source: Ministry of Land, Infrastructure, Transport and Tourism; Cabinet Office, OECD calculations.

StatLink 🔗 *http://dx.doi.org/10.1787/500174833454*

OECD ECONOMIC OUTLOOK 84 – ISBN 978-92-64-05469-1 – © OECD 2008

Japan: **Financial indicators**

	2006	2007	2008	2009	2010
Household saving ratio[1]	3.3	3.1	3.3	3.5	3.2
General government financial balance[2]	-1.4	-2.4	-1.4	-3.3	-3.8
Current account balance[2]	3.9	4.8	3.8	4.3	3.9
Short-term interest rate[3]	0.2	0.7	0.8	0.7	0.4
Long-term interest rate[4]	1.7	1.7	1.5	2.0	2.7

1. As a percentage of disposable income.
2. As a percentage of GDP.
3. 3-month CDs.
4. 10-year government bonds.
Source: OECD Economic Outlook 84 database.

StatLink 📊 *http://dx.doi.org/10.1787/502045044363*

market, which thus far has been largely untouched by the turmoil sweeping through world financial markets, may be negatively affected. In addition, the interest rate spread between government and corporate bonds has widened since mid-September and the number of corporate bond issues has declined.

Fiscal stimulus is being used to limit the downturn...

Output growth is likely to be sustained in the first half of 2009 – albeit at low rates – by residential investment and fiscal stimulus. Housing starts (in terms of area), which collapsed in the second half of 2007 following a revision in the Building Standards Law, have been on an upward trend. The two economic stimulus packages introduced in

Japan: **Demand and output**

	2005	2006	2007	2008	2009	2010
	Current prices ¥ trillion	Percentage changes, volume (2000 prices)				
Private consumption	285.9	2.0	1.5	0.7	0.6	0.7
Government consumption	90.6	-0.4	0.7	0.3	1.4	1.7
Gross fixed investment	116.9	1.3	-0.6	-2.4	-0.1	1.4
Public[1]	22.9	-8.1	-2.5	-4.0	1.1	-4.2
Residential	18.2	0.9	-9.5	-9.2	3.9	2.4
Non-residential	75.7	4.3	2.1	-0.6	-1.2	2.6
Final domestic demand	493.4	1.4	0.9	-0.1	0.6	1.0
Stockbuilding[2]	1.4	0.2	0.1	-0.2	0.0	0.0
Total domestic demand	494.8	1.6	1.0	-0.3	0.6	1.0
Exports of goods and services	71.9	9.7	8.6	5.3	-2.9	0.7
Imports of goods and services	65.0	4.2	1.7	0.9	1.2	3.5
Net exports[2]	7.0	0.8	1.1	0.8	-0.7	-0.4
GDP at market prices	501.7	2.4	2.1	0.5	-0.1	0.6

Note: National accounts are based on official chain-linked data. This introduces a discrepancy in the identity between real demand components and GDP. For further details see *OECD Economic Outlook* Sources and Methods (*http://www.oecd.org/eco/sources-and-methods*).
1. Including public corporations.
2. Contributions to changes in real GDP (percentage of real GDP in previous year), actual amount in the first column.
Source: OECD Economic Outlook 84 database.

StatLink 📊 *http://dx.doi.org/10.1787/502048660064*

Japan: **External indicators**

	2006	2007	2008	2009	2010
	$ billion				
Goods and services exports	702.6	772.1	896.7	923	928
Goods and services imports	648.1	698.9	853.2	828	856
Foreign balance	54.5	73.3	43.4	94	72
Invisibles, net	117.5	138.6	143.8	137	139
Current account balance	172.0	211.8	187.2	231	211
	Percentage changes				
Goods and services export volumes	9.7	8.6	5.3	- 2.9	0.7
Goods and services import volumes	4.2	1.7	0.9	1.2	3.5
Export performance[1]	0.5	1.3	0.5	- 5.7	- 5.3
Terms of trade	- 6.9	- 4.6	- 9.0	10.7	0.0

1. Ratio between export volume and export market of total goods and services.
Source: OECD Economic Outlook 84 database.

StatLink ⟐⟐⟐ http://dx.doi.org/10.1787/502073475202

autumn 2008 will boost public spending by about 1% of GDP, with lump-sum payments to households accounting for almost half of the total. The fiscal stimulus will reverse the downward trend in the primary budget deficit, which had fallen from 6.4% of GDP in 2004 to an estimated 2% in 2008 on a general government basis, excluding one-off factors. In 2009, it is projected to rise to around 3%, making it difficult to achieve the government's fiscal year 2011 target of a primary surplus for the combined central and local governments. Meeting this objective, even if a little later, is a necessary first step to reducing the government debt ratio, which at over 170% is now the highest ever recorded in the OECD area, during the 2010s.

... and the policy interest rate has been cut

Given mounting deflationary pressures and turbulence in international financial markets, the Bank of Japan lowered its policy interest rate from 0.5% to 0.3% in October 2008, the first cut in seven years. Headline inflation is falling from its summer 2008 peak, reflecting the recent decline in oil prices and a stronger yen. Meanwhile, core consumer price inflation (excluding energy and food) has remained around zero since 2007. With rising unemployment, anaemic wage growth and falling unit labour costs, headline and core consumer price inflation are likely to turn slightly negative in 2009. In addition, residential land prices, which stabilised in 2006 after 15 years of decline, appear to have started falling again.

Economic growth is projected to remain sluggish during 2009...

As the fiscal stimulus fades, output growth is projected to stall in the second half of 2009 before picking up in 2010. The external sector is expected to remain a significant drag on activity through 2010, assuming a constant exchange rate. Domestic demand, however, should lead a modest rebound in output growth to around 1% by mid-2010. Consumption spending will be underpinned by gains in real household income in a context of stable prices, smaller falls in employment and a pick-up in wage growth. In addition, the shift to lower-paid part-time workers is likely to end, thus removing a significant drag on wage gains. Moreover, the terms of trade are likely to improve in 2009, for the first time in a decade, and then stabilise in 2010. Stronger consumption growth would in due course help reverse the fall in business investment, which is projected to decline for five consecutive quarters through mid-2009. The continued normalisation of the housing market should make a positive contribution to growth in both 2009 and 2010. Nevertheless, output growth is projected to remain below potential through 2010, with the unemployment rate around 4½ per cent. Consequently, inflation is expected to stay steady at around zero.

... with external and domestic risks mostly on the downside

The exceptional uncertainty about the world economy poses a number of risks. Although the corporate sector's resilience to external shocks has improved since the bubble period and the banking sector is now adequately capitalised, the global financial crisis could disrupt Japan's financial sector, reducing both private consumption and investment. Further yen appreciation would damp exports. There is also a risk that slower growth would push Japan back into deflation. On the other hand, a faster-than-expected resolution to the world financial crisis and a fall in the yen would foster an earlier and stronger economic recovery in Japan.

EURO AREA

The euro area economy has slipped into recession this year, with tighter financial conditions, negative wealth effects, weaker housing market activity and greater uncertainty all reducing domestic demand. Growth is expected to remain below potential until the middle of 2010, before picking-up as the effects of monetary policy easing and the dissipation of stress in global financial markets emerge. Lower commodity prices and the emergence of a sizable negative output gap will dampen inflationary pressures, with headline inflation projected to fall to around 1½ per cent during 2009.

With inflationary pressures already easing, there is scope for additional monetary stimulus, which should be prompt to minimise the downside risks to activity. The loss of tax revenues from financial and housing markets and the costs of emergency actions to alleviate financial turmoil will add to budgetary pressures. Any additional discretionary fiscal measures should be well-targetted and, reflecting the need for medium-term fiscal consolidation, temporary. Growth prospects would be enhanced by implementing measures to strengthen the regulatory and supervisory frameworks in European financial markets.

Economic activity has begun to contract

The euro area economy has slipped into recession, with GDP declining in both the second and third quarters of 2008. In the second quarter, drops in private consumption and business fixed investment reinforced downward pressures from the slump in housing investment. Exports also declined, affected by weaker world demand and the strength of the euro. With heightened turmoil in global financial markets, the near-term outlook for economic growth has weakened considerably, and a protracted slowdown appears increasingly likely. Area-wide industrial production and retail sales both declined in the summer months. Survey data point to further declines in activity, with business sentiment and consumer confidence falling well below their long-term average levels.

Euro area

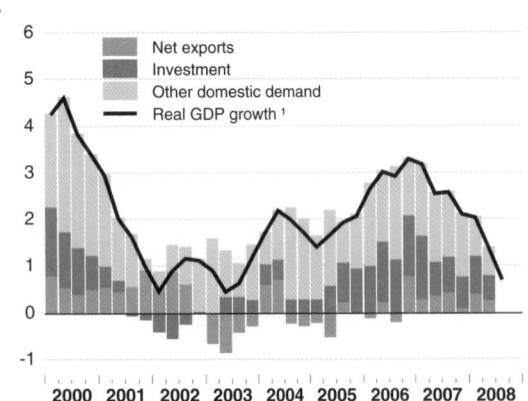

Economic growth continues to weaken
Contribution to real GDP growth

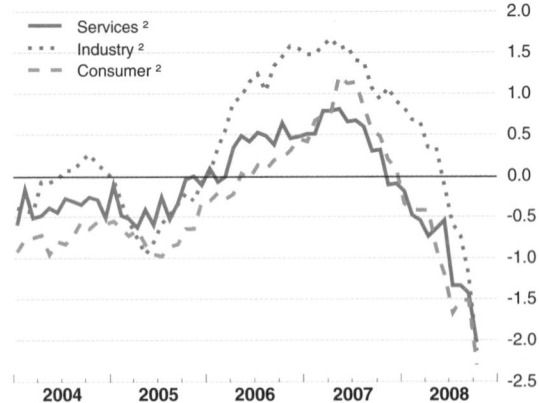

Economic sentiment has declined sharply

1. Year-on-year percentage change.
2. The series are normalised and average 0 over 1999m1-2008m10.

Source: Eurostat and OECD, OECD Economic Outlook 84 database.

StatLink *http://dx.doi.org/10.1787/500234347824*

OECD ECONOMIC OUTLOOK 84 – ISBN 978-92-64-05469-1 – © OECD 2008

Euro area: **Employment, income and inflation**
Percentage changes

	2006	2007	2008	2009	2010
Employment	1.6	1.8	1.0	-0.7	-0.1
Unemployment rate[1]	8.2	7.4	7.4	8.6	9.0
Compensation per employee[2]	2.2	2.4	3.0	2.4	2.1
Labour productivity	1.4	0.8	0.0	0.2	1.2
Unit labour cost	1.1	1.8	3.4	2.7	1.1
Household disposable income	3.7	3.7	4.4	2.4	2.4
GDP deflator	2.0	2.3	2.4	2.0	1.3
Harmonised index of consumer prices	2.2	2.1	3.4	1.4	1.3
Core harmonised index of consumer prices[3]	1.5	1.9	1.8	1.6	1.3
Private consumption deflator	2.2	2.2	3.0	1.4	1.3

Note: The euro area aggregates cover the euro area countries that are members of the OECD.
1. As a percentage of labour force.
2. In the private sector.
3. Harmonised index of consumer prices excluding energy, food, drink and tobacco.
Source: OECD Economic Outlook 84 database.

StatLink 🔗 http://dx.doi.org/10.1787/502088611470

Financial conditions have tightened

Even before recent events, international financial market turmoil had tightened financial conditions. Widening interest rate spreads, more stringent bank lending standards and declining equity prices all raised the cost of financing and generated negative wealth effects on household spending. Credit growth has remained positive this year, but has clearly slowed, especially for households. The euro has depreciated in effective terms by close to 10% since early 2008, but remains above its average over the past decade. More recently, financial pressures on banks, households and companies have intensified, with further increases in spreads and additional falls in equity prices. As a result the household wealth-to-

Euro area

Household net financial wealth is declining

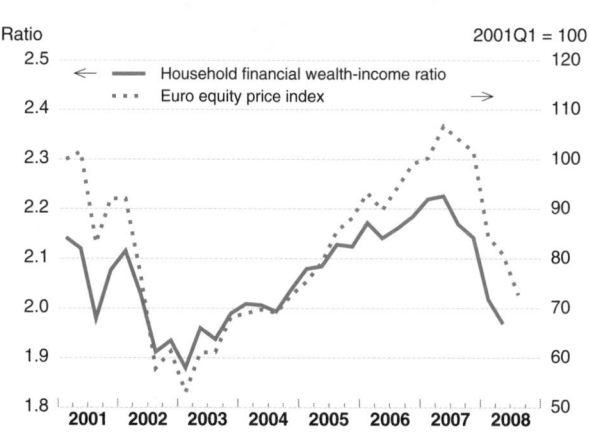

Inflationary pressures have peaked
Contribution to inflation [1]

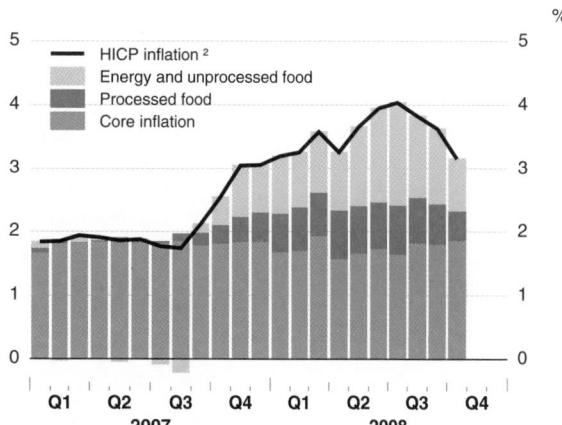

1. Represented by the harmonised consumer price index (HICP).
2. Year-on-year percentage change.
Source: European Central Bank, Datastream and OECD, OECD Economic Outlook 84 database.

StatLink 🔗 http://dx.doi.org/10.1787/500238341334

Euro area: **Financial indicators**

	2006	2007	2008	2009	2010
Household saving ratio[1]	9.3	9.2	9.9	10.6	10.6
General government financial balance[2]	-1.3	-0.6	-1.4	-2.2	-2.5
Current account balance[2]	0.4	0.3	-0.4	-0.1	0.0
Short-term interest rate[3]	3.1	4.3	4.7	2.7	2.6
Long-term interest rate[4]	3.8	4.3	4.4	4.4	4.7

Note: The euro area aggregates cover the euro area countries that are members of the OECD.
1. As a percentage of disposable income.
2. As a percentage of GDP.
3. 3-month interbank rate.
4. 10-year government bonds.
Source: OECD Economic Outlook 84 database.

StatLink ⬛⬛ http://dx.doi.org/10.1787/502117866518

income ratio has declined considerably. Interbank markets have effectively been frozen since mid-September.

Housing markets have turned down

Housing investment peaked in the first quarter of 2007, and has declined by just under half a per cent of GDP since then. House prices have fallen markedly in some countries, and area-wide house price inflation is now around zero, with prices declining in real terms. This will reinforce negative financial wealth effects on private spending, although housing is less widely used as collateral for borrowing in the euro area than in other economies.

Labour market improvements have ended

Unemployment is rising, with the unemployment rate edging up to 7½ per cent in August, from a cyclical trough of 7.2%, close to the structural unemployment rate. Employment has continued to increase, although the growth rate has steadily slowed.

Euro area: **Demand and output**

	2005	2006	2007	2008	2009	2010
	Current prices € billion	Percentage changes, volume (2001 prices)				
Private consumption	4 617.0	2.0	1.6	0.4	0.2	1.2
Government consumption	1 648.7	1.9	2.3	1.8	1.2	1.2
Gross fixed investment	1 662.7	5.8	4.1	0.4	-4.4	1.0
Public	208.6	1.0	3.2	3.0	1.2	1.6
Residential	465.1	6.7	1.4	-3.4	-7.3	-0.7
Non-residential	988.9	6.4	5.5	1.4	-4.3	1.5
Final domestic demand	7 928.4	2.8	2.3	0.7	-0.6	1.1
Stockbuilding[1]	11.6	0.1	0.0	0.2	0.1	0.0
Total domestic demand	7 940.0	2.9	2.3	0.8	-0.5	1.1
Net exports[1]	118.5	0.1	0.3	0.2	0.0	0.1
GDP at market prices	8 058.5	3.0	2.6	1.0	-0.6	1.2

Note: The euro area aggregates cover the euro area countries that are members of the OECD.
1. Contributions to changes in real GDP (percentage of real GDP in previous year), actual amount in the first column.
Source: OECD Economic Outlook 84 database.

StatLink ⬛⬛ http://dx.doi.org/10.1787/502227405885

Euro area: **External indicators**

	2006	2007	2008	2009	2010
			$ billion		
Foreign balance	124.1	181.8	155.5	205	217
Invisibles, net	- 80.9	- 142.5	- 210.1	- 212	- 221
Current account balance	43.2	39.3	- 54.5	- 8	- 4

Note: The euro area aggregates cover the euro area countries that are members of the OECD.
Source: OECD Economic Outlook 84 database.

StatLink ⬛𝒔🔗 http://dx.doi.org/10.1787/502228608072

Inflationary pressures are beginning to recede

Headline inflation fell to 3.2% in October, from a peak of 4% in July, reflecting the decline in global commodity prices. Further sharp declines are likely in late 2008 and the first half of 2009, and headline inflation may well drop below core inflation for some time. Estimates of longer-term inflation expectations in financial markets have also turned down. Core inflation (excluding food, drink, tobacco and energy) has remained under 2% this year although cost growth picked-up in the first half of 2008, pushed by wage indexation clauses in some countries and weakening productivity growth. Nevertheless, the prospect of marked second-round wage and price effects from high headline inflation appears limited. The projected emergence of a sizable negative output gap, rising unemployment and weaker import prices will all moderate wage and price pressures in 2009 and 2010. Both headline and core inflation are projected to be below the medium-term objective of the European Central Bank from mid-2009 onwards.

Monetary policy can ease further

The European Central Bank has already begun to ease its monetary stance, although current financial market tensions have slowed the speed of pass-through into money market and retail interest rates. Policy rates were reduced by 50 basis points in the coordinated cut on 8 October and by a further 50 basis points on 6 November. Additional changes have been made to the refinancing operations of the ECB to alleviate liquidity shortages in financial markets. The prospective dampening of inflationary pressures over the next two years will provide scope for further reductions in policy rates in the coming months. Policy rates are projected to decline to 2% by next spring, and remain at that level for a year. If financial conditions were to deteriorate further, or activity to drop more rapidly than projected, deeper interest rate reductions could prove necessary in the near term. Thereafter, with financial turmoil dissipating and economic activity turning up, modest increases in the policy rate appear appropriate to ensure inflation remains below 2% in the years ahead.

Fiscal pressures are mounting

The ongoing cyclical weakness in the euro area economy, the downturn in revenue-rich financial and housing markets and the area-wide government actions being taken to restore confidence in financial markets will have substantial fiscal costs. The area-wide government deficit is projected to rise by 0.8% of GDP this year and in 2009, reversing much of the decline in 2006-07. Actions to recapitalise financial institutions and enhance deposit guarantees also raise actual and contingent government liabilities. The relatively large automatic stabilisers in Europe will also help to cushion the slowdown. With additional consolidation towards medium-term objectives still needed in many countries, any discretionary fiscal easing should be timely, targeted and temporary and take into account specific challenges of each country.

Further declines in GDP are likely in the near term

Economic activity is projected to decline further until mid-2009. Tighter financial conditions, subdued income growth, negative wealth effects, rising unemployment and enhanced uncertainty about the economic outlook should damp consumption and business investment, augmenting the drag on activity from further declines in residential investment. Export growth will be sluggish, reflecting weak global demand growth.

The eventual pick-up in activity will be slow

These adverse forces should moderate over time, but the pick-up in activity is projected to be only gradual. The drop in headline inflation through 2009, along with a gradual reduction in financial market turmoil and the effects of monetary policy easing, will all help to support an eventual expansion. By the latter half of 2010, activity is projected to rise more rapidly than potential, starting to close the sizable negative output gap that opens up through 2009.

The balance of risks remains on the downside

In the near term, the balance of risks remains on the downside. One notable risk is that the current financial market crisis lasts for longer than assumed. It is also uncertain if monetary policy transmission will work as expected, given the difficulties faced by financial institutions. Euro area activity could also be affected more sharply than projected by the slowdown in the external environment. In some countries, housing market downturns could also be steeper and more protracted than projected.

GERMANY

After a strong start into 2008, activity has contracted reflecting muted consumption and weakening export growth. Activity is projected to contract further in 2009 on the back of falling investment spending and weakness in the main trading partner economies. Private consumption will make a small positive contribution to growth because disinflation increases the purchasing power of past wage settlements. Activity is expected to pick up in late 2009 and return towards trend growth rates in the second half of 2010.

The government balance may be around zero again in 2008 but will turn negative next year as income tax revenues suffer and unemployment spending starts to rise again due to deteriorating labour market conditions. Automatic stabilisers should be allowed to operate but discretionary measures that involve long-term spending programmes should be avoided. A stimulation programme should be timely, well targeted and temporary.

Economic activity is slowing...

Following a very strong first quarter, economic activity declined in the second quarter of 2008. To some extent this reflected temporary factors mainly related to construction investment, but the drop in activity was more broad-based, affecting private consumption and exports. Private consumption fell as rising food and energy prices damped real disposable income growth despite an increase in employment and higher wage settlements in many sectors. Exports also declined in the second quarter, especially to the United States and the United Kingdom, driven by the slowdown in activity in these major export markets and the appreciation of the euro.

... due to weak domestic demand and a negative trade contribution

GDP fell further in the third quarter as weak exports and strong imports overcompensated increases in domestic consumption and a rise in stocks. Private consumption contributed positively to growth, most likely in response to the easing consumer price inflation due to the

Germany

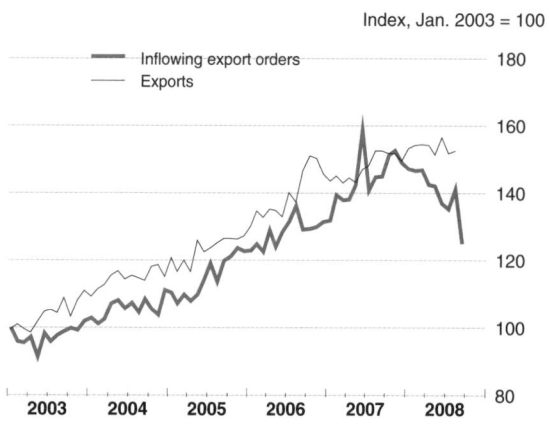

Note: Investment growth is year-on-year growth of quarterly gross fixed capital formation. Ifo data refers to manufacturing, construction, wholesale and retail trade. Exports and export orders are seasonally adjusted volumes.

Source: Deutsche Bundesbank; Ifo Institut für Wirtschaftsforschung; OECD Economic Outlook 84 database.

StatLink ⟶ http://dx.doi.org/10.1787/500321760550

Germany: **Employment, income and inflation**
Percentage changes

	2006	2007	2008	2009	2010
Employment	0.6	1.7	1.3	-0.7	-0.2
Unemployment rate[1]	9.8	8.3	7.4	8.1	8.6
Compensation of employees	1.6	2.9	3.9	1.8	1.6
Unit labour cost	-1.5	0.3	2.4	2.6	0.4
Household disposable income	1.9	1.6	2.6	2.8	2.5
GDP deflator	0.5	1.9	1.6	1.8	1.4
Harmonised index of consumer prices	1.8	2.3	2.9	1.1	1.3
Core harmonised index of consumer prices[2]	0.7	1.9	1.3	1.4	1.3
Private consumption deflator	1.3	1.7	2.1	1.0	1.3

1. As a percentage of labour force, based on national accounts.
2. Harmonised index of consumer prices excluding food, energy, alcohol and tobacco.
Source: OECD Economic Outlook 84 database.

StatLink ⟨⟩ *http://dx.doi.org/10.1787/502241883472*

decline in food and energy prices. However, consumer confidence indicators deteriorated somewhat as strong wage growth in a still-robust labour market was assessed as unlikely to last. Industrial capacity utilisation declined rapidly and business confidence deteriorated markedly, reflecting unfavourable earnings expectations in the wake of the global economic slowdown.

The impact of the financial crisis is intensifying

With the situation in financial markets deteriorating noticeably, the slowdown in activity is set to continue. While credit growth had been holding up well over the past quarters, rising refinancing problems in money and capital markets are leading to tighter credit standards and higher lending rates, thereby restricting lending to companies and

Germany

Wage increases have risen

Consumption has remained weak

Note: Wage growth is the year-on-year growth of quarterly nominal private sector wages. NAIRU is the rate of unemployment consistent with constant price inflation. Private consumption growth is quarter-on-quarter.
Source: OECD Economic Outlook 84 database.

StatLink ⟨⟩ *http://dx.doi.org/10.1787/500386563044*

Germany: **Financial indicators**

	2006	2007	2008	2009	2010
Household saving ratio[1]	10.5	10.8	11.6	12.9	13.0
General government financial balance[2]	-1.5	0.1	0.0	-0.9	-1.0
Current account balance[2]	6.1	7.7	6.4	6.2	6.1
Short-term interest rate[3]	3.1	4.3	4.7	2.7	2.6
Long-term interest rate[4]	3.8	4.2	4.1	4.0	4.4

1. As a percentage of disposable income.
2. As a percentage of GDP.
3. 3-month interbank rate.
4. 10-year government bonds.
Source: OECD Economic Outlook 84 database.

StatLink ᴍᵴᴾ *http://dx.doi.org/10.1787/502262088668*

households. Germany, which is highly dependent on international trade, is expected to be severely hit by the global slowdown *via* lower growth of export markets, especially for investment goods. Rising uncertainty about labour market conditions and the sharp falls in stock markets may temporarily induce consumers to increase their savings rate. On the positive side, the German economy is likely to be less affected by the global housing downturn, as prices and construction did not increase sharply during the previous boom, unlike developments in many other countries.

Germany: **Demand and output**

	2005	2006	2007	2008	2009	2010
	Current prices € billion	Percentage changes, volume (2000 prices)				
Private consumption	1 323.0	1.2	-0.3	-0.6	0.2	1.2
Government consumption	420.0	0.6	2.2	1.9	1.0	1.3
Gross fixed investment	388.9	8.5	4.5	3.6	-2.8	1.2
Public	30.9	3.8	4.4	6.5	3.0	3.1
Residential	116.4	6.5	0.4	1.2	-1.1	1.0
Non-residential	241.6	10.1	6.5	4.4	-4.3	1.0
Final domestic demand	2 131.9	2.4	1.1	0.7	-0.3	1.2
Stockbuilding[1]	- 11.4	-0.1	0.1	0.9	0.4	0.0
Total domestic demand	2 120.4	2.3	1.2	1.7	0.1	1.2
Exports of goods and services	918.6	13.1	7.7	4.2	0.7	3.9
Imports of goods and services	799.7	12.2	5.2	5.4	2.8	4.4
Net exports[1]	118.9	1.0	1.4	-0.2	-0.9	0.0
GDP at market prices	2 239.3	3.2	2.6	1.4	-0.8	1.2
Memorandum items						
GDP without working day adjustments	2 243.2	3.0	2.5	1.7	-0.9	1.3
Investment in machinery and equipmen	186.5	11.4	7.4	5.0	-3.5	1.3
Construction investment	202.3	5.8	1.9	2.4	-2.2	1.1

Note: National accounts are based on official chain-linked data. This introduces a discrepancy in the identity between real demand components and GDP. For further details see *OECD Economic Outlook* Sources and Methods *(http://www.oecd.org/eco/sources-and-methods)*.
1. Contributions to changes in real GDP (percentage of real GDP in previous year), actual amount in the first column.
Source: OECD Economic Outlook 84 database.

StatLink ᴍᵴᴾ *http://dx.doi.org/10.1787/502271343015*

Germany: **External indicators**

	2006	2007	2008	2009	2010
	\$ billion				
Goods and services exports	1 323.9	1 563.4	1 752.1	1 532	1 608
Goods and services imports	1 158.1	1 327.7	1 526.8	1 340	1 410
Foreign balance	165.8	235.8	225.3	192	198
Invisibles, net	12.3	19.5	8.5	2	0
Current account balance	178.2	255.3	233.7	194	198
	Percentage changes				
Goods and services export volumes	13.1	7.7	4.2	0.7	3.9
Goods and services import volumes	12.2	5.2	5.4	2.8	4.4
Export performance[1]	3.6	0.7	0.2	- 0.6	- 0.3
Terms of trade	- 1.3	0.7	- 1.5	1.8	0.3

1. Ratio between export volume and export market of total goods and services.
Source: OECD Economic Outlook 84 database.

StatLink ⟪⟫ http://dx.doi.org/10.1787/502274117182

Automatic stabilisers will lead to a deteriorating budget position in 2009

The general government budget will be roughly in balance in 2008 as the revenue shortfall from the reduction in corporate tax rates and a further cut in the contribution rate of unemployment insurance is offset by higher direct tax receipts from households and lower spending on unemployment benefits. However, the budget is expected to worsen noticeably in 2009. The overall budget deficit is projected to reach 0.9% of GDP in 2009 and remain around this level in 2010. Weakening activity will lower income tax receipts and unemployment related spending will pick up again. Healthcare spending is set to rise more rapidly, owing to a change in the remuneration of outpatient treatment. The announced further cut in the rate of unemployment contributions and the standardisation of the health insurance contribution rate across insurers are expected to roughly offset each other. A fiscal stimulus package is in preparation, mainly in order to mitigate the downturn in investment. It is not included in the projections. The government guarantees offered to banks will have no immediate impact on the public finances; they will become relevant for the budget deficit only if debt assumption takes place. At the same time, gross public debt will be affected by the rescue package to the extent that banks draw on funds that were made available for capital injections through the bank rescue fund.

GDP is expected to contract well into 2009

Real GDP is envisaged to fall sharply during the remainder of 2008 and will continue to decline during the first half of 2009. Unemployment will rise significantly from its current low levels with initial job terminations mainly hitting temporary workers. The decline in activity will be driven by a drop in business investment and a deterioration in the trade balance. Private consumption expenditures will continue to grow moderately, notwithstanding deteriorating credit and labour market conditions, as most of the higher wage settlements of 2008 will reach well into 2009, and lower inflation will increase their real value beyond what had been anticipated. Inflation is projected to slow noticeably to annual rates well below 1½ per cent, reflecting lower oil and food prices as well as the emergence of a sizeable negative output gap. Although the economy is expected to recover beginning in the second half of 2009, annual average growth is projected to fall to –0.8% in 2009. In 2010, the economy is expected to grow at an annual average rate of 1.2%, as quarterly growth is projected to return to trend by mid 2010. These forecasts are adjusted for the number of working days; for both years, however, the adjustment is small.

Downside risks dominate
The projection is surrounded by considerable uncertainty relating to the scale of the direct repercussions of the financial crisis on the real economy, the extent of the economic slowdown in Germany's export markets and the resilience of private consumption. As regards the last, the risk could go either way, speeding up the recovery if consumers start to cut back on savings or delaying it if high uncertainty induces them to save an even higher share of their income. Furthermore, if the fiscal stimulus package is implemented as planned, it may contribute to a stronger recovery once financial conditions normalise; this may also strengthen employers' confidence in the nearer term.

FRANCE

Growth is likely to fall below 1% in 2008 as a whole amid sharply deteriorating global economic conditions in the latter part of the year, due primarily to the financial crisis. The impact of this turbulence will reverberate well into 2009, with negative growth expected until the middle of the year, followed by a gradual pick-up of activity to above-potential rates by mid-2010.

As a result, a significant widening of the general government deficit is expected in both 2009 and 2010, despite the announced tightening of fiscal policy over the next few years, which is projected to result in a modest fall in the underlying deficit. While the government should let the automatic stabilisers operate fully in the short term, the scope for additional discretionary measures is limited by the poor public finance position and prospects. The focus on expenditures control and reform of the public administration should be maintained.

A severe downturn is underway

Real GDP growth will most likely fall below 1% on average in 2008, a significant slowdown relative to the previous year. The gains achieved in the first quarter have been largely erased by a sharp deterioration through the year. All major components of domestic demand have weakened, most notably housing and business investment. Export growth also fell significantly in 2008. Recent information on the business climate and household confidence, combined with indications of a generalised tightening of access to credit, point to a further weakening of activity in the first half of 2009.

Unemployment is on the rise

The downturn in activity is being quickly transmitted to the labour market, with net job losses in the second half of 2008 expected to push the unemployment rate to around 7.5% by year-end. So far, the rise in unemployment has been concentrated among youth and workers hired through temporary work agencies, but it is likely to spread more broadly in the near future. Rising job-market uncertainty, combined with a decline

France

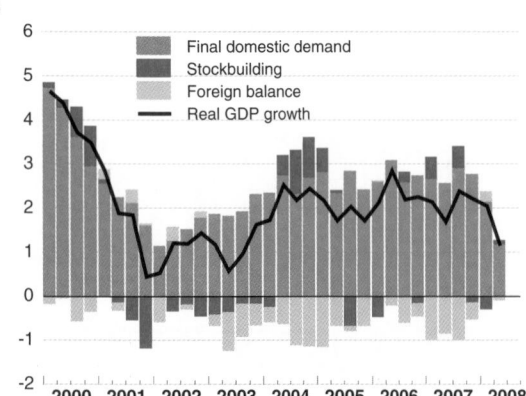

Domestic demand has continued to weaken
Contribution to year-on-year real GDP growth

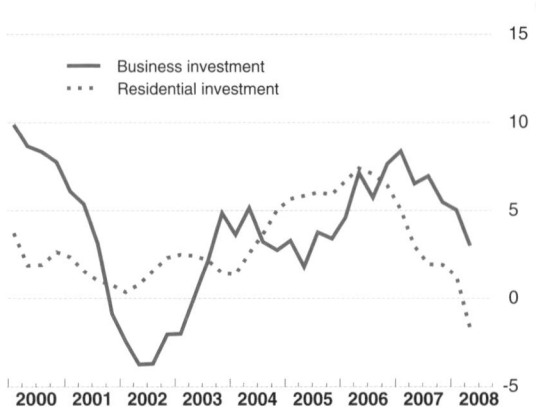

Private investment is leading the slowdown
Year-on-year change

Source: OECD Economic Outlook 84 database.

StatLink ᴍᴙᴩ http://dx.doi.org/10.1787/500408668770

France: **Employment, income and inflation**
Percentage changes

	2006	2007	2008	2009	2010
Employment	0.6	1.8	1.4	-0.6	0.1
Unemployment rate[1]	8.8	8.0	7.3	8.2	8.7
Compensation of employees	4.2	4.3	3.5	1.6	2.3
Unit labour cost	1.8	2.2	2.5	2.0	0.8
Household disposable income	4.7	5.4	4.0	1.8	2.5
GDP deflator	2.5	2.5	2.3	1.7	1.1
Harmonised index of consumer prices	1.9	1.6	3.3	1.0	0.8
Core harmonised index of consumer prices[2]	1.5	1.6	1.7	1.2	0.8
Private consumption deflator	2.2	2.0	2.7	0.9	0.8

1. As a percentage of labour force.
2. Harmonised index of consumer prices excluding food, energy, alcohol and tobacco.
Source: OECD Economic Outlook 84 database.

StatLink http://dx.doi.org/10.1787/502314207172

in wealth associated with housing- and financial-market developments, have induced households to raise their saving rates, despite only modest gains in disposable income. After picking up in the first half of 2008, nominal wage gains are believed to have slowed in the second half, reflecting the rise in unemployment and the decline in corporate profitability. The adverse effect of these developments on household real disposable income is partly cushioned by the rapid decline in headline consumer price inflation in the second half of 2008, reflecting the fall in oil and non-oil commodity prices. With the economy entering a phase of excess capacity, and given the slowdown in unit labour costs and falling profit margins, core inflation has declined – albeit modestly – in recent months.

France

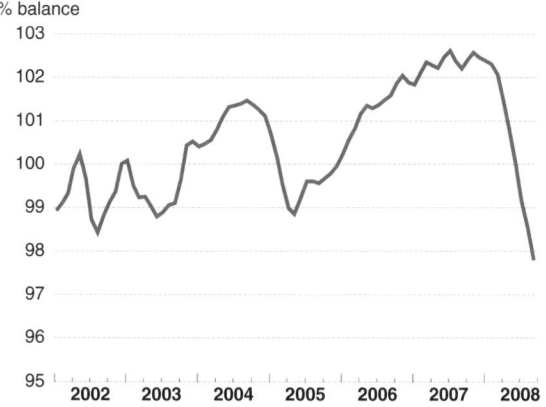

Business confidence is plummeting

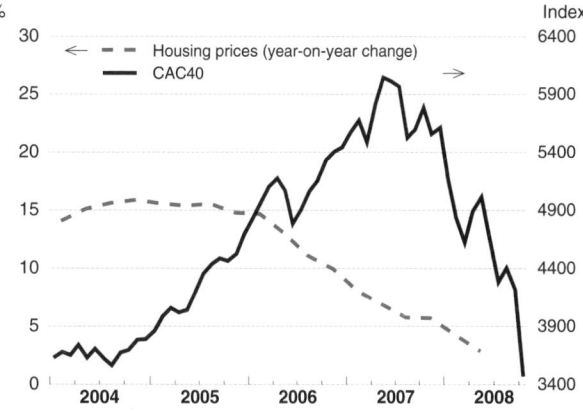

Falling housing and stock markets are bearing down on household wealth

Source: OECD Economic Outlook 84 database.

StatLink http://dx.doi.org/10.1787/500422665213

France: **Financial indicators**

	2006	2007	2008	2009	2010
Household saving ratio[1]	11.7	12.4	12.7	13.3	13.2
General government financial balance[2]	-2.4	-2.7	-2.9	-3.7	-3.9
Current account balance[2]	-0.7	-1.2	-1.6	-1.5	-1.6
Short-term interest rate[3]	3.1	4.3	4.7	2.7	2.6
Long-term interest rate[4]	3.8	4.3	4.3	4.3	4.6

1. As a percentage of disposable income.
2. As a percentage of GDP.
3. 3-month interbank rate.
4. 10-year benchmark government bonds.
Source: OECD Economic Outlook 84 database.

StatLink ᵃˢᵖ *http://dx.doi.org/10.1787/502343026114*

The impact of the financial-market crisis will be protracted

Looking ahead, GDP may contract until the middle of 2009. The aggravation of the financial turbulence during September and October is expected to have a protracted impact on household consumption and, especially private investment, *via* both lower confidence and tighter access to credit. In the case of households, the ongoing consumption retrenchment will be amplified by rising unemployment and the recent fall in house prices, which is expected to continue over the next two years. The housing-market correction will also result in further contraction in residential investment until at least mid-2009. On the external side, weaker activity abroad will slow export market growth significantly, while the loss of export market shares is expected to continue. The underlying fiscal stance is set to tighten somewhat in both 2009 and 2010.

France: **Demand and output**

	2005	2006	2007	2008	2009	2010
	Current prices € billion	Percentage changes, volume (2000 prices)				
Private consumption	980.4	2.5	2.4	0.9	0.3	1.8
Government consumption	408.4	1.4	1.4	1.4	0.8	0.7
Gross fixed investment	343.8	5.0	4.9	0.3	-3.6	2.1
Public	56.9	-2.1	1.7	-0.5	-0.2	1.6
Residential	96.3	6.9	2.9	-2.6	-5.1	0.7
Non-residential	190.6	6.3	6.8	2.0	-3.9	3.0
Final domestic demand	1 732.7	2.7	2.7	0.9	-0.4	1.6
Stockbuilding[1]	5.9	-0.1	0.2	0.0	0.0	0.0
Total domestic demand	1 738.5	2.6	2.9	0.9	-0.4	1.6
Exports of goods and services	448.8	5.6	3.2	2.2	-0.2	2.7
Imports of goods and services	463.5	6.5	5.9	1.9	-0.4	2.9
Net exports[1]	- 14.7	-0.3	-0.8	0.1	0.1	-0.1
GDP at market prices	1 723.8	2.4	2.1	0.9	-0.4	1.5

Note: National accounts are based on official chain-linked data. This introduces a discrepancy in the identity between real demand components and GDP. For further details see *OECD Economic Outlook* Sources and Methods *(http://www.oecd.org/eco/sources-and-methods)*.
1. Contributions to changes in real GDP (percentage of real GDP in previous year), actual amount in the first column.
Source: OECD Economic Outlook 84 database.

StatLink ᵃˢᵖ *http://dx.doi.org/10.1787/502354712165*

France: **External indicators**

	2006	2007	2008	2009	2010
	\$ billion				
Goods and services exports	609.1	689.1	760.9	657	685
Goods and services imports	636.9	739.0	829.1	703	733
Foreign balance	- 27.8	- 49.8	- 68.1	- 45	- 48
Invisibles, net	12.6	18.3	21.3	8	7
Current account balance	- 15.2	- 31.5	- 46.9	- 37	- 41
	Percentage changes				
Goods and services export volumes	5.6	3.2	2.2	- 0.2	2.7
Goods and services import volumes	6.5	5.9	1.9	- 0.4	2.9
Export performance[1]	- 3.3	- 2.6	- 2.0	- 1.9	- 1.7
Terms of trade	- 0.4	0.1	- 1.9	1.7	0.2

1. Ratio between export volume and export market of total goods and services.
Source: OECD Economic Outlook 84 database.

StatLink ⟲🖅 http://dx.doi.org/10.1787/502366141255

The recovery is likely to be only gradual

Following the shrinkage of GDP in the first half of 2009, and as financial markets begin to normalise late in the year, activity will pick up rapidly in 2010 to a rate of growth of 2½ per cent through the year. The excess supply gap is likely to widen to 3% by end-2009, putting substantial downward pressure on core inflation, which is expected to decline gradually from around 1¾ per cent in 2008 to less than 1% in 2010. The fall in inflation will boost household disposable income and, combined with reduced financial-market uncertainty and a stabilising job market, contribute to a sustained pick-up in private consumption through 2010. On the external side, the reduction in the cost of energy and other commodity imports may be largely offset by a further deterioration in the balance of trade in manufactures, leaving little change in the current account deficit of about 1½ per cent of GDP.

The deficit-to-GDP ratio will rise again despite fiscal tightening

The severe downturn in 2008 and 2009 is expected to reduce budgetary revenues significantly, not least taxes on corporate profits which had been particularly buoyant in recent years. At the same time, the rise in unemployment is putting upward pressure on social spending. As a result of these automatic-stabiliser effects, the general government budget deficit is expected to rise steadily from 2.9% of GDP in 2008 to 3.9% in 2010. However, the underlying structural balance is projected to improve slightly in 2009 and 2010, reflecting consolidation measures on the spending side, including the only partial replacement of retiring civil servants. Public debt (Maastricht definition) is projected to rise to over 70% of GDP by 2010.

The main risks are on the downside

Aside from the large uncertainties related to the resolution of the financial-market crisis, one risk to the projection is that the housing market experiences a more severe and long-lasting correction, which would further delay the recovery. Another downside risk is that household and business confidence takes much more time than assumed to return to pre-crisis levels. On the positive side, a more rapid decline in energy and food prices could bring forward the recovery in household consumption.

ITALY

The recession in Italy, which began early this year, is likely to extend through much of 2009, as in many other OECD countries. Global financial turmoil hit an economy already weakened by several years of low productivity growth, deteriorating competitiveness and high public debt, though solid job creation and falling unemployment had been bright spots. Recovering confidence towards the end of 2009 should allow output to accelerate significantly during 2010.

After a substantial reduction in the budget deficit in 2007, the fiscal stance turned somewhat expansionary in 2008. The government's three-year budget plan for 2009-11 recognises that high public debt and rising risk spreads leave little choice but to resume fiscal consolidation and the cyclically adjusted deficit indeed shrinks in these projections. But under current circumstances, the automatic stabilisers should be allowed to operate as the economy weakens. Cuts in public employment foreseen in budget plans should be carefully implemented so as to contribute to improved efficiency as well as fiscal savings.

The economy is in recession

The recessionary forces affecting the whole OECD area came at a bad time for Italy, which was already suffering from a long period of low growth. Following a slowdown in late 2007, activity has remained weak in 2008. Industrial production has been falling, with automobile production particularly affected. Real incomes have risen despite higher inflation but consumers are delaying purchases, and tightening credit conditions may also be making purchases on credit more difficult. Output gains in the service sector are proving insufficient to offset industrial weakness. Confidence indicators declined steeply during the year.

Credit is tightening

Credit conditions reported by banks for housing and consumption loans as well as for companies have continued to tighten in Italy, as in other countries. While house prices still rose in the first half of 2008, the

Italy

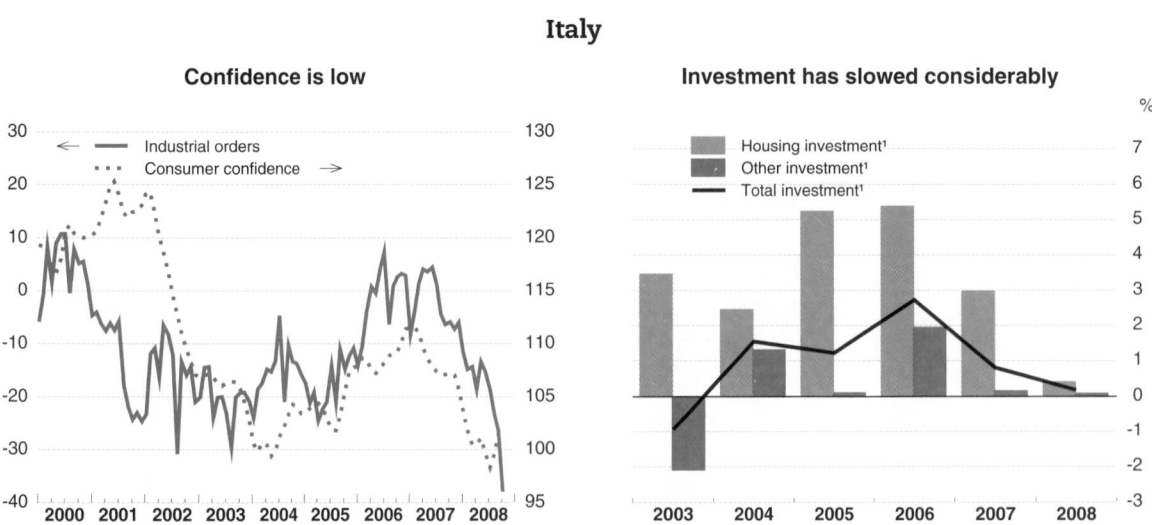

1. Annual growth. For 2008, first semester.
Source: Datastream, Istituto di Studi e Analisi, OECD Economic Outlook 84 database.

StatLink ⟨⟩ http://dx.doi.org/10.1787/500446481632

Italy: **Employment, income and inflation**
Percentage changes

	2006	2007	2008	2009	2010
Employment[1]	2.0	1.1	0.7	-0.4	0.0
Unemployment rate[2]	6.8	6.2	6.9	7.8	8.0
Compensation of employees	4.6	3.5	5.2	1.7	1.9
Unit labour cost	2.7	2.1	5.6	2.7	1.1
Household disposable income	2.9	3.0	4.9	1.3	1.5
GDP deflator	1.7	2.3	3.9	2.5	1.3
Harmonised index of consumer prices	2.2	2.0	3.5	1.5	1.5
Core harmonised index of consumer prices[3]	1.6	1.8	2.2	1.9	1.6
Private consumption deflator	2.7	2.2	3.6	1.7	1.5

1. Data for whole economy employment are from the national accounts. These data include an estimate made by Istat for employment in the underground economy. Total employment according to the national accounts is approximately 2 million, about 10%, higher than employment according to the labour force survey. Following national practice, the unemployment rate is calculated relative to labour force survey data.
2. As a percentage of labour force.
3. Harmonised index of consumer prices excluding food, energy, alcohol and tobacco.
Source: OECD Economic Outlook 84 database.

StatLink ᵐˢ┛ *http://dx.doi.org/10.1787/502371183307*

pace seems to have moderated. Over 70% of Italians own their home, more than in the United Kingdom and the United States, but turnover is low and few mortgage loans exceed half of the purchase price. Statistical evidence suggests that the impact of housing wealth on consumption is quite low. Although the Italian financial sector is not over-exposed to the household property market, its profits fell sharply as a result of financial turmoil, beyond paying higher rates on the inter-bank market. In early October the government announced that funds would be made available to supplement the existing deposit guarantee scheme and to finance Bank

Italy

Public debt[1] remains high

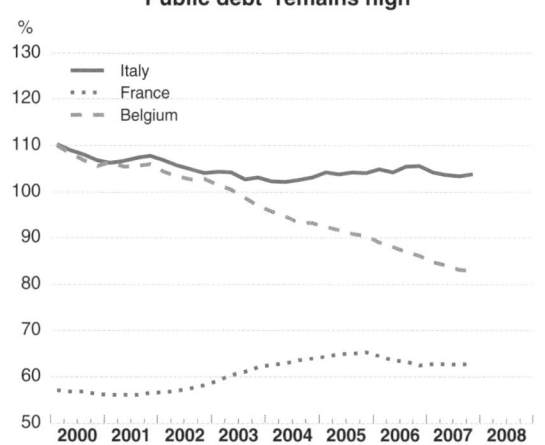

Risk premia[2] on public debt are rising

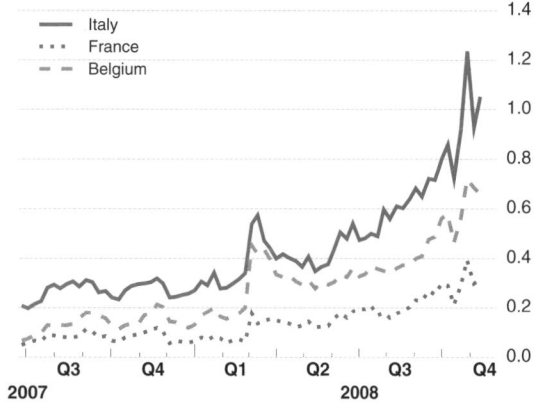

1. As a per cent of GDP.
2. Interest rate differential against German bonds, 10-year maturity.
Source: Datastream, OECD Economic Outlook 84 database.

StatLink ᵐˢ┛ *http://dx.doi.org/10.1787/500447638661*

Italy: **Financial indicators**

	2006	2007	2008	2009	2010
Household saving ratio[1]	9.0	7.9	9.2	9.1	8.4
General government financial balance[2,3,4]	-3.4	-1.5	-2.5	-2.9	-3.1
Current account balance[2]	-2.6	-2.5	-2.6	-2.1	-2.6
Short-term interest rate[5]	3.1	4.3	4.7	2.7	2.6
Long-term interest rate[6]	4.0	4.5	4.7	5.1	5.3

1. As a percentage of disposable income.
2. As a percentage of GDP.
3. The 2006 general government financial balance was revised from -4.4% to -3.4% of GDP following a decision by Eurostat to record VAT reimbursements on company cars in the years when the claims are validated, rather than in 2006 as originally planned.
4. In 2006 includes certain one-off revenues and a railways debt forgiveness operation amounting to 0.9% of GDP. Excluding these extraordinary items, the general government financial balance in 2006 was - 3.0% of GDP.
5. 3-month interbank rate.
6. 10-year government bonds.
Source: OECD Economic Outlook 84 database.

StatLink http://dx.doi.org/10.1787/502452672750

of Italy interventions to provide extraordinary liquidity assistance. Public funds may also be used to recapitalise banks in exchange for preference shares, subject to a government-approved three-year restructuring plan. Italian banks have made significant use of discounting facilities at the European Central Bank, but by end-October the only bank to have raised significant new equity capital did so without any public funds or guarantees.

Italy: **Demand and output**

	2005	2006	2007	2008	2009	2010
	Current prices € billion	Percentage changes, volume (2000 prices)				
Private consumption[1]	842.1	1.1	1.5	-0.5	-0.3	0.8
Government consumption	290.8	0.8	1.2	1.2	0.2	0.1
Gross fixed investment	296.2	2.7	0.8	-1.4	-4.6	2.1
Machinery and equipment	141.9	3.9	-0.5	-1.2	-4.4	2.1
Construction	154.3	1.7	2.0	-1.5	-4.7	2.1
Residential	69.9	5.4	3.0	-1.6	-4.8	2.1
Non-residential	84.4	-1.4	1.2	-1.5	-4.7	2.1
Final domestic demand	1 429.2	1.4	1.3	-0.4	-1.1	0.9
Stockbuilding[2]	0.5	0.4	0.0	-0.5	0.0	0.0
Total domestic demand	1 429.7	1.8	1.3	-0.8	-1.1	0.9
Exports of goods and services	371.2	6.5	4.5	0.4	-0.6	2.0
Imports of goods and services	372.1	6.1	4.0	-1.3	-0.7	2.5
Net exports[2]	- 1.0	0.1	0.1	0.5	0.0	-0.1
GDP at market prices	1 428.7	1.9	1.4	-0.4	-1.0	0.8

Note: National accounts are based on official chain-linked data. This introduces a discrepancy in the identity between real demand components and GDP. For further details see *OECD Economic Outlook* Sources and Methods *(http://www.oecd.org/eco/sources-and-methods)*.
1. Final consumption in the domestic market by households.
2. Contributions to changes in real GDP (percentage of real GDP in previous year), actual amount in the first column.
Source: OECD Economic Outlook 84 database.

StatLink http://dx.doi.org/10.1787/502475136011

Italy: **External indicators**

	2006	2007	2008	2009	2010
	\$ billion				
Goods and services exports	519.4	613.5	681.8	592	610
Goods and services imports	534.4	620.3	674.4	567	591
Foreign balance	- 15.0	- 6.8	7.5	25	18
Invisibles, net	- 33.0	- 45.1	- 69.0	- 67	- 72
Current account balance	- 48.1	- 51.9	- 61.6	- 42	- 53
	Percentage changes				
Goods and services export volumes	6.5	4.5	0.4	- 0.6	2.0
Goods and services import volumes	6.1	4.0	- 1.3	- 0.7	2.5
Export performance[1]	- 3.2	- 2.7	- 4.5	- 2.2	- 2.5
Terms of trade	- 2.9	1.3	0.7	3.0	- 0.7

1. Ratio between export volume and export market of total goods and services.
Source: OECD Economic Outlook 84 database.

StatLink http://dx.doi.org/10.1787/502483875741

Inflation has peaked

Headline inflation rose through much of 2008, peaking in August, but began to decline as world energy and food prices fell. Employment continued to grow quite rapidly in the first half of 2008, though figures for large companies suggest a recent slowing. Unemployment also rose as rising female participation and increasing numbers of immigrant workers swelled the labour force. Wage growth accelerated, as significant catch-up effects came from bi-annual contract renewals; the effect was stronger in the public sector than the private sector. Wage growth will moderate in the second half of 2008 and into 2009. National bargaining links wage increases to "planned" inflation, generally lower than both actual and expected inflation, but with such increases supplemented by local bargaining. Nevertheless, these increases, combined with little or no aggregate productivity growth, have resulted in excessive growth in unit labour costs and a trend deterioration in competitiveness.

Tighter credit and uncertainty play key roles in the outlook

Three key influences will prolong the recession into 2009: tighter domestic credit; global financial turmoil and associated lower activity abroad; and continued losses of cost competitiveness. As stability returns to financial markets and credit flows more freely, the first two of these factors should begin to reverse by late 2009. Recent falls in oil and commodity prices will also bring benefits.

After an expansionary budget in 2008, fiscal policy is set to tighten

The fiscal stance was somewhat expansionary in 2008. Income tax on overtime earnings was reduced and the property tax on owner-occupied dwellings was abolished. The budget for 2009 entails spending curbs and cuts in public employment (including by reducing the size of the teaching workforce by 10% over three years); the three-year budget programme is aiming to balance the budget by 2011. With high public debt, further fiscal tightening is inevitable – the consequences of excessive debt can be clearly seen in the recent widening of sovereign interest rate spreads. The needed fiscal consolidation will nevertheless likely be a drag on demand.

Activity continues to fall into 2009

Against all these headwinds, further falls in GDP can be expected until late 2009. Business and housing investment will decline quite sharply and the share of investment in GDP will recede from the relatively high levels of recent years. Households are likely to remain cautious so that although the saving rate may fall back somewhat following a sharp rise in 2008, growth in private consumption may not resume before late 2009. Depressed activity and falls in import prices will reduce headline inflation quite sharply, and it falls further in 2010. Unemployment will continue to rise through 2009, but continued labour cost growth will slow the decline in underlying inflation and weaken exports, which already suffer from low market growth. By late 2009, a recovery in investment activity should begin, and consumption and export growth will also increase. As confidence improves, growth will accelerate to above potential during 2010. However, poor underlying productivity growth keeps that potential growth rate itself rather low. This period of recession and rising interest payments due to the risk premium on Italian debt will leave public finances weaker despite the planned consolidation, which will improve the underlying fiscal position; the projections assume some, but not full, implementation of announced plans for public expenditure restraint, as the success of past Italian governments in this respect has been rather mixed.

Ambitious public finance targets may not be met

Italy-specific risks in the current outlook include, beyond the financial market turbulence, the degree to which the government succeeds in its fiscal consolidation plans: more successful consolidation than assumed here might bring long-term benefits but be a greater drag on activity in the short term, whereas more slippage could have the opposite effect. An upside risk is an earlier acceleration in consumption if households decide to adjust more quickly to the income gains of 2008, and unwind the increase in the saving rate more quickly.

UNITED KINGDOM

Economic conditions have deteriorated markedly and forward-looking indicators suggest a further sharp weakening in activity over the next quarters. The adjustment in the construction sector is expected to continue, while house prices are likely to fall further. These factors, combined with turmoil in the banking and financial sectors, are already cutting domestic demand. Growth may resume only in late 2009. Unemployment is set to rise rapidly, but should stabilise in 2010. Inflation should recede, reflecting the recent falls in energy and food prices and the increasing output gap.

Given the dramatically weaker outlook and signs that inflation expectations are now declining, the Bank of England should continue to cut its policy rate rapidly, particularly because fiscal policy is constrained by the weak budgetary position. The fiscal rules are likely to be reformulated; it is important to set out a credible plan for putting the public finances on a sound footing as soon as the economy recovers. The comprehensive plan to restore confidence in financial markets is welcome.

Economic growth has stopped

The UK economy stopped growing in the second quarter of 2008 and GDP contracted by 0.5% in the third quarter. House prices are around 15% below their peak of a year ago and mortgage approvals for home purchases are at record low levels, suggesting that dwelling investment will contract further. The labour market has also begun to weaken with the claimant count 14% higher than a year earlier, signalling large increases in the unemployment rate over coming quarters.

Consumer price inflation has overshot the target by a wide margin

Consumer price inflation accelerated over the past year to 5.2% in September, well above the Bank of England's inflation target of 2%. While accelerating inflation has largely reflected higher energy and food prices and a large depreciation of sterling, the elevated headline inflation rate has fed through to higher inflation expectations, which by some measures

United Kingdom

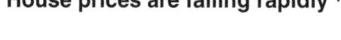

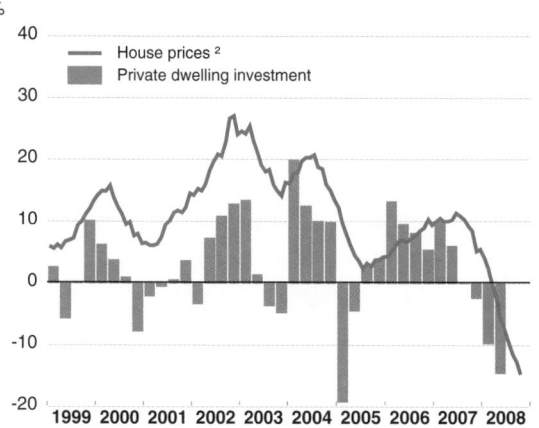

House prices are falling rapidly [1]

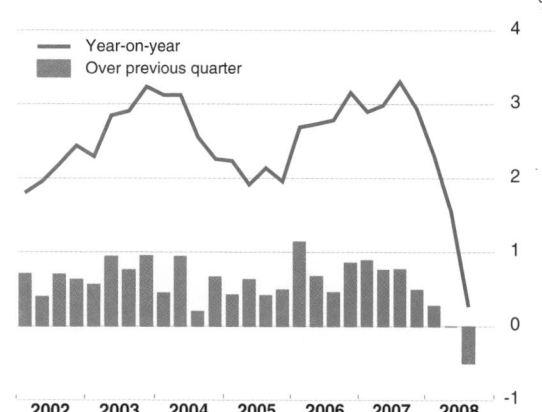

GDP growth has stalled

1. Year-on-year percentage change.
2. Average of the Halifax and Nationwide house price indices.
Source: OECD Economic Outlook 84 database, Nationwide and HBOS plc.

StatLink http://dx.doi.org/10.1787/500482508288

United Kingdom: **Employment, income and inflation**
Percentage changes

	2006	2007	2008	2009	2010
Employment	0.9	0.7	0.8	-1.8	-1.9
Unemployment rate[1]	5.4	5.4	5.5	6.8	8.2
Compensation of employees	4.9	4.1	3.6	1.5	0.0
Unit labour cost	2.0	1.1	2.8	2.7	-0.8
Household disposable income	4.0	2.1	2.9	3.8	2.4
GDP deflator	2.6	2.9	3.3	2.5	1.5
Harmonised index of consumer prices[2]	2.3	2.3	3.7	2.7	1.9
Core harmonised index of consumer prices[3]	1.3	1.6	1.8	2.6	1.9
Private consumption deflator	2.3	2.4	3.3	3.4	2.2

1. As a percentage of labour force.
2. The HICP is known as the Consumer Price Index in the United Kingdom.
3. Harmonised index of consumer prices excluding food, energy, alcohol and tobacco.
Source: OECD Economic Outlook 84 database.

StatLink http://dx.doi.org/10.1787/502622761833

rose to around 4%. However wage inflation has remained moderate, despite strong employment growth, and inflation expectations have now started to decline.

Policy interest rates should be cut further

The Monetary Policy Committee (MPC) cut interest rates by 50 basis points October and then again by 150 basis points in November taking the policy rate down to 3% currently. The focus of the MPC has switched from addressing high inflation expectations, which are now showing clear signs of moderating, to combating the economic downturn. The MPC still has room to reduce interest rates further in coming months and these projections have factored in further cuts over the first half of 2009,

United Kingdom

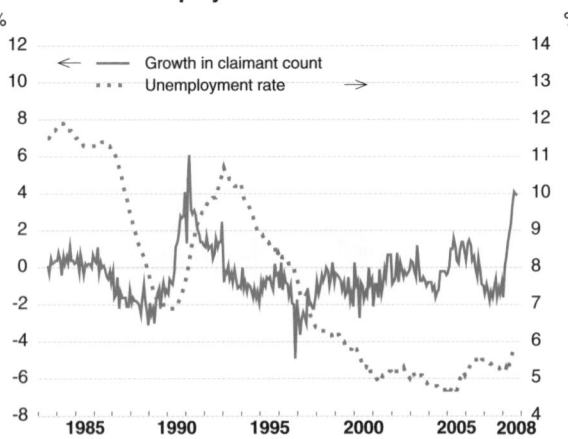

Private house new orders are deteriorating [1]

Unemployment is set to rise [1]

1. Monthly data.
Source: Office for National Statistics.

StatLink http://dx.doi.org/10.1787/500541677735

United Kingdom: **Financial indicators**

	2006	2007	2008	2009	2010
Household saving ratio[1]	4.2	2.5	-0.2	1.1	0.9
General government financial balance[2]	-2.7	-2.8	-3.6	-5.3	-6.5
Current account balance[2]	-3.4	-3.8	-1.9	-1.5	-2.1
Short-term interest rate[3]	4.8	6.0	5.6	2.8	2.7
Long-term interest rate[4]	4.5	5.0	4.7	4.6	5.1

1. As a percentage of disposable income.
2. As a percentage of GDP.
3. 3-month interbank rate.
4. 10-year government bonds.
Source: OECD Economic Outlook 84 database.

StatLink http://dx.doi.org/10.1787/502642285014

bringing the rate down to 2% before beginning to normalise rates towards the end of the projection period.

Restoring confidence in the financial sector

Financial markets are particularly important to the UK economy and the recent severe instability in that sector will therefore have a large impact. The authorities have taken a number of steps to avert a loss of public confidence in the banking sector, including the nationalisation of two mortgage lenders and the coordinated rescue of a bank. The Bank of England has provided liquidity in interbank markets, extended the Special Liquidity Scheme (whereby illiquid mortgage-backed and other securities held by the banking sector can be swapped for UK Treasury Bills), and temporarily extended the types of collateral eligible for repo operations. The recently passed Banking (Special Provisions) Act provides a comprehensive package to address financial market turmoil, giving the

United Kingdom: **Demand and output**

	2005	2006	2007	2008	2009	2010
	Current prices £ billion	Percentage changes, volume (2003 prices)				
Private consumption	810.7	2.1	3.0	1.8	-1.0	0.7
Government consumption	268.6	1.6	1.8	2.3	2.3	2.2
Gross fixed investment	211.3	6.0	7.1	-5.3	-9.0	0.5
Public[1]	8.0	273.5	1.7	4.7	0.9	2.8
Residential	63.8	8.9	3.3	-16.1	-14.3	-0.7
Non-residential	139.5	-7.2	9.8	-2.2	-8.8	0.4
Final domestic demand	1 290.6	2.6	3.4	0.7	-1.7	1.0
Stockbuilding[2]	4.6	0.0	0.2	-0.2	0.1	0.0
Total domestic demand	1 295.2	2.6	3.6	0.5	-1.6	1.0
Exports of goods and services	331.0	11.0	-4.5	1.2	-1.8	0.7
Imports of goods and services	373.7	9.6	-1.9	0.2	-3.4	1.1
Net exports[2]	- 42.7	0.1	-0.7	0.3	0.6	-0.1
GDP at market prices	1 252.5	2.8	3.0	0.8	-1.1	0.9

1. Including nationalised industries and public corporations.
2. Contributions to changes in real GDP (percentage of real GDP in previous year), actual amount in the first column.
Source: OECD Economic Outlook 84 database.

StatLink http://dx.doi.org/10.1787/502687785222

United Kingdom: **External indicators**

	2006	2007	2008	2009	2010
	\$ billion				
Goods and services exports	692.3	737.6	770.3	659	673
Goods and services imports	772.1	832.7	850.3	722	748
Foreign balance	- 79.8	- 95.1	- 80.0	- 62	- 75
Invisibles, net	- 3.5	- 9.9	26.5	27	25
Current account balance	- 83.3	- 105.0	- 53.5	- 35	- 50
	Percentage changes				
Goods and services export volumes	11.0	- 4.5	1.2	- 1.8	0.7
Goods and services import volumes	9.6	- 1.9	0.2	- 3.4	1.1
Export performance[1]	2.3	- 10.2	- 2.4	- 3.2	- 3.4
Terms of trade	0.0	1.5	1.3	- 0.9	- 1.1

1. Ratio between export volume and export market of total goods and services.
Source: OECD Economic Outlook 84 database.

StatLink ᆞᇰᇱ *http://dx.doi.org/10.1787/502727833275*

government special powers to intervene in the banking sector by acquiring equity in troubled institutions. The government has also announced plans to provide up to £ 50 billion of direct recapitalisation assistance to banks, and to bolster the wholesale funds market by guaranteeing the borrowings of eligible institutions against a fee. While the efficacy of these remedies is difficult to judge at this early stage, the government should be commended for taking swift and decisive action.

The fiscal rules will need to be rethought

The government's fiscal position is now expected to deteriorate significantly from the forecasts made in the 2008 budget, leaving only limited room to ease the fiscal stance. As the economy heads into the downturn, revenues will be considerably softer as corporate tax receipts and real estate transaction taxes decline. The government deficit is expected to rise to well above 6% of GDP by 2010. The sustainable investment rule, that government debt should remain below 40% of GDP, is expected to be exceeded by the beginning of 2009 (even excluding the impact of bank nationalisations). The fiscal side of the projections incorporate rough estimates of the recent measures to restore financial stability. The current circumstances mean that the fiscal rules are unlikely to be met going forward, and should be taken as an opportunity for a substantial reformulation. These changes should be expedited so that fiscal policy can be put onto a sound footing again as soon as the recovery gets underway.

An extended period of weakness is expected

Real GDP is projected to grow by just 0.8% in 2008, with output declines beginning in the second half of the year. The depreciation of the pound will help to promote export growth, but will largely be offset by weaker conditions in trading partners. The contraction in GDP is expected to extend into mid-2009, as consumer spending slows sharply with lower house prices, lower net financial wealth, tighter credit conditions and a weakening labour market. House prices are projected to continue to decline over the coming year, falling to about 20% below their peak. This long period of falling house prices and tight credit conditions will cut dwelling investment, with no recovery expected until the second half of 2009. Once house prices stabilise, construction should resume in view of significant underlying demand. The deterioration of the labour market is likely to be muted in comparison to previous downturns, as a substantial reduction of net inflows of European migrant workers is likely. Nevertheless, the unemployment rate is projected to climb to nearly 8% by the end of 2009. Inflation is expected to peak at the end of 2008 and to fall through 2009, as energy and food prices have declined and as activity falls, although headline inflation is not expected to be back to the 2% target until the beginning of 2010.

The duration of the recession is uncertain   The risks around these projections are especially large given the turmoil in financial markets. The negative wealth effects on household consumption from falling house prices and financial wealth may be greater than assumed. The fiscal position is also at risk, particularly because of bank bailout costs, but also because of likely countercyclical fiscal easing. On the upside, the interest rate declines could be even more rapid than projected and any fiscal expansion is likely to provide some stimulus to activity, at least in the short term.

CANADA

The economic downturn that started in 2007, as exports slowed in response to the deflating US housing bubble, continues to worsen. Sharply deteriorating conditions in global financial markets, generalised softness in the US economy and receding commodity prices are amplifying export weakness and dragging down domestic spending. Output has been contracting since August 2008, and slack is projected to grow until the global financial crisis has run its course and external demand bounces back in 2010. The domestic banking and housing sectors are in relatively good shape, however, and no government bail-outs have taken place.

Excess capacity and lower commodity prices are alleviating inflation pressures, allowing the Bank of Canada to boost its expansionary stance. The general government is expected to move into deficit in 2009 and 2010, a largely cyclical outcome that is not alarming and leaves room to absorb eventualities but underlines the need to keep a lid on discretionary expenditure increases.

The export-led slowdown has seeped into domestic demand

The economy has been decelerating since the second quarter of 2007, and activity in the first half of 2008 was basically flat. Exports continue to be the main drag, shaving an average of 2 percentage points from real GDP increases over the three quarters to the second quarter of 2008. Financial market turmoil and recently falling commodity prices are two further factors now weighing on economic activity through income, credit and confidence channels. As a result, domestic demand growth slowed from a pace of 4-5% over the past few years to 2.8% in the first half of 2008, and indicators point to further weakening in the last half of 2008 as a recession takes hold. Total employment has so far held up well, but job creation is slowing. From May to October employment increased by 71 000 jobs, compared to 187 000 over the same period last year. Headline inflation spiked in the third quarter of 2008 (3.4% year-over-year in September) on the back of high oil prices, although the official core measure, at 1.7%, remained within the Bank of Canada's target band.

Canada

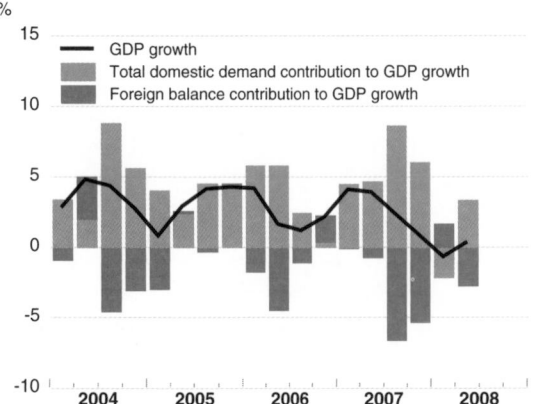

Real GDP has stalled in 2008
Percentage change at annual rates

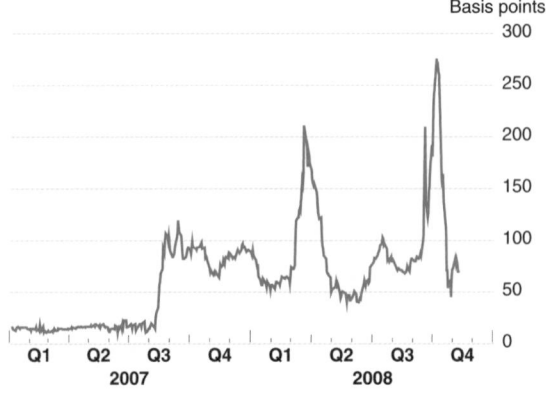

Banks' funding pressures have eased
Three-month bankers' acceptances minus treasury bill yields

Source: Statistics Canada and OECD Economic Outlook 84 database.

StatLink http://dx.doi.org/10.1787/500606208375

Canada: **Employment, income and inflation**
Percentage changes

	2006	2007	2008	2009	2010
Employment	1.9	2.3	1.4	-0.6	0.6
Unemployment rate[1]	6.3	6.0	6.1	7.0	7.5
Compensation of employees	6.9	6.1	4.4	1.1	2.5
Unit labour cost	3.7	3.3	3.9	1.6	0.3
Household disposable income	7.0	5.7	5.3	0.9	2.4
GDP deflator	2.5	3.1	3.3	-1.0	1.0
Consumer price index	2.0	2.1	2.6	1.2	1.0
Core consumer price index[2]	1.9	2.1	1.7	1.6	1.0
Private consumption deflator	1.4	1.6	1.5	0.8	0.9

1. As a percentage of labour force.
2. Consumer price index excluding the eight more volatile items.
Source: OECD Economic Outlook 84 database.

StatLink ᗧᔆᓗ *http://dx.doi.org/10.1787/502764730765*

Stagnant aggregate demand through 2009 and lower commodity prices should ease future inflation pressures. This has allowed the Bank of Canada room to continue cutting rates – including a co-ordinated cut of ½ percentage point on 8 October, followed by a ¼ point cut two weeks later – to help alleviate financial market pressures without risking unhinging well-anchored inflation expectations.

The Canadian banking sector is holding up

Thanks largely to tighter regulation, Canada's banking sector harbours fewer toxic assets and is better capitalised than that of most other OECD countries. Major Canadian banks have an average asset-to-capital ratio of 18, compared with more than 25 in the United States, over 30 for European banks and over 40 for some big global banks. But while

Canada

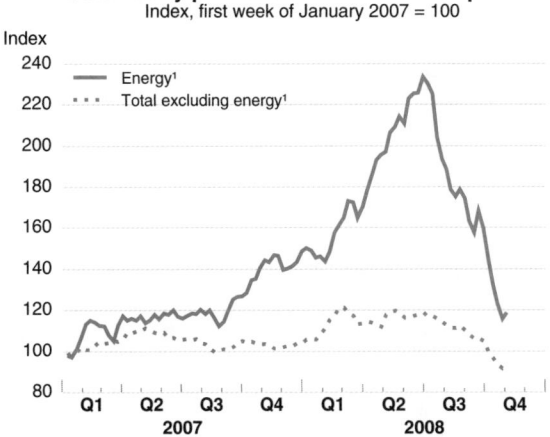

Commodity prices have come off their peaks
Index, first week of January 2007 = 100

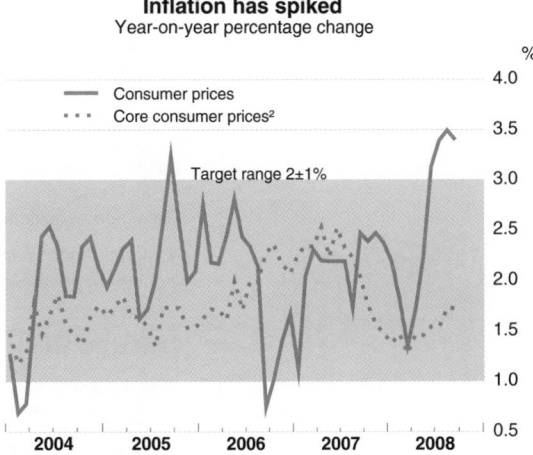

Inflation has spiked
Year-on-year percentage change

1. In US dollar terms based on Canadian production.
2. Bank of Canada definition.
Source: Statistics Canada; Bank of Canada; and OECD Economic Outlook 84 database.

StatLink ᗧᔆᓗ *http://dx.doi.org/10.1787/500615748656*

Canada: **Financial indicators**

	2006	2007	2008	2009	2010
Household saving ratio[1]	3.1	2.7	2.8	3.5	3.2
General government financial balance[2]	1.3	1.4	0.3	-1.3	-1.7
Current account balance[2]	1.4	0.9	0.4	-1.7	-1.4
Short-term interest rate[3]	4.1	4.6	3.5	2.1	2.6
Long-term interest rate[4]	4.2	4.3	3.7	4.1	4.7

1. As a percentage of disposable income.
2. As a percentage of GDP.
3. 3-month deposit rate.
4. 10-year government bonds.
Source: OECD Economic Outlook 84 database.

StatLink http://dx.doi.org/10.1787/502768300744

domestic banks do not need to reduce leverage and may be less dependent on access to foreign capital because of the country's longstanding strong current account position, they have not been immune to global financial-market strains. Volatility has increased, business credit growth has slowed, and banks and non-financial businesses are facing higher borrowing costs. The government has responded with a plan to help ease banks' funding pressures by allowing them to sell some of their mortgages to the Canada Mortgage and Housing Corporation (CMHC), a Crown corporation. In turn, the banks would receive CMHC paper, which they could use as collateral for their own borrowing from other banks. The federal government has also established

Canada: **Demand and output**

	2005	2006	2007	2008	2009	2010
	Current prices CAD billion	Percentage changes, volume (2002 prices)				
Private consumption	759.2	4.3	4.5	3.4	-0.6	1.8
Government consumption	260.2	3.8	3.7	4.3	2.4	2.0
Gross fixed investment	292.3	7.1	3.9	1.0	-2.8	1.3
Public[1]	36.5	6.8	7.9	5.5	3.0	3.0
Residential	90.2	2.2	3.0	-2.2	-3.7	0.5
Non-residential	165.6	9.9	3.5	1.8	-3.8	1.3
Final domestic demand	1 311.7	4.8	4.2	3.0	-0.5	1.8
Stockbuilding[2]	9.9	-0.2	0.2	-0.3	0.1	0.0
Total domestic demand	1 321.6	4.6	4.3	2.7	-0.4	1.8
Exports of goods and services	518.9	0.6	1.0	-4.3	-2.9	2.0
Imports of goods and services	467.9	4.6	5.5	1.9	-2.6	0.9
Net exports[2]	51.1	-1.3	-1.5	-2.1	-0.1	0.4
GDP at market prices	1 372.6	3.1	2.7	0.5	-0.5	2.1

Note: National accounts are based on official chain-linked data. This introduces a discrepancy in the identity
between real demand components and GDP. For further details see OECD Economic Outlook Sources
and Methods (http://www.oecd.org/eco/sources-and-methods).
1. Excluding nationalised industries and public corporations.
2. Contributions to changes in real GDP (percentage of real GDP in previous year), actual amount in the first
column.
Source: OECD Economic Outlook 84 database.

StatLink http://dx.doi.org/10.1787/502807573751

Canada: **External indicators**

	2006	2007	2008	2009	2010
	\$ billion				
Goods and services exports	460.9	496.6	520.7	428	436
Goods and services imports	429.5	469.4	499.1	438	444
Foreign balance	31.4	27.2	21.6	- 10	- 8
Invisibles, net	- 13.6	- 14.9	- 13.9	- 10	- 9
Current account balance	17.8	12.3	7.6	- 21	- 17
	Percentage changes				
Goods and services export volumes	0.6	1.0	- 4.3	- 2.9	2.0
Goods and services import volumes	4.6	5.5	1.9	- 2.6	0.9
Export performance[1]	- 5.7	- 2.0	- 3.6	- 1.8	- 0.5
Terms of trade	0.6	3.1	4.5	- 5.9	- 0.4

1. Ratio between export volume and export market of total goods and services.
Source: OECD Economic Outlook 84 database.

StatLink http://dx.doi.org/10.1787/502831748420

a new Canadian Lenders Assurance Facility to insure the wholesale borrowing of federally regulated deposit-taking institutions. The Bank of Canada has responded to the crisis by providing extra liquidity to the financial system in a series of Term Purchase and Resale Agreements in September and October 2008, and by the aforementioned ¾ point cumulative cut in its target interest rate.

House prices are declining but only modestly

Canada's housing market does not mirror its US counterpart. The US collapse was in large part brought on by overuse of subprime mortgages and easy credit in a low-inflation environment. In Canada, by contrast, such risky mortgages never made up more than 5% of new issuances, compared with 33% in the United States at the peak. The average resale home price started falling year-over-year in June 2008 for the first time in more than nine years, a trend likely to continue in the coming months. But the cooling is unlikely to wipe out all of the gains made during the six-year boom and should leave Canada with relatively healthy sales and price levels compared with other OECD countries. Despite pockets of more extreme overvaluation in some regions, which may therefore entail larger price declines, estimates are that an average nationwide price drop of 5 to 10% would bring the market back into equilibrium. Since such corrections are not unusual, the domestic house-price correction is not a major feature of the outlook.

Weak exports and lower terms of trade drive the projections

The worldwide financial-market crisis is leading to a protracted economic slowdown in the OECD area. For Canada, this means shrinking export volumes through much of 2009, bouncing back only in 2010. And with commodity prices having fallen well below the peaks reached in the early summer, and the recent decline in the exchange rate likely to lower the terms of trade even further, the current account surplus may also be reversed. These forces will affect the domestic economy. If employment drops and the unemployment rate rises as projected to above 7% in 2009, real consumption would shrink in the first half of 2009. Tighter credit conditions and lower profits will hold down business investment, and housing investment may continue its mild downtrend. Declining tax revenues will open up deficits in some provinces, if not at the federal level, and the general government is expected to move into a deficit of up to 1.7% of GDP by 2010. Late in 2009 the gradual recoveries abroad, along with improved Canadian competitiveness, should bolster external demand just as the recent interest-rate cuts stimulate consumption and investment spending. These developments may start closing the output gap in early 2010, though consumer price inflation will continue to edge down thereafter.

Uncertainties around the outlook are greater than usual

Given the importance of commodity and other exports to the economy, the main risks around the projection relate to the depth and length of the downturn in the global economy. A longer or deeper recession in Canada's main export markets than now expected would damp Canadian real GDP growth further through lower export volumes and prices. The reverse, of course, would accelerate the recovery. Domestically, the main risk is that house prices could depreciate more than expected, putting downward pressure on domestic demand and on inflation.

AUSTRALIA

GDP growth could well weaken from 2½ per cent in 2008 to around 1¾ per cent in 2009 before picking up to 2¾ per cent in 2010. This would still imply that, despite the depressed international environment, the impact of the financial crisis and the fall in the terms of trade should be relatively contained. Unemployment is likely to increase, however, and inflation may dip below 3% in 2010.

The expected reduction of inflation due to the current slowdown, along with the need to preserve the stability of the financial system, militates for looser monetary conditions. The recent budget measures, made possible by the significant fiscal leeway built in the previous years, will also support activity, although their effectiveness might be limited if confidence is not restored. It is important for the ongoing reform of industrial relations to preserve labour-market flexibility.

Activity has slowed

GDP growth fell to an annualised rate of 1.1% in the second quarter of 2008. Demand has moderated since the beginning of 2008 under the combined impact of tighter monetary policy, soaring oil prices and the international financial crisis. The slowdown in private consumption has been only partially offset by still-vigorous capital investment and a rebound in exports. Despite weakening activity, the unemployment rate has remained low thanks to the continued dynamism of employment in the mineral-rich states. Inflation has remained high, at a year-on-year rate of 5% in the third quarter of 2008, and underlying inflation was approximately 4½ per cent. An extended period of low growth is probable. Real estate activity is likely to contract, and leading indicators suggest a deterioration in the labour market. Although profit margins are still comfortable, the business climate has worsened, and the expansion of credit, access to which has become more difficult, has slowed.

Australia

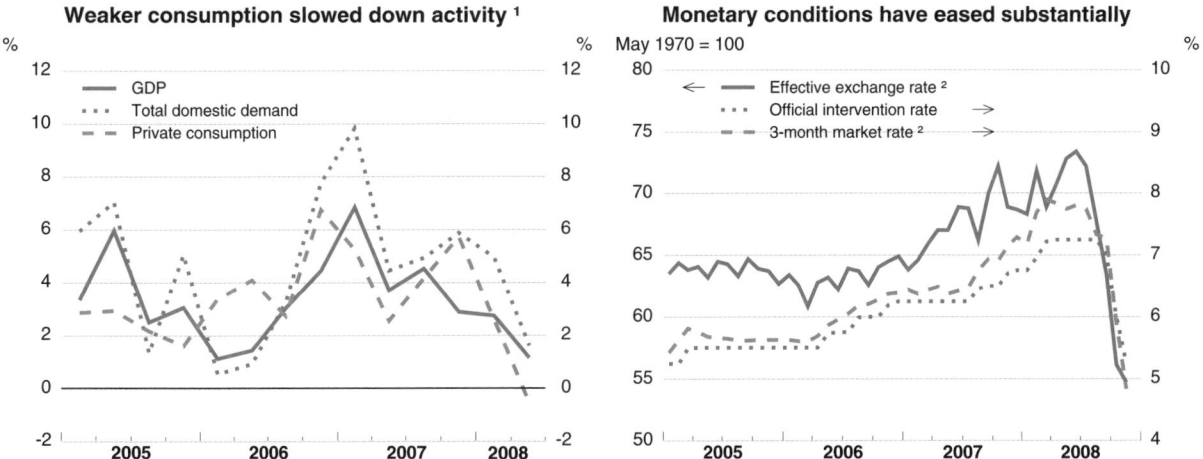

Weaker consumption slowed down activity [1]

- GDP
- Total domestic demand
- Private consumption

Monetary conditions have eased substantially

May 1970 = 100
- Effective exchange rate [2]
- Official intervention rate
- 3-month market rate [2]

1. Percentage change at the annual rate.
2. Daily data (12 November) was used for November 2008.

Source: OECD Economic Outlook 84 database and Reserve Bank of Australia.

StatLink http://dx.doi.org/10.1787/500653268824

Australia: **Demand, output and prices**

	2005	2006	2007	2008	2009	2010
	Current prices AUD billion	Percentage changes, volume (2005/2006 prices)				
Private consumption	533.2	3.1	4.5	2.4	1.7	2.7
Government consumption	167.4	3.2	2.4	3.7	2.4	2.2
Gross fixed capital formation	247.8	4.7	9.4	7.2	2.0	3.2
Final domestic demand	948.4	3.5	5.4	4.0	1.9	2.8
Stockbuilding[1]	2.9	-0.8	0.7	-0.1	-0.1	0.0
Total domestic demand	951.2	2.7	6.2	3.8	1.8	2.8
Exports of goods and services	180.9	3.3	3.1	5.0	3.7	6.9
Imports of goods and services	197.7	7.3	11.2	11.2	3.9	6.3
Net exports[1]	- 16.8	-0.9	-1.9	-1.7	-0.2	-0.2
GDP at market prices	934.4	2.5	4.4	2.5	1.7	2.7
GDP deflator	_	4.9	3.5	5.8	2.1	2.3
Memorandum items						
Consumer price index	_	3.5	2.3	4.6	3.3	2.4
Private consumption deflator	_	2.8	2.6	3.9	3.6	2.4
Unemployment rate	_	4.8	4.4	4.3	5.3	6.0
Household saving ratio[2]	_	0.2	0.9	1.4	3.5	3.1
General government financial balance[3]	_	1.5	1.6	1.8	0.6	0.3
Current account balance[3]	_	-5.3	-6.2	-5.1	-6.8	-7.4

1. Contributions to changes in real GDP (percentage of real GDP in previous year), actual amount in the first column.
2. As a percentage of disposable income.
3. As a percentage of GDP.
Source: OECD Economic Outlook 84 database.

StatLink 📊 http://dx.doi.org/10.1787/502833327110

Monetary policy has been eased substantially

Given the rapid deterioration in the external environment, the fall of commodity prices, and the state of financial markets, restrictive monetary conditions are no longer necessary to slow the pace of growth and inflation. The Reserve Bank of Australia lowered its base rate by 200 basis points, to 5.25%, between September and early November 2008, and the list of bank assets deemed acceptable as collateral for repo operations was expanded. The government has guaranteed bank deposits and the borrowings of financial institutions to facilitate their access to international credit markets. The 25% effective depreciation of the Australian dollar since end-June 2008 has eased monetary conditions further.

A fiscal plan to support activity has been adopted

The budget surplus forecast in May 2008 for the 2008/09 budget was similar to the 2007/08 surplus. However, weaker activity and expansionary fiscal measures are likely to result in a narrowing of the fiscal surplus in 2009. The government has recently adopted measures, amounting to 0.9% of GDP, including pension increases and assistance to families and homebuyers to stimulate activity. In addition, the government announced the accelerated implementation of an infrastructure improvement plan.

Growth is expected to ebb

Growth is projected to slow to 1¾ per cent in 2009 before climbing back to 3¼ per cent, a pace close to potential, toward the end of 2010. The international financial crisis and the delayed impact of the restrictive monetary policy in place up to the third quarter of 2008 should contribute to keeping growth fairly sluggish until mid-2009. With the external environment weakening, it is likely that businesses will have to scale back their ambitious capital investment projects. The recent fiscal measures should however support household demand. Activity is projected to gradually accelerate in the latter half of 2009, with the easing of monetary conditions and the gradual dissipation of global financial turmoil. Exports should also benefit from the drop in the Australian dollar, although the current account deficit could widen because of the fall in the terms of trade. With a negative output gap and the fall of the oil price, inflation should return to the 2-3% range as from year-end 2009, whereas the unemployment rate might reach 6%. A more pessimistic scenario cannot be ruled out, however. An external environment that is less favourable than expected combined with a further decline in the terms of trade would pose significant risks, especially if the global financial crisis continues and brings about a greater weakening of the Chinese economy.

AUSTRIA

Largely as a result of a worsening external environment, growth has declined and the economy is set to contract in 2009 before recovering in 2010. Headline inflation is projected to ease as energy and food prices fall, economic slack increases and import prices decelerate.

The recent fiscal support measures coupled with the working of the automatic fiscal stabilisers will help limit the extent of the slowdown. Preserving wage moderation will be important to avoid competitiveness losses and second-round inflation pressures.

GDP growth softened in the first half of 2008

Activity slowed in the first half of 2008, marking the end of a robust three-year economic expansion. This was primarily due to softer export growth, reflecting both weaker foreign demand and euro appreciation. Private consumption has remained subdued due to sluggish real income growth and deteriorating consumer confidence. Investment growth has moderated, both in the business and in the housing sector, as economic prospects have deteriorated. Spillovers from the global financial turmoil have intensified, with tumbling equity prices, heightened tensions in the banking sector, higher lending rates and corporate loan spreads, and tighter credit standards. In response, the Austrian authorities have raised bank deposit guarantees and introduced a sizeable state aid package to boost banks' capital. These swift measures may help contain contagion effects and negative fallout on the real economy.

Despite tight labour markets inflation has begun to ease

Employment growth was sustained through mid-2008, reflecting past strong output growth. The unemployment rate continued to fall but wage growth was nonetheless contained. Unit labour costs increased, though by less than in most other euro area countries, reflecting the cyclical

Austria

The labour market has remained tight

Export growth has weakened

1. Year-on-year percentage change.
2. Quarter-on-quarter percentage change.
Source: OECD Economic Outlook 84 database.

StatLink ⊙⊙⊙ http://dx.doi.org/10.1787/500685645612

Austria: **Demand, output and prices**

	2005	2006	2007	2008	2009	2010
	Current prices € billion	Percentage changes, volume (2000 prices)				
Private consumption	133.6	2.5	0.9	0.9	0.2	1.2
Government consumption	45.1	2.2	1.9	1.7	0.9	0.7
Gross fixed capital formation	53.4	2.8	3.9	1.9	-3.1	1.0
Final domestic demand	232.1	2.5	1.8	1.3	-0.4	1.1
Stockbuilding[1]	2.5	0.1	-0.2	-0.1	0.0	0.0
Total domestic demand	234.6	2.1	1.9	0.7	-0.6	1.1
Exports of goods and services	132.2	7.3	8.4	3.8	1.0	3.3
Imports of goods and services	122.4	5.4	7.0	3.2	0.6	3.2
Net exports[1]	9.8	1.3	1.1	0.6	0.3	0.2
GDP at market prices	244.4	3.3	3.0	1.9	-0.1	1.2
GDP deflator	_	1.9	2.2	2.6	1.7	1.1
Memorandum items						
Harmonised index of consumer prices	_	1.7	2.2	3.3	1.1	0.8
Private consumption deflator	_	1.8	2.3	3.1	1.2	0.8
Unemployment rate[2]	_	5.6	5.1	4.9	5.7	6.0
Household saving ratio[3]	_	10.8	11.7	11.8	12.2	12.2
General government financial balance[4]	_	-1.7	-0.5	-1.0	-2.7	-3.5
Current account balance[4]	_	2.5	3.1	3.6	3.7	4.0

Note: National accounts are based on official chain-linked data. This introduces a discrepancy in the identity between real demand components and GDP. For further details see *OECD Economic Outlook* Sources and Methods (*http://www.oecd.org/eco/sources-and-methods*).
1. Contributions to changes in real GDP (percentage of real GDP in previous year), actual amount in the first column.
2. See data annex for details.
3. As a percentage of disposable income.
4. As a percentage of GDP.
Source: OECD Economic Outlook 84 database.

StatLink ᵃᵍᵖ *http://dx.doi.org/10.1787/503016477556*

slowdown in productivity. Consumer price inflation, after peaking at 4% in June, has begun to recede thanks to lower food and energy prices.

Export growth is set to weaken

Relatively strong price competitiveness and the high share of trade with fast-growing Central and South-Eastern European countries underpinned Austrian export growth over the past few years. However, the external environment has deteriorated in recent months and exports are expected to slow further into 2009.

Investment and consumption are also set to slow

Investment, after growing robustly in the past three years, is losing momentum following the recent deterioration in business confidence and economic prospects. In addition, the global financial turmoil is likely to increase the cost and lower the availability of credit in Austria. Private consumption is projected to decelerate over the next year due to subdued growth in real income, rising unemployment and falling confidence. Consumer price inflation is expected to continue to ease, reflecting declines in food and energy prices, a negative output gap and slower import price growth. Consequently, real income should improve and, with the recovery of the global economy, consumption and investment should accelerate in 2010.

The fiscal position will deteriorate

Despite the slowdown in activity in the first half of 2008, fiscal revenues (especially direct taxes) grew strongly. However, recent decisions to increase pensions, adjust family allowances and long-term care benefits for past inflation, abolish university fees, cut the value-added tax rate on medication, and support investment by small and medium enterprises will reduce fiscal receipts and add to public spending starting in 2008. These measures, combined with the economic slowdown and a fall in profits of Austrian companies operating in Central and South-Eastern Europe, are expected to result in a significant increase in the general government budget deficit in the next two years, to 3½ per cent of GDP by 2010.

Risks to the outlook are on the downside

Risks to the short-term outlook are skewed to the downside. They primarily relate to foreign demand and to banking sector responses to the intensification of the financial turmoil. Regarding the latter, ensuring financial stability and more international cooperation of financial supervisors are essential, especially in light of the Austrian financial sector's large exposure to Central and South-Eastern European countries and to foreign currency lending. Inflation projections are highly uncertain due to erratic food and energy prices, though there are some upside risks relating to possible demands during the 2009 wage negotiations for compensating higher past inflation.

BELGIUM

Activity is projected to contract slightly and, thereafter, growth may remain below potential well into 2010, before rebounding on the back of easier monetary conditions, renewed growth in real incomes and a recovery in world trade. As a result, unemployment will increase over the projection period. Headline inflation should decline with the fall in energy and food prices, although core inflation should show more persistence.

The automatic stabilisers should be allowed to work fully during the downswing, but securing fiscal sustainability over the longer term will at some point require longer-term structural measures to achieve expenditure restraint at all levels of government. Abolishing the automatic wage indexation would allow for a more rapid decline in core inflation.

Growth has slowed to below its potential rate

Since early 2008, there has been a broad based deceleration of economic activity. Domestically, household spending softened due to sluggish real income growth and a sharp decline in consumer confidence. During the year, housing markets have softened, but by far less than observed in many other European countries. However, residential investment has started to contract. Exports have also slowed as export markets have weakened. Despite slower demand, employment creation has continued, although at a lower pace. The standardised unemployment rate bottomed out over mid-year at just above 6½ per cent, before drifting upwards.

Headline inflation has peaked

Headline consumer price inflation increased sharply until mid-2008, when it reached nearly 6%, before declining as the effects of energy and food prices began to fall. Core inflation had remained stable around 1½ per cent until mid-year, when it started to increase. Upward pressure on core inflation will continue due to the automatic wage indexation, which raised hourly wage growth to around 3½ per cent for the year,

Belgium

Headline inflation has peaked

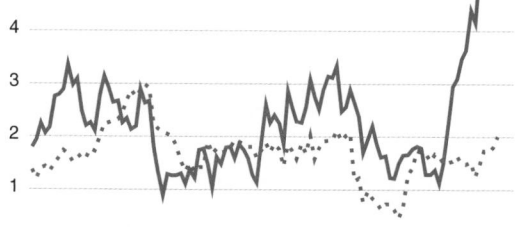

The fall in unemployment has ended
Standardised unemployment rate

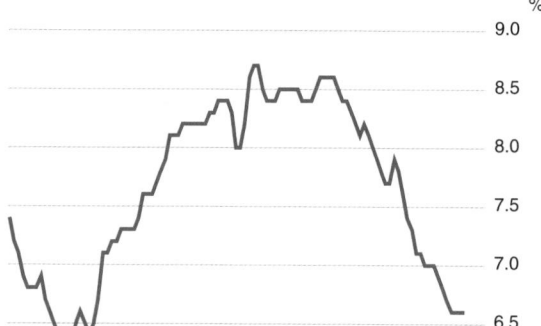

Source: OECD, *Main Economic Indicators.*

StatLink http://dx.doi.org/10.1787/500685675523

Belgium: **Demand, output and prices**

	2005	2006	2007	2008	2009	2010
	Current prices € billion	Percentage changes, volume (2006 prices)				
Private consumption	159.0	2.1	2.0	0.9	0.4	1.4
Government consumption	69.1	0.1	2.3	2.5	1.8	1.5
Gross fixed capital formation	61.6	4.8	6.1	4.9	0.1	3.0
Final domestic demand	289.7	2.2	3.0	2.2	0.7	1.8
Stockbuilding[1]	1.8	0.7	0.1	0.6	0.0	0.0
Total domestic demand	291.5	2.9	3.0	2.7	0.7	1.7
Exports of goods and services	261.9	2.7	3.9	2.7	1.0	3.5
Imports of goods and services	250.8	2.7	4.4	4.4	1.9	4.0
Net exports[1]	11.1	0.1	-0.3	-1.4	-0.8	-0.5
GDP at market prices	302.6	3.0	2.6	1.5	-0.1	1.3
GDP deflator	_	2.3	2.4	2.1	2.3	1.8
Memorandum items						
Harmonised index of consumer prices	_	2.3	1.8	4.6	1.9	1.6
Private consumption deflator	_	2.8	2.8	4.5	1.9	1.6
Unemployment rate	_	8.3	7.4	6.8	7.4	7.8
Household saving ratio[2]	_	8.0	8.6	7.9	8.0	7.9
General government financial balance[3]	_	0.3	-0.3	-0.7	-1.3	-1.6
Current account balance[3]	_	2.7	1.7	-3.3	-2.4	-2.7

Note: National accounts are based on official chain-linked data. This introduces a discrepancy in the identity between real demand components and GDP. For further details see *OECD Economic Outlook* Sources and Methods *(http://www.oecd.org/eco/sources-and-methods)*.
1. Contributions to changes in real GDP (percentage of real GDP in previous year), actual amount in the first column.
2. As a percentage of disposable income.
3. As a percentage of GDP.
Source: OECD Economic Outlook 84 database.

StatLink ᴍ᷑ᴉᴢᴘ *http://dx.doi.org/10.1787/503022006635*

higher than set out in the wage agreements. At the time of writing, this excess wage growth is not expected to be reversed in the wage agreements for 2009-10, which are assumed to broadly follow the expected labour cost trends in the three main trading partners.

Securing fiscal sustainability requires additional measures.

The general government fiscal deficit is estimated to have risen to ¾ per cent of GDP in 2008, reflecting lower-than-expected value-added tax (VAT) receipts, higher-than-expected increases in government wages and transfers due to automatic indexation, and some negative effects from earlier self-reversing fiscal measures. The budget for 2009 is mildly expansionary due to measures to preserve the purchasing power of some consumer groups and regional tax cuts. Together with some reliance on one-off measures and the effects of the automatic stabilisers, the deficit may reach about 1¼ per cent of GDP. The budget deficit is projected to widen by an additional ¼ per cent of GDP in 2010, bringing it further away from the government's revised path towards fiscal sustainability. Over the medium term, this needs to be rectified through structural measures to rein in expenditures at all levels of government.

Growth prospects will brighten only in 2010

Growth is likely to remain sluggish until the second half of 2010. By then, monetary easing, the waning of financial market turbulence, and a recovery in world trade should raise growth above potential. This implies that the output gap will widen over most of the projection period, easing inflationary pressures. The main downside risks to this projection, in addition to increased financial turbulence are that the current wage negotiations may lead to higher wage inflation in Belgium than in the neighbouring countries, hurting cost competitiveness and further reducing export growth, which could also suffer if global markets weaken more than expected. On the upside, decisive action to bolster the financial sector may boost consumer confidence, allowing for a faster recovery.

CZECH REPUBLIC

Growth slowed in the first half of 2008 and is not expected to return to trend again until 2010. The slowdown started with weaker domestic demand in 2008, as the inflation spike eroded consumers' purchasing power, and will continue as export market growth slows. The rebound is projected to be driven by both private consumption and exports. Inflation is expected to decelerate substantially in 2009 as the impact of one-off government measures wears off and global energy and commodity prices fall.

The key impediment to continued high trend growth is a shortage of labour and skills. The government could ease this shortage by further reducing marginal income tax rates and increasing graduation rates from tertiary education. Additional reforms of health care and pension systems are needed to ensure fiscal sustainability and enhance efficiency of public spending.

Growth slowed and inflation peaked in the first half of 2008...

Growth decelerated notably in the first half of 2008, mainly reflecting declining domestic demand. Exports were also somewhat damped by weaker growth of major trading partners and the rapidly appreciating real effective exchange rate. Industrial production weakened during this period, while adjustment in the housing market has so far been gradual, with prices and construction still increasing on an annual basis. Headline consumer price inflation peaked in early 2008 at 7.5% (year-on-year), reflecting rising world energy and food prices, deregulation of rents and a shift from direct to indirect taxes in early 2008. Inflation decelerated in the second quarter, mainly due to falling food and energy prices. The unemployment rate declined to the lowest level of the past ten years and private sector wages continued to increase in the first half of 2008.

Czech Republic

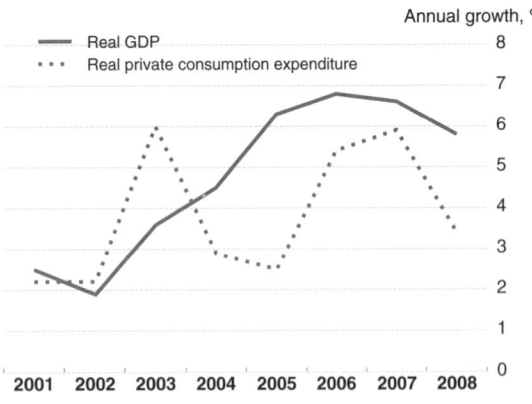

Inflation has peaked

Output deceleration has started with weaker domestic demand

Note: Headline inflation is measured by the consumer price index. Monetary policy relevant inflation as defined by the Czech National Bank is headline inflation adjusted for first-round effects of changes to indirect taxes.
1. GDP and consumption for 2008 are for Q1 and Q2.
Source: Czech National Bank; Czech Statistical Office; OECD, National Accounts database.

StatLink ⟲ http://dx.doi.org/10.1787/500700083423

Czech Republic: **Demand, output and prices**

	2005	2006	2007	2008	2009	2010
	Current prices CZK billion	Percentage changes, volume (2000 prices)				
Private consumption	1 464.2	5.5	5.9	3.3	3.3	4.1
Government consumption	658.5	-0.7	0.5	1.2	1.2	0.8
Gross fixed capital formation	741.9	6.5	5.8	4.1	5.0	5.3
Final domestic demand	2 864.5	4.3	4.6	3.0	3.3	3.7
Stockbuilding[1]	26.0	1.0	1.1	-1.4	-0.4	0.0
Total domestic demand	2 890.5	5.3	5.7	1.5	2.9	3.7
Exports of goods and services	2 150.5	16.4	14.6	10.2	1.8	5.1
Imports of goods and services	2 057.5	14.7	13.8	6.9	2.2	4.3
Net exports[1]	93.0	1.7	1.1	3.0	-0.2	0.9
GDP at market prices	2 983.5	6.8	6.6	4.4	2.5	4.4
GDP deflator	_	0.9	3.6	2.4	2.3	1.8
Memorandum items						
Consumer price index	_	2.6	3.0	6.6	2.0	2.6
Private consumption deflator	_	1.6	2.8	5.4	2.3	2.1
Unemployment rate	_	7.2	5.3	4.5	5.2	5.5
General government financial balance[2]	_	-2.7	-1.0	-1.6	-1.9	-1.7
Current account balance[2]	_	-2.5	-1.7	-2.3	-2.9	-3.3

Note: National accounts are based on official chain-linked data. This introduces a discrepancy in the identity between real demand components and GDP. For further details see *OECD Economic Outlook* Sources and Methods (*http://www.oecd.org/eco/sources-and-methods*).
1. Contributions to changes in real GDP (percentage of real GDP in previous year), actual amount in the first column.
2. As a percentage of GDP.
Source: OECD Economic Outlook 84 database.

StatLink 🔗 *http://dx.doi.org/10.1787/503038438080*

... the exchange rate appreciated and the policy rate was lowered

The Czech koruna appreciated strongly in both nominal and real effective terms in the first half of 2008, partly offsetting domestic inflationary pressures by reducing import prices. At the same time, as wages increased, unit labour costs have soared, weakening competitiveness. In the context of declining headline inflation and reduced inflationary pressures, the Czech National Bank cut its policy interest rate in early August and early November. Since August, the koruna has depreciated relative to the euro.

The 2008 fiscal policy stance has been broadly neutral

While the deficit target for 2008 was almost unchanged from 2007, slower growth and operating of the automatic stabilizers imply deterioration in outcomes in 2008 and 2009 from 2007. The broadly neutral policy stance in 2008 constitutes an improvement over the past several years, when the fiscal policy was procyclical.

Recent tax and labour reforms improve incentives

The recent fiscal reform, which shifted the tax burden from direct to indirect taxation, should stimulate overall labour supply and entrepreneurship. The parliament's approval of a bill raising the retirement age to 65 years will eventually increase the labour supply of workers in this group. Government efforts to attract foreign labour through issuance of green cards should only somewhat ease the labour and skill shortages.

Growth will only accelerate in 2010

Real GDP growth is projected to slow to 4.4% in 2008 and 2.5% in 2009, but rebound to 4.4% in 2010, as private consumption and exports pick up. Given the economy's dependence on external trade, the main risks to this outlook are a greater slowdown than expected in the euro area. Inflation is projected to decline to 2% in 2009 due to subdued domestic demand, the still strong exchange rate, moderate commodity prices, and the waning impact of one-off measures. Higher than projected nominal wage growth constitutes the main risk to the inflation outlook.

DENMARK

After years of strong expansion, the construction boom is now over and falling house prices have put an end to debt-financed consumption growth. As the impact of global financial turmoil materialises, exports are likely to remain weak during 2009, leading businesses to cut back investment.

Denmark enters the slowdown with severe capacity pressures and wages rising much faster than warranted by productivity growth. There is thus little need presently for fiscal demand stimulus, especially since monetary conditions are set to ease along with those of the euro area.

Growth has stalled but wage pressures have intensified

GDP has been essentially flat since the second half of 2007 and, more recently, all major components of demand have weakened. Strong food and energy price inflation cut retail sales, and car sales also weakened. Export orders have declined sharply, and firms indicate that they are trimming investment plans. Nevertheless, employment and hours worked continued to rise in early 2008 and registered unemployment reached a new record low in September. For the private sector as a whole, hourly wage growth rose to nearly 5% in the second quarter of 2008. With productivity growth averaging 1% over the past ten years, this implies overheating and eroding competitiveness. Core inflation, which has gathered momentum, points in the same direction.

Financial turmoil will have a material impact

Credit has expanded strongly in recent years, but with rising defaults, notably by property developers, a couple of small banks have recently been taken over by competitors and a medium-sized bank was taken over and closed down by the central bank in the early autumn. The spread between secured and unsecured interbank interest rates has widened. Tighter credit conditions are likely to weigh on activity well into 2009, notwithstanding the unlimited Government-backed guarantee issued in

Denmark

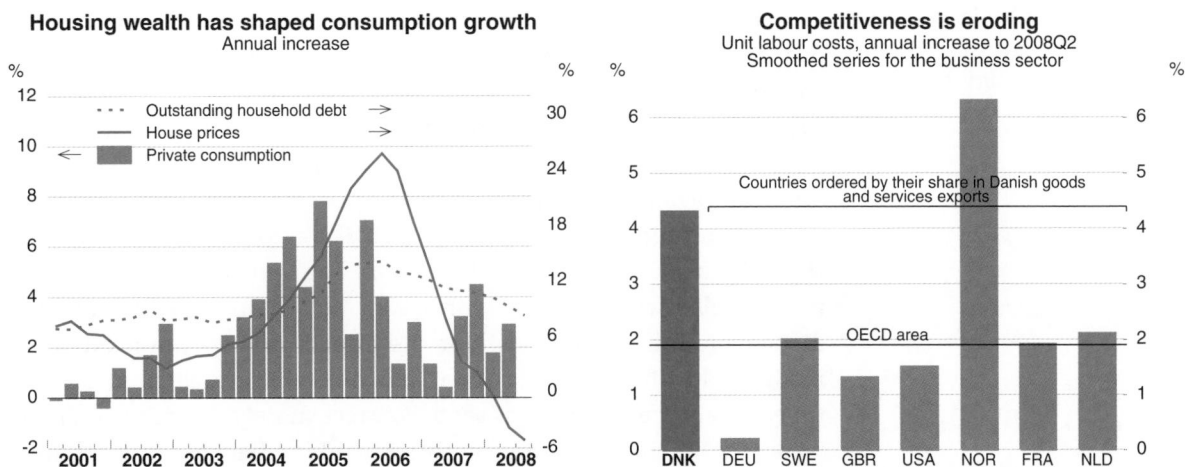

Source: OECD Economic Outlook 84 Database, Nationalbanken and Association of Danish Mortgage Banks; OECD, Monthly Economic Indicators database.

StatLink ᴍᴸᴾ *http://dx.doi.org/10.1787/500702170803*

Denmark: **Demand, output and prices**

	2005	2006	2007	2008	2009	2010
	Current prices DKK billion	Percentage changes, volume (2000 prices)				
Private consumption	759.8	3.8	2.3	1.5	0.3	0.8
Government consumption	401.3	2.0	1.6	0.9	1.5	1.0
Gross fixed capital formation	304.8	14.0	5.9	0.6	-4.3	-2.1
Final domestic demand	1 465.8	5.4	2.9	1.1	-0.5	0.2
Stockbuilding[1]	5.9	0.6	-0.3	-0.3	-0.2	0.0
Total domestic demand	1 471.8	6.0	2.6	0.8	-0.5	0.2
Exports of goods and services	761.6	9.0	1.9	2.6	0.5	3.4
Imports of goods and services	685.2	14.1	3.8	4.0	0.4	2.2
Net exports[1]	76.4	-1.8	-0.9	-0.7	0.1	0.7
GDP at market prices	1 548.2	3.9	1.7	0.2	-0.5	0.9
GDP deflator	_	2.0	1.7	3.4	2.3	2.2
Memorandum items						
Consumer price index	_	1.9	1.7	3.5	1.6	1.6
Private consumption deflator	_	2.1	1.9	2.5	1.5	1.6
Unemployment rate[2]	_	3.9	3.7	3.1	4.0	4.5
Household saving ratio[3]	_	-3.1	-2.8	-1.9	-0.7	1.7
General government financial balance[4]	_	5.0	4.4	2.4	0.1	-0.6
Current account balance[4]	_	2.7	1.1	0.8	0.9	2.0

Note: National accounts are based on official chain-linked data. This introduces a discrepancy in the identity between real demand components and GDP. For further details see *OECD Economic Outlook* Sources and Methods *(http://www.oecd.org/eco/sources-and-methods)*.
1. Contributions to changes in real GDP (percentage of real GDP in previous year), actual amount in the first column.
2. Based on the Labour Force Survey, being ½-1 percentage point above the registered unemployment rate.
3. As a percentage of disposable income, net of household consumption of fixed capital.
4. As a percentage of GDP.
Source: OECD Economic Outlook 84 database.

StatLink http://dx.doi.org/10.1787/503056547021

October, covering all deposits and other bank liabilities except subordinated loan capital.

Housing wealth losses will depress consumption and construction will contract

House prices are now declining and the rate of forced sales has risen over the past year, albeit from a low level. Even only a partial reversal of the spectacular house price gains seen in recent years will entail strong negative wealth effects which will weigh heavily on private consumption. Household borrowing has already slowed as interest rates have increased. With the saving ratio negative over the past four years, the reduction in debt-financed consumption should be expected to continue throughout 2009-10. The acceleration in both private and public sector pay, coupled with tax cuts worth 0.2% of GDP in 2009, will underpin disposable income growth. But the effects on consumption will be moderated by falling employment and general uncertainty. At the same time, housing construction is set to contract sharply. Construction permit issuance has plunged, and with a shrinking backlog of sites under construction, the fall in private residential investment that started in the first half of 2008 is bound to become more pronounced.

The fixed exchange rate requires policy discipline

In late October 2008, capital outflows forced the central bank to hike its interest rate to keep the exchange rate at its central parity. Consequently, the short-term interest rate differential *vis-à-vis* the euro area widened to about 1 percentage point. The tensions are likely to be eased by a large-scale euro lending facility put in place since then. Fiscal policy must also be cautious, however. Aggressive fiscal stimulus to keep unemployment at recent record-low levels would magnify the loss of competitiveness and, ultimately, challenge the stability of the fixed exchange rate regime. This would make it difficult to lower interest rates in line with cuts in the euro area.

With weak growth, capacity pressures will ease

With all major demand components weakening, GDP is projected to contract mildly in 2009. Headline inflation will fall along with global commodity prices. Starting from a situation of acute labour shortages, however, underlying inflation pressures will ease only gradually; the unemployment rate will not exceed its estimated structural level before 2010. The accumulated loss of competitiveness means that recoveries abroad will not feed through fully to Danish export demand. Against this backdrop, business investment is set to decline. Weak activity, low asset prices and falling revenues from North Sea oil production will lead to a fiscal deficit in 2010.

Financial turmoil is the overriding risk

Recent events illustrate the unpredictable nature of financial turmoil. A more dramatic fallout than seen so far, combined with the accumulated loss of competitiveness and imbalances that have built up in the housing market, could prolong the downturn.

FINLAND

Economic activity has slowed substantially, mainly due to a decline in investment. Output growth is projected to be subdued in 2009, before recovering during 2010. Unemployment is likely to drift up during 2009, but should stabilise in 2010. Lower commodity prices and growing slack in the economy should bring down inflation from the current high rate.

The strong fiscal position provides room for fiscal manoeuvre. While the fiscal surplus is likely to fall considerably during 2009, due to weaker activity and sizeable tax cuts, it should remain close to 3% of GDP in 2010, as the recovery takes hold. Labour market mismatches need to be addressed to ensure a further decline in structural unemployment. The closing of the remaining early retirement schemes would raise employment and underpin fiscal sustainability over the medium term.

Domestic demand has slowed considerably

After several years of strong growth, the housing market has turned, reflecting higher interest rates and tighter credit conditions. House prices have started to decline recently. Business investment has plunged, partly due to a downsizing of the pulp and paper industry. Private consumption has remained robust, however, underpinned by rapid wage growth and tax cuts, and export growth was very dynamic until mid-2008. Despite the slowdown in activity, employment has continued to expand and the unemployment rate dropped to close to 6% in August 2008. Inflation has shot up from a low level, in part due to higher food and energy prices. In addition, labour costs have risen sharply, reflecting large wage increases negotiated in the previous wage round.

The fiscal stance is easing

The fiscal stance is easing throughout the projection period, though the surplus could still be close to 3% of GDP in 2010. The 2009 budget proposal anticipates a decline in the budget surplus from 4¾ per cent of GDP in 2008 to 3½ per cent in 2009, largely due to personal income tax

Finland

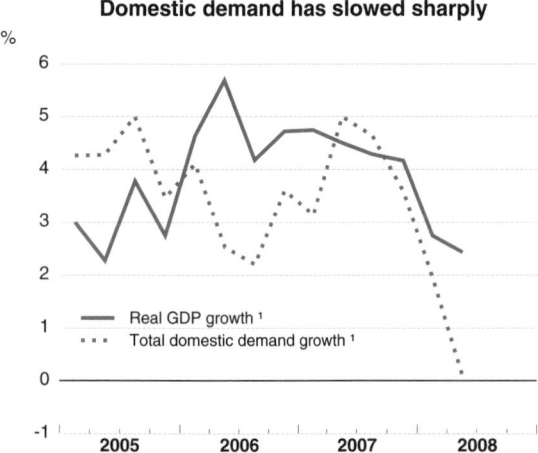

Domestic demand has slowed sharply

Real GDP growth [1]
Total domestic demand growth [1]

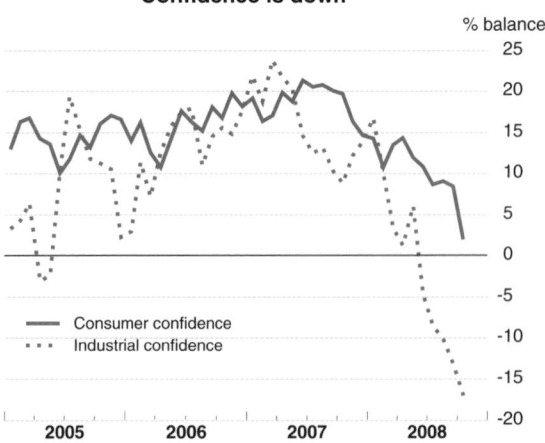

Confidence is down

Consumer confidence
Industrial confidence

1. Year-on-year percentage change.

Source: Eurostat and OECD, OECD Economic Outlook 84 database.

StatLink ⟨⟩ http://dx.doi.org/10.1787/500702726765

Finland: **Demand, output and prices**

	2005	2006	2007	2008	2009	2010
	Current prices € billion	Percentage changes, volume (2000 prices)				
Private consumption	81.3	4.2	3.2	3.3	1.9	1.8
Government consumption	35.0	0.7	1.2	1.5	1.4	1.1
Gross fixed capital formation	29.8	4.8	8.4	0.0	-1.9	1.7
Final domestic demand	146.1	3.5	3.8	2.2	1.0	1.6
Stockbuilding[1,2]	4.2	-0.3	0.3	-1.4	-0.1	0.0
Total domestic demand	150.2	3.1	4.1	0.6	0.9	1.6
Exports of goods and services	65.6	11.9	8.2	5.0	2.1	4.8
Imports of goods and services	58.7	7.8	6.6	1.8	2.6	4.9
Net exports[1]	6.9	2.4	1.4	1.8	0.0	0.5
GDP at market prices	157.2	4.8	4.4	2.1	0.6	1.8
GDP deflator	_	1.5	2.8	3.3	3.3	2.1
Memorandum items						
GDP without working day adjustments	_	4.9	4.5	..	..	..
Harmonised index of consumer prices	_	1.3	1.6	4.0	1.9	1.6
Private consumption deflator	_	1.6	2.2	2.8	1.9	1.7
Unemployment rate	_	7.7	6.9	6.2	6.5	6.8
General government financial balance[3]	_	4.0	5.3	4.6	3.3	2.7
Current account balance[3]	_	4.5	4.3	2.9	2.4	2.5

1. Contributions to changes in real GDP (percentage of real GDP in previous year), actual amount in the first column.
2. Including statistical discrepancy.
3. As a percentage of GDP.
Source: OECD Economic Outlook 84 database.

StatLink ᵃˢˡ http://dx.doi.org/10.1787/503105435305

cuts of more than € 1 billion and weaker activity. The government also announced that the value-added tax rate on food will be cut to 12% in October 2009 as promised prior to the previous election, which will provide an additional fiscal stimulus going into 2010.

Activity will weaken, but should gather momentum again in 2010

GDP growth is projected to slow to 0.6% in 2009 and could then recover to around 2% in 2010. Investment is likely to decline further in 2009. Business investment will suffer from the weakening outlook, tight credit conditions and further downsizing in the capital-intensive pulp and paper industry. Housing investment will also be affected by tighter credit conditions. Export growth is likely to become much less dynamic as world growth slows. An improving growth outlook and lower interest rates should revive investment in 2010. Household consumption will be underpinned by the tax cuts in 2009 and 2010, though a rise in the saving ratio and slower income growth should damp spending. The effect of the slowdown on the unemployment rate is likely to be muted, because labour force growth tends to be cyclical. The unemployment rate may thus rise only a little to 6¾ per cent. Underlying inflation could stay relatively high in the coming quarters, due to the recent wage cost push, but it should ease thereafter. Headline inflation is expected to decline to below 2% by 2010 with the drop in commodity prices and the cut in the VAT rate on food.

Risks are skewed to the downside

House prices have started to decline gently, but a sharp drop cannot be ruled out. This could add to the negative wealth effects of the plunge in share prices. Slower growth elsewhere than projected, especially in the still faster growing emerging economies, would damp export and investment growth.

GREECE

Economic activity has already weakened due to slowing domestic demand. Growth is expected to be subdued until mid-2009 in the context of a sluggish external environment, but to firm gradually thereafter. Inflation is set to decline, but the persistent differential with the euro area is likely to remain.

Despite weaker economic conditions, fiscal consolidation should continue, relying on better control of public spending. A reform of the pension system and greater efficiency in health care and public administration are essential. Recent measures to broaden the tax base are welcome. The strengthening of competition in network industries and a reduction in labour market rigidities would help to reduce inflation and improve long-term growth prospects.

Activity continued to slow and inflation edged up

Real GDP growth continued to slow in 2008, though was still fairly strong at around 3.3% over the first three quarters (year–over–year). Domestic demand decelerated as investment fell, mainly reflecting the continuing decline in residential construction, following a surge in 2006 in response to a change in the tax regime. Despite rising incomes and still rapid credit growth, consumption was weighed down by surging energy and food prices and tighter credit conditions. Export growth remained solid, if moderate by comparison with recent years, but the current account deficit soared to 15½ per cent of GDP in the second quarter of 2008, due to the deterioration in the terms of trade. The unemployment rate declined to around 7¾ per cent in the first half of 2008, which is below the estimated structural rate. Looking forward, indicators, such as retail sales, new car registrations, industrial production and economic sentiment point to a weaker economy. Harmonised inflation reached 5% in May 2008, though it has come down to 4% in October. Core inflation has

Greece

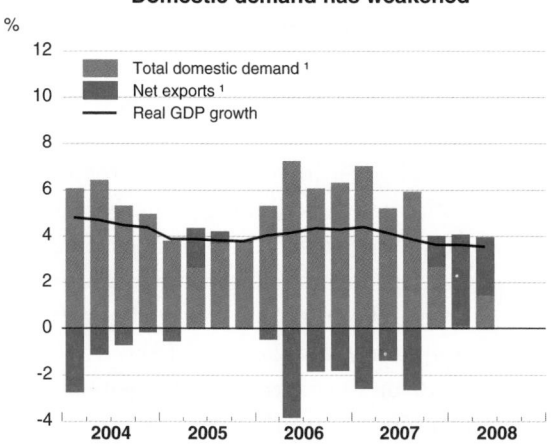

Domestic demand has weakened

- Total domestic demand [1]
- Net exports [1]
- Real GDP growth

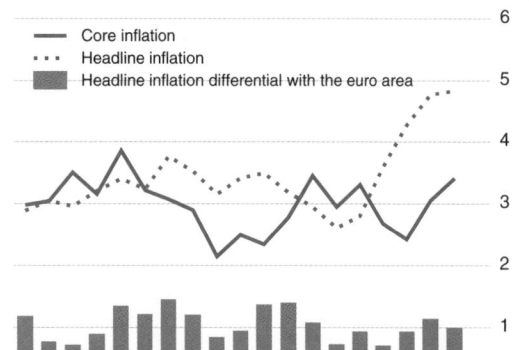

Inflationary pressures have increased [2]

- Core inflation
- Headline inflation
- Headline inflation differential with the euro area

1. Contribution to GDP growth.
2. Year-on-year percentage change of the harmonised consumer price index. Core inflation excludes energy, food, alcohol and tobacco.
Source: OECD, *Main Economic Indicators* and OECD Economic Outlook 84 database.

StatLink ⟨≣⟩ http://dx.doi.org/10.1787/500718712321

Greece: **Demand, output and prices**

	2005	2006	2007	2008	2009	2010
	Current prices € billion	Percentage changes, volume (2000 prices)				
Private consumption	140.8	4.2	3.2	2.4	2.3	2.6
Government consumption	33.0	-0.7	10.3	2.9	1.9	1.5
Gross fixed capital formation	42.7	9.2	4.9	-0.5	1.0	2.7
Final domestic demand	216.5	4.5	4.6	1.8	2.0	2.5
Stockbuilding[1,2]	4.6	1.1	0.1	-0.3	0.4	0.0
Total domestic demand	221.1	5.5	4.5	1.5	2.3	2.4
Exports of goods and services	43.1	5.1	5.9	3.6	3.4	5.8
Imports of goods and services	65.6	8.7	7.0	-3.0	4.2	4.4
Net exports[1]	- 22.5	-2.0	-1.3	1.9	-0.7	-0.3
GDP at market prices	198.6	4.2	4.0	3.2	1.9	2.5
GDP deflator	_	3.4	2.9	3.5	3.8	3.6
Memorandum items						
Harmonised index of consumer prices	_	3.3	3.0	4.5	2.7	2.4
Private consumption deflator	_	3.5	3.1	4.5	2.7	2.4
Unemployment rate	_	8.7	8.1	7.6	8.0	8.2
General government financial balance[3]	_	-3.1	-3.7	-2.8	-2.7	-3.1
Current account balance[4]	_	-11.1	-14.1	-14.5	-13.9	-13.2

1. Contributions to changes in real GDP (percentage of real GDP in previous year), actual amount in the first column.
2. Including statistical discrepancy.
3. National Accounts basis, as a percentage of GDP.
4. On settlement basis, as a percentage of GDP.
Source: OECD Economic Outlook 84 database.

StatLink ᵐˢ⁻ *http://dx.doi.org/10.1787/503106143152*

crept up, reflecting labour cost pressures and the second-round effects from the commodity price rise.

Fiscal policy will be tighter

The general government deficit is likely to narrow to 2.8% of GDP in 2008, including the impact of one-off factors, but could be around one percentage point above the original budget target. The 2009 draft budget aims at a deficit of 2.1% of GDP, in part reflecting new tax measures estimated to raise revenues by 1¼ per cent of GDP for the year. Of this, around ½ per cent of GDP is temporary in nature. The restrictive fiscal stance is justified by the high level of government debt and prospective fiscal costs of ageing, which are estimated to be among the largest in the OECD. The projected deficit for 2009 could exceed the official estimate by around ½ per cent of GDP, due to a less favourable growth scenario and more cautious projections for tax revenues. As some of the fiscal measures adopted in 2009 are temporary, a widening of the deficit to around 3% of GDP is expected in 2010, on the basis of unchanged policies. Strict control of primary public spending and further progress in tackling tax evasion are essential for fiscal sustainability.

Growth should firm gradually as of mid-2009

Economic activity is projected to remain sluggish over the next few quarters reflecting the impact of the financial turmoil and the associated tightening of credit standards, weaker consumer and business confidence, a softer external environment, and the somewhat tighter fiscal stance. Output growth, which could slow to 2% in 2009, should however strengthen gradually and be close to potential by end 2010, outpacing that in the euro area. The upturn is likely to be led by a pick-up in exports and stronger real income gains as inflationary pressures recede. A number of investment-boosting initiatives for the private sector and the deployment of European Union structural funds should provide further impetus. Inflation is expected to decline to below 2½ per cent in 2010 because of lower commodity prices and a negative output gap. As economic growth weakens, unemployment is projected to rise, slightly exceeding 8% by the end of 2009. Although shrinking somewhat, the current account deficit is likely to remain very high, at some 13¼ per cent of GDP.

Risks to activity and the public finances are on the downside

A major uncertainty relates to the strength of foreign demand, and in particular from trading partners in South–East Europe. Weaker activity would make it difficult to achieve the ambitious fiscal targets. Moreover, inflation may not come down as quickly as projected, given a still tight labour market.

HUNGARY

Against the background of global financial turbulence, economic activity is set to decline in 2009, before picking up with the recovery in world trade and with higher confidence following international financing support. Inflation should decelerate towards the 3% target as wage growth remains moderate. The current account deficit should narrow.

Controlling financial vulnerabilities is a key policy priority. The most urgent challenge is to move forward with announced measures to improve banks' risk management (including strengthening stress testing), particularly regarding households' large foreign currency exposure. Efforts to restore the sustainability of public finances should continue and past profligacy in election years avoided, so as to provide room for reducing tax and social security wedges when the financial crisis subsides.

Activity was already weak when the world financial crisis began

Although growth picked up mildly at the very beginning of 2008, this was mainly driven by a rebound in agriculture after a marked contraction in 2007. By contrast, domestic demand had yet to recover from the slowdown induced by the fiscal consolidation in recent years. In addition, industrial activity was still stagnant and, with European activity slowing, there were increasing indications of weakening manufacturing export growth. Helped by falling oil and food prices and currency appreciation, headline inflation fell to 5.7% in September, from 7% at the beginning of the year.

The financial turmoil poses a dilemma for monetary policy

Monetary policy has in principle been conducted more freely since the removal of the exchange rate band in early 2008 allowed it to focus exclusively on the inflation target. However, in practice, financial developments have been constraining this extra flexibility quite markedly. Indeed, sentiment towards forint-denominated assets

Hungary

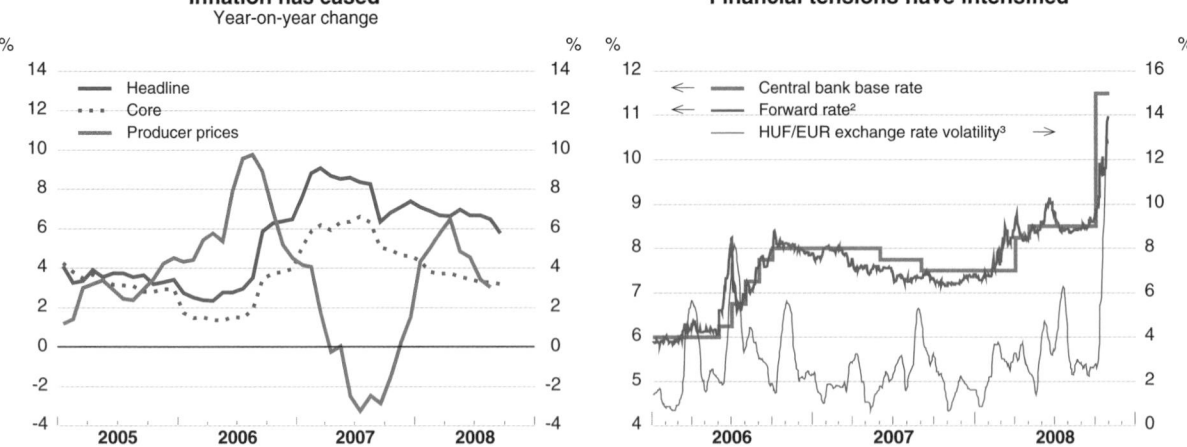

1. Headline and core inflation (excluding food and energy) are represented by the harmonised consumer price index.
2. Average of the forward three month interest rate (one month and three months ahead).
3. Moving standard deviation of a one month window.

Source: Magyar Nemzeti Bank, Datastream and OECD, Main Economic Indicators database.

StatLink ᴹˢᴾ http://dx.doi.org/10.1787/500722576230

Hungary: **Demand, output and prices**

	2005	2006	2007	2008	2009	2010
	Current prices HUF billion	Percentage changes, volume (2000 prices)				
Private consumption	12 124.8	1.7	0.6	1.2	-0.3	0.5
Government consumption	4 958.0	4.3	-7.4	-1.0	-0.1	0.0
Gross fixed capital formation	5 173.5	-6.2	1.5	-0.6	-0.7	1.4
Final domestic demand	22 256.3	0.5	-1.1	0.3	-0.3	0.6
Stockbuilding[1]	147.0	1.4	0.1	0.6	0.1	0.0
Total domestic demand	22 403.3	1.0	-0.4	1.4	-0.1	0.6
Exports of goods and services	14 511.0	18.6	15.9	7.7	3.9	4.7
Imports of goods and services	14 916.9	14.8	13.1	7.5	4.4	4.2
Net exports[1]	-405.9	2.3	2.1	0.3	-0.3	0.5
GDP at market prices	21 997.4	4.1	1.1	1.4	-0.5	1.0
GDP deflator	_	3.9	5.7	5.9	3.6	2.7
Memorandum items						
Consumer price index	_	3.9	8.0	6.4	3.6	3.2
Private consumption deflator	_	3.4	6.4	5.7	4.2	3.1
Unemployment rate	_	7.5	7.4	7.9	8.9	9.2
General government financial balance[2]	_	-9.3	-5.0	-3.4	-3.6	-3.5
Current account balance[2]	_	-7.5	-6.4	-6.1	-6.1	-5.4

Note: National accounts are based on official chain-linked data. This introduces a discrepancy in the identity between real demand components and GDP. For further details see *OECD Economic Outlook* Sources and Methods *(http://www.oecd.org/eco/sources-and-methods)*.
1. Contributions to changes in real GDP (percentage of real GDP in previous year), actual amount in the first column.
2. As a percentage of GDP.
Source: OECD Economic Outlook 84 database.

StatLink ⧉ *http://dx.doi.org/10.1787/503172103088*

deteriorated substantially through October, amid foreign investors' concerns with the rising debt burden of households and their large unhedged exposure to foreign currency loans. Despite a loan of € 5 billion granted by the European Central Bank in mid-October, the central bank of Hungary had to increase its base rate by 300 basis points (to 11.5%) to help attract foreign liquidity. Lending conditions have become increasingly tough. In the projections, policy rates are assumed to start falling from the first quarter of 2009, as foreign investor confidence should begin to recover in the wake of the joint financing package of $25 billion promised at end-October by the International Monetary Fund (IMF), the European Union (EU) and the World Bank (WB). The IMF's Executive Board approved the 17-month Stand-By Arrangement beginning November.

The budget deficit has fallen, but more consolidation is needed

Much of the effort aimed at controlling current vulnerabilities has to fall on fiscal policy. Official interim figures suggest that the 2008 deficit will be around 3.4% of GDP, about 1½ percentage point lower than the preceding year and better than expected. For 2009, the initial draft budget incorporated revenue and spending measures that were outlined before the financial turmoil. The spending side was tightened, reflecting lower spending ceilings for central government ministries while revenue increases were expected from a rise in several excise duties and the introduction of a temporary tax on energy suppliers. To foster fiscal consolidation, the government submitted a revised draft budget on 18 October that has abandoned planned tax reductions (including lower social security contributions) totalling about 0.5% of GDP, and introduced further expenditure restraints. Based on this revised draft budget and taking into account the effects of the worsened economic projections in the OECD outlook, the budget deficit is projected to remain around 3½ per cent of GDP in 2009 and 2010, almost 1 percentage point above government targets. However, the government proposed new tightening measures on 3 November to meet the fiscal deficit target of the IMF stand-by arrangement (2½ per cent of GDP), which have not been built into this projection.

A recession is expected in 2009

Real GDP growth is expected to decelerate sharply, with the economy going into recession in 2009, before recovering during 2010. The slowdown is driven by weakening export demand, which, along with sharply higher interest rates and other financing difficulties, is slowing investment. Even though lower inflation is set to improve consumers' purchasing power, moderate wages and high unemployment imply that private consumption will not start to recover before well into the second half of 2009. Sharply weaker import growth along with market share gains on export markets are projected to result in an improvement in the current account by 2010.

Elections should not be allowed to endanger fiscal consolidation

There is a major short-term uncertainty associated with the outcome of the IMF-EU-WB rescue package, the details of which are unknown at the time of writing. Given Hungary's record of large fiscal budget blow-outs in the run up to elections, the main risk lies in significant fiscal slippage ahead of the 2010 general election. If, by contrast, the good track record of fiscal improvement in recent years is maintained, helped by the new fiscal rules currently debated, monetary policy would not need to remain as restrictive as currently assumed, thereby supporting the recovery in investment and consumption.

ICELAND

After a long period of unbalanced growth, the Icelandic economy has entered a deep recession following the failure of its major banks. The economy is projected to shrink until early 2010 and unemployment to soar over the next two years. Following a large depreciation of the currency, inflation is projected to spike higher, though to fall back sharply once the exchange rate effects have passed through and the effects of substantial economic slack come to bear. The current account deficit should decline markedly.

The authorities are facing very difficult challenges. Apart from remedying the banking crisis, they will need to ensure that inflation does indeed fall quickly. The central bank's task would be facilitated if wage setters were to look through much of the spike in inflation resulting from the depreciation of the exchange rate. Bank regulation will need to be reformed, including through stricter rules on bank governance, to ensure that a similar crisis does not recur.

A broad-based and sharp downturn is underway

Economic growth has slowed sharply, ending the boom that had been underway since 2004. Consumer spending has dropped in response to the squeeze on real incomes resulting from the large depreciation of the exchange rate, tightening credit conditions and a deterioration in the economic outlook. Residential investment has fallen even more sharply, weighed down by a large stock of unsold new housing units, expectations that the large gains in real house prices in recent years will be reversed over the next few years and more limited access to housing finance on costlier terms. Tightening financial conditions and the deteriorating outlook have also weighed on business investment, although part of the decline reflects a temporary hiatus in energy-intensive investment activity. Additional aluminium smelting capacity has underpinned a large increase in exports, attenuating the decline in GDP growth. Employment growth has slowed over the past year and unemployment has begun to rise, albeit from a very low level. Survey evidence points to considerably

Iceland

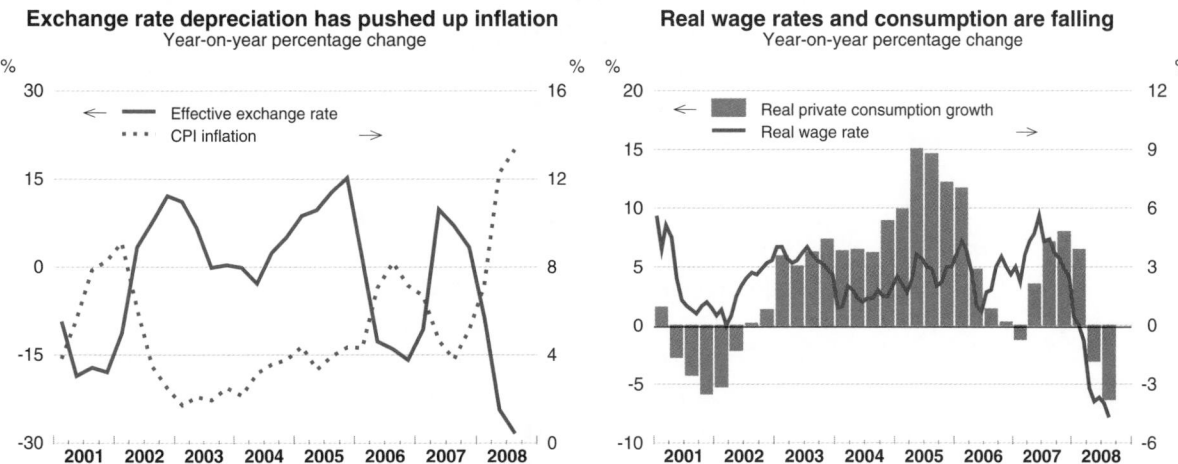

Exchange rate depreciation has pushed up inflation
Year-on-year percentage change

Real wage rates and consumption are falling
Year-on-year percentage change

Source: OECD Economic Outlook 84 database; Statistics Iceland.

StatLink ᴬˡˢ⁴ http://dx.doi.org/10.1787/500737532154

Iceland: **Demand, output and prices**

	2005	2006	2007	2008	2009	2010
	Current prices ISK billion	Percentage changes, volume (2000 prices)				
Private consumption	610.6	4.4	4.3	-4.7	-16.8	-4.2
Government consumption	252.6	4.0	4.2	4.0	2.7	2.0
Gross fixed capital formation	291.3	20.4	-13.7	-22.1	-36.7	-9.4
Final domestic demand	1 154.5	8.3	-0.9	-7.1	-16.5	-3.4
Stockbuilding[1]	- 0.9	1.1	-0.6	-0.2	0.3	0.0
Total domestic demand	1 153.7	9.3	-1.4	-6.6	-15.9	-3.2
Exports of goods and services	324.5	-5.0	18.1	8.9	2.5	4.2
Imports of goods and services	451.7	10.2	-1.4	-9.9	-12.5	-0.9
Net exports[1]	- 127.3	-6.1	6.5	7.6	7.1	2.5
GDP at market prices	1 026.4	4.4	4.9	1.5	-9.3	-0.7
GDP deflator	_	9.0	5.6	9.3	15.2	6.7
Memorandum items						
Consumer price index	_	6.7	5.1	12.1	14.9	6.9
Private consumption deflator	_	7.6	4.7	12.5	15.2	7.1
Unemployment rate	_	2.9	2.3	2.8	7.4	8.6
General government financial balance[2]	_	6.3	5.5	3.2	-1.9	-3.8
Current account balance[2]	_	-25.0	-15.5	-24.0	-13.9	-11.3

Note: National accounts are based on official chain-linked data. This introduces a discrepancy in the identity between real demand components and GDP. For further details see *OECD Economic Outlook* Sources and Methods *(http://www.oecd.org/eco/sources-and-methods).*
1. Contributions to changes in real GDP (percentage of real GDP in previous year), actual amount in the first column.
2. As a percentage of GDP.
Source: OECD Economic Outlook 84 database.

StatLink 🔗 *http://dx.doi.org/10.1787/503173057245*

weaker labour market conditions over coming months and net inflows of foreign workers appear likely to fall sharply. Inflation has soared following the exchange rate depreciation and the rise in commodity prices over the past year.

The financial crisis has worsened

The accentuation of the global financial crisis since mid-September proved fatal for Iceland's three main banks, which have all been placed in receivership under direct government control. The government has guaranteed domestic deposits (which at the end of September were equivalent to around 100% of the GDP in the year to June 2008), and will guarantee foreign retail deposits in line with the requirements of the EU Deposit Insurance Directive; the government is not, however, guaranteeing other bank liabilities. This default on bank debts has curtailed banks' access to international credit markets and seriously disrupted the foreign exchange market, with very negative consequences for the economy. A loan plan from a group of countries led by the International Monetary Fund (IMF) has been agreed that would provide $10 billion (about 100% of GDP at recent onshore exchange rates of 140 kronà to the dollar) over two years (of which approximately $5 billion is in cash, with $2.1 billion coming from the IMF, and the balance being lent by the United Kingdom, the Netherlands and other countries involved to cover the cost of deposit insurance obligations) to support an economic recovery programme and to help Iceland restore confidence in its banking system and stabilise its currency. In this context, the central bank increased the policy interest rate by 6 percentage points to 18% to support the currency and reduce inflationary pressures. Rates are assumed to remain high until late 2009 but to be cut swiftly by the end of 2010 as inflation falls and the effect of the accumulated economic slack mounts. Continued growth in government outlays should somewhat attenuate the contraction in domestic demand, but will result in a large deterioration in the government budget balance over the projection period.

A deep recession is in prospect

The economy is projected to contract very sharply in late 2008-early 2009 and not to begin growing again until mid-2010. Consumption expenditure is likely to shrink markedly as households respond to falling real incomes, rising debt-service costs, tight credit-market conditions, and declining wealth. Sharp declines in private investment are also in prospect. The unemployment rate is likely to move up sharply to around 8½ per cent in 2010. Inflation is projected to increase further into early 2009, but should subsequently decline as the effects of the depreciation pass through and growing slack comes to bear.

Considerable uncertainties on the resolution of the banking crisis

The major risks surrounding this projection are twofold; first, that the exchange rate changes markedly from current values, affecting inflation and household income growth; and second, that wage increases prove higher than projected, pushing up inflation and reducing the gain in cost competitiveness from currency depreciation. The considerable uncertainty about the direct cost to government of guaranteeing domestic bank deposits and other liabilities poses a significant fiscal risk.

IRELAND

Activity is contracting as the severe housing market correction has weakened the wider economy, and the weakness will persist well into 2009. Growth will recover in 2010 as the housing construction cycle bottoms out and the financial turmoil wanes.

To support the stability of the financial system, the ceiling on the deposit guarantee scheme has been raised and the government has introduced a scheme to guarantee bank liabilities. A fiscal deficit has emerged as revenues have slumped. Fiscal policy should be allowed to support demand in the near term but once the recovery is underway substantial measures will be needed to restore medium-term sustainability. Competitiveness needs to be improved; the outline national pay agreement may help but more is required to boost competition in network industries and sheltered service sectors.

The economy is contracting

Economic activity contracted in the first half of 2008, driven by a sharp fall in house building, which is likely to continue. Commencement notices have dropped substantially, house prices are down almost 11% compared with a year ago and housing market transactions are very subdued. Consumption fell sharply in the first half of the year. Business investment is also lower and export growth has weakened.

Unemployment is rising

Employment has fallen and the standardised unemployment rate has increased sharply, mostly owing to layoffs in construction. The severity of the rise in unemployment is likely to be attenuated as the weak economy leads to net outward migration. The number of new Personal Public Service Numbers (PPSNs) issued to migrants from Central and Eastern Europe has dropped significantly.

Ireland

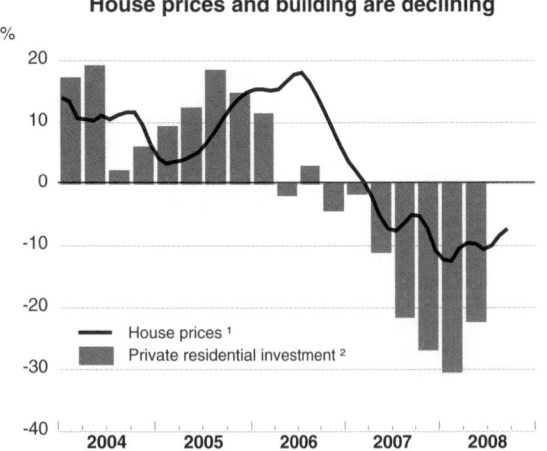

House prices and building are declining

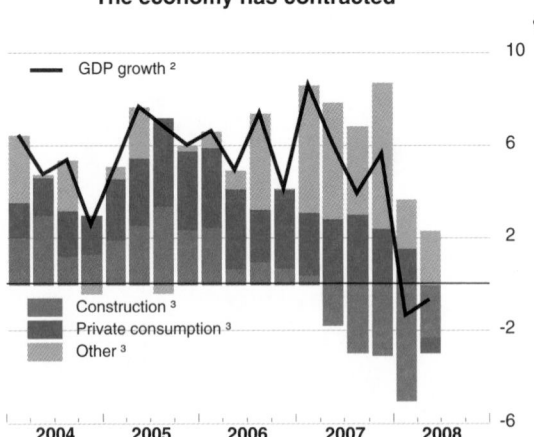

The economy has contracted

1. National house price index, three-month moving average, percentage growth relative to previous three months, annual rate.
2. Year-on-year percentage change.
3. Year-on-year contributions to GDP growth.

Source: OECD Economic Outlook 84 database and permanent tsb.

StatLink http://dx.doi.org/10.1787/500740488776

Ireland: **Demand, output and prices**

	2005	2006	2007	2008	2009	2010
	Current prices € billion	Percentage changes, volume (2006 prices)				
Private consumption	73.8	7.0	6.0	-0.5	0.4	1.6
Government consumption	24.9	5.3	6.8	3.9	2.3	1.5
Gross fixed capital formation	43.1	3.8	1.3	-22.7	-23.8	-2.6
Final domestic demand	141.8	5.7	4.7	-6.3	-4.9	0.8
Stockbuilding[1]	0.8	0.4	-0.8	0.7	0.1	0.0
Total domestic demand	142.6	6.1	3.7	-5.5	-4.7	0.8
Exports of goods and services	132.3	5.7	6.8	1.7	1.4	2.7
Imports of goods and services	112.7	6.4	4.1	-1.6	-1.2	0.5
Net exports[1]	19.6	0.3	2.6	2.5	1.9	1.9
GDP at market prices	162.2	5.7	6.0	-1.8	-1.7	2.6
GDP deflator	_	3.4	1.4	-0.9	0.7	0.3
Memorandum items						
Harmonised index of consumer prices	_	2.7	2.9	3.1	0.9	0.9
Private consumption deflator	_	2.2	3.0	3.4	1.0	1.0
Unemployment rate	_	4.4	4.6	5.9	7.7	7.8
General government financial balance[2]	_	3.0	0.2	-5.6	-7.1	-7.0
Current account balance[2]	_	-3.6	-5.4	-6.2	-6.3	-5.2

Note: National accounts are based on official chain-linked data. This introduces a discrepancy in the identity between real demand components and GDP. For further details see *OECD Economic Outlook* Sources and Methods (*http://www.oecd.org/eco/sources-and-methods*).
1. Contributions to changes in real GDP (percentage of real GDP in previous year), actual amount in the first column.
2. As a percentage of GDP.
Source: OECD Economic Outlook 84 database.

StatLink http://dx.doi.org/10.1787/503176820157

The government has guaranteed bank liabilities

The government has raised the ceiling of the deposit guarantee to € 100 000 and introduced a guarantee scheme for bank liabilities to ensure banks access to funding. Six banks are currently receiving the guarantee. The scheme raises implicit government liabilities by around 2.5 times GNP with the government charging an annual fee based on the estimated impact on public borrowing costs and each institution's long-term credit rating. Banks in the scheme face stricter regulation of their commercial conduct.

Fiscal policy should support activity but medium-term consolidation will be essential

The fiscal balance has deteriorated sharply as revenues have fallen, particularly related to property, while spending has continued to increase at a strong pace. The budget for 2009 raises revenue by 1% of GDP and slows the growth of discretionary spending. While the economy remains weak, fiscal policy should be allowed to support demand. The OECD's projections show the general government deficit rising to around 7% of GDP in 2009. In the medium term, substantial measures will be necessary to close the large deficit that is likely to develop.

Activity will remain weak in the near term

The housing correction will lead GDP to contract further in 2008 and 2009. Consumption growth will remain weak due to falling wealth, employment losses and low consumer confidence. The strong real exchange rate and weakness in the world economy during the financial crisis will constrain exports. Business investment is set to decline with the poor outlook for demand and uncertainty. Weak demand will create a large negative output gap, reducing core inflation. Headline inflation will recede sharply as energy and food prices fall back.

Recovery will begin as the economy rebalances

Growth is likely to return towards the end of 2009 with the stabilisation of housing investment, improving financial conditions and low interest rates. Consumption will pick up as households adjust to lower wealth and the labour market bottoms out. Together with a recovery in business investment and a positive contribution from net trade, growth is likely to recover to above its trend rate by the end of 2010.

Risks surround the depth and duration of the slowdown

The risks of a severe house-building correction and a substantial impact on the wider economy have materialised. But considerable uncertainty remains about the depth and duration of the economic slowdown, which will depend on both developments in the housing market and the impact of the financial crisis on Ireland. A more severe than anticipated slowdown in the world economy would limit the supportive role of exports.

KOREA

Korea has been hard-hit by the global financial crisis and the earlier commodity price shock, which together ended the expansion and pushed up inflation. Sharp won depreciation since mid-September has further clouded the economic outlook. Growth is projected to fall to below 3% in 2009 and then pick up gradually as the world economy improves.

The fiscal stimulus in the 2008 supplementary budget and tax cuts will mitigate the downturn. Monetary policy should focus on supporting activity and financial-market stability until conditions normalise. Foreign exchange market intervention in support of the won is likely to be costly and ineffective in the face of the global financial turbulence, and should therefore be limited to smoothing operations.

The negative impact of the terms-of-trade shock on national income...

Korea, the world's fifth largest oil importer, was negatively affected by the sharp rise in commodity prices, which boosted headline consumer price inflation to 5.5% (year-on-year) in the third quarter of 2008. Core consumer price inflation (excluding food and energy) rose to almost 5%, pointing to significant second-round effects from the terms-of-trade shock. Higher inflation squeezed household and corporate income, damping private consumption and business investment, while residential investment weakened markedly, partly reflecting the impact of recent housing policies. Output growth slowed to a 3% annual rate during the first three quarters of 2008, indicating that the pace of economic activity had weakened markedly even before the global financial crisis intensified in mid-September.

... has been magnified by the global financial crisis

The won depreciated by 13% in trade-weighted terms between mid-September and the end of October, in the context of global financial turbulence, bringing its fall to 27% for the year. Since the last episode of

Korea

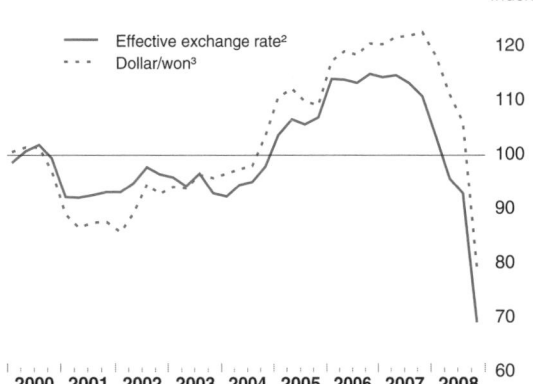

Inflation has risen above the target — Per cent, Annual inflation target zone, Medium-term[1] inflation target zone, (3 ± 1%), (3 ± 0.5%), CPI inflation, Core inflation, 2001–2008

The won has depreciated significantly — Index, Effective exchange rate[2], Dollar/won[3], 2000–2008

1. Since 2004, the target has been a medium-term objective and, in 2007, it was changed from core to overall CPI.
2. Calculated *vis-à-vis* 41 trading partners.
3. The figure for the fourth quarter of 2008 is the rate of 28 October.

Source: Bank of Korea and OECD Economic Outlook 84 database.

StatLink http://dx.doi.org/10.1787/500758063083

Korea: **Demand, output and prices**

	2005	2006	2007	2008	2009	2010
	Current prices KRW trillion	Percentage changes, volume (2000 prices)				
Private consumption	426.7	4.5	4.5	1.7	-1.1	0.4
Government consumption	114.8	6.2	5.8	3.8	3.8	3.7
Gross fixed capital formation	237.2	3.6	4.0	0.6	0.2	1.1
Final domestic demand	778.8	4.4	4.5	1.7	0.0	1.1
Stockbuilding[1]	12.6	-0.2	-0.4	0.5	0.0	0.0
Total domestic demand	791.4	4.2	4.1	2.3	0.0	1.1
Exports of goods and services	342.6	11.8	12.1	9.1	6.4	11.3
Imports of goods and services	323.5	11.3	11.9	6.8	2.7	8.3
Net exports[1]	19.1	1.3	1.3	2.1	2.7	3.2
GDP at market prices	810.5	5.1	5.0	4.2	2.7	4.2
GDP deflator	_	-0.5	1.2	3.6	2.7	0.2
Memorandum items						
Consumer price index	_	2.2	2.5	5.0	3.9	2.9
Private consumption deflator	_	2.1	2.6	5.4	3.9	2.9
Unemployment rate	_	3.5	3.2	3.2	3.6	3.6
Household saving ratio[2]	_	3.4	2.5	3.7	4.2	4.7
General government financial balance[3]	_	3.6	4.5	4.8	3.8	3.6
Current account balance[3]	_	0.6	0.6	-1.1	0.8	1.0

1. Contributions to changes in real GDP (percentage of real GDP in previous year), actual amount in the first column.
2. As a percentage of disposable income.
3. As a percentage of GDP.
Source: OECD Economic Outlook 84 database.

StatLink ᵴᵯ🖳 http://dx.doi.org/10.1787/503226252100

sharp won depreciation during the 1997 crisis, the financial strength of the Korean banking and corporate sector has improved greatly. The current decline is largely explained by net capital outflows from the Korean stock market and the emergence of a current account deficit – of around 1% of GDP – for the first time in a decade. In addition, banks, which rely on overseas markets for about 10% of their funding, are having trouble borrowing in foreign currencies. Financial conditions in Korea have tightened considerably, with corporate bond rates rising by 80 basis points between mid-September and late October, while equity prices have fallen by 25%. Meanwhile, business and household confidence has plummeted.

Despite monetary and fiscal stimulus...

Although inflation is well above the medium-term target of 2.5% to 3.5%, the Bank of Korea cut its policy interest rate by 100 basis points in October, followed by an additional 25 basis points in early November. Intervention in the foreign exchange market has contributed to a decline in Korea's ample foreign exchange reserves by 18% since June (to $212 billion in October), while failing to stabilise the won. The opening of a $30 billion currency swap arrangement with the United States in late October may help calm the foreign exchange market. In addition, the Korean authorities will make available an additional $30 billion of dollar liquidity, using foreign exchange reserves, to domestic banks while guaranteeing their external debt up to $100 billion. Meanwhile, fiscal stimulus is helping to stem the slowdown in activity. A supplementary budget and tax rebates jointly amounting to almost 1% of GDP was approved in September 2008, to be followed by cuts in personal and corporate income tax rates in 2009-10. In early November, the government announced revisions (which are not included in the projections) to the 2009 budget plan that would boost spending by 1.1% of GDP and cut taxes by 0.3% of GDP.

... a strong economic rebound is unlikely before 2010

The economic outlook is highly uncertain given the severity of the shocks to Korea and the problems facing the world economy. Initially, the large depreciation of the won is likely to depress activity by further squeezing household and corporate income and hurting confidence. As a result, growth is projected to fall below 3% in 2009. Weak growth will help bring inflation back within the target zone during 2009. Assuming that the exchange rate remains at its level in late October, Korea would be well placed to increase its share of world trade when the global economy rebounds. An export-led recovery would gradually spread to domestic demand, boosting output growth in 2010 to above 4%.

There are a number of risks

However, continued world financial turmoil may further worsen the short-term outlook by undermining the health of Korean financial institutions, resulting in a credit crunch. There is also a risk that high inflation becomes entrenched, eventually requiring forceful and costly monetary policy tightening to bring it back within the target zone. On the positive side, the large depreciation of the won may lead to a sharper and earlier-than-expected upturn led by buoyant exports. Moreover, the additional fiscal stimulus announced in November is likely to have a positive impact on activity.

LUXEMBOURG

The international financial crisis is sharply reducing economic growth, initially in the financial sector, but subsequently in broader domestic demand. These effects should persist into 2010. Consequently, unemployment will rise further, while core inflation will fall slowly.

The automatic stabilisers should be allowed to operate during the downswing, but the government should aim to improve the structural balance over the medium term to secure fiscal sustainability.

The economy is being battered by international financial storms

Output growth has slowed since end-2007. The international financial crisis forced the financial sector to increase banking provisions and net inflows into investment funds have decreased. As a result, earnings and activity in the sector and exports of service have been depressed. Subsequently, domestic demand slowed from the negative knock-on effects on supporting service sectors. Growth of private consumption weakened as higher inflation eroded real income growth and as consumer confidence fell. Business investment contracted as sentiment in both the construction and manufacturing sector deteriorated and capacity utilisation declined.

Inflationary pressures are underpinned by the automatic wage indexation

Headline inflation peaked at nearly 5% in mid-2008, after which energy and food prices started to fall. Around the same time, core inflation reached nearly 2½ per cent before also beginning to decline. Nevertheless, continued increases in wage growth, due to wage indexation, are likely to slow the decline in core inflation. Employment growth slowed during the year and mostly benefited cross-border workers, leading to a small increase in the standardised unemployment rate. Another factor contributing to higher unemployment was the

Luxembourg

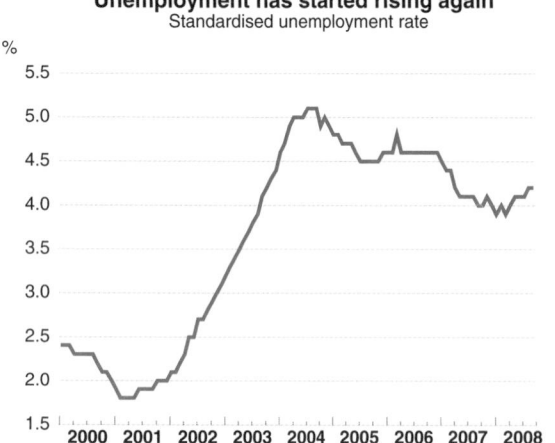

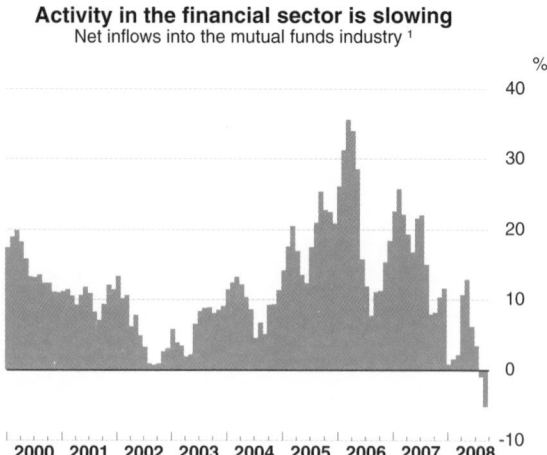

1. Three-month moving average. Inflows are defined as net of variation in financial markets.
Source: OECD, *Main Economic Indicators* and Commission de Surveillance du Secteur Financier.

StatLink http://dx.doi.org/10.1787/500767728577

Luxembourg: **Demand, output and prices**

	2005	2006	2007	2008	2009	2010
	Current prices € billion	Percentage changes, volume (2000 prices)				
Private consumption	10.7	3.0	2.0	2.5	1.2	1.7
Government consumption	5.0	2.8	2.6	1.2	3.7	2.1
Gross fixed capital formation	6.2	2.9	10.1	-3.1	-0.3	2.3
Final domestic demand	21.9	2.9	4.4	0.6	1.4	2.0
Stockbuilding[1]	0.6	-1.0	-0.4	-1.6	-0.7	0.0
Total domestic demand	22.5	1.4	3.7	-1.8	0.4	2.0
Exports of goods and services	47.9	14.7	4.4	2.4	0.9	3.5
Imports of goods and services	40.2	13.5	3.5	-0.7	1.4	3.9
Net exports[1]	7.8	5.3	2.7	5.3	-0.5	0.5
GDP at market prices	30.3	6.5	5.2	2.4	-0.5	1.9
GDP deflator	_	5.1	1.7	1.5	2.4	1.7
Memorandum items						
Harmonised index of consumer prices	_	3.0	2.7	4.5	1.9	1.7
Private consumption deflator	_	2.2	2.1	5.2	1.9	1.7
Unemployment rate	_	4.4	4.4	4.5	6.5	7.0
General government financial balance[2]	_	1.3	3.2	1.6	-0.6	-1.5
Current account balance[2]	_	10.5	9.9	6.6	5.1	6.1

Note: National accounts are based on official chain-linked data. This introduces a discrepancy in the identity between real demand components and GDP. For further details see *OECD Economic Outlook* Sources and Methods *(http://www.oecd.org/eco/sources-and-methods)*.
1. Contributions to changes in real GDP (percentage of real GDP in previous year), actual amount in the first column.
2. As a percentage of GDP.
Source: OECD Economic Outlook 84 database.

StatLink ⫶⫶⫶ *http://dx.doi.org/10.1787/503228874243*

reduced scope of active labour market measures. A sign of the cooling labour market was the declining number of unfilled job vacancies.

A budget deficit could re-emerge over the projection period.

The 2008 general government balance surplus narrowed to 1 ½ per cent of GDP under the impact of slower growth, higher spending on some income transfers and public sector wages (reflecting indexation), lower taxes and measures to compensate consumers' purchasing power for higher inflation. For 2009, the automatic stabilisers will be largely responsible for moving the budget into a deficit of more than ½ per cent of GDP, although other contributing factors are the continued increases in income tax brackets, reductions in corporate taxation, and the introduction of some additional family-oriented measures. On the spending side, a focus is to boost social welfare infrastructure, such as child and old age care facilities. Transfers and public sector wages are set to rise again in March 2009, due to indexation.

Growth is projected to remain below potential until mid-2010

The international financial turbulence will weigh on the financial sector into 2010, when it is assumed to ease. By then, domestic demand should also start to benefit from easier monetary conditions. Unemployment will rise over the projection period, partly because current labour hoarding decisions are likely to be reversed as the downswing continues. However, even as labour market tension eases, wages are projected to accelerate in 2010, when the currently partially suspended wage indexation mechanism is fully restored, triggering two additional wage adjustments during the year. Headline inflation should decelerate over the near-term as lower energy and food prices feed into consumer prices.

The main risk is the financial crisis

The main uncertainty is the duration and severity of the turmoil on the international financial markets, which will govern the extent of the slowdown in the all-important financial sector.

MEXICO

Economic growth is set to fall well below potential in 2008 and 2009, before gradually recovering in 2010. The weak US economy and a fall in oil production will cut exports over the next several quarters, while the effects of the financial turmoil will depress domestic demand growth. Activity will recover through 2010 as global economic conditions improve. Inflation will return to near the target rate as commodity prices fall, activity slows and monetary tightening keeps expectations anchored, although the recent sharp depreciation of the peso will put upward pressure on prices.

Fiscal policy will be supportive in the near term, cushioning the shocks to demand. However, the balanced budget rule has resulted in spending too much of the oil windfall over the past years, and may now constrain fiscal policy if oil prices remain at lower levels. Gradual loosening of the monetary stance is justified unless the recent depreciation of the peso revives inflationary pressures. To boost longer term growth, reforms should focus on enhancing public spending efficiency, product and labour market flexibility, and competition.

Economic activity is weakening

Growth has cooled rapidly in 2008. Private consumption was hit by declining real wages and lower remittances from emigrants in the United States. The strong investment demand early in the year waned in response to the worsening outlook. Exports have been adversely affected by the drop in US industrial production and lower than expected oil output at home. In contrast, public consumption and investment have been robust, boosted by higher oil revenues in the budget. Inflation has jumped above the central bank's target rate due mainly to the rise in world food and energy prices. Prompt tightening of monetary policy coupled with costly gasoline subsidies have kept price expectations in check and avoided second-round effects on wages and other prices. However, the sharp depreciation of the peso since August will put upward pressure on prices. The current account deficit is widening slightly, influenced by declining oil prices and remittances.

Mexico

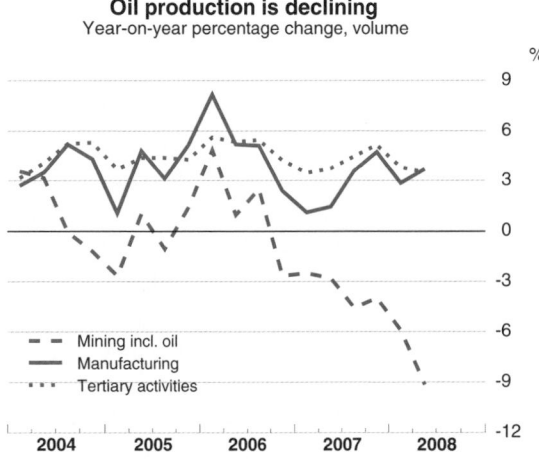

Source: OECD Economic Outlook 84 database; Bank of Mexico.

StatLink http://dx.doi.org/10.1787/500776823034

Mexico: Demand, output and prices

	2005	2006	2007	2008	2009	2010
	Current prices MXN billion	Percentage changes, volume (2003 prices)				
Private consumption	6 140.7	5.6	4.2	2.7	0.9	2.6
Government consumption	996.1	0.3	1.0	4.1	8.2	0.9
Gross fixed capital formation	1 848.8	9.7	5.6	4.9	1.7	2.1
Final domestic demand	8 985.5	5.8	4.2	3.3	1.8	2.3
Stockbuilding[1]	376.0	-0.1	-0.6	-0.4	-0.2	0.0
Total domestic demand	9 361.6	5.6	3.5	3.0	1.6	2.3
Exports of goods and services	2 505.4	10.9	6.1	4.6	-2.7	0.9
Imports of goods and services	2 639.7	12.9	7.0	7.5	1.2	2.6
Net exports[1]	- 134.3	-0.8	-0.4	-1.1	-1.3	-0.6
GDP at market prices	9 227.3	4.9	3.2	1.9	0.4	1.8
GDP deflator	_	6.8	4.7	6.8	4.6	3.4
Memorandum items						
Consumer price index	_	3.6	4.0	4.9	5.3	3.8
Private consumption deflator	_	3.5	4.6	5.2	5.2	3.9
Unemployment rate[2]	_	3.2	3.4	4.1	4.6	4.4
Current account balance[3]	_	-0.2	-0.6	-1.3	-3.1	-3.1

1. Contributions to changes in real GDP (percentage of real GDP in previous year), actual amount in the first column.
2. Based on National Employment Survey.
3. As a percentage of GDP.
Source: OECD Economic Outlook 84 database.

StatLink ᴍᴤᴾ http://dx.doi.org/10.1787/503256752606

The sharp US slowdown will be felt in Mexico

Even though dependence on volatile external financing sources has been sharply reduced, the economy still suffers from longstanding structural weaknesses which reduce resilience to external shocks. The decline in oil output and exports also reflects a failure to undertake structural reforms that would boost productivity and investment in oil exploration by the state-dominated oil company. Against this background, the sharp slowdown in US growth and turmoil in world financial markets are likely to reverberate strongly through the Mexican economy, led by a further worsening of export prospects. Little support to growth can be expected from monetary policy, which has to deal with above-target inflation and downward pressures on the currency. However, a gradual lowering of interest rates will likely be appropriate once inflation pressures subside. A rise in public expenditures, financed by a rise in oil revenues, has helped cushion output, and the focus on increased social spending will smooth the impact of the downturn on low-income groups and mitigate income inequalities. While the increase in the gasoline subsidy has helped to contain prices, it has regressive effects on income distribution, is detrimental to efficient resource allocation, and carries a heavy fiscal cost.

Modest growth in the near term, followed by a rebound in 2010

Weighed down by adverse external market developments and global financial turmoil, the economy is set to grow below potential this year and next. Growth should pick up again in 2010 as the world economy improves, while inflation will come down due to weak activity and lower commodity prices and as monetary policy continues to keep expectations anchored. Low productivity and declining oil production will remain a drag on growth. The current account will worsen during the projection period, reflecting adverse conditions in foreign markets and declines in oil prices.

Developments in the US economy pose the greatest risk

The main downside risk to the Mexican economy is that the downturn in US activity will be deeper or last longer than projected, further affecting Mexico's exports, the inflow of remittances and tourism. A prolonged downturn in the United States and the world economy could also keep oil prices low at a time when Mexico's production and reserves are declining substantially, jeopardising the budget targets in 2009. In addition, sentiment could turn further against emerging markets like Mexico, intensifying downward pressure on the peso.

NETHERLANDS

After coming to a halt in mid 2008, growth will turn negative in 2009. The following year a recovery will get under way as stronger domestic demand is underpinned by easier monetary policy, real income growth is supported by lower inflation, and exporters benefit from stronger world trade. However, a tight labour market will create some persistence in core inflation.

Wage pressure would be eased by introducing measures to increase the labour supply. The budget situation will deteriorate over the short-term, but nevertheless the automatic stabilisers should be allowed to work fully.

Activity slowed in 2008...

After another year of strong expansion in 2007, the Dutch economy slowed during 2008. Private consumption, in particular of durable goods, decelerated in line with weaker real income growth, less impetus from real wealth increases, deteriorating consumer confidence and slower world trade. The reduction in overall demand induced a weakening of private investment.

... but the labour market remained tight

Nevertheless, job vacancies stayed close to historical high levels, and the unemployment rate fell further to a six-year low during the third quarter, before starting to creep up. In response, contractual wages accelerated further to some 3½ per cent. However, as consumer price inflation increased at almost the same pace, real wage growth remained in line with the modest expansion of productivity. Headline inflation was low by international standards, which may be explained by the slow transmission of global oil prices into retail gas prices due to relatively long contract periods. As an implication, headline inflation is likely to remain

Netherlands

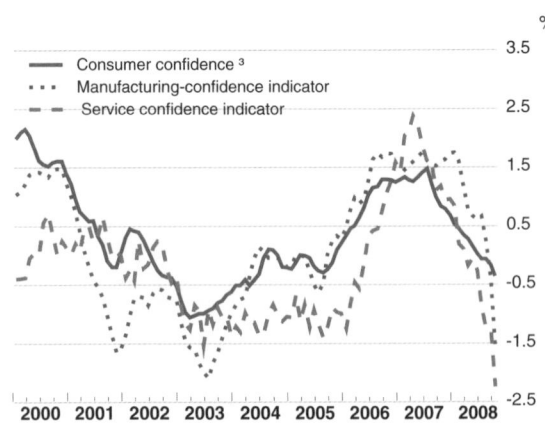

A tight labour market is accompanied by higher inflation

— Consumer price inflation [1]
· · · Core inflation [1]
– – Unemployment rate [2]

Confidence is falling

— Consumer confidence [3]
· · · Manufacturing-confidence indicator
– – Service confidence indicator

1. Inflation indicators are measured by consumer price indices and core inflation excludes food and energy.
2. Standardised unemployment rate.
3. Consumer confidence indicator is standardised over Jan. 1970-Aug. 2008, by subtracting the average and dividing by the standard deviation.

Source: OECD, Main Economic Indicators database.

StatLink http://dx.doi.org/10.1787/500785482242

Netherlands: Demand, output and prices

	2005	2006	2007	2008	2009	2010
	Current prices € billion	Percentage changes, volume (2000 prices)				
Private consumption[1]	250.3	0.0	2.1	1.9	0.0	0.4
Government consumption[1]	121.7	9.0	3.0	0.7	2.0	1.7
Gross fixed capital formation	97.0	7.5	4.9	6.3	-1.5	1.2
Final domestic demand	469.0	3.9	2.9	2.5	0.2	0.9
Stockbuilding[2]	0.6	-0.2	-0.2	0.3	0.0	0.0
Total domestic demand	469.6	3.7	2.7	2.9	0.2	0.9
Exports of goods and services	357.5	7.3	6.5	4.1	1.1	3.8
Imports of goods and services	313.7	8.2	5.7	5.2	1.6	4.4
Net exports[2]	43.8	0.0	1.0	-0.4	-0.2	-0.1
GDP at market prices	513.4	3.4	3.5	2.2	-0.2	0.8
GDP deflator	_	1.7	1.5	1.8	1.5	1.5
Memorandum items						
Harmonised index of consumer prices	_	1.7	1.6	2.3	1.8	1.6
Private consumption deflator	_	1.9	1.6	1.8	1.6	1.6
Unemployment rate	_	4.1	3.3	3.1	3.7	4.1
Household saving ratio[3]	_	5.3	7.3	5.8	5.8	6.1
General government financial balance[4]	_	0.6	0.3	1.0	0.0	-0.9
Current account balance[4]	_	9.3	7.6	7.2	6.8	6.5

Note: National accounts are based on official chain-linked data. This introduces a discrepancy in the identity between real demand components and GDP. For further details see OECD Economic Outlook Sources and Methods (http://www.oecd.org/eco/sources-and-methods).
1. The introduction of a health care insurance reform in 2006 caused, in national accounts, a shift of health care spending from private consumption to public consumption.
2. Contributions to changes in real GDP (percentage of real GDP in previous year), actual amount in the first column.
3. As a percentage of disposable income, including savings in life insurance and pension schemes.
4. As a percentage of GDP.
Source: OECD Economic Outlook 84 database.

StatLink http://dx.doi.org/10.1787/503258484562

higher for longer than in other countries over the near term. Moreover, the tight labour market pushed core inflation up to around 2% during the second half of the year.

The financial crisis has a direct impact on income

The financial crisis has had a direct impact by reducing the value of assets held by pension funds, some of which already announced that payouts will not be increased in line with inflation for 2009, or that contributions will rise. This may further undermine consumer confidence, which has been falling for the past eighteen months, and private consumption. Moreover, insofar as the financial crisis has a permanent effect on pension funds' assets, private savings may increase. On the other hand, the crisis has so far had only a modest impact on housing prices.

The fiscal position is set to deteriorate

The 2008 general government budget surplus should be about 1% of GDP, as a slightly expansionary fiscal stance was offset by higher natural gas related revenues. The 2009 budget provides a discretionary fiscal stimulus with cuts in direct income taxes of euro 2.5 billion (0.4% of GDP). In addition, the government withdrew a plan to increase the value-added tax (VAT) rate from 19% to 20%. Moreover, the increase in gas-related budget income expected in the budget is unlikely to be realised as oil prices are falling faster than expected. Together with the working of automatic stabilisers during the economic slowdown and a reduction in EU contributions, this should result in a balanced budget position in 2009, and in a budget deficit of 0.9% of GDP in 2010. The government's acquisitions in the financial sector may help secure confidence, but will increase gross debt by an estimated 5% of GDP; these operations are set to be reprivatised once markets calm.

Growth will only recover in 2010

The economy should regain strength during 2010. The recovery in world trade will benefit exports and easier monetary policy which will stimulate domestic demand. Falling inflation will lead to higher real income growth, stimulating private consumption. The projected economic slowdown will not be deep enough to substantially reduce labour market tensions in the near term. As a result, wage inflation is expected to persist sustaining core inflation, although at a relatively low rate.

... despite persisting global risks

The main domestic downside risk to the projections is that the financial crisis may have a stronger effect on pension assets, forcing pension funds to hike contribution rates in order to guarantee solvency. This would reduce net income growth, jeopardising a recovery in private consumption, as happened in early 2003. The key external risk is that expected weak world markets will cut exports significantly more than projected. On the upside, labour market tensions may ease faster than projected, easing inflationary risks.

NEW ZEALAND

New Zealand has entered recession ahead of other OECD countries, a victim of simultaneous domestic and foreign shocks. The outlook remains subdued because the large macroeconomic imbalances built up over the past decade – inflation, housing overvaluation, high household debt and a huge current account deficit – will take some time to unwind.

Macroeconomic policies are in a good position to cushion the downturn. Tight monetary policy, in place for some time, is now being eased at a rapid pace, and a fiscal expansion is starting from a point of significant surplus and low debt. It will be important to maintain the strong inflation targeting and fiscal sustainability frameworks and to facilitate the shift of resources to the tradeables sector.

Multiple negative shocks have hit growth

Activity abruptly declined at a 2¼ per cent average annual rate through the first half of 2008, reflecting a housing correction, sharply rising commodities prices, the global credit crunch and domestic drought. In contrast to previous downturns, this one has been led mainly by household demand. Real disposable incomes have been severely squeezed by inflation, which has just peaked at over 5%, and continuing pass-through into mortgages (which are mostly fixed term) of past interest rate hikes plus rising credit spreads. In addition, consumption has been held back by rising employment uncertainty. Moreover, housing investment volumes are contracting sharply, and as a result house price declines are likely to reach 15-20%, which will further crimp consumption. Business investment has held up better, but higher labour, energy and finance costs have reduced profit margins, final demand prospects are poor and business confidence has plunged, suggesting substantial weakness going forward. The drought has sharply curtailed dairy and other farm exports, as well as short-term hydro-electric supply.

New Zealand

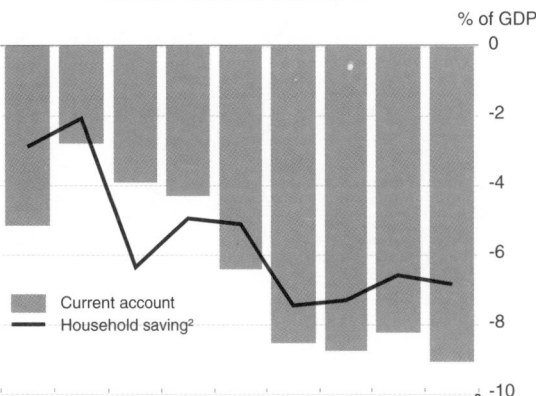

Inflation has been high
Year-on-year percentage change

Household dissaving is driving the current account imbalance

1. Expected inflation in one year.
2. Estimated figures for 2007-08.
3. First half.

Source: Reserve Bank of New Zealand; Statistics New Zealand and OECD Economic Outlook 84 database.

StatLink http://dx.doi.org/10.1787/500786480701

New Zealand: Demand, output and prices

	2005	2006	2007	2008	2009	2010
	Current prices NZD billion	Percentage changes, volume (1995/1996 prices)				
Private consumption	92.1	2.7	4.1	0.0	-0.7	0.7
Government consumption	28.0	4.7	3.6	4.2	4.0	4.0
Gross fixed capital formation	37.5	-1.5	4.7	-0.8	-13.1	3.2
Final domestic demand	157.5	2.0	4.2	0.6	-2.6	1.9
Stockbuilding[1]	0.0	-0.6	0.2	0.3	0.0	0.0
Total domestic demand	158.4	1.2	4.5	1.1	-2.5	1.9
Exports of goods and services	43.4	1.7	3.3	0.2	1.9	4.4
Imports of goods and services	46.7	-2.6	8.7	5.9	-4.6	4.4
Net exports[1]	- 3.2	1.3	-1.7	-1.7	2.1	0.0
GDP at market prices	155.2	2.5	3.0	-0.5	-0.4	1.9
GDP deflator	_	2.4	4.3	3.6	1.7	2.4
Memorandum items						
GDP (production)	_	2.0	3.2	0.5	-0.3	1.9
Consumer price index	_	3.4	2.4	4.0	2.3	2.1
Private consumption deflator	_	2.8	1.7	3.5	2.3	1.1
Unemployment rate	_	3.8	3.6	4.0	5.4	6.0
General government financial balance[2]	_	3.7	3.7	2.5	-0.6	-1.6
Current account balance[2]	_	-8.7	-8.2	-9.5	-7.6	-6.6

Note: National accounts are based on official chain-linked data. This introduces a discrepancy in the identity between real demand components and GDP. For further details see *OECD Economic Outlook* Sources and Methods *(http://www.oecd.org/eco/sources-and-methods).*
1. Contributions to changes in real GDP (percentage of real GDP in previous year), actual amount in the first column.
2. As a percentage of GDP.
Source: OECD Economic Outlook 84 database.

StatLink ⟨⟨⟨ *http://dx.doi.org/10.1787/503301141245*

Policy rate cuts are being frontloaded

The Reserve Bank decided to bring forward its planned reductions in the overnight cash rate (OCR), judging that weakening demand will suffice to bring inflation inside the 1-3% target band over the medium term. The OCR fell from 8¼ to 6½ per cent between July and October 2008, with further cuts signalled. Declining interest rates have tended to reinforce the ongoing currency depreciation, lending support to growth and eventual current account adjustment. However, for the time being monetary easing may not prove very effective in spurring domestic demand as the transmission mechanism's effectiveness may have been damaged by financial strains. The mostly foreign-owned banks are well capitalised, with little direct exposure to other countries' troubled assets. Nevertheless, they are vulnerable insofar as one third of lending is financed by overseas borrowing, most of it short-term, which has become more expensive and harder to obtain. Several non-banks, mainly engaged in property development, have failed. In line with developments in other countries, most notably Australia, opt-in guarantee schemes have been introduced for all retail deposits and wholesale funding of qualifying bank and non-bank financial institutions.

Fiscal deficits are looming

The automatic stabilisers and significant medium-term discretionary expansion (4% of GDP) will mean budget deficits and rising indebtedness for the first time since the 1980s. The weak growth picture implies lower tax receipts and increased social expenditure. Household tax cuts have just entered into force, while recent corporate tax cuts have helped to ease firms' financial pressures. Finally, recently introduced measures (Kiwi Saver and free early childhood education) have been more expensive than originally estimated due to their high uptake and treaty settlements have become more costly. Although new spending promises have been made ahead of the November 2008 elections, both major parties have committed to keeping the allowance for new spending to that indicated in the 2008 budget.

Macroeconomic imbalances should unwind

Despite a near-term boost from tax cuts and bounce-back from drought, only modest macroeconomic improvement is projected until mid-2010. The main growth drivers will be public spending and exports, while demand from households is expected to be very weak. Business investment will eventually recover thanks to real interest rate declines, wage moderation, competitiveness gains and a pick-up in foreign demand. Inflation should fall to within the target band by mid-2009 thanks to lower oil prices and persisting economic slack. The current account deficit should shrink in line with household deleveraging and weak business investment that will more than offset renewed government dissaving.

Risks are stacked on the downside

The main risk is the possibility of increased costs of offshore funding and, in particular, the heightened risk aversion which could cause further reductions in the carry trade, unwanted currency depreciation and higher inflation. The new carbon emissions permit trading scheme to be rolled out in 2010 also carries risks for inflation expectations and investor confidence.

NORWAY

After the remarkable performance of the past few years, the Norwegian economy is now slowing toward its potential rate of growth. Domestic demand is moderating as a result of the increased cost of borrowing, falling house prices and declining terms of trade. Nonetheless, inflation remains higher than desirable and rising labour costs are undermining competitiveness.

The central bank should continue to monitor inflation pressures but pay increasing attention to the impact of financial turbulence on the real economy, as it did recently with successive cuts in policy rates. The structural budget deficit is likely to exceed the 4% rule in 2009 due to adverse stock market effects on the value of the Government Pension Fund. While this is appropriate in current cyclical conditions, fiscal stimulus should remain temporary in view of long-term budgetary challenges.

The economy has started to slow

Activity slowed markedly this year, reflecting weaker private consumption and residential investment. Despite the moderation of growth, capacity utilisation remains high, notably in the manufacturing sector. Though unemployment has started to rise, it remains well below the estimated structural rate of unemployment. Labour market tightening and mediocre productivity growth have underpinned rising unit labour costs and domestically generated inflation. A deterioration of cost competitiveness and currency appreciation in the first half of the year led to a slowdown in exports of traditional goods. While the persistence of above-target inflation had justified a tightening of monetary conditions over the first half of the year, the central bank cut policy rates twice in October to facilitate financial normalization, in line with the policies of Norway's trading partners.

Norway

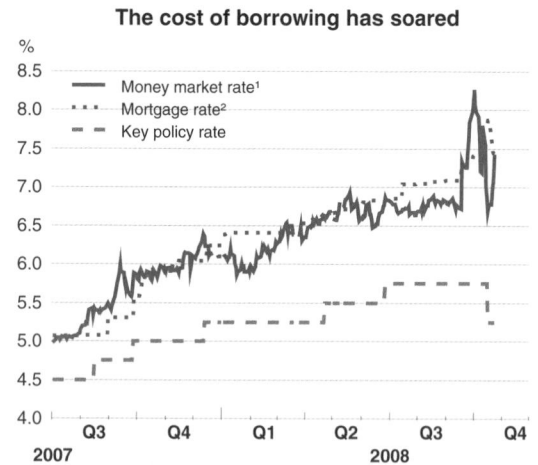

The cost of borrowing has soared

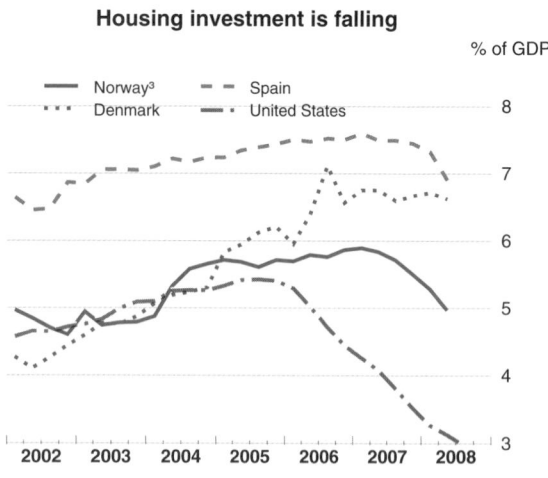

Housing investment is falling

1. Three-month NIBOR.
2. Interest rates on new mortgage loans of NOK 1 million, up to 60% of purchase price, with floating interest rate. Figures for the 20 largest banks, weighted according to market share.
3. In percentage of mainland gross domestic product.

Source: Norsk familieØkonomi AS and Norges Bank, OECD Economic Outlook 84 database.

StatLink ⟡ *http://dx.doi.org/10.1787/500803081371*

Norway: **Demand, output and prices**

	2005	2006	2007	2008	2009	2010
	Current prices NOK billion	Percentage changes, volume (2005 prices)				
Private consumption	826.2	4.7	6.4	2.4	1.8	1.6
Government consumption	387.2	2.9	3.6	3.5	3.6	3.2
Gross fixed capital formation	365.6	7.3	9.3	3.5	-2.4	1.1
Final domestic demand	1 579.0	4.9	6.4	2.9	1.2	1.9
Stockbuilding[1]	46.5	0.7	-0.3	1.1	0.3	0.0
Total domestic demand	1 625.4	5.5	5.8	4.3	1.5	1.8
Exports of goods and services	868.4	0.4	2.8	2.0	0.6	0.4
Imports of goods and services	548.1	8.1	8.7	5.8	0.6	0.7
Net exports[1]	320.3	-2.1	-1.2	-0.9	0.1	0.0
GDP at market prices	1 945.7	2.5	3.7	2.7	1.3	1.6
GDP deflator	–	8.4	1.6	6.2	-4.8	2.6
Memorandum items						
Mainland GDP at market prices[2]	–	4.8	6.2	2.9	1.2	1.7
Consumer price index	–	2.3	0.7	3.6	2.5	1.8
Private consumption deflator	–	2.1	0.7	3.5	2.7	1.8
Unemployment rate	–	3.4	2.5	2.6	3.0	3.3
Household saving ratio[3]	–	0.1	-0.3	2.0	5.2	7.0
General government financial balance[4]	–	18.5	17.4	20.0	14.0	13.1
Current account balance[4]	–	17.3	15.6	16.2	13.3	14.3

Note: National accounts are based on official chain-linked data. This introduces a discrepancy in the identity between real demand components and GDP. For further details see *OECD Economic Outlook* Sources and Methods *(http://www.oecd.org/eco/sources-and-methods)*.
1. Contributions to changes in real GDP (percentage of real GDP in previous year), actual amount in the first column.
2. GDP excluding oil and shipping.
3. As a percentage of disposable income.
4. As a percentage of GDP.
Source: OECD Economic Outlook 84 database.

StatLink ⟨⟩ http://dx.doi.org/10.1787/503306148405

Adverse conditions are partly offset by expansionary fiscal policy

Several developments are likely to weigh on activity in the short term. The housing market entered a downturn, with falling house prices and a sharp contraction of residential investment, which is expected to persist for most of 2009. This will depress output directly through weaker construction activity, and indirectly through a negative wealth on consumer spending. The sharp drop in equity markets is expected to have similar consequences. The liquidity problems facing financial institutions and the resulting strong increase in bank lending margins will reduce non-oil investment. Inflation expectations will start to moderate soon and, although actual inflation will not undershoot the target over the next year, it is likely to fall below 2% in 2010, leaving room for the central bank to reduce interest rates during 2009. In addition, fiscal policy will remain supportive in 2009-10, with a further increase in the cyclically-adjusted non-oil central government deficit, essentially through increasing welfare spending, while remaining within the limits permitted by the 4% rule.*

* According to this rule, the 4% expected real return on the outstanding value of the Government Pension Fund Global (GPF) is transferred to the budget every year, subject to certain possible adjustments for the business cycle and unusual changes to the value of the GPF.

Growth will be weak in 2009, but should rebound in 2010

Weak overall demand will limit the growth of mainland activity in 2009. The off-shore sector will however continue to support mainland demand, through spill-over from oil investment, even if the latter may be weakened by the recent fall in oil prices. Labour market pressures will ease and productivity is expected to gently rise towards its trend growth, resulting in a deceleration of unit labour cost growth. Both headline and underlying inflation will move below the Norges Bank's target in 2010, despite renewed increases in import prices. While financial markets are expected to remain under stress in the near term, their gradual normalization and cuts in policy rates will reopen access to liquidity and credit, allowing headwinds to ease in 2010.

Uncertainty will haunt private sector prospects

The main risks to the projections pertain to the uncertainty about the effects of financial market turmoil and inflation prospects. The private non-oil sector has borrowed abroad extensively in recent years, partially offsetting outflows through the Pension Fund (Global); the resulting dependence of Norway's money market on international ones may make the persistence or the deepening of financial turbulence more disruptive than now expected. Norwegian banks may face even greater difficulties in accessing US dollar lending, one of their main source of financing, requiring the central bank to reinforce its support for the market in dollar/ krone swaps. This may create exchange rate volatility, as observed just recently. Further depreciation of the currency might feed inflation, near-term expectations for which are not fully stabilised. Continuing deterioration in the terms of trade through further falls in oil and metal prices would depress real incomes. On the other hand, currency depreciation could offset weaker domestic demand.

POLAND

The pace of expansion decelerated moderately in the first half of 2008 and recent data point to a further weakening of activity. Amidst the global slowdown, growth is projected to fall below potential, although income tax cuts should support private consumption. With declining oil prices and persisting, albeit abating, demand pressures in labour and product markets, core inflation is expected to subside more gradually than headline inflation.

Fiscal policy has been somewhat expansionary in 2008, though significant underspending on infrastructure investment has led to an unexpectedly low central government budget deficit. The debate over the adoption of the single currency has intensified. A structural improvement in the fiscal balance and a permanent reduction in inflation are key hurdles en route to meeting the Maastricht criteria.

Economic activity has been slowing

Private consumption has fuelled the expansion, supported by substantial real disposable income gains. So far, all forms of investment activity have also added significantly to GDP growth. Despite earlier currency appreciation, exports have remained fairly robust. However, economic activity eased slightly in the first half of 2008, with real GDP increasing by around 6% (year-on-year), about a half point above its estimated potential rate. Data for the third quarter suggest further deceleration, with lower industrial production, retail sales and construction activity.

Labour market tightness has eased

Unemployment has continued to fall very rapidly, mainly driven by the strong, if slowing, pace of job creation in the business sector. Coupled with growing indications of return migration and weakening labour demand, pressures for higher wage compensation have slightly diminished, though unit labour costs have continued to surge.

Poland

Manufacturing output and confidence have deteriorated
Seasonally adjusted

Non-residential construction has dropped
Contribution to year-on-year investment growth

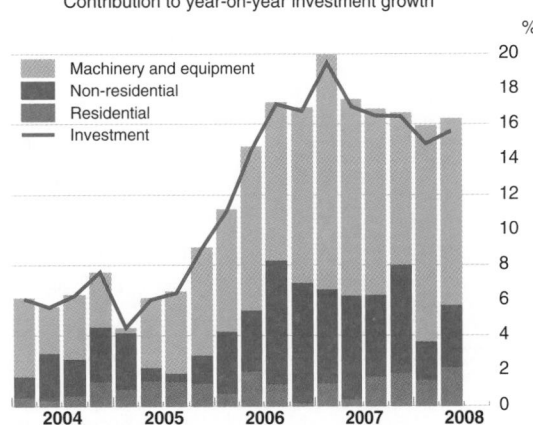

1. Year-on-year percentage change, three-month moving average.

Source: OECD Economic Outlook 84 database and *Main Economic Indicators.*

StatLink http://dx.doi.org/10.1787/500817503316

Poland: **Demand, output and prices**

	2005	2006	2007	2008	2009	2010
	Current prices PLZ billion	Percentage changes, volume (2000 prices)				
Private consumption	623.4	5.0	5.0	4.9	3.9	4.1
Government consumption	177.8	6.1	3.7	0.1	1.8	2.0
Gross fixed capital formation	179.2	14.9	17.3	13.6	4.0	3.2
Final domestic demand	980.3	7.0	7.1	5.9	3.6	3.6
Stockbuilding[1]	10.3	0.4	1.6	-0.1	-0.1	0.0
Total domestic demand	990.6	7.3	8.6	5.7	3.4	3.5
Exports of goods and services	364.7	14.6	9.1	6.5	1.3	1.9
Imports of goods and services	371.9	17.4	13.5	6.8	3.6	2.1
Net exports[1]	- 7.3	-1.1	-2.0	-0.3	-1.0	-0.1
GDP at market prices	983.3	6.2	6.7	5.4	3.0	3.5
GDP deflator	_	1.5	3.9	3.4	3.7	3.5
Memorandum items						
Consumer price index	_	1.3	2.5	4.2	3.2	3.6
Private consumption deflator	_	1.2	2.4	4.1	2.9	3.5
Unemployment rate	_	13.8	9.6	7.2	7.1	7.6
General government financial balance[2,3]	_	-3.8	-2.0	-2.3	-2.7	-2.9
Current account balance[2]	_	-2.7	-4.7	-5.3	-6.3	-6.3

Note: National accounts are based on official chain-linked data. This introduces a discrepancy in the identity between real demand components and GDP. For further details see *OECD Economic Outlook* Sources and Methods *(http://www.oecd.org/eco/sources-and-methods)*.
1. Contributions to changes in real GDP (percentage of real GDP in previous year), actual amount in the first column.
2. As a percentage of GDP.
3. With private pension funds (OFE) classified outside the general government sector.
Source: OECD Economic Outlook 84 database.

StatLink http://dx.doi.org/10.1787/503327253358

Meeting the Maastricht criteria will require tighter fiscal discipline...

The government and the central bank have advanced plans to join the euro area by announcing their intention to enter the European Union exchange-rate mechanism before mid-2009, judging that Poland could fulfil all the Maastricht criteria as early as 2011. In this perspective, fiscal consolidation actions are even more pressing. Although the general government deficit was reduced to 2% of GDP in 2007, fiscal policy has been somewhat expansionary in 2008, with the stimulus being limited only by underspending on much needed infrastructure investments. A sustainable deficit-reduction plan should aim instead to contain social spending, notably by pursuing efforts to eliminate most early retirement schemes and to merge the farmers' pension scheme with the general pension system. Taxing income from farming and introducing a cadastral tax on property would be additional steps in the right direction.

... and sustainably lower inflation

As headline inflation continued to rise in the spring, the central bank increased its key policy rate to 6% in June. The earlier trend appreciation of the currency had already tightened monetary conditions, though the exchange rate has been more volatile of late. Inflation peaked in the summer and then began to reverse with falling commodity prices. Despite prospects of significantly weaker oil prices and activity in 2009, core inflation is projected to remain higher than its headline counterpart as wage-induced cost-push and demand-pull factors subside only gradually. Bringing headline inflation back to the official target of 2.5% will probably be the minimum necessary to satisfy the Maastricht inflation criterion for adopting the euro and should remain the key objective. Indeed, further monetary policy tightening would have been warranted if the global financial crisis had not intensified. These projections assume an unchanged policy rate over the projection horizon.

Growth will fall below potential

Growth is projected to fall below potential rates over the next two years and recover slowly in 2010. Private consumption is expected to sustain economic activity to some extent, while investment growth will remain subdued under the weight of tighter monetary conditions and credit standards, much weaker confidence, deteriorating corporate financial positions, lower FDI inflows and a slowdown in construction. Improved absorption of EU funds could support growth, however. Much weaker growth prospects in the euro area will dampen trade volumes in 2009, followed by a modest upswing in 2010.

Currency stability under the ERM2 may prove difficult

In the context of the financial crisis spreading to emerging markets, it is fortunate that Poland has stronger fundamentals than other such economies. However, the external position is weakening and a possible outflow of capital could put the financing of the large current account deficit under stress. This would render the stability of the currency following the required entry into the ERM2 all the more difficult.

PORTUGAL

Economic activity moderated in the first half of 2008, as investment and export growth softened. In line with the recent intensification of the financial crisis and expectations of a significant slowing in Portugal's export markets, activity is expected to contract until the second half of 2009, before recovering slowly in 2010. The unemployment rate is set to increase from its already high level. The sizeable negative output gap and lower food and energy prices will reduce inflation.

The fiscal position is likely to deteriorate in 2009 and 2010 as weaker economic conditions reduce revenue growth. Further fiscal consolidation and structural reforms are required in the medium term to strengthen economic performance. Greater public sector efficiency and a more favourable business environment would foster private sector confidence and economic growth.

Economic activity has softened

Economic activity moderated in the first half of 2008, as solid consumption growth was offset by weaker investment and export growth. Portuguese banks continue to tighten lending standards as the global financial crisis has intensified. Despite the softening in activity, conditions in the labour market improved in the first half of the year, with unemployment falling below 7.5%. Although food and energy prices have fallen significantly from their mid-year highs, headline inflation was still 2.5% in October 2008. Unit labour cost growth has picked up in recent quarters, though core inflation remains contained.

The budget deficit is likely to rise again

The 2008 budget deficit is likely to be 2.2% of GDP, slightly less than in 2007. Despite the government's announcement of additional revenue measures in its recent budget proposals for 2009, the deterioration in economic activity means that the budget deficit could well rise to just under 3% of GDP next year. Without further reductions in government outlays, or a more rapid economic upturn, the budget deficit could rise above 3% in 2010.

Portugal

Economic activity has slowed

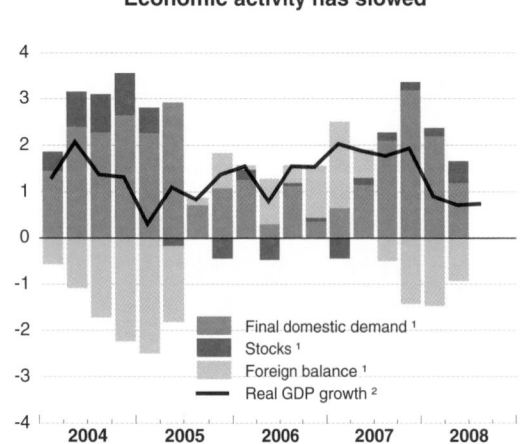

Weak growth is likely to continue

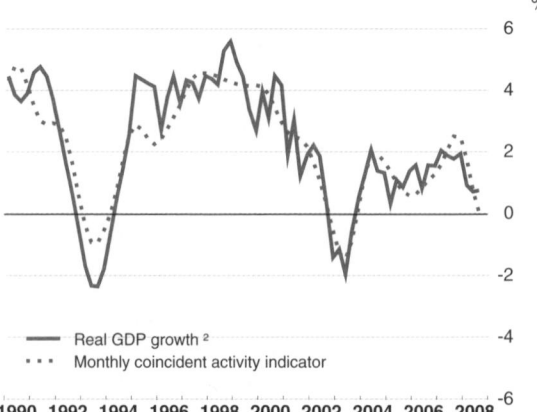

1. Year-on-year contribution to GDP growth.
2. Year-on-year percentage change.

Source: Bank of Portugal and OECD Economic Outlook 84 database.

StatLink http://dx.doi.org/10.1787/500820786306

OECD ECONOMIC OUTLOOK 84 – ISBN 978-92-64-05469-1 – © OECD 2008

Portugal: **Demand, output and prices**

	2005	2006	2007	2008	2009	2010
	Current prices € billion	Percentage changes, volume (2000 prices)				
Private consumption	96.7	1.9	1.6	1.2	-0.2	0.6
Government consumption	32.0	-1.4	0.0	-0.2	0.2	0.5
Gross fixed capital formation	33.1	-0.7	3.1	0.7	-1.2	0.5
Final domestic demand	161.8	0.7	1.6	0.8	-0.4	0.5
Stockbuilding[1]	0.6	0.0	0.0	0.0	0.0	0.0
Total domestic demand	162.3	0.7	1.6	0.9	-0.4	0.5
Exports of goods and services	42.6	8.7	7.5	2.0	-0.5	1.6
Imports of goods and services	55.8	5.1	5.6	2.4	-0.9	1.3
Net exports[1]	- 13.2	0.6	0.1	-0.4	0.2	0.0
GDP at market prices	149.1	1.4	1.9	0.5	-0.2	0.6
GDP deflator	_	2.8	2.9	2.2	2.3	1.8
Memorandum items						
Harmonised index of consumer prices	_	3.0	2.4	2.8	1.3	1.6
Private consumption deflator	_	3.1	2.7	2.8	1.4	1.6
Unemployment rate	_	7.7	8.0	7.6	8.5	8.8
Household saving ratio[2]	_	8.1	6.6	6.9	7.3	7.4
General government financial balance[3,4]	_	-3.9	-2.7	-2.2	-2.9	-3.1
Current account balance[3]	_	-10.1	-9.8	-10.9	-10.2	-10.1

1. Contributions to changes in real GDP (percentage of real GDP in previous year), actual amount in the first column.
2. As a percentage of disposable income.
3. As a percentage of GDP.
4. Based on national accounts definition.
Source: OECD Economic Outlook 84 database.

StatLink 🔗 *http://dx.doi.org/10.1787/503456226076*

Activity is expected to contract in 2009

Real GDP is projected to fall by ¼ per cent in 2009. Very tight credit conditions, a softening labour market and low levels of consumer confidence will constrain consumption. The same factors should keep residential investment weak, though Portugal is less exposed to an abrupt downturn because its housing market has been soft for many years. Falling activity in a number of Portugal's major export markets, particularly Spain, points to very weak near-term exports. Weak exports, tighter credit conditions and subdued internal demand are projected to depress business investment in 2009 and lead to labour shedding in the next few quarters and an increase in the unemployment rate. In late 2009, activity is projected to recover along with global growth, and unemployment should begin to come down again toward the end of 2010 as domestic activity gathers pace. Lower food and energy prices, weak economic growth, and a high unemployment rate are expected to keep increases in private sector wages moderate, and help to reduce core inflation towards the euro area average.

The risks are to the downside

The recent intensification of stress in global financial markets and the deterioration of economic conditions in Portugal's largest export markets mean that risks are firmly on the downside for activity and government finances.

SLOVAK REPUBLIC

Although the Slovak Republic will continue to maintain the highest growth rate among OECD countries over the next two years, activity is expected to decelerate significantly in 2009. In particular investment spending and trade growth are likely to be adversely affected by the effects of the financial crisis. Growth is envisaged to return to close to its potential rate towards the end of the projection horizon. Inflation rates should decline from their currently high levels, but to stay above euro area levels.

Dealing with the adoption of the euro, which will take place on 1st January 2009, will determine policy priorities. Although the expected slowdown will damp the danger of a boom-bust cycle induced by low real interest rates, fiscal policy should be used cautiously. Rising house prices and household indebtedness should be closely watched.

Growth has remained robust...

After growing by 10.4% in 2007, the highest growth rate since independence, economic activity has continued at a robust pace since the start of the year. Private consumption was strong, despite a marked increase in inflation rates, as unemployment continued to decline. Growth in fixed investment continued to benefit from low real interest rates and strong foreign direct investment inflows. At the same time, export growth has slowed somewhat, reflecting in part the appreciation of the exchange rate by around 10% *vis-à-vis* the euro since the beginning of the year and ahead of the publication of the final euro conversion rate prior to euro area entry in early July.

... but has decelerated

However, activity has been slowing somewhat over the summer months. The first effects of the turmoil in international financial markets are visible, as government bond spreads *vis-à-vis* Germany have soared. In addition, foreign car companies seem to have become more cautious with respect to their investment plans in the Slovak Republic. Against this

Slovak Republic

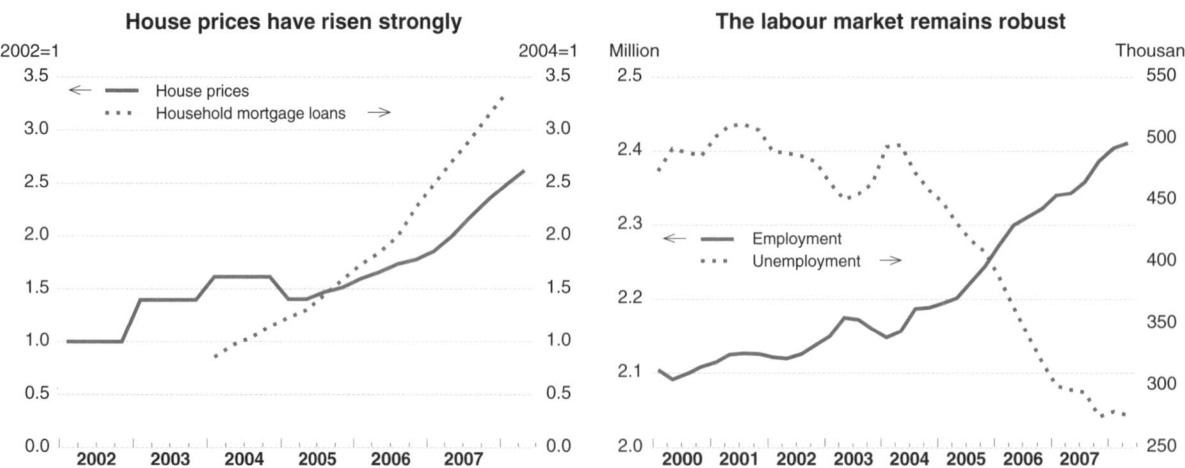

Source: ECB, BIS and OECD Economic Outlook 84 database.

StatLink 🔗 http://dx.doi.org/10.1787/500825176015

OECD ECONOMIC OUTLOOK 84 – ISBN 978-92-64-05469-1 – © OECD 2008

Slovak Republic: **Demand, output and prices**

	2005	2006	2007	2008	2009	2010
	Current prices SKK billion	Percentage changes, volume (2000 prices)				
Private consumption	851.7	5.6	7.1	6.2	3.8	5.1
Government consumption	272.8	10.1	0.7	5.5	3.5	2.5
Gross fixed capital formation	394.3	8.4	7.9	6.7	3.8	6.6
Final domestic demand	1 518.8	7.1	6.1	6.2	3.8	5.0
Stockbuilding[1]	34.6	-0.5	-0.1	0.4	-0.1	0.0
Total domestic demand	1 553.4	6.5	5.9	6.5	3.6	4.9
Exports of goods and services	1 132.8	21.0	16.0	6.6	1.6	7.8
Imports of goods and services	1 201.0	17.7	10.4	8.3	1.6	7.0
Net exports[1]	- 68.1	1.7	4.3	-1.5	0.0	0.7
GDP at market prices	1 485.3	8.5	10.4	7.3	4.0	5.6
GDP deflator	_	2.9	1.1	4.9	3.5	2.6
Memorandum items						
Consumer price index	_	4.5	2.8	4.4	2.8	2.8
Private consumption deflator	_	4.9	2.6	4.0	2.7	2.8
Unemployment rate	_	13.3	11.0	9.7	9.4	9.0
General government financial balance[2]	_	-3.5	-2.0	-2.1	-2.0	-1.5
Current account balance[2]	_	-7.1	-5.3	-5.0	-4.1	-2.2

Note: National accounts are based on official chain-linked data. This introduces a discrepancy in the identity between real demand components and GDP. For further details see *OECD Economic Outlook* Sources and Methods *(http://www.oecd.org/eco/sources-and-methods)*.
1. Contributions to changes in real GDP (percentage of real GDP in previous year), actual amount in the first column.
2. As a percentage of GDP.
Source: OECD Economic Outlook 84 database.

StatLink ⌐🔗 *http://dx.doi.org/10.1787/503467605664*

background, business as well as consumer sentiment has started to deteriorate. While retail sales have remained fairly stable, industrial production appears to be levelling off.

Euro area entry poses challenges

As a catching-up country within the euro area, Slovakia is likely to experience a higher equilibrium inflation rate and consequently lower real interest rates than other euro area members. In addition, increased integration with euro area financial markets will foster desirable financial development, but also lead to rising indebtedness. Experience from other euro area countries suggests that such conditions can lead to an overshooting of aggregate demand. Although slowing economic activity will limit this risk in the short term, a key policy challenge over the medium term will be to avoid such a boom-bust-cycle. In this respect, the continued growth in house prices and household indebtedness should be watched carefully.

The financial crisis will affect the economy

Following a temporary deceleration of economic activity related to the international financial crisis, growth is envisaged to be 4% in 2009 before picking up to 5.6%, near its trend rate, in 2010. Until then, weaker demand from main trading partners will significantly reduce export growth, in particular as the economy is highly exposed to a deterioration of automobile demand. Investment growth is also likely to slow sharply due to worsening earnings expectations and tighter lending standards of banks. Restricted credit is also likely to constrain the further growth of house prices, although the absence of an earlier country-wide construction boom may limit the downside risks in this sector. Private consumption is projected to remain fairly robust as consumers have not borrowed against their higher housing wealth, another factor limiting the downside risk from falling house prices. Although inflation is likely to be muted due to the slowdown in economic activity and the lower energy and food prices, it will stay above the euro area average, driven by the catching-up process. Unemployment is expected to continue falling, albeit less so than in the past.

Risks to the outlook lie on the downside

The projection of an only temporary slowing of the economy and continued growth at potential rates thereafter is surrounded by considerable uncertainty. Apart from a stronger adverse impact of the financial crisis or the downturn of the international automotive cycle, a boom-bust cycle following euro area entry remains the biggest risk over the medium term.

SPAIN

GDP is projected to fall in 2009, as residential construction continues to contract, before recovering modestly in 2010. Unemployment will continue to increase substantially. Inflation should recede as a large negative output gap opens up and commodity prices moderate, while falling imports should significantly reduce the current account deficit.

Discretionary fiscal policy easing of around 1½ per cent of GDP has been supporting growth in 2008. The automatic stabilisers should also be allowed to operate in 2009 and 2010. Steps will then need to be taken to curb spending pressures in the longer term. Eliminating the indexation of wages to past inflation would preserve competitiveness, mitigating the downward cycle. With potential growth expected to decline in line with lower immigration flows and slowing rises in female participation, further steps to nurture competition in product and services markets need to be taken to increase productivity growth.

Activity is declining

GDP has contracted, as private consumption weakened and investment fell, led by very large and steepening declines in residential construction. Confidence indicators in services, manufacturing and consumers continue to deteriorate. The unemployment rate is rising, reflecting a large increase in labour supply and falling employment. Headline inflation is abating, reaching 3.6% in October, due to lower oil prices; core inflation also fell, to 2.9%.

The fiscal stance will turn neutral

The government has taken a number of measures that, together with tax reductions legislated earlier, amount to a discretionary fiscal stimulus of around 1.5% of GDP in 2008. Automatic stabilisers are also having a significant impact, as unemployment-related spending has risen and unusually strong revenue growth in recent years is reversing. In 2009,

Spain

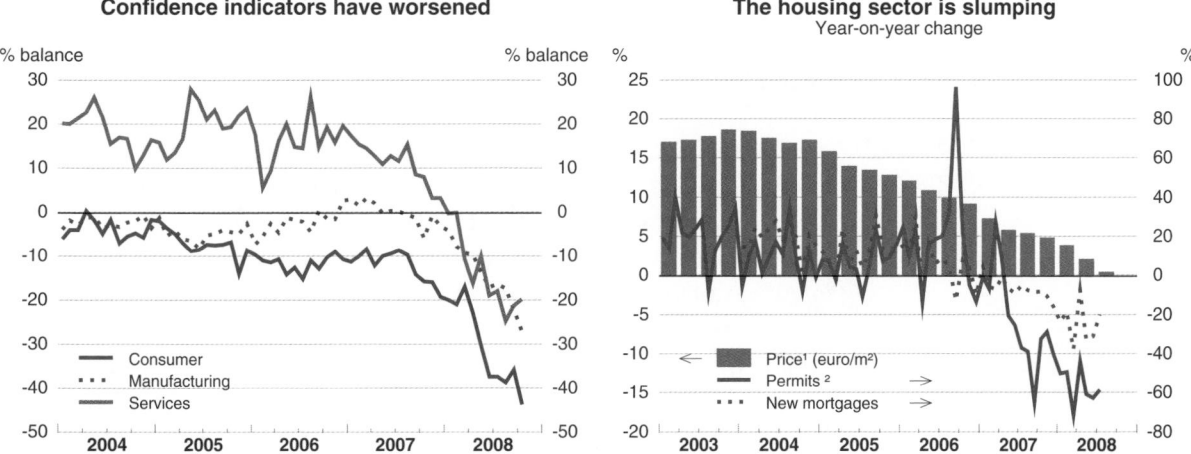

1. Excluding social housing.
2. Data in September 2006 and 2007 as well as March 2007 and 2008 are affected by the introduction of a new building code, raising construction costs.

Source: Eurostat, Ministerio de Vivienda and Bank of Spain.

StatLink 🔗 *http://dx.doi.org/10.1787/501002745688*

Spain: Demand, output and prices

	2005	2006	2007	2008	2009	2010
	Current prices € billion	Percentage changes, volume (2000 prices)				
Private consumption	525.1	3.9	3.5	1.2	-0.4	0.2
Government consumption	163.7	4.6	4.9	3.6	3.4	3.1
Gross fixed capital formation	267.0	7.1	5.3	-2.0	-9.2	-2.7
Final domestic demand	955.9	4.9	4.2	0.7	-2.2	0.0
Stockbuilding[1]	0.9	0.2	-0.1	0.0	-0.1	0.0
Total domestic demand	956.8	5.1	4.2	0.7	-2.3	0.0
Exports of goods and services	233.4	6.7	4.9	3.2	3.7	5.6
Imports of goods and services	281.4	10.3	6.2	0.9	-1.6	2.6
Net exports[1]	- 48.0	-1.5	-0.8	0.6	1.5	0.7
GDP at market prices	908.8	3.9	3.7	1.3	-0.9	0.8
GDP deflator	_	4.0	3.2	3.4	2.5	1.1
Memorandum items						
Harmonised index of consumer prices	_	3.6	2.8	4.4	1.8	1.5
Private consumption deflator	_	3.4	3.2	4.3	1.8	1.5
Unemployment rate	_	8.5	8.3	10.9	14.2	14.8
Household saving ratio	_	11.2	10.2	11.2	12.7	13.8
General government financial balance[2]	_	2.0	2.2	-1.5	-2.9	-3.8
Current account balance[2]	_	-8.9	-10.1	-9.7	-7.4	-6.4

Note: National accounts are based on official chain-linked data. This introduces a discrepancy in the identity between real demand components and GDP. For further details see *OECD Economic Outlook* Sources and Methods *(http://www.oecd.org/eco/sources-and-methods)*.
1. Contributions to changes in real GDP (percentage of real GDP in previous year), actual amount in the first column.
2. As a percentage of GDP.
Source: OECD Economic Outlook 84 database.

StatLink ᴍᴤ🖵 *http://dx.doi.org/10.1787/503468203426*

revenue losses from the elimination of the wealth tax will be offset by spending cuts by the central government. Budgetary policy may face a dilemma in 2010, since slowing construction-related revenues are likely to require spending cuts at the local level to satisfy budgetary rules, and conforming with the SGP commitments may require a pro-cyclical tightening.

Financial conditions will remain tight

Financial conditions have tightened, as past rises in short-term interest rates have fed into mortgage rates and lending has slowed. Banks are well capitalised and profitable, but heavy exposure to the residential construction sector will lead to a further rise in non-performing loans and might restrict future credit growth. This is especially the case for savings banks, which are subject to restrictions on their ability to raise external capital. On the other hand, the expected further fall in short-term interest rates, as well as lower energy prices will provide some relief to highly indebted households. The government has increased the public guarantee for bank deposits fivefold to € 100 000, and a fund was established with up to € 50 billion (around 4.5% of GDP) to improve banks' liquidity by buying highly-rated bond issues from banks, which are facing difficulties in bond markets. In addition, the government stands ready to guarantee banks' new issues of bills and bonds of up to €100 billion in 2008.

The economy will contract in 2009 before recovering in 2010

The sharp contraction in residential construction is set to persist for some time and house prices will continue to fall in reaction to weaker demand and a significant overhang of unsold units. Private consumption growth will be slowed by declines in housing and stock market wealth, more restrictive financial conditions and employment losses. The slowdown in demand, tighter credit standards and falling profits are projected to result in a sharp fall in business investment. Sluggish world trade in 2009 should limit export growth, although the fall in imports and in oil prices should reduce the current account deficit significantly. The unemployment rate is expected to rise to near 15%, even as much lower projected immigration moderates labour supply growth. In 2010, growth is projected to begin to pick up again as declines in housing investment ease, financial turmoil recedes and world growth resumes. Indeed, exports are expected to be the main driver of Spanish growth in 2010, which would help to further lessen the current account deficit. Core and headline inflation will fall to around 1¾ per cent as significant slack opens up and recent oil and food price decreases are passed through. The inflation differential with the euro area should fall below ¼ percentage point.

Housing and financial markets pose risks

Credit constraints could tighten further due to a rise in non-performing loans, especially if employment losses and house price falls are large, and if the international financial crisis persists. Given the high level of household and business indebtedness and the prevalence of variable-rate mortgages, activity remains particularly sensitive to changes in short-term interest rates.

SWEDEN

The Swedish economy stalled in the first half of 2008 and is expected to weaken in the near term, as the effects of the international financial crisis take their toll. Consumption is projected to pick up late next year as the turmoil subsides and thanks to further income tax cuts and lower interest rates. Export growth should gradually recover as Sweden's export markets expand again.

With widening slack and lower commodity prices, the Riksbank has scope to continue to cut interest rates. The announced fiscal easing in 2009 will support demand and is structured to contribute, over time, to improving supply.

Activity stalled in the first half of 2008

With virtually no growth in real GDP in the first half of 2008, the output gap was probably already negative by mid-year. Private consumption slowed, investment lost momentum and export growth remained weak. Retail trade, motor vehicle registrations, new industrial orders and industrial production are all lower than they were a year ago. The purchasing managers' index and consumer and business confidence have continued to fall, pointing to ongoing weakness in coming quarters.

Financial market turbulence affects the real economy

International financial market turmoil has affected the Swedish financial system, in particular through higher and more volatile interest rates in the interbank and mortgage bond markets. By the end of October, two financial institutions had taken out special loans from the Riksbank to ease liquidity constraints and, in early November, one of them was taken over by the Government. Equity prices have fallen significantly since the start of the year. Consumer confidence has dropped to levels well below those recorded during the 2001-03 downturn. Business

Sweden

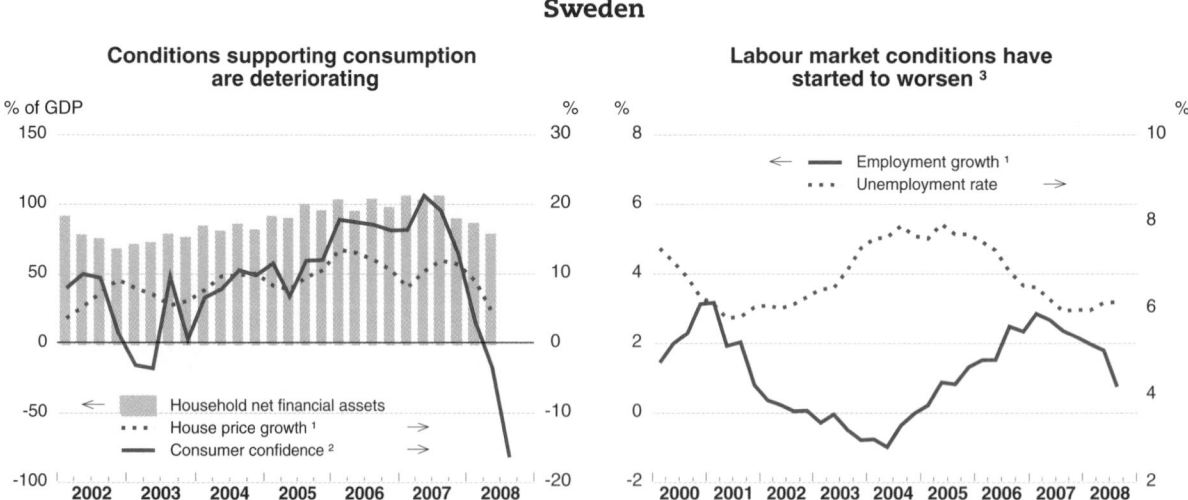

1. Change from same period of previous year.
2. Quarterly averages of the monthly values.
3. Based on the definition of unemployment which covers 15-to-74-year-olds and classifies job-seeking full-time students as unemployed.

Source: OECD Economic Outlook 84 database, National Institute of Economic Research and Statistics Sweden.

StatLink 🔗 *http://dx.doi.org/10.1787/501014372343*

Sweden: **Demand, output and prices**

	2005	2006	2007	2008	2009	2010
	Current prices SEK billion	Percentage changes, volume (2000 prices)				
Private consumption	1 328.4	2.5	3.0	1.9	0.7	2.5
Government consumption	722.7	1.5	1.1	0.6	1.0	0.5
Gross fixed capital formation	475.9	7.7	8.0	3.0	-2.7	2.0
Final domestic demand	2 526.9	3.2	3.4	1.8	0.1	1.8
Stockbuilding[1]	- 4.2	0.2	0.7	0.3	0.2	0.0
Total domestic demand	2 522.7	3.4	4.2	2.1	0.3	1.8
Exports of goods and services	1 333.4	8.7	6.3	3.3	0.3	3.8
Imports of goods and services	1 120.9	8.2	9.9	4.2	0.3	3.3
Net exports[1]	212.5	0.9	-1.1	-0.2	0.0	0.5
GDP at market prices	2 735.2	4.4	2.9	0.8	0.0	2.2
GDP deflator	_	1.5	2.9	3.7	2.5	1.6
Memorandum items						
Consumer price index	_	1.4	2.2	3.5	1.5	1.1
Private consumption deflator	_	0.9	1.3	2.4	1.3	1.0
Unemployment rate[2]	_	7.1	6.1	6.1	7.0	7.7
Household saving ratio[3]	_	7.1	8.3	9.2	10.3	9.2
General government financial balance[4]	_	2.2	3.5	2.8	0.5	0.4
Current account balance[4]	_	8.5	8.4	6.5	6.5	6.9

Note: National accounts are based on official chain-linked data. This introduces a discrepancy in the identity between real demand components and GDP. For further details see *OECD Economic Outlook* Sources and Methods *(http://www.oecd.org/eco/sources-and-methods).*
1. Contributions to changes in real GDP (percentage of real GDP in previous year), actual amount in the first column.
2. Historical data and projections are based on the definition of unemployment which covers 15 to 74 year olds and classifies job-seeking full-time students as unemployed.
3. As a percentage of disposable income.
4. As a percentage of GDP.
Source: OECD Economic Outlook 84 database.

StatLink http://dx.doi.org/10.1787/503475057612

confidence was slower to turn down, but is now well below average and firms are scaling back production, investment and hiring plans. The value of household net financial assets fell by 12% in the first half of the year and has plummeted further since. House prices have decelerated and may yet fall, constraining the use of mortgage equity to finance consumption. Lending to households and businesses has slowed almost as much as in the euro area, but significantly less than in the United States. Ongoing turbulence is expected to lead to a further slowdown in lending.

The monetary stance should be eased further

Subdued growth and lower commodity prices should reduce inflation, allowing the Riksbank to cut interest rates further, following the 100 basis points of cuts implemented in October. The recently announced fiscal stimulus, amounting to almost 1% of GDP in 2009, will not undermine fiscal sustainability and most of the measures should be beneficial for growth in the longer term. The strong fiscal position provides scope for further easing if the outlook deteriorates further, but it should be temporary and designed to avoid negative long-term fiscal implications.

Recovery in GDP growth is not expected before late 2009

Domestic demand is projected to contract at the end of 2008 and in early 2009 and to recover gradually thereafter. Further income tax and interest rate cuts, and a return to more normal financial conditions in late 2009, should spur a recovery in consumer spending. Export growth is likely to remain weak in the near term, before picking up in line with Sweden's export markets by 2010. Business investment is expected to fall sharply but then rebound along with exports. Residential investment is expected to contract, with weaker house prices and confidence compounding unfavourable demographic patterns. Employment and labour force participation are both expected to decline, and the unemployment rate is set to exceed its estimated structural rate. Labour productivity growth is expected to remain weak in the coming quarters, but should pick up as activity regains momentum.

A prolonged slowdown cannot be ruled out

Given the turmoil in the global financial markets, the slowdown may turn out to be deeper or longer than currently anticipated. A number of measures have been introduced to support Swedish financial markets. However, the potential for further spill-over of deteriorating financial conditions in other countries remains. This could come through problems accessing funding in foreign markets, as has recently been the case with Iceland, or through write-downs in the value of foreign assets owned by Swedish institutions, some of which are exposed in the Baltic States. Also, domestic developments, notably a weaker housing market, might feed back into the financial markets, compounding financial stress.

SWITZERLAND

Economic activity is expected to contract somewhat in 2009, due to poorer export prospects and a diminished contribution of financial services, followed by a rebound in 2010 as global financial market turbulence abates. Inflation is projected to fall back to 1%, reflecting lower oil prices, the opening of an output gap and wage moderation.

A further reduction in policy interest rates may be needed, but monetary policy stimulus will have to be withdrawn in the course of 2010. Fiscal policy should allow automatic stabilizers to operate.

Activity is decelerating as export growth is weakening

GDP growth slowed as exports of goods decelerated and foreign commission income of banks declined because of a diminishing volume of securities trading, weighing on services exports. Reduced profits of Swiss multinationals abroad, including in the financial sector, are narrowing the current account surplus. Private consumption growth benefited from the expansion of employment on the back of a large inflow of mostly well-qualified foreign workers. However, business investment appears to be losing momentum, with diminishing order stocks in manufacturing and stagnant sales of consumer durables. By contrast, the number of new residential construction permits has risen, suggesting some rebound from subdued residential construction activity in recent years. Consumer price inflation has been high by historical standards, reaching 2.6% in October, mostly reflecting high oil prices.

Monetary policy is supporting credit conditions

Following the onset of international financial market turbulence, the central bank stabilized the interbank interest rate, the operational target of monetary policy, allowing overnight interest rates for repurchase operations to fall significantly. This monetary stimulus notwithstanding, the trade-weighted effective exchange rate has remained broadly

Switzerland

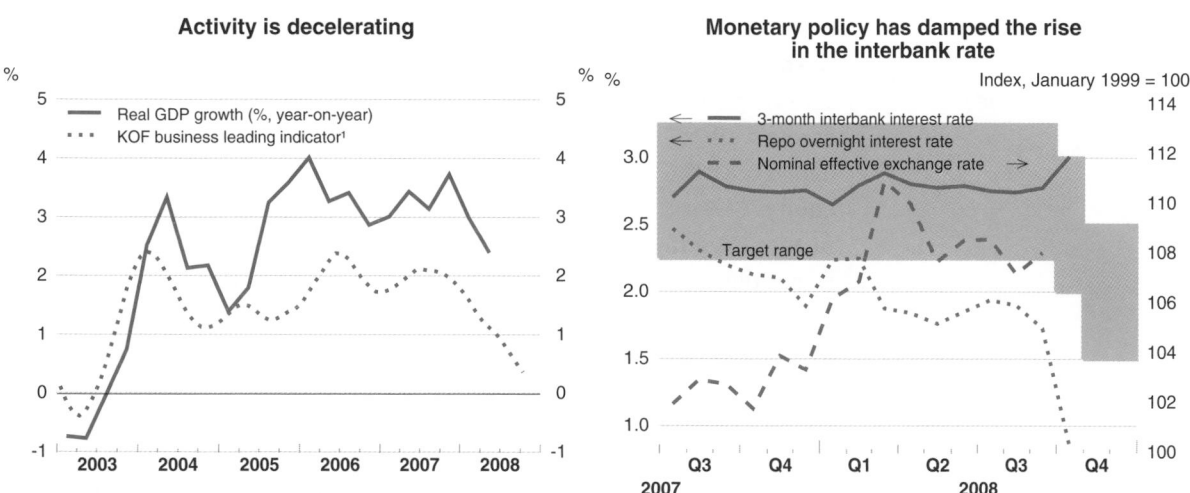

1. Composite leading indicator of business cycle trends in manufacturing, private consumption, financial services, construction and EU export markets.

Source: KOF institute (Swiss Federal Institute of Technology); Swiss National Bank and OECD Economic Outlook 84 database.

StatLink ⟨⟩ *http://dx.doi.org/10.1787/501026877414*

Switzerland: **Demand, output and prices**

	2005	2006	2007	2008	2009	2010
	Current prices CHF billion	Percentage changes, volume (2000 prices)				
Private consumption	278.6	1.6	2.1	2.0	1.2	1.3
Government consumption	54.2	-0.9	-1.1	-0.8	0.9	1.1
Gross fixed capital formation	98.2	4.7	5.4	-0.7	-3.2	2.4
Final domestic demand	431.0	2.0	1.9	1.6	0.2	1.5
Stockbuilding[1]	1.9	-0.5	-0.7	-1.2	-0.1	0.0
Total domestic demand	433.0	1.4	1.1	0.3	0.1	1.5
Exports of goods and services	226.2	9.9	9.4	5.2	2.1	3.6
Imports of goods and services	196.1	6.5	5.9	2.6	3.0	3.9
Net exports[1]	30.2	2.1	2.3	1.7	-0.2	0.2
GDP at market prices	463.1	3.4	3.3	1.9	-0.2	1.6
GDP deflator	_	1.7	1.8	2.7	2.0	1.3
Memorandum items						
Consumer price index	_	1.1	0.7	2.5	1.0	1.1
Private consumption deflator	_	1.3	1.1	1.5	0.6	1.1
Unemployment rate	_	4.0	3.6	3.5	3.9	4.2
General government financial balance[2]	_	1.0	1.3	1.1	0.3	0.0
Current account balance[2]	_	14.5	13.4	8.0	9.4	9.8

1. Contributions to changes in real GDP (percentage of real GDP in previous year), actual amount in the first column.
2. As a percentage of GDP.
Source: OECD Economic Outlook 84 database.

StatLink http://dx.doi.org/10.1787/503482246177

unchanged over the past six months. Moreover, the central bank lowered its target range for the three-month interbank rate by three quarters of a point in October and early November, to between 1.5% and 2.5%, and announced its intention to move the interbank rate close to the centre of this range. It has decided to provide a loan worth up to $54 billion (equivalent to 70% of official foreign currency reserves) to a fund that will purchase illiquid assets (at no more than mark-to-market value) from a major domestic bank, UBS, which faced large asset write-offs. This operation has no monetary policy implications, but the central bank's net foreign asset position might be affected if the value of the purchased assets were to fall significantly. The federal government has also supplied a loan of CHF 6 billion (1.1% of GDP) to UBS, which may be converted into equity. Given the significant deterioration of the external environment, further lowering of the target range of policy interest rates may be needed to support activity. Some of the significant monetary policy stimulus would have to be withdrawn in 2010, however, as economic growth picks up again.

Fiscal policy remains neutral

Government revenue growth has remained buoyant so far. However, the decline in profits of financial intermediaries is likely to have significant lagged effects on revenues in 2009 and 2010, resulting in a marked deterioration of the general government budget surplus, notwithstanding continued restraint in central government payroll spending. Budget outcomes have significantly exceeded the requirements of the budgetary rules in recent years, leaving room for the automatic stabilizers to operate. The budgetary impact of an increase in the standard value-added tax rate by a quarter percentage point will in part be offset by a reform of personal income taxation, which reduces the tax burden on the second wage earner in two-earner couples in 2010.

Unemployment will rise and the current account surplus fall significantly

Economic activity is expected to shrink by 0.2% in 2009, mostly on account of diminished export prospects and poorer business conditions in the financial sector, pushing the unemployment rate above 4% in the following year. In 2010, with financial market activity expected to recover, GDP growth may reach 1½ per cent, led by net exports. Inflation may decline to 1%. The current account surplus is expected to fall from 13% to around 8% of GDP in 2008, recovering subsequently, while the general government surplus may disappear by 2010.

The large weight of financial services in GDP entails risks to growth

As financial services contribute 12½ per cent to Swiss GDP, significantly more than in most OECD countries, a prolonged decline in global activity in this sector would have a more marked direct effect on economic growth and tax revenues.

TURKEY

The economy slowed in 2008 as weakness in domestic demand was compounded by the international slowdown in the wake of financial market turbulence. Growth is expected to decline to below 2% in 2009 before recovering to 4¼ per cent in 2010, in line with the global recovery.

As the current account deficit is large and the volatility of the exchange rate has considerably increased, supporting investor confidence is crucial. Fuller fiscal transparency and implementing credible spending rules would facilitate the operation of automatic stabilisers without undermining confidence. If systemic liquidity risks emerge in the financial system, the government should be prepared to introduce contingency support mechanisms to preserve the hard-won stability of the financial sector.

Domestic demand has weakened

GDP growth continued to decline in the first half of 2008, reflecting weaker domestic demand. The rise of interest rates as a result of monetary policy tightening and higher risk premia in the deteriorating international environment has dampened domestic demand. Market share losses due to competition from low-cost countries and real currency appreciation resulted in large job losses in labour-intensive sectors such as textiles and clothing. The unfavourable political environment has undermined business and consumer confidence.

Inflation has probably peaked but second round effects persist

Inflation, which has been well above the official target of 4% since mid-2007, peaked at 12% in July 2008, but has receded since then. Oil and food prices largely explained changes in inflation (Turkey imports almost all its primary energy inputs, and food and tobacco represent 34% of the consumer price index basket). There were also price pressures in the sectors sheltered from foreign competition such as rental housing and public utilities. Core inflation increased from 4.3% in February 2008 to

Turkey

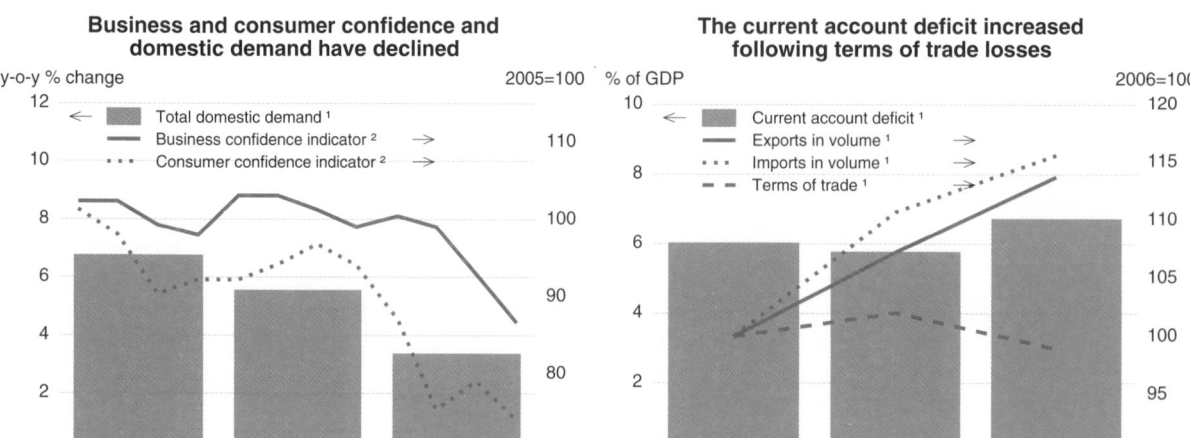

1. In part forecasts for 2008.
2. For 2008 Q4, October figure.
Source: OECD Economic Outlook 84 database and OECD, *Main Economic Indicators.*

StatLink ᴍ͡ˢ http://dx.doi.org/10.1787/501035110047

OECD ECONOMIC OUTLOOK 84 – ISBN 978-92-64-05469-1 – © OECD 2008

Turkey: **Demand, output and prices**

	2005	2006	2007	2008	2009	2010
	Current prices TRL billion	Percentage changes, volume (1998 prices)				
Private consumption	465.4	4.6	4.1	3.2	1.1	3.9
Government consumption	76.5	8.4	6.5	4.2	2.8	2.7
Gross fixed capital formation	136.5	13.3	5.5	3.7	2.7	6.8
Final domestic demand	678.4	6.8	4.7	3.4	1.6	4.4
Stockbuilding[1]	- 6.8	-0.1	0.9	-0.1	0.1	0.0
Total domestic demand	671.6	6.7	5.5	3.4	1.7	4.4
Exports of goods and services	141.8	6.6	7.3	6.0	3.8	9.4
Imports of goods and services	164.5	6.9	10.7	4.4	3.6	9.0
Net exports[1]	- 22.7	-0.3	-1.3	0.1	-0.2	-0.3
GDP at market prices	648.9	6.9	4.6	3.3	1.6	4.2
GDP deflator	_	9.3	7.6	12.7	9.1	8.1
Memorandum items						
Consumer price index	_	9.6	8.8	10.3	8.3	7.6
Private consumption deflator	_	9.8	8.6	13.0	8.9	7.6
Unemployment rate	_	9.7	9.6	9.7	10.5	10.6
Current account balance[2]	_	-6.0	-5.8	-6.7	-6.1	-5.7

Note: National accounts are based on official chain-linked data. This introduces a discrepancy in the identity between real demand components and GDP. For further details see *OECD Economic Outlook* Sources and Methods (http://www.oecd.org/eco/sources-and-methods).
1. Contributions to changes in real GDP (percentage of real GDP in previous year), actual amount in the first column.
2. As a percentage of GDP.
Source: OECD Economic Outlook 84 database.

StatLink ᵃᵐˢ⁴ http://dx.doi.org/10.1787/503621738862

7.4% in September and households' inflation expectations one and two years ahead are still above the inflation target.

Employment growth has slowed but the current account deficit remained large

In the first half of 2008, despite strong employment growth notwithstanding the GDP slowdown, the unemployment rate edged up to 9.0% in June 2008. The current account deficit widened as a result of increases in oil prices and is expected to reach about 6½ per cent of GDP in 2008. The non-energy trade balance, however, remained stable at around 4% of GDP. The current account deficit has been funded by capital inflows, including continuing foreign direct investment and private commercial credits, but this could prove a source of weakness given global financial strains.

Macroeconomic policy remains conservative

Fiscal policy adheres to the medium-term plan announced in May 2008. The primary surplus of the "consolidated government sector" (complete general government accounts are not available) should stay above 4% of GDP this year, at the same level as in 2007, despite the slowdown. The 2009 budget proposal is expected to target a similar surplus, but using a significantly stronger growth assumption than projected in this Outlook. If the institutional framework for fiscal policy were strengthened, including with multi-year spending rules and full fiscal transparency according to international standards, letting automatic stabilisers work fully would be less challenging for fiscal credibility. Monetary policy remains tight, which is needed to re-gain credibility for the (upwardly revised) inflation targets of 7.5% for 2009 and 6.5% for 2010, especially since the impact of falling oil and food prices may be offset by the exchange rate depreciation. The Central Bank will likely hesitate to lower its reference rates substantially, which stood at 16.25% in mid-November, as long as inflation expectations remain above target.

Supporting investor confidence will be essential in the international turmoil

Like other emerging markets, Turkey has been strongly affected by the international turmoil. The Turkish Lira has depreciated, the Istanbul Stock Exchange has fallen and the sovereign risk premium has increased substantially. As Turkey continues to depend on foreign capital to finance its large external deficit and to roll over its external debt, accessing foreign resources may become more difficult and costly in the months ahead. Supporting investor confidence will therefore be crucial. The authorities should monitor closely the impacts of increased exchange and interest-rate volatility on the stability of the financial system, and be ready to phase in adequate contingency support mechanisms to offset any emerging systemic risks. The evolution of domestic business and household confidence, which reached historical lows in fall 2008, will weigh heavily on investment and consumption outcomes and on growth.

Growth will weaken before picking up in 2010

Growth is expected to fall below 2% in 2009, before picking up in 2010 as financial strains ease and the global economy recovers. Risks are on the downside in the short-term, but more balanced in the medium-term. If there is any serious fiscal drift or political tensions before the Spring 2009 municipal elections, exchange and interest rate volatility may increase, hindering growth and financial stability. On the other hand, a sharper decline of inflation in response to steeper decreases in oil and food prices might permit additional reductions in policy and market interest-rates and stimulate growth, together with a further consolidation of investor confidence.

ISBN 978-92-64-05469-1
OECD Economic Outlook 84
© OECD 2008

Chapter 3

DEVELOPMENTS IN SELECTED NON-MEMBER ECONOMIES

BRAZIL

The expansion that gathered pace during 2007 was sustained in the first half of 2008, although activity appears to be slackening owing to a worsening of financial conditions. Domestic demand has been the main driver of growth. The trade surplus is shrinking, essentially due to buoyant demand for imports, and the current account has shifted into deficit. Dynamism in the labour market continued to deliver robust job creation. Inflation picked up considerably through mid-year.

Further monetary tightening is expected in the near term, despite a falling output gap in 2009, to quell the inflationary pressures arising from a sharp exchange rate depreciation. The primary budget surplus target is expected to be met, although the 2009 draft budget law calls for further increases in expenditure. Reversing the trend of increasing public spending is among Brazil's main macroeconomic policy challenges.

Growth remains strong but is losing steam

GDP grew by 6.1% on a year-on-year basis in the second quarter, a pace of expansion little changed since end-2007. Domestic demand continued to outpace GDP growth, supported by vigorous private consumption and strong investment spending. Rising imports have narrowed the trade surplus. This is widening the current account deficit (coupled with record-high investment income payments), following five years of surpluses. Export performance has remained robust, buttressed by still vigorous external demand and price gains, and despite a strong, albeit declining, exchange rate. Job creation has been particularly robust in labour-intensive sectors, such as construction, supported by dynamic investment demand. Unemployment fell marginally during the first semester and remains at historically low levels. From the supply side, agriculture and manufacturing continue to lead the expansion. Recent indicators, such as sales, capacity utilisation and industrial production, nevertheless point to a deceleration in activity in the coming months.

Brazil

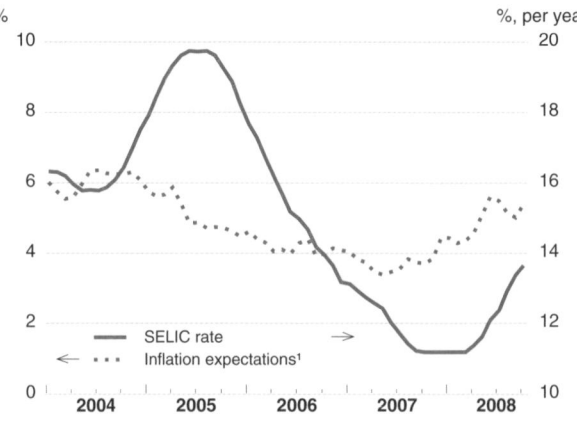

Domestic demand growth remains robust
Year-on-year percentage change

Monetary tightening is ongoing

1. 12-month ahead, year-on-year percentage change.
Source: Central Bank of Brazil and IBGE.

StatLink http://dx.doi.org/10.1787/501054502653

Brazil: **Macroeconomic indicators**

	2006	2007	2008	2009	2010
Real GDP growth	3.8	5.4	5.3	3.0	4.5
Inflation (CPI)	3.1	4.5	6.3	5.3	4.5
Fiscal balance (per cent of GDP)	-3.0	-2.3	-2.0	-1.8	-0.9
Primary fiscal balance (per cent of GDP)	3.9	4.0	4.3	3.8	3.8
Current account balance (per cent of GDP)	1.3	0.1	-1.7	-2.2	-2.4

Note: Real GDP growth and inflation are defined in percentage change from the previous period. Inflation refers to the end-year consumer price index (IPCA).
Source: Figures for 2006-07 are from national sources. Figures for 2008-10 are OECD projections.

StatLink ᵐˢᵖ *http://dx.doi.org/10.1787/503626103581*

Monetary policy continues to be tightened

Inflation rose considerably in mid-year and remains well above the central target. Rising food and energy prices contributed, but strong demand growth has been the main source of inflationary pressures. The authorities responded with a cumulative 250-basis-point policy-rate hike since April to 13.75% in September, and left the rate unchanged in October. Wholesale-price inflation began to recede in August, reflecting global trends in commodity prices, but gathered pace again from October owing to a sharp depreciation of the *real* in September/October. The 6.5% ceiling of the end-year target range is unlikely to be breached, but the exchange rate depreciation will exert upward pressure on prices over the coming months.

External credit conditions have deteriorated

The economy has not been immune to the deteriorating global financial environment. External financial conditions tightened considerably in the third quarter, with a steep increase in sovereign risk premia. Domestic bank credit growth remains healthy but is losing steam. The central bank relaxed reserve requirements in September/October to

Brazil

Fiscal policy is on track
Consolidated public sector[1]

The external current account has shifted into deficit[1]
USD billion

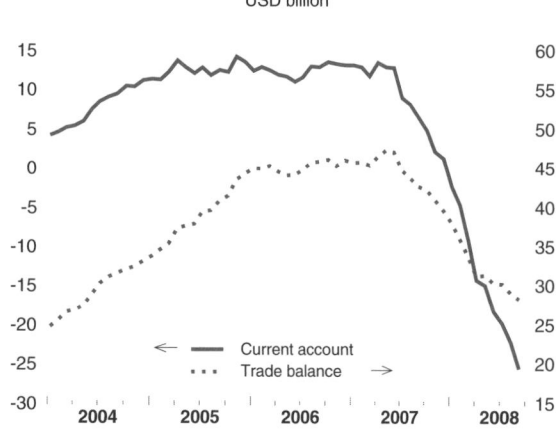

1. Cumulated 12-month flows.
Source: IBGE and Central Bank of Brazil.

StatLink ᵐˢᵖ *http://dx.doi.org/10.1787/501057786157*

Brazil: **External indicators**

	2006	2007	2008	2009	2010
	\$ billion				
Goods exports	137.8	160.6	203.5	207.5	219.0
Goods imports	91.4	120.6	176.6	189.1	207.3
Trade balance	46.5	40.0	26.9	18.4	11.7
Services, net	- 9.6	- 13.4	- 17.6	- 18.6	- 19.2
Invisibles, net	- 23.3	- 25.2	- 36.3	- 34.9	- 34.4
Current account balance	13.5	1.5	- 27.0	- 35.0	- 42.0
	Percentage changes				
Goods export volumes	3.3	5.5	3.0	3.5	4.0
Goods import volumes	16.1	22.0	22.0	6.0	7.0
Terms of trade	5.3	2.1	2.5	- 2.5	- 1.0

Source: Figures for 2006-07 are from national sources. Figures for 2008-10 are OECD projections.

StatLink ⟶ http://dx.doi.org/10.1787/503627603622

alleviate pressure in the interbank market and took measures to tackle liquidity shortages in second and third-tier banks. Most recently, a temporary \$30 billion swap facility was set up between the Brazilian and US central banks. The performance of domestic equity and corporate bond markets has suffered as the global appetite for risk has diminished.

Fiscal policy is on track...

Fiscal performance has been solid, with the consolidated primary budget surplus at about 4.4% of GDP on a 12-month cumulative basis in August. This outturn has been aided in part by cyclical revenue gains, which have more than compensated for the losses associated with the non-renewal of the bank debit tax (CPMF) at end-2007. A strong labour market is boosting formal employment, thus raising social security revenues and reducing the payment of social benefits. Capital outlays are on the rise, including disbursements under the federal investment package (PAC) launched in 2007. But federal payroll spending is trending up as a result of recent wide-ranging changes in career streams and hikes in compensation. The public debt-to-GDP ratio continues to fall, although ongoing monetary tightening is putting upward pressure on the interest bill.

... but expenditure is again being raised

The 2009 draft federal budget law, submitted to Congress in August, maintains the primary budget surplus target at 3.8% of GDP. An additional surplus of 0.5% of GDP, if it materialises, is expected to be earmarked to finance deposits in Brazil's soon-to-be-created sovereign wealth fund. The draft budget is predicated on additional revenue gains and a proposed 12% increase in the minimum wage, well ahead of expected labour productivity growth, as well as further increases in civil service compensation and outlays on social benefits. The primary budget surplus target is expected to be met, despite these increases in expenditure and the adverse impact of the deceleration of economic activity on revenue.

OECD ECONOMIC OUTLOOK 84 – ISBN 978-92-64-05469-1 – © OECD 2008

Adoption of an overall budget balance target is being discussed

The government announced its intention to shift the current fiscal target from a primary surplus to an overall balance from 2010. A band would be defined around this balance to deal with uncertainty about fluctuations in the interest bill arising from changes in the monetary stance. Brazil's still high, although declining, share of floating-rate securities in the government debt stock makes its debt dynamics particularly sensitive to monetary policy moves. The authorities also announced their intention to shift the public accounts gradually to full accruals from the current cash-flow basis, although the timeframe for implementation has not been announced.

Growth is poised to ebb in the near term

Activity is expected to lose impetus in the first half of 2009, due to ongoing credit tightening, but to regain strength towards year-end and into 2010. Domestic demand will in all likelihood continue to drive growth. The current account deficit is set to widen on the back of solid, albeit weakening, import growth, while export growth weakens along with global demand. Moreover, the terms of trade are already deteriorating as a result of falling commodity prices. With the positive output gap gradually shrinking in 2009, and once the second-round effects on prices of a weaker exchange rate have began to fade, inflation is poised to converge to the 4.5% central target over the forecast period. Further monetary tightening is projected in the coming months, possibly at a slower pace than in the recent past, but is unlikely after mid-2009, once disinflation has been secured.

The balance of risks continues to be tilted to external sources

A further deterioration of the global financial environment and global demand is the main source of risk to the Brazilian economy. A further sharp decline in commodity prices may raise concern among market participants about the resilience of Brazil's external accounts, especially in an environment of heightened risk aversion. On the domestic front, disinflation may prove to be more gradual than envisaged as a result of a weaker *real*. In this case, the monetary tightening cycle may be longer than projected.

CHINA

GDP growth has fallen, from a peak of nearly 12% to a pace in the high single digits. Export growth is weakening and, with slower capital formation, domestic demand is also projected to ease in 2009, before recovering in 2010. Disinflation is on course to continue, in part due to moderating commodity prices but also reflecting slower output growth.

The fiscal position is healthy and, even though the government has already introduced a package to stimulate demand, income tax cuts could also be considered. With headline inflation declining, monetary policy has scope to further offset the impact of the global downturn, following recent interest rate cuts. Lower inflation also provides an opportunity to re-align energy prices with underlying costs; major hikes in electricity prices are required to alleviate shortages and stimulate much-needed investment spending in the sector.

GDP growth continues to moderate

Growth has moderated for seven quarters in a row. Reflecting the global downturn and increasing domestic costs, real exports have been losing momentum since mid-2007, which has resulted in a marked fall in the growth of imports used in export processing industries over recent months. The trade balance has been broadly stable for the past 18 months at around $200 billion at an annual rate.

Domestic demand rebalances away from investment

Domestic demand growth has also softened since late 2007. Growth in real fixed investment continues to trend downwards, largely reflecting a slump in real estate investment driven at least partly by the tightening in monetary policy through to mid-2008. In a number of cities in China's coastal manufacturing regions, residential property prices have fallen considerably. Nationally, real house prices have declined by 3.5% from their end-2007 peak. Industrial production has also slowed in 2008, reflecting *inter alia* the re-emergence of electricity shortages and restrictions imposed for the Olympics. Profit growth has fallen by half to

China

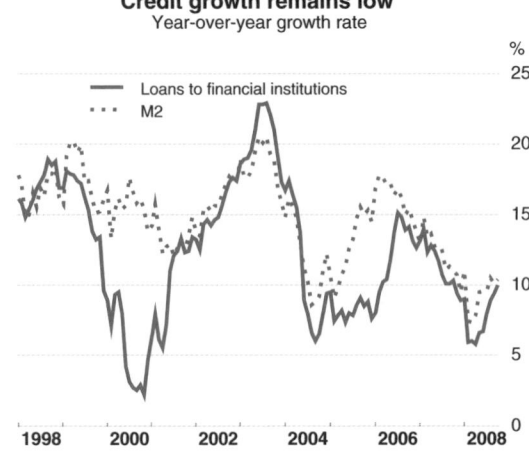

No sign of stress in the interbank market
3-month moving average

Credit growth remains low
Year-over-year growth rate

Source: CEIC.

StatLink http://dx.doi.org/10.1787/501064282703

China: **Macroeconomic indicators**

	2006	2007	2008	2009	2010
Real GDP growth	11.6	11.9	9.5	8.0	9.2
Domestic demand growth	11.4	11.4	9.4	8.1	9.2
Inflation[1]	3.3	5.2	5.0	2.5	2.7
Consumer price index[2]	1.6	4.8	6.1	3.0	2.5
Fiscal balance (per cent of GDP)[3]	0.5	2.1	2.0	0.8	1.0
Current account balance (per cent of GDP)	9.4	11.3	9.7	9.4	9.1

Note: Real GDP growth and domestic demand growth are percentage changes from the previous year.
1. Percentage change in GDP deflator from previous period.
2. Change in Laspeyres fixed-base-year index (base year 2005).
3. Consolidated budgetary and extrabudgetary accounts on a national accounts basis.
Source: National sources and OECD projections.

StatLink ᵃ🔗 *http://dx.doi.org/10.1787/503633774276*

20% in 2008 compared to 2007. Although nominal wage growth has been strong, high inflation during the year to Spring 2008 has eroded the gains in purchasing power. On the other hand, buoyant real retail sales in recent months indicate ongoing resilience in consumption spending.

Inflation is falling as food prices moderate

Even with increases in regulated energy prices, consumer price inflation declined rapidly from a peak of 8.7% in February 2008 to 4% by October. Disinflation has been driven by lower food prices. Non-food price inflation continues to increase gradually and is currently running at just over 2%. Upstream pricing pressures have also moderated but remain somewhat elevated, with producer prices up by 6.6% in October.

Monetary policy has changed focus from inflation to growth

Faced with heightened volatility in asset markets and extreme global uncertainty, the People's Bank of China has signalled its intention to support growth. Accordingly, since mid-September it has cut the

China

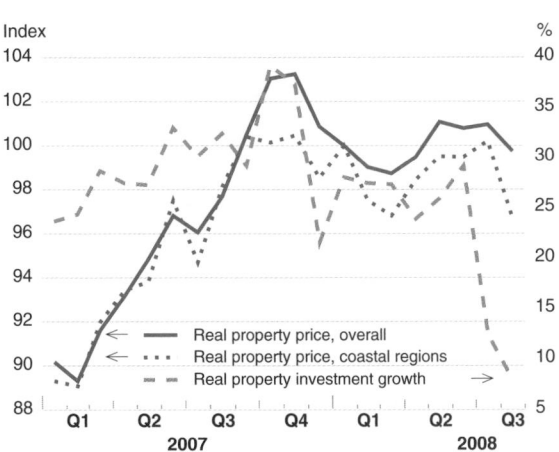

The real estate sector is under strain

Domestic demand has slowed
Year-over-year growth rate

Source: CEIC.

StatLink ᵃ🔗 *http://dx.doi.org/10.1787/501070022752*

China: **External indicators**

	2006	2007	2008	2009	2010
	\$ billion				
Goods and services exports	1 061.7	1 342.2	1 620.9	1 772.7	1 998.3
Goods and services imports	852.8	1 034.8	1 298.3	1 418.8	1 624.0
Foreign balance	208.9	307.4	322.5	353.8	374.3
Net investment income and transfers	41.0	64.4	76.1	83.4	98.1
Current account balance	249.8	371.8	398.6	437.2	472.4
	Percentage changes				
Goods and services export volumes	23.8	19.9	9.4	5.7	10.7
Goods and services import volumes	15.9	13.7	7.9	9.3	12.7
Export performance[1]	14.7	13.3	5.5	4.1	5.7
Terms of trade	- 0.9	- 1.2	- 5.1	3.5	0.3

1. Ratio between export volume and export market of total goods and services.
Source: OECD Economic Outlook 84 database.

StatLink ═╗═ http://dx.doi.org/10.1787/503736881488

benchmark lending rate three times and the benchmark deposit rate twice, in 27 basis point steps. In addition, the lower bound on commercial bank lending rates has been cut from 90% to 70% of the benchmark lending rate for home loans. The People's Bank has also cut the reserve requirements of the smaller banks – which tend to serve small and medium-sized enterprises – by 100 basis points and of the top-tier banks by 50 basis points. The interbank market remains insulated from the turmoil in global money markets and interest rates have been relatively stable. From end-July the appreciation of the renminbi *vis-à-vis* the US dollar has been brought to a halt. However, given the strengthening of the US dollar, the renminbi's effective exchange rate has appreciated. Reflecting greater global risk aversion and flat net exports, foreign exchange reserve accumulation has slowed sharply. Growth in M2 and bank lending remains low, leading to the removal of credit quotas by the People's Bank.

The fiscal position is sound   The government accounts remain healthy, with a budget surplus and a low debt-to-GDP ratio. Partly as a result of windfall revenues from the special tax on crude oil production, government revenues were buoyant over the first half of 2008, growing three percentage points faster than expenditure. They have slowed somewhat since, however, in line with moderating economic growth. Overall, it would seem that the fiscal surplus is running at around the same level so far in 2008 as in 2007. Against this backdrop of a strong fiscal position, the government has announced a stimulus package designed to support growth. A number of infrastructure projects have been approved and brought forward and social spending increased. In an effort to stimulate investment the government has also moved to cut the cost of capital by making the value-added tax on investment goods fully deductible. The export tax rebate on selected goods has also been increased and the State Council has established a fund to finance low-cost housing.

A soft landing remains the most likely outcome

Looking forward, growth is likely to moderate further, and the annualised quarter-on-quarter growth rate is projected to fall below 8% in the near term. Global uncertainties and the correction in the domestic housing market will restrain investment spending, keeping domestic demand soft into the first half of 2009 before it recovers gradually into 2010. Export growth is projected to remain subdued in 2009 and then to pick up in 2010. China's export market share is likely to expand at a slower pace than in the past as unit labour costs are rising markedly. Import growth is projected to gather pace as domestic demand increases, leading to some decline in the current account surplus as a share of GDP in 2010, despite the improvement in the terms-of-trade. Lower commodity prices coupled with a spell of subpar growth should ensure that inflation continues to ease during 2009 and then stabilises in 2010.

Macroeconomic policy must walk a fine line

The rebalancing of growth away from net exports towards domestic demand, with an emphasis on stimulating investment spending, is set to continue. This transition entails stresses in some sectors of the economy, particularly the export-oriented ones. A risk to growth is that exports prove to be more sensitive to falling foreign demand than assumed in the projections or that exporters do not cut prices. Also, if consumption were to react more than expected to the erosion in wealth, the slowdown in growth could be larger than projected. On the other hand, although the exact stimulus flowing from the November 10 package is uncertain, and has not been included in the baseline projections, it is clear that the package represents a major upside factor for the development of the economy over the next two years. Capital formation is likely to be boosted both in the government sector, through accelerated outlays on infrastructure, and in the company sector, through the change in the value-added tax regime. This latter reform will significantly lower the user cost of capital for firms, so stimulating their investment.

INDIA

Growth has continued to slacken to under 8% by the second quarter of 2008. Inflation is high, driven by commodity prices, but the peak appears to have passed. The current account deficit has risen substantially and there is downward pressure on the exchange rate. The economy is projected to slow further over the next year and to recover in tandem with the world economy in 2010.

Unchecked fiscal spending during the expansion has left the Indian authorities with little room for manoeuvre in the ongoing slowdown. At the same time, foreign institutions have become more reluctant to invest in India. A period of fiscal retrenchment seems desirable, focussed on making government subsidies available only to those in real need.

The economy continues to slow

From a peak growth rate of 11% during 2006, the economy slowed markedly, to 7.9% by the second quarter of 2008. Private consumption and investment have both lost momentum, and the drag from foreign trade has become more pronounced. Government consumption, however, has picked up. The slowdown continued in the third quarter of 2008, with industrial production up only 4.5% in July-August over a year earlier.

The external deficit has widened

Since mid-2007, the nominal value of imports of goods and services has increasingly outpaced exports, notably due to previously rising oil prices and slowing software sales. Accordingly, the current account deficit widened to 2% of GDP in the first half of 2008, against only 0.5% a year earlier.

But inflation is beginning to ease

Inflation, as measured by the 12-month rate of change in the wholesale price index, has run at a double-digit pace since June 2008. However, and notwithstanding the serious problems plaguing this index (as well as the various consumer price indices), the inflation peak seems to have passed. Indeed, the quarterly rate of inflation has eased

India

Interest rates are high and volatile

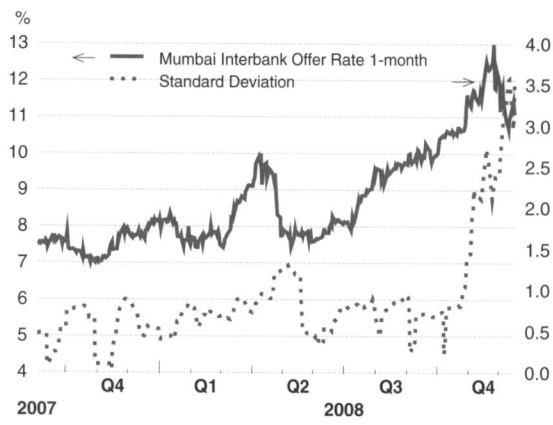

Reserves are being used to defend the rupee

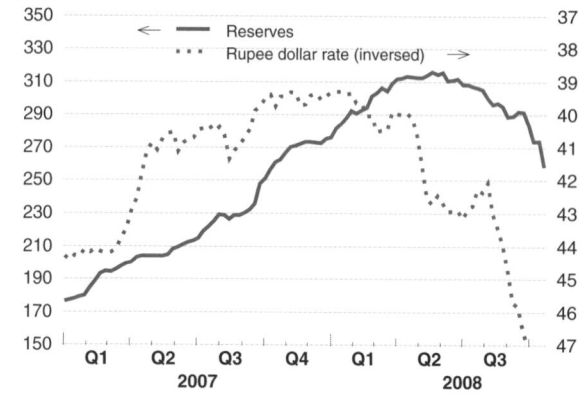

Source: Centre for Monitoring the Indian Economy.

StatLink 🔗 http://dx.doi.org/10.1787/501108787482

India: **Macroeconomic indicators**

	2006	2007	2008	2009	2010
Real GDP growth	9.6	9.0	7.0	7.3	8.3
Inflation[1]	5.6	4.3	10.4	5.0	4.0
Consumer price index[2]	6.7	6.2	10.3	6.0	4.5
Wholesale price index (WPI)[3]	5.4	4.7	11.6	6.3	5.2
Short-term interest rate[4]	8.2	8.9	10.2	8.7	7.5
Long-term interest rate[5]	7.8	7.9	8.6	7.8	8.1
Fiscal balance (per cent of GDP[6]	-7.4	-6.1	-9.5	-10.0	-9.5
Current account balance (per cent of GDP)	-1.1	-1.2	-3.2	-2.0	-2.0

Note: Data refer to fiscal years starting in April.
1. Percentage change in GDP deflator from previous period.
2. Consumer price index for industrial workers.
3. All commodities.
4. Mumbai three month offered rate.
5. 10 year government bond.
6. Gross fiscal balance for central and state governments, includes net lending and transfers to oil, food and fertiliser companies and recurrent Pay Commission awards, but not backpay nor debt write-offs for small farmers.
Source: CMIE and OECD projections.

StatLink http://dx.doi.org/10.1787/503744818245

considerably in recent months, despite substantial effective exchange rate depreciation. This largely reflects the very sharp deceleration in the prices of metals and petroleum. Going forward, all indicators of inflation are expected to ease, in a context of lower commodity prices and slower growth.

Capital outflows are causing stress

Pressure on the exchange rate has stemmed from a marked re-assessment of the Indian stock market by foreign investors, leading to a negative swing in portfolio investment of 6% of GDP in the year to second quarter of 2008. The Reserve Bank increased rupee purchases and

India

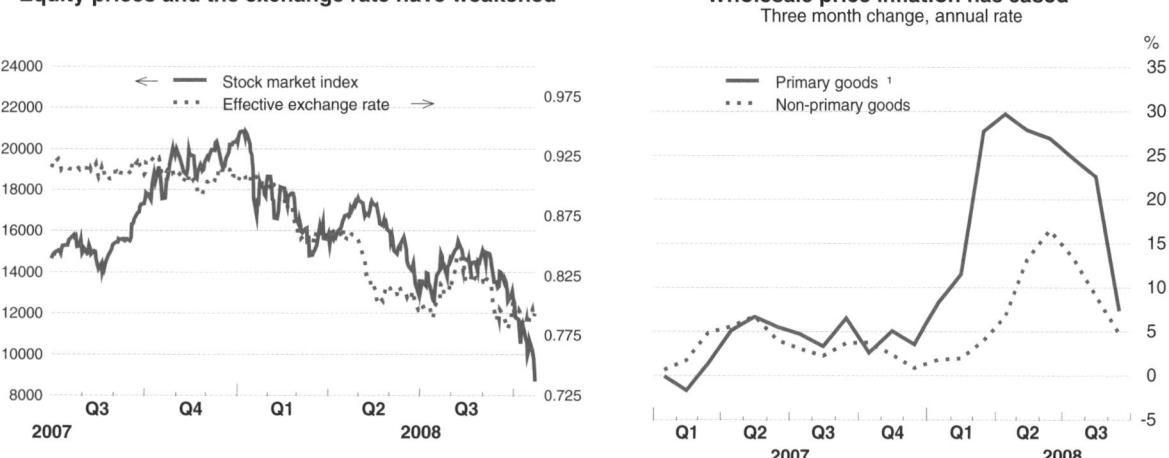

1. Primary products include agricultural, food and energy products, metals and cement.
Source: Centre for Monitoring the Indian Economy.

StatLink http://dx.doi.org/10.1787/501123678227

India: **External indicators**

	2006	2007	2008	2009	2010
	\$ billion				
Goods and services exports	204.3	252.7	308.2	331.2	365.1
Goods and services imports	235.6	301.4	380.2	389.8	427.7
Foreign balance	- 31.4	- 48.8	- 72.0	- 58.6	- 62.6
Net investment income	- 6.0	- 4.3	- 6.5	- 7.4	- 8.0
Transfers	27.6	38.9	40.0	41.0	42.0
Current account balance	-9.8	-14.1	-38.5	-25.0	-28.6
	Percentage changes				
Goods and services export volumes	18.9	7.5	7.0	6.8	8.5
Goods and services import volumes	24.5	7.7	6.0	6.5	8.0
Terms of trade	5.2	-0.6	-4.2	4.5	0.0

Note: Data refer to fiscal years starting in April.
Source: National sources and OECD projections.

StatLink ⟨▭⟩ http://dx.doi.org/10.1787/503783320077

hiked interest rates, but the exchange rate slide continued in the third quarter. Despite controls on short-term capital flows, volatility in domestic interest rates shot up from mid-year onwards. With the intensification of the global financial crisis in September, the stock market continued to weaken and by end-October equity prices were 53% below their January 2008 peak. To mitigate the impact of slower world growth, the Reserve Bank reduced the cash reserve ratio for banks by 350 basis points, to 5.5%, thereby injecting liquidity equivalent to 4% of GDP into the banking system, and lowered its repo rate by 150 basis points, to 7.5%.

Fiscal consolidation appears to have been abandoned

Fiscal consolidation efforts have been greatly relaxed. The on-budget fiscal data show impressive deficit reductions at both the central and state levels since the introduction of the Fiscal Responsibility and Budget Management Act (FRBMA) in 2004 and its subsequent generalisation in the states. So far this fiscal year, however, total central government receipts have fallen while expenditure grew slightly. In addition, off-budget spending and unfunded commitments have risen. Pay increases for public sector employees, as set by the Pay Commission, and the waiver of loans for small farmers introduced in the previous budget look set to add an additional 1% of GDP to the central government fiscal deficit in 2008 and more to the deficits of state governments. Moreover, while the government has so far only committed to reimburse the banks one third of the cost of the latter initiative, the projections assume that the government will shoulder all of the cost during the projection period (1.4% of GDP). In addition, off-budget outlays on food, fertiliser and oil subsidies could amount to an additional 3% of GDP in the current fiscal year, or even more according to official estimates. All in all, it would seem that the constraints imposed by the FRBMA have led to soaring off-budget expenditure, bringing the consolidated fiscal deficit (including off-budget items) to 10% of GDP in fiscal year 2009.

Growth is to be more subdued this year and next

The projections for the Indian economy are predicated on a gradual return to normal conditions in global financial markets beginning in late 2009 and on a constant nominal exchange rate. Even in these circumstances, pressure on the currency may limit the room for further cuts in interest rates, so that the real rates facing consumers and firms will rise markedly, weighing on domestic demand. Moreover, the recent fall in the exchange rate may only be sufficient to offset the slowing of world trade. With lower commodity prices and subpar growth, inflationary pressures should ease. Falling oil prices will not directly affect the price level, due the subsidisation and regulation of energy prices. However, they will reduce the toll on public spending. Overall, growth is projected to drop to around 7% in 2008 and 2009 before recovering to over 8% in 2010 as world growth picks up.

High fiscal deficits might deter foreign investment

The Indian economy faces the risk of a loss of confidence on the part of international investors. This is linked to a global flight towards the safest assets, but also to the serious loss of fiscal discipline that has led some credit agencies to downgrade India's sovereign debt. As debt issuance increases, the risk premium on Indian paper could rise, further depressing stock market prices. This could trigger additional withdrawals of foreign equity and put further downward pressure on the exchange rate. In turn, non-resident Indians may delay transfer payments, which are an essential source of finance for the current account. On the upside, however, the likely decline in inflation could help restore confidence more rapidly than envisaged, which would support demand and activity.

RUSSIAN FEDERATION

The fallout from the global financial crisis will sharply reduce real GDP growth in Russia through 2009, with a pick-up expected in 2010. With a reversal in the substantial rise in oil and metal prices, the pattern of terms of trade gains fuelling rapid growth in domestic demand has come to an end. Inflation has risen strongly, but may now have peaked and should decline in 2009-10. Fiscal and current account balances are expected to worsen sharply.

Policy challenges will multiply in a new environment of more binding fiscal constraints. At a minimum, less economically efficient forms of stimulus, like reducing the rate of value-added tax, should be resisted. As to monetary policy, countering the effects of short-term speculative capital outflows on the exchange rate is justifiable, but reserves should not be run down to postpone adjustments warranted by fundamentals. The authorities have responded decisively to threats to banking system stability, but further action, including improved coordination with foreign regulators given the global scale of the problem, may be needed.

Growth has been strong, but is decelerating

GDP growth remained rapid at 8% year-on-year in the first half of 2008, supported by further terms of trade gains. Private consumption continued to expand at double-digit rates, in line with strong, albeit decelerating, growth in real wages and consumer credit. Investment growth showed some signs of a slowdown but remained high. On the supply side, construction and market services continued to expand, but growth in construction has been falling since January and many projects have recently been put on hold due to financing constraints. Manufacturing activity has slowed down somewhat, while resource extraction has continued to stagnate. A range of official and survey data beyond the second quarter, together with the financial crisis that struck in September, suggest a marked slowdown in the second half of 2008.

Russian Federation

The falling oil price has been the main factor in the stock market decline

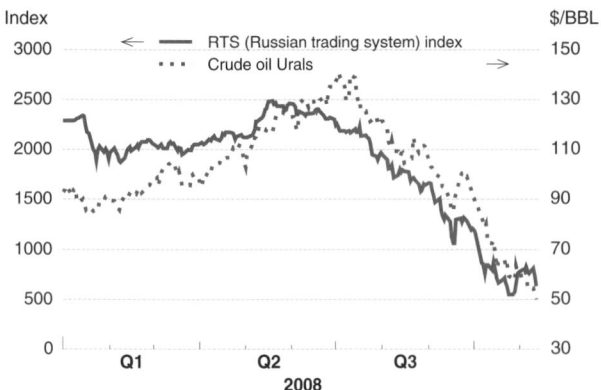

The exchange rate is still managed, but within wider bands

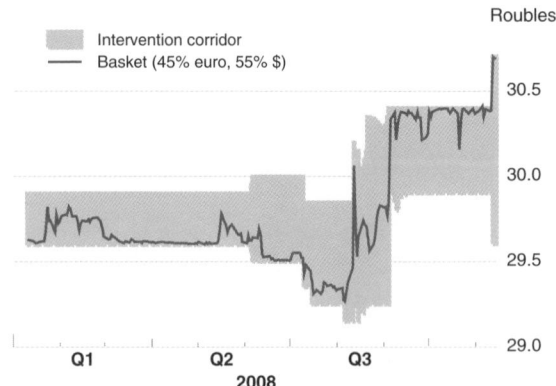

Source: Datastream and OECD estimates.

StatLink http://dx.doi.org/10.1787/501164656621

Russian Federation: **Macroeconomic indicators**

	2006	2007	2008	2009	2010
Real GDP growth	7.4	8.1	6.5	2.3	5.6
Inflation [1]	9.0	11.9	13.6	7.5	6.5
Fiscal balance (per cent of GDP)[2]	8.4	6.1	5.5	-1.8	-1.2
Current account balance (per cent of GDP)	9.5	5.9	6.5	0.5	-0.8

1. End-of-period.
2. Consolidated budget.
Source: Data for 2006-07 are from national sources. Data for 2008-10 are OECD estimates and projections.

StatLink ᴴᴴ *http://dx.doi.org/10.1787/503800321524*

Inflation remains high but inflationary pressures have eased

Inflation has risen to about 15% and will finish the year well above the authorities' (upwardly-revised) objective of 11.8% for 2008. Beyond rising food and energy prices, this surge reflected strong domestic demand and the policy of the Central Bank of Russia (CBR) to target the nominal exchange rate (versus a basket of the US dollar and the euro) in the face of large balance of payments inflows, which resulted in very rapid money supply growth. Food and energy prices have recently begun to weaken, while money supply growth has been slowed by the fall in commodity prices and a reversal of net capital inflows.

Weakening net capital flows have brought changes in monetary policy

Monetary policy has been undergoing significant changes, a result of both long-term planning by the CBR and shifts in the balance of payments. Under the quasi-fixed-exchange-rate regime in place for the past several years, central bank interventions in the foreign exchange market were the dominant factor in the growth of monetary aggregates. Large current account surpluses driven by high oil prices, combined with a shift over the years from net private capital outflows to inflows, yielded

Russian Federation

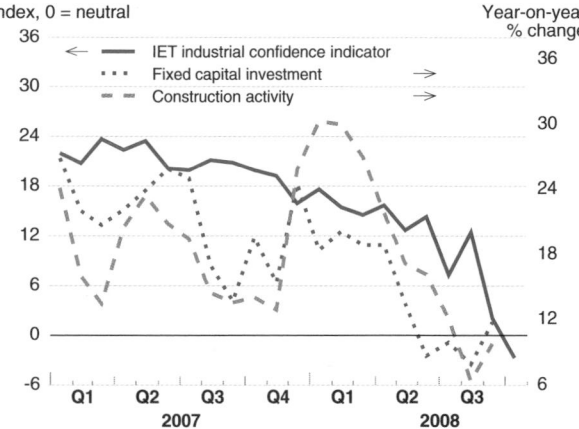

A shift to net private capital outflows is bringing down money supply growth

Several indicators are signalling a slowdown

Source: OECD calculations based on Central Bank of Russia, Russian Federal Service for State Statistics and Institute for the Economy in Transition.

StatLink ᴴᴴ *http://dx.doi.org/10.1787/501175835452*

Russian Federation: **External indicators**

	2006	2007	2008	2009	2010
	\$ billion				
Goods and services exports	335	394	520	410	435
Goods and services imports	209	283	350	350	400
Foreign balance	126	111	170	60	35
Invisibles, net	-31	-35	-54	-52	-50
Current account balance	94	76	116	8	-15
	Percentage changes				
Goods and services export volumes	7.3	6.4	6.0	2.0	4.5
Goods and services import volumes	21.9	27.3	23.0	8.0	13.0
Terms of trade	11.4	4.2	23.7	- 16.5	0.4

Source: National sources and OECD projections.

StatLink ⫘⫘ http://dx.doi.org/10.1787/503804440683

very rapid money supply growth; real interest rates have been negative for many years. In May 2008 the CBR widened its foreign exchange market intervention bands to permit more day-to-day volatility, flagging this change as a step in the direction of a long-term shift to inflation targeting.

The financial crisis elicited strong supportive action

The financial system has been shaken by the effects of the international financial crisis and related external factors. By late-October the Russia stock market index had fallen by more than 75% from its peak in May 2008, with disorderly price declines triggering market closures on several occasions, as investors withdrew from emerging market assets generally and concern about Russia-specific factors, including the falling oil price, grew. A cycle of margin calls and forced equity sales sparked a liquidity crisis in a range of small and medium-sized banks. The government and the CBR responded with relaxed reserve requirements, stepped-up overnight repos, the placing of large government deposits normally held at the central bank, and more generous deposit insurance.

The long string of budget surpluses is likely to end in 2009

Growth in public spending slowed in the first half of 2008, while surging oil prices brought further revenue windfalls. The central government surplus ran at 8.8% of GDP through August, compared with the 2008 budget target of 4.6%. Assets in the two funds created in February 2008 from the previous Stabilisation Fund reached \$190 billion at end-September. In October, the government amended the rules regarding management of the National Welfare Fund's resources to permit it to invest in domestic assets. The decision to cut the value-added tax rate has been postponed, but pressures are growing for the budget to do more to support activity. Even with unchanged expenditures, the budget is likely to move into deficit in 2009 as a result of weaker oil and gas revenues.

Growth is projected to slow markedly in 2009 before picking up in 2010

With terms of trade gains projected to reverse and given a negative environment in international capital markets and the worsening outlook for other major economies (itself a factor in the weakness of commodities prices), growth of domestic demand will slow. Real GDP growth should decline sharply in 2009 before recovering somewhat in 2010. Household consumption will continue to expand, albeit at a slower pace, while investment growth will be hard-hit by the tighter credit conditions and the less favourable outlook for demand. Although inflation remains an important challenge, the recent falls in energy and food prices and the slowdown in money supply and economic growth should ease pressures. The current account is set to swing sharply, probably moving into deficit for the first time since 1997.

The global crisis carries risks including the risk of overreacting

The deterioration in the external climate carries substantial risks for Russia, less through financial channels – given still underdeveloped intermediation – than *via* further falls in the price of oil and other export commodities. The vigorous action already taken to protect banking, corporate and financial markets from the effects of global financial turmoil should limit spill-over to real economic activity, though further action may be necessary. At the same time, the scale of the response (announced liquidity support measures are around 14% of GDP) suggests that vigilance will be needed to prevent accommodating misallocation of resources which could rekindle a renewed upsurge in inflation when credit growth resumes. Renewing efforts to step up long-needed structural reforms would strengthen trend growth and bolster confidence.

CHILE

After several years of robust expansion, activity is projected to moderate and inflation to recede. The slowing world economy, tighter financial conditions and lower investments in mining and energy will all slow growth. Inflation will decline gradually as second-round wage increases from high commodity prices wear off and expectations are re-anchored to the central bank's target. Past current account surpluses have disappeared as copper prices have retreated from high levels.

To ensure an orderly decline in inflation, policies should remain prudent. Depending on world macroeconomic and financial developments, a gradual loosening of the monetary policy stance may be warranted unless the recent depreciation of the peso revives inflationary pressures. The fiscal rule provides an appropriate mild countercyclical cushion to activity.

Growth is now moderating but inflation is high

Activity was robust and broad-based during the first half of 2008. Consumer spending, especially of durable goods, was sustained by rapid employment gains, while investments in mining and energy were boosted by high commodity prices. However, the economic environment has recently weakened significantly. Lower copper prices and strikes in the copper mines have slowed export growth and the current account has swung into deficit. Together with the central bank's interventions in foreign exchange markets from April to September to accumulate reserves, this contributed to a sharp depreciation of the currency. Economic prospects dimmed further in October as the turmoil in world financial markets intensified. Both headline and core inflation have risen since April as second-round effects propagated the initial impact of spikes in world food and energy prices. Employment has been growing at close to 3% year-on-year so far in 2008, and the resulting tight labour market conditions have contributed to strong nominal wage growth. Inflation expectations are well above the central bank's target of 2-4% but have

Chile

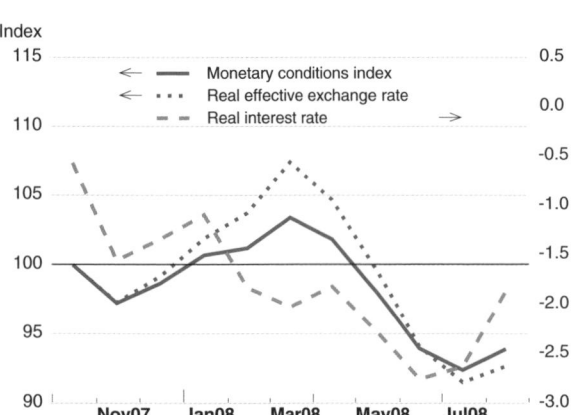

Monetary conditions have eased

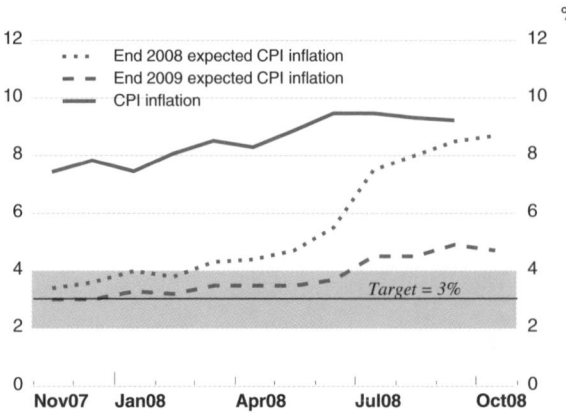

Inflation expectations are not well anchored[1]

1. Central Bank of Chile Survey.

Source: OECD Economic Outlook 84 database; Central Bank of Chile.

StatLink http://dx.doi.org/10.1787/501206520000

Chile: **Macroeconomic indicators**

	2006	2007	2008	2009	2010
Real GDP growth	4.3	5.1	3.9	2.6	3.1
Inflation[1]	3.4	4.4	8.0	5.6	3.8
Fiscal balance[2]	7.7	8.8	7.0	1.5	1.6
Structural fiscal balance[2]	1.0	1.0	0.5	0.5	0.5
Current account balance[2]	5.0	4.0	-1.6	-2.9	-2.6

1. Inflation refers to average consumer price index.
2. In percent of GDP.
Source: National sources and OECD projections.

StatLink ⬛⬛ *http://dx.doi.org/10.1787/503815784202*

receded recently during the turmoil on world financial markets. The financial sector is well capitalised but has been affected by US dollar liquidity restrictions.

The central bank has tightened the stance of monetary policy

The combination of high inflation, slowing growth, pressures on the currency and a stressed financial sector make for difficult macroeconomic policy choices. While much of the acceleration in inflation reflects the pass-through of world food and energy price increases, strong aggregate demand is likely to have contributed to the propagation of price pressures throughout the economy. To deal with these pressures, the central bank increased its policy rate to 8.25% in four successive 50 basis points increases from June to September. In October, however, in the wake of the worsening financial turmoil, slowing activity and falling commodity prices, the central bank interrupted the monetary policy tightening. A gradual loosening may be appropriate to support activity, unless the recent depreciation of the currency revives inflationary pressures. Fiscal policy has been expansionary and, going forward, the implementation of the fiscal rule will result again in a mildly countercyclical stance in 2009, with government spending rising by 5.7% in real terms.

Growth is projected to slow

Growth is projected to moderate from recent peaks as world activity decelerates, tighter monetary policy bites into demand, and investment activity wears off. The economy should rebound in 2010 as Chile's export markets start to recover and global financial market turmoil subsides. Weakening activity, in combination with lower world commodity prices, is expected to bring consumer price inflation near the central bank's target, with a gradual decline from some 8% at end 2008 towards 3% by end 2010.

Downside risk to growth, upside risk to inflation

The growth projection is subject to significant downside risks, as the terms of trade deterioration and world slump may be worse than anticipated. Inflation may revert to the target more slowly than projected if the recent depreciation of the currency is passed through to domestic prices and upcoming public and private sector wage negotiations result in real wage increases in excess of productivity growth.

ESTONIA

Real GDP will continue to decline through to the end of 2008, reflecting mostly a sharp drop in domestic demand. Growth is projected to gradually pick up by the end of 2009 and into 2010, driven by stronger exports. Currently high inflationary pressures are expected to weaken in 2009, but the past real exchange rate appreciation will make the desired export driven recovery challenging.

The currency board and the government's commitment to the balanced budget rule limit macroeconomic policy options to support the recovery. Labour market flexibility, in particular more rapid wage adjustment and higher regional mobility, would be desirable in this context.

A loan financed boom is ending in a bust

Strong domestic demand, in particular household consumption and investment in real estate, have driven the exceptionally rapid economic growth of recent years. Private consumption and investment were financed by borrowing from foreign banks at low or even negative real interest rates, while strong labour shortages led to high wage increases. Growth peaked in mid-2007 as international financial market problems began and lending conditions tightened. Real GDP declined in the first half of 2008 by almost 2%. The output decline has been fastest in the real estate and construction sectors, and has been accompanied by house price decreases. However, inflation has remained high due to the lagged response in the labour market.

Wage increases have exceeded labour productivity growth

Wages rose by about 20% in 2007 and continued to increase in the first half of 2008 by around 15%. The hike in wages led to a widening gap between real wages and labour productivity and fuelled a strong real exchange rate appreciation, which has weakened competitiveness. These developments will make moving towards an export driven economy more challenging.

Estonia

Demand and output are now falling

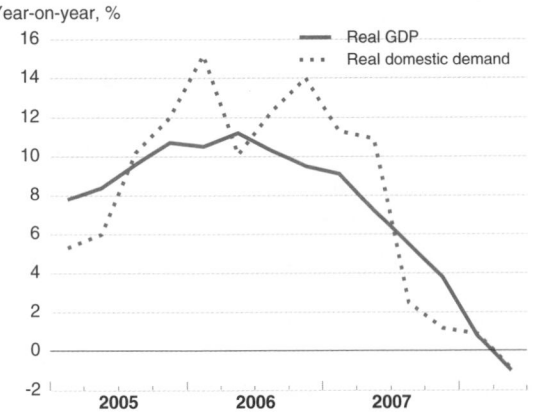

The current account has been increasingly financed by external credit

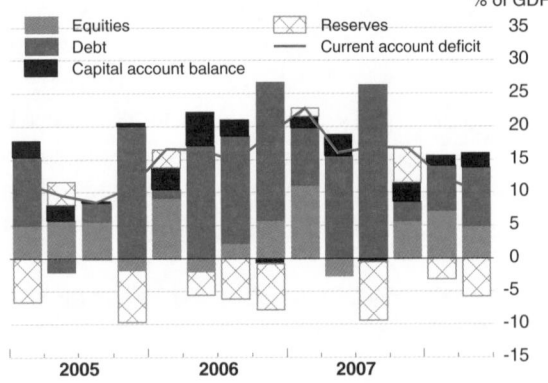

Note: In the decomposition of the current account deficit, negative numbers indicate an increase in reserves. The financial account balance is decomposed into equities (net direct investment plus net equities in portfolio investment) and debt. Net errors and omissions have been added to the capital account balance.

Source: Bank of Estonia; OECD Economic Outlook 84 database.

StatLink ⟡⟡ *http://dx.doi.org/10.1787/501236857414*

Estonia: **Demand, output and prices**

	2005	2006	2007	2008	2009	2010
	Current prices EEK billion	Percentage changes, volume (2000 prices)				
Private consumption	96.6	12.7	7.9	-1.5	-1.6	2.2
Government consumption	30.0	1.8	3.9	3.6	-0.2	0.1
Gross fixed capital formation	53.3	19.5	4.9	-1.4	-6.4	3.0
Final domestic demand	179.8	12.9	6.3	-0.7	-2.7	2.0
Stockbuilding[1]	4.7	1.4	1.8	-3.7	0.9	0.0
Total domestic demand	184.5	13.9	7.5	-3.9	-1.8	2.0
Exports of goods and services	138.9	11.6	0.0	-3.2	0.6	4.7
Imports of goods and services	149.8	20.4	4.2	-6.4	-1.0	3.4
Net exports[1]	- 11.0	-8.3	-3.9	3.1	1.2	0.9
GDP at market prices	173.5	10.4	6.3	-1.9	-2.0	2.9
GDP deflator	_	7.0	9.6	10.0	6.8	5.7
Memorandum items						
Harmonised index of consumer prices	_	4.4	6.7	10.7	5.1	3.2
Private consumption deflator	_	4.1	7.8	10.0	5.9	4.2
General government financial balance[2]	_	2.9	2.7	-0.7	-2.4	-1.4

Note: National accounts are based on official chain-linked data. This introduces a discrepancy in the identity between real demand components and GDP. For further details see *OECD Economic Outlook* Sources and Methods *(http://www.oecd.org/eco/sources-and-methods).*
1. Contributions to changes in real GDP (percentage of real GDP in previous year), actual amount in the first column.
2. As a percentage of GDP.
Source: OECD Economic Outlook 84 database.

StatLink http://dx.doi.org/10.1787/503830260434

Fiscal policy is pro-cyclical

The commitment to the balanced budget rule makes fiscal policy pro-cyclical and limits policy adjustment to mitigate the effects of the down turn. The planned cut in the income tax rate from 21 to 20% in 2009 has been postponed and the lower reduced-rate of value added tax has been increased from 5 to 9%. On the spending-side, the government envisages staff and wage cuts as well as partial reversals of many recently introduced expenditure increases.

Labour market reform raises flexibility but risks reducing work incentives

The new labour law, currently under consideration in parliament, proposes some measures that will raise labour market flexibility, in particular shortening the notice period for layoffs and cutting severance payments. The law, in combination with business-friendly product market regulations, would facilitate economic recovery. However, the simultaneously expanded unemployment insurance will have to be well managed. Increasing replacement rates risks a reduction in incentives to search for and take a job.

The sharp fall in growth will continue

The economy is estimated to have entered a recession in 2008, with GDP falling by 1.9%. This fall is driven mainly by a drop in domestic demand, particularly private consumption and real estate investment. By end-2009, real GDP growth is expected to turn positive again, mainly reflecting stronger exports as the world economy reverses. Currently strong inflation is expected to ease in 2009 and fall further in 2010 to close to 3% as the impact of the tax hikes fades, and falls in food and energy prices are passed through.

The still high current account deficit creates risks for the recovery

While the current account deficit has narrowed, the risk of an accelerated reversal of capital flows remains. Weaker than expected economic growth in Estonia's main trade partners is a downside risk to the export driven growth recovery.

OECD ECONOMIC OUTLOOK 84 – ISBN 978-92-64-05469-1 – © OECD 2008

INDONESIA

Strong domestic demand continued to underpin growth in the first half of 2008. Investment was particularly robust. Imports are growing faster than exports, but the trade and current accounts are still in healthy surpluses. Inflation rose substantially following a hike in regulated domestic fuel prices in May.

Monetary policy is being tightened and measures to tackle worsening credit conditions are being taken. Outlays on fuel-price subsidies are being contained but the budget will continue to be vulnerable to fluctuations in international energy costs in the absence of a formal mechanism for adjusting domestic fuel prices.

Activity remains vigorous but is decelerating

Real GDP grew by 6.4% on a year-on-year basis in the second quarter, a mild deceleration from the first quarter. Domestic demand continued to be the main driver, although private consumption lost some impetus in the second quarter because of rising fuel and food prices. Investment growth was particularly solid. Export performance has been strong reflecting still-supportive external demand, but buoyant import growth is narrowing the sizeable, current account surplus.

Monetary tightening was halted in October

Inflation spiked during June-August following a policy-induced upward adjustment in domestic fuel prices by nearly 30% at the end of May. Bank Indonesia responded to the ensuing inflationary pressures, a concomitant deterioration in expectations and rising food prices by hiking the policy rate by a total of 100 basis points, to 9.5% in October. Inflation is showing signs of moderation, as the effects of the fuel-price hike wear off, but remains well above the end-year target range of 4-6%. Credit conditions have deteriorated on the heels of the worsening global financial environment. Bank reserve requirements have been lowered and additional liquidity-boosting measures have been taken. The central bank is continuing to intervene in the foreign-exchange market to tame excessive exchange-rate volatility. In line with growing global risk

Indonesia

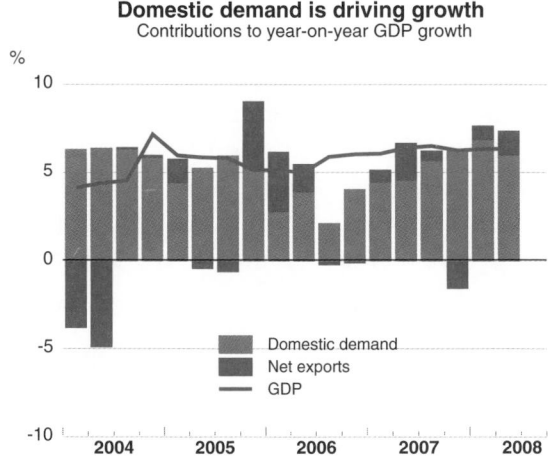

Domestic demand is driving growth
Contributions to year-on-year GDP growth

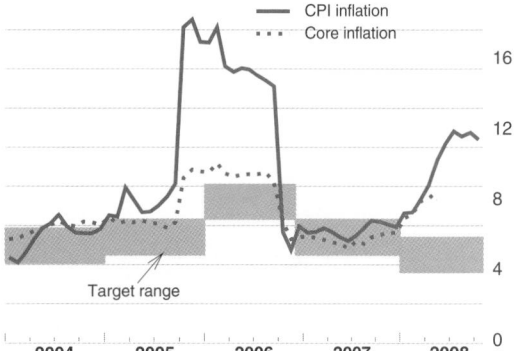

Inflation remains high
Year-on-year percentage change

Source: OECD, *Main Economic Indicators*, and Statistics Indonesia (BPS).

StatLink http://dx.doi.org/10.1787/501237438201

Indonesia: **Macroeconomic indicators**

	2006	2007	2008	2009	2010
Real GDP growth	5.5	6.3	6.2	5.4	6.0
Inflation	6.6	6.6	12.0	7.0	6.0
Fiscal balance (per cent of GDP)	-1.0	-1.2	-1.3	-1.5	-1.5
Current account balance ($ billion)	10.8	10.4	4.0	3.0	2.0
Current account balance (per cent of GDP)	3.0	2.4	0.8	0.5	0.3

Note: Real GDP growth and inflation are defined in percentage change from the previous period.
Inflation refers to the end-year consumer price index.
Source: Figures for 2006-07 are from national sources. Figures for 2008-10 are OECD projections.

StatLink ⟨≣⟩ http://dx.doi.org/10.1787/503846582614

aversion, the *rupiah* has depreciated since mid-year, especially in October, and the domestic yield curve has steepened.

The domestic fuel price hike relieved budgetary pressures

Budget revisions following the May fuel-price hike point to a deficit of 1.3% of GDP in 2008, marginally higher than in 2007. Despite the price adjustment, energy subsidies still account for a large share of total central government expenditure. The public debt is likely to fall to within the 30-35% of GDP target range for 2009. Legislation was approved in September reducing marginal personal income tax rates from 2009; the top personal tax rate will fall by 5 percentage points to 30%. A flat corporate tax rate of 28% will be introduced in 2009, with a further reduction to 25% in 2010. Small and medium-sized enterprises will be granted additional tax relief. The law provides incentives for firms to list in the stock exchange by reducing their corporate tax rate by 5 percentage points. The tax rate on dividend income will also be lowered. The package is foreseen to cost about 0.7% of GDP in 2009.

Growth may regain strength towards end-2009

Activity is expected to lose steam in the coming months and then regain momentum from the second half of 2009. Domestic demand, especially private consumption, is set to remain the main driver of growth. Exports are also likely to continue to perform reasonably well, despite the slowdown in global demand and falling commodity prices. A moderation in demand for imports in line with slackening activity should sustain the trade surplus. Inflation is set to move toward the target range in 2009-10 as monetary policy continues to be tightened and commodity prices remain contained. Fiscal policy is expected to remain on track, with low international fuel prices providing relief to the budget. Nevertheless, in the absence of an automatic adjustment mechanism for domestic fuel prices, fiscal policy will remain vulnerable to movements in global energy prices.

The main risks stem from external sources

A slower-than-expected recovery in global demand, coupled with a faster-than-anticipated fall in commodity prices, would take a toll on export growth. At the same time, heightened volatility in international financial markets would pose challenges for the conduct of monetary policy and for budget financing. On the domestic front, meeting the inflation target may take longer than expected, causing the current monetary tightening cycle to be more protracted.

ISRAEL

Global financial turmoil is deepening the slowdown, with the pace of economic activity not expected to pick up substantially before the latter part of 2009. The central bank has already cut its policy rate in reaction to the crisis in financial markets.

Monetary policy should remain biased towards easing in the near term. Further ahead, assuming a relatively trouble-free recovery from the financial crisis, the policy stance should tighten. Consideration of an increase in the fiscal spending ceiling should be put on hold in light of the increased economic uncertainty.

A slowdown in economic activity is already underway

A rapid pace of export-led growth in recent years (over 5% on average each year from 2004 to 2007) has for some time generated expectations of a slowdown as output had almost certainly risen above potential levels. Real GDP growth eased in the spring of this year, in part because first-quarter growth had been boosted by extra vehicle sales prompted by tax and regulatory changes. There are signs of a substantial slackening in activity for the balance of the year: the Bank of Israel's State-of-the-Economy index, credit-card purchases and consumer confidence all point to weakening demand and output.

Thus far, domestic banking has stood up well

Recent events in global financial markets are probably already deepening the slowdown. So far, the Israeli banking sector has not encountered serious difficulties, but the economy is inevitably exposed to global developments. In the initial weeks following the acceleration of the global financial crisis in mid-September Israeli equity prices fell sharply, and wealth effects will probably affect consumption. Tightening credit

Israel[1]

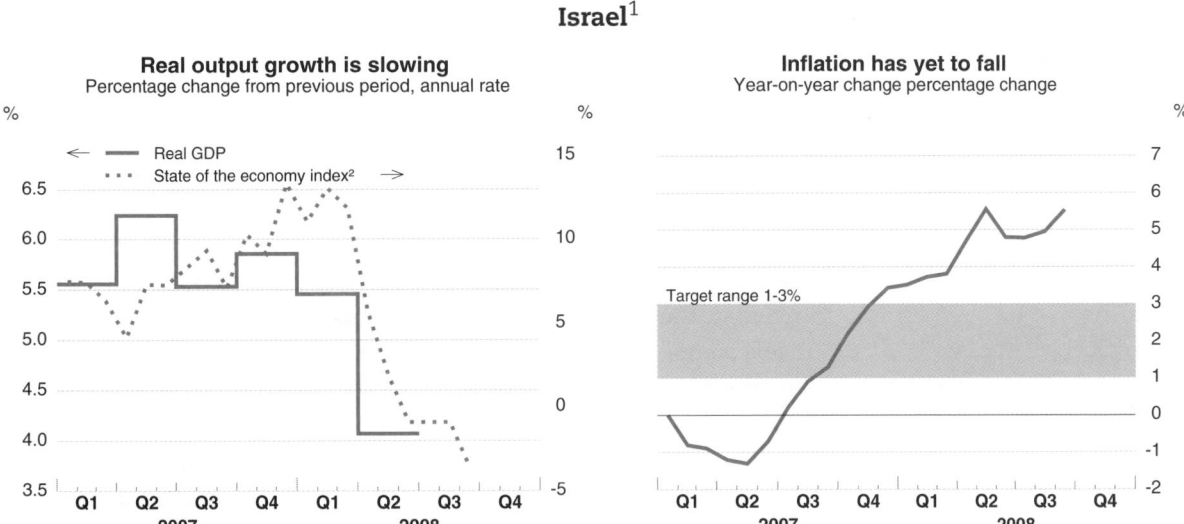

1. For technical reasons, these figures use Israel's official statistics, which include data relating to the Golan Heights, East Jerusalem and Israeli settlements in the West Bank.
2. The State of the Economy index is calculated by the Bank of Israel each month and comprises six indicators covering: industrial production, employment, revenues in service sectors, goods imports and exports, and services exports.

Source: Central Bureau of Statistics and Bank of Israel.

StatLink http://dx.doi.org/10.1787/501244841868

Israel: **Demand, output and prices**

	2005	2006	2007	2008	2009	2010
	Current prices ILS billion	Percentage changes, volume (2005 prices)				
Private consumption	333.5	4.0	6.9	4.2	2.1	3.8
Government consumption	153.5	2.7	2.9	0.9	1.9	1.5
Gross fixed capital formation	97.8	9.9	15.3	6.4	1.7	6.5
Final domestic demand	584.9	4.6	7.3	3.8	2.0	3.7
Stockbuilding[1]	14.7	-0.4	-0.5	-0.4	0.2	0.0
Total domestic demand	599.6	4.1	6.7	3.4	2.1	3.7
Exports of goods and services	256.6	6.1	8.6	7.5	0.9	5.2
Imports of goods and services	258.5	3.6	11.7	5.3	1.3	5.0
Net exports[1]	- 1.8	1.1	-1.3	0.9	-0.2	0.0
GDP at market prices	597.8	5.2	5.4	4.7	2.0	3.8
GDP deflator	_	1.9	-0.2	2.4	3.3	1.5
Memorandum items						
Inflation (CPI), Average increase		2.1	0.5	4.8	3.0	1.5
Inflation (CPI), December-to-December increase		-0.1	3.4	5.0	1.5	1.5
Private consumption deflator		1.8	0.6	5.6	3.0	1.5
General government financial balance[2]		-0.9	-0.4	-1.5	-1.9	-1.3
Current account balance[2]		6.1	3.0	2.6	3.0	3.1

Note: National accounts are based on official chain-linked data. This introduces a discrepancy in the identity between real demand components and GDP. For further details see *OECD Economic Outlook* Sources and Methods *(http://www.oecd.org/eco/sources-and-methods).* For technical reasons this table uses Israel's official statistics, which include data relating to the Golan Heights, East Jerusalem and Israeli settlements in the West Bank.
1. Contributions to changes in real GDP (percentage of real GDP in previous year), actual amount in the first column.
2. As a percentage of GDP.
Source: OECD Economic Outlook 84 database and Israel's Central Bureau of Statistics.

StatLink 🔗 *http://dx.doi.org/10.1787/503873465165*

conditions and further weakening of external demand are also likely channels through which the crisis will affect the real economy.

The central bank has cut its policy rate in reaction to the financial crisis

Inflation has been above the central bank's target range (1 to 3% consumer price index growth) since late-2007, largely due to hikes in world food and commodity prices. Until recently, monetary policy was being tightened in response. Inflationary pressures are now abating with the most recent month-on-month figures showing small increases or falls in key components of the consumer price index, and indicators of inflationary expectations are favourable. This has given the Bank leeway to react to the crisis in financial markets; the policy rate was cut by 50 basis points, effective in October and by 25 points and then 50 points in November, bringing the rate to 3.0%. The first reduction prompted a temporary stock-market rally but also further depreciation of the currency. Against the dollar, the shekel has been trading some 5-10% below mid-year levels. Since March this year, the central bank has been implicitly favouring depreciation through a programme of announced foreign currency purchases that are primarily aimed at increasing reserves, which had for some time been seen as below optimal levels.

Weak tax revenues are pushing the government balance back into deficit

Robust growth in recent years, combined with spending and deficit ceilings, yielded a large fiscal improvement despite a series of tax cuts. Indeed, last year's outturn saw a small surplus, and general-government debt has fallen from 100% of GDP in 2004 to 80%. This year, however, growth in tax receipts has dropped significantly, and a return to deficit is expected. Weaker GDP growth and completion of the schedule of tax cuts imply that revenue increases will also be low in 2009 and 2010.

Real GDP growth is projected to drop significantly in 2009

Despite recent weakness, growth is not expected to fall by much for 2008 as a whole but is projected to drop to around 2% in 2009. Output is not likely to pick up significantly until the second half of next year. Although, export growth will dip, the current account surplus will increase slightly, thanks to improved terms of trade. A fiscal deficit of 1.5% of GDP is projected for 2008, and this is expected to widen in 2009 before narrowing again in 2010 as activity recovers. Inflation is expected to fall back into the central bank's target range around mid-2009.

The greatest domestic risk is an increase in public spending ceiling

The impact of the global credit crunch on the economy could be more pronounced than projected. Another risk relates to the increase in the ceiling on government expenditure growth, which has been widely discussed. Under robust growth prospects, a modest increase could be warranted. However, debt reduction needs to remain a priority and given the current economic climate such proposals should be put to one side. In any case, significant changes in policy will no doubt have to await the outcome of the February general elections.

SLOVENIA

Economic activity is likely to slow significantly in 2009, driven in particular by a sharp deceleration in investment in construction. The following year, economic growth should return toward trend as both investment and private consumption recover. Headline inflation is expected to subside due to falling commodity prices, although planned public wage increases will exert upward pressure on core inflation.

With European Central Bank monetary policy likely to remain accommodating for Slovenia during the projection period, the fiscal policy stance should remain at least neutral to avoid adding to inflationary pressures. Competition in product markets needs to be nurtured to help reduce prices and improve productivity.

Growth is tilting to the downside

After having the strongest growth performance in the euro area in 2007 (6.8%), activity started to decelerate over the course of 2008. On the business side, construction spending has decreased while manufactures' order books reveal that deteriorating international conditions damped exports. More broadly, business sentiment has been falling since the peak in mid-2007. Private consumption is being dragged down by the negative effects of higher inflation on real incomes and, with consumer confidence plummeting, there is little prospect of a revival in the short-term. Reflecting past strong growth, the registered unemployment rate has reached its lowest level in a decade.

Public wage policy will affect the pace of disinflation

Headline inflation increased during 2008 to 7% in June, the highest in the euro area. However, it has started to decline as energy and food prices have fallen. Nevertheless, core inflation remains high and is likely to recede only gradually because the government has started implementing

Slovenia

Growth is slowing down[1]

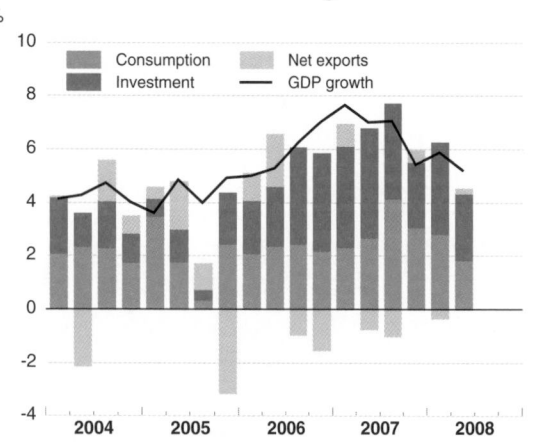

Monetary policy has become accommodating[2]

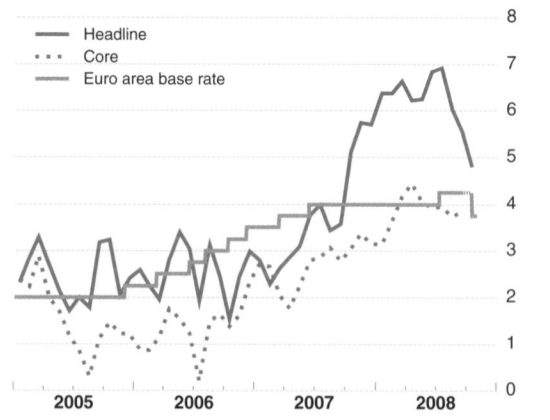

1. Contribution to GDP growth for all series except GDP itself. GDP growth can deviate from the sum of the components shown because stock building is excluded.
2. Inflation is measured by the year-on-year change in the harmonised consumer price index. Core inflation excludes food and energy.
Source: Eurostat and OECD Economic Outlook 84 database.

StatLink ⟨⟩ http://dx.doi.org/10.1787/501284221166

Slovenia: **Demand, output and prices**

	2005	2006	2007	2008	2009	2010
	Current prices € billion	Percentage changes, volume (1995 prices)				
Private consumption	15.6	2.9	5.0	3.3	3.0	3.2
Government consumption	5.5	4.1	2.5	2.8	2.3	2.0
Gross fixed capital formation	7.3	10.4	11.9	8.4	1.6	3.7
Final domestic demand	28.3	5.0	6.4	4.6	2.5	3.1
Stockbuilding[1]	0.5	0.8	1.8	0.5	-0.8	0.0
Total domestic demand	28.8	5.7	6.9	4.9	1.6	3.0
Exports of goods and services	17.9	12.5	13.8	6.3	3.6	6.1
Imports of goods and services	18.0	12.2	15.7	6.8	3.1	5.3
Net exports[1]	- 0.1	0.2	-1.3	-0.5	0.3	0.4
GDP at market prices	28.7	5.9	6.8	4.8	2.1	3.5
GDP deflator	_	2.0	4.1	4.0	3.4	2.7
Memorandum items						
Consumer price index	_	2.5	3.8	4.9	3.0	2.8
Private consumption deflator	_	2.4	4.1	5.2	2.9	2.8
General government financial balance[2]	_	-1.2	-0.1	0.3	-0.7	-0.4

Note: National accounts are based on official chain-linked data. This introduces a discrepancy in the identity
   between real demand components and GDP. For further details see *OECD Economic Outlook* Sources
   and Methods *(http://www.oecd.org/eco/sources-and-methods)*.
1. Contributions to changes in real GDP (percentage of real GDP in previous year), actual amount in the first
   column.
2. As a percentage of GDP.
Source: OECD Economic Outlook 84 database.

StatLink ᵐˢᴾ *http://dx.doi.org/10.1787/503885515482*

a catch-up policy for public sector wages, which may in turn fuel higher wage demands in the private sector. Wage growth is likely to exceed productivity growth in the coming years, eroding competitiveness.

Accommodating monetary policy requires an appropriate fiscal stance

European Central Bank monetary policy is likely to remain accommodative for Slovenia during the projection period. In this context, the authorities' restrictive fiscal stance, as laid out in their Stability Programme, seems appropriate in view of inflationary pressures. However, with the planned phasing out of the payroll tax (cumulated loss of revenue of about 2% of GDP by 2009), the policy of public sector salary catch-ups and possible reversal of the strong revenue growth experienced in recent years, the actual fiscal position is likely to deteriorate. Hence, renewed efforts to control expenditures may be necessary to maintain the targeted improvement in the structural fiscal balance.

Disinflation and railway projects will bring the economy back to trend

In 2009, GDP growth is projected to be subdued, though still positive, owing to weak private consumption, the decrease in road construction investment and the global downturn. The following year, growth should return to trend as lower inflation should help increase real incomes and allow private consumption growth to return to trend by the end of 2010. Investment will be boosted by new railway projects, and exporters should benefit from the recovery in international trade. The current account deficit widened to about 6% of GDP in 2008, but should narrow progressively.

Second-round effect on wages poses a risk

The main risk to the projections is the upward price pressures emerging from potential spill-over of strong public sector wage increases to higher wage demands in the private sector. On the other hand, inflationary pressures may be less pronounced if recent measures to reduce the tax wedge significantly increase labour supply.

SOUTH AFRICA

This year's economic slowdown is projected to continue, reflecting weaker consumption growth and worsening terms of trade. Real GDP growth is expected to fall to about 3% in 2009 before rebounding to above 4% in 2010, with the FIFA World Cup providing a fillip to activity. Inflation is expected to turn down, returning to the central bank's target range in 2010, as a result of the monetary tightening over the past two years and falling food and energy prices. Current account deficits will remain large with lower export prices broadly offsetting weaker import volume growth.

The projected move back into budget deficits is not worrisome, but fiscal policy should more than claw back the cyclical easing over the medium term, in order to get to cyclically adjusted balance. Monetary policy should continue to focus on price stability, but with food and energy prices falling, some easing may be possible earlier than previously envisaged. Prospects for long-term growth and meeting official employment targets would be improved by strengthening product market competition, with lighter regulation and less costly compliance being high priorities.

Growth has slowed

Having averaged 5% a year between 2004 and 2007, real GDP growth slowed to 4.2% in the first half of 2008. This was a function mostly of electricity supply disruptions in the first quarter, but also reflected weaker growth of domestic demand, especially private consumption. Substantial terms of trade gains and favourable domestic and international credit conditions in recent years have fuelled aggregate demand, resulting in very large current account deficits. This process has reversed course, however, with a progressive tightening of monetary policy, rising spreads on emerging market assets this year and a sharp weakening in the prices of South Africa's key export commodities since the second quarter.

Inflation remains high, however

Inflation trended upwards from early 2006 through late-2008, and has exceeded the upper end of the central bank's target range of 3-6% since

South Africa

The credit crunch has hit asset prices hard

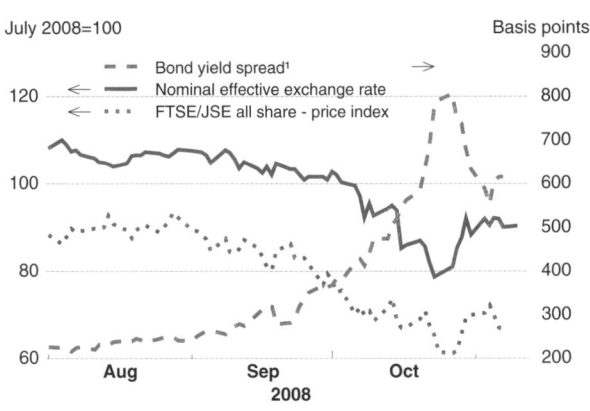

The long rise in food prices, one driver of high inflation, has turned
Year-on-year percentage change

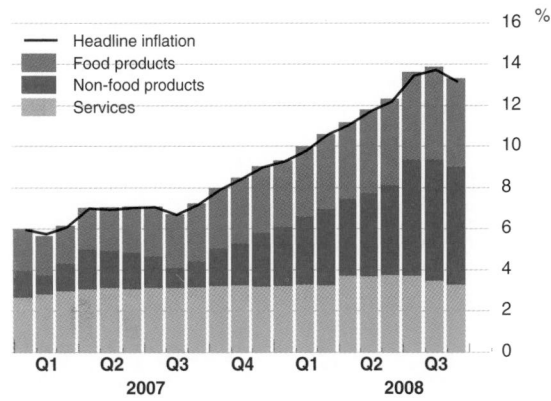

1. JP Morgan EMBI+ stripped spread.

Source: OECD calculations based on Statistics South Africa, South Africa Reserve Bank and Datastream.

StatLink http://dx.doi.org/10.1787/501324886582

South Africa: **Macroeconomic indicators**

	2006	2007	2008	2009	2010
Real GDP growth	5.4	5.1	3.3	3.0	4.2
Inflation	4.6	6.5	11.4	6.9	5.7
Fiscal balance (per cent of GDP)	0.2	1.3	0.1	-1.6	-1.1
Unemployment (per cent)	23.1	23.6	23.3	23.1	22.5
Current account balance (per cent of GDP)	-6.5	-7.3	-7.7	-6.5	-5.8

Source: National sources and OECD projections.

StatLink ᘉᔉ http://dx.doi.org/10.1787/504016778110

April 2007. It reached 13.6% in August 2008 before subsiding somewhat in September. Food and energy accounted for more than half the increase from the low point, and the big upward step in electricity tariffs in mid-year to address serious shortages provided another impetus. However, there have also been signs of second-round effects, as medium-term inflation expectations have risen to around 7%, and wage demands have picked up.

Global economic turmoil has hit export prices

The downturn in the terms of trade is a threat to domestic demand growth. Rising commodity prices had fuelled investment, government spending (via buoyant tax revenues, easing the public finance constraint), and consumption (via strong real wage gains), while attracting foreign capital inflows, which have further fed demand. This sequence is now reversing.

Political uncertainty has increased

Events surrounding the unexpected forced resignation of President Thabo Mbeki aggravated divisions within the ruling African National Congress (ANC), signaling political uncertainty ahead of the 2009 presidential elections, at a time when appetite for emerging market assets has ebbed with an increase in risk aversion.

Growth will be slower but still solid

A slowdown in domestic demand driven by tighter credit conditions both domestically and abroad, as well as a deterioration in the terms of trade, should see real GDP growth decline to 3.3% in 2008 and somewhat further in 2009. The main support to growth will be investment, particularly public infrastructure spending on the 2010 World Cup and expanding electricity supply. Growth should rebound to around potential in 2010 as financial turmoil fades and global economic activity recovers.

The target measure of inflation will fall substantially in 2009

The easing of fuel and food prices suggests that year-on-year inflation will continue to fall in coming months, notwithstanding the recent weakness of the rand. The further slowdown in economic growth in 2009 should reinforce the downtrend, and a rebasing and reweighting of the consumer price index will bring a step decrease in the target inflation measure in the first quarter of 2009. Nonetheless, inflation is not expected to return to the central bank's target zone until 2010.

A sudden stop of capital inflows is now a more immediate risk

South Africa's large current account deficits have been a locus of macroeconomic vulnerability for several years. Now, with sentiment towards emerging market assets having worsened and international lending flows shrinking, the risk that the private capital inflows needed to finance those deficits will dry up has become more acute. A scenario with a forced contraction of imports and much weaker growth, while still less likely than the central scenario, has become a more immediate possibility.

ISBN 978-92-64-05469-1
OECD Economic Outlook 84
© OECD 2008

Chapter 4

RESPONSES TO INFLATION SHOCKS: DO G7 COUNTRIES BEHAVE DIFFERENTLY?

Monetary policy responses to global inflation shocks have varied across countries

After declining steadily since the early 1980s, domestic inflation picked up again in the early 2000s in most OECD countries and has accelerated significantly over the past year before receding very recently (Chapter 1) These movements can to a large extent be related to import prices and more specifically the commodity components of imports (Figure 4.1). Between 2000 and July 2008, oil prices expressed in US dollars and yen increased fivefold and non-energy commodity prices have more than doubled.[1] Since then, commodity prices (in particular oil prices) have declined but still remain above their level in early 2007. The monetary policy responses to higher inflationary pressures have differed across industrialised economies even using benchmarks that take into account the relative cyclical positions of the major economies. Some central banks have appeared more "hawkish" on inflation, while others, where the acceleration of commodity prices inflation coincided with the beginning of financial turmoil, have appeared more dovish.

Different exposure to global price shocks and propagation mechanisms...

These different behaviours could reflect a number of factors including: i) differences in the exposure to global price shocks as a result of differences in the commodity intensity of production and consumption; ii) differences in the propagation of shocks due to differences in inflation and wage dynamics.[2] In order to assess the role played by these factors, this chapter compares the exposure of the main OECD economies to recent global inflation shocks and the way in which the latter tend to pass into domestic inflation.[3] First, economies' exposure to price shocks is assessed by calculating the direct mechanical impact of recent commodity price and exchange rate developments on domestic inflation. The propagation of price shocks to inflation dynamics is then examined by means of estimated relationships for domestic price and wage inflation.[4]

1. In line with these developments, the acceleration of inflation has mainly concerned headline inflation, while measures of underlying inflation (whether statistical or exclusion-based) have remained comparatively stable.
2. A large body of research has addressed other factors conditioning monetary policy reactions such as policy objectives, monetary policy transmission, and the role of domestic and global shocks for selected countries or economic regions. Overall, it suggests that policy objectives and transmission channels have been rather similar on both sides of the Atlantic, whereas the two regions have been hit by different shocks, prompting stronger interest rate adjustments in the United States. See notably the comparison by Smets and Wouters (2005) and Sahuc and Smets (2008) using dynamic general equilibrium models (DSGE).
3. The chapter covers G7 economies, but with a focus on the differences between the United States and the euro area.
4. The main technical details of the underlying data, calculations, and estimates are reported in the Appendix. More details can also be found in Vogel *et al.* (2009).

Figure 4.1. **Import price inflation and its components in the G7 economies**

Year-on-year growth rate, in percentage

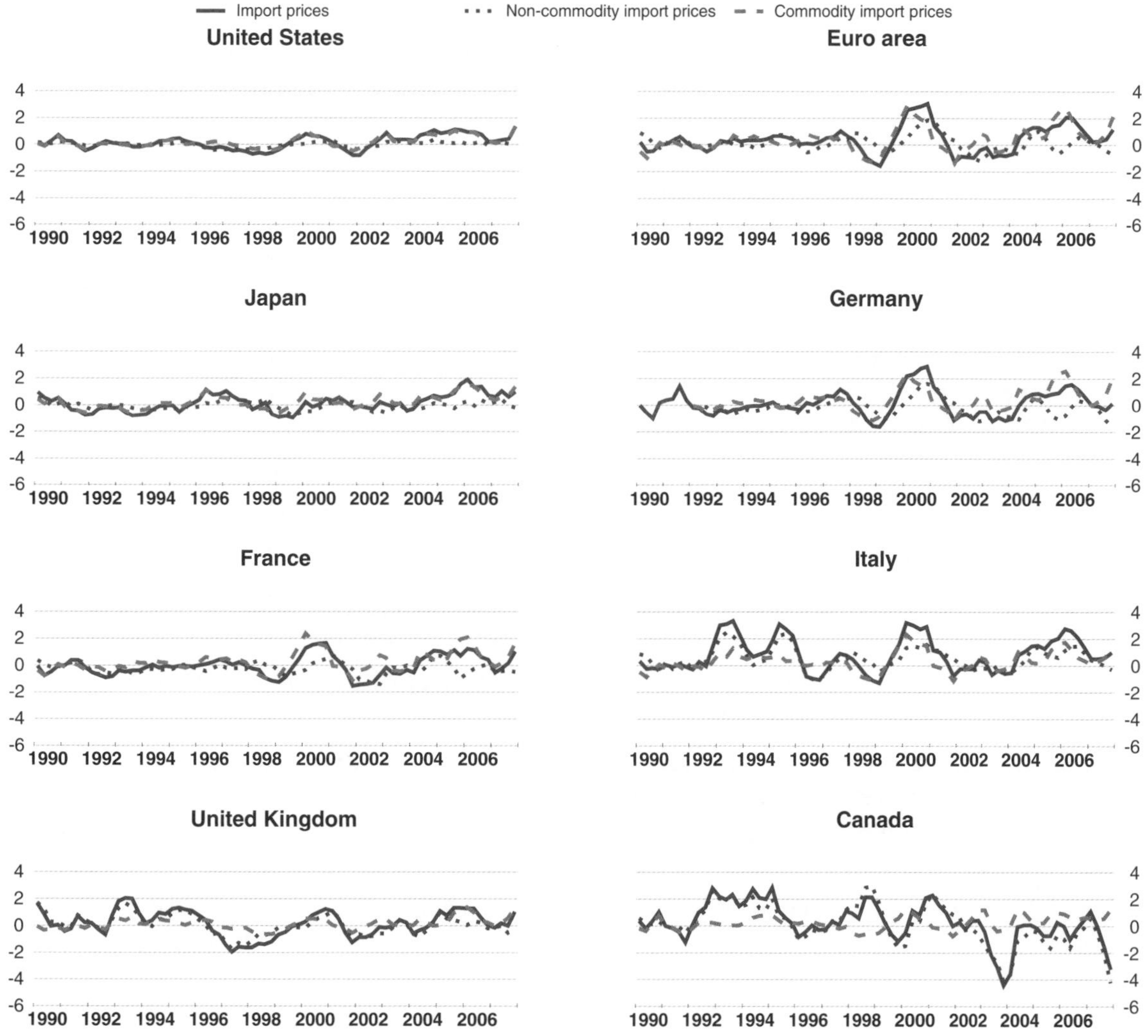

—— Import prices ···· Non-commodity import prices – – Commodity import prices

United States

Euro area

Japan

Germany

France

Italy

United Kingdom

Canada

Note: Import price inflation is weighted by the share of the respective imports in total domestic demand. Euro area data are not corrected for intra-area trade. Import prices do not disentangle price changes for a given basket of imports and changes in import composition.

Source: OECD Economic Outlook 84 database.

StatLink ⬛⬛⬛ http://dx.doi.org/10.1787/501408682317

... may have contributed to the differences in policy stance:

The main finding of the chapter is that explanations related to exposure to global commodity prices shock and their propagation to prices and wages may have contributed to the differences in policy stances observed during the boom of commodity prices, but cannot explain them all. In particular:

The initial shock faced by the euro area was smaller...

● The increase in commodity prices from 2000 to mid-2008 has had a larger direct impact on domestic inflation in the United States than in the euro area reflecting both dollar depreciation and a higher energy intensity of the US economy. This impact has been even larger in the case of Japan.

... but oil prices seem to have a larger long-term effect on domestic prices

- On the other hand, and despite the higher oil intensity of the US economy, estimated past behaviour suggests that, for given wage developments, the long-term effect of oil prices on domestic prices is stronger in the euro area than in Japan and the United States.

Other price and wage dynamics are more similar across countries

- Repercussions from non-oil commodity prices on domestic prices are more similar among G7 countries and in particular relatively comparable in the euro area and the United States. Similarly, based on evidence over the past decade, wages do not appear more susceptible to react to inflationary impulses in consumer prices in the euro area than in the United States or Japan.

Risks of inflationary wage developments were also assessed differently

A price shock of the magnitude recently observed has not been experienced since the last oil shock, implying a risk that wages could react more than in the past decade to the increase in commodity prices. The extent to which this risk has affected the policy stance may have varied and may be a key factor behind the differences in policy stance, notably across the Atlantic. Moreover, the fall in commodity prices since mid-2008 and the decline in economic activity are likely to have sharply reduced this risk and any associated reason for policy divergence.

Measuring the direct impact of recent international price shocks

The commodity price shocks were stronger for United States and Japan

The immediate exposure of an economy to the inflation effects of commodity price shocks depends on the share of the corresponding commodity in total demand and the respective rates of commodity price inflation in local currency.[5] According to back-of-the-envelope calculations reported in Table 4.1, the inflation impact has, on the whole and since 2001, been substantially larger for the United States and Japan than for the euro area. Since 2006, when prices of food and a number of other commodities, including metals, began to increase sharply, the mechanical contribution of commodity prices to inflation has gone up significantly but remains larger in the United States and Japan than in the euro area.

This reflects a higher use of oil in the United States and exchange rate movements

While greater exposure of the United States results partly from a larger use of oil in production and consumption, currency movements have also contributed to cross-country differences.[6] The appreciation of the

5. More precisely, the direct inflationary effects of various commodity prices can be calculated by multiplying the share of the corresponding commodity in total demand by the respective rates of commodity price inflation relative to domestic inflation.

6. The estimated commodity price effects are expressed in local currency terms, combining the direct effect on import prices at constant exchange rates with the full impact of exchange rate movements. It is realistic to assume an approximately full pass-through of exchange rate movements to corresponding domestic currency prices of imported commodities. However, such an assumption is less straightforward for those commodities, *e.g.* gas, for which a world market price does not prevail. This analysis does take into account possible interactions between commodity prices and exchange rates, nor the effects of indirect taxation on the pass-through of commodity prices into retail prices.

Table 4.1. **The direct impact of higher commodity prices on domestic inflation**

Annual average, percentage points (domestic currency terms)

	Energy	Food	Other commodities	Total	Headline – core inflation
2001-08[1]					
United States	0.5	0.2	0.1	0.7	0.8
Japan	0.5	0.4	0.2	1.1	2.1
Euro 3[2]	0.2	0.1	0.0	0.4	0.5
Germany	0.3	0.1	0.0	0.4	0.7
France	0.2	0.1	0.0	0.3	0.4
Italy	0.2	0.1	0.0	0.3	0.3
United Kingdom	0.3	0.2	0.1	0.6	0.6
Canada	0.2	0.1	0.1	0.4	0.2
2006-08					
United States	0.7	0.4	0.1	1.2	0.7
Japan	0.7	0.9	0.3	2.0	2.0
Euro 3[2]	0.4	0.4	0.1	0.9	0.6
Germany	0.4	0.4	0.1	0.9	0.8
France	0.4	0.3	0.1	0.8	0.4
Italy	0.4	0.5	0.2	1.0	0.5
United Kingdom	0.6	0.7	0.2	1.4	0.9
Canada	0.4	0.4	0.2	1.0	0.0

Note: These estimates combine the movements in individual commodity prices and exchange rates, weighted by the relevant shares in total demand.
1. For the rest of 2008, commodity prices and domestic inflation are assumed to be in line with the projections presented in this *OECD Economic Outlook*.
2. GDP weighted average of France, Germany and Italy.
Source: IEA Energy Statistics of OECD countries, OECD Economic Outlook 84 database, OECD STAN database and OECD calculations.

StatLink http://dx.doi.org/10.1787/504025240156

European and Canadian currencies against the US dollar has significantly cushioned the inflationary impact of the *commodity* price shocks. For instance, in the euro area oil prices in local currency rose by a factor of three between 2001 and mid-2008 (compared with five in the United States).

The impact of exchange rate movements on non-commodity import prices...

Exchange rate movements have also contributed to cross-country differences via their impact on *non-commodity* import prices. The pass-through of exchange rate movements to non-commodity imports is significantly weaker than the near one-to-one pass-through that prevails for commodity imports, and there are important cross-country differences. Table 4.2 reports the direct mechanical impact of nominal effective exchange rate developments on non-commodity imports prices based on recent pass-through estimates (see Box 4.1). The final column reports the corresponding impacts on domestic inflation, taking into account the import content of demand in the G7 economies and assuming no changes in profit margins.

... has been limited by partial pass-through

Overall, recent exchange rate developments and their impact on non-commodity import prices account for differentials in inflation rates of at most 0.2 percentage points between the euro area and the United States, with the lower US pass-through serving to significantly moderate the

Table 4.2. **The direct impact of exchange-rate movements on domestic prices via non-commodity import prices**

	Nominal effective exchange rate variation (per cent)[1]	Impact on non-commodity import prices (in domestic currency terms) (per cent)[2]	Impact on domestic prices (percentage points)[3]
2001-08[4]			
United States	-1.6	0.3	0.0
Japan	-0.2	0.1	0.0
Euro 3[5]	1.3	-0.5	-0.1
Germany	1.4	-0.5	-0.2
France	1.2	-0.1	0.0
Italy	1.3	-0.8	-0.2
United Kingdom	-1.5	0.9	0.2
Canada	2.8	-1.8	-0.6
2006-08[4]			
United States	-1.1	0.2	0.0
Japan	3.8	-2.1	-0.2
Euro 3[5]	0.8	-0.3	-0.1
Germany	0.8	-0.3	-0.1
France	0.8	-0.1	0.0
Italy	0.8	-0.5	-0.1
United Kingdom	-3.9	2.2	0.5
Canada	-1.0	0.7	0.2

1. An increase means an appreciation of the nominal effective exchange rate. Annual average rates.
2. The estimated impact is based on the pass-through estimates for non-commodity imports shown in the figure of Box 4.1.
3. Based on the share of non-commodity imports in total demand.
4. For the rest of 2008, nominal exchange rates are those assumed in the projections for this Economic Outlook.
5. GDP weighted average of France, Germany and Italy.
Source OECD calculations.

StatLink ᵃᵍˢ⥤ http://dx.doi.org/10.1787/504033401823

potential inflationary impact of the dollar depreciation. More generally, compared with the impact of higher commodity prices, such estimates also point to limited additional inflationary pressure in other depreciating countries and disinflationary pressure in appreciating countries. A notable exception is the United Kingdom, where sterling depreciation over the past year is estimated to have added up to a full percentage point of inflation *via* its impact on non-commodity import prices alone.[7]

Assessing the overall impact of import prices on domestic inflation

Domestic costs still dominate consumer price levels

A second source of cross-country differences in inflation effects from commodity prices and exchange rate changes may come from differences in the propagation of global price shocks to domestic inflation including through indirect or second-round effects captured by inflation dynamics. Long-run relationships between consumer prices, key commodity and non-commodity import prices and domestic labour costs, derived from

7. Most of the average contribution for the United Kingdom shown in Table 4.2 for 2006-08 has in fact occurred during the past year.

Box 4.1. **Exchange rate pass-through into import prices varies across the G7 economies**

The exchange rate pass-through represents the impact of changes in the nominal exchange rate on import prices in the local currency of the destination market. The strength of the pass-through varies across countries and sectors, depending on a number of factors (Goldberg and Hellerstein, 2008):

- Incomplete pass-through may result from mark-ups and marginal production costs varying with exchange rate appreciation or depreciation.

  ❖ Mark-up fluctuations occur when the price elasticity of demand depends on the sales price and of competitors' sales prices. If the industry is competitive, exporting firms may absorb a proportion of the exchange rate change so as not to lose market share.

  ❖ Situations where marginal production costs depend on the exchange rate are: the presence of local, non-traded costs in the destination market; the use of imported inputs in the production of export goods; decreasing returns to scale, where marginal costs depend on the quantity produced.

- Nominal price stickiness due to menu costs or contract duration leads prices to respond less to current changes in the economic environment. It may also reduce pass-through if changes in the exchange rate are expected to be short-lived, so that exporters chose not to adjust sales prices in the country of destination.

Recent empirical research summarised in Goldberg and Hellerstein (2008) finds a large role for non-traded local costs in the destination country and for imported inputs in explaining incomplete pass-through of exchange rate changes to import prices. Nominal price stickiness, on the other hand, is primarily found to delay the transmission of exchange rate fluctuations into import prices.

Elasticity of total import and non-commodity import prices to exchange rate variations

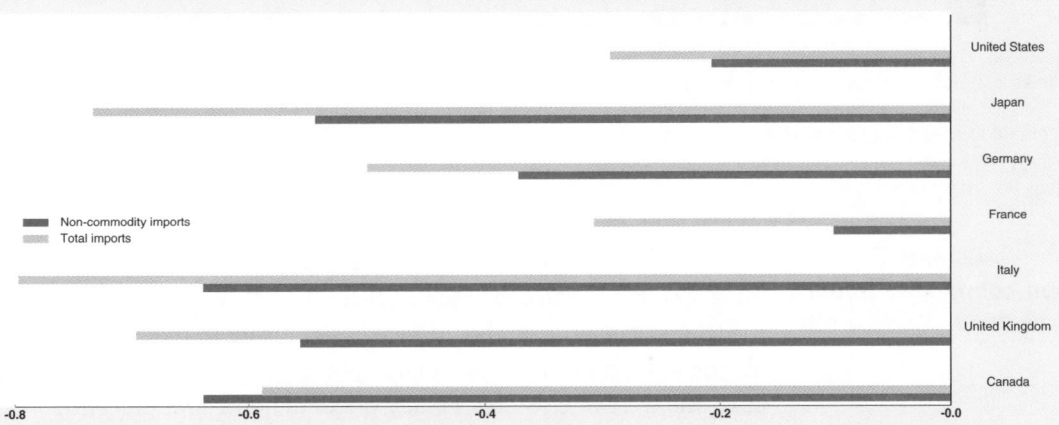

Note: The estimated pass-through measures the cumulative response of import prices in local currency in the first year after a change in the exchange rate. See Vogel *et al.* (2009) for more details.

Source: OECD estimates

StatLink ᴍˢᴾ http://dx.doi.org/10.1787/501513773068

The figure presents estimates of the pass-through in the G7 economies for total import and non-commodity import prices.[1] Overall, the rates of pass-through are generally below unity in the G7. The estimates also display substantial heterogeneity of the estimates across countries, however, with notably lower pass-through rates in France and the United States and higher ones in Canada, Italy, Japan and the United Kingdom.[2]

1. This work is based on conventional pass-through equations estimated on quarterly data for the period 1993-2007. For more details see Vogel *et al.* (2009).
2. The high pass-through for Canada is partly artificial, and due to assumptions made by the Canadian Statistical Office in the construction of import price series.

Phillips curve estimates, show that consumer price levels are still, in the long run, largely driven by the domestic cost component, with between 20% and 100% of a change in the level of unit labour costs (used as proxy for domestic non-commodity factor costs) passing through into consumer prices in the long run[8] (Figure 4.2). The euro area as a whole appears at the top of the range, with Japan and to some extent the United States and the United Kingdom at lower levels of pass-through, suggesting that risks of a wage-price feedback loop are slightly higher in the euro area.

Figure 4.2. **The long-run impact of commodities, import prices and labour costs on consumer prices**

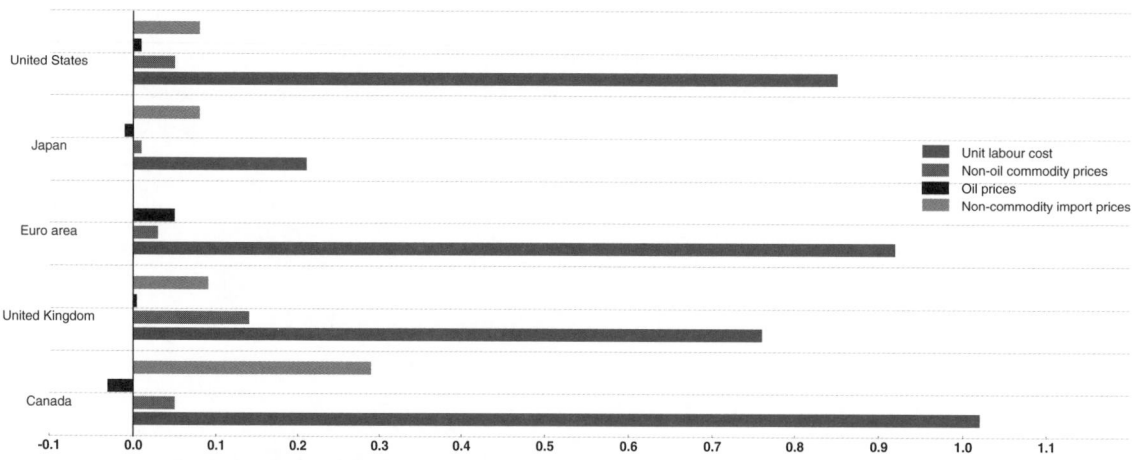

Note: These estimates correspond to the estimated long-run price responses to changes in individual factors obtained for the period 1990-2007. Thus, for example, for the United States, the long-run response elasticities of consumer prices to unit labour costs, oil, non-oil commodities and non-commodity import prices are 0.85, 0.01, 0.08 and 0.05 respectively. See the appendix for more details.
Source: OECD estimates.

StatLink http://dx.doi.org/10.1787/501425082186

Commodity and non-commodity import prices do also play a role

Non-oil commodity import prices appear to have a very significant impact on long-term consumer price levels in the United States, Canada and the United Kingdom, and only weakly significant in the euro area. Oil prices also have a significant impact on long-term consumer price levels in the euro area, and the United States. Finally, prices of non-commodity imports, which by far account for most of total imports, are found to have a robust long-run effect on consumer price levels in the United States and Canada.[9]

8. The methodology used to assess the impact of import prices on domestic price inflation in a Phillips curve framework follows Pain *et al.* (2006) and Sekine (2006). It is based on an error-correction model relating domestic prices to unit labour costs, import prices and measures of output gaps. An innovation considered here is to separately identify the relative importance of non-commodity, energy and non-energy commodity imports as distinct sources of inflationary/disinflationary pressures. See the Appendix and Vogel *et al.* (2009).
9. Estimations on the three largest euro area countries presented in Vogel *et al.* (2008) show noticeable cross-country differences within the euro area, with notably oil prices having a very significant impact on long-term consumer price level in Germany, non-oil commodity prices having a very significant impact on long-term consumer price levels in France and Italy and non-commodity import price playing a role in France only.

OECD ECONOMIC OUTLOOK 84 – ISBN 978-92-64-05469-1 – © OECD 2008

There are noticeable cross-country differences in the transmission of oil prices shocks

Cross-country differences in the long-term impact of non-oil commodity prices are limited and long-term responses to non-oil commodity prices are not statistically different between the euro area and the United States. On the other hand, in sharp contrast with priors associated with the higher oil intensity of the US economy and the possible buffer role played by higher indirect taxes in the euro area, the impact of an oil-price shock seems stronger in the euro area than in the United States. These differences in oil-price effects may not have shown up in the context of the recent run-up in oil prices because the oil price increase faced by the United States was much stronger (because of the dollar depreciation *vis-à-vis* the euro) and the speed of adjustment is slightly slower in the euro area. But to the extent these differences are real, they might be seen to justify greater caution from the European Central Bank on inflation risks from higher oil prices.

Second round effects could come from wage dynamics

Much of the inflation risk and uncertainty associated with recent commodity price shocks has been associated with potential second-round effects via wages and the possibility of a wage-price spiral, often judged to be more likely in Europe. Europe may indeed have a lower ability to absorb adverse terms-of-trade shocks because of automatic wage indexation still present in a few countries and collective bargaining institutions that may lead to real wage rigidity.[10]

Wage resistance seems to have disappeared in all regions...

However, based on various empirical estimates on wage behaviour there seems to be no compelling evidence of significant real wage resistance (*i.e.* a situation where workers resist the loss in purchasing power of their wages resulting from adverse terms-of-trade shocks) over the recent period neither in the euro area as a whole and its three largest member countries, nor in the United States and Japan. Rolling estimations show that real wage resistance, as captured by the long-run effect of commodity shocks on real wage costs, has declined noticeably after the oil price shocks of the 1970s in the United States, the euro area and Japan (Figure 4.3).[11] It increased, however, in the United States in the aftermath of the strong dollar depreciation in the second part of the 1980s.

... but could have come back as a result of the large commodity price shock

While the apparent absence of real wage resistance since the mid-1990s may be due to structural changes (associated with labour market reforms and central bank credibility), it may also reflect the absence of large adverse shocks between then and the recent past. The recent commodity price shock is of a magnitude not experienced since the two oil-price shocks. As concerns oil and commodities strong demand from

---

10. See Du Caju *et al.* (2008) for recent information on wage bargaining institutions in Europe and comparison with the United States.
11. Within the euro area, similar analysis shows that Germany appears to have experienced very little real wage resistance even in the 1970s. In contrast, France and the Italy exhibited real wage resistance in the 1970s and 1980s, but not later. Results are not reproduced here but reported in Vogel *et al.* (2009).

Figure 4.3. **The evolution of wage resistance over time**

United States

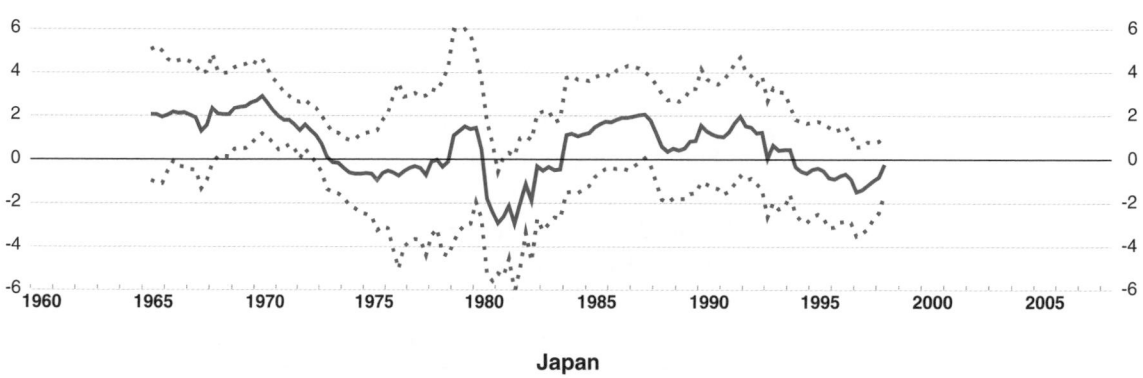

Japan

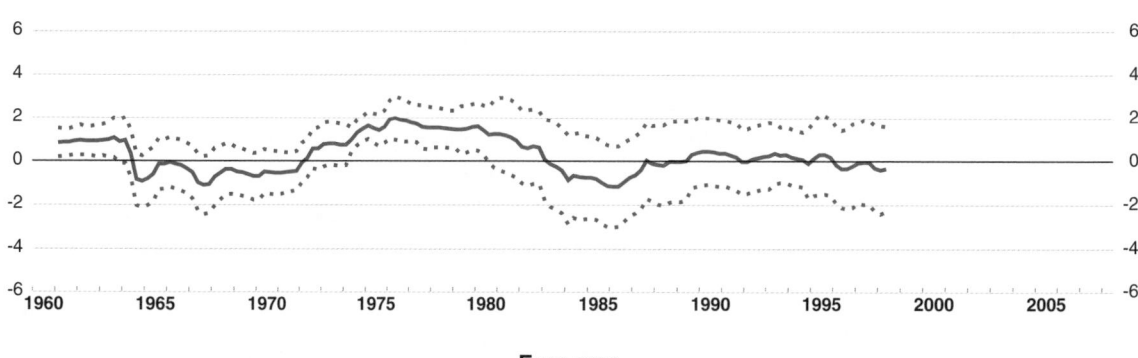

Euro area

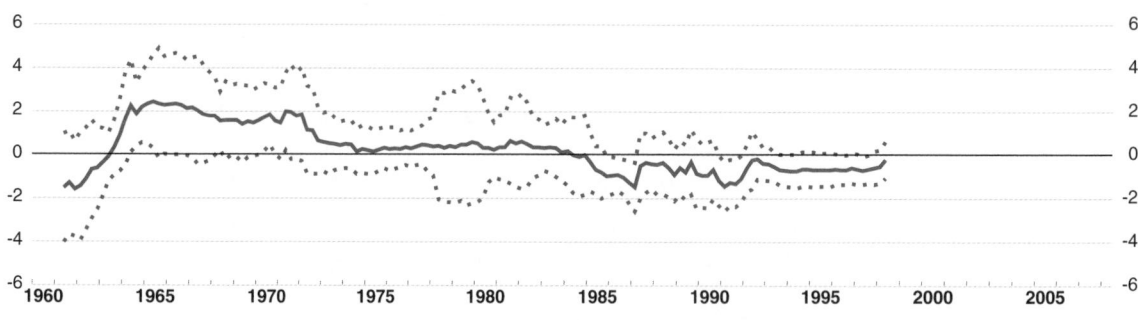

Note: Long-run effect of the wedge between consumer and output prices on real wage costs and 95% confidence interval. The dates on the horizontal axis correspond to the start of the 10-year estimation window. See appendix for more details.

Source: OECD Economic Outlook 84 database; and OECD calculations.

StatLink ⫘ http://dx.doi.org/10.1787/501500253874

emerging market countries implies that recent increases are less likely to be reversed to the extent they did in past episodes.

Different assessments of risks have contributed to policy divergence

Overall, in addition to stronger concern for activity associated with financial turmoil in the United States, an apparently stronger long-term impact of oil prices on inflation and greater concern that wages could react more than in the past decade to the increase in commodity prices are likely to have contributed to a tighter monetary stance in the euro area

OECD ECONOMIC OUTLOOK 84 – ISBN 978-92-64-05469-1 – © OECD 2008

than in the United States. However, the recent fall in commodity prices and the global slowdown in economic activity have sharply reduced inflation risks and, thereby, reasons for policy divergence.

Implications of falling commodity prices for inflation

Since they peaked at an historic high around $150 a barrel in mid-July, oil prices have more than halved and non-oil commodity prices have also declined sharply. Looking forward, these falls and especially much weaker oil prices should result in a lower commodity import prices and should bring headline inflation below core inflation in coming quarters in most OECD countries. The effect on the euro area should be less than in the United States and Japan because of the recent depreciation of the euro against the US dollar.

APPENDIX 4.A1

Supporting analytical material

This appendix describes the general methods and more detailed empirical estimates underlying the analysis of inflation responses to price shocks discussed in the main text of the chapter. It first describes the calculation of the direct impact of higher commodity prices on domestic inflation and then presents background information on price and wage inflation estimates.

Assessing the direct impact of rising commodity prices on inflation in the G7 over the recent past

Back-of-the-envelope calculations of the direct impact of commodity prices shocks...

Consistent with previous OECD work (see Pain *et al.*, 2006) the analysis of the direct impact of commodity import prices was done within a simple accounting framework, where the impact of energy, food and other commodity prices has been considered separately. The *ex ante* inflationary pressure from commodity prices is determined multiplying commodity price inflation (relative to domestic inflation) by the share of the corresponding commodity category in total demand.

... using data from various sources

The shares of the various commodities in total demand were based on the share of net imports plus domestic value added using the OECD Structural Analysis (STAN) Database.[12] The prices of energy commodities were proxied by the international (Brent) price of crude oil, and the price of food by the Hamburg Institute of International Economics (HWWA) food index. Non-food non-energy commodity import prices were computed as the import weighted average of three HWWA international prices (tropical beverages, agricultural raw materials and minerals, ores and metals). All commodity import prices were expressed in local currency terms, so that the direct measure of inflationary pressures

---

12. Data updated to 2006 were available for all countries except the United Kingdom, Canada and Japan, for which data were taken from the 2005 version of STAN stopping in 2003. For missing years, the share of energy was extrapolated on the basis of the shares of crude oil in total demand, with the shares of other commodities assumed to be stable. Given the absence of data on the value-added of energy commodities as well as metals and minerals in France, only imports were considered here.

combines the direct effect on import prices at constant exchange rates and the impact of exchange rate fluctuations.

Estimating the impact of import prices on inflation within a Phillips curve framework

A Phillips curve framework...

The methodology used to assess the impact of import prices on domestic price inflation[13] in a Phillips curve framework follows Pain *et al.* (2006) and Sekine (2006). More precisely, an error correction model relating domestic prices to unit labour costs, import prices and measures of output gaps is estimated in order to assess simultaneously the short-term dynamics and the long-run price level effects of shifts in prices both of manufactured imports and of commodity imports. Batini *et al.* (2005) show how such an empirical specification can be derived from models of staggered price setting.[14]

... including commodity import prices...

An innovation considered here is the disaggregation in non-commodity, energy and non-energy commodity imports as separate sources of inflationary/disinflationary pressure. The different effect of commodity and non-commodity import penetration on consumer price inflation has also been taken into account by interacting the long-run price coefficients with the respective share of these factors in domestic demand. The general equation specification underlying the estimates is:

$$\Delta \ln P_t = c + A(L)\Delta \ln P_{t-1} + B(L)\Delta \ln P_t^{M,oil} + C(L)\Delta \ln P_t^{M,noil} +$$
$$D(L)\Delta \ln P_t^{M,non-com} + E(L)\Delta \ln ULC_t - \lambda(\ln P_{t-1} - \alpha M_{t-1}^{SH,oil} \ln P_{t-1}^{M,oil} -$$
$$\beta M_{t-1}^{SH,noil} \ln P_{t-1}^{M,noil} - \gamma M_{t-1}^{SH,non-com} \ln P_{t-1}^{M,non-com} - \delta (1 - M_{t-1}^{SH,oil} - M_{t-1}^{SH,noil}$$
$$- M_{t-1}^{SH,non-com}) \ln ULC_{t-1}) + \xi GAP_t + \varepsilon_t \qquad [1]$$

where P represents the domestic price level measured by the private consumption expenditure deflator, $P_t^{M,oil}$ the oil import price measured in local currency, $P_t^{M,noil}$ the non-oil commodity import price in local currency, $P_t^{M,non-com}$ the non-commodity import prices, ULC the domestic unit labour costs and GAP the domestic output gap.[15] $M_{t-1}^{SH,oil}$, $M_{t-1}^{SH,noil}$ and $M_{t-1}^{SH,non-com}$ indicate the shares of oil supply, non-energy and non-

13. The literature sometimes refers to the link between import and consumer prices as *second-stage* pass-through, in distinction from the *first-stage* pass-through of foreign price and exchange rate movements to import prices measured in the currency of the destination country (Sekine, 2006).

14. Ihrig *et al.* (2007) use an identical specification to assess both the pass-through from foreign production costs to destination-currency import prices and from import prices to the aggregate CPI. Integrating import prices in a Phillips curve framework seems a richer approach, however, as it allows a more explicit testing of theoretical hypotheses and also provides additional information on the long-run relationship between import prices, domestic production costs and domestic consumer prices.

15. The foreign output gap – a trade-weighted average of foreign output gaps for each country – was also tested, but the respective coefficient has never been significantly different from zero. Inflation expectations could not be included because of limited data availability outside the United States.

commodity imports in total demand, respectively. All data come from the *Economic Outlook* database, with the exception of oil-supply data taken from the IEA *World Energy Statistics and Balances* database. A(L), B(L), C(L), D(L) and E(L) denote polynomial functions of the lag operator.

... with a focus on cross-country differences

A system of equation including the United States, Japan, the euro area, the United Kingdom and Canada has been estimated by the seemingly unrelated regression method (SUR) and following a general-to-specific approach. The estimations were done over the period 1990Q1-2007Q4 as tests for parameter stability initially carried out on estimates over a much longer period suggested changes in inflation dynamics around 1990 in several countries. The restriction of static homogeneity of degree one, which implies the mark-up of prices over costs to be independent of the price level, was found to hold for all countries but Canada and Japan, and assumed only for the United States, the euro area and the United Kingdom.[16] Corresponding estimates of the error-correction terms are reported in Table 4.3. The existence of significant long-run co-integration relationships in the error-correction model has been tested and accepted in all cases. Details on the dynamics are available in Vogel *et al.* (2009) and show that most, but not all, changes in imports prices were rightly signed and had a significant impact on short term inflation. They also show an only very weak impact of domestic output gaps on inflation.

Table 4.3. **Consumer price Phillips curves-long-run specification**

	ECM term	Non-commodity imports (-1)	Oil imports (-1)	Non-oil commodity imports (-1)	Unit labour cost (-1)	adj. R^2
United States	-0.11	-0.08	-0.01	-0.05	-0.85	0.63
	(0.00)	(0.04)	(0.13)	(0.00)		
Japan	-0.16	-0.08	0.01	-0.01	-0.21	0.46
	(0.01)	(0.21)	(0.41)	(0.58)	(0.07)	
Euro area	-0.08	0.00	-0.05	-0.03	-0.92	0.63
	(0.00)		(0.00)	(0.26)		
United Kingdom	-0.11	-0.09	0.00	-0.14	-0.76	0.63
	(0.00)	(0.28)	(0.84)	(0.00)		
Canada	-0.12	-0.29	0.03	-0.05	-1.02	0.30
	(0.00)	(0.00)	(0.29)	(0.06)	(0.00)	

Note: These estimates correspond to the estimated long-run error correction mechanism (ECM) relationships (see equation [1] in the appendix) for the period 1990-2007. P-values of a t-test on the significance of estimated coefficients are provided in brackets. For details on the dynamics part of the equation see Vogel et al. (2009).

Source: OECD estimates.

StatLink ⟶ http://dx.doi.org/10.1787/504066226760

16. Moreover, the parameter estimates for the long-run impact of non-commodity import prices in the equation for the euro area, which was clearly not significant but had counterintuitive signs, has been constrained to zero.

Real wage resistance in response to commodity price shocks

*Gauging workers'
resistance to losses in
purchasing power from
terms-of-trade shocks*

To examine the issue of how the response of real wages to commodity price shocks may have changed in the United States, the euro area, Japan and selected European countries, the following simple autoregressive distributed lag equation is estimated in a rolling ten-year window:[17]

$$\Delta ulc_t = c + \sum_{i=1}^{m} \alpha_i \Delta ulc_{t-i} + \sum_{i=0}^{n} \beta_i \Delta wedge_{t-i}$$
$$+ \sum_{i=0}^{w} \pi_i \Delta unempgap_{t-i} + \varepsilon_t \qquad [2]$$

where *ulc* is the log of the total economy unit labour cost, *wedge* is the log of the private consumption deflator to GDP deflator ratio and *unempgap* is the unemployment gap (the unemployment rate-NAIRU). The *wedge* term is inserted to capture commodity price shocks as the consumption deflator is expected to increase by a greater amount than the GDP deflator in response to an increase in commodity prices. This will drive the real consumption wage below the real production wage, potentially generating real wage resistance. If there is real wage resistance to a commodity price increase (decrease) then the initial fall (rise) in the real consumption wage will provoke a compensating increase (decrease) in nominal wages and hence real wage costs. The magnitude of this effect should be captured by the long-run elasticity:

$$\theta = \frac{\sum_{i=0}^{n} \beta_i}{1 - \sum_{i=1}^{m} \alpha_i} \qquad [3]$$

*Results are robust to
changes in methodology*

As a sensitivity check, the exercise has been repeated but with real wages (compensation per employee relative to the GDP deflator) instead of unit labour costs as the dependent variable in Equation 2 and productivity growth (contemporaneous and lagged) included as a separate regressor. The results regarding the size and significance of the wedge variable were similar. Estimating a more comprehensive wage equation does not change the main conclusions.

---

17. This equation is not a "comprehensive" wage equation, but rather specified to examine a particular feature of wage setting, *i.e.* how real wage resistance to commodity price shocks may be changing over time.

Bibliography

Batini, N., B. Jackson and S. Nickell (2005), "An Open-Economy New Keynesian Phillips Curve for the U.K", *Journal of Monetary Economics*, Vol. 52, No. 6.

Du Caju, P., E. Gautier, D. Momferatou and M. Ward-Warmedinger (2008) "Institutional features of wage bargaining in 22 EU countries, the US and Japan" presented at ECB conference Wage Dynamics in Europe: Findings from the Wage Dynamics Network.

Goldberg, P. and R. Hellerstein (2008), "A Structural Approach to Explaining Incomplete Exchange-Rate Pass-Through and Pricing-to-Market", *American Economic Review*, Vol. 98, No. 2.

Ihrig, J., S. Kamin, D. Lindner and J. Marquez (2007), "Some Simple Tests of the Globalization and Inflation Hypothesis", *Board of Governors of the Federal Reserve System International Finance Discussion Papers*, No. 891.

Pain, N., I. Koske and M. Sollie (2006), "Globalisation and Inflation in the OECD Economies", *OECD Economics Department Working Papers*, No. 524.

Sekine, T. (2006), "Time-Varying Exchange Rate Pass-Through: Experiences of Some Industrial Countries", *BIS Working Papers*, No. 202.

Sahuc, J.-G. and F. Smets (2008), "Differences in Interest Rate Policy at the ECB and the Fed: An Investigation with a Medium-Scale DSGE Model", *Journal of Money, Credit and Banking*, Vol. 40, No. 2-3.

Smets, F. and R. Wouters (2005), "Comparing Shocks and Frictions in US and Euro Area Business Cycles: A Bayesian DSGE Approach", *Journal of Applied Econometrics*, Vol. 20, No. 2.

Vogel, L., E. Rusticelli, P. Richardson, S. Guichard, C. Gianella (2009), "Inflation responses to recent shocks: do G7 countries behave differently?", *OECD Economics Department Working Papers*, forthcoming.

Special chapters in recent issues of OECD Economic Outlook

No. 82, December 2007

Corporate saving and investment: recent trends and prospects

No. 81, June 2007

Making the most of globalisation

Fiscal consolidation: lessons from pas experiences

No. 80, December 2006

Has the rise in debt made households more vulnerable?

No. 79, June 2006

Future budget pressures arising from spending on health and long-term care

No. 78, December 2006

Recent house price developments: the role of fundamentals

No. 77, June 2005

Measurign and assessing underlying inflation

No. 76, December 2004

Oil price developments: drivers, economic consequences and policy responses

Saving behaviour and the effectiveness of fiscal policy

No. 75, June 2004

Housing markets, wealth and the business cycle

The challenges of narrowing the US current account deficit

Asset price cycles, "one-off" factors and structural budget balances

Enhancing income convergence in central Europe after EU accession

No. 74, December 2003

Fiscal stance over the cycle: the role of debt, institutions, and budget constraints

Fiscal relations across levels of government

Enhancing the cost effectiveness of public spending

ISBN 978-92-64-05469-1
OECD Economic Outlook 84
© OECD 2008

STATISTICAL ANNEX

This annex contains data on some main economic series which are intended to provide a background to the recent economic developments in the OECD area described in the main body of this report. Data for 2008 to 2010 are OECD estimates and projections. The data on some of the tables have been adjusted to internationally agreed concepts and definitions in order to make them more comparable as between countries, as well as consistent with historical data shown in other OECD publications. Regional totals and sub-totals are based on those countries in the table for which data are shown. Aggregate measures contained in the Annex, except the series for the euro area (see below), are computed on the basis of 2000 GDP weights expressed in 2000 purchasing power parities (see following page for weights). Aggregate measures for external trade and payments statistics, on the other hand, are based on current year exchange rates for values and base-year exchange rates for volumes.

The OECD projection methods and underlying statistical concepts and sources are described in detail in documentation that can be downloaded from the OECD Internet site:

● *OECD Economic Outlook* Sources and Methods (*www.oecd.org/eco/sources-and-methods*).

● *OECD Economic Outlook* Database Inventory (*www.oecd.org/pdf/M00024000/M00024521.pdf*).

● "The construction of macroeconomic data series of the euro area" (*www.oecd.org/pdf/M00017000/M00017861.pdf*).

Corrigenda for the current and earlier issues, as applicable, can be found at *www.oecd.org/document/53/0,2340,en_2649_33733_37352309_1_1_1_1,00.html*.

NOTE ON NEW FORECASTING FREQUENCIES

OECD is now making quarterly projections on a seasonal and working day-adjusted basis for selected key variables. This implies that differences between adjusted and unadjusted annual data may occur, though these in general are quite small. In some countries, official forecasts of annual figures do not include working-day adjustment. Even when official forecasts do adjust for working days, the size of the adjustment may in some cases differ from that used by the OECD. The cut-off date for information used in the compilation of the projections is 14 November 2008.

Country classification

OECD	
Seven major OECD countries	Canada, France, Germany, Italy, Japan, United Kingdom and United States.
Euro area OECD countries	Austria, Belgium, Finland, France, Germany, Greece, Ireland, Italy, Luxembourg, Netherlands, Portugal and Spain.

Non-OECD	
Africa and the Middle East	Africa and the following countries (Middle East): Bahrain, Cyprus, Iran, Iraq, Jordan, Kuwait, Lebanon, Oman, Qatar, Saudi Arabia, Syrian Arab Republic, United Arab Emirates and Yemen.
Dynamic Asian Economies (DAEs)	Chinese Taipei; Hong Kong, China; Indonesia; Malaysia; the Philippines; Singapore and Thailand.
Other Asia	Non-OECD Asia and Oceania, excluding China, the DAEs and the Middle East.
Latin America	Central and South America.
Central and Eastern Europe	Albania, Bulgaria, Romania, the Newly Independent States of the former Soviet Union, and the Baltic States.

Weighting scheme for aggregate measures

Per cent

Australia	1.85	Mexico	3.58
Austria	0.84	Netherlands	1.70
Belgium	1.02	New Zealand	0.29
Canada	3.17	Norway	0.59
Czech Republic	0.56	Poland	1.47
Denmark	0.56	Portugal	0.63
Finland	0.48	Slovak Republic	0.21
France	5.57	Spain	3.11
Germany	7.73	Sweden	0.89
Greece	0.73	Switzerland	0.83
Hungary	0.45	Turkey	2.14
Iceland	0.03	United Kingdom	5.57
Ireland	0.40	United States	35.64
Italy	5.29	Total OECD	100.00
Japan	11.78	Memorandum items:	
Korea	2.81	Euro area	27.59
Luxembourg	0.08		

Note: Based on 2000 GDP and purchasing power parities (PPPs).

Irrevocable euro conversion rates

National currency unit per euro

Austria	13.7603	Ireland	0.787564
Belgium	40.3399	Italy	1 936.27
Finland	5.94573	Luxembourg	40.3399
France	6.55957	Netherlands	2.20371
Germany	1.95583	Portugal	200.482
Greece	340.750	Spain	166.386

Source: European Central Bank.

National accounts reporting systems, base-years and latest data updates

In the present edition of the OECD Economic Outlook, *the status of national accounts in the OECD countries is as follows :*

	Expenditure accounts	Household accounts	Government accounts	Use of chain weighted price indices	Benchmark/ base year
Australia	SNA93 (1959q3-2008q2)	SNA93 (1959q3-2008q2)	SNA93 (1959q3-2008q2)	NO	2005/2006
Austria	ESA95 (1996q1-2008q2)	ESA95 (1995-2007)	ESA95 (1976-2007)	YES	2000
Belgium	ESA95 (1995q1-2008q2)	ESA95 (1985-2007)	ESA95 (1985-2007)	YES	2006
Canada	SNA93 (1961q1-2008q2)	SNA93 (1961q1-2008q2)	SNA93 (1961q1-2008q2)	YES	2002
Czech Republic	SNA93 (1996q1-2008q2)	SNA93 (1995-2007)	SNA93 (1995-2007)	YES	2000
Denmark	ESA95 (1990q1-2008q2)	ESA95 (1990-2006)	ESA95 (1990-2007)	YES	2000
Finland	ESA95 (1990q1-2008q2)	ESA95 (1995-2007)	ESA95 (1975-2007)	NO	2000
France	ESA95 (1978q1-2008q2)	ESA95 (1978q1-2008q2)	ESA95 (1978-2007)	YES	2000
Germany[1]	ESA95 (1991q1-2008q2)	ESA95 (1991-2007)	ESA95 (1991-2007)	YES	2000
Greece	ESA95 (2000q1-2008q2)	..	ESA95 (2000-2007)	NO	2000
Hungary	SNA93 (2000q1-2008q2)	ESA95 (2000-2006)	SNA93 (2000-2007)	YES	2000
Iceland	SNA93 (1997q1-2008q2)	..	SNA93 (1998-2007)	YES	2000
Ireland	ESA95 (2000q1-2008q2)	ESA95 (2002-2007)	ESA95 (1990-2007)	YES	2006
Italy	ESA95 (1981q1-2008q2)	ESA95 (1990-2007)	ESA95 (1980-2007)	YES	2000
Japan	SNA93 (1994q1-2008q2)	SNA93 (1980-2006)	SNA93 (1980-2006)	YES	2000
Korea	SNA93 (1970q1-2008q3)	SNA93 (1975-2007)	SNA93 (1975-2006)	NO	2000
Luxembourg	ESA95 (1995q1-2008q2)	..	ESA95 (1990-2007)	YES	2000
Mexico	SNA93 (1978q1-2008q2)	..	..	NO	2003
Netherlands	ESA95 (1987q1-2008q2)	ESA95 (1980-2007)	ESA95 (1969-2007)	YES	2000
New Zealand	SNA93 (1987q2-2008q2)	..	SNA93 (1986-2005)	YES	1995/1996
Norway	SNA93 (1978q1-2008q2)	SNA93 (1978-2007)	SNA93 (1991-2007)	YES	2005
Poland	SNA93 (1995q1-2008q2)	SNA93 (1995-2006)	SNA93 (1999-2007)	YES	2000
Portugal	ESA95 (1995q1-2008q2)	ESA95 (2000-2007)	ESA95 (1999-2007)	NO	2000
Slovak Republic	SNA93 (1997q1-2008q2)	SNA93 (1995q1-2006q4)	SNA93 (1993-2007)	YES	2000
Spain	ESA95 (1995q1-2008q2)	ESA95 (2000-2007)	ESA95 (1995-2007)	YES	2000
Sweden	ESA95 (1993q1-2008q2)	ESA95 (1993q1-2008q2)	ESA95 (1993-2007)	YES	2000
Switzerland	SNA93 (1981q1-2008q2)	SNA93 (1990-2006)	SNA93 (1990-2006)	YES	2000
Turkey	SNA93 (1998q1-2008q2)	..	..	YES	1998
United Kingdom	ESA95 (1955q1-2008q2)	ESA95 (1987q1-2008q2)	ESA95 (1987q1-2008q2)	YES	2003
United-States	NIPA (SNA93) (1960q1-2008q3)	NIPA (SNA93) (1960q1-2008q3)	NIPA (SNA93) (1960q1-2008q2)	YES	2000

Note: SNA: System of National Accounts. ESA: European Standardised Accounts. NIPA: National Income and Product Accounts. GFS: Government Financial Statistics. The numbers in brackets indicate the starting year for the time series and the latest available historical data included in this Outlook database.
1. Data prior to 1991 refer to the new SNA93/ESA95 accounts for western Germany data.

Annex Tables

Demand and Output

Wages, Costs, Unemployment and Inflation

Key Supply-Side Data

Saving

Fiscal Balances and Public Indebtedness

OECD ECONOMIC OUTLOOK 84 – ISBN 978-92-64-05469-1 – © OECD 2008

Annex Table 1. Real GDP

Percentage change from previous year

	Average 1984-94	1995	1996	1997	1998	1999	2000	2001	2002	2003	2004	2005	2006	2007	2008	2009	2010	Fourth quarter 2008	2009	2010
Australia	3.2	3.9	4.1	3.9	5.1	4.4	3.6	2.1	4.0	3.4	3.2	3.2	2.5	4.4	2.5	1.7	2.7	1.6	2.0	3.1
Austria	2.6	2.4	2.3	2.4	3.7	3.7	3.3	0.9	1.4	0.8	2.5	3.3	3.3	3.0	1.9	-0.1	1.2	0.9	-0.1	2.0
Belgium	2.3	2.4	0.9	3.7	1.7	3.4	3.8	0.8	1.5	1.0	2.8	2.2	3.0	2.6	1.5	-0.1	1.3	0.8	-0.2	2.2
Canada	2.5	2.8	1.6	4.2	4.1	5.5	5.2	1.8	2.9	1.9	3.1	2.9	3.1	2.7	0.5	-0.5	2.1	-0.5	0.2	2.9
Czech Republic	..	5.9	4.2	-0.7	-0.8	1.3	3.7	2.5	1.9	3.6	4.5	6.3	6.8	6.6	4.4	2.5	4.4	3.4	2.6	5.2
Denmark	2.0	3.1	2.8	3.2	2.2	2.6	3.5	0.7	0.5	0.4	2.3	2.5	3.9	1.7	0.2	-0.5	0.9	0.1	-0.7	1.6
Finland	1.2	3.8	3.7	6.1	5.2	3.9	5.0	2.5	1.6	1.9	3.8	2.9	4.8	4.4	2.1	0.6	1.8	1.1	0.8	2.4
France	2.2	2.2	1.0	2.2	3.6	3.2	4.1	1.8	1.1	1.1	2.2	1.9	2.4	2.1	0.9	-0.4	1.5	-0.1	0.1	2.3
Germany	2.8	2.0	1.0	1.9	1.8	1.9	3.5	1.4	0.0	-0.2	0.7	0.9	3.2	2.6	1.4	-0.8	1.2	0.2	-0.1	1.8
Greece	1.3	2.1	2.4	3.6	3.4	3.4	4.5	4.5	3.9	5.0	4.6	3.8	4.2	4.0	3.2	1.9	2.5	2.9	1.8	3.0
Hungary	..	1.5	1.3	4.6	4.9	4.2	5.2	4.1	4.1	4.2	4.8	4.0	4.1	1.1	1.4	-0.5	1.0	1.8	-1.5	2.6
Iceland	2.0	0.1	4.8	4.9	6.3	4.1	4.3	3.9	0.1	2.4	7.7	7.5	4.4	4.9	1.5	-9.3	-0.7	-3.2	-7.9	2.6
Ireland	4.0	9.6	8.1	11.5	8.4	10.7	9.2	5.8	6.4	4.5	4.7	6.4	5.7	6.0	-1.8	-1.7	2.6	-3.1	0.3	4.0
Italy	2.2	2.9	1.0	1.9	1.3	1.4	3.9	1.7	0.5	0.0	1.4	0.7	1.9	1.4	-0.4	-1.0	0.8	-0.7	-0.5	1.5
Japan	3.5	2.0	2.7	1.6	-2.0	-0.1	2.9	0.2	0.3	1.4	2.7	1.9	2.4	2.1	0.5	-0.1	0.6	-0.4	0.3	0.9
Korea	8.5	9.2	7.0	4.7	-6.9	9.5	8.5	3.8	7.0	3.1	4.7	4.2	5.1	5.0	4.2	2.7	4.2	2.5	3.4	4.5
Luxembourg	5.8	1.4	1.6	5.9	6.5	8.4	8.4	2.6	4.1	1.6	4.5	5.2	6.5	5.2	2.4	-0.5	1.9	..	..	..
Mexico	2.5	-6.2	5.1	6.8	4.9	3.9	6.6	-0.2	0.8	1.4	4.0	3.1	4.9	3.2	1.9	0.4	1.8	0.7	0.3	2.6
Netherlands	2.8	3.1	3.4	4.3	3.9	4.7	3.9	1.9	0.1	0.3	2.2	2.0	3.4	3.5	2.2	-0.2	0.8	0.5	-0.1	1.5
New Zealand	1.6	4.3	3.3	2.9	0.8	4.7	3.8	2.4	4.7	4.4	4.3	2.7	2.5	3.0	-0.5	-0.4	1.9	-1.8	0.6	2.4
Norway	2.8	4.2	5.1	5.4	2.7	2.0	3.3	2.0	1.5	1.0	3.9	2.7	2.5	3.7	2.7	1.3	1.6	1.8	0.9	1.9
Poland	..	7.0	6.2	7.1	5.0	4.5	4.3	1.2	1.4	3.9	5.3	3.6	6.2	6.7	5.4	3.0	3.5	4.2	2.8	3.8
Portugal	3.5	4.3	3.6	4.2	4.9	3.8	3.9	2.0	0.8	-0.8	1.5	0.9	1.4	1.9	0.5	-0.2	0.6	-0.1	0.0	1.0
Slovak Republic	..	5.8	6.9	5.7	4.4	0.0	1.4	3.4	4.8	4.8	5.2	6.6	8.5	10.4	7.3	4.0	5.6	5.7	4.2	6.0
Spain	2.9	2.8	2.4	3.9	4.5	4.7	5.0	3.6	2.7	3.1	3.3	3.6	3.9	3.7	1.3	-0.9	0.8	0.0	-0.6	1.5
Sweden	1.4	4.2	1.5	2.7	3.7	4.3	4.5	1.2	2.4	2.1	3.5	3.3	4.4	2.9	0.8	0.0	2.2	-0.1	0.5	3.1
Switzerland	1.8	0.4	0.6	2.1	2.6	1.3	3.6	1.2	0.4	-0.2	2.5	2.5	3.4	3.3	1.9	-0.2	1.6	0.6	0.1	2.2
Turkey	4.1	7.2	7.0	7.5	3.1	-3.4	6.8	-5.7	6.2	5.3	9.4	8.4	6.9	4.6	3.3	1.6	4.2	-0.7	..	..
United Kingdom	2.5	3.0	2.9	3.3	3.6	3.5	3.9	2.5	2.1	2.8	2.8	2.1	2.8	3.0	0.8	-1.1	0.9	0.5	-0.5	1.7
United States	3.0	2.5	3.7	4.5	4.2	4.4	3.7	0.8	1.6	2.5	3.6	2.9	2.8	2.0	1.4	-0.9	1.6	0.1	-0.3	2.3
Euro area	2.5	2.5	1.5	2.6	2.7	2.8	4.0	1.9	0.9	0.8	1.9	1.8	3.0	2.6	1.0	-0.6	1.2	0.0	-0.1	1.9
Total OECD	3.0	2.6	3.1	3.7	2.7	3.3	4.0	1.1	1.6	1.9	3.2	2.7	3.1	2.6	1.4	-0.4	1.5	0.2	0.2	2.2

Note: The adoption of new National Accounts systems, SNA93 or ESA95, has been proceeding at an uneven pace among OECD member countries, both with respect to variables and the time period covered. As a consequence, there are breaks in many national series. Moreover, most countries are using chain-weighted price indices to calculate real GDP and expenditures components. See Table "National Accounts Reporting Systems and Base-years" at the beginning of the Statistical Annex and *OECD Economic Outlook* Sources and Methods (*http://www.oecd.org/eco/sources-and-methods*). These numbers are working-day adjusted and hence may differ from the basis used for official projections.

Source: OECD Economic Outlook 84 database.

StatLink http://dx.doi.org/10.1787/504066715648

Annex Table 2. Nominal GDP
Percentage change from previous year

	Average 1984-94	1995	1996	1997	1998	1999	2000	2001	2002	2003	2004	2005	2006	2007	2008	2009	2010	Fourth quarter 2008	2009	2010
Australia	8.0	5.6	6.3	5.4	5.4	4.9	8.0	6.1	7.1	6.3	7.5	7.5	7.5	8.1	8.4	3.8	5.0	7.5	3.4	5.5
Austria	5.6	4.3	3.3	2.1	3.8	3.9	4.8	2.5	2.8	2.1	4.1	5.1	5.3	5.3	4.5	1.6	2.3	3.5	1.2	3.0
Belgium	5.5	3.6	1.4	4.8	3.8	3.7	5.7	2.8	3.4	2.7	5.2	4.7	5.3	5.0	3.5	2.2	3.2	3.4	1.9	4.0
Canada	5.5	5.1	3.3	5.5	3.7	7.4	9.6	2.9	4.0	5.2	6.4	6.3	5.7	5.9	3.8	-1.5	3.1	0.5	0.8	4.2
Czech Republic	..	16.8	14.8	7.6	10.2	4.2	5.3	7.4	4.8	4.6	9.2	6.0	7.8	10.4	6.9	4.9	6.2	6.0	4.2	7.4
Denmark	5.0	4.4	4.9	5.3	3.4	4.3	6.6	3.2	2.8	2.0	4.7	5.6	6.0	3.3	3.6	1.9	3.1	2.7	1.9	3.5
Finland	5.3	9.1	3.6	7.9	9.1	4.8	7.7	5.5	2.9	1.5	4.6	3.1	6.4	7.3	5.4	3.9	3.9	4.2	3.8	4.2
France	5.2	3.6	2.7	3.2	4.5	3.2	5.5	3.8	3.5	3.0	3.8	4.0	4.9	4.6	3.2	1.3	2.7	2.0	1.6	3.3
Germany	5.7	3.9	1.5	2.2	2.4	2.2	2.8	2.6	1.4	0.9	1.7	1.6	3.7	4.5	3.0	1.0	2.5	2.4	1.2	3.2
Greece	18.0	12.1	9.9	10.7	8.8	6.5	8.0	7.3	7.7	8.7	8.2	7.2	7.8	7.0	6.8	5.8	6.1	6.9	5.8	6.2
Hungary	..	28.6	22.8	23.9	18.1	12.9	15.6	12.9	12.3	10.3	9.4	6.3	8.1	6.9	7.4	3.0	3.8	7.3	1.5	5.1
Iceland	17.3	3.1	7.4	8.0	11.8	7.5	8.1	12.9	5.8	3.0	10.4	10.5	13.8	10.7	11.0	4.5	6.0	10.0	3.1	7.8
Ireland	7.5	13.0	10.6	15.8	15.6	15.1	15.9	11.6	11.3	7.1	6.9	8.8	8.9	7.5	-2.7	-1.0	3.0	-2.9	0.7	4.1
Italy	8.7	8.0	5.8	4.6	3.9	3.2	5.9	4.8	3.7	3.2	4.0	2.8	3.7	3.7	3.5	1.5	2.0	4.4	0.6	2.8
Japan	4.9	1.4	2.2	2.2	-2.0	-1.4	1.1	-1.0	-1.3	-0.2	1.6	0.7	1.4	1.3	-0.5	1.1	0.3	0.5	0.2	0.6
Korea	16.3	17.2	12.5	9.5	-1.4	9.4	9.3	7.5	10.0	5.9	7.5	4.0	4.6	6.3	7.9	5.5	4.4	8.6	3.9	4.5
Luxembourg	8.7	3.8	4.5	4.2	6.9	13.4	9.7	3.7	5.6	7.6	7.5	9.4	11.9	7.0	3.9	1.9	3.6	..	..	..
Mexico	46.6	29.3	37.5	25.7	21.1	19.6	19.5	5.7	7.8	10.0	13.4	7.7	12.1	8.1	8.9	5.0	5.3	6.4	4.3	5.7
Netherlands	4.3	5.2	4.7	7.0	5.9	6.5	8.2	7.1	3.9	2.5	3.0	4.5	5.2	5.0	4.0	1.4	2.3	2.4	1.5	3.0
New Zealand	8.2	6.6	5.9	3.5	1.5	5.1	6.5	6.8	5.9	5.9	8.2	4.6	4.9	7.4	3.0	1.3	4.4	-0.7	3.2	4.7
Norway	5.8	7.4	9.5	8.3	1.9	8.8	19.4	3.8	-0.3	4.0	9.4	11.6	11.1	5.3	9.1	-3.5	4.2	-2.3	3.8	3.4
Poland	..	36.9	25.3	22.0	16.6	10.8	11.8	4.7	3.7	4.3	9.7	6.4	7.8	10.9	9.0	6.8	7.1	8.1	6.5	7.4
Portugal	16.2	7.9	6.3	8.2	8.8	7.2	7.1	5.8	4.7	2.3	4.0	3.5	4.2	4.9	2.8	2.1	2.3	2.0	1.8	2.8
Slovak Republic	..	16.3	11.3	10.9	9.7	7.4	10.9	8.6	8.8	10.3	11.4	9.1	11.7	11.6	12.6	7.6	8.4	12.3	6.1	9.0
Spain	9.9	7.8	6.0	6.3	7.1	7.5	8.7	8.0	7.1	7.4	7.4	8.1	8.1	7.0	4.8	1.6	1.8	3.2	1.5	2.2
Sweden	7.1	7.8	2.3	4.0	4.4	5.6	5.9	3.4	4.1	3.9	4.4	4.2	6.0	5.9	4.5	2.5	3.8	4.2	1.5	3.8
Switzerland	4.8	1.1	0.8	1.9	2.9	1.9	4.8	2.0	0.9	0.8	3.1	2.6	5.2	5.2	4.7	1.8	2.9	3.5	1.8	3.4
Turkey	67.7	100.7	90.3	95.2	81.1	49.0	59.3	44.1	45.9	29.8	22.9	16.1	16.9	12.6	16.4	10.8	12.7	..	..	..
United Kingdom	7.7	5.8	6.6	6.2	5.9	5.6	5.1	4.6	5.3	6.0	5.3	4.3	5.5	6.0	4.1	1.3	2.3	2.9	1.4	3.1
United States	6.0	4.6	5.7	6.2	5.3	6.0	5.9	3.2	3.4	4.7	6.6	6.3	6.1	4.8	3.6	0.9	3.1	2.4	1.3	3.8
Euro area	6.8	5.3	3.4	4.1	4.3	3.9	5.4	4.4	3.5	3.0	3.8	3.8	5.0	4.9	3.5	1.5	2.5	2.9	1.4	3.2
Total OECD	9.8	8.5	8.0	8.0	6.3	6.1	7.2	4.4	4.3	4.5	5.8	5.0	5.7	5.1	4.0	1.7	3.0	3.1	1.8	3.6

Note: The adoption of new National Accounts systems, SNA93 or ESA95, has been proceeding at an uneven pace among OECD member countries, both with respect to variables and the time period covered. As a consequence, there are breaks in many national series. See Table "National Accounts Reporting Systems and Base-years" at the beginning of the Statistical Annex and *OECD Economic Outlook* Sources and Methods (http://www.oecd.org/eco/sources-and-methods). Working-day adjusted -- see note to Table on Real GDP.

Source: OECD Economic Outlook 84 database.

StatLink ⟹ http://dx.doi.org/10.1787/504105754573

Annex Table 3. Real private consumption expenditure
Percentage change from previous year

	Average 1984-94	1995	1996	1997	1998	1999	2000	2001	2002	2003	2004	2005	2006	2007	2008	2009	2010	Fourth quarter 2008	2009	2010
Australia	2.7	4.8	2.8	3.7	4.4	5.2	3.9	2.9	3.8	3.6	5.9	3.0	3.1	4.5	2.4	1.7	2.7	1.2	2.1	3.1
Austria	2.9	0.9	2.9	0.0	2.0	1.9	2.7	0.3	1.6	1.2	2.0	2.6	2.5	0.9	0.9	0.2	1.2	0.7	0.4	1.7
Belgium	2.1	0.9	1.1	2.1	2.7	2.1	3.7	1.1	0.6	0.9	1.1	1.5	2.1	2.0	0.9	0.4	1.4	0.6	0.6	1.9
Canada	2.6	2.1	2.6	4.6	2.8	3.8	4.0	2.3	3.6	3.0	3.3	3.7	4.3	4.5	3.4	-0.6	1.8	0.7	0.1	2.6
Czech Republic	..	5.9	8.9	2.2	-0.8	2.6	1.4	2.1	2.2	6.0	2.9	2.5	5.5	5.9	3.3	3.3	4.1	3.9	3.2	4.7
Denmark	1.8	1.6	2.2	3.0	2.3	-0.4	0.2	0.1	1.5	1.0	4.7	5.2	3.8	2.3	1.5	0.3	0.8	-0.3	0.2	1.1
Finland	1.2	4.0	3.9	3.0	4.3	3.1	2.2	2.8	2.3	4.7	2.8	3.7	4.2	3.2	3.3	1.9	1.8	3.1	1.7	2.0
France	2.0	1.8	1.7	0.4	3.9	3.5	3.6	2.6	2.3	2.0	2.4	2.5	2.5	2.4	0.9	0.3	1.8	0.0	0.6	2.7
Germany	2.9	2.3	1.3	0.9	1.4	2.9	2.5	1.9	-0.8	0.1	-0.2	0.2	1.2	-0.3	-0.6	0.2	1.2	-0.9	0.5	1.7
Greece	2.3	2.6	2.4	2.7	3.5	2.5	2.2	4.5	4.2	5.0	4.7	4.2	4.2	3.2	2.4	2.3	2.6	..	..	..
Hungary	..	-7.1	-3.5	1.9	4.9	5.6	3.6	6.2	10.6	8.3	2.7	3.4	1.7	0.6	1.2	-0.3	0.5	1.1	-0.7	1.6
Iceland	1.2	2.2	5.7	6.3	10.2	7.9	4.2	-2.8	-1.5	6.1	7.0	12.9	4.4	4.3	-4.7	-16.8	-4.2	-13.6	-14.7	1.7
Ireland	3.4	3.4	6.8	7.8	7.5	8.9	9.6	4.9	3.9	2.9	3.7	7.2	7.0	6.0	-0.5	0.4	1.6	-2.3	1.0	2.3
Italy	2.3	1.5	1.0	3.2	3.5	2.6	2.3	0.7	0.2	1.0	0.8	0.9	1.1	1.5	-0.5	-0.3	0.8	-0.6	0.0	1.3
Japan	3.5	1.9	2.5	0.7	-0.9	1.0	0.7	1.6	1.1	0.4	1.6	1.3	2.0	1.5	0.7	0.6	0.7	0.4	0.6	1.3
Korea	8.0	9.9	6.7	3.3	-13.4	11.5	8.4	4.9	7.9	-1.2	-0.3	3.6	4.5	4.5	1.7	-1.1	0.4	0.0	-1.0	0.9
Luxembourg	3.5	1.9	2.9	3.9	5.6	3.5	5.3	3.3	5.8	-5.3	2.5	2.0	3.0	2.0	2.5	1.2	1.7	..	..	..
Mexico	3.1	-9.5	2.2	6.5	5.5	4.3	8.2	2.5	1.6	2.3	5.6	4.8	5.6	4.2	2.7	0.9	2.6	1.6	1.1	3.5
Netherlands	2.0	2.7	4.3	3.5	5.1	5.3	3.7	1.8	0.9	-0.2	1.0	1.0	0.0	2.1	1.9	0.0	0.4	0.8	-0.1	0.9
New Zealand	1.8	4.5	4.9	2.5	2.7	3.6	1.8	2.0	4.5	5.9	5.8	4.9	2.7	4.1	0.0	-0.7	0.7	-1.2	-0.2	1.1
Norway	2.1	3.6	6.3	3.1	2.8	3.7	4.2	2.1	3.1	2.8	5.6	4.0	4.7	6.4	2.4	1.8	1.6	2.0	1.1	2.0
Poland	..	3.7	8.8	7.2	5.0	5.7	3.1	2.2	3.4	2.1	4.7	2.1	5.0	5.0	4.9	3.9	4.1	5.0	3.8	4.3
Portugal	3.9	0.6	3.2	3.7	5.0	5.3	3.7	1.3	1.3	-0.1	2.5	2.0	1.9	1.6	1.2	-0.2	0.6	0.4	0.0	0.9
Slovak Republic	..	5.4	9.3	7.3	6.6	0.3	2.3	5.4	5.5	1.7	4.6	6.5	5.6	7.1	6.2	3.8	5.1	5.1	4.3	5.2
Spain	2.9	1.7	2.3	3.2	4.8	5.3	5.0	3.4	2.8	2.9	4.2	4.2	3.9	3.5	1.2	-0.4	0.2	0.2	-0.4	0.4
Sweden	1.5	1.0	1.7	2.6	3.0	4.1	5.1	0.4	2.6	2.0	2.6	2.7	2.5	3.0	1.9	0.7	2.5	1.3	0.9	3.3
Switzerland	1.7	0.6	1.1	1.4	2.2	2.3	2.4	2.3	0.1	0.9	1.6	1.8	1.6	2.1	2.0	1.2	1.3	1.8	0.8	1.7
Turkey	2.6	4.8	8.5	8.4	0.6	0.1	5.9	-6.6	4.7	10.2	11.0	7.9	4.6	4.1	3.2	1.1	3.9	..	..	..
United Kingdom	3.2	1.9	3.9	3.8	4.3	5.2	4.7	3.1	3.5	2.9	2.9	1.9	2.1	3.0	1.8	-1.0	0.7	0.0	-0.7	1.6
United States	3.2	2.7	3.4	3.8	5.0	5.1	4.7	2.5	2.7	2.8	3.6	3.0	3.0	2.8	0.4	-1.2	1.2	-1.0	0.0	1.6
Euro area	2.5	2.0	1.7	1.8	3.1	3.3	3.1	2.0	0.9	1.2	1.5	1.8	2.0	1.6	0.4	0.2	1.2	-0.1	0.4	1.7
Total OECD	3.1	2.1	3.1	3.1	3.0	4.1	3.9	2.2	2.3	2.1	2.9	2.6	2.8	2.8	1.0	-0.2	1.3	-0.1	0.3	1.9

Note: The adoption of new National Accounts systems, SNA93 or ESA95, has been proceeding at an uneven pace among OECD member countries, both with respect to variables and the time period covered. As a consequence, there are breaks in many national series. Moreover, most countries are using chain-weighted price indices to calculate real GDP and expenditures components. See Table "National Accounts Reporting Systems and Base-years" at the beginning of the Statistical Annex and *OECD Economic Outlook Sources and Methods (http://www.oecd.org/eco/sources-and-methods).* Working-day adjusted -- see note to Table on Real GDP.

Source: OECD Economic Outlook 84 database.

StatLink ᵐˢᵖ *http://dx.doi.org/10.1787/504120236168*

Annex Table 4. Real public consumption expenditure
Percentage change from previous year

	Average 1984-94	1995	1996	1997	1998	1999	2000	2001	2002	2003	2004	2005	2006	2007	2008	2009	2010	Fourth quarter 2008	2009	2010
Australia	3.0	4.1	3.2	3.0	3.2	3.2	4.4	1.7	3.0	3.7	3.9	3.0	3.2	2.4	3.7	2.4	2.2	2.9	2.2	2.2
Austria	1.9	2.9	2.0	3.5	3.1	3.4	0.2	-0.6	0.7	1.0	1.1	1.5	2.2	1.9	1.7	0.9	0.7	0.9	0.2	1.0
Belgium	1.3	1.5	1.6	0.4	0.9	3.3	2.9	2.4	2.9	2.1	1.8	0.4	0.1	2.3	2.5	1.8	1.5	3.0	0.8	2.0
Canada	2.1	-0.6	-1.2	-1.0	3.2	2.1	3.1	3.9	2.5	3.1	2.0	1.5	3.8	3.7	4.3	2.4	2.0	3.3	2.0	2.0
Czech Republic	..	-4.3	1.5	3.0	-1.6	3.7	0.7	3.6	6.7	7.1	-3.5	2.9	-0.7	0.5	1.2	1.2	0.8	0.1	1.0	0.7
Denmark	1.3	2.4	3.6	0.7	3.5	2.4	2.3	2.2	2.1	0.7	1.8	0.9	2.0	1.6	0.9	1.5	1.0	1.0	0.8	1.0
Finland	1.3	2.2	2.7	1.7	1.7	1.6	0.8	0.6	2.3	1.6	2.6	1.6	0.7	1.2	1.5	1.4	1.1	2.2	0.9	1.2
France	2.7	0.0	2.0	1.2	-0.6	1.4	2.0	1.1	1.9	2.0	2.2	1.3	1.4	1.4	1.4	0.8	0.7	1.5	0.4	1.0
Germany	1.6	1.9	2.1	0.5	1.8	1.2	1.4	0.5	1.5	0.4	-0.7	0.4	0.6	2.2	1.9	1.0	1.3	2.0	1.1	1.2
Greece	0.0	5.6	0.9	3.0	1.7	2.1	14.8	0.4	7.3	-1.0	2.7	1.4	-0.7	10.3	2.9	1.9	1.5	..	..	..
Hungary	..	-5.7	-2.4	3.1	1.7	1.5	-2.0	2.1	5.8	5.3	1.8	2.4	4.3	-7.4	-1.0	-0.1	0.0	-2.3	-4.5	2.7
Iceland	4.1	1.7	1.0	2.6	4.2	4.4	3.8	4.6	5.3	1.8	2.2	3.5	4.0	4.2	4.0	2.7	2.1	3.7	2.0	2.0
Ireland	0.8	3.9	3.1	5.5	5.6	5.8	9.2	10.4	7.0	1.8	2.3	3.1	5.3	6.8	3.9	2.3	1.5	4.4	1.2	1.8
Italy	1.6	-3.3	0.8	0.5	0.4	1.4	2.2	3.9	2.4	1.9	2.2	1.9	0.8	1.2	1.2	0.2	0.1	1.3	-0.3	0.2
Japan	3.1	3.9	2.9	0.8	1.8	4.2	4.3	3.0	2.4	2.3	1.9	1.6	-0.4	0.7	0.3	1.4	1.7	-0.2	2.0	1.4
Korea	7.1	5.0	8.0	2.6	2.3	2.9	1.6	4.9	6.0	3.8	3.7	5.0	6.2	5.8	3.8	3.8	3.7	3.0	4.0	3.5
Luxembourg	5.0	4.7	6.0	3.6	1.5	8.2	4.7	6.4	4.6	4.1	4.1	3.8	2.8	2.6	1.2	3.7	2.1	1.2	4.4	0.2
Mexico	1.8	-1.8	-0.2	2.6	2.5	4.5	2.6	-2.4	-0.2	1.0	-2.8	3.5	0.3	1.0	4.1	8.2	0.9	8.2	4.4	0.2
Netherlands	2.9	2.5	-0.7	2.5	2.5	2.8	2.0	4.6	3.3	2.9	-0.1	0.5	9.0	3.0	0.7	2.0	1.7	1.2	2.0	1.5
New Zealand	1.3	4.5	2.0	6.2	-0.3	6.8	-2.4	4.1	1.4	3.4	5.6	4.1	4.7	3.6	4.2	4.0	4.0	4.1	4.1	4.0
Norway	3.1	0.6	2.7	3.3	3.4	3.1	1.9	4.6	3.1	1.7	1.5	0.7	2.9	3.6	3.5	3.6	3.2	3.2	3.7	3.0
Poland	..	4.8	2.2	3.1	1.9	2.5	2.1	2.7	1.4	4.9	3.1	5.2	6.1	3.7	0.1	1.8	2.0	0.0	2.0	2.0
Portugal	4.9	1.0	3.8	2.0	6.2	4.1	3.5	3.3	2.6	0.2	2.6	3.2	-1.4	0.0	-0.2	0.2	0.5	-0.9	0.9	0.4
Slovak Republic	..	3.6	11.1	0.2	5.9	-7.4	4.7	5.4	4.0	4.2	-2.0	3.5	10.1	0.7	5.5	3.5	2.5	5.2	2.6	2.5
Spain	4.9	2.4	1.3	2.5	3.5	4.0	5.3	3.9	4.5	4.8	6.3	5.5	4.6	4.9	3.6	3.4	3.1	3.5	3.2	3.0
Sweden	1.6	-0.4	0.7	-0.8	3.4	1.7	-1.2	0.8	2.2	0.4	-0.2	0.4	1.5	1.1	0.6	1.0	0.5	0.4	1.4	0.0
Switzerland	3.2	0.2	1.6	0.4	-1.1	0.5	2.3	4.5	1.2	1.9	0.8	1.0	-0.9	-1.1	-0.8	0.9	1.1	1.4	1.0	1.2
Turkey	4.9	6.8	8.6	4.1	7.8	4.0	5.7	-1.1	5.8	-2.6	6.0	2.5	8.4	6.5	4.2	2.8	2.7	..	..	..
United Kingdom	0.8	1.3	0.7	-0.5	1.1	3.6	3.1	2.4	3.4	3.5	3.4	1.7	1.6	1.8	2.3	2.3	2.2	2.8	2.0	2.5
United States	2.1	0.2	0.4	1.8	1.6	3.1	1.7	3.1	4.3	2.5	1.5	0.3	1.6	1.9	2.8	2.3	1.4	3.4	1.5	1.5
Euro area	2.2	0.8	1.7	1.2	1.2	1.9	2.4	2.0	2.4	1.7	1.6	1.5	1.9	2.3	1.8	1.2	1.2	1.9	0.9	1.3
Total OECD	2.4	1.2	1.5	1.4	1.8	2.9	2.5	2.5	3.2	2.3	1.7	1.4	1.9	2.1	2.3	2.1	1.5	2.7	1.6	1.6

Note: The adoption of new National Accounts systems, SNA93 or ESA95, has been proceeding at an uneven pace among OECD member countries, both with respect to variables and the time period covered. As a consequence, there are breaks in many national series. Moreover, most countries are using chain-weighted price indices to calculate real GDP and expenditures components. See Table "National Accounts Reporting Systems and Base-years" at the beginning of the Statistical Annex and *OECD Economic Outlook Sources and Methods* (*http://www.oecd.org/eco/sources-and-methods*). Working-day adjusted -- see note to Table on Real GDP.

Source: OECD Economic Outlook 84 database.

StatLink ⟶ http://dx.doi.org/10.1787/504144574321

Annex Table 5. Real total gross fixed capital formation
Percentage change from previous year

	Average 1984-94	1995	1996	1997	1998	1999	2000	2001	2002	2003	2004	2005	2006	2007	2008	2009	2010	Fourth quarter 2008	2009	2010
Australia	3.2	3.0	6.1	10.7	5.6	5.7	1.6	-4.8	17.0	9.4	6.9	8.9	4.7	9.4	7.2	2.0	3.2	5.9	1.7	3.9
Austria	4.1	0.6	1.6	0.8	2.4	2.4	3.6	-1.1	-2.9	2.2	2.0	2.5	2.8	3.9	1.9	-3.1	1.0	0.1	-2.8	2.3
Belgium	4.2	4.2	0.5	7.5	3.4	4.2	4.2	0.2	-2.2	-0.6	6.8	7.3	4.8	6.1	4.9	0.1	3.0	1.9	0.7	4.7
Canada	3.1	-2.1	4.4	15.2	2.4	7.3	4.7	4.0	1.6	6.2	7.8	9.2	7.1	3.9	1.0	-2.8	1.3	-1.8	-1.8	2.7
Czech Republic	..	19.8	7.6	-5.7	-0.9	-3.3	5.1	6.6	5.1	0.4	3.9	1.8	6.5	5.8	4.1	5.0	5.3	2.4	4.7	5.7
Denmark	2.9	11.9	5.8	10.3	8.1	-0.1	7.6	-1.4	0.1	-0.2	3.9	6.2	14.0	5.9	0.6	-4.3	-2.1	-0.8	-5.5	-0.2
Finland	-3.0	13.1	6.2	13.5	11.3	2.9	5.9	4.1	-3.1	4.0	3.6	3.6	4.8	8.4	0.0	-1.9	1.7	-4.4	-1.1	3.3
France	2.4	2.1	0.6	0.3	7.2	8.1	7.5	2.3	-1.6	2.2	3.3	4.5	5.0	4.9	0.3	-3.6	2.1	-3.0	-1.6	3.4
Germany	3.6	0.1	-0.5	0.8	3.6	4.4	3.7	-3.4	-6.2	-0.3	-1.3	1.3	8.5	4.5	3.6	-2.8	1.2	0.6	-1.7	2.3
Greece	1.0	4.1	8.4	6.8	10.6	11.0	8.0	4.8	9.5	13.2	1.9	-0.5	9.2	4.9	-0.5	1.0	2.7	..	..	..
Hungary	..	-4.3	6.8	9.2	13.2	5.9	7.7	5.2	9.8	2.2	7.9	8.5	-6.2	1.5	-0.6	-0.7	1.4	1.0	-2.3	2.6
Iceland	-0.8	-1.7	25.0	9.3	34.4	-4.1	11.8	-4.3	-14.0	11.1	28.1	35.7	20.4	-13.7	-22.1	-36.7	-9.4	-29.0	-30.9	0.1
Ireland	1.4	15.8	15.9	17.4	14.3	14.4	6.3	0.1	8.6	4.6	6.3	12.3	3.8	1.3	-22.7	-23.8	-2.6	-31.2	-11.3	0.7
Italy	1.2	7.3	1.8	1.9	3.6	3.7	7.1	2.4	3.7	-0.9	1.6	1.2	2.7	0.8	-1.4	-4.6	2.1	-4.2	-2.3	4.7
Japan	4.4	0.9	4.6	-0.3	-7.2	-0.8	1.2	-0.9	-4.9	-0.5	1.4	3.1	1.3	-0.6	-2.4	-0.1	1.4	-1.3	0.6	1.9
Korea	12.3	13.1	8.4	-2.3	-22.9	8.3	12.2	-0.2	6.6	4.0	2.1	2.4	3.6	4.0	0.6	0.2	1.1	0.0	-0.2	2.1
Luxembourg	7.9	-1.5	6.3	8.6	9.0	17.9	-2.2	8.1	4.8	7.6	-0.5	3.0	2.9	10.1	-3.1	-0.3	2.3	..	..	..
Mexico	4.7	-29.0	16.3	21.1	10.5	7.7	11.4	-5.6	-0.7	0.4	8.0	6.4	9.7	5.6	4.9	1.7	2.1	3.9	1.6	2.7
Netherlands	2.9	5.9	8.5	8.5	6.8	8.7	0.6	0.2	-4.5	-1.5	-1.6	3.7	7.5	4.9	6.3	-1.5	1.2	4.1	-0.3	2.1
New Zealand	1.3	12.4	7.2	1.2	-3.4	6.8	8.4	-1.1	10.8	10.2	13.3	3.6	-1.5	4.7	-0.8	-13.1	3.2	-9.1	-7.9	6.9
Norway	-0.9	3.9	10.2	15.8	13.6	-5.4	-3.5	-1.1	6.6	0.2	10.2	13.3	7.3	9.3	3.5	-2.4	1.1	-4.6	-1.6	2.5
Poland	..	16.6	19.7	21.8	14.0	6.6	2.7	-9.7	-6.3	-0.1	6.4	6.5	14.9	17.3	13.6	4.0	3.2	10.6	2.1	4.1
Portugal	5.4	6.6	5.6	14.3	11.7	6.2	3.5	1.0	-3.5	-7.4	0.2	-0.9	-0.7	3.1	0.7	-1.2	0.5	-2.6	-0.7	1.4
Slovak Republic	..	0.6	30.1	14.0	9.4	-15.7	-9.6	12.9	0.2	-2.7	4.8	17.6	8.4	7.9	6.7	3.8	6.6	4.9	4.7	7.1
Spain	4.9	7.7	2.6	5.0	11.3	10.4	6.6	4.8	3.4	5.9	5.1	7.0	7.1	5.3	-2.0	-9.2	-2.7	-6.7	-7.5	-0.5
Sweden	0.3	10.0	4.7	-0.1	8.1	8.5	6.3	-0.5	-1.8	1.4	5.7	8.9	7.7	8.0	3.0	-2.7	2.0	0.0	-1.6	3.8
Switzerland	2.3	4.8	-1.7	2.1	6.4	1.5	4.2	-3.5	-0.5	-1.2	4.5	3.8	4.7	5.4	-0.7	-3.2	2.4	-2.3	-1.4	3.7
Turkey	8.8	9.1	14.1	14.8	-3.9	-16.2	17.5	-30.0	14.7	14.2	28.4	17.4	13.3	5.5	3.7	2.7	6.8	-12.1	..	..
United Kingdom	2.8	2.9	5.4	6.8	13.7	3.0	2.7	2.6	3.6	1.1	4.9	2.2	6.0	7.1	-5.3	-9.0	0.5	-5.3	-4.4	2.3
United States	2.9	5.7	8.1	8.0	9.1	8.2	6.1	-1.7	-3.5	3.2	6.1	5.8	2.0	-2.0	-3.1	-7.3	1.4	-5.3	-5.5	4.9
Euro area	2.9	3.1	1.4	2.8	5.7	6.1	5.3	0.6	-1.3	1.2	1.8	3.4	5.8	4.1	0.4	-4.4	1.0	-2.9	-2.7	2.6
Total OECD	3.5	3.3	6.1	6.2	4.9	5.3	5.4	-1.4	-1.1	2.3	4.8	5.0	4.3	2.0	-0.9	-4.3	1.5	-3.2	-2.9	3.6

Note: The adoption of new National Accounts systems, SNA93 or ESA95, has been proceeding at an uneven pace among OECD member countries, both with respect to variables and the time period covered. As a consequence, there are breaks in many national series. Moreover, most countries are using chain-weighted price indices to calculate real GDP and expenditures components. See Table "National Accounts Reporting Systems and Base-years" at the beginning of the Statistical Annex and *OECD Economic Outlook Sources and Methods (http://www.oecd.org/eco/sources-and-methods).* Working-day adjusted -- see note to Table on Real GDP.

Source: OECD Economic Outlook 84 database.

StatLink ⟨⟩ http://dx.doi.org/10.1787/504146357417

Annex Table 6. Real gross private non-residential fixed capital formation
Percentage change from previous year

	Average 1984-94	1995	1996	1997	1998	1999	2000	2001	2002	2003	2004	2005	2006	2007	2008	2009	2010	Fourth quarter 2008	2009	2010
Australia	2.8	10.7	15.2	9.4	3.2	5.3	0.3	-3.1	14.7	13.4	8.5	14.6	7.2	11.4	8.0	1.8	3.0	6.4	1.3	3.8
Austria	5.0	-1.4	2.6	8.0	5.4	4.9	8.2	2.6	-3.3	4.7	3.1	2.4	2.4	4.4	2.3	-3.4	1.4	-0.1	-2.5	2.4
Belgium	4.3	5.3	5.2	7.3	5.2	2.2	5.4	3.2	-2.9	-2.2	6.5	5.2	5.8	6.8	7.6	0.2	3.5	3.1	0.4	6.0
Canada	3.3	4.8	4.4	22.6	5.3	7.2	4.7	0.2	-4.1	6.9	8.2	12.1	9.9	3.5	1.8	-3.8	1.3	-1.4	-2.8	3.1
Denmark	5.0	12.3	5.2	12.1	11.9	-1.5	6.7	-0.3	0.7	-3.0	-0.3	1.3	14.6	8.8	2.3	-2.2	0.0	1.3	-3.5	1.8
Finland	-3.5	26.7	6.5	10.5	15.4	1.0	8.5	10.6	-7.1	0.6	0.7	6.7	6.7	12.8	1.2	-2.3	1.7	-5.8	-1.3	3.5
France	2.9	3.9	0.8	2.0	10.4	9.1	8.6	3.4	-3.0	1.2	3.7	3.1	6.3	6.8	2.0	-3.9	3.0	-1.6	-1.9	4.9
Germany	3.2	2.0	-0.2	2.8	6.0	5.8	7.9	-2.6	-7.0	0.7	0.7	4.4	10.1	6.5	4.4	-4.3	1.0	-0.2	-3.5	2.8
Greece	4.1	3.0	20.9	5.1	13.0	20.7	13.3	5.8	9.4	13.3	2.7	4.7	-2.4	14.5	3.3	5.9	5.9	..	..	..
Iceland	-3.0	9.6	49.2	17.6	46.2	-7.4	11.1	-11.3	-20.2	20.9	33.9	60.2	21.1	-26.0	-24.2	-46.3	-15.2	-27.3	-41.9	-0.1
Ireland	1.8	18.5	16.1	19.9	20.0	14.3	2.5	-8.8	12.6	1.5	6.6	14.9	5.8	20.4	-28.9	-29.5	-11.5	-41.3	-17.9	-10.2
Italy	2.0	12.2	1.5	3.4	4.0	4.1	8.4	2.0	4.5	-3.4	1.1	-0.5	2.2	0.1	-2.3	-5.9	2.6	-5.7	-3.0	5.9
Japan	4.6	3.0	1.6	8.4	-6.5	-4.3	7.5	1.3	-5.2	4.4	5.6	9.2	4.3	2.1	-0.6	-1.2	2.6	-2.2	0.6	3.1
Korea	12.5	15.7	8.5	-3.4	-29.2	13.8	18.9	-4.7	7.6	2.1	1.9	3.4	7.7	5.5	0.9	-0.1	0.7	0.8	-1.1	2.0
Netherlands	3.5	9.3	10.4	13.5	8.3	11.3	-2.0	-3.0	-7.6	-1.0	-2.7	2.2	10.4	4.8	8.8	-2.8	1.6	5.2	-0.7	2.9
New Zealand	3.0	15.5	6.5	-5.9	-1.1	7.0	19.4	-3.0	-1.0	13.0	13.3	11.0	-1.6	7.7	8.4	-15.7	3.9	-3.4	-10.7	9.0
Norway	-1.3	2.3	13.1	16.1	16.0	-8.3	-3.9	-4.3	-1.9	-2.9	10.3	17.3	7.0	11.0	8.1	-2.9	1.2	0.6	-2.2	3.1
Spain	5.4	12.4	3.9	6.5	11.4	11.7	7.9	3.2	1.2	5.3	6.8	7.7	7.8	5.7	-0.2	-5.8	-0.4	-3.7	-4.6	1.6
Sweden	1.6	20.7	8.3	4.6	9.8	9.0	9.0	-2.0	-6.0	1.6	4.8	8.9	6.4	8.9	3.4	-4.0	1.3	1.0	-4.3	4.6
Switzerland	..	8.9	0.8	2.5	8.2	4.4	5.4	-2.3	-0.5	-4.4	4.7	6.4	7.2	7.3	-0.9	-4.4	2.3	-2.9	-2.4	3.9
United Kingdom	3.3	7.8	10.4	10.0	19.3	4.1	4.4	1.5	1.2	-1.0	1.0	17.3	-7.2	9.8	-2.2	-8.8	0.4	-9.5	-5.2	2.7
United States	3.0	10.5	9.3	12.1	11.1	9.2	8.7	-4.2	-9.2	1.0	5.8	7.2	7.5	4.9	2.4	-7.6	1.7	-2.5	-6.4	6.3
Euro area	3.2	6.0	2.2	4.9	7.8	7.2	7.3	0.9	-2.2	0.6	2.4	3.6	6.4	5.5	1.4	-4.3	1.5	-2.4	-2.7	3.5
Total OECD	3.6	8.1	6.1	8.9	6.5	6.3	7.8	-1.4	-4.6	1.7	4.5	7.7	6.3	5.3	1.5	-5.2	1.7	-2.5	-3.8	4.4

Note: The adoption of new national account systems, SNA93 or ESA95, has been proceeding at an uneven pace among OECD member countries, both with respect to variables and the time period covered. As a consequence, there are breaks in many national series. Moreover, most countries are using chain-weighted price indices to calculate real GDP and expenditures components. Some countries, United States, Canada and France use hedonic price indices to deflate current-price values of investment in certain information and communication technology products such as computers. See Table "National Account Reporting Systems and Base-years" at the beginning of the Statistical Annex. National account data do not always have a sectoral breakdown of investment expenditures, and for some countries data are estimated by the OECD. See also *OECD Economic Outlook Sources and Methods, (http://www.oecd.org/eco/sources-and-methods).* Working-day

Source: OECD Economic Outlook 84 database.

StatLink http://dx.doi.org/10.1787/504147641162

Annex Table 7. Real gross residential fixed capital formation
Percentage change from previous year

	Average 1984-94	1995	1996	1997	1998	1999	2000	2001	2002	2003	2004	2005	2006	2007	2008	2009	2010	Fourth quarter 2008	2009	2010
Australia	3.7	-7.6	-9.5	16.5	11.6	5.7	1.5	-10.9	25.7	4.7	2.9	-3.6	-2.1	3.1	1.2	0.5	2.7	0.8	1.2	3.4
Austria	3.2	8.7	2.5	-1.7	-3.0	-2.0	-4.9	-6.5	-5.0	-3.8	-0.3	2.4	5.9	4.0	0.7	-2.9	0.2	0.3	-4.4	2.8
Belgium	7.9	4.3	-8.4	9.8	-0.2	5.0	1.3	-4.4	-0.9	3.6	10.0	10.1	7.4	5.3	0.6	-1.4	1.7	-1.1	-0.5	2.9
Canada	2.0	-14.9	9.7	8.2	-3.6	3.6	5.2	10.5	14.1	5.4	7.5	3.5	2.2	3.0	-2.2	-3.7	0.5	-5.0	-2.3	1.7
Denmark	-2.3	14.5	6.7	9.7	1.9	4.3	10.3	-9.3	0.8	11.8	11.9	18.7	12.2	4.5	-2.2	-11.2	-9.2	-5.1	-12.7	-6.4
Finland	-3.9	-3.2	4.4	20.1	9.0	9.5	5.9	-10.2	0.5	9.5	9.7	5.7	6.3	0.0	-2.1	-2.7	1.3	-2.1	-2.1	3.2
France	0.3	2.3	0.5	1.0	3.7	7.1	2.5	1.4	1.3	2.1	3.2	5.8	6.9	2.9	-2.6	-5.1	0.7	-6.4	-2.2	1.3
Germany	4.4	0.8	-0.3	0.1	0.2	1.6	-1.8	-5.9	-6.0	-0.9	-3.6	-3.7	6.5	0.4	1.2	-1.1	1.0	0.7	0.4	1.3
Greece	-0.7	2.6	-1.2	6.6	8.8	3.8	-4.3	4.3	15.2	12.3	-1.9	0.0	29.1	-6.8	-7.7	-2.3	0.6	..	..	..
Iceland	-0.9	-8.7	7.1	-9.3	1.0	0.6	12.8	12.3	12.4	3.7	14.2	11.9	16.5	13.2	-31.4	-44.3	-9.4	-47.3	-37.3	0.5
Ireland	3.2	14.5	18.3	15.8	6.4	12.9	7.6	1.9	5.4	18.3	10.7	13.7	1.8	-15.2	-28.7	-28.6	3.0	-33.3	-11.1	8.8
Italy	0.4	0.5	-3.1	-2.4	-1.2	1.3	5.1	1.5	2.5	3.5	2.5	5.2	5.4	3.0	-1.6	-4.8	2.1	-4.7	-2.3	4.7
Japan	4.1	-4.8	11.8	-12.1	-14.3	0.2	0.9	-5.3	-4.0	-1.0	1.9	-1.5	0.9	-9.5	-9.2	3.9	2.4	5.4	3.1	2.1
Korea	13.9	9.9	2.8	-4.9	-13.4	-6.1	-9.3	12.9	11.4	9.0	4.7	2.2	-3.5	-1.8	-5.3	-2.4	0.0	-7.2	-0.9	0.6
Netherlands	2.4	0.1	3.9	5.6	3.0	2.8	1.6	3.2	-6.5	-3.7	4.1	5.0	5.0	5.0	3.9	-1.2	0.4	3.4	-1.0	0.9
New Zealand	2.9	3.5	5.2	6.8	-12.8	7.5	0.5	-11.7	21.3	19.8	5.4	-4.5	-3.8	5.6	-17.2	-21.2	0.7	-28.4	-10.2	3.5
Norway	-3.5	10.5	2.8	12.1	7.7	3.0	5.6	8.2	-0.7	1.9	16.3	10.8	6.6	5.5	-11.6	-6.1	-1.0	-13.8	-2.3	-0.5
Spain	2.3	7.1	12.3	2.2	10.9	11.4	10.3	7.5	7.0	9.3	5.9	6.1	6.0	3.8	-9.8	-25.6	-14.8	-19.5	-23.3	-11.2
Sweden	-7.1	-23.9	8.9	-11.5	-0.6	10.8	10.0	4.2	10.5	5.4	15.4	15.7	13.8	8.7	-0.3	-2.3	1.6	-1.4	-1.5	3.5
Switzerland	..	-2.0	-8.7	-0.1	2.8	-5.5	-2.7	-4.1	-3.7	14.4	7.0	1.1	-1.6	0.1	-1.6	0.0	3.8	..	..	..
United Kingdom	0.6	-0.8	7.2	7.0	3.7	1.7	0.6	0.3	6.9	1.2	13.1	-4.7	8.9	3.3	-16.1	-14.3	-0.7	-21.2	-6.8	1.7
United States	2.2	-3.2	8.0	1.9	7.6	6.0	0.8	0.4	4.8	8.4	10.0	6.3	-7.1	-17.9	-21.3	-16.8	0.7	-20.8	-10.3	5.1
Euro area	2.4	1.8	0.5	1.2	1.9	3.7	1.5	-1.1	-0.8	2.7	1.8	3.3	6.7	1.4	-3.4	-7.3	-0.7	-6.6	-4.6	0.8
Total OECD	2.7	-1.8	5.6	0.8	1.8	4.0	1.2	-0.4	3.1	4.8	6.4	3.5	0.0	-7.3	-11.6	-9.5	0.4	-11.3	-5.6	2.8

Note: The adoption of new national account systems, SNA93 or ESA95, has been proceeding at an uneven pace among OECD member countries, both with respect to variables and the time period covered. As a consequence, there are breaks in many national series. Moreover, most countries are using chain-weighted price indices to calculate real GDP and expenditures components. See Table "National Account Reporting Systems and Base-years" at the beginning of the Statistical Annex and *OECD Economic Outlook Sources and Methods (http://www.oecd.org/eco/sources-and-methods)*. Working-day adjusted -- see note to Table on Real GDP.

Source: OECD Economic Outlook 84 database.

StatLink http://dx.doi.org/10.1787/504158232050

Annex Table 8. Real total domestic demand
Percentage change from previous year

	Average 1984-94	1995	1996	1997	1998	1999	2000	2001	2002	2003	2004	2005	2006	2007	2008	2009	2010	Fourth quarter 2008	2009	2010
Australia	2.8	4.6	3.5	3.6	5.9	5.2	2.9	0.6	6.3	6.1	5.3	4.6	2.7	6.2	3.8	1.8	2.8	2.5	2.0	3.2
Austria	2.8	2.1	2.6	1.3	2.4	3.0	2.1	0.6	0.0	1.4	2.3	2.8	2.1	1.9	0.7	-0.6	1.1	-0.2	-0.4	1.7
Belgium	2.8	3.3	0.8	2.4	2.1	2.9	4.1	0.1	0.5	1.1	2.5	2.7	2.9	3.0	2.7	0.7	1.7	1.8	0.7	2.5
Canada	2.6	1.8	1.3	6.1	2.5	4.2	4.7	1.3	3.2	4.5	4.1	4.8	4.6	4.3	2.7	-0.4	1.8	0.0	0.1	2.5
Czech Republic	..	8.2	7.8	-1.0	-1.3	1.2	3.6	3.7	3.8	4.2	3.1	1.7	5.3	5.7	1.5	2.9	3.7	3.1	3.1	4.1
Denmark	1.8	4.5	2.5	4.7	3.7	-0.6	3.2	0.0	1.7	0.2	4.3	3.4	6.0	2.6	0.8	-0.5	0.2	0.0	-0.9	0.8
Finland	0.5	5.4	2.0	4.7	5.8	1.9	3.7	1.7	1.3	3.7	3.6	4.2	3.1	4.1	0.6	0.9	1.6	0.3	0.9	2.1
France	2.2	1.9	0.7	1.0	4.2	3.7	4.4	1.7	1.2	1.7	3.1	2.6	2.6	2.9	0.9	-0.4	1.6	0.0	0.0	2.4
Germany	2.9	2.0	0.4	0.9	2.2	2.6	2.4	-0.4	-2.0	0.6	-0.6	0.2	2.3	1.2	1.7	0.1	1.2	1.9	0.1	1.7
Greece	1.7	3.5	3.2	3.4	4.4	3.7	5.6	2.6	5.1	6.7	4.9	3.0	5.5	4.5	1.5	2.3	2.4	..	..	..
Hungary	..	-5.2	0.3	4.9	8.2	5.1	4.5	2.2	6.5	6.2	3.8	1.5	1.0	-0.4	1.4	-0.1	0.6	2.8	-1.8	2.0
Iceland	1.5	1.9	6.9	5.5	13.8	4.2	5.9	-2.1	-2.3	5.8	9.9	15.8	9.3	-1.4	-6.6	-15.9	-3.2	-11.3	-13.3	1.4
Ireland	2.5	6.3	7.9	9.7	9.1	8.9	9.0	4.0	5.8	3.6	3.6	8.1	6.1	3.7	-5.5	-4.7	0.8	-9.7	-1.2	1.8
Italy	2.1	1.9	0.6	2.6	2.8	2.7	3.2	1.5	1.3	0.8	1.2	0.9	1.8	1.3	-0.8	-1.1	0.9	-1.2	-0.5	1.8
Japan	3.7	2.6	3.3	0.5	-2.4	0.0	2.4	1.0	-0.4	0.8	1.9	1.7	1.6	1.0	-0.3	0.6	1.0	-0.3	0.9	1.4
Korea	9.0	9.9	8.1	0.4	-17.2	13.2	8.5	3.5	7.4	0.6	1.5	3.2	4.2	4.1	2.3	0.0	1.1	0.7	0.0	1.6
Luxembourg	4.4	1.2	4.6	6.1	6.4	8.1	4.3	4.6	2.6	0.4	3.3	4.9	1.4	3.7	-1.8	0.4	2.0	..	..	..
Mexico	3.2	-12.0	5.4	8.8	5.8	4.2	7.9	0.3	0.8	0.8	3.9	3.7	5.6	3.5	3.0	1.6	2.3	1.8	1.6	2.9
Netherlands	2.4	3.3	3.9	4.5	5.1	4.9	2.7	2.3	-0.4	0.4	0.5	1.3	3.7	2.7	2.9	0.2	0.9	1.8	0.4	1.3
New Zealand	1.5	5.8	4.4	2.5	0.5	5.9	1.9	1.7	5.7	6.2	7.6	4.2	1.2	4.5	1.1	-2.5	1.9	-1.4	-0.9	2.8
Norway	1.7	4.4	4.4	6.8	5.8	0.4	2.9	0.6	2.3	1.7	6.7	5.5	5.5	5.8	4.3	1.5	1.8	1.2	1.0	2.2
Poland	..	7.4	9.6	9.3	6.4	5.2	3.1	-1.3	1.0	2.8	6.2	2.5	7.3	8.6	5.7	3.4	3.5	4.9	3.0	3.8
Portugal	4.4	4.1	3.6	5.5	7.0	5.7	3.3	1.7	0.0	-2.1	2.7	1.6	0.7	1.6	0.9	-0.4	0.5	-0.6	0.0	0.9
Slovak Republic	..	9.9	17.2	6.1	4.8	-6.2	1.2	8.2	4.1	-0.7	6.0	8.5	6.5	5.9	6.5	3.6	4.9	2.2	4.0	5.1
Spain	3.7	3.1	2.1	3.4	6.2	6.4	5.3	3.8	3.2	3.8	4.8	5.1	5.1	4.2	0.7	-2.3	0.0	-1.3	-1.6	0.7
Sweden	1.4	2.2	1.0	1.3	4.3	3.6	4.0	0.0	1.4	1.7	2.0	3.1	3.4	4.2	2.1	0.3	1.8	2.1	0.5	2.4
Switzerland	2.0	1.4	0.6	0.6	3.7	0.2	2.2	2.0	0.1	0.5	1.9	1.9	1.4	1.1	0.3	0.1	1.5	-1.5	0.3	2.1
Turkey	4.5	10.5	7.8	8.9	0.9	-1.9	7.8	-11.5	8.7	8.6	11.5	9.2	6.7	5.5	3.4	1.7	4.4	..	..	..
United Kingdom	2.6	1.9	3.1	3.5	5.2	4.6	3.9	3.0	3.2	2.9	3.4	1.9	2.6	3.6	0.5	-1.6	1.0	-1.7	-0.7	1.9
United States	2.9	2.4	3.8	4.8	5.3	5.3	4.4	0.9	2.2	2.8	4.1	3.0	2.6	1.4	-0.1	-1.6	1.3	-1.2	-0.7	2.2
Euro area	2.6	2.3	1.2	2.1	3.5	3.5	3.6	1.3	0.4	1.4	1.8	2.0	2.9	2.3	0.8	-0.5	1.1	0.2	-0.2	1.8
Total OECD	3.0	2.3	3.2	3.5	3.0	4.0	4.1	0.9	1.8	2.3	3.3	2.8	3.0	2.3	0.8	-0.6	1.4	-0.2	0.0	2.1

Note: The adoption of new National Accounts systems, SNA93 or ESA95, has been proceeding at an uneven pace among OECD member countries, both with respect to variables and the time period covered. As a consequence, there are breaks in many national series. Moreover, most countries are using chain-weighted price indices to calculate real GDP and expenditures components. See Table "National Accounts Reporting Systems and Base-years" at the beginning of the Statistical Annex and *OECD Economic Outlook Sources and Methods* (*http://www.oecd.org/eco/sources-and-methods*). Working-day adjusted – see note to Table on Real GDP.

Source: OECD Economic Outlook 84 database.

StatLink http://dx.doi.org/10.1787/504163284543

OECD ECONOMIC OUTLOOK 84 – ISBN 978-92-64-05469-1 – © OECD 2008

Annex Table 9. Foreign balance contributions to changes in real GDP

Per cent

	Average 1984-94	1995	1996	1997	1998	1999	2000	2001	2002	2003	2004	2005	2006	2007	2008	2009	2010	Fourth quarter[1] 2008	2009	2010
Australia	0.5	-0.1	0.9	0.9	-1.0	-0.5	0.9	1.2	-1.7	-2.2	-1.8	-1.2	-0.9	-1.9	-1.7	-0.2	-0.2	-0.5	-0.1	-0.3
Austria	-0.2	-0.3	-0.5	1.4	1.1	0.6	1.3	0.5	1.5	0.6	-0.3	0.1	1.3	1.1	0.6	0.3	0.2	0.2	-0.1	0.7
Belgium	-0.3	0.4	0.3	1.0	-0.4	0.6	0.0	0.6	0.8	0.1	0.4	-0.6	0.1	-0.3	-1.4	-0.8	-0.5	-0.6	-0.6	-0.5
Canada	-0.1	1.0	0.3	-1.7	1.7	1.4	0.6	0.7	-0.1	-2.5	-0.9	-1.7	-1.3	-1.5	-2.1	-0.1	0.4	1.7	0.4	0.7
Czech Republic	-3.9	-2.7	-3.9	0.3	0.7	0.1	0.1	-1.4	-2.0	-0.6	1.3	4.7	1.7	1.1	3.0	-0.2	0.9	-0.8	0.3	1.4
Denmark	0.2	-1.2	0.5	-1.3	-1.4	3.2	0.5	0.7	-1.1	0.2	-1.8	-0.8	-1.8	-0.9	-0.7	0.1	0.7	-0.1	0.6	0.8
Finland	0.2	0.6	0.1	1.4	0.9	3.0	1.1	0.2	0.1	-1.7	1.1	-1.2	2.4	1.4	1.8	0.0	0.5	-1.5	0.5	1.0
France	-0.1	0.4	0.4	1.2	-0.5	-0.4	-0.3	0.1	-0.1	-0.6	-0.8	-0.6	-0.3	-0.8	0.1	0.1	-0.1	0.4	-0.1	-0.2
Germany	0.1	0.0	0.6	0.9	-0.3	-0.6	1.1	1.8	2.0	-0.8	1.3	0.8	1.0	1.4	-0.2	-0.9	0.0	0.1	-0.2	0.2
Greece	-0.5	-1.7	-1.2	-0.4	-1.7	-1.1	-2.0	1.5	-1.7	-2.4	-1.1	0.4	-2.0	-1.3	1.9	-0.7	-0.3	..	..	..
Hungary	0.5	5.0	1.2	-0.2	-3.0	-0.8	0.7	1.8	-2.2	-2.2	0.3	2.5	2.3	2.1	0.3	-0.3	0.5	-0.5	0.3	0.7
Iceland	0.4	-1.9	-1.7	-0.8	-7.5	-0.3	-1.9	6.2	2.5	-3.3	-2.5	-9.2	-6.1	6.5	7.6	7.1	2.5	4.0	3.5	0.6
Ireland	1.7	4.2	1.4	2.7	0.0	4.2	1.6	2.6	3.0	1.7	0.6	-1.2	0.3	2.6	2.5	1.9	1.9	1.4	1.5	2.6
Italy	0.1	1.0	0.4	-0.6	-1.4	-1.2	0.8	0.2	-0.8	-0.8	0.1	-0.2	0.1	0.1	0.5	0.0	-0.1	0.3	0.0	-0.3
Japan	-0.2	-0.5	-0.5	1.0	0.4	-0.1	0.5	-0.8	0.7	0.7	0.8	0.3	0.8	1.1	0.8	-0.7	-0.4	-1.6	-0.3	-0.5
Korea	-0.9	-1.5	-1.8	4.2	11.3	-2.9	0.3	0.5	-0.2	2.5	3.3	1.3	1.3	1.3	2.1	2.7	3.2	1.5	3.5	3.0
Luxembourg	1.8	1.2	-1.7	0.5	1.1	1.8	5.6	-1.7	2.0	1.2	2.5	1.1	5.3	2.7	5.3	-0.5	0.5	..	..	..
Mexico	-0.7	6.2	-0.1	-1.8	-0.8	-0.3	-1.3	-0.5	0.0	0.5	0.0	-0.6	-0.8	-0.4	-1.1	-1.3	-0.6	-1.7	-0.6	-0.8
Netherlands	0.4	0.0	-0.2	0.0	-0.9	0.1	1.3	-0.2	0.5	-0.1	1.7	0.8	0.0	1.0	-0.4	-0.2	-0.1	-0.1	-0.3	-0.5
New Zealand	0.1	-1.3	-1.0	0.5	0.1	-1.2	2.2	0.5	-0.9	-1.9	-2.8	-1.7	1.3	-1.7	-1.7	2.1	0.0	6.1	0.0	-0.6
Norway	1.3	0.0	1.0	-0.8	-2.6	1.6	0.6	1.5	-0.4	-0.5	-2.0	-2.0	-2.1	-1.2	-0.9	0.1	0.0	0.6	0.1	-0.3
Poland	0.5	0.2	-2.8	-2.3	-1.7	-1.1	0.9	2.6	0.5	1.0	-1.0	1.1	-1.1	-2.0	-0.3	-1.0	-0.1	-1.0	-0.1	-0.1
Portugal	-0.9	-0.1	-0.2	-1.6	-2.6	-2.5	0.3	0.2	0.7	1.5	-1.4	-0.8	0.6	0.1	-0.4	0.2	0.0	0.2	0.0	0.1
Slovak Republic	11.2	-3.6	-10.5	-1.2	-0.8	6.9	0.1	-5.0	0.4	5.5	-0.9	-2.1	1.7	4.3	-1.5	0.0	0.7	-0.1	0.5	1.1
Spain	-1.2	-0.3	0.3	0.5	-1.7	-1.7	-0.4	-0.2	-0.6	-0.8	-1.7	-1.7	-1.5	-0.8	0.6	1.5	0.7	2.0	0.6	0.9
Sweden	0.0	1.7	0.5	1.2	-0.3	1.4	0.7	1.1	1.0	0.3	2.1	0.8	0.9	-1.1	-0.2	0.0	0.5	0.1	0.2	1.0
Switzerland	0.0	-1.0	0.0	1.4	-0.9	1.1	1.4	-0.7	0.4	-0.8	0.6	0.7	2.1	2.3	1.7	-0.2	0.2	-0.6	0.1	0.4
Turkey	0.2	-2.9	0.2	-0.9	2.1	-1.5	-1.1	6.5	-3.0	-3.8	-2.4	-1.3	-0.3	-1.3	0.1	-0.2	-0.3	..	..	..
United Kingdom	0.0	0.9	0.0	-0.2	-1.4	-1.0	0.0	-0.5	-1.1	-0.1	-0.7	0.1	0.1	-0.7	0.3	0.6	-0.1	1.0	0.1	0.2
United States	0.1	0.1	-0.1	-0.4	-1.2	-1.0	-0.8	-0.2	-0.7	-0.4	-0.7	-0.2	0.0	0.6	1.4	0.8	0.2	0.7	0.3	0.0
Euro area	0.0	0.2	0.3	0.6	-0.7	-0.6	0.4	0.7	0.5	-0.6	0.1	-0.2	0.1	0.3	0.2	0.0	0.1	0.4	0.0	0.2
Total OECD	0.0	0.2	-0.1	0.1	-0.4	-0.6	-0.1	0.2	-0.2	-0.4	-0.2	-0.1	0.1	0.3	0.6	0.2	0.1	0.2	0.2	0.1

Note: The adoption of new National Accounts systems, SNA93 or ESA95, has been proceeding at an uneven pace among OECD member countries, both with respect to variables and the time period covered. As a consequence, there are breaks in many national series. Moreover, most countries are using chain-weighted price indices to calculate real GDP and expenditures components. See Table "National Accounts Reporting Systems and Base-years" at the beginning of the Statistical Annex and *OECD Economic Outlook* Sources and Methods (*http://www.oecd.org/eco/sources-and-methods*). Working-day adjusted -- see note to Table on Real GDP.

1. Contributions to per cent change in the previous quarter, seasonally adjusted at annual rates

Source: OECD Economic Outlook 84 database.

StatLink ⟶ *http://dx.doi.org/10.1787/504166114236*

Annex Table 10. Output gaps

Deviations of actual GDP from potential GDP as a per cent of potential GDP

	1991	1992	1993	1994	1995	1996	1997	1998	1999	2000	2001	2002	2003	2004	2005	2006	2007	2008	2009	2010
Australia	-2.3	-2.7	-1.9	-0.6	-0.6	-0.7	-1.0	0.0	0.4	0.1	-1.3	-0.7	-0.5	-0.1	0.3	-0.2	1.0	0.3	-1.2	-1.6
Austria	1.5	1.1	-1.3	-1.1	-0.9	-0.8	-0.8	0.6	1.8	2.6	0.9	-0.3	-1.9	-1.8	-0.8	0.2	0.9	0.4	-2.1	-3.1
Belgium	1.4	1.0	-2.0	-0.8	-0.4	-1.6	-0.1	-0.5	0.7	2.3	0.9	0.2	-0.9	-0.1	-0.1	0.7	1.1	0.3	-1.9	-2.6
Canada	-3.0	-4.2	-4.2	-2.0	-2.0	-3.4	-2.4	-1.5	0.7	2.6	1.2	1.2	0.3	0.6	0.8	1.3	1.6	-0.3	-3.1	-3.2
Czech Republic	..	..	..	-0.9	2.4	4.3	1.5	-1.1	-1.9	-0.8	-1.1	-2.4	-2.6	-2.3	-0.5	1.3	2.4	1.8	-0.1	-0.2
Denmark	-1.6	-1.6	-3.8	-0.9	-0.4	-0.2	0.5	0.4	0.7	2.1	0.9	-0.4	-1.7	-1.1	-0.4	1.7	1.9	0.9	-0.5	-0.6
Finland	-2.8	-7.6	-9.4	-7.6	-6.1	-5.0	-1.9	0.1	0.8	2.5	1.5	0.0	-1.3	-0.5	-0.6	1.1	2.2	1.2	-1.1	-2.1
France	1.7	1.1	-1.3	-1.0	-0.7	-1.7	-1.6	-0.3	0.5	1.9	1.2	0.1	-0.7	-0.3	-0.1	0.7	0.9	0.0	-2.2	-2.5
Germany	1.2	1.0	-1.7	-0.7	-0.5	-1.2	-1.0	-0.8	-0.4	1.6	1.6	0.3	-1.2	-1.6	-1.8	0.1	1.2	1.1	-1.1	-1.5
Greece	1.4	0.8	-2.0	-1.6	-1.7	-1.9	-1.4	-1.2	-1.5	-1.1	-0.7	-0.8	0.2	1.0	1.2	1.5	1.4	0.8	-1.1	-2.3
Hungary	..	..	-1.3	0.1	-0.3	-1.5	-0.5	0.3	0.1	0.6	0.1	0.0	0.2	1.1	1.4	2.1	0.1	-1.4	-4.9	-6.8
Iceland	-2.4	-6.7	-6.2	-3.6	-4.7	-1.9	-0.2	1.8	1.5	1.3	2.0	-0.2	-0.5	3.3	5.8	2.8	1.9	-0.4	-10.3	-12.4
Ireland	0.5	-1.6	-4.1	-4.5	-2.2	-1.6	1.3	1.1	3.4	4.6	2.9	2.3	0.9	0.3	1.2	1.7	2.8	-3.4	-8.1	-8.6
Italy	0.9	-0.2	-2.9	-2.5	-1.5	-2.3	-2.0	-2.1	-2.2	0.1	0.6	0.0	-0.9	-0.5	-0.8	-0.2	0.2	-1.2	-3.5	-4.0
Japan	4.2	2.7	0.9	0.3	0.5	1.8	2.2	-1.1	-2.4	-0.6	-1.6	-2.5	-2.4	-1.2	-0.5	0.7	1.6	0.9	-0.4	-1.1
Luxembourg	7.1	3.3	2.3	1.3	-2.0	-5.0	-4.0	-2.7	0.4	3.6	1.3	1.1	-1.4	-1.3	-0.7	0.8	1.2	-0.7	-5.3	-7.2
Netherlands	0.7	-0.4	-2.0	-1.9	-1.7	-1.3	-0.1	0.9	2.5	3.6	2.8	0.3	-1.6	-1.5	-1.6	-0.4	0.9	1.2	-0.7	-1.6
New Zealand	-4.2	-5.3	-2.8	-0.1	0.8	1.4	0.4	-2.4	-1.0	-0.3	-0.7	0.6	1.0	2.1	1.9	1.1	1.7	-0.3	-3.0	-3.3
Norway	-5.4	-4.5	-3.4	-2.2	-1.6	-0.5	1.5	2.9	2.5	2.2	1.5	0.0	-1.7	-0.5	0.6	1.4	3.4	2.5	-0.1	-1.5
Poland	..	..	..	..	-1.0	-0.6	0.9	0.2	0.0	0.3	-2.0	-3.4	-2.4	-0.3	-0.1	1.9	3.2	3.0	0.8	-0.5
Portugal	5.9	3.9	-1.1	-3.0	-1.8	-1.1	0.1	1.9	3.0	4.4	3.9	2.3	-0.6	-0.7	-1.3	-1.2	-0.7	-1.4	-2.7	-3.2
Spain	3.8	1.6	-2.5	-3.0	-3.3	-4.0	-3.3	-2.0	-0.5	1.0	1.0	0.0	-0.6	-0.8	-0.6	-0.1	0.4	-1.2	-4.7	-6.2
Sweden	0.1	-2.4	-5.5	-3.5	-1.4	-1.8	-1.4	-0.3	1.3	2.8	0.9	0.2	-0.9	-0.7	-0.5	1.0	0.9	-1.2	-3.7	-3.9
Switzerland	0.5	-1.0	-2.2	-1.9	-2.3	-2.6	-1.4	0.1	0.1	2.0	1.4	0.1	-1.9	-1.2	-0.5	0.7	1.3	0.6	-1.7	-2.1
United Kingdom	0.1	-1.8	-2.1	-0.9	-0.9	-1.1	-0.8	-0.2	0.2	1.1	0.7	0.1	0.3	0.5	0.0	0.4	1.3	0.3	-2.4	-3.3
United States	-1.7	-1.4	-2.0	-1.3	-2.2	-1.9	-0.9	0.0	1.3	2.2	0.3	-0.5	-0.5	0.6	1.0	1.2	0.7	-0.4	-3.6	-4.2
Euro area	1.5	0.7	-2.0	-1.6	-1.2	-1.8	-1.4	-0.8	-0.1	1.6	1.3	0.2	-0.9	-0.9	-0.9	0.2	0.8	-0.1	-2.4	-3.1
Total OECD	0.2	-0.4	-1.8	-1.2	-1.3	-1.3	-0.6	-0.4	0.2	1.5	0.4	-0.5	-0.9	-0.2	0.1	0.8	1.0	0.0	-2.5	-3.2

Note: Potential output for countries where data availability permits follows the methodology outlined in Beffy, P.O., Olivaud, P., Richardson, P., and F. Sedillot (2006), "New OECD Methods for Supply-Side and Medium-Term Assessments: A Capital Services Approach", Economics Department Working Papers No. 482, ECO/WKP(2006)10. This combines a production function with some smoothing of its components using a statistical filter. The smoothing is both country and component specific. In countries where extensive data are not available, more simplified methodologies are used that essentially apply statistical filters to whatever data are available. The smoothed series from all these procedures are then used to generate a measure of potential output that determines the output gap – which signals the presence, or absence, of inflationary pressure.

1. Mainland Norway.

Source: OECD Economic Outlook 84 database.

StatLink http://dx.doi.org/10.1787/504171446030

OECD ECONOMIC OUTLOOK 84 – ISBN 978-92-64-05469-1 – © OECD 2008

Annex Table 11. Compensation per employee in the private sector
Percentage change from previous period

	Average 1981-1991	1992	1993	1994	1995	1996	1997	1998	1999	2000	2001	2002	2003	2004	2005	2006	2007	2008	2009	2010
Australia	7.3	4.7	2.7	2.9	3.1	5.5	4.6	3.0	3.4	3.1	4.5	3.1	3.8	6.4	5.3	5.4	5.3	4.9	4.5	4.0
Austria	4.9	5.7	4.5	3.5	1.4	1.3	1.2	2.8	1.9	2.4	2.1	2.1	1.9	1.9	2.5	3.3	2.3	2.3	1.8	2.1
Belgium	5.8	4.9	4.1	3.8	1.9	1.2	3.2	1.1	3.6	1.7	3.7	3.5	1.5	2.1	1.8	3.6	4.4	3.5	2.6	2.1
Canada	5.4	3.5	2.1	0.3	1.9	2.8	5.8	2.6	3.3	5.3	2.1	0.8	1.8	5.2	4.9	4.5	4.6	3.7	1.9	2.0
Czech Republic	..	..	..	..	..	16.5	9.2	9.7	7.9	7.4	7.2	7.0	8.7	6.1	4.8	6.6	7.5	7.5	6.0	7.1
Denmark	6.6	5.3	1.9	1.7	2.2	4.0	3.8	4.0	3.7	3.1	4.1	3.7	3.5	3.2	4.3	3.8	4.7	4.2	4.5	4.4
Finland	8.7	1.8	2.0	5.1	4.6	2.1	2.6	4.4	2.4	4.1	4.9	1.5	2.7	3.4	3.4	3.0	3.3	5.6	4.1	3.9
France	6.5	3.7	2.1	1.1	1.4	1.4	1.4	1.4	1.9	2.3	2.4	3.4	3.0	3.9	3.0	3.4	2.9	2.9	2.2	1.9
Germany	3.5	10.3	3.6	2.9	3.4	1.0	0.6	0.8	1.0	2.0	1.6	1.3	1.6	0.1	-0.1	1.3	1.3	2.3	2.6	1.9
Greece	18.7	12.6	8.9	11.6	12.6	10.8	11.6	4.8	6.8	5.6	7.7	5.2	5.8	3.2	7.9	7.1	6.5	6.8	6.5	6.2
Hungary	..	..	..	..	24.2	21.4	18.7	12.4	1.7	15.5	13.8	10.2	6.9	13.6	7.4	4.3	6.4	8.3	6.3	6.9
Iceland	31.6	0.6	-3.7	3.7	4.9	5.1	3.8	9.4	8.5	10.0	5.5	7.6	0.6	12.4	10.8	9.2	5.5	8.1	10.6	6.5
Ireland	7.1	7.9	4.9	1.5	3.4	4.3	4.2	4.9	4.0	8.6	6.6	3.1	5.0	4.7	6.4	5.2	6.2	5.6	2.1	1.6
Italy	10.0	5.8	4.3	4.4	5.4	4.2	3.6	-1.0	1.9	1.9	2.4	1.8	1.8	3.2	2.7	1.8	2.4	3.9	1.8	1.8
Japan	3.5	0.7	0.5	1.4	1.0	-0.2	1.1	-1.2	-1.6	0.1	-1.2	-2.1	-1.2	-0.9	0.0	0.0	-0.8	0.7	0.1	0.1
Korea	12.2	11.8	12.9	12.0	15.0	12.0	4.0	4.4	2.1	3.2	6.6	4.8	7.0	4.2	3.9	2.9	4.1	7.5	3.8	3.3
Luxembourg	5.2	6.5	5.5	4.1	0.2	1.0	2.0	1.4	4.6	6.1	3.5	2.4	0.5	3.5	3.6	3.1	4.8	2.7	2.3	5.6
Mexico	..	20.5	10.3	9.3	8.1	19.1	23.4	16.1	17.8	11.6	9.2	3.9	3.6	2.4	5.6	3.0	4.4	4.5	3.7	3.5
Netherlands	3.5	4.1	2.7	1.9	0.3	1.9	2.5	4.2	3.5	4.8	4.8	4.4	3.2	3.4	0.8	2.7	3.1	3.4	2.2	1.9
Norway	7.6	4.3	2.7	3.1	3.2	2.5	2.5	7.5	6.1	4.5	7.0	3.9	2.5	4.4	5.5	7.7	5.7	6.2	4.7	4.8
Poland	..	..	..	..	..	29.0	20.5	14.7	12.6	10.2	9.5	0.5	0.3	1.6	0.5	0.8	7.3	9.4	6.1	5.1
Portugal	16.9	16.2	7.2	6.0	6.8	7.2	6.7	2.4	2.3	4.0	2.9	2.8	5.3	1.6	3.3	2.1	5.3	3.6	2.0	2.1
Slovak Republic	..	..	..	..	..	11.8	18.6	9.6	7.1	15.7	4.6	7.8	8.5	9.9	12.1	7.3	9.5	7.9	5.6	7.3
Spain	9.9	10.4	8.3	4.0	3.5	5.2	3.6	1.3	1.9	2.9	4.1	3.5	2.7	1.8	2.8	2.2	2.9	4.1	3.0	2.4
Sweden	8.4	1.7	6.4	6.9	2.2	7.2	5.5	2.8	1.2	6.8	4.1	2.6	2.5	4.6	3.2	2.1	5.1	3.5	2.9	3.6
Switzerland	4.7	4.0	2.8	2.5	2.6	0.6	2.9	0.3	1.6	2.7	3.8	1.4	-0.5	-0.9	3.3	3.8	3.8	2.2	1.6	2.1
United Kingdom	7.7	4.8	2.3	3.4	2.6	2.2	4.0	7.2	4.5	5.8	4.8	2.8	4.6	3.6	3.8	4.0	3.6	2.5	3.2	1.8
United States	4.5	6.2	2.0	1.8	2.3	3.0	4.0	5.4	4.5	6.7	2.6	3.3	3.3	4.5	3.4	3.9	4.0	3.5	3.0	2.2
Euro area	6.5	7.5	3.9	3.1	3.0	1.9	2.0	1.1	1.7	2.4	2.5	2.2	2.3	1.6	1.5	2.2	2.4	3.0	2.4	2.1
Total OECD	5.5	6.3	3.1	2.9	3.1	3.8	4.2	3.9	3.4	4.7	2.9	2.3	2.6	2.9	2.7	2.9	3.1	3.3	2.6	2.1

Note: The private sector is in the OECD terminology defined as total economy less the public sector. Hence business sector employees are defined as total employees less public sector employees. See also *OECD Economic Outlook Sources and Methods (http://www.oecd.org/eco/sources-and-methods)*.

Source: OECD Economic Outlook 84 database.

StatLink http://dx.doi.org/10.1787/504181352277

Annex Table 12. Labour productivity for the total economy
Percentage change from previous period

	Average 1981-1991	1992	1993	1994	1995	1996	1997	1998	1999	2000	2001	2002	2003	2004	2005	2006	2007	2008	2009	2010
Australia	0.8	3.0	3.5	1.9	-0.3	2.8	2.9	3.3	2.7	0.9	0.9	2.1	1.1	1.4	0.0	0.4	1.5	0.4	1.1	1.9
Austria	2.2	1.8	0.9	2.6	2.5	2.0	1.7	2.7	2.0	1.9	0.3	1.4	0.6	2.5	2.2	2.1	1.5	0.3	-0.2	0.9
Belgium	1.8	1.7	-0.3	3.6	1.7	0.6	3.2	0.2	2.0	1.8	-0.6	1.6	1.0	2.1	0.9	1.7	0.9	-0.1	0.1	1.1
Canada	0.9	1.9	1.8	2.7	1.0	0.7	2.1	1.6	2.9	2.7	0.6	0.5	-0.5	1.3	1.5	1.1	0.4	-1.0	0.1	1.5
Czech Republic	..	..	..	1.3	5.2	3.2	-0.9	0.8	4.9	3.9	2.0	1.3	5.0	4.1	5.2	5.1	4.7	3.1	3.1	4.4
Denmark	1.8	3.1	1.4	3.8	2.3	1.9	1.8	0.7	1.7	3.0	-0.2	0.4	1.5	2.9	1.6	2.2	0.0	-0.9	1.5	2.1
Finland	2.5	3.4	5.3	5.0	2.0	2.3	2.8	3.2	1.4	2.7	1.0	0.6	1.8	3.2	1.5	3.0	2.3	0.4	0.3	1.6
France	2.1	1.8	0.5	2.0	1.3	0.7	1.7	2.0	1.1	1.3	0.0	0.5	1.0	2.1	1.4	1.4	0.7	0.3	0.3	1.4
Germany	1.7	3.4	0.5	2.8	1.7	1.3	2.0	0.6	0.5	1.5	0.9	0.6	0.7	0.3	1.0	2.5	0.9	0.1	0.0	1.4
Greece	0.9	-0.8	-2.4	0.1	1.2	2.8	4.2	-0.7	3.4	4.6	4.4	1.6	4.0	2.2	2.9	2.1	2.7	1.9	1.5	1.9
Hungary	..	..	..	..	5.1	1.8	4.4	3.0	0.7	3.8	3.8	4.1	2.9	5.6	4.0	3.4	1.2	3.2	0.8	1.3
Iceland	1.0	-3.4	1.5	2.8	-2.9	4.8	4.9	2.1	0.4	2.3	2.2	1.6	2.3	8.3	4.0	-0.7	0.3	0.1	-4.2	0.9
Ireland	3.4	2.8	1.2	2.4	4.5	4.4	5.6	-0.2	4.2	4.4	2.7	4.6	2.5	1.6	1.6	1.4	2.4	-1.9	0.4	2.1
Italy	1.7	1.4	1.8	4.0	3.1	0.4	1.6	0.3	0.3	1.9	-0.3	-1.2	-1.4	0.9	0.1	-0.1	0.2	-1.0	-0.6	0.7
Japan	2.6	-0.1	0.0	1.0	1.9	2.3	0.5	-1.4	0.7	3.1	0.7	1.5	1.6	2.5	1.5	2.0	1.6	0.8	0.6	0.8
Korea	6.0	3.9	4.9	5.2	6.1	4.7	2.9	-0.9	7.6	4.0	1.8	4.1	3.2	2.8	2.8	3.8	3.7	3.5	2.6	3.4
Luxembourg	3.7	-0.7	2.4	1.2	-2.0	-0.9	2.8	1.9	3.2	2.7	-2.8	0.8	-0.2	2.2	2.3	2.7	0.8	-1.6	0.2	1.0
Mexico	..	0.0	-1.6	0.9	-5.4	1.0	1.0	2.2	2.7	4.3	-0.4	-1.5	0.5	0.5	2.5	1.4	1.5	0.6	0.1	0.6
Netherlands	0.8	0.4	0.9	2.3	0.8	1.2	1.2	1.3	2.1	1.7	-0.1	-0.4	0.8	3.1	1.4	1.5	1.1	0.8	-0.1	0.7
New Zealand	1.3	0.4	3.1	1.5	-0.2	0.7	1.7	0.5	2.7	2.1	0.1	2.0	1.8	1.1	0.0	-0.2	1.4	0.3	1.0	1.8
Norway	2.3	3.8	2.8	3.5	1.9	2.5	2.4	0.2	1.6	2.8	1.6	1.1	1.8	3.6	2.1	-0.7	0.2	-0.5	0.4	0.5
Poland	..	..	7.0	7.0	6.0	5.0	5.6	3.8	8.8	5.9	3.5	4.6	5.1	4.0	1.3	2.7	2.2	1.7	2.1	3.0
Portugal	1.8	0.2	0.0	1.1	4.9	3.1	2.3	2.3	2.4	1.6	0.2	0.1	-0.3	1.4	0.8	0.7	1.8	-0.3	0.3	0.6
Slovak Republic	..	..	..	..	4.0	4.8	6.9	4.9	2.6	3.4	2.8	4.7	3.6	5.5	5.1	6.1	8.1	4.9	3.1	4.5
Spain	1.8	2.4	1.9	2.9	0.9	0.7	0.3	0.0	0.2	0.0	0.5	0.3	0.0	-0.3	-0.5	0.0	0.6	1.2	1.3	1.4
Sweden	1.5	3.4	3.4	4.8	2.5	2.3	4.0	2.0	2.2	2.0	-0.9	2.4	2.6	4.2	3.0	2.7	0.6	-0.2	1.3	3.2
Switzerland	0.1	0.5	0.6	1.9	0.4	0.7	2.0	1.2	0.5	2.5	-0.5	-0.1	0.2	2.2	1.7	0.9	0.8	-0.1	-0.4	1.4
Turkey	2.9	5.1	13.5	-12.4	4.2	4.0	7.5	0.4	-4.5	9.0	-5.7	6.5	6.1	7.3	6.8	5.5	3.2	1.5	0.9	2.5
United Kingdom	2.0	2.6	3.2	3.5	1.8	1.9	1.5	2.6	2.1	2.7	1.6	1.3	1.9	1.7	1.9	2.3	2.3	0.1	0.7	2.8
United States	1.3	3.3	0.7	1.0	0.2	1.8	2.1	1.9	2.4	1.9	0.9	2.8	2.5	2.6	1.3	1.0	1.1	1.6	0.0	1.1
Euro area	1.9	2.1	0.9	2.9	1.8	0.9	1.9	0.9	0.9	1.5	0.3	0.2	0.4	0.9	0.7	1.4	0.8	0.0	0.2	1.2
Total OECD	1.8	2.3	1.3	1.7	1.2	1.7	2.0	1.2	1.9	2.4	0.6	1.7	1.7	2.1	1.4	1.5	1.3	0.9	0.4	1.4

Note: See also OECD *Economic Outlook* Sources and Methods (*http://www.oecd.org/eco/sources-and-methods*).
Source: OECD Economic Outlook 84 database.

StatLink ᴍᴙ http://dx.doi.org/10.1787/504208516862

Annex Table 13. Unemployment rates: commonly used definitions

Per cent of labour force

	2005 Unemployment thousands	1995	1996	1997	1998	1999	2000	2001	2002	2003	2004	2005	2006	2007	2008	2009	2010	Fourth quarter 2008	2009	2010
Australia	531	8.2	8.2	8.2	7.7	6.9	6.3	6.7	6.3	5.9	5.4	5.0	4.8	4.4	4.3	5.3	6.0	4.5	5.8	6.0
Austria	253	5.5	5.9	5.9	5.9	5.5	4.8	4.9	5.6	5.8	5.9	6.0	5.6	5.1	4.9	5.7	6.0	5.1	6.0	6.0
Belgium	397	9.7	9.6	9.2	9.3	8.5	6.8	6.6	7.5	8.2	8.4	8.5	8.3	7.4	6.8	7.4	7.8	6.8	7.7	7.9
Canada	1 172	9.5	9.6	9.1	8.3	7.6	6.8	7.2	7.6	7.6	7.2	6.8	6.3	6.0	6.1	7.0	7.5	6.4	7.3	7.4
Czech Republic	410	4.1	3.9	4.8	6.5	8.8	8.9	8.2	7.3	7.8	8.3	7.9	7.2	5.3	4.5	5.2	5.5	4.6	5.5	5.5
Denmark	139	6.7	6.3	5.2	4.8	5.0	4.3	4.4	4.5	5.3	5.5	4.8	3.9	3.7	3.1	4.0	4.5	3.2	4.3	4.6
Finland	220	16.7	15.9	12.7	11.4	10.3	9.8	9.2	9.1	9.0	8.9	8.4	7.7	6.9	6.2	6.5	6.8	6.3	6.6	6.9
France	2 428	10.1	10.6	10.8	10.3	10.0	8.6	7.8	7.9	8.5	8.8	8.8	8.8	8.0	7.3	8.2	8.7	7.6	8.6	8.6
Germany	4 573	7.9	8.6	9.3	8.9	8.2	7.4	7.5	8.3	9.2	9.7	10.5	9.8	8.3	7.4	8.1	8.6	7.4	8.4	8.6
Greece	467	8.3	9.0	8.9	10.6	11.6	11.0	10.5	9.8	10.0	9.5	9.3	8.7	8.1	7.6	8.0	8.2	:	:	:
Hungary	304	10.4	10.1	8.9	7.9	7.1	6.5	5.8	5.9	5.9	6.2	7.3	7.5	7.4	7.9	8.9	9.2	8.0	9.3	9.0
Iceland	4	4.7	3.7	3.9	2.7	2.0	2.3	2.3	2.9	3.4	3.1	2.6	2.9	2.3	2.8	7.4	8.6	3.5	9.0	8.1
Ireland	89	12.3	11.8	10.7	7.6	5.6	4.3	3.9	4.4	4.6	4.5	4.3	4.4	4.6	5.9	7.7	7.8	7.3	7.8	7.6
Italy	1 881	11.3	11.3	11.4	11.5	11.1	10.2	9.2	8.8	8.6	8.1	7.8	6.8	6.2	6.9	7.8	8.0	7.2	8.2	7.8
Japan	2 943	3.1	3.4	3.4	4.1	4.7	4.7	5.0	5.4	5.3	4.7	4.4	4.1	3.9	4.1	4.4	4.4	4.3	4.4	4.4
Korea	887	2.1	2.0	2.6	7.0	6.6	4.4	4.0	3.3	3.6	3.7	3.7	3.5	3.2	3.2	3.6	3.6	3.4	3.7	3.5
Luxembourg	10	3.0	3.3	3.6	3.1	2.9	2.6	2.5	2.9	3.7	4.2	4.7	4.4	4.4	4.5	6.5	7.0	4.9	7.3	6.8
Mexico[1]	1 470	6.9	5.2	4.1	3.6	2.5	2.6	2.5	2.9	3.0	3.7	3.5	3.2	3.4	4.1	4.6	4.4	4.5	4.6	4.2
Netherlands	427	7.2	6.6	5.7	4.5	3.7	2.8	2.5	2.9	4.0	4.9	4.9	4.1	3.3	3.1	3.7	4.1	3.2	3.9	4.2
New Zealand	80	6.2	6.1	6.6	7.5	6.8	6.0	5.3	5.2	4.7	3.9	3.7	3.8	3.6	4.0	5.4	6.0	4.3	6.0	6.1
Norway	110	4.9	4.8	4.0	3.2	3.2	3.4	3.5	3.9	4.5	4.5	4.6	3.4	2.5	2.6	3.0	3.3	2.6	3.2	3.3
Poland	3 045	13.3	12.3	11.2	10.6	14.0	16.1	18.2	19.9	19.6	19.0	17.7	13.8	9.6	7.2	7.1	7.6	6.8	7.3	7.8
Portugal	422	7.2	7.3	6.7	5.0	4.4	4.0	4.0	5.0	6.3	6.7	7.7	7.7	8.0	7.6	8.5	8.8	7.8	8.8	8.7
Slovak Republic	427	13.1	11.3	11.9	12.6	16.4	18.8	19.3	18.6	17.5	18.1	16.1	13.3	11.0	9.7	9.4	9.0	9.0	9.5	8.8
Spain	1 913	18.7	17.5	16.3	14.6	12.2	10.8	10.1	11.0	11.0	10.5	9.2	8.5	8.3	10.9	14.2	14.8	12.4	14.8	14.7
Sweden	364	10.6	11.6	11.8	9.9	8.3	6.9	5.9	6.1	6.8	7.7	7.7	7.1	6.1	6.1	7.0	7.7	6.4	7.4	7.7
Switzerland	187	3.5	3.9	4.2	3.5	3.0	2.6	2.6	3.2	4.3	4.4	4.4	4.0	3.6	3.5	3.9	4.2	3.6	4.1	4.2
Turkey	2 343	7.5	6.5	6.7	6.7	7.5	6.3	8.2	10.1	10.3	10.0	10.0	9.7	9.6	9.7	10.5	10.6	:	:	:
United Kingdom	1 465	8.6	8.1	7.0	6.3	6.0	5.5	5.1	5.2	5.0	4.8	4.8	5.4	5.4	5.5	6.8	8.2	6.0	7.3	8.3
United States	7 580	5.6	5.4	4.9	4.5	4.2	4.0	4.8	5.8	6.0	5.5	5.1	4.6	4.6	5.7	7.3	7.5	6.5	7.5	7.4
Euro area	13 079	10.3	10.4	10.4	9.9	9.1	8.1	7.7	8.1	8.6	8.8	8.8	8.2	7.4	7.4	8.6	9.0	7.8	9.0	9.0
Total OECD	36 539	7.2	7.0	6.7	6.6	6.4	5.9	6.2	6.7	6.9	6.8	6.6	6.0	5.6	5.9	6.9	7.2	6.3	7.2	7.2

Note: Labour market data are subject to differences in definitions across countries and to many series breaks, though the latter are often of a minor nature. For information about definitions, sources, data coverage, breaks in series and rebasings, see *OECD Economic Outlook Sources and Methods* (*http://www.oecd.org/eco/sources-and-methods*).

1. Based on National Employment Survey.

Source: OECD Economic Outlook 84 database.

StatLink http://dx.doi.org/10.1787/504265451240

Annex Table 14. Standardised unemployment rates

Per cent of civilian labour force

	1989	1990	1991	1992	1993	1994	1995	1996	1997	1998	1999	2000	2001	2002	2003	2004	2005	2006	2007
Australia	6.0	6.7	9.3	10.5	10.6	9.5	8.2	8.2	8.3	7.7	6.9	6.3	6.7	6.4	5.9	5.4	5.1	4.8	4.4
Austria	..	..	..	..	3.9	3.8	3.9	4.4	4.4	4.5	3.9	3.7	3.6	4.2	4.3	4.8	5.2	4.7	4.4
Belgium	7.4	6.6	6.4	7.1	8.6	9.8	9.7	9.6	9.2	9.3	8.5	6.9	6.6	7.5	8.2	8.4	8.5	8.3	7.5
Canada	7.5	8.1	10.3	11.2	11.4	10.4	9.5	9.6	9.1	8.3	7.6	6.8	7.2	7.7	7.6	7.2	6.8	6.3	6.0
Czech Republic	..	..	..	..	4.4	4.3	4.1	3.9	4.8	6.4	8.6	8.7	8.0	7.3	7.8	8.3	7.9	7.2	5.3
Denmark	6.8	7.2	7.9	8.6	9.5	7.7	6.8	6.3	5.2	4.9	5.1	4.3	4.5	4.6	5.4	5.5	4.8	3.9	3.8
Finland	3.1	3.2	6.7	11.6	16.2	16.8	15.1	14.9	12.7	11.4	10.3	9.6	9.1	9.1	9.1	8.8	8.4	7.7	6.8
France	8.8	8.4	8.9	9.8	11.0	11.6	11.0	11.5	11.4	11.0	10.4	9.0	8.3	8.6	9.0	9.3	9.3	9.2	8.3
Germany[1]	5.6	4.8	4.2	6.3	7.6	8.2	8.0	8.7	9.4	9.0	8.3	7.5	7.6	8.4	9.3	9.8	10.6	9.8	8.4
Greece	6.7	6.3	6.9	7.8	8.6	8.8	9.0	9.7	9.6	11.1	12.0	11.3	10.7	10.3	9.7	10.5	9.9	8.9	8.3
Hungary	..	..	..	10.0	12.1	11.0	10.4	9.6	9.0	8.4	6.9	6.4	5.8	5.8	5.9	6.1	7.2	7.4	7.3
Ireland	14.7	13.4	14.7	15.4	15.6	14.4	12.3	11.6	9.9	7.6	5.7	4.3	3.9	4.5	4.7	4.5	4.4	4.5	4.6
Italy	9.7	8.9	8.5	8.8	9.8	10.6	11.2	11.2	11.2	11.4	11.0	10.1	9.1	8.7	8.5	8.1	7.7	6.8	6.2
Japan	2.3	2.1	2.1	2.2	2.5	2.9	3.1	3.4	3.4	4.1	4.7	4.7	5.0	5.4	5.3	4.7	4.4	4.1	3.9
Korea	2.6	2.4	2.4	2.5	2.9	2.5	2.1	2.0	2.6	7.0	6.6	4.4	4.0	3.3	3.6	3.7	3.7	3.5	3.2
Luxembourg	1.8	1.7	1.6	2.1	2.6	3.2	2.9	2.9	2.7	2.7	2.4	2.3	1.9	2.6	3.8	4.9	4.6	4.6	4.2
Netherlands	6.6	5.9	5.5	5.3	6.2	6.8	6.6	6.0	4.9	3.8	3.2	2.8	2.2	2.8	3.7	4.6	4.7	3.9	3.2
New Zealand	7.1	7.8	10.3	10.4	9.5	8.1	6.3	6.1	6.6	7.4	6.8	6.0	5.3	5.2	4.6	3.9	3.7	3.8	3.6
Norway	5.4	5.8	5.8	6.5	6.6	6.0	5.5	4.8	4.0	3.2	3.2	3.4	3.6	3.9	4.5	4.4	4.6	3.5	2.6
Poland	..	..	..	..	16.3	16.9	15.4	14.1	10.9	10.2	13.4	16.2	18.3	20.0	19.7	19.0	17.8	13.9	9.6
Portugal	5.2	4.8	4.2	4.1	5.5	6.8	7.2	7.2	6.7	5.0	4.5	4.0	4.0	5.1	6.4	6.8	7.7	7.8	8.1
Slovak Republic	..	..	..	..	..	13.7	13.1	11.3	11.9	12.7	16.3	18.8	19.3	18.7	17.6	18.2	16.3	13.4	11.2
Spain	13.9	13.0	13.0	14.7	18.3	19.5	18.4	17.8	16.7	15.0	12.5	11.1	10.4	11.1	11.1	10.6	9.2	8.5	8.3
Sweden	1.6	1.7	3.1	5.6	9.1	9.4	8.8	9.6	9.9	8.2	6.7	5.6	4.9	5.0	5.6	6.3	7.3	7.0	6.2
Switzerland	..	..	1.9	3.1	4.0	3.8	3.5	3.9	4.2	3.5	3.0	2.6	2.6	3.2	4.3	4.4	4.4	4.0	3.6
United Kingdom	7.1	6.9	8.6	9.8	10.2	9.3	8.5	7.9	6.8	6.1	5.9	5.4	5.0	5.1	5.0	4.7	4.8	5.4	5.3
United States	5.3	5.6	6.8	7.5	6.9	6.1	5.6	5.4	4.9	4.5	4.2	4.0	4.7	5.8	6.0	5.5	5.1	4.6	4.6
Euro area	..	..	7.8	8.5	10.0	10.7	10.4	10.6	10.5	10.0	9.2	8.3	7.8	8.2	8.7	8.8	8.8	8.2	7.4
Total OECD	6.2	6.1	6.8	7.4	7.8	7.6	7.2	7.2	6.9	6.8	6.7	6.2	6.4	6.9	7.1	6.9	6.7	6.1	5.6

Note: In so far as possible, the data have been adjusted to ensure comparability over time and to conform to the guidelines of the International Labour Office. All series are benchmarked to labour-force-survey-based estimates. In countries with annual surveys, monthly estimates are obtained by interpolation/extrapolation and by incorporating trends in administrative data, where available. The annual figures are then calculated by averaging the monthly estimates (for both unemployed and the labour force). For countries with monthly or quarterly surveys, the annual estimates are obtained by averaging the monthly or quarterly estimates, respectively. For several countries, the adjustment procedure used is similar to that of the Bureau of Labor Statistics, U.S. Department of Labor. For EU countries, the procedures are similar to those used in deriving the Comparable Unemployment Rates (CURs) of the Statistical Office of the European Communities. Minor differences may appear mainly because of various methods of calculating and applying adjustment factors, and because EU estimates are based on the civilian labour force. See technical notes in OECD Quarterly Labour Force Statistics.

Source: OECD Main Economic Indicators.

1. Prior to July 1991 data refers to Western Germany.

StatLink http://dx.doi.org/10.1787/504306614103

Annex Table 15. Labour force, employment and unemployment

Millions

	1992	1993	1994	1995	1996	1997	1998	1999	2000	2001	2002	2003	2004	2005	2006	2007	2008	2009	2010
Labour force																			
Major seven countries	325.4	326.6	329.0	330.8	333.7	337.5	340.0	342.7	347.2	349.2	351.0	353.4	355.3	358.4	361.6	364.3	366.9	368.4	370.2
Total of smaller countries[1]	138.9	166.3	172.4	175.0	177.4	180.3	182.6	184.4	186.4	188.6	191.7	193.0	196.7	199.2	202.4	205.3	208.4	210.2	211.9
Euro area	132.6	132.6	133.3	133.9	135.0	135.9	137.6	139.1	140.9	142.5	144.2	145.5	147.2	148.9	150.3	151.7	153.3	154.2	154.8
Total OECD[1]	464.3	492.9	501.4	505.8	511.1	517.8	522.6	527.2	533.5	537.8	542.7	546.4	552.0	557.7	564.0	569.6	575.3	578.6	582.0
Employment																			
Major seven countries	303.1	303.6	306.4	309.1	311.7	315.9	318.9	322.2	327.8	328.9	328.5	330.0	332.8	336.4	340.8	344.6	345.6	342.9	343.3
Total of smaller countries[1]	129.9	152.7	158.0	160.2	163.6	167.2	169.2	171.2	174.0	175.6	177.6	178.5	181.8	184.7	189.2	193.1	195.7	195.5	196.7
Euro area	121.7	119.7	119.3	120.2	120.9	121.8	124.0	126.4	129.4	131.5	132.5	133.0	134.3	135.8	138.0	140.5	141.9	140.9	140.8
Total OECD[1]	433.0	456.3	464.5	469.3	475.3	483.1	488.1	493.4	501.8	504.5	506.1	508.5	514.6	521.1	530.0	537.8	541.3	538.5	540.0
Unemployment																			
Major seven countries	22.3	23.0	22.5	21.7	22.0	21.6	21.1	20.6	19.3	20.3	22.5	23.3	22.5	22.0	20.9	19.7	21.3	25.5	26.9
Total of smaller countries[1]	9.0	13.6	14.4	14.8	13.8	13.1	13.4	13.2	12.4	13.0	14.1	14.5	14.9	14.5	13.2	12.1	12.7	14.7	15.2
Euro area	10.8	12.8	14.0	13.8	14.1	14.1	13.6	12.7	11.5	11.0	11.7	12.6	12.9	13.1	12.3	11.2	11.4	13.3	14.0
Total OECD[1]	31.3	36.6	36.9	36.5	35.8	34.7	34.5	33.8	31.7	33.3	36.6	37.8	37.4	36.5	34.0	31.9	34.0	40.1	42.1

1. The aggregate measures include Mexico as of 1991. There is a potential bias in the aggregates thereafter because of the limited coverage of the Mexican National Survey of Urban Employment.
Source: OECD Economic Outlook 84 database.

StatLink ⬛⬛ http://dx.doi.org/10.1787/504340357170

Annex Table 16. GDP deflators
Percentage change from previous year

	Average 1984-94	1995	1996	1997	1998	1999	2000	2001	2002	2003	2004	2005	2006	2007	2008	2009	2010	Fourth quarter 2008	2009	2010
Australia	4.6	1.6	2.2	1.5	0.3	0.5	4.2	3.9	2.9	2.8	4.1	4.1	4.9	3.5	5.8	2.1	2.3	5.8	1.4	2.3
Austria	2.9	1.9	1.0	-0.3	0.1	0.2	1.4	1.6	1.3	1.3	1.6	1.8	1.9	2.2	2.6	1.7	1.1	2.5	1.3	0.9
Belgium	3.1	1.2	0.5	1.1	2.0	0.3	1.9	2.1	1.8	1.6	2.3	2.5	2.3	2.4	2.1	2.3	1.8	2.6	2.1	1.7
Canada	3.0	2.3	1.6	1.2	-0.4	1.7	4.1	1.1	1.1	3.3	3.2	3.4	2.5	3.1	3.3	-1.0	1.0	1.0	0.6	1.2
Czech Republic	..	10.2	10.2	8.4	11.1	2.8	1.5	4.9	2.8	0.9	4.5	-0.3	0.9	3.6	2.4	2.3	1.8	2.5	1.6	2.0
Denmark	3.0	1.3	2.0	2.0	1.2	1.7	3.0	2.5	2.3	1.6	2.3	3.1	2.0	1.7	3.4	2.3	2.2	2.6	2.6	1.9
Finland	4.0	5.1	-0.1	1.6	3.6	0.8	2.6	2.9	1.3	-0.4	0.8	0.1	1.5	2.8	3.3	3.3	2.1	3.1	2.9	1.7
France	3.0	1.3	1.6	1.0	0.9	0.0	1.4	2.0	2.4	1.9	1.6	2.0	2.5	2.5	2.3	1.7	1.1	2.1	1.5	1.0
Germany	2.8	1.9	0.5	0.3	0.6	0.3	-0.7	1.2	1.4	1.2	1.0	0.7	0.5	1.9	1.6	1.8	1.4	2.3	1.3	1.4
Greece	16.5	9.8	7.4	6.8	5.2	3.0	3.4	2.7	3.7	3.5	3.4	3.3	3.4	2.9	3.5	3.8	3.6	3.9	4.0	3.2
Hungary	..	26.7	21.2	18.5	12.6	8.4	9.9	8.4	7.8	5.8	4.4	2.2	3.9	5.7	5.9	3.6	2.7	5.4	3.1	2.4
Iceland	15.0	3.0	2.5	2.9	5.1	3.3	3.6	8.6	5.6	0.6	2.5	2.8	9.0	5.6	9.3	15.2	6.7	13.6	12.0	5.1
Ireland	3.3	3.0	2.3	3.8	6.6	4.0	6.1	5.5	4.6	2.5	2.1	2.3	3.4	1.4	-0.9	0.7	0.3	0.2	0.4	0.1
Italy	6.3	5.0	4.8	2.6	2.6	1.8	1.9	3.0	3.3	3.1	2.6	2.1	1.7	2.3	3.9	2.5	1.3	5.2	1.1	1.3
Japan	1.4	-0.5	-0.6	0.6	0.0	-1.3	-1.7	-1.2	-1.5	-1.6	-1.1	-1.2	-1.0	-0.8	-1.0	1.3	-0.3	1.0	-0.2	-0.3
Korea	7.2	7.4	5.1	4.6	5.8	-0.1	0.7	3.5	2.8	2.7	2.7	-0.2	-0.5	1.2	3.6	2.7	0.2	5.9	0.5	0.0
Luxembourg	2.7	2.3	2.9	-1.6	0.4	4.7	1.2	1.1	1.5	5.8	2.8	4.1	5.1	1.7	1.5	2.4	1.7	..	..	..
Mexico	43.0	37.8	30.7	17.7	15.4	15.1	12.1	5.9	6.9	8.5	9.1	4.4	6.8	4.7	6.8	4.6	3.4	5.7	4.0	3.0
Netherlands	1.5	2.1	1.3	2.6	1.9	1.8	4.1	5.1	3.8	2.2	0.7	2.4	1.7	1.5	1.8	1.5	1.5	1.9	1.7	1.5
New Zealand	6.5	2.2	2.5	0.6	0.8	0.4	2.5	4.3	1.1	1.4	3.8	1.8	2.4	4.3	3.6	1.7	2.4	1.1	2.6	2.3
Norway	2.9	3.0	4.2	2.8	-0.8	6.6	15.7	1.7	-1.8	3.0	5.3	8.7	8.4	1.6	6.2	-4.8	2.6	-4.1	2.9	1.5
Poland	..	28.0	17.9	13.9	11.1	6.0	7.3	3.5	2.2	0.4	4.1	2.6	1.5	3.9	3.4	3.7	3.5	3.7	3.6	3.4
Portugal	12.2	3.4	2.6	3.8	3.8	3.3	3.0	3.7	3.9	3.2	2.4	2.5	2.8	2.9	2.2	2.3	1.8	2.1	1.8	1.8
Slovak Republic	..	9.9	4.1	4.9	5.0	7.4	9.4	5.0	3.9	5.3	5.9	2.4	2.9	1.1	4.9	3.5	2.6	6.3	1.9	2.9
Spain	6.7	4.9	3.5	2.4	2.5	2.6	3.5	4.2	4.3	4.1	4.0	4.3	4.0	3.2	3.4	2.5	1.1	3.2	2.1	0.8
Sweden	5.6	3.4	0.9	1.3	0.7	1.2	1.4	2.1	1.6	1.8	0.8	0.9	1.5	2.9	3.7	2.5	1.6	4.3	1.0	2.0
Switzerland	2.9	0.7	0.2	-0.1	0.3	0.6	1.1	0.8	0.5	1.0	0.6	0.1	1.7	1.8	2.7	2.0	1.3	2.9	1.7	1.1
Turkey	61.1	87.2	77.8	81.5	75.7	54.2	49.2	52.9	37.4	23.3	12.4	7.1	9.3	7.6	12.7	9.1	8.1	..	..	..
United Kingdom	5.0	2.7	3.6	2.8	2.2	2.1	1.2	2.1	3.1	3.1	2.5	2.2	2.6	2.9	3.3	2.5	1.5	3.7	1.9	1.3
United States	2.9	2.0	1.9	1.7	1.1	1.4	2.2	2.4	1.7	2.1	2.9	3.3	3.2	2.7	2.2	1.8	1.5	2.3	1.6	1.5
Euro area	4.2	2.7	1.9	1.4	1.6	1.0	1.4	2.4	2.6	2.2	1.9	2.0	2.0	2.3	2.4	2.0	1.3	2.8	1.6	1.2
Total OECD	6.6	5.8	4.8	4.2	3.6	2.7	3.1	3.2	2.7	2.5	2.6	2.3	2.5	2.4	2.6	2.1	1.5	2.9	1.6	1.4

Note: The adoption of new National Accounts systems, SNA93 or ESA95, has been proceeding at an uneven pace among OECD member countries, both with respect to variables and the time period covered. As a consequence, there are breaks in many national series. See Table "National Accounts Reporting Systems and Base-years" at the beginning of the Statistical Annex and *OECD Economic Outlook* Sources and Methods (*http://www.oecd.org/eco/sources-and-methods*).

Source: OECD Economic Outlook 84 database.

StatLink ᔖ *http://dx.doi.org/10.1787/504371303541*

Annex Table 17. Private consumption deflators
Percentage change from previous year

	Average 1984-94	1995	1996	1997	1998	1999	2000	2001	2002	2003	2004	2005	2006	2007	2008	2009	2010	Fourth quarter 2008	2009	2010
Australia	5.4	2.2	2.1	1.7	1.3	0.5	2.9	3.7	2.7	2.2	1.2	1.7	2.8	2.6	3.9	3.6	2.4	4.4	2.9	2.2
Austria	2.7	2.1	1.9	1.5	0.5	0.5	2.5	1.8	0.7	1.6	2.0	2.2	1.8	2.3	3.1	1.2	0.8	2.5	0.8	0.8
Belgium	2.9	2.1	1.0	1.5	1.2	0.1	3.5	2.2	1.3	1.6	2.6	2.9	2.8	2.8	4.5	1.9	1.6	3.6	1.8	1.5
Canada	3.5	1.3	1.6	1.6	1.2	1.7	2.2	1.8	2.0	1.6	1.5	1.7	1.4	1.6	1.5	0.8	0.9	1.2	1.1	0.8
Czech Republic	..	9.2	7.7	9.0	8.9	1.9	3.2	3.9	1.2	-0.4	3.3	0.8	1.6	2.8	5.4	2.3	2.1	3.8	2.1	2.1
Denmark	2.8	1.8	1.6	2.0	1.4	1.9	2.7	2.3	1.7	1.3	1.3	2.1	2.1	1.9	2.5	1.5	1.6	2.2	1.8	1.4
Finland	4.2	1.2	0.4	2.2	2.1	1.4	4.3	2.7	2.1	-0.3	1.0	0.5	1.6	2.2	2.8	1.9	1.7	2.7	1.7	1.7
France	3.0	1.0	1.6	0.9	0.2	-0.5	2.3	1.7	1.0	1.9	1.9	1.8	2.2	1.7	2.7	0.9	0.8	2.0	0.8	0.7
Germany	2.2	1.3	0.9	1.4	0.5	0.3	0.9	1.8	1.2	1.5	1.3	1.5	1.3	1.7	2.1	1.0	1.3	1.6	1.1	1.3
Greece	16.8	9.0	8.2	5.6	4.5	2.3	3.1	2.7	2.5	2.7	2.4	3.3	3.5	3.1	4.5	2.7	2.4	4.5	..	..
Hungary	..	28.3	22.9	18.0	13.6	10.2	11.0	8.2	3.9	4.1	4.6	3.8	3.4	6.4	5.7	4.2	3.1	5.1	3.4	3.1
Iceland	15.1	2.2	2.5	0.8	1.5	2.8	5.0	7.8	4.8	1.3	3.0	1.9	7.6	4.7	12.5	15.2	7.1	16.1	13.4	4.7
Ireland	3.2	2.8	2.6	2.6	3.6	2.6	6.3	4.2	5.1	3.9	1.6	1.5	2.2	3.0	3.4	1.0	1.0	2.4	0.8	1.2
Italy	6.2	6.0	4.1	2.2	1.8	1.8	3.4	2.6	2.9	2.8	2.6	2.3	2.7	2.2	3.6	1.7	1.5	3.1	1.5	1.4
Japan	1.3	-0.2	0.0	1.3	0.2	-0.5	-1.1	-1.1	-1.4	-0.9	-0.7	-0.8	-0.3	-0.5	0.4	-0.2	-0.3	0.2	-0.2	-0.3
Korea	6.7	6.6	6.2	6.0	6.7	3.3	4.8	4.8	2.8	3.4	3.5	2.6	2.1	2.6	5.4	3.9	2.9	6.2	2.7	3.0
Luxembourg	2.9	2.0	1.0	1.8	1.7	2.5	3.7	2.3	0.5	2.2	2.1	3.1	2.2	2.1	5.2	1.9	1.7	..	..	..
Mexico	44.2	34.0	30.9	16.6	20.4	14.0	10.3	7.1	5.3	7.1	6.5	3.4	3.5	4.6	5.2	5.2	3.9	5.6	4.8	3.5
Netherlands	1.9	2.1	2.0	2.3	2.0	1.9	3.8	4.5	3.0	2.4	1.0	2.1	1.9	1.6	1.8	1.6	1.6	1.6	1.8	1.5
New Zealand	6.6	2.1	2.4	1.8	1.9	0.7	2.2	2.3	1.9	0.5	1.1	1.7	2.8	1.7	3.5	2.3	1.1	4.0	1.4	1.0
Norway	4.5	2.3	1.3	2.4	2.5	2.0	2.9	2.2	1.4	3.0	0.7	1.1	2.1	0.7	3.5	2.7	1.8	3.3	2.4	1.8
Poland	..	27.2	18.6	14.7	10.5	6.1	10.0	3.8	3.3	0.4	3.0	2.1	1.2	2.4	4.1	2.9	3.5	3.5	3.5	3.4
Portugal	11.2	4.3	2.9	2.9	2.3	2.2	3.4	3.4	3.0	2.9	2.5	2.7	3.1	2.7	2.8	1.4	1.6	2.1	1.6	1.6
Slovak Republic	..	9.2	4.0	4.8	5.7	9.9	8.2	5.6	2.8	6.5	7.4	2.6	4.9	2.6	4.0	2.7	2.8	3.5	2.6	2.8
Spain	6.4	4.8	3.2	2.7	1.9	2.3	3.7	3.4	2.8	3.1	3.6	3.4	3.4	3.2	4.3	1.8	1.5	3.4	1.4	1.5
Sweden	6.2	3.0	1.0	1.5	0.5	1.4	1.0	2.2	1.7	1.7	0.9	1.2	0.9	1.3	2.4	1.3	1.0	2.3	1.1	1.1
Switzerland	2.7	1.4	1.3	0.8	-0.1	0.4	0.8	0.7	0.9	0.4	0.8	0.5	1.3	1.1	1.5	0.6	1.1	1.0	0.9	1.0
Turkey	62.2	92.4	67.8	82.1	83.0	53.4	54.9	49.7	38.5	23.4	10.8	8.3	9.8	8.6	13.0	8.9	7.6	13.0	..	..
United Kingdom	5.0	3.2	3.5	2.5	2.4	1.2	1.1	2.0	2.0	1.9	1.6	2.5	2.3	2.4	3.3	3.4	2.2	4.4	2.7	1.8
United States	3.3	2.1	2.2	1.7	0.9	1.7	2.5	2.1	1.4	2.0	2.6	2.9	2.8	2.6	3.6	1.2	1.3	2.8	1.1	1.2
Euro area	4.1	2.6	2.1	1.8	1.1	0.8	2.4	2.4	1.8	2.1	2.0	2.1	2.2	2.2	3.0	1.4	1.3	2.4	1.3	1.3
Total OECD	6.8	5.8	4.8	4.4	3.8	2.8	3.6	3.1	2.3	2.3	2.3	2.2	2.3	2.3	3.3	1.7	1.5	2.9	1.5	1.4

Note: The adoption of new National Accounts systems, SNA93 or ESA95, has been proceeding at an uneven pace among OECD member countries, both with respect to variables and the time period covered. As a consequence, there are breaks in many national series. See Table "National Accounts Reporting Systems and Base-years" at the beginning of the Statistical Annex and *OECD Economic Outlook* Sources and Methods (*http://www.oecd.org/eco/sources-and-methods*).

Source: OECD Economic Outlook 84 database.

StatLink http://dx.doi.org/10.1787/504387070345

Annex Table 18. Consumer price indices
Percentage change from previous year

	Average 1984-94	1995	1996	1997	1998	1999	2000	2001	2002	2003	2004	2005	2006	2007	2008	2009	2010	Fourth quarter 2008	2009	2010
Australia	5.4	4.6	2.6	0.3	0.9	1.5	4.5	4.4	3.0	2.8	2.3	2.7	3.5	2.3	4.6	3.3	2.4	4.8	2.8	2.2
Austria	..	1.6	1.8	1.2	0.8	0.5	2.0	2.3	1.7	1.3	2.0	2.1	1.7	2.2	3.3	1.1	0.8	2.4	0.8	0.8
Belgium	..	1.3	1.8	1.5	0.9	1.1	2.7	2.4	1.6	1.5	1.9	2.5	2.3	1.8	4.6	1.9	1.6	3.8	1.8	1.5
Canada	3.5	2.1	1.6	1.6	1.0	1.7	2.7	2.5	2.3	2.8	1.9	2.2	2.0	2.1	2.6	1.2	1.0	2.7	1.2	0.9
Czech Republic	..	9.1	8.8	8.5	10.7	2.1	3.9	4.7	1.8	0.1	2.8	1.9	2.6	3.0	6.6	2.0	2.6	5.5	2.2	2.7
Denmark	3.2	2.1	2.1	2.2	1.8	2.5	2.9	2.3	2.4	2.1	1.2	1.8	1.9	1.7	3.5	1.6	1.6	3.1	1.8	1.4
Finland	..	0.4	1.1	1.2	1.3	1.3	2.9	2.7	2.0	1.3	0.1	0.8	1.3	1.6	4.0	1.9	1.6	4.1	1.6	1.5
France	..	1.8	2.1	1.3	0.7	0.6	1.8	1.8	1.9	2.2	2.3	1.9	1.9	1.6	3.3	1.0	0.8	2.5	0.9	0.7
Germany	..	..	1.2	1.5	0.6	0.6	1.4	1.9	1.4	1.0	1.8	1.9	1.8	2.3	2.9	1.1	1.3	2.1	1.1	1.3
Greece	16.6	8.9	7.9	5.4	4.5	2.1	2.9	3.7	3.9	3.4	3.0	3.5	3.3	3.0	4.5	2.7	2.4	4.0	2.3	2.3
Hungary	..	28.3	23.5	18.3	14.2	10.0	9.8	9.1	5.3	4.7	6.7	3.6	3.9	8.0	6.4	3.6	3.2	5.7	3.3	3.3
Iceland[1]	14.6	1.7	2.3	1.8	1.7	3.2	5.1	6.4	5.2	2.1	3.2	4.0	6.7	5.1	12.1	14.9	6.9	15.0	13.4	4.7
Ireland	..	..	2.2	1.3	2.1	2.5	5.3	4.0	4.7	4.0	2.3	2.2	2.7	2.9	3.1	0.9	0.9	2.1	1.0	1.1
Italy	..	5.4	4.0	1.9	2.0	1.7	2.6	2.3	2.6	2.8	2.3	2.2	2.2	2.0	3.5	1.5	1.5	2.9	1.5	1.4
Japan	1.6	-0.1	0.0	1.7	0.7	-0.3	-0.5	-0.8	-0.9	-0.2	0.0	-0.6	0.2	0.1	1.4	0.3	-0.1	1.4	-0.2	-0.1
Korea	5.6	4.5	4.9	4.4	7.5	0.8	2.3	4.1	2.7	3.6	3.6	2.8	2.2	2.5	5.0	3.9	2.9	5.7	2.7	3.0
Luxembourg	..	..	1.2	1.4	1.0	1.0	3.8	2.4	2.1	2.5	3.2	3.8	3.0	2.7	4.5	1.9	1.7	..	..	..
Mexico	43.4	35.0	34.4	20.6	15.9	16.6	9.5	6.4	5.0	4.5	4.7	4.0	3.6	4.0	4.9	5.3	3.8	5.2	5.0	3.2
Netherlands	..	1.4	1.4	1.9	1.8	2.0	2.3	5.1	3.9	2.2	1.4	1.5	1.7	1.6	2.3	1.8	1.6	2.2	1.8	1.5
New Zealand	6.8	3.8	2.3	1.2	1.3	-0.1	2.6	2.6	2.7	1.8	2.3	3.0	3.4	2.4	4.0	2.3	2.1	3.7	2.1	2.0
Norway	4.6	2.4	1.2	2.6	2.3	2.3	3.1	3.0	1.3	2.5	0.5	1.5	2.3	0.7	3.6	2.5	1.8	3.0	2.4	1.8
Poland	..	28.0	19.8	14.9	11.6	7.2	9.9	5.4	1.9	0.7	3.4	2.2	1.3	2.5	4.2	3.2	3.6	3.7	3.6	3.5
Portugal	..	4.0	2.9	1.9	2.2	2.2	2.8	4.4	3.7	3.3	2.5	2.1	3.0	2.4	2.8	1.3	1.6	2.1	1.6	1.5
Slovak Republic	..	9.8	5.8	6.1	6.7	10.6	12.0	7.3	3.1	8.6	7.5	2.7	4.5	2.8	4.4	2.8	2.8	4.0	2.6	2.8
Spain	6.2	4.6	3.6	1.9	1.8	2.2	3.5	2.8	3.6	3.1	3.1	3.4	3.6	2.8	4.4	1.8	1.5	3.5	1.4	1.5
Sweden	5.7	2.5	0.5	0.7	-0.3	0.5	0.9	2.4	2.2	1.9	0.4	0.5	1.4	2.2	3.5	1.5	1.1	2.5	1.2	1.1
Switzerland	3.0	1.8	0.8	0.5	0.0	0.8	1.6	1.0	0.6	0.6	0.8	1.2	1.1	0.7	2.5	1.0	1.1	1.9	1.0	1.0
Turkey	60.7	89.1	80.4	85.7	84.6	64.9	54.9	54.4	45.0	21.6	8.6	8.2	9.6	8.8	10.3	8.3	7.6	..	..	..
United Kingdom[2]	..	2.7	2.5	1.8	1.6	1.3	0.8	1.2	1.3	1.4	1.3	2.0	2.3	2.3	3.7	2.7	1.9	4.2	2.1	1.8
United States[3]	3.6	2.8	2.9	2.3	1.5	2.2	3.4	2.8	1.6	2.3	2.7	3.4	3.2	2.9	4.3	1.6	1.5	3.6	1.3	1.4
Euro area	..	3.0	2.3	1.7	1.2	1.1	2.1	2.4	2.3	2.1	2.2	2.2	2.2	2.1	3.4	1.4	1.3	2.7	1.3	1.3

Note: Consumer price index. For the euro area countries, the euro area aggregate and the United Kingdom: harmonised index of consumer prices (HICP).
1. Excluding rent, but including imputed rent.
2. Known as the CPI in the United Kingdom.
3. The methodology for calculating the Consumer Price Index has changed considerably over the past years, lowering measured inflation substantially.
Source: OECD Economic Outlook 84 database.

StatLink ⟍⟋ http://dx.doi.org/10.1787/504454501551

Annex Table 19. Oil and other primary commodity markets

	1993	1994	1995	1996	1997	1998	1999	2000	2001	2002	2003	2004	2005	2006	2007	2008	2009	2010
Oil market conditions[1]																		
Demand																		
							Million barrels per day											
OECD[2]	43.3	44.4	44.9	46.0	46.7	46.9	47.8	47.9	47.9	47.9	48.6	49.4	49.7	49.3	49.2	47.8	47.1	..
of which: North America	21.1	21.7	21.6	22.2	22.7	23.1	23.8	24.1	24.0	24.1	24.5	25.4	25.5	25.3	25.5	24.4	24.0	..
Europe[3]	14.3	14.4	14.7	15.0	15.1	15.4	15.3	15.2	15.4	15.3	15.4	15.5	15.6	15.6	15.3	15.2	15.0	..
Pacific	8.0	8.4	8.6	8.8	8.9	8.4	8.7	8.6	8.5	8.5	8.6	8.5	8.6	8.4	8.3	8.2	8.1	..
Non-OECD[4]	24.6	24.2	25.2	26.0	26.9	27.3	28.0	28.6	29.2	29.8	30.7	33.0	34.1	35.5	36.9	38.4	39.5	..
Total	67.9	68.6	70.1	72.0	73.6	74.2	75.8	76.5	77.1	77.7	79.3	82.3	83.7	84.9	86.1	86.2	86.5	..
Supply																		
OECD[2]	20.0	20.8	21.1	21.7	22.1	21.9	21.5	21.9	21.8	21.9	21.6	21.2	20.3	20.0	19.8	19.3	19.1	..
OPEC total	27.2	27.6	27.9	28.7	30.2	31.0	29.6	31.0	30.5	28.9	30.8	33.1	34.2	34.3	35.5	..	..	..
Former USSR	7.9	7.3	7.1	7.1	7.2	7.3	7.5	7.9	8.6	9.4	10.3	11.2	11.6	12.2	12.8	12.8	13.0	..
Other non-OECD[4]	12.6	13.4	14.5	15.0	15.4	15.7	16.0	16.2	16.4	16.9	17.1	17.7	18.2	18.8	17.5	..	..	..
Total	67.7	69.1	70.6	72.5	74.8	75.9	74.5	77.1	77.3	77.0	79.8	83.2	84.4	85.4	85.6	..	..	..
Trade																		
OECD net imports[2]	23.5	23.8	23.5	24.3	25.0	25.4	25.6	26.1	26.4	25.8	27.3	28.3	29.5	29.6	29.2	28.7	28.0	..
Former USSR net exports	2.0	2.7	2.8	3.1	3.4	3.6	3.9	4.3	4.9	5.9	6.7	7.5	7.8	8.2	8.6	8.5	8.7	..
Other non-OECD net exports[4]	21.5	21.1	20.7	21.1	21.5	21.8	21.7	21.8	21.5	19.9	20.5	20.8	21.7	21.4	20.5	20.1	19.3	..
Prices[5]																		
							cif, $ per bl											
Brent crude oil import price	17.0	15.8	17.0	20.7	19.1	12.7	17.9	28.4	24.5	25.0	28.8	38.2	54.4	65.1	72.5	99.3	60.0	60.0
Prices of other primary commodities[5]																		
							$ indices											
Food and tropical beverages	113	146	151	156	159	133	108	100	93	104	112	125	126	139	174	242	197	192
Agricultural raw materials	99	120	141	118	113	97	94	100	86	85	104	114	115	129	156	157	143	141
Minerals, ores and metals	87	103	122	108	110	93	89	100	91	89	102	140	172	248	280	308	224	224
Total[6]	109	128	139	143	139	116	100	100	92	99	111	128	127	148	186	241	192	188

1. Based on data published in in varoius issues of International Energy Agency, Oil Market Report and Annual Statistical Supplement, August 2008.
2. Excluding Czech Republic, Hungary, Korea, Mexico and Poland.
3. European Union countries and Iceland, Norway, Switzerland and Turkey.
4. Including Czech Republic, Hungary, Korea, Mexico and Poland.
5. Indices through 2007 are based on data compiled by International Energy Agency for oil and by Hamburg Institute for Economic Research for the prices of other primary commodities; OECD estimates and projections for 2008 to 2010.
6. OECD calculations. The total price index for non-energy primary commodities is a weighted average of the individual HWWA non-oil commodities indices with the weights drawn from the commodities' share in total non-energy commodities world trade.

Source: OECD Economic Outlook 84 database.

StatLink http://dx.doi.org/10.1787/504461267035

Annex Table 20. Employment rates, participation rates and labour force

| | Employment rates | | | | | | Labour force participation rates | | | | | | Labour force | | | | | |
| | Per cent | | | | | | Per cent | | | | | | Percentage change | | | | | |
	Average 1987-89	Average 1997-99	2007	2008	2009	2010	Average 1987-89	Average 1997-99	2007	2008	2009	2010	Average 1987-96	Average 1997-06	2007	2008	2009	2010
Australia	67.7	69.2	74.1	74.3	73.4	72.6	72.7	74.8	77.5	77.6	77.5	77.3	1.8	1.7	2.5	2.0	1.6	1.5
Austria	69.9	71.1	73.1	74.0	73.7	73.6	73.0	75.5	77.1	77.8	78.2	78.3	0.7	0.7	1.1	1.3	0.9	0.6
Belgium	57.2	59.7	63.1	63.3	62.6	62.2	62.7	65.6	68.2	67.9	67.7	67.5	0.5	1.0	0.9	0.8	0.5	0.6
Canada	70.8	70.0	75.2	75.4	74.2	73.9	76.9	76.4	80.0	80.4	79.8	79.9	1.0	1.7	2.0	1.5	0.3	1.1
Czech Republic	..	67.5	66.8	67.4	67.1	67.0	..	72.4	70.5	70.6	70.7	70.9	..	0.1	0.0	0.4	0.2	0.3
Denmark	77.7	76.5	79.2	79.9	78.5	77.7	82.4	80.5	82.2	82.5	81.8	81.4	0.0	0.3	1.4	0.5	-1.0	-0.6
Finland	72.7	64.5	70.5	71.7	71.8	71.7	76.3	72.9	75.7	76.5	76.8	77.0	-0.3	0.7	1.0	1.3	-0.5	0.4
France	61.7	61.2	63.7	64.2	63.5	63.1	67.6	68.3	69.2	69.3	69.2	69.2	0.4	0.7	0.8	0.7	0.4	0.6
Germany	67.3	67.8	73.0	74.1	73.8	73.6	71.3	74.3	79.6	80.0	80.3	80.5	0.8	0.5	0.1	0.3	0.0	0.3
Greece	60.2	60.0	65.2	65.8	65.9	66.1	64.5	67.0	71.0	71.3	71.6	72.0	0.9	1.4	0.7	0.8	0.8	0.8
Hungary	..	52.4	56.2	55.4	54.7	54.6	..	56.9	60.7	60.1	60.1	60.1	..	0.8	0.0	-1.0	-0.1	0.0
Iceland	87.1	83.1	84.4	84.2	80.5	78.8	88.6	85.6	86.4	86.7	87.0	86.2	0.2	1.9	3.9	2.0	-0.7	-0.3
Ireland	53.7	62.3	70.8	69.4	67.7	68.1	64.1	67.6	74.1	73.8	73.3	73.9	1.3	3.2	3.8	1.3	-0.4	0.6
Italy	54.2	52.1	59.3	59.7	59.6	59.6	60.4	58.8	63.2	64.2	64.7	64.8	-0.3	0.9	0.3	1.6	0.7	0.2
Japan	70.8	74.9	77.2	77.6	77.7	77.9	72.6	78.1	80.3	80.9	81.3	81.5	1.1	-0.2	0.2	-0.1	-0.4	-0.2
Korea	59.2	61.9	67.1	67.1	66.6	66.6	60.9	65.4	69.4	69.3	69.1	69.1	2.6	1.1	1.0	0.6	0.5	0.7
Luxembourg	60.4	61.0	64.7	65.5	64.2	63.6	61.4	63.0	67.7	68.6	68.7	68.4	1.1	2.2	2.2	2.6	1.0	0.5
Mexico	..	62.4	62.3	..	..	..	..	64.6	64.5	..	..	..	..	1.8	1.9	2.1	0.8	0.9
Netherlands	62.3	72.4	77.8	78.8	78.6	78.5	67.4	75.9	80.5	81.3	81.6	81.9	1.7	1.0	1.7	1.2	0.6	0.6
New Zealand	72.5	70.7	76.6	..	..	..	76.8	76.0	79.5	..	..	..	1.1	1.7	1.6	0.7	0.2	0.7
Norway	77.0	78.0	78.5	80.5	81.1	81.6	79.7	80.8	80.5	82.7	83.6	84.4	0.4	0.7	2.5	3.2	1.4	1.4
Poland	..	58.2	56.4	58.2	58.4	58.1	..	66.0	62.4	62.7	62.8	62.9	..	-0.1	-0.5	1.0	0.7	1.0
Portugal	65.8	69.8	72.0	72.4	71.9	71.8	70.1	73.8	78.3	78.4	78.6	78.8	1.0	1.1	0.5	0.4	0.5	0.3
Slovak Republic	..	59.5	60.6	61.8	62.3	62.9	..	68.9	68.1	68.5	68.8	69.2	..	0.7	-0.2	0.9	0.7	0.6
Spain	49.5	53.0	67.1	66.0	63.7	62.8	58.0	61.9	73.1	74.1	74.2	73.8	1.2	3.3	2.8	2.9	1.4	0.2
Sweden	82.5	72.1	75.6	..	..	..	84.4	80.1	80.5	..	..	..	0.1	0.5	1.5	1.2	-0.3	-0.3
Switzerland	79.4	80.5	81.9	82.8	82.5	82.2	79.9	83.4	85.0	85.8	85.8	85.7	1.3	0.8	1.9	1.8	0.7	0.6
Turkey	53.7	49.7	44.4	44.4	44.0	44.0	58.5	53.4	49.1	49.2	49.1	49.2	1.9	1.0	1.4	1.8	1.6	1.7
United Kingdom	69.8	70.7	72.2	72.3	70.8	69.1	76.4	75.6	76.3	76.6	76.0	75.2	0.1	0.8	0.6	1.0	-0.4	-0.5
United States	71.0	72.4	72.0	..	..	..	75.2	75.8	75.5	..	..	..	1.2	1.2	1.1	0.9	1.0	0.9
Euro area	60.1	61.3	67.3	67.8	67.1	66.8	65.7	68.0	72.7	73.2	73.4	73.5	0.6	1.1	0.9	1.1	0.5	0.4
Total OECD	61.3	66.2	68.1	67.5	66.9	66.6	65.3	70.8	72.1	72.0	72.0	72.0	1.1	1.0	1.0	1.0	0.6	0.6

Note: Employment rates are calculated as the ratio of total employment to the population of working age. The working age population concept used here and in the labour force participation rate is defined as all persons of the age 15 to 64 years (16 to 64 years for Spain). This definition does not correspond to the commonly-used working age population concepts for Mexico (15 years and above), the United States and New Zealand (16 years and above) and Sweden (15-74). Hence for these countries no projections are available. For information about sources and definitions, see OECD *Economic Outlook* Sources and Methods (*http://www.oecd.org/eco/sources-and-methods*).

Source: OECD Economic Outlook 84 database.

StatLink http://dx.doi.org/10.1787/504477453157

Annex Table 21. Potential GDP, employment and capital stock

Percentage change from previous period

	Potential GDP						Employment						Capital stock[1]					
	Average 1987-96	Average 1997-06	2007	2008	2009	2010	Average 1987-96	Average 1997-06	2007	2008	2009	2010	Average 1987-96	Average 1997-06	2007	2008	2009	2010
Australia	3.2	3.4	3.1	3.2	3.2	3.2	1.8	2.1	2.9	2.1	0.5	0.8	3.2	4.2	4.2	4.2	4.2	4.2
Austria	2.4	2.4	2.3	2.4	2.4	2.4	0.6	0.8	1.5	1.5	0.0	0.3	2.9	2.5	2.2	2.2	2.2	2.2
Belgium	2.0	2.1	2.3	2.2	2.1	2.0	0.5	1.1	1.8	1.5	-0.2	0.2	3.0	2.6	2.5	2.5	2.5	2.5
Canada	2.5	3.0	2.4	2.4	2.3	2.2	0.9	2.1	2.3	1.4	-0.6	0.6	4.8	4.5	4.2	4.2	4.2	4.2
Czech Republic	..	3.3	5.4	5.0	4.6	4.4	..	-0.2	2.0	1.3	-0.4	0.0	..	..	..	..	..	..
Denmark	2.1	1.9	1.5	1.1	0.9	1.0	-0.2	0.5	1.6	1.1	-1.9	-1.2	3.6	3.9	3.6	3.5	3.4	3.3
Finland	1.9	3.2	3.4	3.1	2.9	2.8	-1.6	1.3	2.0	2.0	0.2	0.1	2.7	2.3	2.3	2.3	2.3	2.3
France	2.0	2.1	1.8	1.9	1.9	1.8	0.2	1.0	1.8	1.4	-0.6	0.1	2.9	3.2	2.9	2.9	2.9	2.9
Germany	2.2	1.3	1.4	1.5	1.4	1.6	0.7	0.5	1.7	1.3	-0.7	-0.2	2.8	1.9	1.6	1.6	1.7	1.8
Greece	1.7	3.8	4.1	3.9	3.8	3.7	0.6	1.4	1.3	1.3	0.4	0.6	2.7	4.5	4.0	4.0	4.0	4.0
Hungary	..	4.1	3.2	3.0	3.1	3.2	..	1.0	0.1	-1.5	-1.3	-0.3	..	..	..	..	..	..
Iceland	1.7	4.2	5.8	3.8	0.7	1.7	-0.1	2.0	4.5	1.5	-5.4	-1.6	..	..	..	..	..	..
Ireland	5.4	6.8	4.9	4.5	3.4	3.1	2.0	4.0	3.6	-0.1	-2.3	0.5	2.8	7.8	5.6	5.5	5.5	5.5
Italy	2.1	1.2	1.0	1.1	1.3	1.3	-0.4	1.4	1.0	0.8	-0.4	0.0	3.1	3.0	2.8	2.9	3.0	3.0
Japan	2.5	1.2	1.2	1.2	1.2	1.3	1.0	-0.3	0.5	-0.3	-0.7	-0.2	4.3	1.7	0.9	0.9	0.9	0.9
Korea	..	..	..	..	..	..	2.7	1.0	1.2	0.6	0.1	0.7	..	..	..	..	..	..
Luxembourg	5.5	4.7	4.8	4.4	4.3	4.0	0.9	2.1	2.2	2.5	-1.2	-0.1	..	..	..	..	..	..
Mexico	..	2.5	2.1	2.0	1.7	1.7	..	1.9	1.7	1.4	0.3	1.2	..	..	..	..	..	..
Netherlands	2.9	2.5	2.1	2.0	1.7	1.7	1.8	1.2	2.5	1.5	0.0	0.1	3.2	2.9	2.1	2.1	2.0	2.0
New Zealand	2.1	3.1	2.6	2.6	2.4	2.3	0.8	2.1	1.8	0.2	-1.3	0.1	3.4	4.7	4.5	4.5	4.5	4.5
Norway	1.9	3.1	4.2	3.8	3.7	3.1	0.0	0.8	3.4	3.2	1.0	1.1	..	..	..	..	..	..
Poland	..	3.8	5.3	5.6	5.2	4.8	..	-0.4	4.4	3.7	0.8	0.4	..	..	..	..	..	..
Portugal	2.9	2.2	1.4	1.3	1.1	1.1	1.0	1.0	0.1	0.9	-0.5	0.0	3.7	3.7	2.1	2.0	2.0	2.0
Slovak Republic	..	3.4	3.2	3.0	2.8	2.4	..	0.5	2.4	2.4	1.0	1.0	..	..	..	..	..	..
Spain	3.0	3.4	3.2	3.0	2.8	2.4	1.0	4.4	3.1	-0.1	-2.3	-0.6	5.0	5.5	4.8	4.7	4.7	4.6
Sweden	1.8	3.0	3.0	3.0	2.6	2.4	-1.0	1.1	2.5	1.2	-1.2	-1.0	3.7	3.7	3.3	3.3	3.3	3.3
Switzerland	1.8	1.7	2.7	2.6	2.2	2.1	0.9	0.8	2.3	1.9	0.4	0.3	..	..	..	..	..	..
Turkey	2.1	..	..	..	..	..	2.1	0.6	1.4	1.7	0.7	1.6	..	..	..	..	..	..
United Kingdom	2.4	2.7	2.2	1.8	1.6	1.9	0.4	1.0	0.7	0.8	-1.8	-1.9	4.5	4.6	3.7	3.6	3.5	3.5
United States	3.1	2.7	2.6	2.5	2.3	2.3	1.3	1.2	1.1	-0.3	-0.7	0.7	4.5	4.4	3.6	3.6	3.6	3.6
Euro area	2.3	2.0	1.9	1.9	1.9	1.8	0.5	1.4	1.8	1.0	-0.7	-0.1	..	..	..	..	..	..
Total OECD	2.7	2.4	2.2	2.2	2.1	2.1	1.1	1.0	1.5	0.7	-0.5	0.3	4.1	3.6	3.0	3.0	3.0	3.0

Note: Potential output is estimated using a Cobb-Douglas production function approach. For information about definitions, sources and data coverage, see *OECD Economic Outlook* Sources and Methods (*http://www.oecd.org/eco/sources-and-methods*).

1. Smooth value, total economy less housing.

Source: OECD Economic Outlook 84 database.

StatLink http://dx.doi.org/10.1787/504507208270

Annex Table 22. Structural unemployment and unit labor costs

	Structural unemployment rate (Per cent)									Unit labour costs[1] (Percentage change)								
	Average 1984-86	Average 1994-96	2004	2005	2006	2007	2008	2009	2010	Average 1984-93	Average 1994-03	2004	2005	2006	2007	2008	2009	2010
Australia	7.5	7.9	5.5	5.3	5.2	5.1	5.1	5.1	5.1	4.3	1.9	4.0	4.7	4.5	3.4	4.3	3.9	2.6
Austria	3.4	4.9	5.3	5.2	5.2	5.2	5.2	5.2	5.2	3.4	0.2	-0.5	0.3	1.3	1.3	2.4	2.1	1.2
Belgium	7.7	8.2	8.0	8.0	8.0	7.9	7.9	7.9	7.9	3.1	1.6	0.0	1.2	1.7	3.1	3.5	2.4	1.0
Canada	8.8	8.5	7.0	6.8	6.6	6.5	6.4	6.2	6.1	3.5	1.5	2.6	2.8	3.7	3.3	3.9	1.6	0.3
Czech Republic	..	..	..	..	..	..	..	..	..	..	6.2	1.9	0.5	1.1	2.3	5.0	4.3	2.1
Denmark	6.2	6.4	4.8	4.6	4.5	4.4	4.3	4.2	4.2	3.4	2.5	0.7	2.0	1.7	3.7	5.4	3.4	2.3
Finland	3.9	12.0	8.0	7.9	7.8	7.5	7.2	7.0	6.9	4.0	1.4	0.2	2.3	-0.2	1.2	5.3	3.9	2.2
France	8.1	9.8	8.6	8.6	8.5	8.3	8.1	8.0	8.0	2.7	1.5	1.2	1.7	1.8	2.2	2.5	2.0	0.8
Germany	5.5	7.5	8.5	8.7	8.6	8.4	8.3	8.2	8.2	2.7	0.4	-0.3	-1.5	-1.5	0.3	2.4	2.6	0.4
Greece	6.0	8.3	9.5	9.3	9.1	8.9	8.9	8.8	8.8	16.2	6.3	5.2	3.7	4.8	3.9	4.6	5.1	4.9
Hungary	..	..	..	..	..	..	..	..	..	..	11.3	4.4	3.8	2.5	5.2	5.6	4.2	3.8
Iceland	1.5	4.1	2.8	2.8	2.8	2.8	2.8	2.8	2.8	18.1	5.6	1.8	5.7	9.3	6.6	7.9	16.1	5.8
Ireland	15.0	12.0	4.9	4.8	4.7	4.7	4.7	4.7	4.7	2.7	2.1	3.8	5.5	3.9	2.6	8.1	2.5	-2.6
Italy	7.6	9.6	7.3	6.9	6.6	6.3	6.2	6.2	6.2	6.1	2.4	2.2	4.1	2.7	2.1	5.6	2.7	1.1
Japan	2.5	3.2	4.3	4.2	4.1	4.1	4.1	4.0	4.0	1.4	-1.2	-3.5	-1.1	-0.8	-1.8	0.8	0.0	-0.5
Korea	..	..	..	..	..	..	..	..	..	8.8	3.1	2.8	1.7	0.3	1.6	4.5	0.5	0.1
Luxembourg	..	..	..	..	..	..	..	..	..	2.5	2.1	1.6	1.6	0.6	3.9	4.4	2.8	4.9
Mexico	..	..	..	..	..	..	..	..	..	48.3	14.9	2.9	4.2	3.0	2.5	4.2	4.1	2.8
Netherlands	7.1	5.8	3.7	3.7	3.6	3.6	3.5	3.5	3.5	1.5	2.7	-0.1	-0.6	0.6	2.1	2.8	2.4	1.4
New Zealand	4.8	7.3	4.7	4.3	4.1	4.0	4.0	4.0	4.0	1.6	1.9	3.3	4.2	6.0	3.8	4.8	2.9	1.1
Norway	2.9	4.6	3.9	3.8	3.6	3.3	3.3	3.3	3.3	3.7	3.2	0.9	3.1	6.0	6.3	6.6	3.7	4.0
Poland	..	12.9	18.1	18.0	16.9	14.7	12.3	10.7	9.8	..	9.3	-1.4	1.6	0.6	1.6	6.7	4.6	3.2
Portugal	7.1	6.2	6.5	6.7	6.8	6.9	6.9	6.9	6.8	13.0	3.6	1.7	3.9	1.8	1.3	4.8	1.9	1.2
Slovak Republic	..	..	..	..	..	..	..	..	..	..	5.2	0.4	3.5	1.7	0.0	2.8	3.0	2.6
Spain	11.9	14.0	10.2	9.7	9.1	8.9	8.9	8.9	8.9	7.9	3.2	2.6	3.7	3.7	3.3	3.5	4.2	2.3
Sweden	4.0	7.7	7.3	7.3	7.2	7.2	7.0	6.8	6.7	5.7	2.0	-0.4	0.1	-0.5	4.4	4.1	2.5	0.4
Switzerland	1.0	3.0	3.7	3.7	3.7	3.7	3.7	3.7	3.7	3.8	1.0	-2.4	1.2	1.8	1.9	1.8	2.5	1.2
Turkey	10.1	8.2	5.3	5.3	5.3	5.3	5.3	5.3	5.3	64.2	60.0	10.2	5.6	9.1	9.0	12.1	9.0	6.0
United Kingdom	6.7	5.7	5.1	5.0	5.0	4.9	4.9	4.9	4.9	5.4	2.7	2.2	2.0	2.0	1.1	2.8	2.7	-0.8
United States	5.5	5.1	5.1	5.0	5.0	4.9	4.9	4.9	4.9	2.9	2.1	2.0	2.3	2.9	3.1	2.2	3.4	1.4
Euro area	7.4	9.0	8.1	8.0	7.8	7.6	7.5	7.5	7.5	4.0	1.5	0.9	1.2	1.1	1.8	3.4	2.7	1.1
Total OECD	6.5	6.8	6.2	6.1	6.0	5.9	5.8	5.7	5.7	6.8	3.5	1.2	1.8	2.0	2.2	3.0	2.8	1.1

Note: The structural unemployment rate corresponds to "NAIRU" and is estimated on the basis of the methods outlined in Richardson et al (2000), "The concept, policy use and measurement of structural unemployment", OECD Economics Department Working Paper No 250. The most recent updates of the OECD's estimates are described in Gianella et al (2008) "What drives the NAIRU? Evidence from a panel of OECD countries", OECD Economics Department Working Paper No. 649. For more information about sources and definitions, see *OECD Economic Outlook Sources and Methods* (http://www.oecd.org/eco/sources-and-methods).

1. Total economy.

Source: OECD Economic Outlook 84 database.

StatLink http://dx.doi.org/10.1787/504522185303

OECD ECONOMIC OUTLOOK 84 – ISBN 978-92-64-05469-1 – © OECD 2008

Annex Table 23. Household saving rates
Per cent of disposable household income

	1991	1992	1993	1994	1995	1996	1997	1998	1999	2000	2001	2002	2003	2004	2005	2006	2007	2008	2009	2010
Net savings																				
Australia	5.1	5.1	5.4	6.9	6.4	7.0	4.5	1.8	1.9	1.8	2.0	-2.3	-3.1	-2.6	-0.8	0.2	0.9	1.4	3.5	3.1
Austria	13.3	12.1	12.4	12.3	12.1	9.5	7.9	8.7	9.9	9.3	8.1	8.1	9.2	9.4	9.8	10.8	11.7	11.8	12.2	12.2
Belgium	12.7	13.9	15.2	14.9	16.0	14.2	13.2	12.4	12.7	10.9	11.9	11.2	9.6	8.1	7.5	8.0	8.6	7.9	8.0	7.9
Canada	13.3	13.0	11.9	9.5	9.2	7.0	4.9	4.9	4.0	4.7	5.2	3.5	2.6	3.2	2.0	3.1	2.7	2.8	3.5	3.2
Czech Republic	..	..	6.4	1.2	10.0	6.1	6.0	4.1	3.4	3.3	2.2	3.0	2.4	0.5	3.2	4.5	4.3	3.3	4.2	4.4
Denmark	1.8	1.5	2.6	-1.6	1.3	0.9	-1.6	0.0	-3.3	-1.9	3.7	4.1	4.1	0.7	-4.0	-3.1	-2.8	-1.9	-0.7	1.7
Finland	7.3	10.2	7.8	1.3	4.1	0.3	1.5	0.4	1.7	-1.7	-0.7	0.2	1.2	2.3	0.3	-2.4	-2.8	-2.7	-1.7	-1.2
France	10.4	11.4	12.2	11.6	12.8	11.9	12.8	12.4	12.1	12.0	12.7	13.8	12.7	12.6	11.7	11.7	12.4	12.7	13.3	13.2
Germany	12.9	12.7	12.1	11.4	11.0	10.5	10.1	10.1	9.5	9.2	9.4	9.9	10.3	10.4	10.6	10.5	10.8	11.6	12.9	13.0
Hungary	..	..	..	..	..	..	..	..	..	8.9	8.7	6.6	4.4	7.0	6.9	7.3	7.6	7.1	8.5	8.8
Ireland	..	..	..	..	..	..	..	..	..	..	..	5.4	5.4	8.3	5.6	3.8	5.3	10.6	11.4	9.3
Italy	21.4	20.2	19.5	18.1	17.0	17.9	15.1	11.4	10.2	8.4	10.5	11.3	10.3	10.2	9.9	9.0	7.9	9.2	9.1	8.4
Japan	15.0	14.2	13.7	12.6	11.9	10.6	10.3	11.3	10.0	8.6	5.0	4.9	3.9	3.5	3.9	3.3	3.1	3.3	3.5	3.2
Korea	24.6	23.4	21.8	20.7	17.5	17.5	16.1	24.9	17.5	10.7	6.4	2.2	3.9	6.3	4.7	3.4	2.5	3.7	4.2	4.7
Netherlands	14.5	16.6	14.1	14.4	14.3	12.7	13.3	12.2	9.0	6.9	9.7	8.7	7.6	7.4	6.4	5.3	7.3	5.8	5.8	6.1
Norway	3.4	5.3	6.4	5.4	4.8	2.6	3.0	5.7	4.7	4.3	3.1	8.2	8.9	7.2	10.1	0.1	-0.3	2.0	5.2	7.0
Poland	..	..	..	..	14.6	11.7	11.7	12.1	10.6	8.4	9.9	6.0	5.2	4.7	4.7	4.0	6.0	8.1	7.8	5.7
Sweden	7.1	11.0	11.2	9.8	9.5	7.3	4.9	4.0	3.6	4.8	9.3	9.1	9.0	7.7	6.8	7.1	8.3	9.2	10.3	9.2
Switzerland	13.1	13.1	13.0	12.4	12.7	10.9	10.7	10.7	10.8	11.7	11.9	10.7	9.4	9.0	9.9	12.0	13.0	12.6	12.8	13.1
United States	7.3	7.7	5.8	4.8	4.6	4.0	3.6	4.3	2.4	2.3	1.8	2.4	2.1	2.1	0.4	0.7	0.6	1.6	2.8	2.5
Gross savings																				
Portugal	14.6	13.2	..	..	13.1	11.9	10.8	10.5	9.8	10.2	10.9	10.6	10.5	9.7	9.2	8.1	6.6	6.9	7.3	7.4
Spain	10.3	13.2	15.5	13.1	17.5	17.4	16.0	14.4	12.7	11.1	11.1	11.4	12.0	11.3	11.3	11.2	10.2	11.2	12.7	13.8
United Kingdom	10.3	11.7	10.8	10.3	10.3	9.4	9.6	7.4	5.2	4.7	4.8	4.8	5.1	4.0	5.1	4.2	2.5	-0.2	1.1	0.9

Note: The adoption of new national account systems, SNA93 or ESA95, has been proceeding at an uneven pace among OECD member countries, both with respect to variables and the time period covered. As a consequence, there are breaks in many national series. See Table "National Accounts Reporting Systems and Base-years" at the beginning of the Statistical Annex and *OECD Economic Outlook* Sources and Methods *(http://www.oecd.org/eco/sources-and-methods).* Countries differ in the way household disposable income is reported (in particular whether private pension benefits less pension contributions are included in disposable income or not), but the calculation of household saving is adjusted for this difference. Most countries are reporting household saving on a net basis (i.e. excluding consumption of fixed capital by households and unincorporated businesses). In most countries the households' saving include saving by non-profit institutions (in some cases referred to as personal saving). Other countries (Czech Republic, Finland, France, Japan and New Zealand) report saving of households only.

Source: OECD Economic Outlook 84 database.

StatLink http://dx.doi.org/10.1787/504526711431

Annex Table 24. Gross national saving
Per cent of nominal GDP

	1988	1989	1990	1991	1992	1993	1994	1995	1996	1997	1998	1999	2000	2001	2002	2003	2004	2005	2006	2007
Australia	23.8	22.8	18.6	16.2	18.0	19.6	18.5	18.7	19.9	20.1	19.4	20.3	19.7	20.4	20.1	20.7	20.2	21.4	21.6	..
Austria	23.0	23.4	23.6	23.2	22.0	21.3	20.8	22.2	22.1	22.7	23.3	23.1	23.6	23.0	24.8	24.5	25.0	25.0	25.0	26.1
Belgium	22.1	23.3	23.6	22.7	23.2	24.3	25.5	25.4	24.5	25.9	25.6	26.3	26.0	24.6	24.2	23.6	24.0	23.7	24.6	25.0
Canada	20.5	19.8	17.3	14.7	13.4	14.0	16.2	18.3	18.8	19.6	19.1	20.7	23.6	22.2	21.2	21.4	23.0	23.8	24.4	23.7
Czech Republic	..	..	..	..	28.6	28.7	28.4	29.0	27.0	24.4	26.3	24.6	24.8	24.2	22.4	20.7	22.0	23.9	24.3	25.0
Denmark	18.7	19.1	20.3	19.5	20.0	19.1	19.3	20.4	20.5	21.4	20.7	21.7	22.6	23.5	22.9	23.1	23.4	25.2	25.2	23.6
Finland	26.3	25.8	24.0	16.5	13.9	15.0	18.2	21.9	20.9	24.2	25.5	26.9	28.8	29.3	28.4	24.5	26.6	25.7	26.8	28.6
France	19.8	20.7	20.8	20.2	19.6	18.3	18.7	19.1	18.7	19.9	21.0	21.8	21.6	21.3	19.8	19.1	19.0	18.5	19.1	19.3
Germany	24.7	25.7	25.3	22.6	22.3	21.2	20.9	21.0	20.5	20.7	20.9	20.3	20.2	19.5	19.4	19.5	22.0	22.2	23.9	25.9
Greece	11.0	11.0	10.7	10.7	10.9	10.9	11.0	11.3	11.4	11.2	11.3	11.3	11.3	11.8	9.6	11.7	12.3	10.3	10.2	8.6
Iceland	17.4	17.5	16.9	16.0	15.7	17.6	17.9	17.1	17.2	17.9	17.4	15.0	13.1	17.0	19.7	15.0	13.6	12.2	9.5	12.1
Ireland	14.5	14.8	17.7	17.3	15.3	17.4	17.7	20.3	21.7	23.4	25.0	24.0	24.2	22.2	21.1	23.4	24.0	24.0	24.8	21.8
Italy	21.8	21.1	20.8	20.0	19.1	19.7	19.9	22.0	22.2	22.2	21.6	21.1	20.6	20.9	20.8	19.8	20.3	19.6	19.6	19.7
Japan	32.8	33.0	33.2	33.9	33.2	31.9	30.1	29.3	29.7	29.8	28.8	27.2	27.5	25.8	25.2	25.4	25.8	26.8	26.6	..
Korea	40.6	37.7	37.7	37.7	36.9	36.8	36.3	36.2	35.3	35.4	37.2	35.0	33.6	31.6	31.2	32.6	34.8	32.7	31.2	30.6
Mexico	23.9	23.2	23.6	21.4	18.6	16.5	16.0	21.1	25.7	28.1	23.3	23.6	23.8	20.1	20.9	21.6	23.8	23.3	25.5	..
Netherlands	25.8	27.1	26.0	25.6	24.8	25.0	26.1	27.2	26.7	28.1	25.2	27.1	28.4	26.7	25.8	25.4	27.6	26.5	29.4	29.5
New Zealand	19.1	18.3	16.8	13.8	14.6	17.2	18.0	17.9	16.9	16.5	16.1	15.9	17.1	19.2	18.8	18.8	17.5	15.3	15.1	..
Norway	24.5	25.6	25.2	24.0	23.1	23.3	24.2	25.9	27.9	29.6	26.3	28.5	35.4	35.1	31.5	30.5	32.7	37.4	39.0	38.5
Poland	..	..	..	4.0	4.0	4.2	5.6	6.0	5.7	6.4	7.7	6.6	6.1	4.8	2.9	3.3	2.8	5.1	5.4	7.1
Portugal	26.5	26.8	25.4	22.5	21.5	19.0	18.2	20.2	19.5	19.3	19.8	18.9	17.0	16.7	16.7	16.4	15.3	12.8	11.7	12.1
Slovak Republic	..	..	..	..	..	23.8	26.4	26.8	24.6	25.1	24.2	24.1	23.5	22.4	21.7	18.3	19.7	20.2	20.4	22.8
Spain	22.7	22.2	22.2	21.6	20.0	20.0	19.5	21.7	21.5	22.2	22.4	22.4	22.3	22.0	22.9	23.4	22.4	22.0	21.9	21.1
Sweden	25.3	26.2	24.2	20.3	16.6	14.3	17.8	20.9	20.4	20.7	21.5	21.8	22.8	22.6	22.3	23.4	23.1	23.4	26.7	28.1
Switzerland	..	..	33.1	31.1	28.6	29.7	29.3	29.6	28.8	30.8	32.0	32.9	34.7	31.4	29.0	33.1	32.9	35.8	36.6	..
United Kingdom	17.5	17.4	16.5	15.6	14.5	14.3	15.9	16.2	16.3	17.4	18.3	16.0	15.4	15.6	15.8	15.7	15.9	15.1	14.2	14.5
United States	16.9	16.3	15.3	15.3	14.2	13.8	14.6	15.5	16.1	17.3	18.0	17.8	17.7	16.1	13.9	12.9	13.4	14.4	15.0	13.7

Note: Based on SNA93 or ESA95.
Source: National accounts of OECD countries database.

StatLink http://dx.doi.org/10.1787/504537567731

Annex Table 25. General government total outlays
Per cent of nominal GDP

	1991	1992	1993	1994	1995	1996	1997	1998	1999	2000	2001	2002	2003	2004	2005	2006	2007	2008	2009	2010
Australia	37.7	38.3	37.8	38.2	38.2	37.2	36.3	35.2	34.8	35.2	35.9	35.4	34.6	35.1	34.8	34.5	33.8	33.7	35.1	35.0
Austria	52.9	53.4	56.5	56.1	56.5	56.0	53.6	54.0	53.6	52.1	51.5	51.0	51.5	54.1	49.9	49.4	48.4	48.4	49.4	49.8
Belgium	53.4	53.7	54.8	52.5	52.0	52.5	51.1	50.4	50.2	49.2	49.2	49.9	51.2	49.5	52.0	48.3	48.4	48.9	49.6	50.0
Canada	52.3	53.3	52.2	49.7	48.5	46.6	44.3	44.8	42.7	41.1	42.0	41.2	41.2	39.9	39.3	39.3	39.1	39.6	41.4	41.5
Czech Republic	..	..	..	..	54.0	42.4	43.2	43.1	42.2	41.7	44.2	46.2	47.1	44.8	44.6	43.2	41.5	41.5	42.0	41.2
Denmark	56.5	57.0	60.1	60.0	59.1	58.7	56.4	56.0	55.1	53.3	53.9	54.2	54.7	54.3	52.3	50.9	50.4	50.4	51.9	52.6
Finland	56.6	61.9	64.6	63.9	61.4	59.8	56.3	52.5	51.5	48.4	47.9	48.9	50.1	50.2	50.5	48.8	47.3	47.3	47.8	48.0
France	50.6	52.0	54.9	54.2	54.4	54.5	54.1	52.7	52.6	51.6	51.6	52.6	53.2	53.3	53.5	52.7	52.4	52.5	53.2	53.4
Germany	46.1	47.3	48.3	47.9	54.8	49.3	48.3	48.1	48.2	45.1	47.5	48.0	48.4	47.3	46.9	45.3	43.8	43.4	43.9	44.0
Greece	41.8	44.3	46.6	44.8	45.8	44.1	45.0	44.4	44.4	46.7	45.3	44.8	45.0	45.5	43.1	42.0	43.5	43.2	43.3	43.5
Hungary	55.8	59.7	59.3	62.8	55.3	52.0	49.9	51.5	48.6	46.5	47.2	51.3	49.1	48.9	50.1	51.9	49.8	48.6	48.6	48.5
Iceland	42.9	43.8	43.6	43.4	42.7	42.2	40.7	41.3	42.0	41.9	42.6	44.3	45.6	44.1	42.2	41.7	42.8	43.9	51.3	52.5
Ireland	44.5	44.9	44.7	44.0	41.2	39.2	36.7	34.5	34.1	31.5	33.3	33.6	33.3	33.7	33.7	33.8	35.4	39.6	41.5	41.3
Italy	54.0	55.4	56.4	53.5	52.5	52.5	50.2	49.3	48.2	46.1	48.0	47.4	48.3	47.8	48.2	48.8	48.2	48.4	48.8	48.8
Japan	31.6	32.5	34.3	35.5	36.5	36.8	35.7	42.5	38.6	39.0	38.6	38.8	38.4	37.0	38.4	36.0	35.8	36.4	37.2	37.5
Korea	20.9	22.0	21.6	21.0	20.8	21.7	22.4	24.7	23.9	23.9	25.0	24.8	30.9	28.1	28.9	30.2	30.7	30.9	31.7	31.8
Luxembourg	38.5	40.1	39.9	39.1	39.8	41.2	40.7	40.7	39.1	37.9	38.0	41.6	41.9	42.3	41.5	38.7	37.9	39.2	41.2	42.1
Netherlands	54.9	55.7	55.7	53.5	56.4	49.4	47.5	46.7	46.0	44.2	45.4	46.2	47.1	46.1	44.8	45.6	45.3	45.1	45.9	46.3
New Zealand	50.3	49.4	45.7	42.9	42.0	41.0	41.7	41.4	41.0	39.6	38.5	38.4	38.8	38.6	40.4	40.9	41.5	42.6	44.6	45.1
Norway	54.5	55.7	54.6	53.7	50.9	48.5	46.9	49.2	47.7	42.3	44.2	47.1	48.3	45.6	42.3	40.6	41.0	40.5	44.9	45.8
Poland	..	..	..	..	47.7	51.0	46.4	44.3	42.7	41.1	43.8	44.2	44.6	42.6	43.3	43.8	42.0	41.2	41.4	41.3
Portugal	43.4	44.5	46.1	44.3	43.4	44.1	43.2	42.8	43.2	43.1	44.4	44.3	45.5	46.5	47.6	46.3	45.8	46.3	48.2	49.2
Slovak Republic	..	..	..	56.1	48.7	53.8	49.1	45.9	47.9	51.0	44.6	45.1	40.1	37.8	38.1	37.1	34.6	33.9	34.5	34.8
Spain	44.3	45.4	49.0	46.7	44.4	43.2	41.6	41.1	39.9	39.1	38.6	38.9	38.4	38.9	38.4	38.5	38.8	39.7	40.6	40.9
Sweden	61.1	69.3	70.9	68.4	65.3	62.9	60.7	58.5	60.2	57.0	61.2	55.8	56.0	54.4	54.0	53.1	51.4	51.2	52.3	52.1
Switzerland	32.1	34.2	35.1	35.2	35.0	35.3	35.5	35.8	34.3	35.1	34.8	36.2	36.4	35.9	35.3	33.7	32.9	32.6	33.2	33.3
United Kingdom	43.2	45.2	45.3	44.6	44.1	42.2	40.6	39.5	38.8	36.6	39.9	40.9	42.4	43.2	44.2	44.3	44.5	45.4	47.7	48.9
United States[1]	37.8	38.5	38.0	37.0	37.0	36.5	35.4	34.7	34.3	34.2	35.3	36.3	36.8	36.4	36.6	36.5	37.4	38.6	39.8	39.9
Euro area	49.3	50.5	52.3	51.0	53.2	50.7	49.4	48.6	48.2	46.3	47.3	47.6	48.1	47.7	47.4	46.7	46.1	46.3	46.9	47.1
Total OECD	41.3	42.4	42.9	42.2	42.9	41.8	40.8	40.8	39.9	39.1	40.1	40.6	41.2	40.6	40.2	40.2	40.3	40.9	42.0	42.2

Note: Data refer to the general government sector, which is a consolidation of accounts for the central, state and local governments plus social security. Total outlays are defined as current outlays plus capital outlays. For more details see OECD Economic Outlook Sources and Methods (http://www.oecd.org/eco/sources-and-methods).
1. These data include outlays net of operating surpluses of public enterprises.
Source: OECD Economic Outlook 84 database.

StatLink http://dx.doi.org/10.1787/504605611231

Annex Table 26. General government total tax and non-tax receipts
Per cent of nominal GDP

	1991	1992	1993	1994	1995	1996	1997	1998	1999	2000	2001	2002	2003	2004	2005	2006	2007	2008	2009	2010
Australia	33.0	32.8	33.4	33.8	34.5	34.9	35.6	36.8	36.9	36.1	35.8	36.7	36.3	36.1	36.3	36.0	35.4	35.5	35.6	35.3
Austria	49.9	51.4	52.1	51.2	50.6	51.9	51.7	51.5	51.2	50.3	51.4	50.1	49.9	49.6	48.2	47.7	47.9	47.4	46.6	46.4
Belgium	46.0	45.6	47.4	47.4	47.5	48.5	49.0	49.5	49.6	49.1	49.6	49.8	51.1	49.2	49.3	48.6	48.1	48.2	48.3	48.4
Canada	43.9	44.2	43.5	43.0	43.2	43.8	44.5	44.3	44.3	43.3	42.6	41.1	41.1	40.7	40.8	40.7	40.5	39.9	40.1	39.8
Czech Republic	..	..	..	..	40.5	39.1	39.4	38.1	38.5	37.9	38.5	39.4	40.5	41.9	41.1	40.5	40.5	39.9	40.1	39.5
Denmark	53.6	54.5	56.3	56.7	56.2	56.7	55.9	56.0	56.5	55.5	55.0	54.5	54.6	56.1	57.4	55.9	54.9	52.9	52.0	52.0
Finland	55.6	56.5	56.3	57.1	55.3	56.3	55.1	54.2	53.1	55.3	52.9	53.1	52.5	52.4	53.2	52.8	52.7	51.9	51.1	50.7
France	47.6	47.4	48.5	48.7	48.9	50.4	50.8	50.0	50.8	50.1	50.0	49.4	49.1	49.6	50.5	50.3	49.7	49.6	49.4	49.4
Germany	43.3	44.8	45.3	45.6	45.1	46.0	45.7	45.9	46.7	46.4	44.7	44.4	44.4	43.5	43.6	43.8	43.9	43.4	43.0	43.0
Greece	31.9	33.3	34.6	36.5	36.7	37.5	39.1	40.5	41.3	43.0	40.9	40.0	39.3	38.1	37.9	39.0	39.8	40.4	40.7	40.4
Hungary	52.7	52.4	52.6	51.5	47.6	46.0	42.5	43.1	43.3	43.6	43.2	42.4	42.0	42.5	42.3	42.6	44.9	45.2	45.0	44.9
Iceland	40.0	41.0	39.1	38.7	39.8	40.6	40.7	40.9	43.2	43.6	41.9	41.7	42.8	44.1	47.1	48.0	48.2	47.1	49.4	48.8
Ireland	41.6	41.9	42.0	42.0	39.1	39.1	38.1	36.8	36.7	36.2	34.3	33.3	33.8	35.1	35.4	36.8	35.7	34.0	34.4	34.3
Italy	42.6	45.0	46.3	44.4	45.1	45.5	47.6	46.2	46.5	45.3	44.9	44.4	44.8	44.2	43.8	45.4	46.6	45.9	45.9	45.7
Japan	33.4	33.3	32.0	31.4	31.4	31.7	31.7	31.3	31.2	31.4	32.2	30.8	30.5	30.9	31.7	34.6	33.4	35.0	33.9	33.7
Korea	22.7	23.4	23.9	23.8	24.6	25.1	25.6	26.4	26.6	29.3	29.6	30.2	31.3	30.6	31.9	33.8	35.2	35.7	35.5	35.4
Luxembourg	39.2	39.9	41.3	41.5	42.2	42.4	44.3	44.1	42.5	43.9	44.1	43.8	42.4	41.1	41.4	40.0	41.1	40.7	40.5	40.6
Netherlands	52.3	51.5	52.9	50.0	47.2	47.5	46.3	45.8	46.4	46.1	45.1	44.1	43.9	44.3	44.5	46.2	45.6	46.0	45.9	45.4
New Zealand	46.8	46.4	45.3	46.0	44.9	43.9	43.3	41.5	40.8	41.2	40.6	41.6	42.6	42.9	44.9	44.7	45.2	45.1	44.0	43.5
Norway	54.6	53.9	53.2	54.0	54.2	54.8	54.5	52.5	53.7	57.7	57.5	56.3	55.5	56.7	57.3	59.1	58.4	60.5	58.8	58.9
Poland	..	..	..	..	43.3	46.1	41.8	40.1	40.4	38.1	38.6	39.2	38.4	36.9	39.0	40.0	40.0	38.9	38.7	38.4
Portugal	36.5	40.4	38.6	37.1	38.4	39.7	39.7	39.4	40.5	40.2	40.1	41.4	42.5	43.1	41.6	42.3	43.2	44.1	45.3	46.0
Slovak Republic	..	..	..	47.3	45.3	43.9	42.7	40.5	40.5	38.7	38.1	36.9	37.4	35.4	35.3	33.5	32.7	31.7	32.5	33.4
Spain	39.5	41.4	41.7	40.0	38.0	38.4	38.2	37.8	38.4	38.1	38.0	38.4	38.2	38.5	39.4	40.5	41.0	38.2	37.7	37.1
Sweden	61.0	60.5	59.8	59.4	58.0	59.6	59.0	59.7	61.4	60.7	62.9	54.3	54.8	55.0	56.1	55.3	54.9	54.0	52.8	52.5
Switzerland	30.3	31.1	31.6	32.4	33.0	33.5	32.7	33.8	33.8	35.2	34.7	35.0	34.6	34.2	34.6	34.7	34.2	33.7	33.5	33.3
United Kingdom	39.8	38.7	37.3	37.8	38.2	38.0	38.4	39.4	39.8	40.3	40.6	39.0	38.7	39.5	40.8	41.6	41.7	41.9	42.4	42.4
United States[1]	32.9	32.8	33.0	33.4	33.8	34.3	34.6	35.1	35.2	35.8	34.9	32.5	31.9	32.1	33.4	34.2	34.5	33.3	33.0	33.1
Euro area	44.7	45.8	46.6	46.0	45.6	46.4	46.7	46.3	46.8	46.3	45.4	45.0	45.0	44.7	44.9	45.4	45.5	44.9	44.7	44.6
Total OECD	37.6	37.9	37.9	37.9	38.1	38.6	38.8	38.9	39.1	39.3	38.8	37.4	37.1	37.1	38.0	38.9	38.9	38.5	38.2	38.1

Note: Data refer to the general government sector, which is a consolidation of accounts for central, state and local governments plus social security. Non-tax receipts consist of property income (including dividends and other transfers from public enterprises), fees, charges, sales, fines, capital tranfers received by the general government, etc. For more details see OECD Economic Outlook Sources and Methods (http://www.oecd.org/eco/sources-and-methods).

1. Excludes the operating surpluses of public enterprises.

Source: OECD Economic Outlook 84 database.

StatLink http://dx.doi.org/10.1787/504606040136

Annex Table 27. General government financial balances
Surplus (+) or deficit (-) as a per cent of nominal GDP

	1991	1992	1993	1994	1995	1996	1997	1998	1999	2000	2001	2002	2003	2004	2005	2006	2007	2008	2009	2010
Australia	-4.7	-5.5	-4.4	-4.5	-3.7	-2.4	-0.7	1.6	2.0	0.9	-0.1	1.3	1.8	1.1	1.5	1.5	1.6	1.8	0.6	0.3
Austria	-3.0	-2.0	-4.4	-4.9	-5.9	-4.1	-1.9	-2.5	-2.4	-1.9	-0.2	-0.9	-1.6	-4.5	-1.6	-1.7	-0.5	-1.0	-2.7	-3.5
Belgium	-7.4	-8.1	-7.4	-5.1	-4.5	-4.0	-2.2	-0.9	-0.6	0.0	0.4	-0.1	-0.1	-0.3	-2.7	0.3	-0.3	-0.7	-1.3	-1.6
Canada	-8.4	-9.1	-8.7	-6.7	-5.3	-2.8	0.2	0.1	1.6	2.9	0.7	-0.1	-0.1	0.9	1.5	1.3	1.4	0.3	-1.3	-1.7
Czech Republic	..	..	..	..	-13.4	-3.3	-3.8	-5.0	-3.7	-3.7	-5.7	-6.8	-6.6	-2.9	-3.6	-2.7	-1.0	-1.6	-1.9	-1.7
Denmark	-2.9	-2.6	-3.8	-3.3	-2.9	-1.9	-0.5	0.0	1.4	2.3	1.2	0.2	-0.1	1.9	5.1	5.0	4.4	2.4	0.1	-0.6
Finland	-1.0	-5.4	-8.3	-6.7	-6.2	-3.5	-1.2	1.7	1.6	6.9	5.0	4.2	2.4	2.2	2.7	4.0	5.3	4.6	3.3	2.7
France	-2.9	-4.5	-6.4	-5.5	-5.5	-4.0	-3.3	-2.6	-1.8	-1.5	-1.6	-3.2	-4.1	-3.6	-3.0	-2.4	-2.7	-2.9	-3.7	-3.9
Germany	-2.8	-2.5	-3.0	-2.3	-9.7	-3.3	-2.6	-2.2	-1.5	1.3	-2.8	-3.6	-4.0	-3.8	-3.3	-1.5	0.1	0.0	-0.9	-1.0
Greece	-9.9	-10.9	-11.9	-8.3	-9.1	-6.6	-5.9	-3.8	-3.1	-3.7	-4.4	-4.8	-5.8	-7.4	-5.2	-3.1	-3.7	-2.8	-2.7	-3.1
Hungary	-3.1	-7.3	-6.8	-11.4	-7.7	-6.0	-7.4	-8.4	-5.3	-2.9	-4.1	-9.0	-7.2	-6.4	-7.8	-9.3	-5.0	-3.4	-3.6	-3.5
Iceland	-2.9	-2.8	-4.5	-4.7	-3.0	-1.6	0.0	-0.4	1.1	1.7	-0.7	-2.6	-2.8	0.0	4.9	6.3	5.5	3.2	-1.9	-3.8
Ireland	-2.8	-2.9	-2.7	-2.0	-2.1	-0.1	1.4	2.3	2.6	4.7	1.0	-0.3	0.5	1.4	1.7	3.0	0.2	-5.6	-7.1	-7.0
Italy	-11.4	-10.4	-10.1	-9.1	-7.4	-7.0	-2.7	-3.1	-1.8	-0.9	-3.1	-3.0	-3.5	-3.6	-4.4	-3.4	-1.5	-2.5	-2.9	-3.1
Japan	1.8	0.8	-2.4	-4.2	-5.1	-5.1	-4.0	-11.2	-7.4	-7.6	-6.3	-8.0	-7.9	-6.2	-6.7	-1.4	-2.4	-1.4	-3.3	-3.8
Korea	1.7	1.4	2.2	2.9	3.8	3.4	3.3	1.6	2.7	5.4	4.6	5.4	0.4	2.5	3.0	3.6	4.5	4.8	3.8	3.6
Luxembourg	0.7	-0.2	1.5	2.5	2.4	1.2	3.7	3.3	3.4	6.0	6.1	2.1	0.5	-1.2	-0.1	1.3	3.2	1.6	-0.6	-1.5
Netherlands	-2.7	-4.2	-2.8	-3.5	-9.2	-1.9	-1.2	-0.9	0.4	2.0	-0.3	-2.1	-3.2	-1.8	-0.3	0.6	0.3	1.0	0.0	-0.9
New Zealand	-3.5	-3.0	-0.4	3.1	2.9	2.9	1.7	0.1	-0.2	1.6	2.1	3.2	3.8	4.3	4.5	3.7	3.7	2.5	-0.6	-1.6
Norway	0.1	-1.9	-1.4	0.3	3.2	6.3	7.6	3.3	6.0	15.4	13.3	9.2	7.3	11.1	15.1	18.5	17.4	20.0	14.0	13.1
Poland	..	..	..	..	-4.4	-4.9	-4.6	-4.3	-2.3	-3.0	-5.1	-5.0	-6.3	-5.7	-4.3	-3.8	-2.0	-2.3	-2.7	-2.9
Portugal	-6.9	-4.2	-7.5	-7.2	-5.0	-4.5	-3.5	-3.4	-2.8	-3.0	-4.3	-2.9	-3.0	-3.4	-6.1	-3.9	-2.7	-2.2	-2.9	-3.1
Slovak Republic	..	..	..	-8.8	-3.4	-9.9	-6.3	-5.3	-7.4	-12.3	-6.5	-8.2	-2.7	-2.3	-2.8	-3.5	-2.0	-2.1	-2.0	-1.5
Spain	-4.8	-4.0	-7.3	-6.8	-6.5	-4.9	-3.4	-3.2	-1.4	-1.0	-0.7	-0.5	-0.2	-0.4	1.0	2.0	2.2	-1.5	-2.9	-3.8
Sweden	-0.1	-8.8	-11.2	-9.1	-7.3	-3.3	-1.6	1.2	1.2	3.7	1.7	-1.4	-1.2	0.6	2.1	2.2	3.5	2.8	0.5	0.4
Switzerland	-1.8	-3.1	-3.5	-2.8	-2.0	-1.8	-2.8	-1.9	-0.5	0.1	-0.1	-1.2	-1.7	-1.8	-0.7	1.0	1.3	1.1	0.3	0.0
United Kingdom	-3.4	-6.5	-8.0	-6.8	-5.8	-4.2	-2.2	-0.1	0.9	3.7	0.6	-2.0	-3.7	-3.7	-3.3	-2.7	-2.8	-3.6	-5.3	-6.5
United States	-4.9	-5.8	-4.9	-3.6	-3.1	-2.2	-0.8	0.4	0.9	1.6	-0.4	-3.8	-4.8	-4.4	-3.3	-2.2	-2.9	-5.3	-6.7	-6.8
Euro area	-4.6	-4.7	-5.7	-4.9	-7.6	-4.3	-2.7	-2.3	-1.4	0.0	-1.8	-2.6	-3.1	-3.0	-2.5	-1.3	-0.6	-1.4	-2.2	-2.5
Total OECD	-3.7	-4.5	-4.9	-4.2	-4.8	-3.2	-1.8	-2.0	-0.8	0.2	-1.3	-3.3	-4.0	-3.4	-2.8	-1.3	-1.4	-2.5	-3.8	-4.1
Memorandum items																				
General government financial balances excluding social security																				
United States	-5.8	-6.6	-5.6	-4.4	-3.9	-3.1	-1.9	-0.8	-0.6	0.1	-2.0	-5.4	-6.2	-5.7	-4.6	-3.7	-4.3	-6.7	-8.1	-8.3
Japan	-0.9	-1.7	-4.6	-6.2	-7.0	-6.9	-5.8	-12.5	-8.5	-8.2	-6.5	-7.9	-8.0	-6.6	-7.0	-1.4	-2.2	-1.2	-3.5	-4.1

Note: Financial balances include one-off factors such as those resulting from the sale of the mobile telephone licenses. As data are on a national account basis (SNA93/ESA95), the government financial balances may differ from the numbers reported to the European Commission under the Excessive Deficit Procedure for some EU countries. For more details see footnotes to Annex Tables 25 and 26 and *OECD Economic Outlook* Sources and Methods (*http://www.oecd.org/eco/sources-and-methods*).

Source: OECD Economic Outlook 84 database.

StatLink http://dx.doi.org/10.1787/504646514481

Annex Table 28. General government cyclically-adjusted balances

Surplus (+) or deficit (-) as a per cent of potential GDP

	1991	1992	1993	1994	1995	1996	1997	1998	1999	2000	2001	2002	2003	2004	2005	2006	2007	2008	2009	2010
Australia	-4.0	-4.3	-3.5	-4.1	-3.5	-2.0	-0.3	1.8	2.0	0.7	0.1	1.6	2.0	1.1	1.4	1.5	1.2	1.5	0.9	1.0
Austria	-3.5	-2.5	-3.9	-4.2	-5.3	-3.6	-1.4	-2.4	-3.0	-3.4	-0.9	-0.8	-0.8	-3.5	-1.0	-1.6	-0.9	-1.3	-2.1	-2.1
Belgium	-8.5	-8.8	-6.3	-4.4	-3.9	-2.9	-1.9	-0.4	-0.8	-1.4	-0.5	-0.3	0.3	-0.1	-2.5	0.0	-0.9	-1.1	-0.5	-0.4
Canada	-7.2	-7.0	-6.6	-5.5	-4.4	-1.5	1.3	0.8	1.5	2.1	0.2	-0.5	-0.2	0.7	1.3	0.9	0.8	0.2	-0.3	-0.4
Czech Republic	..	..	..	..	..	..	..	..	-3.0	-3.4	-5.3	-5.8	-5.5	-2.0	-3.3	-3.1	-1.9	-2.3	-1.9	-1.6
Denmark	-2.0	-1.5	-1.7	-2.2	-2.5	-1.8	-0.8	-0.4	1.0	1.2	0.2	0.1	0.7	2.7	5.4	4.4	3.4	1.5	0.0	-0.2
Finland	0.2	-1.5	-3.1	-2.5	-2.8	-0.8	-0.2	1.8	1.3	6.1	4.5	4.2	3.0	2.5	3.0	3.6	4.5	4.0	3.5	3.3
France	-3.9	-5.1	-5.9	-4.8	-5.0	-3.2	-2.4	-2.2	-1.8	-2.2	-2.5	-3.5	-3.9	-3.4	-2.9	-2.5	-3.1	-3.2	-3.0	-2.7
Germany	-3.2	-3.0	-2.3	-1.8	-9.3	-2.7	-2.0	-1.7	-1.2	-1.9	-3.6	-3.8	-3.5	-2.9	-2.3	-1.3	-0.3	-0.6	-0.5	-0.3
Greece	-10.4	-11.2	-11.1	-7.6	-8.4	-5.9	-5.3	-3.3	-2.4	-3.2	-4.6	-4.5	-5.8	-7.9	-5.7	-3.7	-4.4	-3.2	-2.3	-2.2
Hungary	..	..	-6.2	-11.3	-7.6	-5.3	-7.1	-8.5	-5.4	-3.2	-4.2	-9.0	-7.3	-6.8	-8.4	-10.2	-5.1	-2.9	-1.7	-0.6
Iceland	-2.1	-0.5	-2.1	-3.2	-1.3	-0.7	0.2	-0.9	0.5	1.2	-1.4	-2.6	-2.6	-0.8	3.1	5.1	4.7	3.2	1.3	1.0
Ireland	-3.3	-2.3	-1.0	0.0	-1.0	0.6	1.3	1.8	1.4	3.1	-0.3	-1.4	0.0	1.2	1.3	2.4	-0.7	-4.5	-3.7	-3.2
Italy	-12.0	-10.4	-8.6	-7.5	-6.4	-5.7	-1.5	-1.9	-0.5	-1.7	-3.3	-3.0	-3.1	-3.2	-3.9	-3.2	-1.6	-2.0	-1.2	-0.8
Japan	0.8	-0.2	-2.8	-4.3	-5.2	-5.7	-4.7	-10.9	-6.6	-7.3	-5.7	-7.1	-7.0	-5.7	-6.5	-1.6	-2.8	-1.7	-3.2	-3.4
Luxembourg	-1.9	-1.9	0.4	1.9	2.9	3.1	5.6	4.7	3.6	4.9	5.2	1.6	0.8	-0.6	0.3	1.1	2.8	1.7	1.3	1.6
Netherlands	-3.4	-4.5	-2.1	-2.3	-8.0	-1.0	-0.9	-1.1	-0.5	-0.4	-2.1	-3.0	-2.7	-0.8	0.7	1.2	0.1	0.4	0.0	-0.2
New Zealand	-1.6	-0.8	0.7	3.2	2.5	2.3	1.5	1.0	0.2	1.7	2.3	3.0	3.4	3.4	3.7	3.3	3.0	2.6	0.8	0.0
Norway[1]	-3.6	-5.7	-6.0	-4.7	-1.6	-1.4	-0.9	-2.3	-1.1	1.0	0.1	-2.2	-3.9	-1.9	-0.8	1.3	2.8	3.3	0.2	0.2
Poland	..	..	..	..	..	-4.6	-5.0	-4.4	-2.3	-3.1	-4.4	-3.8	-5.4	-5.6	-4.3	-4.5	-3.2	-3.4	-3.0	-2.8
Portugal	-9.4	-5.9	-7.2	-6.0	-4.2	-3.9	-3.5	-4.2	-4.1	-5.3	-6.2	-4.0	-2.7	-3.1	-5.4	-3.3	-2.2	-1.6	-1.6	-1.5
Spain	-6.8	-5.0	-6.4	-5.0	-4.7	-2.9	-1.7	-2.1	-1.2	-1.8	-1.3	-0.6	0.0	0.0	1.1	2.0	2.0	-0.9	-0.7	-0.6
Sweden	-0.5	-7.5	-7.6	-6.7	-6.3	-2.0	-0.6	1.6	0.7	2.4	1.0	-1.7	-0.8	0.9	2.4	1.7	3.0	3.2	2.2	2.2
Switzerland	-2.1	-2.7	-2.6	-2.0	-1.2	-0.9	-2.1	-1.9	-0.5	-0.7	-0.8	-1.3	-1.1	-1.3	-0.4	0.9	1.0	0.9	0.8	0.7
United Kingdom	-3.8	-5.8	-7.0	-6.3	-5.4	-3.7	-1.9	0.0	0.9	1.0	0.3	-2.1	-3.8	-3.9	-3.4	-2.9	-3.3	-3.8	-4.4	-4.8
United States	-4.5	-5.2	-4.2	-3.1	-2.5	-1.6	-0.5	0.4	0.4	0.9	-0.7	-3.6	-4.6	-4.4	-3.6	-2.6	-3.2	-5.1	-5.5	-5.1
Euro area	-5.4	-5.1	-4.6	-4.1	-6.9	-3.3	-2.0	-1.9	-1.3	-1.8	-2.5	-2.7	-2.6	-2.5	-2.1	-1.4	-1.0	-1.3	-1.0	-1.1
Total OECD	-4.0	-4.5	-4.4	-3.9	-4.5	-2.8	-1.6	-1.9	-1.0	-1.0	-1.9	-3.4	-3.9	-3.5	-3.1	-1.8	-2.0	-2.8	-3.2	-3.1

Note: Cyclically-adjusted balances exclude one-off revenues from the sale of mobile telephone licenses. For more details on the methodology used for estimating the cyclical component of government balances see *OECD Economic Outlook* Sources and Methods (*http://www.oecd.org/eco/sources-and-methods*).

1. As a percentage of mainland potential GDP. The financial balances shown are adjusted to exclude net revenues from petroleum activities.

Source: OECD Economic Outlook 84 database.

StatLink ⟨⟩ http://dx.doi.org/10.1787/504660104343

Annex Table 29. General government underlying balances
Surplus (+) or deficit (-) as a per cent of potential GDP

	1991	1992	1993	1994	1995	1996	1997	1998	1999	2000	2001	2002	2003	2004	2005	2006	2007	2008	2009	2010
Australia	-3.6	-4.1	-3.4	-4.1	-3.4	-2.0	-0.4	1.6	1.8	0.5	0.5	1.8	1.7	1.2	1.5	1.7	1.4	1.4	0.7	0.8
Austria	-3.5	-2.6	-3.9	-4.3	-5.7	-3.8	-1.6	-2.1	-3.1	-3.4	-0.8	-1.1	-1.2	-0.4	-1.3	-1.8	-1.1	-1.7	-2.2	-2.3
Belgium	-8.7	-8.8	-6.1	-4.3	-4.0	-2.9	-1.6	-0.2	-0.7	-1.2	-0.6	-0.5	-1.1	-0.7	-0.6	-0.3	-0.9	-1.1	-0.5	-0.4
Canada	-7.1	-7.0	-6.7	-5.7	-4.4	-1.5	1.0	0.6	1.2	2.1	0.1	-0.5	-0.2	0.8	1.4	1.1	0.9	0.3	-0.3	-0.4
Czech Republic	..	..	..	..	..	..	..	..	-4.3	-5.0	-4.0	-4.0	-4.6	-2.0	-2.9	-3.2	-2.3	-2.2	-1.6	-1.1
Denmark	-1.9	-1.2	-1.5	-1.9	-2.3	-1.6	-0.6	-0.2	1.1	1.3	0.4	0.1	0.7	2.5	5.3	4.3	3.4	1.5	0.1	-0.1
Finland	0.0	-2.0	-2.5	-1.6	-0.9	-0.2	-0.8	1.3	1.3	5.7	4.3	4.0	2.7	2.3	2.9	3.5	4.6	4.1	3.7	3.5
France	-4.1	-5.1	-5.5	-4.6	-4.5	-3.3	-2.8	-2.1	-1.6	-2.3	-2.4	-3.6	-4.1	-3.5	-3.4	-2.5	-3.1	-3.1	-2.8	-2.5
Germany	-3.5	-3.6	-3.0	-2.6	-3.6	-3.4	-2.6	-2.1	-1.6	-1.9	-3.4	-3.7	-3.2	-2.8	-2.1	-1.3	-0.3	-0.5	-0.5	-0.2
Greece	-9.9	-10.1	-9.5	-8.5	-9.1	-6.7	-5.5	-3.5	-1.7	-4.0	-3.9	-4.1	-5.5	-6.8	-5.5	-4.6	-4.8	-4.1	-2.6	-1.8
Hungary	..	..	-9.7	-13.8	-4.2	-3.1	-6.4	-6.6	-5.1	-2.8	-3.9	-7.5	-7.6	-7.9	-9.4	-10.8	-5.4	-3.1	-1.8	-0.4
Iceland	-1.6	-0.6	-2.6	-3.1	-2.0	-1.1	-0.4	-1.0	0.5	1.2	-1.1	-2.6	-2.3	-0.7	3.3	5.1	4.8	3.3	1.2	0.9
Ireland	-3.8	-2.7	-1.4	0.4	-0.9	0.5	0.9	1.5	2.9	3.0	-0.2	-1.4	-0.1	1.2	1.2	2.3	-0.3	-4.6	-3.7	-3.2
Italy	-11.8	-12.1	-8.9	-7.5	-5.8	-5.5	-2.2	-2.0	-0.5	-1.7	-3.0	-2.6	-3.9	-3.6	-3.7	-2.0	-1.3	-1.8	-1.1	-0.9
Japan	0.5	-0.5	-3.0	-4.7	-5.5	-5.7	-5.2	-5.6	-6.9	-7.0	-6.3	-7.3	-6.8	-6.8	-5.3	-3.7	-3.1	-2.7	-3.1	-2.7
Luxembourg	-1.6	-1.5	0.4	2.1	3.0	3.1	5.6	4.5	3.4	4.9	3.6	1.6	0.9	-0.3	0.5	1.5	2.7	1.8	1.5	1.8
Netherlands	-3.9	-5.2	-2.9	-3.0	-3.5	-2.1	-1.4	-1.6	-0.9	-0.5	-1.7	-2.8	-2.5	-0.8	0.6	0.9	0.2	0.5	0.1	0.0
New Zealand	-3.5	-2.0	0.0	2.5	2.3	2.3	1.5	0.9	0.4	1.9	2.4	3.4	3.6	3.5	3.9	3.4	3.1	2.7	0.8	0.1
Norway[1]	-3.4	-5.4	-5.9	-4.4	-1.4	-1.5	-1.0	-2.6	-1.1	1.6	0.0	-2.1	-3.9	-2.0	-0.8	1.3	2.8	3.3	0.2	0.1
Poland	..	..	..	..	..	-4.2	-5.1	-4.2	-2.7	-3.3	-4.3	-3.8	-4.8	-5.5	-4.3	-4.4	-3.2	-3.5	-3.1	-2.9
Portugal	-9.5	-6.0	-7.2	-6.3	-4.4	-4.0	-3.5	-3.5	-3.7	-4.7	-5.9	-5.3	-5.1	-4.6	-4.8	-2.8	-1.2	-1.7	-1.8	-1.6
Spain	-7.2	-5.3	-5.4	-4.8	-4.8	-3.4	-2.0	-2.0	-1.2	-1.3	-1.2	-0.5	-0.2	0.2	1.0	1.9	2.1	-0.2	-0.6	-0.5
Sweden	-1.8	-4.3	-5.9	-6.4	-6.3	-2.5	-0.5	0.4	0.5	2.1	0.9	-1.8	-0.8	0.8	2.6	1.8	3.1	3.2	2.2	2.3
Switzerland	-2.1	-2.7	-2.6	-2.2	-1.4	-1.2	-2.6	-1.7	-1.0	0.7	-0.3	-0.7	-1.1	-1.3	-0.5	0.7	0.8	0.8	0.7	0.6
United Kingdom	-3.5	-5.7	-6.8	-6.3	-5.1	-3.6	-1.9	-0.1	0.7	0.8	0.3	-2.1	-3.7	-3.9	-3.5	-2.6	-3.1	-3.6	-4.4	-4.9
United States	-4.4	-5.1	-4.2	-3.0	-2.6	-1.6	-0.6	0.3	0.4	0.8	-0.8	-3.6	-4.5	-4.3	-3.5	-2.7	-3.0	-5.2	-5.5	-5.2
Euro area	-5.5	-5.6	-4.7	-4.4	-4.4	-3.6	-2.5	-2.1	-1.4	-1.8	-2.3	-2.6	-2.9	-2.5	-2.1	-1.2	-0.9	-1.2	-1.0	-1.0
Total OECD	-4.0	-4.7	-4.4	-4.1	-3.8	-2.9	-1.9	-1.3	-1.1	-1.1	-1.9	-3.4	-3.9	-3.7	-2.9	-2.1	-2.0	-2.9	-3.1	-3.0

Note: The underlying balances are adjusted for the cycle and for one-offs. For more details see *OECD Economic Outlook* Sources and Methods (*http://www.oecd.org/eco/sources-and-methods*).
1. As a percentage of mainland potential GDP. The financial balances shown are adjusted to exclude net revenues from petroleum activities.
Source: OECD Economic Outlook 84 database.

StatLink http://dx.doi.org/10.1787/504660675245

Annex Table 30. **General government underlying primary balances**

Surplus (+) or deficit (−) as a per cent of potential GDP

	1991	1992	1993	1994	1995	1996	1997	1998	1999	2000	2001	2002	2003	2004	2005	2006	2007	2008	2009	2010
Australia	-0.6	-1.1	-1.0	-0.5	0.3	1.0	2.1	3.6	3.6	2.3	2.1	3.4	3.1	2.5	2.7	2.7	2.5	2.3	1.5	1.5
Austria	-0.7	0.4	-0.8	-1.3	-2.4	-0.4	1.6	1.0	-0.2	-0.5	1.9	1.4	1.1	1.7	0.9	0.3	1.0	0.4	-0.2	-0.1
Belgium	2.1	1.7	4.0	4.4	4.5	5.1	5.8	6.9	5.9	5.3	5.6	5.0	4.0	4.0	3.6	3.5	2.8	2.6	3.0	3.0
Canada	-2.0	-1.9	-1.6	-0.6	1.1	3.6	5.7	5.3	5.5	5.2	3.0	2.1	1.7	2.4	2.5	1.8	1.6	0.7	0.3	0.1
Czech Republic	..	..	..	..	..	..	..	..	-3.9	-5.0	-4.1	-4.0	-4.4	-1.7	-2.4	-2.9	-2.0	-1.9	-1.3	-0.8
Denmark	2.8	2.3	2.2	1.7	1.2	1.6	2.3	2.5	3.5	3.4	2.2	1.8	2.2	3.7	6.2	4.9	3.8	1.8	0.3	0.0
Finland	-2.0	-3.8	-2.9	-0.7	-0.1	1.1	1.1	2.9	2.8	6.7	4.8	4.0	2.7	2.3	2.7	3.2	4.0	3.4	3.1	2.9
France	-1.7	-2.6	-2.8	-1.8	-1.5	-0.3	0.2	0.8	1.1	0.3	0.3	-0.9	-1.6	-1.0	-1.0	-0.2	-0.6	-0.6	-0.4	-0.1
Germany	-1.5	-1.2	-0.5	-0.1	-0.7	-0.5	0.2	0.8	1.1	0.8	-0.8	-1.2	-0.7	-0.4	0.2	1.1	2.1	1.9	2.0	2.2
Greece	-1.4	0.0	1.3	3.4	1.6	3.4	2.7	4.1	5.0	2.6	2.0	1.1	-0.8	-2.1	-1.1	-0.5	-0.7	0.1	1.4	2.1
Hungary	..	..	-6.2	-7.0	4.2	4.8	0.8	-0.3	1.0	1.8	0.1	-3.9	-3.9	-3.9	-5.5	-7.1	-1.6	0.5	1.6	2.8
Iceland	-0.6	0.2	-1.5	-1.9	-0.6	0.2	0.7	0.0	1.4	1.9	-0.6	-2.2	-1.7	-0.4	2.9	4.4	3.8	2.9	1.3	1.5
Ireland	1.8	2.4	3.1	4.7	3.0	3.5	3.5	3.8	4.3	3.9	0.0	-1.2	0.1	1.3	1.3	2.2	-0.4	-4.6	-3.7	-3.2
Italy	-0.9	-0.5	2.8	2.7	4.6	4.7	6.1	5.3	5.3	4.1	2.7	2.5	0.6	0.7	0.4	2.1	3.1	2.6	3.4	3.7
Japan	1.7	0.6	-1.8	-3.5	-4.2	-4.4	-3.8	-4.1	-5.4	-5.5	-4.9	-5.9	-5.5	-5.7	-4.5	-3.0	-2.4	-1.9	-2.1	-1.4
Luxembourg	-4.3	-3.9	-1.5	0.5	1.7	2.0	4.6	3.5	2.6	3.6	2.3	0.5	0.0	-1.0	-0.2	0.7	2.0	1.2	0.9	1.2
Netherlands	0.5	-0.8	1.5	1.1	0.9	2.3	2.8	2.4	2.8	2.5	0.7	-0.7	-0.5	1.0	2.4	2.6	1.8	2.0	1.6	1.5
New Zealand	-0.8	0.7	2.2	3.7	3.7	3.0	2.3	1.5	0.5	2.3	2.4	3.4	3.5	3.1	3.3	2.7	2.2	1.8	-0.2	-0.9
Norway[1]	-7.5	-9.2	-9.0	-6.9	-5.4	-7.3	-8.1	-7.3	-7.4	-10.9	-11.1	-11.7	-13.6	-12.9	-13.4	-13.4	-11.9	-13.3	-13.0	-13.2
Poland	..	..	..	..	..	-0.1	-1.3	-0.5	-0.3	-0.9	-1.7	-1.9	-2.6	-3.6	-2.5	-2.6	-1.6	-1.9	-1.5	-1.4
Portugal	-0.9	2.2	-0.1	-0.3	1.3	1.0	0.4	-0.2	-0.6	-1.5	-2.7	-2.4	-2.4	-2.0	-2.3	0.0	1.6	1.2	1.0	1.1
Spain	-4.0	-1.9	-1.0	-0.6	-0.3	1.1	2.1	1.7	2.0	1.6	1.5	1.8	1.8	2.0	2.4	3.1	3.3	1.0	0.6	0.8
Sweden	-2.5	-5.3	-6.3	-5.8	-5.0	-0.9	1.4	1.8	1.9	3.1	1.6	-0.6	-0.6	0.7	2.1	1.4	2.5	2.6	1.5	1.5
Switzerland	-1.7	-2.1	-2.0	-1.4	-0.6	-0.5	-1.7	-0.7	0.1	1.7	0.6	0.3	-0.1	-0.3	0.4	1.5	1.6	1.5	1.4	1.3
United Kingdom	-1.2	-3.4	-4.4	-3.7	-2.1	-0.6	1.2	2.9	3.1	3.1	2.3	-0.4	-2.0	-2.2	-1.6	-0.8	-1.1	-1.8	-2.6	-3.3
United States	-0.8	-1.6	-0.9	0.3	0.9	1.7	2.6	3.4	3.1	3.4	1.5	-1.6	-2.6	-2.5	-1.5	-0.7	-1.0	-3.1	-3.3	-3.0
Euro area	-1.3	-1.0	0.1	0.2	0.3	1.1	1.8	2.0	2.2	1.6	0.9	0.4	0.0	0.2	0.4	1.2	1.6	1.3	1.5	1.6
Total OECD	-0.7	-1.3	-1.1	-0.7	-0.2	0.5	1.3	1.8	1.6	1.5	0.4	-1.3	-1.9	-1.8	-1.1	-0.3	-0.2	-1.2	-1.3	-1.1

Note: Adjusted for the cycle and for one-offs and excludes the impact of net interest payments on the underlying balance. For more details see *OECD Economic Outlook* Sources and Methods
  (*http://www.oecd.org/eco/sources-and-methods*).
1. As a percentage of mainland potential GDP. The financial balances shown are adjusted to exclude net revenues from petroleum activities.
Source: OECD Economic Outlook 84 database.

StatLink http://dx.doi.org/10.1787/504701374057

Annex Table 31. General government net debt interest payments
Per cent of nominal GDP

	1991	1992	1993	1994	1995	1996	1997	1998	1999	2000	2001	2002	2003	2004	2005	2006	2007	2008	2009	2010
Australia	3.0	3.1	2.5	3.6	3.7	3.1	2.5	2.0	1.9	1.7	1.6	1.6	1.4	1.3	1.1	1.0	1.0	0.9	0.8	0.7
Austria	2.8	2.9	3.2	3.1	3.4	3.4	3.2	3.1	2.9	2.8	2.7	2.5	2.4	2.2	2.2	2.1	2.1	2.1	2.1	2.2
Belgium	10.6	10.4	10.3	8.8	8.5	8.1	7.4	7.1	6.6	6.4	6.2	5.5	5.1	4.6	4.1	3.8	3.7	3.6	3.6	3.5
Canada	5.3	5.3	5.3	5.2	5.7	5.3	4.8	4.8	4.3	3.1	2.9	2.6	1.8	1.6	1.1	0.7	0.7	0.4	0.6	0.5
Czech Republic	..	..	..	..	0.0	0.4	0.3	0.4	0.4	0.0	-0.1	0.0	0.2	0.3	0.4	0.3	0.3	0.3	0.3	0.3
Denmark	4.7	3.6	3.9	3.6	3.5	3.2	2.9	2.6	2.4	2.1	1.8	1.7	1.5	1.2	0.9	0.6	0.4	0.3	0.2	0.1
Finland	-2.0	-2.0	-0.4	1.0	0.8	1.4	1.9	1.6	1.5	1.0	0.5	0.0	0.0	0.0	-0.1	-0.3	-0.6	-0.6	-0.6	-0.6
France	2.3	2.5	2.7	2.9	3.0	3.1	3.0	2.9	2.7	2.6	2.6	2.6	2.5	2.5	2.4	2.3	2.5	2.5	2.5	2.5
Germany	2.0	2.4	2.5	2.5	2.9	2.9	2.9	2.9	2.7	2.7	2.6	2.5	2.6	2.5	2.4	2.4	2.4	2.4	2.4	2.4
Greece	8.4	10.1	11.0	12.1	10.9	10.3	8.3	7.6	6.7	6.7	6.0	5.2	4.7	4.6	4.3	4.1	4.1	4.1	4.0	4.0
Hungary	1.7	4.0	3.5	6.7	8.4	8.1	7.3	6.3	6.0	4.5	3.9	3.6	3.7	4.0	3.9	3.7	3.8	3.7	3.6	3.4
Iceland	1.0	0.9	1.1	1.2	1.5	1.4	1.1	1.0	0.9	0.7	0.5	0.3	0.6	0.3	-0.4	-0.7	-0.9	-0.4	0.1	0.6
Ireland	5.6	5.1	4.8	4.5	3.9	3.1	2.6	2.3	1.4	0.9	0.2	0.2	0.2	0.1	0.1	-0.1	-0.1	-0.1	0.0	0.0
Italy	10.8	11.6	12.0	10.5	10.5	10.5	8.5	7.6	5.9	5.8	5.7	5.0	4.6	4.3	4.1	4.1	4.4	4.5	4.6	4.8
Japan	1.1	1.1	1.2	1.2	1.3	1.3	1.3	1.5	1.5	1.5	1.4	1.4	1.3	1.2	0.8	0.6	0.7	0.8	1.0	1.3
Korea	-0.6	-0.7	-0.6	-0.6	-0.7	-0.9	-1.0	-1.3	-1.2	-1.5	-1.2	-1.3	-1.2	-1.3	-1.3	-1.6	-1.5	-1.6	-1.6	-1.6
Luxembourg	-2.5	-2.3	-1.9	-1.6	-1.4	-1.1	-1.0	-1.0	-0.9	-1.2	-1.3	-1.1	-0.9	-0.7	-0.6	-0.7	-0.7	-0.6	-0.6	-0.6
Netherlands	4.3	4.4	4.4	4.2	4.4	4.4	4.2	4.0	3.6	2.9	2.4	2.2	2.0	1.9	1.8	1.7	1.7	1.5	1.5	1.5
New Zealand	2.8	2.8	2.3	1.2	1.4	0.7	0.7	0.7	0.2	0.4	0.0	0.0	-0.1	-0.4	-0.6	-0.7	-0.9	-0.9	-1.1	-1.0
Norway	-3.6	-3.4	-2.8	-2.2	-3.5	-4.8	-5.7	-4.0	-5.2	-9.2	-8.4	-7.7	-7.9	-8.5	-9.3	-10.6	-10.7	-12.0	-10.5	-10.8
Poland	..	7.9	7.2	6.1	5.1	4.2	3.8	3.7	2.4	2.4	2.7	1.9	2.2	1.9	1.8	1.7	1.6	1.6	1.6	1.5
Portugal	8.1	..	..	..	5.8	5.0	3.9	3.2	3.0	3.1	3.0	2.9	2.8	2.7	2.6	2.8	2.9	2.9	2.8	2.8
Slovak Republic	..	..	..	1.1	0.6	0.7	1.2	1.5	1.5	1.9	2.2	2.8	1.2	0.5	-0.2	-0.1	-0.1	0.0	-0.2	-0.3
Spain	3.1	3.4	4.5	4.4	4.6	4.7	4.2	3.8	3.2	2.9	2.6	2.3	2.0	1.7	1.4	1.2	1.1	1.2	1.3	1.4
Sweden	-0.7	-1.0	-0.4	0.7	1.4	1.6	1.9	1.3	1.3	1.0	0.7	1.1	0.2	-0.1	-0.5	-0.4	-0.6	-0.6	-0.8	-0.8
Switzerland	0.4	0.6	0.7	0.8	0.8	0.8	0.9	0.9	1.1	1.0	0.9	1.0	1.0	1.0	0.9	0.8	0.8	0.7	0.7	0.7
United Kingdom	2.3	2.3	2.4	2.6	3.0	3.0	3.1	3.0	2.5	2.3	2.0	1.7	1.7	1.7	1.9	1.8	1.9	1.8	1.8	1.7
United States	3.6	3.5	3.4	3.4	3.6	3.4	3.2	3.1	2.7	2.5	2.3	2.1	1.9	1.8	1.9	2.0	2.1	2.1	2.2	2.3
Euro area	4.2	4.6	4.9	4.6	4.8	4.9	4.4	4.1	3.6	3.4	3.2	3.0	2.9	2.7	2.6	2.5	2.5	2.5	2.6	2.6
Total OECD	3.2	3.3	3.3	3.3	3.5	3.4	3.1	3.0	2.6	2.4	2.2	2.1	1.9	1.8	1.7	1.6	1.7	1.7	1.8	1.8

Note: In the case of Ireland and New Zealand where net interest payments are not available, net property income paid is used as a proxy. For Denmark, net interest payments include dividends received. See *OECD Economic Outlook* Sources and Methods (*http://www.oecd.org/eco/sources-and-methods*).

Source: OECD Economic Outlook 84 database.

StatLink ᡒᡓ http://dx.doi.org/10.1787/504752855046

Annex Table 32. General government gross financial liabilities
Per cent of nominal GDP

	1991	1992	1993	1994	1995	1996	1997	1998	1999	2000	2001	2002	2003	2004	2005	2006	2007	2008	2009	2010
Australia	23.2	27.4	30.6	40.1	41.9	39.1	37.4	32.3	28.0	25.0	22.2	20.1	18.8	17.0	16.7	16.1	15.4	14.2	13.4	13.3
Austria	57.7	57.4	62.3	65.3	69.8	70.2	66.6	68.4	71.2	71.0	72.0	73.2	71.3	70.8	70.3	65.9	61.9	62.6	64.8	67.7
Belgium[1]	127.3	136.5	140.6	137.7	135.3	133.4	128.0	122.9	119.5	113.5	111.8	108.3	103.5	98.6	95.7	91.2	87.6	92.2	92.3	92.1
Canada	82.3	90.2	96.3	98.0	101.6	101.7	96.3	95.2	91.4	82.1	82.7	80.6	76.6	72.6	71.1	68.0	64.1	63.0	65.6	66.9
Czech Republic	..	..	..	..	..	..	..	..	..	..	..	33.1	34.9	34.7	34.9	34.7	38.4	36.1	35.1	34.8
Denmark	67.2	71.1	85.0	78.9	79.3	76.6	72.1	69.7	64.1	57.1	55.0	55.4	53.6	50.1	42.3	37.4	31.0	28.4	28.5	29.5
Finland	24.6	44.3	57.6	60.9	65.2	65.9	64.6	60.9	54.7	52.4	49.8	49.5	51.3	51.4	48.4	44.8	41.5	39.6	38.8	39.2
France	39.5	43.9	51.0	60.2	63.0	66.7	69.1	70.7	67.1	65.9	64.4	67.4	71.5	74.1	76.0	71.5	70.1	72.5	75.9	79.0
Germany[2]	37.7	40.9	46.2	46.5	55.7	58.8	60.3	62.2	61.5	60.4	59.7	62.1	65.3	68.7	71.1	69.4	65.5	64.8	66.3	66.3
Greece	..	..	..	..	101.2	103.1	100.0	97.6	101.1	114.9	117.9	116.3	112.5	114.4	112.3	105.8	102.3	100.8	99.8	99.1
Hungary	79.2	81.1	92.0	91.8	88.5	76.1	66.7	64.9	66.2	60.1	59.7	61.0	61.4	65.3	68.7	71.9	72.0	71.8	73.6	75.3
Iceland	38.4	46.2	53.1	55.7	58.9	56.3	53.1	47.9	43.4	41.0	45.9	42.1	40.8	34.5	25.4	30.1	24.0	24.8	122.4	126.7
Ireland	..	..	..	..	..	..	..	62.2	51.3	40.1	37.4	35.2	34.1	32.7	32.6	28.8	27.9	32.8	40.9	48.4
Italy	100.4	106.9	116.2	120.9	122.5	128.9	130.3	132.6	126.4	121.6	120.8	119.4	116.8	117.3	119.9	117.1	113.2	113.0	114.4	115.9
Japan[3]	64.1	67.9	73.9	79.4	86.7	94.0	100.5	113.2	127.0	135.4	143.7	152.3	158.0	165.5	175.3	171.9	170.6	173.0	174.1	177.0
Korea	6.7	6.4	5.6	5.2	5.5	5.9	7.5	13.1	15.6	16.3	17.4	16.6	18.4	22.6	24.7	27.6	28.9	32.6	31.5	33.3
Luxembourg	..	..	..	..	9.5	10.1	10.2	11.1	10.0	9.3	8.2	8.5	7.9	8.5	7.6	10.4	9.9	18.1	17.3	20.2
Netherlands	88.6	92.1	96.7	86.7	89.6	88.1	82.2	80.8	71.6	63.9	59.4	60.3	61.4	61.9	60.5	54.2	51.7	54.5	54.2	54.7
New Zealand	..	..	..	57.4	51.3	44.9	42.3	42.2	39.6	37.4	35.4	33.5	31.4	28.6	27.5	27.1	25.3	25.3	28.4	32.8
Norway	27.8	32.4	40.8	37.3	40.9	36.5	32.0	30.8	30.8	34.0	32.9	40.5	49.3	52.7	49.1	60.9	57.9	45.4	52.7	57.4
Poland	..	..	..	..	51.6	51.4	48.3	43.8	46.6	45.4	43.8	55.0	55.3	54.6	56.4	55.9	52.5	52.8	54.0	55.5
Portugal	..	..	..	..	68.8	68.4	67.4	65.2	62.0	61.1	62.6	66.1	67.2	69.5	73.0	72.0	70.1	70.9	72.9	75.1
Slovak Republic	..	..	..	..	38.2	37.7	39.0	41.2	53.5	57.6	57.2	50.3	48.3	47.3	38.7	34.7	36.5	38.0	39.0	40.0
Spain	49.6	52.1	65.5	64.3	69.3	76.0	75.0	75.3	69.4	66.5	61.9	60.2	55.3	53.4	50.8	46.6	42.7	44.2	47.7	51.8
Sweden	54.7	72.9	78.2	82.5	81.0	84.4	83.2	82.5	73.7	64.7	63.4	60.5	59.8	59.5	59.7	52.5	47.0	44.6	41.3	40.5
Switzerland	33.3	38.4	42.9	45.5	47.7	50.1	52.1	54.9	51.9	52.5	51.3	57.2	57.0	57.9	56.5	50.6	48.6	48.1	47.5	47.3
United Kingdom	32.8	39.0	48.7	46.8	51.6	51.2	52.0	52.5	47.4	45.1	40.4	40.8	41.2	43.5	46.1	46.0	46.9	58.7	63.6	69.4
United States	67.7	70.2	71.9	71.1	70.7	70.0	67.6	64.5	61.0	55.2	55.2	57.6	60.9	61.9	62.3	61.7	62.9	73.2	78.1	82.5
Euro area	59.2	60.7	65.9	69.1	ǀ72.4	77.5	79.6	80.3	78.5	75.3	73.9	74.2	75.1	75.9	77.0	74.7	71.4	70.7	73.2	74.7
Total OECD	59.7	62.6	66.7	68.2	ǀ70.0	72.0	72.3	72.9	72.2	69.5	69.8	71.7	74.0	75.6	77.4	76.0	75.0	79.7	82.8	85.8

StatLink http://dx.doi.org/10.1787/504764530263

Note: Gross debt data are not always comparable across countries due to different definitions or treatment of debt components. Notably, they include the funded portion of government employee pension liabilities for some OECD countries, including Australia and the United States. The debt position of these countries is thus overstated relative to countries that have large unfunded liabilities for such pensions which according to ESA95/SNA93 are not counted in the debt figures, but rather as a memorandum item to the debt. Maastricht debt for European Union countries is shown in Annex Table 62.
For more details see *OECD Economic Outlook* Sources and Methods (*http://www.oecd.org/eco/sources-and-methods*) from 2005 onwards.
1. Includes the debt of the Belgium National Railways Company (SNCB) from 2005 onwards.
2. Includes the debt of the Inherited Debt Fund from 1995 onwards.
3. Includes the debt of the Japan Railway Settlement Corporation and the National Forest Special Account from 1998 onwards.
Source: OECD Economic Outlook 84 database.

Annex Table 33. General government net financial liabilities
Per cent of nominal GDP

	1991	1992	1993	1994	1995	1996	1997	1998	1999	2000	2001	2002	2003	2004	2005	2006	2007	2008	2009	2010
Australia	11.2	15.7	21.3	25.7	26.3	20.9	21.1	16.0	14.9	8.8	6.4	4.4	2.7	0.7	-0.8	-4.1	-6.0	-7.5	-8.2	-8.2
Austria	28.6	29.6	33.4	35.2	38.8	40.3	36.5	36.8	35.8	34.8	35.6	37.1	36.1	37.9	37.6	33.2	30.7	30.4	32.7	35.4
Belgium[1]	108.0	113.1	115.0	114.4	114.5	115.5	110.9	107.5	102.9	97.3	94.8	93.1	90.3	84.0	81.9	76.9	73.0	71.2	70.9	70.4
Canada	50.5	59.1	64.2	67.9	70.7	70.0	64.7	60.8	55.8	46.2	44.3	42.6	38.7	35.2	30.7	26.5	23.4	22.3	23.9	24.8
Czech Republic	..	..	..	..	..	..	..	..	..	..	..	-15.9	-7.2	-9.4	-10.7	-9.9	-8.0	-5.9	-3.7	-1.8
Denmark	25.7	28.1	31.1	31.5	36.0	36.2	33.8	36.3	30.6	25.7	21.9	20.4	17.7	12.1	8.9	2.6	-3.1	-5.4	-5.4	-4.6
Finland[2]	-33.4	-24.4	-15.9	-16.3	-4.0	-6.7	-7.5	-14.5	-50.1	-31.1	-31.6	-31.5	-39.6	-45.8	-57.8	-67.3	-71.2	-72.2	-72.8	-72.7
France	18.5	20.0	26.8	29.7	37.5	41.8	42.3	40.5	33.5	35.1	36.7	41.8	44.2	45.3	43.2	37.5	34.4	36.2	39.5	42.4
Germany[3]	8.7	15.1	18.5	19.3	30.3	33.2	33.0	36.7	35.2	34.4	36.7	40.8	43.5	47.5	49.8	48.1	44.5	43.2	43.7	43.5
Greece	..	..	..	..	81.4	81.8	77.1	72.8	70.4	88.9	93.2	94.1	87.8	88.0	83.8	76.3	68.5	67.0	66.0	65.3
Hungary	-59.2	-47.4	-19.3	3.3	24.3	25.3	24.9	31.8	33.6	31.9	32.0	36.8	37.3	41.7	46.2	51.7	52.7	52.5	54.6	56.1
Iceland	19.7	26.5	34.6	37.6	39.5	39.3	37.3	31.3	24.4	24.3	25.3	22.0	23.2	20.8	9.4	7.8	1.6	-1.8	0.2	3.9
Ireland	..	..	..	..	..	..	..	42.5	27.6	16.8	13.2	14.3	11.7	9.2	7.0	1.7	0.3	6.0	13.1	19.8
Italy	86.2	93.2	100.5	104.5	99.0	104.5	104.7	107.0	101.1	95.6	96.3	95.7	92.7	92.5	93.6	90.5	87.6	87.2	88.8	90.1
Japan[4]	12.6	13.9	17.2	20.0	24.1	29.3	34.8	46.2	53.8	60.4	66.3	72.6	76.5	82.7	84.6	84.6	85.9	87.8	90.1	93.7
Korea	-15.3	-14.7	-15.5	-16.1	-17.4	-19.0	-21.5	-23.1	-23.9	-27.0	-30.0	-31.8	-30.0	-29.8	-34.3	-35.3	-37.7	-39.7	-41.5	-43.3
Luxembourg	..	..	..	..	-37.8	-41.1	-41.6	-46.4	-47.7	-51.0	-58.0	-55.7	-56.9	-51.9	-48.6	-44.7	-45.0	-44.9	-43.4	-40.4
Netherlands	34.5	40.3	44.8	44.6	54.1	52.8	49.7	48.2	36.7	34.9	33.0	34.9	36.2	37.6	35.0	31.6	29.7	27.6	27.3	27.5
New Zealand	..	..	..	44.4	38.0	32.8	30.2	28.2	25.8	23.7	21.4	17.1	11.1	4.9	-1.5	-8.3	-13.4	-15.5	-14.6	-12.4
Norway	-37.4	-35.1	-32.0	-30.6	-36.1	-41.4	-48.9	-52.0	-58.4	-68.4	-85.9	-81.8	-96.5	-105.5	-123.5	-137.6	-144.0	-152.0	-171.5	-177.7
Poland	..	..	..	..	-15.0	-5.7	0.3	6.3	13.4	15.5	18.5	22.1	22.7	20.8	21.8	20.4	20.7	21.3	22.6	24.0
Portugal	..	..	..	..	25.1	27.3	32.1	33.3	30.8	27.4	29.5	34.0	36.3	40.2	43.9	43.0	43.1	44.2	46.2	48.3
Slovak Republic	..	..	..	..	-30.7	-18.3	-12.3	-3.9	0.9	12.7	10.5	1.7	1.6	5.7	1.7	4.0	5.5	7.0	8.5	9.3
Spain	33.3	35.2	43.5	46.4	51.6	55.5	54.2	53.7	47.7	44.2	41.6	40.2	36.8	34.5	30.4	24.1	19.1	19.7	22.4	25.8
Sweden	-5.0	4.6	10.5	20.7	25.6	26.6	24.7	22.1	12.5	5.5	1.3	6.5	3.3	0.7	-4.1	-16.1	-20.9	-22.8	-22.7	-22.3
Switzerland	..	..	..	..	..	..	..	..	12.6	11.4	10.9	15.7	15.9	17.7	16.7	13.6	11.6	9.9	9.4	9.2
United Kingdom	14.9	21.8	31.5	32.1	37.8	39.8	41.9	43.4	38.7	35.6	32.3	33.0	33.4	35.7	29.4	29.2	30.2	32.6	37.4	43.0
United States	48.9	52.4	54.9	54.4	53.8	52.0	49.0	45.2	40.6	36.0	35.3	37.9	41.2	42.8	43.2	42.4	43.0	46.2	52.6	57.8
Euro area	36.3	36.9	40.6	42.9	46.4	51.6	53.1	53.3	50.2	47.3	47.6	49.5	50.5	51.0	50.9	47.8	44.1	42.7	44.1	45.4
Total OECD	33.8	36.6	40.2	41.5	42.3	43.9	43.8	43.8	41.3	38.6	38.6	40.7	42.6	43.9	43.4	41.7	40.7	41.7	45.0	48.1

Note: Net debt measures are not always comparable across countries due to different definitions or treatment of debt (and asset) components. First, the treatment of government liabilities in respect of their employee pension plans may be different (see note to Annex Table 32). Second, the range of items included as general government assets differs across countries. For example, equity holdings are excluded from government assets in some countries whereas foreign exchange, gold and SDR holdings are considered as assets in the United States and the United Kingdom. For details see *OECD Economic Outlook* Sources and Methods *(http://www.oecd.org/eco/sources-and-methods).*

1. Includes the debt of the Belgium National Railways Company (SNCB) from 2005 onwards.
2. From 1995 onwards housing corporation shares are no longer classified as financial assets.
3. Includes the debt of the Inherited Debt Fund from 1995 onwards.
4. Includes the debt of the Japan Railway Settlement Corporation and the National Forest Special Account from 1998 onwards.

Source: OECD Economic Outlook 84 database.

StatLink ᴍꜱᴘ *http://dx.doi.org/10.1787/504837115051*

Annex Table 34. Short-term interest rates
Per cent, per annum

	1994	1995	1996	1997	1998	1999	2000	2001	2002	2003	2004	2005	2006	2007	2008	2009	2010	Fourth quarter 2008	2009	2010
Australia	5.7	7.7	7.2	5.4	5.0	5.0	6.2	4.9	4.7	4.9	5.5	5.6	6.0	6.7	7.1	4.3	5.0	5.6	4.2	5.5
Austria	5.1	4.6	3.4	3.5	3.6															
Belgium	5.7	4.8	3.2	3.4	3.6															
Canada	5.6	7.1	4.5	3.6	5.1	4.9	5.7	4.0	2.6	3.0	2.4	2.8	4.1	4.6	3.5	2.1	2.6	3.1	2.4	3.1
Czech Republic	9.1	10.9	12.0	16.0	14.3	6.9	5.4	5.2	3.5	2.3	2.4	2.0	2.3	3.1	4.0	3.9	3.8	3.9	3.8	3.8
Denmark	6.1	6.1	3.9	3.7	4.1	3.3	4.9	4.6	3.5	2.4	2.1	2.2	3.1	4.3	5.1	3.2	2.7	5.8	2.8	2.9
Finland	5.4	5.8	3.6	3.2	3.6															
France	5.8	6.6	3.9	3.5	3.6															
Germany	5.4	4.5	3.3	3.3	3.5															
Greece	19.3	15.5	12.8	10.4	11.6	8.9	4.4													
Hungary	26.9	32.0	24.0	20.1	18.0	14.7	11.0	10.8	8.9	8.2	11.3	7.0	6.9	7.6	8.9	8.3	7.2	10.5	7.8	7.0
Iceland	4.9	7.0	7.0	7.1	7.5	9.3	11.2	12.0	9.0	5.3	6.3	9.4	12.4	14.3	16.0	17.1	12.6	18.0	15.1	11.1
Ireland	5.9	6.2	5.4	6.1	5.4															
Italy	8.5	10.5	8.8	6.9	5.0															
Japan	2.2	1.2	0.6	0.6	0.7	0.2	0.2	0.1	0.1	0.0	0.0	0.0	0.2	0.7	0.8	0.7	0.4	0.9	0.6	0.4
Korea	13.3	14.1	12.6	13.4	15.2	6.8	7.1	5.3	4.8	4.3	3.8	3.6	4.5	5.2	5.3	4.1	4.9	4.7	4.3	5.3
Luxembourg	5.7	4.8	3.2	3.4	3.6															
Mexico	14.6	48.2	32.9	21.3	26.2	22.4	16.2	12.2	7.5	6.5	7.1	9.3	7.3	7.4	7.9	7.1	5.9	8.3	6.3	5.8
Netherlands	5.2	4.4	3.0	3.3	3.5															
New Zealand	6.7	9.0	9.3	7.7	7.3	4.8	6.5	5.7	5.7	5.4	6.1	7.1	7.5	8.3	8.3	4.9	5.5	7.4	4.4	5.9
Norway	5.9	5.5	4.9	3.7	5.8	6.5	6.7	7.2	6.9	4.1	2.0	2.2	3.1	5.0	6.1	4.8	4.3	5.6	4.5	4.3
Poland	31.8	27.7	21.3	23.1	19.9	14.7	18.9	15.7	8.8	5.7	6.2	5.2	4.2	4.8	6.4	6.6	6.6	6.6	6.6	6.6
Portugal	11.1	9.8	7.4	5.7	4.3															
Slovak Republic	..	8.4	12.0	22.4	21.1	15.7	8.6	7.8	7.8	6.2	4.7	2.9	4.3	4.3	4.2	2.7	2.6	3.8	2.6	2.8
Spain	8.0	9.4	7.5	5.4	4.2															
Sweden	7.4	8.7	5.8	4.1	4.2	3.1	4.0	4.0	4.1	3.0	2.1	1.7	2.3	3.6	3.9	2.1	2.2	2.9	1.9	2.7
Switzerland	4.2	2.9	2.0	1.6	1.5	1.4	3.2	2.9	1.1	0.3	0.5	0.8	1.6	2.6	2.7	1.7	1.9	2.4	1.7	2.0
Turkey	..	..	..	..	..	..	38.9	92.4	59.5	38.5	23.8	15.6	17.9	18.3	18.3	15.5	13.7	17.7	15.3	13.0
United Kingdom	5.5	6.7	6.0	6.8	7.3	5.4	6.1	5.0	4.0	3.7	4.6	4.7	4.8	6.0	5.6	2.8	2.7	5.0	2.7	2.8
United States	4.7	6.0	5.4	5.7	5.5	5.4	6.5	3.7	1.8	1.2	1.6	3.5	5.2	5.3	3.3	1.7	2.0	3.6	2.0	2.5
Euro area	6.3	6.5	4.8	4.3	3.9	3.0	4.4	4.3	3.3	2.3	2.1	2.2	3.1	4.3	4.7	2.7	2.6	4.6	2.6	2.8

Note: Three-month money market rates where available, or rates on proximately similar financial instruments. See *OECD Economic Outlook* Sources and Methods (*http://www.oecd.org/eco/sources-and-methods*). Individual euro area countries are not shown after 1998 (2000 for Greece) since their short term interest rates are equal to the euro area rate.

Source: OECD Economic Outlook 84 database.

StatLink http://dx.doi.org/10.1787/504873037420

Annex Table 35. Long-term interest rates
Per cent, per annum

	1994	1995	1996	1997	1998	1999	2000	2001	2002	2003	2004	2005	2006	2007	2008	2009	2010	Fourth quarter 2008	Fourth quarter 2009	Fourth quarter 2010
Australia	8.9	9.2	8.2	7.0	5.5	6.0	6.3	5.6	5.8	5.4	5.6	5.3	5.6	6.0	5.9	5.5	6.1	5.4	5.7	6.3
Austria	7.0	7.1	6.3	5.7	4.7	4.7	5.6	5.1	5.0	4.2	4.2	3.4	3.8	4.3	4.3	4.4	4.7	4.2	4.5	4.8
Belgium	7.7	7.4	6.3	5.6	4.7	4.7	5.6	5.1	4.9	4.1	4.1	3.4	3.8	4.3	4.4	4.4	4.7	4.3	4.5	4.8
Canada	8.4	8.2	7.2	6.1	5.3	5.5	5.9	5.5	5.3	4.8	4.6	4.1	4.2	4.3	3.7	4.1	4.7	3.7	4.4	5.0
Czech Republic	..	..	..	..	..	..	6.3	6.3	4.9	4.1	4.8	3.5	3.8	4.3	4.7	4.8	4.9	4.8	4.9	4.9
Denmark	7.8	8.3	7.2	6.3	5.0	4.9	5.7	5.1	5.1	4.3	4.3	3.4	3.8	4.3	4.3	4.1	4.5	4.1	4.3	4.7
Finland	9.0	8.8	7.1	6.0	4.8	4.7	5.5	5.0	5.0	4.1	4.1	3.4	3.8	4.3	4.3	4.3	4.6	4.1	4.3	4.8
France	7.2	7.5	6.3	5.6	4.6	4.6	5.4	4.9	4.9	4.1	4.1	3.4	3.8	4.3	4.3	4.3	4.6	4.1	4.4	4.8
Germany	6.9	6.9	6.2	5.7	4.6	4.5	5.3	4.8	4.8	4.1	4.0	3.4	3.8	4.2	4.1	4.0	4.4	3.8	4.2	4.6
Greece	..	..	..	9.8	8.5	6.3	6.1	5.3	5.1	4.3	4.3	3.6	4.1	4.5	4.8	5.2	5.3	5.1	5.3	5.3
Hungary	..	..	..	..	..	..	8.6	7.9	7.1	6.8	8.3	6.6	7.1	6.7	8.0	8.3	8.2	8.3	8.3	8.2
Iceland	7.0	9.7	9.2	8.7	7.7	8.5	11.2	10.4	8.0	6.7	7.5	7.7	9.3	9.8	11.3	12.6	9.3	14.0	11.0	8.9
Ireland	8.0	8.2	7.2	6.3	4.7	4.8	5.5	5.0	5.0	4.1	4.1	3.3	3.8	4.3	4.5	4.4	4.5	4.5	4.4	4.7
Italy	10.5	12.2	9.4	6.9	4.9	4.7	5.6	5.2	5.0	4.3	4.3	3.6	4.0	4.5	4.7	5.1	5.3	4.9	5.2	5.3
Japan	4.4	3.4	3.1	2.4	1.5	1.7	1.7	1.3	1.3	1.0	1.5	1.4	1.7	1.7	1.5	2.0	2.7	1.6	2.3	3.0
Korea	12.3	12.4	10.9	11.7	12.8	8.7	8.5	6.9	6.6	5.0	4.7	5.0	5.2	5.4	5.5	5.3	5.8	5.2	5.5	6.0
Luxembourg	7.2	7.2	6.3	5.6	4.7	4.7	5.5	4.9	4.7	3.3	2.8	2.4	3.3	4.4	4.7	4.5	4.8	4.5	4.7	5.0
Mexico	13.8	39.9	34.4	22.4	24.8	24.1	16.9	13.8	8.5	7.4	7.7	9.3	7.5	7.6	8.3	7.3	6.8	9.0	6.3	7.0
Netherlands	6.9	6.9	6.2	5.6	4.6	4.6	5.4	5.0	4.9	4.1	4.1	3.4	3.8	4.3	4.3	4.3	4.6	4.1	4.4	4.8
New Zealand	7.6	7.8	7.9	7.2	6.3	6.4	6.9	6.4	6.5	5.9	6.1	5.9	5.8	6.3	6.1	4.8	5.4	5.6	4.9	5.8
Norway	7.4	7.4	6.8	5.9	5.4	5.5	6.2	6.2	6.4	5.0	4.4	3.7	4.1	4.8	4.5	4.2	4.5	4.2	4.3	4.5
Portugal	10.5	11.5	8.6	6.4	4.9	4.8	5.6	5.2	5.0	4.2	4.1	3.4	3.9	4.4	4.6	4.7	5.0	4.6	4.8	5.1
Slovak Republic	..	..	9.7	9.4	21.7	16.2	9.8	8.0	6.9	5.0	5.0	3.5	4.4	4.5	4.7	5.0	5.1	4.8	5.1	5.1
Spain	10.0	11.3	8.7	6.4	4.8	4.7	5.5	5.1	5.0	4.1	4.1	3.4	3.8	4.3	4.4	4.6	4.9	4.4	4.7	4.9
Sweden	9.5	10.2	8.0	6.6	5.0	5.0	5.4	5.1	5.3	4.6	4.4	3.4	3.7	4.2	4.0	3.9	4.5	3.6	4.2	4.8
Switzerland	5.0	4.5	4.0	3.4	3.0	3.0	3.9	3.4	3.2	2.7	2.7	2.1	2.5	2.9	3.0	2.2	2.9	2.6	2.2	3.4
Turkey	..	..	..	..	..	..	37.7	99.6	63.5	44.1	24.9	16.2	18.0	18.3	19.0	15.9	13.9	19.5	14.6	13.4
United Kingdom	8.1	8.2	7.8	7.1	5.6	5.1	5.3	4.9	4.9	4.5	4.9	4.4	4.5	5.0	4.7	4.6	5.1	4.4	4.8	5.3
United States	7.1	6.6	6.4	6.4	5.3	5.6	6.0	5.0	4.6	4.0	4.3	4.3	4.8	4.6	3.8	4.1	4.8	3.8	4.4	5.0
Euro area	8.0	8.4	7.1	6.0	4.8	4.7	5.4	5.0	4.9	4.1	4.1	3.4	3.8	4.3	4.4	4.4	4.7	4.3	4.6	4.9

Note: 10-year benchmark government bond yields where available or yield on proximately similar financial instruments (for Korea a 5-year bond is used). See also *OECD Economic Outlook* Sources and Methods (*http://www.oecd.org/eco/sources-and-methods*).
Source: OECD Economic Outlook 84 database.

StatLink ⏩ http://dx.doi.org/10.1787/50500206218

Annex Table 36. Nominal exchange rates (*vis-à-vis* the US dollar)
Average of daily rates

	Monetary unit	1998	1999	1999	2000	2001	2002	2003	2004	2005	2006	2007	Estimates and assumptions[1] 2008	2009	2010
Australia	Dollar	1.592	1.550	1.550	1.727	1.935	1.841	1.542	1.359	1.313	1.328	1.195	1.214	1.601	1.601
Austria	Schilling	12.38	12.91												
Belgium	Franc	36.30	37.86												
Canada	Dollar	1.483	1.486	1.486	1.485	1.548	1.570	1.400	1.301	1.212	1.134	1.074	1.080	1.295	1.295
Czech Republic	Koruny	32.28	34.59	34.59	38.64	38.02	32.73	28.13	25.69	23.95	22.59	20.29	17.06	19.45	19.453
Denmark	Krone	6.699	6.980	6.980	8.088	8.321	7.884	6.577	5.988	5.996	5.943	5.443	5.147	5.974	5.974
Finland	Markka	5.345	5.580												
France	Franc	5.899	6.156												
Germany	Deutschemark	1.759	1.836												
Greece	Drachma	295.3	319.8												
Hungary	Forint	214.3	237.1	237.1	282.3	286.5	257.9	224.3	202.6	199.5	210.4	183.6	173.8	209.9	209.9
Iceland	Krona	71.17	72.43	72.43	78.84	97.67	91.59	76.69	70.19	62.88	69.90	64.07	86.80	122.20	122.20
Ireland	Pound	0.703	0.739												
Italy	Lira	1736	1817												
Japan	Yen	130.9	113.9	113.9	107.8	121.5	125.3	115.9	108.1	110.1	116.4	117.8	103.6	95.7	95.7
Korea	Won	1 400.5	1 186.7	1 186.7	1 130.6	1 290.4	1 251.0	1 191.0	1 145.2	1 024.2	951.8	929.5	1 116.6	1 467.9	1 467.9
Luxembourg	Franc	36.30	37.86												
Mexico	Peso	9.153	9.553	9.553	9.453	9.344	9.660	10.790	11.281	10.890	10.903	10.929	11.177	13.366	13.366
Netherlands	Guilder	1.983	2.068												
New Zealand	Dollar	1.869	1.892	1.892	2.205	2.382	2.163	1.724	1.509	1.421	1.542	1.361	1.430	1.806	1.806
Norway	Krone	7.545	7.797	7.797	8.797	8.993	7.986	7.078	6.739	6.441	6.415	5.858	5.639	6.909	6.909
Poland	Zloty	3.492	3.964	3.964	4.346	4.097	4.082	3.888	3.651	3.234	3.103	2.765	2.412	2.952	2.952
Portugal	Escudo	180.1	188.2												
Slovak Republic	Koruna	35.2	41.36	41.36	46.23	48.35	45.30	36.76	32.23	31.04	29.65	24.68	21.58	24.44	24.437
Spain	Peseta	149.4	156.2												
Sweden	Krona	7.947	8.262	8.262	9.161	10.338	9.721	8.078	7.346	7.472	7.373	6.758	6.609	8.042	8.042
Switzerland	Franc	1.450	1.503	1.503	1.688	1.687	1.557	1.345	1.243	1.246	1.253	1.200	1.082	1.161	1.161
Turkey	Lira	0.260	0.419	0.419	0.624	1.228	1.512	1.503	1.426	1.341	1.430	1.300	1.320	1.686	1.686
United Kingdom	Pound	0.604	0.618	0.618	0.661	0.694	0.667	0.612	0.546	0.550	0.543	0.500	0.543	0.643	0.643
United States	Dollar	1.000	1.000	1.000	1.000	1.000	1.000	1.000	1.000	1.000	1.000	1.000	1.000	1.000	1.000
Euro area	Euro	..	0.939	0.939	1.085	1.117	1.061	0.885	0.805	0.805	0.797	0.730	0.690	0.802	0.802
	SDR	0.737	0.731	0.731	0.758	0.785	0.773	0.714	0.675	0.677	0.680	0.653	0.635	0.675	0.675

Note: No rates are shown for individual euro area countries after 1999.
1. On the technical assumption that exchange rates remain at their levels of 28 October 2008.
Source: OECD Economic Outlook 84 database.

StatLink ⬛⬛ http://dx.doi.org/10.1787/505008140551

Annex Table 37. **Effective exchange rates**
Indices 2000 = 100, average of daily rates

	1995	1996	1997	1998	1999	2000	2001	2002	2003	2004	2005	2006	2007	Estimates and assumptions[1] 2008	2009	2010
Australia	103.9	113.9	115.4	107.4	107.6	100.0	93.7	97.2	108.6	117.1	120.0	118.3	125.7	122.3	98.1	98.1
Austria	102.5	101.5	99.6	101.6	102.3	100.0	100.4	101.0	104.4	105.5	104.7	104.8	105.4	105.8	105.0	105.0
Belgium	107.9	106.2	102.0	104.4	104.1	100.0	101.2	103.0	108.3	110.2	109.7	109.8	111.3	113.5	111.4	111.4
Canada	102.0	103.9	104.3	99.4	99.1	100.0	97.0	95.5	105.5	112.0	119.8	127.7	133.6	132.2	111.9	111.9
Czech Republic	98.8	100.4	97.4	99.1	98.7	100.0	105.0	117.0	116.7	117.0	124.3	130.5	133.3	149.8	151.4	151.4
Denmark	105.7	104.7	102.3	104.9	104.2	100.0	101.8	103.3	108.1	109.5	108.6	108.4	109.8	111.6	109.8	109.8
Finland	103.6	101.1	98.9	101.7	104.7	100.0	102.1	104.2	110.3	112.4	111.5	111.3	113.0	115.2	111.9	111.9
France	104.5	104.9	102.1	104.5	103.8	100.0	100.9	102.5	109.4	109.0	108.4	108.5	109.9	111.8	110.1	110.1
Germany	106.0	104.5	100.9	104.6	104.5	100.0	101.2	103.1	109.4	111.6	110.3	110.3	111.8	113.2	110.8	110.8
Greece	113.8	111.9	109.9	106.6	107.0	100.0	101.0	102.8	107.8	109.5	108.5	108.6	110.1	112.5	111.2	111.2
Hungary	153.0	130.3	120.7	109.3	105.4	100.0	101.9	108.9	108.3	110.4	111.1	104.0	110.0	110.8	104.5	104.5
Iceland	93.3	92.8	94.8	97.4	99.0	100.0	85.2	87.9	92.0	93.1	103.5	92.7	93.7	69.2	54.4	54.4
Ireland	111.2	114.1	113.9	110.5	107.3	100.0	101.2	103.6	112.6	115.1	114.9	115.1	118.1	123.4	119.2	119.2
Italy	91.3	100.5	101.8	104.0	103.8	100.0	101.3	103.2	108.3	110.1	109.2	109.3	110.7	112.3	110.7	110.7
Japan	92.5	80.6	77.1	80.0	91.9	100.0	92.3	88.4	91.5	95.3	92.4	85.4	80.5	90.2	106.5	106.5
Korea	119.5	121.4	112.4	81.3	93.3	100.0	92.4	95.4	94.8	94.8	105.6	113.9	113.2	90.9	70.3	70.3
Luxembourg	105.4	104.3	102.0	103.0	102.8	100.0	100.4	101.5	104.9	106.1	105.5	105.5	106.6	107.5	105.9	105.9
Mexico	138.6	117.7	115.5	102.6	97.9	100.0	102.8	99.7	87.1	81.9	84.3	83.8	82.2	80.1	68.3	68.3
Netherlands	108.8	107.3	102.1	105.7	105.4	100.0	101.4	103.7	110.8	113.4	112.7	112.6	114.7	116.5	112.5	112.5
New Zealand	116.9	124.3	127.3	114.3	110.3	100.0	98.7	106.8	121.5	129.7	135.8	125.4	133.9	125.2	110.9	110.9
Norway	104.5	104.6	105.6	102.4	102.2	100.0	103.3	112.1	109.7	106.0	110.6	109.9	111.6	111.5	102.4	102.4
Poland	122.7	114.4	106.3	104.0	97.0	100.0	110.2	105.4	94.8	92.7	103.6	106.8	110.4	120.6	113.3	113.3
Portugal	104.9	104.5	103.1	103.0	102.4	100.0	100.9	102.0	104.8	105.5	104.9	105.0	105.7	107.1	107.3	107.3
Slovak Republic	100.4	101.3	106.0	105.9	98.3	100.0	97.6	98.0	103.6	108.0	110.1	113.4	125.0	133.4	136.0	136.0
Spain	106.0	107.1	102.8	104.0	103.1	100.0	101.1	102.5	106.3	107.5	106.9	107.0	108.0	109.7	108.5	108.5
Sweden	94.0	103.5	100.2	99.9	99.7	100.0	91.9	94.1	99.5	101.3	98.7	99.1	100.2	98.8	92.7	92.7
Switzerland	104.0	102.7	96.9	101.0	101.8	100.0	104.0	109.3	111.1	111.5	110.6	108.9	106.0	112.5	118.5	118.5
Turkey	991	581.1	345.5	207.8	137.2	100.0	56.3	41.8	36.8	35.9	37.7	35.1	35.9	34.2	30.2	30.2
United Kingdom	76.4	78.1	91.1	97.0	97.4	100.0	99.0	100.2	96.3	100.8	99.3	99.8	101.4	89.4	84.5	84.5
United States	78.5	82.9	88.8	98.0	97.6	100.0	105.3	105.8	99.6	95.1	92.6	91.0	87.0	84.6	94.4	94.4
Euro area	109.5	111.7	104.6	110.8	109.9	100.0	102.5	106.4	119.3	123.8	121.8	121.9	125.6	129.6	123.1	123.1

Note: For details on the method of calculation, see the section on exchange rates and competitiveness indicators in *OECD Economic Outlook Sources and Methods* (*http://www.oecd.org/eco/sources-and-methods*).

1. On the technical assumption that exchange rates remain at their levels of 28 October 2008.

Source: OECD Economic Outlook 84 database.

StatLink http://dx.doi.org/10.1787/505012733154

Annex Table 38. Export volumes of goods and services
National accounts basis, percentage changes from previous year

	1991	1992	1993	1994	1995	1996	1997	1998	1999	2000	2001	2002	2003	2004	2005	2006	2007	2008	2009	2010
Australia	13.1	5.5	8.4	9.3	5.0	10.7	12.0	0.1	4.4	10.2	2.2	0.2	-1.6	4.6	2.4	3.3	3.1	5.0	3.7	6.9
Austria	4.4	1.3	-1.6	5.4	6.3	5.0	11.7	8.3	6.6	13.0	6.2	3.4	4.8	8.0	6.4	7.3	8.4	3.8	1.0	3.3
Belgium	3.1	3.7	-0.4	8.3	5.0	2.4	6.8	6.0	4.8	8.3	1.1	1.2	3.0	6.1	3.9	2.7	3.9	2.7	1.0	3.5
Canada	1.8	7.2	10.8	12.7	8.5	5.6	8.3	9.1	10.7	8.9	-3.0	1.2	-2.3	5.0	1.8	0.6	1.0	-4.3	-2.9	2.0
Czech Republic	..	..	..	0.2	16.7	5.7	8.2	10.4	4.9	17.8	11.0	1.9	7.2	20.3	11.7	16.4	14.6	10.2	1.8	5.1
Denmark	6.5	0.5	1.0	8.4	3.1	4.2	4.9	4.1	11.6	12.7	3.1	4.1	-1.0	2.8	8.3	9.0	1.9	2.6	0.5	3.4
Finland[1]	-7.2	9.4	16.4	13.5	8.6	5.8	14.0	9.3	11.1	17.3	2.1	2.8	-1.7	8.6	7.0	11.9	8.2	5.0	2.1	4.8
France[1]	5.6	5.5	0.5	8.3	8.8	3.3	13.1	8.1	4.2	13.1	2.5	1.3	-0.7	3.0	3.5	5.6	3.2	2.2	-0.2	2.7
Germany	11.1	-2.0	-4.8	8.1	6.6	6.2	11.8	7.4	5.6	14.1	6.8	4.3	2.4	9.4	7.9	13.1	7.7	4.2	0.7	3.9
Greece	4.1	10.0	-2.6	7.4	3.0	3.5	20.0	5.3	18.1	14.1	-2.7	-7.7	2.5	12.6	2.7	5.1	5.9	3.6	3.4	5.8
Hungary	..	..	13.7	13.7	36.4	12.1	22.3	17.6	12.2	22.0	8.1	3.9	6.2	15.0	11.3	18.6	15.9	7.7	3.9	4.7
Iceland	-5.9	-2.0	6.5	9.3	-2.3	9.9	5.6	2.5	4.0	4.2	7.4	3.8	1.6	8.4	7.2	-5.0	18.1	8.9	2.5	4.2
Ireland	5.7	13.9	9.7	15.1	20.0	12.5	17.6	23.1	15.5	20.2	8.7	5.2	0.4	7.5	5.2	5.7	6.8	1.7	1.4	2.7
Italy	-2.1	6.4	8.7	10.6	12.7	0.6	5.7	1.7	-0.6	13.0	2.2	-2.8	-1.6	3.8	1.8	6.5	4.5	0.4	-0.6	2.0
Japan	4.1	3.9	-0.1	3.6	4.3	5.9	11.1	-2.7	1.9	12.7	-6.9	7.5	9.2	13.9	7.0	9.7	8.6	5.3	-2.9	0.7
Korea	11.1	12.2	12.2	16.3	24.4	12.2	21.6	12.7	14.6	19.1	-2.7	13.3	15.6	19.6	8.5	11.8	12.1	9.1	6.4	11.3
Luxembourg	9.2	2.7	4.8	7.7	4.6	2.7	10.8	10.9	14.2	13.5	3.9	2.1	6.8	11.3	5.9	14.7	4.4	2.4	0.9	3.5
Mexico	5.1	5.0	8.1	17.7	30.2	18.2	10.6	12.3	12.3	16.3	-3.5	1.4	2.7	11.5	6.7	10.9	6.1	4.6	-2.7	0.9
Netherlands	6.6	2.9	4.0	8.7	9.2	4.4	10.9	6.8	8.7	13.5	1.9	0.9	1.5	7.9	6.0	7.3	6.5	4.1	1.1	3.8
New Zealand	10.6	3.8	4.8	9.9	3.8	3.8	3.9	1.5	7.9	7.0	3.3	6.4	2.2	5.9	-0.4	1.7	3.3	0.2	1.9	4.4
Norway	6.1	4.8	3.1	8.4	5.0	10.0	7.8	0.7	2.8	3.2	4.3	-0.3	-0.2	1.1	1.1	0.4	2.8	2.0	0.6	0.4
Poland	..	..	..	13.1	22.9	12.8	12.2	14.4	-2.4	23.1	3.1	4.8	14.2	14.0	7.9	14.6	9.1	6.5	1.3	1.9
Portugal	1.2	3.2	-3.3	8.4	8.8	5.7	6.1	8.5	3.0	8.4	1.8	1.5	3.9	4.0	2.0	8.7	7.5	2.0	-0.5	1.6
Slovak Republic	..	..	..	14.8	4.5	-1.4	10.0	21.0	12.2	8.9	6.8	5.4	15.9	7.4	13.9	21.0	16.0	6.6	1.6	7.8
Spain	8.3	7.5	7.8	16.7	9.4	10.3	15.0	8.0	7.5	10.2	4.2	2.0	3.7	4.2	2.5	6.7	4.9	3.2	3.7	5.6
Sweden	-1.9	2.2	8.3	13.6	11.0	4.5	13.2	8.5	7.5	11.5	0.9	1.2	3.9	10.7	7.0	8.7	6.3	3.3	0.3	3.8
Switzerland	-1.1	3.3	1.4	1.9	0.6	3.7	11.2	4.3	6.5	12.5	0.5	-0.1	-0.5	7.9	7.3	9.9	9.4	5.2	2.1	3.6
Turkey	3.7	11.0	7.7	15.2	8.0	22.0	19.1	12.0	-10.7	16.0	3.9	6.9	6.9	11.2	7.9	6.6	7.3	6.0	3.8	9.4
United Kingdom	-0.2	4.2	4.5	9.2	9.4	8.8	8.1	3.1	3.7	9.1	3.0	1.0	1.8	4.8	8.1	11.0	-4.5	1.2	-1.8	0.7
United States[1]	6.6	6.9	3.2	8.7	10.1	8.4	11.9	2.4	4.3	8.7	-5.4	-2.3	1.3	9.7	7.0	9.1	8.4	8.5	2.8	3.8
Total OECD	4.9	4.5	2.9	8.9	9.2	6.8	11.1	5.2	5.5	11.9	0.1	1.9	2.7	8.6	6.1	8.8	6.2	4.5	0.8	3.6

Note: Regional aggregates are calculated inclusive of intra-regional trade as the sum of volumes expressed in 2000 $.
1. Volume data use hedonic price deflators for certain components.
Source: OECD Economic Outlook 84 database.

StatLink ⟶ http://dx.doi.org/10.1787/505016501805

OECD ECONOMIC OUTLOOK 84 – ISBN 978-92-64-05469-1 – © OECD 2008

Annex Table 39. Import volumes of goods and services
National accounts basis, percentage changes from previous year

	1991	1992	1993	1994	1995	1996	1997	1998	1999	2000	2001	2002	2003	2004	2005	2006	2007	2008	2009	2010
Australia	-2.5	7.1	4.4	14.3	8.0	8.1	10.4	6.5	8.9	7.4	-4.2	10.9	10.7	15.3	8.5	7.3	11.2	11.2	3.9	6.3
Austria	6.5	1.8	-0.7	8.3	7.0	6.3	7.5	5.4	5.1	10.2	5.3	0.2	4.0	9.5	6.9	5.4	7.0	3.2	0.6	3.2
Belgium	2.9	4.1	-0.4	7.3	4.7	2.1	5.7	6.9	4.2	8.8	0.3	0.3	3.0	6.0	4.9	2.7	4.4	4.4	1.9	4.0
Canada	2.5	4.7	7.4	8.1	5.7	5.1	14.2	5.1	7.8	8.1	-5.1	1.7	4.1	8.0	7.1	4.6	5.5	1.9	-2.6	0.9
Czech Republic	..	..	..	7.8	21.2	12.2	6.8	8.3	4.5	17.3	12.6	4.9	8.0	17.6	5.0	14.7	13.8	6.9	2.2	4.3
Denmark	3.6	0.1	-1.1	12.8	7.2	3.3	9.5	8.5	3.5	13.0	1.9	7.5	-1.6	7.7	11.3	14.1	3.8	4.0	0.4	2.2
Finland	-13.4	0.5	1.3	13.0	7.8	6.5	11.4	8.2	3.6	18.7	2.2	3.2	3.0	7.2	11.8	7.8	6.6	1.8	2.6	4.9
France[1]	2.6	1.4	-2.9	8.6	7.2	1.8	8.3	11.5	6.4	15.4	2.3	1.6	1.5	6.4	6.0	6.5	5.9	1.9	-0.4	2.9
Germany	10.9	1.7	-4.6	8.3	6.8	3.7	8.3	9.0	8.3	10.7	1.5	-1.4	5.3	6.5	6.7	12.2	5.2	5.4	2.8	4.4
Greece	5.8	1.1	0.6	1.5	8.9	7.0	14.2	9.2	15.0	15.1	-5.8	-0.2	8.7	10.7	0.4	8.7	7.0	-3.0	4.2	4.4
Hungary	..	..	..	8.8	15.1	9.4	23.1	23.8	13.3	19.9	5.3	6.8	9.3	13.7	7.0	14.8	13.1	7.5	4.4	4.2
Iceland	5.3	-6.0	-7.5	3.8	3.6	16.5	8.0	23.4	4.4	8.6	-9.1	-2.5	10.8	14.5	29.4	10.2	-1.4	-9.9	-12.5	-0.9
Ireland	2.4	8.2	7.5	15.5	16.4	12.5	16.7	27.6	12.4	21.8	7.1	2.7	-1.7	8.5	8.2	6.4	4.1	-1.6	-1.2	0.5
Italy	2.2	6.5	-11.6	8.7	9.7	-1.2	9.8	8.6	4.7	10.7	1.4	0.2	1.5	3.3	2.7	6.1	4.0	-1.3	-0.7	2.5
Japan	-1.1	-0.7	-1.4	7.9	13.3	13.4	0.5	-6.8	3.6	9.2	0.6	0.9	3.9	8.1	5.8	4.2	1.7	0.9	1.2	3.5
Korea	18.6	5.4	6.0	21.3	23.0	14.3	3.5	-21.8	27.8	20.1	-4.2	15.2	10.1	13.9	7.3	11.3	11.9	6.8	2.7	8.3
Luxembourg	9.1	-3.1	5.2	6.7	4.2	5.3	12.6	11.7	14.7	10.9	5.9	0.8	6.9	11.6	6.2	13.5	3.5	-0.7	1.4	3.9
Mexico	15.3	19.9	1.9	21.2	-15.1	22.7	22.7	16.8	13.9	21.6	-1.5	1.4	0.7	10.7	8.4	12.9	7.0	7.5	1.2	2.6
Netherlands	6.3	2.9	0.4	9.0	10.2	5.3	11.9	9.0	9.3	12.2	2.5	0.3	1.8	5.7	5.4	8.2	5.7	5.2	1.6	4.4
New Zealand	-5.2	8.3	5.4	13.1	8.7	7.6	2.1	1.3	12.1	-0.4	2.0	9.6	8.4	15.9	5.4	-2.6	8.7	5.9	-4.6	4.4
Norway	0.4	1.7	4.8	5.8	5.8	8.8	12.5	8.8	-1.6	2.0	1.7	1.0	1.4	8.8	8.7	8.1	8.7	5.8	0.6	0.7
Poland	..	10.7	..	11.3	24.2	27.2	21.1	18.7	1.6	15.5	-5.3	2.8	9.6	15.7	4.7	17.4	13.5	6.8	3.6	2.1
Portugal	7.2	10.7	-3.3	8.8	7.4	5.2	9.8	14.2	8.6	5.3	0.9	-0.7	-0.8	6.7	3.5	5.1	5.6	2.4	-0.9	1.3
Slovak Republic	..	..	..	-4.7	11.6	17.3	10.2	19.1	0.4	8.2	13.5	4.4	7.4	8.3	16.1	17.7	10.4	8.3	1.6	7.0
Spain	10.3	6.8	-5.2	11.4	11.1	8.8	13.3	14.8	13.7	10.8	4.5	3.7	6.2	9.6	7.7	10.3	6.2	0.9	-1.6	2.6
Sweden	-4.9	1.5	-2.2	12.6	7.1	3.8	12.0	11.2	5.1	11.5	-1.7	-1.3	3.8	7.2	6.3	8.2	9.9	4.2	0.3	3.3
Switzerland	-1.3	-3.3	-0.1	7.7	4.0	4.0	8.1	7.4	4.1	10.3	2.3	-1.1	1.3	7.3	6.6	6.5	5.9	2.6	3.0	3.9
Turkey	-5.2	10.9	35.8	-21.9	29.6	20.5	22.4	2.3	-3.7	21.8	-24.8	20.9	23.5	20.8	12.2	6.9	10.7	4.4	3.6	9.0
United Kingdom[1]	-4.4	6.8	3.3	5.9	5.5	9.7	9.7	9.3	7.9	8.9	4.8	4.9	2.2	6.8	7.0	9.6	-1.9	0.2	-3.4	1.1
United States[1]	-0.6	6.9	8.7	11.9	8.0	8.7	13.6	11.6	11.5	13.1	-2.7	3.4	4.1	11.3	5.9	6.0	2.2	-2.3	-2.1	1.6
Total OECD	2.5	4.2	1.4	9.5	8.3	7.6	10.1	7.5	8.6	12.1	-0.1	2.6	4.0	9.0	6.4	7.8	4.6	1.9	0.1	3.1

Note: Regional aggregates are calculated inclusive of intra-regional trade as the sum of volumes expressed in 2000 $.
1. Volume data use hedonic price deflators for certain components.
Source: OECD Economic Outlook 84 database.

StatLink http://dx.doi.org/10.1787/505021877183

Annex Table 40. Export prices of goods and services

National accounts basis, percentage changes from previous year, national currency terms

	1991	1992	1993	1994	1995	1996	1997	1998	1999	2000	2001	2002	2003	2004	2005	2006	2007	2008	2009	2010
Australia	-5.2	2.0	0.9	-4.0	5.9	-2.5	-0.2	2.4	-4.2	13.2	6.7	-1.8	-5.4	3.9	12.4	12.2	0.7	19.8	9.3	-0.7
Austria	0.6	0.6	-0.2	1.0	1.8	1.1	0.9	0.1	0.6	1.4	0.6	0.3	-0.4	1.0	2.1	2.7	1.8	1.6	1.8	1.2
Belgium	-0.6	-1.1	-1.3	1.3	1.6	1.4	4.6	-1.0	-0.2	9.4	2.1	-0.5	-2.2	2.4	4.1	3.4	3.0	3.2	1.7	1.6
Canada	-3.6	2.9	4.4	5.9	6.4	0.6	0.2	-0.3	1.1	6.2	1.3	-1.9	-1.3	2.2	2.8	0.1	0.8	9.4	2.4	-0.1
Czech Republic	..	..	..	5.2	6.4	4.9	5.6	4.0	1.1	3.3	-0.4	-5.5	0.1	2.7	-2.2	-1.3	0.2	-6.3	0.9	2.6
Denmark	1.3	1.3	-1.7	-0.3	1.0	1.5	2.7	-2.1	-0.5	8.2	1.6	-1.3	-1.1	1.9	5.8	2.6	2.1	5.6	0.9	1.6
Finland	0.2	4.3	6.5	1.3	4.8	-0.1	-1.0	-1.0	-5.0	3.2	-1.4	-2.5	-1.4	-0.4	1.0	2.7	0.5	2.1	0.7	0.2
France[1]	-0.9	-2.3	-2.2	-0.5	-0.5	0.9	1.4	-1.5	-1.6	2.4	-0.2	-1.7	-1.7	0.6	2.1	2.2	0.5	1.6	1.2	1.5
Germany	1.4	1.0	0.1	0.8	1.2	-0.5	0.9	-0.9	-0.9	2.5	0.4	-0.2	-1.7	0.0	0.7	1.4	0.5	1.2	1.5	1.0
Greece	14.0	10.1	9.1	8.6	8.7	5.6	3.6	4.1	1.9	8.0	6.4	2.5	2.3	3.0	4.1	3.4	2.3	2.7	-3.3	1.7
Hungary	..	..	..	18.5	45.5	19.0	15.2	12.8	4.5	9.9	3.0	-4.0	0.1	-1.1	-0.3	6.5	-4.0	2.6	3.3	1.1
Iceland	6.9	-1.3	4.8	6.2	4.8	-0.2	2.1	4.5	0.0	3.8	21.5	-1.7	-7.1	1.3	-4.5	21.4	2.2	22.2	19.6	5.4
Ireland	-0.3	-2.0	6.8	0.2	1.9	-0.3	1.2	2.7	2.3	6.1	4.6	-0.4	-5.0	-0.6	0.6	1.3	0.1	-1.6	0.7	0.0
Italy	3.9	0.7	10.4	3.4	8.2	0.3	1.3	1.4	0.7	4.4	2.3	1.4	0.4	2.6	4.0	4.6	3.6	4.2	2.0	1.0
Japan	-2.3	-2.5	-6.6	-3.1	-2.1	3.5	1.8	0.9	-8.8	-4.1	2.2	-1.2	-3.4	-1.2	1.4	3.7	2.3	-2.9	-2.0	-0.1
Korea	2.7	2.5	0.4	1.1	2.0	-3.1	4.7	24.7	-19.3	-4.2	2.4	-9.4	-1.4	4.3	-7.9	-4.8	0.5	22.2	9.2	-1.9
Luxembourg	1.2	1.8	5.7	3.1	1.5	6.2	2.1	0.6	5.2	9.4	-3.7	-0.1	-1.8	6.1	8.2	8.5	5.1	-0.2	-0.8	1.4
Mexico	7.5	5.2	3.3	5.9	79.5	23.0	7.2	9.3	6.6	3.4	-2.3	3.3	11.2	6.7	3.0	4.5	2.7	4.5	-0.7	2.7
Netherlands	0.3	-1.9	-2.5	0.6	0.7	0.8	2.5	-2.0	-1.2	6.0	0.9	-1.8	-0.8	0.6	3.4	2.9	1.2	3.6	-1.3	1.5
New Zealand	-2.8	5.5	2.1	-2.6	-0.5	-2.5	-2.4	4.9	-0.1	14.3	7.2	-7.2	-7.3	-0.1	1.2	7.0	1.7	13.5	9.6	3.5
Norway	-1.2	-7.0	2.1	-2.8	1.8	6.9	2.0	-7.9	10.7	36.7	-2.2	-10.2	2.1	12.9	17.3	15.3	0.9	8.0	-12.3	3.7
Poland	..	..	..	31.7	19.6	6.8	14.1	13.1	5.7	1.9	1.3	4.7	6.2	8.3	-2.5	2.3	2.7	0.7	1.4	0.7
Portugal	3.4	0.5	4.9	6.4	5.6	-0.9	3.4	1.6	0.3	5.3	0.8	-0.1	-1.4	1.5	1.9	4.2	2.7	2.8	1.8	1.5
Slovak Republic	..	..	..	10.7	8.4	4.3	6.5	-4.8	-1.1	17.3	4.9	1.0	1.5	1.8	-1.9	2.2	-1.6	4.3	0.1	1.3
Spain	1.5	2.9	5.0	4.6	5.9	1.4	3.0	0.5	0.0	7.3	1.8	0.7	-0.2	1.6	4.3	4.0	2.4	3.4	2.2	1.8
Sweden	1.6	-2.8	9.0	3.5	6.9	-5.1	0.4	-1.4	-1.7	2.5	2.4	-1.5	-1.7	-0.3	2.5	2.9	1.6	3.9	2.7	2.0
Switzerland	2.6	0.8	2.0	-0.4	-0.3	-1.1	0.7	-0.3	-0.8	2.9	0.3	-2.4	0.5	0.5	0.9	2.7	2.5	2.0	1.4	1.1
Turkey	61.0	62.5	59.9	164.8	73.0	69.0	87.0	60.1	52.0	42.0	89.4	25.4	10.7	13.3	-0.2	13.7	2.1	15.4	7.1	3.0
United Kingdom[1]	1.7	0.7	9.1	1.2	3.3	1.6	-4.1	-4.7	0.3	1.9	-0.4	0.3	1.7	-0.4	0.9	2.4	2.5	11.4	4.0	1.3
United States[1]	1.3	-0.4	0.0	1.1	2.3	-1.3	-1.7	-2.3	-0.6	1.7	-0.4	-0.4	2.2	3.5	3.6	3.5	3.5	6.7	0.9	1.4
Total OECD	1.2	0.6	1.9	2.4	5.1	1.6	1.5	0.7	-1.1	3.5	1.4	-0.8	0.0	1.8	2.3	3.0	1.9	4.9	1.4	1.1

Note: Regional aggregates are calculated inclusive of intra-regional trade. They are calculated as the geometric averages of prices weighted by trade volumes expressed in 2000 $.
1. Certain components are estimated on a hedonic basis.
Source: OECD Economic Outlook 84 database.

StatLink http://dx.doi.org/10.1787/505032405120

Annex Table 41. Import prices of goods and services

National accounts basis, percentage changes from previous year, national currency terms

	1991	1992	1993	1994	1995	1996	1997	1998	1999	2000	2001	2002	2003	2004	2005	2006	2007	2008	2009	2010
Australia	1.3	4.2	5.7	-4.3	3.5	-6.5	-1.6	6.8	-4.6	7.5	5.6	-4.0	-8.6	-5.0	0.7	4.2	-3.8	8.2	18.6	0.6
Austria	-0.2	0.8	-3.8	2.7	0.6	0.6	1.7	0.3	0.5	2.9	0.5	-1.1	-0.6	1.3	2.8	3.3	1.8	2.6	1.4	1.2
Belgium	-0.7	-2.8	-2.8	1.8	1.7	2.5	5.3	-1.9	0.4	11.8	2.0	-1.2	-2.0	2.8	4.3	4.3	2.5	6.4	1.6	1.5
Canada	-1.6	4.4	6.4	6.6	3.4	-1.1	0.8	3.7	-0.2	2.1	3.0	0.6	-6.5	-2.2	-0.8	-0.5	-2.2	4.7	8.7	0.3
Czech Republic	..	..	..	2.6	5.8	1.8	5.3	-1.7	1.7	6.0	-2.6	-8.4	-0.4	1.4	-0.5	-0.1	-1.0	-4.1	1.4	2.2
Denmark	2.1	-1.1	-1.3	0.5	0.5	-0.1	2.4	-2.1	-0.5	7.2	1.5	-2.5	-2.0	0.7	3.7	3.1	3.3	4.3	0.4	1.0
Finland	4.0	6.7	8.9	-1.3	0.6	-0.7	-0.1	-2.7	-2.0	7.1	-2.9	-2.8	0.1	2.2	4.6	6.1	2.0	3.5	-1.3	0.2
France[1]	0.8	-3.8	-2.2	-0.4	-0.4	0.8	0.6	-2.8	-1.7	5.5	-0.9	-4.3	-1.5	1.4	3.1	2.7	0.4	3.6	-0.5	1.3
Germany	2.8	-2.1	-1.8	-0.1	-0.3	0.2	3.1	-2.4	-1.4	7.7	0.5	-2.2	-2.6	0.2	2.1	2.7	-0.1	2.7	-0.2	0.7
Greece	12.3	12.3	7.4	5.6	7.5	5.0	2.8	3.8	1.7	9.3	5.8	-0.2	0.2	1.0	3.1	3.5	2.7	4.4	-5.3	0.4
Hungary	..	..	..	15.6	41.1	20.7	13.4	11.7	5.5	12.7	2.4	-5.4	0.3	-1.0	1.3	8.0	-4.3	2.5	3.3	1.1
Iceland	3.4	-0.7	8.7	5.9	3.7	3.1	0.0	-0.7	0.6	6.3	21.1	-2.3	-3.2	2.6	-5.4	17.4	2.1	30.8	18.3	5.4
Ireland	2.4	-1.2	4.5	2.4	3.8	-0.5	0.8	2.5	2.6	7.1	3.9	-1.3	-4.0	0.1	1.8	2.2	2.7	1.6	1.5	0.6
Italy	0.0	1.7	15.4	4.8	11.4	-2.6	1.7	-1.6	0.7	11.2	1.4	-0.3	-1.3	2.7	6.2	7.6	2.3	3.5	-0.9	1.7
Japan	-5.1	-5.1	-8.3	-4.5	-1.8	8.4	6.5	-2.7	-8.5	1.5	2.4	-0.9	-0.8	2.9	8.3	11.4	7.1	6.7	-11.5	-0.1
Korea	1.9	3.5	0.3	1.1	4.2	3.0	11.4	27.2	-16.8	5.9	5.8	-8.9	1.0	5.5	-2.6	-0.9	1.0	29.3	10.3	0.5
Luxembourg	2.5	2.7	3.2	2.1	1.3	5.7	5.2	1.5	3.0	12.7	-3.3	-1.0	-5.8	7.5	7.8	7.3	6.2	1.6	-1.4	1.4
Mexico	9.0	4.0	3.7	5.1	95.1	21.4	3.6	12.0	3.7	0.1	-2.8	2.0	12.5	8.4	0.3	1.8	3.0	1.7	-0.7	1.8
Netherlands	0.1	-1.4	-2.4	0.3	0.3	0.7	1.5	-2.4	-0.9	5.8	-0.4	-2.9	-0.9	1.4	2.7	3.4	1.3	4.1	-1.5	1.5
New Zealand	2.3	6.3	-1.6	-3.8	-1.8	-3.7	-0.4	5.7	0.7	15.4	2.2	-5.9	-11.4	-4.3	1.0	10.0	-4.8	9.9	10.5	0.5
Norway	-0.4	-1.8	1.6	0.7	0.6	0.8	0.3	1.2	-1.1	7.5	-0.1	-5.0	1.1	4.8	1.5	3.3	3.1	2.4	2.8	2.6
Poland	..	..	..	27.0	18.0	11.0	16.0	10.8	6.5	7.9	1.3	5.4	6.7	4.9	-3.5	2.4	1.1	0.5	-0.9	0.6
Portugal	1.0	-4.2	4.4	4.3	3.9	1.5	2.6	-1.4	-0.7	8.5	0.3	-1.7	-1.8	2.2	3.2	4.0	1.4	3.7	-0.3	1.3
Slovak Republic	..	..	..	12.3	7.3	9.4	3.6	-2.4	0.3	14.1	6.0	1.0	1.9	2.1	-1.6	3.6	-0.5	0.7	-0.5	1.2
Spain	-1.5	1.2	6.1	5.8	4.4	0.4	3.4	-1.5	0.3	10.6	-0.2	-2.0	-1.5	2.2	3.7	3.8	2.1	3.1	-1.3	1.6
Sweden	0.3	-2.4	13.7	3.3	4.7	-4.4	0.7	-1.1	1.1	4.3	3.8	0.1	-2.0	0.5	5.2	3.3	-0.2	3.7	2.0	2.1
Switzerland	0.5	1.9	-1.4	-4.5	-2.6	-0.4	3.8	-1.6	-0.1	5.8	0.5	-5.9	-1.4	1.2	3.3	4.4	3.6	1.7	-1.1	0.6
Turkey	60.2	63.1	48.9	163.3	85.0	80.4	74.1	62.5	47.9	56.7	93.4	22.1	7.1	10.8	0.2	19.0	0.1	19.0	3.5	1.6
United Kingdom	0.3	0.0	8.6	3.0	5.9	0.1	-7.0	-5.7	-1.1	3.1	-0.2	-2.2	0.4	-0.7	3.9	2.4	1.0	9.9	5.0	2.5
United States[1]	-0.4	0.1	-0.9	0.9	2.7	-1.8	-3.6	-5.4	0.6	4.2	-2.5	-1.2	3.5	4.9	6.3	4.3	3.7	12.5	-1.1	0.7
Total OECD	0.8	0.2	1.5	2.5	5.6	1.7	1.3	-0.6	-0.9	5.9	0.8	-1.6	0.1	2.4	3.8	4.1	2.0	7.3	0.1	1.0

Note: Regional aggregates are calculated inclusive of intra-regional trade. They are calculated as the geometric averages of prices weighted by trade volumes expressed in 2000 $.
1. Certain components are estimated on a hedonic basis.
Source: OECD Economic Outlook 84 database.

StatLink http://dx.doi.org/10.1787/505060406781

Annex Table 42. Competitive positions: relative consumer prices

Indices, 2000 = 100

	1991	1992	1993	1994	1995	1996	1997	1998	1999	2000	2001	2002	2003	2004	2005	2006	2007	2008
Australia	121.2	109.4	101.0	106.0	104.3	114.1	113.1	103.7	104.7	100.0	96.2	101.6	114.9	124.4	128.2	127.9	135.9	132.6
Austria	103.5	104.9	106.2	106.4	109.4	106.9	103.3	103.6	102.6	100.0	100.2	100.6	103.4	104.2	103.7	103.1	103.4	103.3
Belgium	106.4	107.0	106.8	108.6	112.3	109.6	104.3	105.3	104.0	100.0	100.9	102.2	106.9	108.8	109.0	108.6	109.4	112.4
Canada	137.7	127.3	118.6	109.0	106.7	106.8	106.0	100.1	99.4	100.0	96.9	96.1	106.8	112.6	119.5	126.2	131.2	127.8
Czech Republic	..	..	77.0	80.8	83.6	89.1	90.6	99.3	98.0	100.0	106.7	118.5	115.9	116.7	123.8	130.5	134.0	154.9
Denmark	100.4	101.0	101.8	101.5	105.2	103.7	101.0	103.4	103.6	100.0	101.5	103.4	108.5	109.2	108.1	107.7	108.3	109.9
Estonia	141.3	122.0	102.0	105.9	113.7	107.0	103.1	104.5	104.4	100.0	101.4	102.5	106.8	106.7	104.1	103.0	104.4	106.5
Finland	106.2	107.7	108.7	108.6	110.9	110.2	105.9	106.8	104.6	100.0	99.9	101.2	106.1	107.7	106.7	106.2	106.5	107.2
France	104.4	109.0	112.6	113.3	117.6	112.9	107.5	108.8	106.4	100.0	100.0	100.7	105.6	107.0	105.0	104.2	105.3	104.9
Germany	96.6	99.1	99.8	100.6	103.9	106.7	107.5	106.2	106.8	100.0	101.0	103.7	109.8	112.2	112.7	113.7	115.8	118.7
Greece	..	..	95.6	93.4	88.7	89.5	95.1	95.8	98.6	100.0	108.2	119.2	121.8	129.8	132.4	126.2	140.8	145.0
Hungary	104.1	103.9	97.7	91.6	90.3	89.6	91.2	93.6	96.2	100.0	88.8	94.8	99.6	102.3	116.1	108.6	113.0	90.0
Iceland	113.6	116.8	108.0	107.9	109.1	110.9	109.9	107.1	103.8	100.0	103.8	109.4	120.8	123.8	123.7	126.0	132.5	138.9
Ireland	123.8	121.7	102.7	99.9	92.7	102.6	103.2	104.8	103.9	100.0	101.3	103.4	109.1	110.8	109.6	109.5	110.1	111.1
Italy	79.8	82.1	95.2	102.7	104.5	87.4	82.6	83.7	94.5	100.0	89.5	83.9	85.1	86.3	81.3	73.5	67.3	72.4
Japan	116.5	109.5	106.4	107.6	108.9	112.8	106.4	81.2	92.8	100.0	94.6	99.6	101.2	102.9	115.7	125.3	124.6	100.8
Korea	103.6	104.5	104.4	105.7	108.3	105.7	102.6	102.9	102.1	100.0	100.7	101.9	105.7	107.1	106.8	107.6	108.8	109.4
Luxembourg	86.0	93.2	99.5	95.2	64.5	72.0	83.3	84.2	92.1	100.0	106.6	106.9	95.5	91.7	95.2	95.2	94.5	92.6
Mexico	105.4	107.2	107.6	107.7	111.8	108.8	103.0	106.1	105.6	100.0	103.0	106.8	114.3	116.0	114.5	113.2	114.2	114.5
Netherlands	114.2	103.4	105.8	111.5	119.5	126.7	129.1	115.5	110.1	100.0	98.9	108.3	123.2	131.8	139.2	129.5	137.6	128.1
New Zealand	107.4	107.3	103.1	100.5	103.0	101.7	103.1	100.6	101.1	100.0	103.9	112.0	110.2	105.3	109.6	109.5	109.3	109.8
Norway	..	..	73.2	74.0	79.0	84.8	87.8	93.3	90.7	100.0	112.9	107.7	95.6	94.6	105.8	108.1	111.7	122.3
Poland	95.1	103.5	100.3	98.8	102.3	102.2	101.0	101.9	102.0	100.0	102.5	104.8	108.7	109.5	108.8	109.5	110.2	110.2
Portugal	..	..	85.1	84.2	86.1	85.9	90.7	91.8	90.7	100.0	101.2	102.5	115.6	126.6	129.7	136.6	150.6	161.2
Slovak Republic	120.7	120.3	107.1	102.3	103.8	105.5	101.0	102.0	102.0	100.0	102.2	104.6	109.6	111.8	112.6	114.3	115.9	118.2
Slovenia	129.0	129.0	105.9	104.5	103.7	111.6	106.1	103.2	101.4	100.0	91.7	94.1	99.5	99.7	95.6	95.1	96.1	94.5
Spain	103.5	101.6	103.4	108.2	114.7	110.6	102.2	104.0	102.9	100.0	102.2	105.9	106.3	105.3	103.4	100.6	96.2	100.8
Sweden	87.1	83.6	89.7	65.9	71.5	72.2	77.2	84.9	89.3	100.0	81.5	88.7	93.4	96.4	107.3	106.8	115.7	116.5
Switzerland	96.2	93.2	83.8	83.7	80.1	81.4	94.1	99.5	99.2	100.0	97.4	97.6	93.2	96.8	95.2	95.7	97.1	85.5
Turkey	85.2	83.4	84.5	84.7	83.5	86.1	90.5	97.9	96.8	100.0	105.8	106.0	99.9	95.7	94.3	93.6	89.7	87.6
United Kingdom	122.2	126.8	118.9	118.6	123.0	121.8	111.4	114.6	110.9	100.0	102.0	105.9	118.7	122.8	120.5	120.1	122.9	125.2

StatLink ⟦⟧ http://dx.doi.org/10.1787/505064117506

Note: Competitiveness-weighted relative consumer prices in dollar terms. Competitiveness weights take into account the structure of competition in both export and import markets of the manufacturing sector of 42 countries. An increase in the index indicates a real effective appreciation and a corresponding deterioration of the competitive position. For details on the method of calculation see Durand, M., C. Madaschi and F. Terribile (1998), "Trends in OECD Countries' International Competitiveness: The Influence of Emerging Market Economies", OECD Economics Department Working Papers, No. 195. See also OECD Economic Outlook Sources and Methods (http://www.oecd.org/eco/sources-and-methods).

Source: OECD Economic Outlook 84 database.

Annex Table 43. Competitive positions: relative unit labour costs

Indices, 2000 = 100

	1991	1992	1993	1994	1995	1996	1997	1998	1999	2000	2001	2002	2003	2004	2005	2006	2007	2008
Australia	103.9	98.1	88.9	92.9	97.9	108.9	109.9	100.8	106.5	100.0	92.2	97.4	112.5	126.6	138.2	139.0	148.6	145.3
Austria	112.1	113.7	115.0	115.4	113.3	107.1	104.5	106.4	105.2	100.0	98.6	99.2	103.2	104.3	103.8	101.0	101.4	101.4
Belgium	106.9	108.5	110.8	114.8	116.1	111.3	103.3	104.4	105.7	100.0	102.4	104.4	110.4	111.0	111.0	111.0	112.7	110.0
Canada	133.0	122.7	110.8	103.2	106.0	110.3	110.0	104.9	103.7	100.0	100.9	103.8	119.0	132.2	142.4	151.3	158.9	162.6
Czech Republic	..	..	91.3	88.8	88.4	96.6	98.7	109.5	101.3	100.0	112.5	126.3	130.4	127.2	129.3	130.4	129.2	143.1
Denmark	95.3	96.3	98.6	95.6	100.1	101.6	98.5	102.6	103.3	100.0	102.3	106.9	114.3	117.7	122.2	122.3	124.0	127.9
Estonia	170.6	134.7	103.0	110.4	125.3	118.2	111.0	111.6	111.7	100.0	99.3	97.6	100.3	100.0	98.2	92.5	88.1	89.2
Finland	117.2	115.6	115.5	115.3	116.0	114.4	109.1	106.8	105.3	100.0	98.7	100.5	102.6	104.7	103.7	104.7	106.6	107.7
France	92.3	100.7	104.7	104.6	114.4	112.4	103.8	106.6	106.3	100.0	98.5	100.6	105.2	104.9	100.4	97.2	95.1	93.2
Germany	87.7	89.5	97.9	100.1	105.0	107.3	114.8	110.3	107.0	100.0	94.3	97.9	100.9	112.2	107.4	112.1	116.8	121.8
Greece	..	..	146.1	130.3	118.1	109.2	107.7	99.8	96.0	100.0	108.1	116.4	113.5	124.3	127.7	117.4	125.1	126.9
Hungary	79.6	80.7	74.1	71.8	72.7	72.3	75.9	82.9	92.1	100.0	87.3	93.0	98.1	101.2	117.7	113.9	123.9	96.5
Iceland	153.9	154.2	147.7	144.5	135.4	134.3	127.1	115.2	106.2	100.0	97.5	90.8	99.9	102.2	102.7	99.9	101.9	103.4
Ireland	124.6	119.4	98.9	93.6	85.4	97.7	101.1	102.7	103.9	100.0	102.0	106.9	118.9	124.1	125.9	129.7	134.6	141.2
Italy	76.9	79.4	92.5	105.0	103.9	85.6	81.8	85.2	97.4	100.0	91.6	86.4	81.0	79.2	71.3	62.0	55.5	60.2
Japan	129.9	122.1	117.4	119.8	133.3	144.7	128.6	89.9	93.4	100.0	92.7	97.3	96.9	98.6	110.0	114.8	112.7	84.8
Korea	117.8	116.3	111.3	111.4	115.8	112.4	108.9	105.5	100.9	100.0	105.8	106.9	113.3	113.8	118.7	122.5	127.5	131.5
Luxembourg	79.7	88.8	97.5	94.5	58.8	62.1	75.1	76.5	86.6	100.0	112.8	117.3	106.3	103.2	104.1	101.3	100.8	95.2
Mexico	109.9	112.7	110.5	107.3	110.5	107.0	104.1	108.0	107.3	100.0	101.9	106.4	115.7	117.0	115.1	114.0	116.6	120.9
Netherlands	113.9	99.2	100.2	108.7	114.5	124.7	130.1	118.1	113.2	100.0	102.0	111.9	129.8	144.4	152.5	142.2	156.7	152.7
New Zealand	79.2	79.9	78.2	80.7	85.6	85.8	90.8	93.8	98.7	100.0	102.8	114.1	109.4	105.9	111.8	115.0	122.1	128.3
Norway	..	..	77.3	81.9	88.2	94.1	97.1	103.5	97.6	100.0	105.3	92.4	75.1	70.9	79.4	76.9	79.2	88.1
Poland	93.6	104.0	100.4	100.1	101.7	98.0	96.3	99.3	101.8	100.0	100.1	101.9	103.5	105.1	106.8	107.7	105.6	104.6
Portugal	..	..	77.0	92.5	97.7	97.0	100.7	96.9	90.5	100.0	95.5	100.4	104.9	107.9	101.6	98.8	98.8	99.0
Slovak Republic	112.8	115.8	107.1	101.8	102.6	105.1	102.9	103.3	100.8	100.0	101.2	104.0	110.4	114.5	117.3	119.6	122.2	127.5
Slovenia	167.3	163.8	120.5	112.1	107.8	121.1	113.4	107.0	99.4	100.0	95.7	92.8	94.7	91.3	85.8	83.7	87.1	86.7
Sweden	119.6	109.6	102.3	71.1	60.5	59.2	66.7	72.7	94.2	100.0	76.1	76.4	74.9	77.6	85.4	82.1	86.7	88.6
Switzerland	80.9	75.1	67.7	70.3	68.7	70.2	84.6	94.6	96.8	100.0	97.5	100.2	96.9	102.2	101.0	103.2	105.8	93.5
Turkey	93.9	91.8	91.6	89.7	85.2	86.4	89.3	95.6	95.6	100.0	101.7	97.4	91.6	84.1	81.6	81.2	77.3	74.6
United Kingdom	118.4	124.5	117.3	114.9	121.0	122.2	111.0	113.5	112.2	100.0	99.7	105.2	119.6	125.1	122.5	122.3	125.2	129.0

Note: Competitiveness-weighted relative unit labour costs in the manufacturing sector in dollar terms. Competitiveness weights take into account the structure of competition in both export and import markets of the manufacturing sector of 42 countries. An increase in the index indicates a real effective appreciation and a corresponding deterioration of the competitive position. For details on the method of calculation see Durand, M., C. Madaschi and F. Terrible (1998), "Trends in OECD Countries' International Competitiveness: The Influence of Emerging Market Economies", OECD Economics Department Working Papers, No. 195. See also *OECD Economic Outlook* Sources and Methods (*http://www.oecd.org/eco/sources-and-methods*).

Source: OECD Economic Outlook 84 database.

StatLink http://dx.doi.org/10.1787/505134438284

Annex Table 44. Export performance for total goods and services

Percentage changes from previous year

	1991	1992	1993	1994	1995	1996	1997	1998	1999	2000	2001	2002	2003	2004	2005	2006	2007	2008	2009	2010
Australia	8.6	-0.7	2.8	-1.6	-6.9	1.6	5.5	3.5	-3.7	-2.0	2.7	-5.8	-9.0	-7.9	-6.4	-4.8	-3.5	0.1	0.8	0.6
Austria	2.5	2.5	-0.8	-2.5	-2.1	-0.3	2.0	0.7	0.3	0.6	3.8	1.3	-0.8	-1.4	-1.2	-3.4	0.7	-1.4	-0.9	-1.2
Belgium	-0.7	0.9	-0.4	-0.1	-3.1	-2.8	-2.9	-2.4	-2.3	-3.4	-0.6	-0.8	-1.1	-2.4	-3.3	-6.2	-1.6	-0.9	-0.2	-0.4
Canada	1.5	0.5	3.0	1.0	0.3	-3.0	-3.9	-0.8	0.1	-3.7	-0.9	-2.2	-6.4	-5.7	-4.4	-5.7	-2.0	-3.6	-1.8	-0.5
Czech Republic	..	..	..	-6.7	7.6	-0.5	-1.4	1.2	-1.0	5.4	8.1	0.2	1.7	10.4	3.4	4.4	6.6	4.7	0.1	0.7
Denmark	5.0	-1.6	0.1	-0.7	-5.0	-2.1	-4.8	-3.5	5.0	1.2	2.2	2.2	-5.3	-5.9	0.6	-0.3	-4.4	-1.3	-0.6	-0.5
Finland	-5.9	16.6	14.3	5.0	-0.2	-0.3	3.8	3.3	6.5	4.0	-0.4	-1.1	-7.7	-2.5	-2.0	0.4	-1.5	-1.4	0.4	-0.2
France	1.8	2.2	0.1	0.4	0.5	-2.6	2.9	1.1	-2.3	1.7	1.1	-1.4	-5.4	-6.0	-3.9	-3.3	-2.6	-2.0	-1.9	-1.7
Germany	10.1	-3.7	-6.4	-0.3	-2.2	-0.3	1.5	0.2	-0.6	1.4	5.1	1.0	-2.5	-0.8	0.2	3.6	0.7	0.2	-0.6	-0.3
Greece	0.9	9.3	-5.0	1.0	-5.2	-2.5	8.3	-0.6	13.3	2.1	-3.7	-10.7	-2.8	1.4	-5.9	-4.4	-1.6	-2.4	1.2	0.7
Hungary	..	..	..	5.8	25.5	5.9	12.0	9.8	6.5	8.5	5.0	1.4	0.3	4.7	2.9	6.7	7.1	2.1	2.3	0.1
Iceland	-8.8	-4.0	6.3	0.7	-9.5	3.2	-3.8	-5.4	-3.2	-6.4	5.3	1.2	-2.1	-0.1	0.0	-13.3	12.7	5.6	2.0	0.8
Ireland	3.6	9.2	8.5	6.0	11.4	5.8	7.3	14.5	7.3	7.9	7.6	2.5	-3.4	-1.1	-1.4	-2.2	2.7	-0.7	1.1	-0.7
Italy	-4.6	6.5	6.9	2.7	3.9	-5.4	-4.0	-5.0	-6.2	0.5	0.5	-5.7	-6.6	-6.1	-6.0	-3.2	-2.7	-4.5	-2.2	-2.5
Japan	-2.8	-4.3	-7.7	-7.6	-7.0	-1.6	1.5	-1.7	-7.3	-2.2	-5.1	0.9	0.7	-0.4	-1.8	0.5	1.3	0.5	-5.7	-5.3
Korea	6.0	5.2	4.8	5.4	11.3	3.0	11.6	12.3	6.2	4.3	-2.5	6.2	5.3	4.3	-1.2	1.7	4.0	3.6	2.4	4.1
Luxembourg	5.3	-0.2	6.6	-0.7	-3.0	-1.7	1.6	2.5	7.3	1.9	2.3	0.9	3.0	3.5	-0.7	5.7	-0.8	-0.9	-0.2	-0.2
Mexico	4.6	-2.1	-0.2	5.4	19.9	9.1	-2.4	1.5	2.0	3.2	-1.2	-1.5	-1.4	0.1	0.2	4.2	2.9	5.7	-1.3	-1.2
Netherlands	3.0	0.4	4.3	0.4	1.2	-0.8	1.5	-0.9	2.0	1.6	0.5	-1.1	-2.8	-0.8	-1.2	-1.8	0.6	0.1	-0.3	-0.2
New Zealand	7.6	-2.3	-0.1	-1.3	-6.1	-4.1	-4.2	-0.1	-0.2	-4.1	4.9	0.4	-4.8	-6.2	-8.6	-6.3	-3.5	-5.2	-0.3	-1.1
Norway	4.7	1.1	1.7	-0.4	-2.7	3.5	-2.2	-6.9	-4.1	-7.6	3.0	-2.8	-3.6	-6.8	-5.8	-7.9	-1.4	-0.9	0.6	-2.7
Poland	..	..	..	5.0	13.2	7.3	2.6	6.4	-7.3	9.5	-0.1	2.4	8.0	3.9	-0.3	2.7	0.5	0.6	-0.2	-2.5
Portugal	-3.7	..	-2.5	-0.1	0.5	-0.2	-4.1	-0.8	-4.2	-2.8	-0.4	-0.8	-0.3	-4.5	-5.3	-0.6	1.7	-1.4	-1.2	-2.0
Slovak Republic	..	..	..	6.2	-5.1	-7.5	0.2	11.3	6.0	-3.7	3.2	2.9	9.4	-3.0	6.4	8.4	6.5	1.1	-0.2	3.5
Spain	4.7	3.3	7.8	7.9	1.4	4.7	4.2	-0.7	1.7	-1.1	2.6	0.4	0.4	-4.0	-4.4	-2.1	-0.9	-0.7	2.6	1.8
Sweden	-3.4	0.4	6.0	4.5	2.5	-2.0	2.6	1.2	2.0	0.1	-0.4	-1.9	-0.4	0.8	-1.4	-0.8	-0.1	-1.0	-1.0	-0.1
Switzerland	-5.0	0.0	1.1	-6.4	-7.7	-2.0	1.5	-2.2	-0.5	0.5	-0.5	-2.5	-5.3	-1.6	-0.5	0.4	3.1	1.3	0.5	-0.8
Turkey	1.6	14.5	7.8	8.1	0.2	15.7	8.6	5.4	-14.9	3.7	0.8	3.1	1.3	0.7	-0.9	-3.8	-0.8	-0.3	1.7	4.2
United Kingdom	-3.7	0.9	2.5	0.0	0.3	2.3	-2.0	-4.1	-3.3	-3.0	2.4	-1.8	-2.6	-4.8	0.2	2.3	-10.2	-2.4	-3.2	-3.4
United States	1.1	0.0	-1.4	-1.7	2.4	0.0	0.6	-1.3	-2.1	-3.4	-4.6	-4.6	-3.3	-1.1	-1.7	0.0	1.2	2.8	0.9	-0.6
Total OECD	1.6	0.5	0.0	-0.4	0.3	-0.1	0.7	-0.7	-1.5	-0.6	-0.3	-1.3	-2.4	-1.9	-1.8	-0.3	-0.2	0.3	-0.7	-0.8
Memorandum items																				
China	3.8	12.7	5.2	17.7	-3.7	10.0	13.7	6.6	4.5	12.4	7.7	20.9	19.4	10.3	14.4	14.7	13.3	5.5	4.0	5.7
Dynamic Asia[1]	6.6	3.7	3.3	1.9	0.6	-3.6	-1.5	-0.6	-0.2	2.0	-3.9	0.4	0.1	1.0	-0.4	-0.2	-0.6	1.2	0.0	0.4
Other Asia	8.7	6.8	5.6	6.2	8.0	0.4	-3.0	6.0	4.7	0.4	6.5	9.5	3.2	6.3	4.8	7.1	-0.3	-0.1	2.1	0.9
Latin America	-2.5	1.6	5.8	-3.1	-4.3	-0.8	-3.7	0.5	-1.8	-4.8	4.1	2.0	2.3	0.5	0.8	-4.0	-1.8	0.6	1.3	0.2
Africa and Middle-East	-4.7	3.4	2.9	-3.9	-6.7	-3.3	0.2	0.0	-6.3	-0.8	1.8	-3.0	2.5	-3.2	-3.9	-5.1	-1.2	-0.7	-0.6	-1.0
Central & Eastern Europe	..	..	..	..	..	-0.2	-3.7	-1.8	-1.4	3.5	4.8	1.9	-0.4	-1.9	-3.1	-3.1	-3.4	-1.3	-0.9	1.5

Note: Regional aggregates are calculated inclusive of intra-regional trade. Export performance is the ratio between export volumes and export markets for total goods and services. The calculation of export markets is based on a weighted average of import volumes in each exporting country's markets, with weights based on trade flows in 2000.
1. Dynamic Asia includes Chinese Taipei; Hong Kong, China; Indonesia; Malaysia; Philippines; Singapore and Thailand.
Source: OECD Economic Outlook 84 database.

StatLink ⟳ http://dx.doi.org/10.1787/505140445154

Annex Table 45. **Shares in world exports and imports**
Percentage, values for goods and services, national accounts basis

	1994	1995	1996	1997	1998	1999	2000	2001	2002	2003	2004	2005	2006	2007	2008	2009	2010
A. Exports																	
Canada	3.6	3.5	3.5	3.6	3.7	4.0	4.2	4.1	3.8	3.5	3.4	3.3	3.1	2.9	2.6	2.3	2.2
France	5.6	5.6	5.4	5.3	5.6	5.3	4.8	4.9	4.9	4.9	4.7	4.3	4.1	4.0	3.8	3.6	3.5
Germany	9.3	9.5	9.1	8.6	9.1	8.8	8.0	8.6	9.0	9.3	9.3	8.9	8.9	9.1	8.8	8.4	8.3
Italy	4.5	4.6	4.6	4.3	4.5	4.1	3.8	4.0	3.9	4.0	3.8	3.6	3.5	3.6	3.4	3.2	3.1
Japan	8.1	7.6	6.8	6.7	6.2	6.3	6.5	5.7	5.5	5.4	5.4	5.1	4.7	4.5	4.5	5.0	4.8
United Kingdom	5.3	5.1	5.3	5.6	5.6	5.5	5.2	5.2	5.2	5.1	4.9	4.7	4.7	4.3	3.9	3.6	3.5
United States	13.5	12.8	13.0	13.7	14.0	13.9	13.8	13.5	12.5	11.1	10.4	10.2	10.0	9.7	9.7	10.9	10.8
Other OECD countries	24.7	25.7	25.6	25.2	26.3	26.3	25.6	26.3	26.6	27.2	27.2	26.5	26.1	26.5	26.3	24.6	24.6
Total OECD	74.6	74.4	73.5	72.9	75.1	74.4	71.8	72.2	71.5	70.6	69.1	66.6	65.2	64.5	63.0	61.7	60.8
Non-OECD Asia	14.5	14.9	15.3	15.8	14.8	15.2	16.3	16.0	16.8	17.1	17.7	18.5	19.2	19.7	20.0	23.2	24.2
Latin America	2.8	2.8	2.8	3.0	2.9	2.7	2.9	2.9	2.8	2.7	2.9	3.1	3.3	3.2	3.1	3.4	3.3
Other non-OECD countries	8.0	7.9	8.5	8.3	7.2	7.7	9.0	8.8	8.9	9.6	10.3	11.8	12.3	12.6	13.8	11.7	11.7
Total of non-OECD countrie	25.3	25.6	26.5	27.1	24.9	25.6	28.2	27.8	28.5	29.4	30.9	33.4	34.8	35.5	37.0	38.3	39.2
B. Imports																	
Canada	3.5	3.2	3.2	3.5	3.6	3.7	3.6	3.5	3.4	3.2	3.0	3.0	2.9	2.8	2.6	2.4	2.3
France	5.5	5.4	5.2	4.8	5.2	4.9	4.6	4.7	4.6	4.8	4.7	4.5	4.4	4.4	4.3	3.9	3.8
Germany	9.4	9.5	8.9	8.3	8.8	8.6	7.9	8.1	7.9	8.4	8.1	7.8	7.9	7.9	7.9	7.5	7.4
Italy	3.9	4.0	3.8	3.8	4.0	3.8	3.6	3.7	3.8	3.9	3.8	3.6	3.7	3.7	3.5	3.2	3.1
Japan	6.4	6.5	6.6	6.1	5.2	5.4	5.6	5.3	4.9	4.7	4.6	4.6	4.4	4.2	4.4	4.6	4.5
United Kingdom	5.4	5.2	5.4	5.6	5.9	5.9	5.5	5.6	5.8	5.6	5.5	5.3	5.3	5.0	4.4	4.0	3.9
United States	15.5	14.4	14.6	15.5	16.5	17.7	18.6	18.2	17.8	16.6	16.0	15.9	15.3	14.1	13.5	14.1	13.5
Other OECD countries	24.2	24.7	25.0	24.5	25.4	25.4	24.9	25.0	25.4	26.2	26.3	25.9	26.0	26.7	26.6	24.6	24.5
Total OECD	73.8	73.0	72.7	72.1	74.5	75.5	74.5	74.2	73.6	73.3	71.9	70.7	69.9	68.7	67.0	64.3	63.1
Non-OECD Asia	14.9	15.5	15.7	15.8	13.8	14.2	15.4	15.0	15.6	15.9	16.9	17.3	17.5	17.9	18.5	20.5	21.4
Latin America	3.0	3.1	3.1	3.5	3.6	3.0	2.9	3.0	2.5	2.3	2.3	2.6	2.7	2.9	3.0	3.4	3.4
Other non-OECD countries	8.1	8.3	8.4	8.6	8.2	7.4	7.2	7.8	8.3	8.5	8.9	9.4	9.9	10.5	11.4	11.8	12.0
Total of non-OECD countrie	26.1	27.0	27.3	27.9	25.5	24.5	25.5	25.8	26.4	26.7	28.1	29.3	30.1	31.3	33.0	35.7	36.9

Note: Regional aggregates are calculated inclusive of intra-regional trade.
Source: OECD Economic Outlook 84 database.

StatLink ⬛⬛🖎 http://dx.dx.doi.org/10.1787/505203300253

Annex Table 46. Geographical structure of world trade growth
Average of export and import volumes

	1994	1995	1996	1997	1998	1999	2000	2001	2002	2003	2004	2005	2006	2007	2008	2009	2010
A. Trade growth by main regions																	
						percentage changes from previous year											
NAFTA[1]	11.1	8.3	8.9	12.8	7.9	8.9	11.5	-3.7	1.1	2.4	10.0	6.2	7.0	4.7	2.2	-0.4	2.3
OECD Europe	8.5	8.3	5.5	10.3	8.3	6.1	12.1	2.8	1.7	2.7	7.2	6.2	9.0	5.1	3.1	0.6	3.3
OECD Asia & Pacific[2]	8.6	11.0	10.2	7.4	-4.0	7.2	12.7	-3.0	7.1	8.2	12.8	6.7	8.2	7.9	5.5	1.2	5.2
Total OECD	9.2	8.7	7.2	10.6	6.3	7.1	12.0	0.0	2.2	3.4	8.8	6.3	8.3	5.4	3.2	0.4	3.3
Non-OECD Asia	15.3	14.9	6.8	8.0	-4.8	10.2	18.5	-2.2	11.9	14.4	19.0	13.3	13.0	10.3	7.0	5.2	8.8
Latin America	10.0	11.9	5.9	13.7	7.2	-4.8	7.4	2.9	-4.2	4.5	14.2	12.9	9.6	11.3	9.6	5.2	5.1
Other non-OECD countries	2.6	5.9	5.3	8.2	0.8	0.3	12.1	5.0	6.2	9.1	12.1	9.4	9.5	10.2	9.2	3.3	6.7
Non-OECD	11.0	11.9	6.2	8.7	-1.6	5.1	15.2	0.5	8.3	11.8	16.5	12.2	11.7	10.4	7.8	4.7	7.9
World	9.7	9.6	6.9	10.1	4.1	6.5	12.8	0.1	3.9	5.7	11.1	8.1	9.4	7.0	4.8	1.9	5.0
B. Contribution to World Trade growth by main regions																	
						percentage points											
NAFTA[1]	2.3	1.7	1.8	2.7	1.7	2.0	2.6	-0.8	0.2	0.5	2.0	1.2	1.4	0.9	0.4	-0.1	0.4
OECD Europe	3.5	3.4	2.2	4.1	3.3	2.5	5.0	1.1	0.7	1.1	2.9	2.4	3.4	1.9	1.1	0.2	1.2
OECD Asia & Pacific[2]	0.9	1.2	1.1	0.8	-0.4	0.7	1.3	-0.3	0.7	0.8	1.3	0.7	0.8	0.8	0.6	0.1	0.5
Total OECD	6.7	6.3	5.1	7.6	4.5	5.2	8.8	0.0	1.6	2.4	6.2	4.3	5.6	3.6	2.1	0.3	2.1
Non-OECD Asia	2.3	2.3	1.1	1.3	-0.8	1.5	2.8	-0.4	1.8	2.4	3.4	2.6	2.6	2.2	1.5	1.1	2.0
Latin America	0.3	0.4	0.2	0.4	0.2	-0.2	0.2	0.1	-0.1	0.1	0.4	0.4	0.3	0.3	0.3	0.2	0.2
Other non-OECD countries	0.3	0.6	0.5	0.7	0.1	0.0	1.0	0.4	0.5	0.8	1.1	0.9	0.9	0.9	0.9	0.3	0.7
Non-OECD	3.1	3.3	1.8	2.5	-0.5	1.3	4.0	0.1	2.2	3.3	4.9	3.8	3.8	3.4	2.7	1.6	2.8
World	9.7	9.6	6.9	10.1	4.1	6.5	12.8	0.1	3.9	5.7	11.1	8.1	9.4	7.0	4.8	1.9	5.0

Note: Regional aggregates are calculated inclusive of intra-regional trade as the sum of volumes expressed in 2000 $.
1. Canada, Mexico and United States.
2. Australia, Japan, Korea and New Zealand.
Source: OECD Economic Outlook 84 database.

StatLink http://dx.doi.org/10.1787/505203682401

Annex Table 47. Trade balances for goods and services
$ billion, national accounts basis

	1991	1992	1993	1994	1995	1996	1997	1998	1999	2000	2001	2002	2003	2004	2005	2006	2007	2008	2009	2010
Australia	1.1	-0.9	-1.4	-4.3	-5.1	-0.4	2.0	-6.2	-9.6	-3.9	2.5	-4.3	-13.5	-17.5	-12.8	-8.7	-16.0	-8.1	-25.5	-28.8
Austria	-1.0	-1.6	0.4	-2.7	-2.7	-3.3	-0.7	1.5	2.8	3.6	4.5	9.2	12.6	12.8	12.2	15.8	21.7	23.3	22.0	23.3
Belgium	4.2	6.5	7.9	9.7	12.1	10.8	11.0	11.2	11.2	6.7	8.3	12.0	14.1	16.0	13.9	12.0	13.6	-6.0	-8.8	-11.0
Canada	-3.4	-2.2	0.0	6.7	18.9	24.7	12.6	12.3	24.2	41.6	41.2	32.4	32.5	42.7	42.4	31.4	27.2	21.6	-10.4	-7.8
Czech Republic	..	..	0.0	-1.1	-2.4	-3.6	-3.1	-0.7	-0.8	-1.7	-1.5	-1.6	-2.1	0.0	3.9	5.1	9.0	12.1	9.7	12.2
Denmark	7.5	9.4	9.4	8.1	7.4	9.1	6.3	3.7	8.8	9.6	10.7	10.2	13.3	11.9	12.8	7.6	3.9	4.4	4.7	7.9
Finland	-1.1	0.6	3.6	5.4	9.3	9.4	9.9	11.5	13.1	11.8	12.2	12.8	11.7	13.2	8.7	10.3	12.3	16.0	15.5	16.1
France	-13.4	2.5	11.1	11.5	18.6	24.2	41.3	37.4	30.0	12.4	15.5	25.4	18.9	0.6	-18.2	-27.8	-49.8	-68.1	-45.4	-47.9
Germany	-6.4	-9.2	-0.9	2.7	11.9	22.0	27.0	29.7	18.0	7.0	38.3	93.3	97.9	138.6	148.3	165.8	235.8	225.3	191.6	198.1
Greece	-11.9	-11.6	-10.7	-9.3	-12.4	-14.1	-13.1	-14.7	-15.0	-17.0	-15.3	-17.7	-24.7	-28.5	-27.9	-33.8	-41.4	-40.8	-33.5	-33.2
Hungary	..	..	-3.1	-2.7	-0.1	0.3	0.5	-0.6	-1.3	-1.7	-0.6	-1.4	-3.3	-3.4	-2.0	-0.8	2.1	2.9	2.0	2.7
Iceland	-0.1	0.0	0.2	0.3	0.3	0.0	0.0	-0.4	-0.4	-0.6	-0.1	0.1	-0.3	-0.7	-2.0	-3.0	-2.1	-1.2	0.2	0.5
Ireland	2.5	4.3	5.4	5.6	7.8	8.9	10.6	10.4	13.5	12.9	16.4	21.4	25.6	28.0	24.5	24.0	27.9	30.0	29.1	32.5
Italy	1.4	-1.4	31.4	36.1	43.2	58.5	46.3	37.1	22.1	10.5	15.3	11.6	8.9	11.6	-1.1	-15.0	-6.8	7.5	24.8	18.4
Japan	56.2	82.2	97.0	96.5	74.8	23.4	47.4	72.3	69.4	68.0	26.1	51.2	69.3	89.0	63.3	54.5	73.3	43.4	94.3	71.8
Korea	-8.2	-3.9	1.4	-3.1	-5.7	-19.2	-4.5	44.2	29.8	16.1	11.1	7.5	14.6	28.9	18.7	8.2	8.1	-8.8	3.8	5.7
Luxembourg	1.7	2.5	2.8	3.6	4.4	4.2	3.2	3.2	4.1	4.2	3.6	4.4	7.0	8.4	9.6	13.5	16.0	18.3	15.8	16.3
Mexico	-9.1	-18.3	-15.8	-20.1	7.8	7.2	0.0	-8.5	-7.6	-11.3	-13.7	-11.4	-10.1	-13.2	-12.3	-12.1	-16.5	-17.9	-25.2	-28.5
Netherlands	12.6	12.7	17.7	19.8	23.8	22.1	21.9	18.9	17.4	21.3	23.2	28.8	33.9	45.1	54.5	54.5	66.9	67.6	55.9	56.0
New Zealand	1.3	0.7	1.2	1.1	0.7	0.3	0.3	0.2	-0.6	0.4	1.5	0.8	0.7	-0.5	-2.3	-1.8	-1.5	-2.6	-0.2	0.9
Norway	9.4	8.7	7.6	7.6	9.2	14.3	13.0	2.8	11.6	28.6	29.0	25.8	29.2	35.1	49.7	61.3	61.2	74.3	35.3	37.6
Poland	..	..	0.8	2.1	3.0	-2.2	-6.1	-8.3	-9.9	-11.0	-7.0	-6.9	-5.8	-5.8	-2.2	-6.2	-12.1	-15.1	-12.4	-12.7
Portugal	-6.3	-7.7	-6.4	-6.7	-7.3	-8.2	-9.0	-10.6	-12.4	-12.3	-11.6	-10.6	-10.3	-14.0	-16.4	-16.0	-16.6	-19.8	-15.0	-15.0
Slovak Republic	..	..	-0.6	0.8	0.4	-2.3	-2.1	-2.4	-0.9	-0.5	-1.7	-1.8	-0.6	-1.1	-2.2	-2.1	-0.4	1.1	1.4	2.2
Spain	-17.2	-16.4	-3.2	0.1	0.0	3.3	5.0	-1.4	-11.3	-18.2	-15.4	-14.7	-21.1	-41.8	-59.5	-79.2	-97.8	-97.7	-47.4	-36.6
Sweden	4.2	4.6	7.6	9.9	17.5	18.4	18.9	16.8	16.6	15.4	15.2	16.9	21.3	29.1	28.4	32.3	34.7	36.2	32.0	34.6
Switzerland	5.9	10.9	14.4	14.6	16.1	14.7	14.1	13.1	14.9	14.6	12.6	18.4	21.4	25.1	24.2	29.9	39.3	53.2	55.0	57.8
Turkey	0.3	0.2	-4.8	6.1	-0.1	-3.1	-1.1	2.7	0.8	-8.0	7.8	3.8	-3.2	-10.4	-16.9	-26.0	-33.9	-43.7	-31.2	-31.6
United Kingdom	-7.0	-11.8	-7.4	-4.5	-1.4	1.0	7.3	-11.3	-21.9	-27.2	-34.6	-42.2	-42.7	-60.0	-77.5	-79.8	-95.1	-80.0	-62.3	-74.8
United States	-27.5	-33.3	-65.0	-93.6	-91.4	-96.3	#####	-160.0	-260.5	-379.5	-367.0	-424.4	-499.4	-615.4	-713.6	-757.3	-707.9	-683.0	-526.7	-480.1
Euro area	-34.7	-18.7	59.1	75.8	108.9	137.8	153.3	134.2	93.5	43.0	94.9	175.8	174.5	189.9	148.5	124.1	181.8	155.5	204.6	217.0
Total OECD	-4.1	27.6	100.6	100.3	158.9	124.2	157.2	103.8	-43.9	-208.0	-173.7	-151.0	-204.0	-276.5	-452.1	-543.6	-444.9	-455.7	-250.9	-213.4

Source: OECD Economic Outlook 84 database.

StatLink http://dx.doi.org/10.1787/505206530533

Annex Table 48. Investment income, net
$ billion

	1991	1992	1993	1994	1995	1996	1997	1998	1999	2000	2001	2002	2003	2004	2005	2006	2007	2008	2009	2010
Australia	-12.2	-10.1	-8.1	-12.4	-14.0	-15.2	-13.8	-11.4	-11.6	-10.8	-9.9	-11.5	-14.9	-21.4	-27.7	-31.1	-40.6	-41.3	-26.5	-30.5
Austria	-1.4	-1.4	-1.5	-1.7	-2.4	-0.9	-1.5	-2.0	-2.9	-2.5	-3.1	-1.6	-1.2	-1.3	-1.9	-3.7	-5.1	-4.4	-4.4	-4.1
Belgium[1]	5.7	6.4	6.9	7.4	7.3	6.8	6.3	6.9	6.7	6.3	4.6	4.5	6.5	5.7	5.3	7.6	6.0	2.3	5.4	6.7
Canada	-17.4	-17.5	-20.8	-18.9	-22.7	-21.5	-20.9	-20.0	-22.6	-22.3	-25.4	-19.3	-21.3	-18.6	-18.5	-11.8	-13.0	-11.8	-8.3	-7.4
Czech Republic	..	..	-0.1	0.0	-0.1	-0.7	-0.8	-1.1	-1.4	-1.4	-2.2	-3.5	-4.3	-6.1	-6.0	-8.0	-10.9	-18.2	-16.8	-20.4
Denmark	-5.1	-4.9	-3.8	-3.8	-3.8	-3.7	-3.4	-2.8	-2.6	-3.6	-3.6	-2.7	-2.6	-2.2	1.6	2.7	2.2	1.4	1.0	1.3
Finland	-4.7	-5.4	-4.9	-4.4	-4.4	-3.7	-2.4	-3.1	-2.0	-1.7	-1.0	-0.6	-2.6	0.2	-0.3	0.8	0.8	-6.3	-7.0	-7.0
France	-3.6	-6.4	-7.0	-6.2	-8.4	-1.9	7.1	8.7	22.9	19.4	19.5	8.7	14.9	22.5	25.0	35.9	39.1	49.2	39.1	37.7
Germany	18.0	18.2	11.5	1.4	-2.8	0.8	-2.7	-10.8	-12.4	-8.9	-10.0	-17.3	-17.1	25.1	31.4	47.4	58.7	47.5	34.4	32.5
Greece	-2.0	-2.4	-1.6	-1.4	-1.8	-2.1	-1.7	-1.6	-0.7	-0.9	-1.8	-2.0	-4.5	-5.4	-7.0	-8.9	-12.5	-14.5	-15.5	-16.5
Hungary	..	..	-1.5	-1.6	-1.7	-2.0	-2.7	-3.0	-2.9	-2.6	-2.9	-3.6	-4.2	-5.4	-6.3	-7.0	-10.1	-11.0	-9.4	-9.5
Iceland	-0.2	-0.2	-0.1	-0.2	-0.2	-0.2	-0.2	-0.2	-0.2	-0.2	-0.3	0.0	-0.2	-0.6	-0.6	-1.2	-1.1	-3.3	-2.1	-2.2
Ireland	-4.6	-5.6	-5.2	-5.4	-7.3	-8.2	-9.7	-10.5	-13.7	-13.5	-16.4	-22.4	-24.8	-28.0	-31.0	-30.2	-39.2	-41.2	-35.9	-36.8
Italy	-17.5	-22.0	-17.4	-16.9	-15.8	-15.3	-10.1	-11.0	-11.1	-11.9	-10.4	-14.6	-20.5	-18.7	-16.7	-16.9	-27.9	-42.9	-44.2	-49.2
Japan	26.0	35.6	40.7	40.6	44.2	53.3	58.1	54.8	58.0	60.6	69.4	66.0	71.8	86.2	103.3	118.0	138.8	143.6	137.2	139.9
Korea	-0.2	-0.4	-0.4	-0.5	-1.3	-1.8	-2.5	-5.6	-5.2	-2.4	-1.2	0.4	0.3	1.1	-1.6	0.5	0.8	1.8	2.3	2.4
Luxembourg	..	..	..	..	1.6	1.3	0.5	0.2	-0.5	-1.3	-1.6	-3.4	-4.0	-4.3	-6.7	-10.6	-15.0	-14.2	-10.8	-10.7
Mexico	-8.6	-9.6	-11.4	-13.0	-13.3	-13.9	-12.8	-13.3	-12.9	-15.0	-13.9	-12.7	-12.3	-10.3	-13.6	-14.5	-14.1	-20.6	-24.9	-24.0
Netherlands	0.4	-1.0	0.9	3.6	7.3	3.5	7.0	-2.7	3.5	-2.3	-0.2	0.1	1.2	11.3	3.9	18.3	4.7	6.3	6.0	5.8
New Zealand	-2.5	-2.5	-2.9	-3.4	-4.0	-4.7	-4.9	-2.6	-3.1	-3.4	-3.1	-3.2	-4.2	-5.9	-7.4	-7.9	-9.5	-10.4	-8.4	-8.7
Norway	-2.7	-3.4	-3.3	-2.2	-1.9	-1.9	-1.7	-1.2	-1.3	-2.3	0.2	0.6	1.4	0.5	2.1	-0.5	2.3	3.1	10.4	13.5
Poland	..	..	..	-2.6	-2.0	-1.1	-1.1	-1.2	-1.0	-0.7	-0.6	-1.1	-2.5	-8.2	-6.7	-9.7	-16.3	-21.1	-27.2	-33.5
Portugal	0.2	0.7	0.3	-0.5	0.2	-0.9	-1.3	-1.5	-1.6	-2.4	-3.5	-3.0	-2.6	-3.7	-4.8	-8.0	-10.1	-11.7	-10.4	-10.8
Slovak Republic	..	..	0.0	-0.1	0.0	0.0	-0.1	-0.2	-0.3	-0.4	-0.3	-0.5	-0.1	-0.4	-2.0	-2.1	-3.2	-3.5	-4.0	-3.8
Spain	-4.3	-5.8	-3.6	-7.8	-5.4	-7.5	-7.4	-8.6	-9.5	-6.9	-11.3	-11.6	-11.7	-15.1	-21.3	-25.9	-43.2	-54.5	-53.5	-57.2
Sweden	-6.4	-10.0	-8.7	-5.9	-5.5	-6.3	-4.9	-3.2	-2.0	-1.4	-1.4	-1.8	3.9	-0.4	2.8	7.4	10.7	1.5	0.2	0.4
Switzerland	7.9	7.4	8.2	6.9	10.7	11.6	15.3	17.0	19.4	21.2	13.8	10.7	25.9	27.2	37.9	31.4	21.9	-6.4	-1.3	-0.1
Turkey	-2.7	-2.6	-2.7	-3.3	-3.2	-2.9	-3.0	-3.0	-3.5	-4.0	-5.0	-4.6	-5.6	-5.5	-5.9	-6.7	-7.1	-9.1	-11.7	-13.0
United Kingdom	-10.1	-1.8	-3.8	2.0	-1.4	-3.8	0.5	19.6	-1.7	3.0	13.6	27.6	28.7	32.8	40.1	18.5	17.6	53.1	50.7	48.2
United States	24.1	24.2	25.3	17.1	20.9	22.3	12.6	4.3	13.9	21.1	31.7	27.4	45.3	67.2	72.4	57.2	81.8	112.6	92.7	75.4
Euro area	-13.7	-24.6	-21.7	-31.8	-32.1	-28.2	-16.1	-36.1	-21.5	-26.5	-35.2	-63.2	-66.4	-11.8	-24.0	5.7	-43.8	-84.3	-96.9	-109.6
Total OECD	-23.7	-20.4	-15.3	-32.9	-31.3	-20.7	-2.3	-9.1	-2.3	8.8	23.7	5.0	38.9	118.3	139.9	140.9	106.5	76.1	57.1	18.2

Note: The classification of non-factor services and investment income is affected by the change in reporting system to the International Monetary Fund, Fifth Balance of Payments Manual.
1. Including Luxembourg until 1994.
Source: OECD Economic Outlook 84 database.

StatLink http://dx.doi.org/10.1787/505212710332

Annex Table 49. Total transfers, net
$ billion

	1991	1992	1993	1994	1995	1996	1997	1998	1999	2000	2001	2002	2003	2004	2005	2006	2007	2008	2009	2010
Australia	0.1	-0.1	-0.1	-0.2	-0.1	0.1	0.0	-0.3	0.0	0.0	0.1	0.0	-0.1	-0.2	-0.4	-0.3	-0.2	-0.2	-0.1	-0.1
Austria	-0.1	-1.0	-1.0	-1.1	-1.7	-1.8	-1.7	-1.9	-2.0	-1.3	-1.2	-1.8	-2.3	-2.8	-2.6	-1.4	-1.4	-1.9	-1.4	-1.5
Belgium[1]	-2.1	-2.5	-2.6	-3.3	-4.2	-4.1	-3.7	-4.3	-4.6	-3.9	-4.1	-4.4	-6.4	-6.5	-6.3	-6.6	-6.9	-7.1	-6.2	-6.9
Canada	-1.1	-0.9	-0.6	-0.3	-0.1	0.5	0.5	0.6	0.5	0.8	1.0	0.0	-0.2	-0.5	-1.1	-1.0	-1.0	-1.2	-1.2	-1.2
Czech Republic	..	..	0.1	0.1	0.6	0.4	0.4	0.5	0.6	0.4	0.5	0.9	0.6	0.2	0.3	-0.6	-0.9	0.5	0.1	0.1
Denmark	-1.6	-1.7	-1.7	-2.0	-2.4	-2.6	-1.8	-2.3	-2.9	-3.0	-2.6	-2.6	-3.7	-4.6	-4.2	-4.6	-5.0	-6.0	-5.1	-5.1
Finland	-1.0	-0.8	-0.4	-0.5	-0.4	-0.9	-0.7	-1.0	-1.0	-0.7	-0.7	-0.8	-1.1	-1.1	-1.5	-1.7	-1.9	-1.7	-1.8	-1.8
France	-15.4	-18.9	-10.2	-13.3	-5.9	-7.4	-13.2	-12.1	-13.2	-14.0	-14.8	-14.2	-19.2	-21.8	-27.3	-27.1	-30.3	-33.6	-30.7	-30.7
Germany	-35.5	-32.5	-33.0	-36.6	-38.8	-34.0	-30.5	-30.2	-26.4	-25.6	-23.9	-26.0	-34.7	-35.1	-36.0	-33.9	-42.2	-34.7	-27.6	-27.6
Greece[2]	6.2	6.5	6.5	6.9	8.0	8.0	8.3	7.9	3.9	3.3	3.5	3.6	4.3	4.5	3.9	4.3	2.2	4.3	4.3	4.3
Hungary	..	0.2	0.2	0.2	0.2	0.0	0.2	0.2	0.4	0.4	0.4	0.5	0.7	-0.5	-0.7	-0.5	-0.7	-1.4	-0.7	-0.7
Iceland	0.0	0.0	0.0	0.0	0.0	0.0	0.0	0.0	0.0	0.0	0.0	0.0	0.0	0.5	0.0	0.0	-0.1	0.0	0.0	0.0
Ireland	2.6	2.1	1.9	1.7	1.8	2.2	2.0	1.5	1.3	0.9	0.3	0.7	0.5	0.5	0.3	-0.6	-1.7	-3.0	-3.5	-3.7
Italy	-7.6	-7.8	-7.3	-7.2	-4.2	-6.6	-4.2	-7.4	-5.4	-4.3	-5.8	-5.5	-8.1	-10.3	-12.3	-16.9	-18.9	-29.0	-24.8	-24.8
Japan	-8.3	-3.9	-5.3	-6.1	-7.8	-9.1	-8.8	-8.8	-10.8	-9.8	-8.1	-8.5	-7.7	-8.0	-7.6	-10.6	-11.6	-12.3	-13.6	-13.6
Korea	0.8	1.1	1.2	1.3	0.0	0.0	0.6	3.3	1.9	0.6	-0.4	-1.6	-2.9	-2.4	-2.5	-4.1	-3.6	-3.0	..	..
Luxembourg	..	..	..	..	-0.6	-0.6	-0.5	-0.4	-0.6	-0.5	-0.5	-0.3	-0.6	-1.1	-1.2	-1.3	-2.4	-3.0	-2.6	-2.6
Mexico	3.0	3.4	3.6	3.8	4.0	4.5	5.2	6.0	6.3	7.0	9.3	10.3	14.1	17.2	20.7	24.1	24.3	23.3	20.5	20.4
Netherlands	-4.1	-4.4	-4.5	-5.2	-6.4	-6.8	-6.1	-7.2	-6.4	-6.3	-6.7	-6.5	-7.2	-10.4	-11.8	-13.0	-12.3	-13.5	-11.5	-11.8
New Zealand	0.2	0.2	0.2	0.3	0.3	0.6	0.3	0.3	0.2	0.2	0.2	0.1	0.1	0.1	0.3	0.5	0.4	0.8	0.6	0.6
Norway	-1.5	-1.8	-1.4	-1.7	-2.1	-1.5	-1.4	-1.5	-1.4	-1.3	-1.6	-2.2	-2.9	-2.6	-2.7	-2.3	-2.6	-3.4	0.1	0.1
Poland	..	..	6.8	1.3	1.0	1.7	2.0	2.9	2.2	1.3	1.5	2.0	2.5	3.7	5.0	6.6	8.5	9.5	13.4	17.9
Portugal[2]	6.0	7.9	6.8	5.4	7.3	4.4	3.8	4.0	3.8	3.4	3.4	2.8	3.3	3.5	2.8	3.2	3.6	3.8	3.4	3.4
Slovak Republic	..	..	0.1	0.1	0.1	0.2	0.2	0.4	0.2	0.1	0.2	0.2	0.2	0.1	0.0	-0.1	-0.4	-0.5	0.7	1.3
Spain	2.6	2.1	1.3	1.2	4.8	3.2	2.9	3.2	3.0	1.6	1.3	2.4	-0.6	-0.1	-4.2	-7.9	-9.3	-12.9	-11.8	-11.8
Sweden	-1.1	-1.4	-1.2	-1.2	-2.6	-1.9	-2.4	-2.5	-2.7	-2.5	-2.5	-2.9	-2.4	-4.7	-4.6	-4.9	-6.2	-5.6	-5.5	-5.7
Switzerland	-2.6	-3.0	-3.0	-3.5	-4.4	-4.3	-4.1	-4.6	-5.3	-4.5	-5.5	-5.9	-5.5	-6.3	-11.9	-9.3	-9.4	-12.9	-14.6	-15.2
Turkey	5.1	3.9	3.7	3.0	4.4	4.1	4.5	5.5	4.9	4.8	3.0	2.4	1.0	1.1	1.5	1.9	2.2	1.9	1.9	1.9
United Kingdom	-1.7	-9.3	-7.6	-7.9	-11.6	-7.1	-9.4	-13.6	-11.8	-14.7	-9.4	-13.3	-16.1	-18.8	-21.5	-22.0	-27.5	-27.6	-23.3	-23.3
United States	9.9	-35.1	-39.8	-40.3	-38.1	-43.0	-45.1	-53.2	-50.4	-58.6	-51.3	-64.9	-71.8	-84.5	-89.8	-92.0	-112.7	-122.3	-124.3	-128.3
Euro area	-48.4	-49.4	-42.6	-51.8	-40.2	-44.4	-43.6	-47.9	-47.4	-47.3	-49.4	-50.1	-72.2	-80.6	-96.1	-102.9	-121.5	-132.1	-114.3	-115.5
Total OECD	-47.2	-98.2	-94.2	-105.1	-99.0	-101.9	-102.5	-115.0	-115.7	-126.4	-114.6	-135.7	-166.2	-191.5	-215.3	-222.2	-267.8	-292.6	-265.5	-266.5

1. Including Luxembourg until 1994.
2. Breaks between 1998 and 1999 for Greece and between 1995 and 1996 for Portugal, reflecting change in methodology to the International Monetary Fund, Fifth Balance of Payments Manual (capital transfers from European Union are excluded from the current account).
Source: OECD Economic Outlook 84 database.

StatLink ᔖᕙ http://dx.doi.org/10.1787/505231500781

Annex Table 50. Current account balances
$ billion

	1991	1992	1993	1994	1995	1996	1997	1998	1999	2000	2001	2002	2003	2004	2005	2006	2007	2008	2009	2010
Australia	-11.0	-11.1	-9.7	-17.1	-19.3	-15.5	-11.8	-17.8	-21.3	-14.7	-7.4	-15.7	-28.4	-39.2	-40.9	-40.2	-56.8	-49.5	-52.1	-59.5
Austria	0.1	-0.7	-1.4	-3.3	-6.2	-5.4	-6.5	-5.2	-6.7	-5.0	-3.7	0.7	-0.5	1.3	3.4	8.1	11.6	14.8	13.3	14.8
Belgium[1]	7.2	9.9	13.0	14.2	15.3	13.8	13.8	13.3	12.9	9.4	7.9	11.7	12.9	12.6	9.9	10.8	7.4	-17.4	-10.8	-12.3
Canada	-22.4	-21.1	-21.7	-13.0	-4.4	3.4	-8.2	-7.7	1.7	19.7	16.3	12.6	10.6	22.9	22.1	17.8	12.3	7.6	-20.6	-17.2
Czech Republic	..	..	0.5	-0.8	-1.4	-4.1	-3.6	-1.3	-1.5	-2.7	-3.3	-4.2	-5.8	-5.7	-1.7	-3.6	-3.0	-5.1	-6.0	-7.1
Denmark	1.2	3.2	3.9	2.3	1.2	2.7	0.7	-1.5	3.4	2.5	4.2	5.0	7.3	5.7	11.1	7.4	3.5	2.7	2.8	6.3
Finland	-6.8	-5.1	-1.1	1.0	5.4	5.1	6.8	7.3	8.1	9.9	10.8	12.0	8.5	12.4	7.1	9.4	10.6	8.0	5.8	6.3
France	-12.1	-3.4	7.2	5.4	11.0	20.8	37.2	38.9	45.6	22.2	26.3	19.2	15.6	11.5	-13.7	-15.2	-31.5	-46.9	-37.0	-40.8
Germany	-24.0	-22.0	-19.5	-30.8	-29.5	-13.8	-10.1	-16.9	-27.8	-33.6	0.5	41.2	45.5	125.8	144.9	178.2	255.3	233.7	193.7	198.4
Greece[2]	-2.6	-3.6	-1.9	-1.4	-4.5	-6.4	-5.3	-3.8	-7.4	-9.8	-9.5	-10.1	-12.8	-13.3	-17.8	-29.7	-44.6	-51.6	-44.7	-45.3
Hungary	-0.3	-0.2	-3.7	-4.2	-1.6	-1.7	-2.0	-3.4	-3.8	-4.0	-3.2	-4.7	-6.7	-8.8	-8.3	-8.5	-8.9	-9.6	-8.2	-7.5
Iceland	-0.3	-0.2	0.0	0.1	0.1	-0.1	-0.1	-0.6	-0.6	-0.9	-0.4	0.1	-0.5	-1.3	-2.6	-4.2	-3.2	-4.2	-1.7	-1.5
Ireland	0.3	0.5	1.8	1.5	1.7	2.0	1.9	0.7	0.3	-0.3	-0.7	-1.2	0.0	-1.1	-7.0	-7.9	-14.2	-16.6	-14.5	-12.2
Italy	-24.3	-30.2	7.9	12.5	25.0	39.2	33.7	22.9	8.2	-5.7	-0.7	-9.7	-19.7	-16.4	-28.7	-48.1	-51.9	-61.6	-41.8	-53.2
Japan	72.7	108.3	130.0	130.6	114.3	64.8	97.0	119.7	115.6	118.7	88.4	112.3	136.4	170.9	166.6	172.0	211.8	187.2	230.9	211.0
Korea	-8.4	-4.1	0.8	-4.0	-8.7	-23.1	-8.3	40.4	24.5	12.3	8.0	5.4	11.9	28.2	15.0	5.4	6.0	-10.2	5.6	7.6
Luxembourg	..	..	..	..	2.5	2.3	1.9	1.8	1.8	2.7	1.8	2.3	2.4	4.1	4.1	4.4	4.9	3.6	2.5	3.0
Mexico	-14.6	-24.4	-23.4	-29.7	-1.6	-2.5	-7.7	-16.0	-13.9	-18.7	-17.7	-14.1	-8.6	-6.6	-5.2	-2.2	-5.8	-14.1	-29.5	-31.5
Netherlands	7.4	6.9	13.2	17.3	25.8	21.5	25.1	13.0	15.7	7.2	9.8	11.1	29.9	46.0	46.5	63.2	59.2	62.3	50.4	49.9
New Zealand	-1.2	-1.7	-1.7	-2.0	-3.0	-3.9	-4.3	-2.1	-3.5	-2.7	-1.4	-2.3	-3.4	-6.3	-9.3	-9.3	-10.5	-12.1	-7.7	-6.9
Norway	5.0	3.0	2.2	3.8	5.2	10.9	10.0	0.0	8.9	25.1	27.5	24.2	27.7	32.9	49.2	58.5	60.8	74.0	46.2	51.6
Poland	..	..	..	1.0	0.9	-3.3	-5.7	-6.9	-12.5	-10.3	-5.9	-5.5	-5.5	-10.1	-3.7	-9.4	-20.1	-28.0	-29.3	-31.3
Portugal[2]	-0.7	-0.3	0.3	-2.3	-0.2	-4.9	-6.6	-8.4	-10.3	-11.6	-11.5	-10.3	-9.6	-13.6	-17.6	-19.7	-22.1	-26.8	-21.7	-22.1
Slovak Republic	..	..	-0.6	0.8	0.5	-2.0	-1.8	-2.0	-1.0	-0.7	-1.7	-1.9	-0.3	-1.4	-4.1	-3.9	-4.0	-4.9	-3.7	-2.2
Spain	-19.9	-21.6	-5.6	-6.5	-1.7	-1.5	-0.6	-7.2	-17.9	-23.0	-24.0	-22.5	-31.1	-54.9	-83.1	-110.4	-145.6	-156.1	-102.8	-90.7
Sweden	-3.7	-7.5	-2.6	2.5	8.4	9.8	10.3	9.7	10.7	9.4	8.5	9.8	22.3	24.0	24.8	33.3	38.5	32.0	26.7	29.3
Switzerland	10.1	14.7	18.9	17.0	20.6	21.3	24.7	25.0	29.0	30.1	19.7	23.6	42.0	46.9	51.0	56.4	57.1	39.5	44.3	47.7
Turkey	0.2	-1.0	-6.4	2.6	-2.3	-2.4	-2.6	2.0	-1.3	-9.8	3.4	-1.5	-8.0	-15.5	-22.1	-31.8	-38.1	-50.6	-40.0	-41.7
United Kingdom	-18.9	-23.0	-18.7	-10.4	-14.3	-9.8	-1.6	-5.3	-35.4	-38.9	-30.4	-27.9	-30.0	-46.1	-58.9	-83.3	-105.0	-53.5	-34.9	-50.0
United States	2.9	-50.1	-84.8	-121.6	-113.6	-124.8	-140.7	-215.1	-301.6	-417.4	-384.7	-461.3	-523.4	-625.0	-729.0	-788.1	-731.2	-696.4	-562.3	-537.0
Euro area	-75.4	-69.6	13.9	7.7	44.7	72.8	91.4	56.3	22.4	-37.6	7.0	44.3	41.1	114.4	48.0	43.2	39.3	-54.5	-7.6	-4.3
Total OECD	-63.7	-84.6	-3.2	-34.5	25.8	-7.6	35.5	-26.4	-180.2	-340.7	-273.1	-302.0	-321.4	-320.1	-498.0	-590.6	-557.3	-649.7	-447.1	-444.1

Note: The balance-of-payments data in this table are based on the concepts and definition of the International Monetary Fund, Fifth Balance of Payments Manual.
1. Including Luxembourg until 1994.
2. Breaks between 1998 and 1999 for Greece and between 1995 and 1996 for Portugal, reflecting change in methodology to the International Monetary Fund, Fifth Balance of Payments Manual (capital transfers from European Union are excluded from the current account).
Source: OECD Economic Outlook 84 database.

StatLink ⟐⟐⟐ http://dx.doi.org/10.1787/550530886503

Annex Table 51. Current account balances as a percentage of GDP

	1991	1992	1993	1994	1995	1996	1997	1998	1999	2000	2001	2002	2003	2004	2005	2006	2007	2008	2009	2010
Australia	-3.4	-3.6	-3.2	-4.9	-5.2	-3.7	-2.9	-4.8	-5.3	-3.7	-2.0	-3.8	-5.4	-6.1	-5.7	-5.3	-6.2	-5.1	-6.8	-7.4
Austria	0.1	-0.4	-0.8	-1.6	-2.6	-2.3	-3.1	-2.5	-3.2	-2.6	-1.9	0.3	-0.2	0.5	1.2	2.5	3.1	3.6	3.7	4.0
Belgium[1]	3.5	4.2	5.8	5.9	5.4	5.0	5.5	5.2	5.1	4.0	3.4	4.6	4.1	3.5	2.6	2.7	1.7	-3.3	-2.4	-2.7
Canada	-3.7	-3.6	-3.9	-2.3	-0.8	0.5	-1.3	-1.2	0.3	2.7	2.3	1.7	1.2	2.3	1.9	1.4	0.9	0.4	-1.7	-1.4
Czech Republic	..	..	1.2	-1.8	-2.5	-6.6	-6.2	-2.0	-2.4	-4.8	-5.3	-5.5	-6.2	-5.2	-1.3	-2.5	-1.7	-2.3	-2.9	-3.3
Denmark	0.9	2.1	2.8	1.5	0.7	1.4	0.4	-0.9	1.9	1.6	2.6	2.9	3.4	2.3	4.3	2.7	1.1	0.8	0.9	2.0
Finland	-5.3	-4.6	-1.3	1.1	4.1	4.0	5.6	5.6	6.2	8.1	8.6	8.8	5.2	6.5	3.6	4.5	4.3	2.9	2.4	2.5
France	-1.0	-0.2	0.6	0.4	0.7	1.3	2.6	2.6	3.1	1.7	2.0	1.3	0.9	0.6	-0.6	-0.7	-1.2	-1.6	-1.5	-1.6
Germany	-1.3	-1.1	-1.0	-1.4	-1.2	-0.6	-0.5	-0.8	-1.3	-1.8	0.0	2.0	1.8	4.6	5.2	6.1	7.7	6.4	6.2	6.1
Greece[2]	-2.5	-3.2	-1.9	-1.2	-3.4	-4.6	-3.9	-2.8	-5.6	-7.8	-7.3	-6.8	-6.6	-5.8	-7.2	-11.1	-14.1	-14.5	-13.9	-13.2
Hungary	..	..	-9.4	-9.9	-3.3	-3.8	-4.3	-7.0	-7.6	-8.4	-6.0	-7.0	-8.0	-8.6	-7.5	-7.5	-6.4	-6.1	-6.1	-5.4
Iceland	-4.0	-2.4	0.7	1.9	0.7	-1.8	-1.7	-6.7	-6.7	-10.2	-4.3	1.5	-4.8	-9.8	-16.1	-25.0	-15.5	-24.0	-13.9	-11.3
Ireland	0.7	1.0	3.6	2.7	2.6	2.7	2.4	0.8	0.3	-0.4	-0.6	-1.0	0.0	-0.6	-3.5	-3.6	-5.4	-6.2	-6.3	-5.2
Italy	-2.0	-2.4	0.8	1.2	2.2	3.1	2.8	1.9	0.7	-0.5	-0.1	-0.8	-1.3	-0.9	-1.6	-2.6	-2.5	-2.6	-2.1	-2.6
Japan	2.1	2.8	3.0	2.8	2.2	1.4	2.3	3.1	2.6	2.5	2.2	2.9	3.2	3.7	3.7	3.9	4.8	3.8	4.3	3.9
Korea	-2.7	-1.2	0.2	-1.0	-1.7	-4.2	-1.3	11.8	5.5	2.4	1.7	1.0	2.0	4.2	1.9	0.6	0.6	-1.1	0.8	1.0
Luxembourg	..	..	..	..	12.2	11.3	10.4	9.1	8.3	13.3	8.7	10.6	8.2	11.8	11.0	10.5	9.9	6.6	5.1	6.1
Mexico	-4.3	-6.1	-5.3	-6.4	-0.5	-0.7	-1.8	-3.5	-2.6	-2.9	-2.6	-2.0	-1.2	-0.9	-0.6	-0.2	-0.6	-1.3	-3.1	-3.1
Netherlands	2.4	2.0	4.0	4.9	6.2	5.1	6.5	3.2	3.8	1.9	2.4	2.5	5.5	7.5	7.3	9.3	7.6	7.2	6.8	6.5
New Zealand	-2.8	-4.2	-3.9	-3.9	-5.0	-5.8	-6.4	-3.9	-6.2	-5.1	-2.8	-3.9	-4.3	-6.4	-8.5	-8.7	-8.2	-9.5	-7.6	-6.6
Norway	4.3	2.3	1.8	3.0	3.5	6.8	6.3	0.0	5.6	15.0	16.1	12.6	12.3	12.7	16.3	17.3	15.6	16.2	13.3	14.3
Poland	..	..	..	0.9	0.6	-2.1	-3.7	-4.0	-7.5	-6.0	-3.1	-2.8	-2.5	-4.0	-1.2	-2.7	-4.7	-5.3	-6.3	-6.3
Portugal[2]	-0.8	-0.2	0.4	-2.3	-0.1	-4.2	-5.9	-7.0	-8.5	-10.2	-9.9	-8.1	-6.1	-7.6	-9.5	-10.1	-9.8	-10.9	-10.2	-10.1
Slovak Republic	..	..	-4.6	4.8	2.6	-9.3	-8.4	-8.8	-4.8	-3.6	-8.3	-7.9	-0.9	-3.5	-8.6	-7.1	-5.3	-5.0	-4.1	-2.2
Spain	-3.6	-3.5	-1.1	-1.2	-0.3	-0.2	-0.1	-1.2	-2.9	-4.0	-3.9	-3.3	-3.5	-5.3	-7.4	-8.9	-10.1	-9.7	-7.4	-6.4
Sweden	-1.4	-2.8	-1.3	1.1	3.3	3.5	4.1	3.8	4.2	3.8	3.8	4.0	7.1	6.7	6.8	8.5	8.4	6.5	6.5	6.9
Switzerland	4.2	5.8	7.7	6.3	6.5	7.0	9.3	9.2	10.8	12.0	7.7	8.3	12.9	12.9	13.7	14.5	13.4	8.0	9.4	9.8
Turkey	0.1	-0.4	-2.6	2.0	-1.2	-1.0	-1.0	0.9	-0.8	-3.7	1.8	-0.7	-2.7	-4.0	-4.6	-6.0	-5.8	-6.7	-6.1	-5.7
United Kingdom	-1.8	-2.1	-1.9	-1.0	-1.2	-0.8	-0.1	-0.4	-2.4	-2.6	-2.1	-1.7	-1.6	-2.1	-2.6	-3.4	-3.8	-1.9	-1.5	-2.1
United States	0.0	-0.8	-1.3	-1.7	-1.5	-1.6	-1.7	-2.5	-3.3	-4.3	-3.8	-4.4	-4.8	-5.3	-5.9	-6.0	-5.3	-4.9	-3.9	-3.6
Euro area	-1.3	-1.1	0.2	0.1	0.6	1.0	1.4	0.8	0.3	-0.6	0.1	0.6	0.5	1.2	0.5	0.4	0.3	-0.4	-0.1	0.0
Total OECD	-0.3	-0.4	0.0	-0.2	0.1	0.0	0.1	-0.1	-0.7	-1.3	-1.1	-1.1	-1.1	-1.0	-1.4	-1.6	-1.4	-1.5	-1.1	-1.1

1. Including Luxembourg until 1994.
2. Breaks between 1998 and 1999 for Greece and between 1995 and 1996 for Portugal, reflecting change in methodology to the International Monetary Fund, Fifth Balance of Payments Manual (capital transfers from European Union are excluded from the current account).

Source: OECD Economic Outlook 84 database.

StatLink http://dx.doi.org/10.1787/505324652651

Annex Table 52. Structure of current account balances of major world regions
$ billion

	1994	1995	1996	1997	1998	1999	2000	2001	2002	2003	2004	2005	2006	2007	2008	2009	2010
Goods and services trade balance[1]																	
OECD	100	159	124	157	104	-44	-208	-174	-151	-204	-276	-452	-544	-445	-456	-251	-213
Non-OECD of which:	-29	-64	-19	-19	-20	88	212	142	184	270	341	569	761	849	957	593	586
China	7	12	18	41	42	31	29	28	37	36	49	125	209	307	323	354	374
Dynamic Asia[2]	0	-15	-2	4	62	70	62	64	80	99	93	96	137	179	181	284	324
Other Asia	-18	-25	-28	-25	-21	-22	-19	-15	-13	-13	-34	-49	-57	-92	-112	-70	-83
Latin America	-7	-19	-17	-31	-45	-16	-3	-9	22	42	60	76	89	63	35	-3	-14
Africa and Middle-East	-11	-16	8	0	-52	4	96	48	34	74	121	241	288	333	437	-11	-55
Central and Eastern Europe	0	0	3	-7	-7	21	47	26	23	30	52	80	94	59	93	38	40
World[3]	71	95	105	138	83	44	4	-32	33	66	65	117	217	404	501	342	373
Investment income, net																	
OECD	-33	-31	-21	-2	-9	-2	9	24	5	39	118	140	141	106	76	57	18
Non-OECD of which:	-41	-56	-66	-75	-81	-87	-97	-92	-101	-110	-136	-146	-158	-150	-161	-156	-150
China	-1	-12	-12	-16	-17	-14	-15	-19	-15	-8	-4	11	12	26	35	48	62
Dynamic Asia[2]	-2	-2	-6	-4	-4	-11	-13	-7	-12	-7	-16	-22	-18	-14	-10	-3	5
Other Asia	-6	-6	-6	-7	-7	-7	-8	-8	-7	-8	-9	-12	-14	-13	-13	-15	-20
Latin America	-24	-28	-29	-36	-38	-38	-39	-41	-40	-45	-57	-64	-74	-74	-77	-78	-78
Africa and Middle-East	-8	-4	-6	-3	-1	-7	-12	-10	-18	-24	-28	-27	-12	-12	-15	-18	-20
Central and Eastern Europe	..	-4	-7	-11	-14	-10	-11	-7	-10	-18	-22	-33	-52	-63	-83	-91	-100
World[3]	-74	-87	-87	-78	-90	-89	-88	-68	-96	-72	-17	-7	-17	-43	-85	-99	-132
Net transfers, net																	
OECD	-105	-99	-102	-103	-115	-116	-126	-115	-136	-166	-191	-215	-222	-268	-293	-266	-266
Non-OECD of which:	25	29	36	39	37	47	50	60	75	96	112	135	161	194	214	226	235
China	1	1	1	5	4	5	6	8	13	18	23	25	29	39	41	36	37
Dynamic Asia[2]	1	-2	-2	-4	-4	1	1	1	2	3	2	9	10	11	11	11	11
Other Asia	15	16	21	21	19	22	23	27	31	37	38	46	54	71	85	98	105
Latin America	9	11	10	10	11	13	13	16	18	21	24	29	35	38	38	42	42
Africa and Middle-East	-1	-1	4	2	1	0	-1	0	2	6	10	13	15	16	16	16	16
Central and Eastern Europe	..	4	4	4	5	6	8	8	9	12	15	17	20	22	23	25	25
World[3]	-80	-70	-66	-64	-78	-69	-77	-54	-61	-70	-79	-80	-62	-74	-79	-39	-32
Current balance																	
OECD	-34	26	-8	36	-26	-180	-341	-273	-302	-321	-320	-498	-591	-557	-650	-447	-444
Non-OECD of which:	-45	-90	-49	-55	-64	48	165	110	157	255	317	557	763	894	1009	663	670
China	8	2	7	30	29	21	21	17	35	46	69	161	250	372	399	437	472
Dynamic Asia[2]	-2	-20	-10	-4	54	61	50	58	70	96	78	81	129	175	182	292	340
Other Asia	-9	-15	-14	-11	-9	-6	-3	5	10	16	-5	-15	-17	-34	-40	14	2
Latin America	-22	-36	-36	-57	-72	-41	-29	-34	0	18	27	41	50	27	-3	-38	-49
Africa and Middle-East	-21	-21	4	-1	-52	-3	83	38	19	56	103	224	289	336	438	-13	-59
Central and Eastern Europe	..	-1	0	-13	-15	17	42	26	23	24	46	65	63	18	33	-28	-35
World[3]	-80	-65	-57	-20	-91	-132	-176	-163	-144	-70	-3	59	173	336	360	216	226

StatLink http://dx.doi.org/10.1787/505352361230

Note: Historical data for the OECD area are aggregates of reported balance-of-payments data of each individual country. Because of various statistical problems as well as a large number of non-reporters among non-OECD countries, trade and current account balances estimated on the basis of these countries' own balance-of-payments records may differ from corresponding estimates shown in this table.
1. National accounts basis for OECD countries and balance-of-payments basis for the non-OECD regions.
2. Dynamic Asia includes Chinese Taipei; Hong Kong, China; Indonesia; Malaysia; Philippines; Singapore and Thailand.
3. Reflects statistical errors and asymmetries. Given the very large gross flows of world balance-of-payments transactions, statistical errors and asymmetries easily give rise to world totals (balances) that are significantly different from zero.
Source: OECD Economic Outlook 84 database.

OECD ECONOMIC OUTLOOK 84 – ISBN 978-92-64-05469-1 – © OECD 2008

Annex Table 53. Export market growth in goods and services
Percentage changes from previous year

	1991	1992	1993	1994	1995	1996	1997	1998	1999	2000	2001	2002	2003	2004	2005	2006	2007	2008	2009	2010
Australia	4.2	6.2	5.4	11.0	12.8	9.0	6.1	-3.3	8.4	12.4	-0.5	6.3	8.2	13.6	9.4	8.5	6.9	4.9	2.9	6.3
Austria	1.9	-1.2	-0.7	8.1	8.5	5.3	9.5	7.5	6.2	12.3	2.3	2.1	5.7	9.5	7.8	11.1	7.6	5.2	1.9	4.6
Belgium	3.7	2.7	0.0	8.5	8.4	5.4	10.0	8.5	7.2	12.1	1.7	2.0	4.2	8.7	7.4	9.5	5.6	3.6	1.1	4.0
Canada	0.3	6.7	7.6	11.6	8.1	8.8	12.8	10.0	10.6	13.1	-2.1	3.5	4.4	11.4	6.5	6.7	3.1	-0.7	-1.1	2.4
Czech Republic	..	..	..	7.4	8.4	6.2	9.8	9.1	5.9	11.8	2.7	1.7	5.4	8.9	8.0	11.4	7.5	5.3	1.7	4.4
Denmark	1.4	2.1	0.9	9.2	8.4	6.4	10.2	7.8	6.3	11.4	0.9	1.9	4.6	9.2	7.6	9.3	6.6	4.0	1.1	3.9
Finland	-1.4	-6.1	1.9	8.1	8.8	6.1	9.9	5.8	4.4	12.8	2.6	3.9	6.5	11.4	9.1	11.4	9.8	6.4	1.6	5.0
France	3.8	3.2	0.4	7.8	8.3	6.1	9.9	6.9	6.6	11.3	1.3	2.8	4.9	9.6	7.7	9.3	6.0	4.3	1.7	4.4
Germany	0.9	1.8	1.7	8.4	9.0	6.6	10.2	7.2	6.3	12.6	1.6	3.3	4.9	10.2	7.7	9.1	7.0	4.0	1.2	4.2
Greece	3.2	0.6	2.5	6.3	8.6	6.2	10.9	5.8	4.2	11.7	1.0	3.4	5.4	11.1	9.1	9.9	7.6	6.2	2.3	5.0
Hungary	..	..	..	7.5	8.7	5.8	9.2	7.1	5.4	12.4	2.9	2.4	5.8	9.9	8.1	11.2	8.3	5.5	1.6	4.6
Iceland	3.1	2.1	0.2	8.5	8.0	6.5	9.8	8.4	7.4	11.3	2.0	2.5	3.8	8.5	7.2	9.5	4.8	3.2	0.5	3.4
Ireland	2.1	4.3	1.1	8.6	7.7	6.3	9.5	7.5	7.7	11.3	1.1	2.7	3.9	8.7	6.7	8.1	3.9	2.4	0.3	3.4
Italy	2.6	-0.1	1.7	7.7	8.5	6.4	10.1	7.0	6.0	12.4	1.7	3.0	5.4	10.5	8.3	10.0	7.4	5.1	1.7	4.6
Japan	7.2	8.5	8.3	12.0	12.2	7.6	9.4	-1.1	9.9	15.2	-1.9	6.6	8.5	14.4	8.9	9.1	7.3	4.8	3.0	6.3
Korea	4.8	6.6	7.0	10.3	11.7	9.0	9.0	0.3	7.9	14.2	-0.3	6.6	9.7	14.6	9.9	10.0	7.8	5.3	3.9	6.9
Luxembourg	3.7	3.0	-1.8	8.4	7.8	4.5	9.0	8.2	6.4	11.4	1.6	1.1	3.6	7.6	6.6	8.5	5.2	3.3	1.0	3.7
Mexico	0.4	7.2	8.4	11.7	8.6	8.3	13.4	10.7	10.2	12.8	-2.3	2.9	4.2	11.3	6.5	6.5	3.1	-1.0	-1.4	2.1
Netherlands	3.5	2.5	-0.4	8.2	7.9	5.2	9.3	7.7	6.5	11.6	1.5	2.0	4.5	8.7	7.3	9.3	5.8	4.1	1.4	4.0
New Zealand	2.8	6.2	4.8	11.3	10.5	8.2	8.5	1.6	8.1	11.6	-1.4	5.9	7.3	12.9	9.0	8.6	7.0	5.7	2.6	5.5
Norway	1.4	3.6	1.4	8.9	8.0	6.3	10.2	8.2	7.3	11.6	1.3	2.6	3.5	8.5	7.3	9.0	4.3	2.8	0.1	3.2
Poland	..	..	..	7.6	8.5	5.1	9.4	7.6	5.2	12.4	3.3	2.4	5.7	9.7	8.2	11.6	8.6	5.8	1.6	4.6
Portugal	5.1	4.2	-0.8	8.1	8.3	5.9	10.7	9.4	7.5	11.5	2.2	2.3	4.2	8.9	7.7	9.4	5.7	3.5	0.7	3.7
Slovak Republic	..	..	..	8.1	10.1	6.6	9.8	8.7	5.9	13.2	3.5	2.4	6.0	10.7	7.0	11.6	8.9	5.4	1.8	4.2
Spain	3.4	4.1	0.1	8.1	7.9	5.4	10.4	8.8	5.7	11.4	1.6	1.5	3.3	8.5	7.3	9.0	5.8	4.0	1.1	3.7
Sweden	1.6	1.8	2.2	8.7	8.3	6.6	10.3	7.2	5.4	11.4	1.3	3.2	4.2	9.9	8.5	9.6	6.4	4.3	1.3	3.9
Switzerland	4.2	3.4	0.3	8.9	9.0	5.8	9.6	6.6	7.0	11.9	1.0	2.5	5.1	9.7	7.9	9.5	6.1	3.9	1.6	4.4
Turkey	2.1	-3.1	-0.1	6.6	7.7	5.5	9.7	6.3	4.9	11.8	3.1	3.6	5.5	10.4	8.9	10.9	8.2	6.4	2.0	5.0
United Kingdom	3.6	3.2	1.9	9.1	9.1	6.3	10.3	7.5	7.3	12.5	0.6	2.8	4.5	10.2	7.9	8.5	6.3	3.7	1.5	4.2
United States	5.5	6.9	4.7	10.6	7.5	8.4	11.3	3.8	6.6	12.6	-0.8	2.4	4.8	11.0	8.8	9.1	7.2	5.5	1.9	4.4
Total OECD	3.3	3.9	2.9	9.3	8.8	6.9	10.3	5.9	7.1	12.5	0.4	3.2	5.3	10.7	8.0	9.1	6.5	4.1	1.5	4.4
Memorandum items																				
China	4.5	4.9	5.7	10.8	11.5	7.1	8.3	-0.3	8.0	13.6	-2.0	4.3	5.9	12.5	8.2	7.9	5.8	3.7	1.6	4.7
Dynamic Asia[1]	6.2	8.3	7.8	11.7	13.1	8.6	7.9	-2.4	9.4	14.9	-1.1	7.4	10.0	15.0	9.7	9.6	7.5	5.1	3.9	7.1
Other Asia	4.7	5.6	4.6	9.5	10.4	7.3	8.9	2.1	7.5	12.4	-0.4	5.1	6.8	12.5	9.3	9.1	6.4	4.8	2.7	5.6
Latin America	4.3	7.3	6.8	10.8	10.4	7.6	12.6	6.9	4.7	12.0	-0.1	1.1	4.8	11.9	9.0	9.4	7.4	4.6	2.1	4.4
Africa and Middle-East	5.0	4.9	3.0	9.2	11.1	7.9	8.2	0.8	7.8	12.6	-0.3	4.9	6.5	11.8	8.6	8.7	6.5	4.5	2.6	5.6
Central & Eastern Europe	-2.5	-8.4	2.3	6.5	10.1	6.3	10.0	5.1	3.7	14.1	3.0	5.1	8.0	12.4	9.7	12.2	10.9	6.9	2.2	5.7

Note: Regional aggregates are calculated inclusive of intra-regional trade. The calculation of export markets is based on a weighted average of import volumes in each exporting country's market, with weights based on goods and services trade flows in 2000.

1. Dynamic Asia includes Chinese Taipei; Hong Kong, China; Indonesia; Malaysia; Philippines; Singapore and Thailand.

Source: OECD Economic Outlook 84 database.

StatLink http://dx.doi.org/10.1787/505361727201

Annex Table 54. Import penetration
Goods and services import volume as a percentage of total final expenditure, constant prices

	1991	1992	1993	1994	1995	1996	1997	1998	1999	2000	2001	2002	2003	2004	2005	2006	2007	2008	2009	2010
Australia	10.5	11.0	11.1	11.9	12.3	12.7	13.4	13.6	14.1	14.5	13.8	14.5	15.4	16.8	17.5	18.3	19.2	20.6	20.9	21.5
Austria	25.0	25.1	24.9	25.9	26.9	27.7	28.7	29.0	29.4	30.9	31.9	31.4	31.8	33.5	34.4	34.8	35.7	36.0	36.2	36.7
Belgium	38.9	39.5	39.6	40.5	40.8	41.0	41.6	42.9	43.1	44.2	44.1	43.9	44.3	45.1	45.8	45.7	46.1	46.9	47.4	48.0
Canada	22.5	23.1	24.0	24.6	25.1	25.8	27.6	27.8	28.2	28.8	27.3	27.1	27.5	28.5	29.4	29.7	30.3	30.6	30.1	29.9
Czech Republic	..	..	27.7	28.6	31.3	32.8	34.3	36.3	37.0	40.0	42.3	43.0	44.1	47.3	47.0	49.0	50.8	51.5	51.4	51.4
Denmark	23.1	22.8	22.6	23.8	24.5	24.6	25.7	26.9	27.0	28.8	29.1	30.5	30.1	31.2	33.0	35.2	35.7	36.6	36.8	37.2
Finland	18.6	19.3	19.7	21.2	21.5	22.2	23.0	23.3	23.1	25.4	25.5	25.9	26.1	26.6	28.4	28.9	29.2	29.2	29.5	30.2
France	16.1	16.2	15.9	16.7	17.4	17.5	18.3	19.5	19.9	21.7	21.8	21.8	21.9	22.6	23.3	24.1	24.7	24.9	24.9	25.2
Germany	18.9	18.9	18.3	19.1	19.9	20.3	21.3	22.5	23.6	24.8	24.9	24.6	25.6	26.7	27.8	29.6	30.1	31.0	31.8	32.5
Greece	18.9	18.9	19.3	19.2	20.3	21.0	22.7	23.7	25.8	27.7	25.7	24.9	25.6	26.7	26.0	26.8	27.4	26.1	26.5	26.9
Hungary	..	..	25.3	26.5	29.4	30.8	34.3	38.0	39.9	43.1	43.4	44.0	45.3	47.5	48.3	51.2	54.4	56.3	57.8	58.7
Iceland	24.4	23.9	22.3	22.3	22.9	24.8	25.3	28.1	28.2	29.0	26.3	25.8	27.4	28.6	32.5	33.8	32.4	30.2	29.6	29.5
Ireland	29.3	29.9	30.8	32.5	33.7	34.4	35.4	39.0	39.1	41.5	41.8	40.6	39.2	40.3	40.9	41.0	40.6	40.8	41.1	40.6
Italy	16.4	17.3	15.6	16.5	17.4	17.1	18.1	19.2	19.7	20.8	20.7	20.7	20.9	21.2	21.6	22.3	22.7	22.6	22.6	22.9
Japan	6.7	6.6	6.5	7.0	7.7	8.4	8.3	8.0	8.2	8.7	8.7	8.8	9.0	9.4	9.7	9.9	9.8	9.9	10.0	10.2
Korea	20.8	20.7	20.7	22.6	24.8	26.0	25.8	22.6	25.4	27.4	25.8	27.2	28.6	30.3	30.9	32.1	33.6	34.1	34.1	35.0
Luxembourg	..	..	..	..	50.5	51.4	53.1	54.4	55.8	56.3	57.2	56.4	57.7	59.3	59.7	61.3	60.9	59.8	60.1	60.6
Mexico	10.7	12.2	12.2	13.9	12.7	14.5	16.3	17.9	19.3	21.4	21.2	21.3	21.1	22.2	23.1	24.4	25.1	26.1	26.2	26.4
Netherlands	30.7	30.9	30.8	32.0	33.4	33.8	35.3	36.4	37.4	39.2	39.3	39.4	39.8	40.6	41.4	42.6	43.2	43.9	44.4	45.3
New Zealand	18.8	20.3	20.2	21.2	21.9	22.6	22.4	22.6	23.8	23.0	23.0	23.8	24.5	26.6	27.1	26.0	27.2	28.6	27.6	28.1
Norway	18.4	18.1	18.4	18.5	18.7	19.2	20.2	21.1	20.5	20.3	20.3	20.2	20.3	21.0	22.0	22.9	23.8	24.3	24.2	24.0
Poland	..	..	14.2	15.0	16.9	19.5	21.6	23.7	23.2	25.1	23.9	24.1	25.1	26.9	27.1	29.1	30.4	30.6	30.8	30.5
Portugal	21.5	23.1	22.9	24.2	24.8	25.0	26.0	27.7	28.6	28.9	28.7	28.4	28.4	29.4	29.9	30.7	31.4	31.8	31.7	31.9
Slovak Republic	..	..	35.5	33.2	34.3	36.5	37.5	40.5	40.6	42.2	44.5	44.4	45.0	45.8	48.0	50.2	50.1	51.0	50.4	50.8
Spain	15.6	16.4	15.7	16.9	18.0	19.0	20.3	21.9	23.3	24.3	24.5	24.7	25.3	26.4	27.2	28.5	29.0	28.9	28.8	29.2
Sweden	21.3	21.9	21.9	23.3	23.8	24.2	25.9	27.3	27.4	28.7	28.1	27.4	27.8	28.4	28.9	29.8	31.2	31.7	31.7	31.9
Switzerland	23.3	22.7	22.7	23.8	24.4	25.1	26.2	27.1	27.6	28.9	29.1	28.8	29.1	30.1	31.0	31.6	32.1	32.3	32.9	33.4
Turkey	11.0	11.5	13.8	11.8	13.9	15.2	16.9	16.8	16.7	18.7	15.4	17.2	19.7	21.3	21.9	22.0	23.0	23.1	23.5	24.3
United Kingdom	15.4	16.2	16.4	16.6	17.0	17.9	18.8	19.6	20.3	21.0	21.4	21.9	21.7	22.4	23.3	24.4	23.5	23.4	23.0	23.0
United States	7.9	8.1	8.5	9.1	9.6	10.0	10.7	11.4	12.1	13.1	12.7	12.9	13.0	13.9	14.2	14.6	14.6	14.2	14.0	14.0
Total OECD	12.9	13.1	13.2	14.0	14.6	15.2	16.0	16.7	17.4	18.5	18.4	18.5	18.8	19.7	20.3	21.1	21.4	21.6	21.6	21.9

Note: Regional aggregate is calculated inclusive of intra-regional trade as the sum of import volumes expressed in 2000 $ divided by the sum of total final expenditure expressed in 2000 $.
Source: OECD Economic Outlook 84 database.

StatLink ᵃᵖˢ http://dx.doi.org/10.1787/505405754773

Annex Table 55. **Quarterly demand and output projections**

Percentage changes from previous period, seasonally adjusted at annual rates, volume

	2008	2009	2010	2008 Q4	2009 Q1	Q2	Q3	2010 Q4	Q1	Q2	Q3	Q4	Fourth quarter[1] 2008	2009	2010
Private consumption															
Canada	3.4	-0.6	1.8	-3.5	-1.2	-0.2	0.5	1.5	2.0	2.5	2.7	3.0	0.7	0.1	2.6
France	0.9	0.3	1.8	0.0	0.2	0.4	0.6	1.0	1.8	2.4	3.0	3.5	0.0	0.6	2.7
Germany	-0.6	0.2	1.2	0.1	0.2	0.4	0.6	0.9	1.2	1.6	1.8	2.2	-0.9	0.5	1.7
Italy	-0.5	-0.3	0.8	0.0	-0.2	-0.3	0.0	0.4	0.7	1.2	1.6	1.9	-0.6	0.0	1.3
Japan	0.7	0.6	0.7	0.2	2.2	1.6	-1.2	-0.2	1.3	1.3	1.3	1.3	0.4	0.6	1.3
United Kingdom	1.8	-1.0	0.7	-1.8	-0.9	-0.9	-0.7	-0.4	1.2	1.6	1.6	2.0	0.0	-0.7	1.6
United States	0.4	-1.2	1.2	-2.8	-1.5	-0.5	0.8	1.1	1.2	1.6	1.8	2.0	-1.0	0.0	1.6
Euro area	0.4	0.2	1.2	0.1	0.1	0.2	0.4	0.7	1.1	1.5	1.9	2.3	-0.1	0.4	1.7
Total OECD	1.0	-0.2	1.3	-1.0	-0.2	0.2	0.5	0.9	1.4	1.8	2.0	2.2	-0.1	0.3	1.9
Public consumption															
Canada	4.3	2.4	2.0	2.0	2.0	2.0	2.0	2.0	2.0	2.0	2.0	2.0	3.3	2.0	2.0
France	1.4	0.8	0.7	1.0	0.4	0.2	0.4	0.4	0.8	0.8	1.2	1.2	1.5	0.4	1.0
Germany	1.9	1.0	1.3	0.5	0.4	1.2	1.4	1.4	1.2	1.2	1.2	1.2	2.0	1.1	1.2
Italy	1.2	0.2	0.1	1.0	-0.2	-0.7	-0.3	0.0	0.2	0.2	0.2	0.2	1.3	-0.3	0.2
Japan	0.3	1.4	1.7	1.2	1.3	2.3	2.2	2.2	1.3	1.4	1.4	1.4	-0.2	2.0	1.4
United Kingdom	2.3	2.3	2.2	2.6	2.6	1.8	1.6	1.8	2.3	2.4	2.4	2.8	2.8	2.0	2.5
United States	2.8	2.3	1.4	2.3	1.8	1.8	1.3	1.3	1.5	1.3	1.6	1.8	3.4	1.5	1.5
Euro area	1.8	1.2	1.2	1.4	0.8	0.9	1.0	1.1	1.2	1.2	1.3	1.3	1.9	0.9	1.3
Total OECD	2.3	2.1	1.5	2.4	1.7	1.7	1.5	1.5	1.5	1.5	1.6	1.8	2.7	1.6	1.6
Business investment															
Canada	1.8	-3.8	1.3	-8.0	-5.0	-5.0	-2.0	1.0	2.0	3.0	3.5	4.0	-1.4	-2.8	3.1
France	2.0	-3.9	3.0	-9.3	-7.0	-2.0	0.0	1.6	3.6	4.5	5.7	5.7	-1.6	-1.9	4.9
Germany	4.4	-4.3	1.0	-6.1	-7.3	-5.8	-1.4	0.6	1.7	2.3	2.8	4.2	-0.2	-3.5	2.8
Italy	-2.3	-5.9	2.6	-10.1	-6.2	-3.9	-3.2	1.7	2.0	5.1	7.8	8.8	-5.7	-3.0	5.9
Japan	-0.6	-1.2	2.6	-1.8	-1.9	0.0	1.8	2.7	2.7	3.2	3.2	3.2	-2.2	0.6	3.1
United Kingdom	-2.2	-8.8	0.4	-15.1	-9.6	-6.8	-3.9	0.0	1.0	2.8	3.2	3.6	-9.5	-5.2	2.7
United States	2.4	-7.6	1.7	-13.1	-11.3	-8.0	-4.7	-1.5	2.5	5.1	8.4	9.1	-2.5	-6.4	6.3
Euro area	1.4	-4.3	1.5	-7.0	-6.2	-3.6	-1.4	0.6	1.8	3.1	4.2	5.0	-2.4	-2.7	3.5
Total OECD	1.5	-5.2	1.7	-9.0	-7.6	-5.1	-2.5	0.0	2.2	3.8	5.6	6.1	-2.5	-3.8	4.4
Total investment															
Canada	1.0	-2.8	1.3	-5.9	-3.6	-3.5	-1.0	1.0	1.8	2.5	2.9	3.4	-1.8	-1.8	2.7
France	0.3	-3.6	2.1	-7.4	-5.6	-2.1	0.2	1.3	2.6	3.2	4.0	4.0	-3.0	-1.6	3.4
Germany	3.6	-2.8	1.2	-3.7	-4.4	-3.2	-0.4	1.0	1.5	2.0	2.3	3.3	0.6	-1.7	2.3
Italy	-1.4	-4.6	2.1	-7.8	-5.0	-3.0	-2.5	1.4	1.6	4.1	6.1	7.0	-4.2	-2.3	4.7
Japan	-2.4	-0.1	1.4	0.9	1.0	0.4	0.0	1.2	1.4	2.0	2.1	2.1	-1.3	0.6	1.9
United Kingdom	-5.3	-9.0	0.5	-14.1	-8.5	-5.5	-3.7	0.6	1.1	2.2	2.7	3.2	-12.1	-4.4	2.3
United States	-3.1	-7.3	1.4	-12.7	-10.4	-7.3	-3.5	-0.7	2.0	3.9	6.7	7.2	-5.3	-5.5	4.9
Euro area	0.4	-4.4	1.0	-6.6	-5.8	-3.5	-1.5	0.2	1.2	2.3	3.2	3.8	-2.9	-2.7	2.6
Total OECD	-0.9	-4.3	1.5	-7.1	-6.0	-4.0	-1.8	0.3	1.9	3.1	4.5	4.9	-3.2	-2.9	3.6

Note: The adoption of new national account systems, SNA93 or ESA95, has been proceeding at an uneven pace among OECD member countries, both with respect to variables and the time period covered. As a consequence, there are breaks in many national series. Moreover, some countries are using chain-weighted price indices to calculate real GDP and expenditures components. See Table "National Account Reporting Systems and Base-years" at the beginning of the Statistical Annex and *OECD Economic Outlook* Sources and Methods *(http://www.oecd.org/eco/sources-and-methods)*.

1. Year-on -year growth rates in per cent.
Source: OECD Economic Outlook 84 database.

StatLink http://dx.doi.org/10.1787/505420435326

Annex Table 55. **Quarterly demand and output projections** *(cont'd)*
Percentage changes from previous period, seasonally adjusted at annual rates, volume

	2008	2009	2010	2008 Q4	2009 Q1	Q2	Q3	Q4	2010 Q1	Q2	Q3	Q4	Fourth quarter[1] 2008	2009	2010
Total domestic demand															
Canada	2.7	-0.4	1.8	-3.4	-1.1	-0.5	0.5	1.5	2.0	2.4	2.6	2.9	0.0	0.1	2.5
France	0.9	-0.4	1.6	-1.5	-1.2	-0.2	0.5	0.9	1.7	2.2	2.8	3.1	0.0	0.0	2.4
Germany	1.7	0.1	1.2	-1.2	-0.9	-0.2	0.6	1.0	1.2	1.6	1.8	2.2	1.9	0.1	1.7
Italy	-0.8	-1.1	0.9	-1.4	-1.2	-0.9	-0.6	0.5	0.8	1.5	2.2	2.5	-1.2	-0.5	1.8
Japan	-0.3	0.6	1.0	0.6	1.7	1.4	-0.3	0.5	1.3	1.5	1.5	1.5	-0.3	0.9	1.4
United Kingdom	0.5	-1.6	1.0	-3.0	-1.4	-1.1	-0.7	0.2	1.4	1.8	1.9	2.4	-1.7	-0.7	1.9
United States	-0.1	-1.6	1.3	-3.4	-2.5	-1.2	0.2	0.9	1.4	1.9	2.5	2.8	-1.2	-0.7	2.2
Euro area	0.8	-0.5	1.1	-1.4	-1.2	-0.5	0.1	0.7	1.2	1.6	2.0	2.4	0.2	-0.2	1.8
Total OECD	0.8	-0.6	1.4	-1.6	-1.0	-0.3	0.3	0.9	1.5	1.9	2.4	2.6	-0.2	0.0	2.1
Export of goods and services															
Canada	-4.3	-2.9	2.0	-4.0	-4.0	-1.5	0.0	1.0	2.0	3.0	4.0	5.0	-4.5	-1.1	3.5
France	2.2	-0.2	2.7	-0.2	-0.4	0.4	1.2	2.0	2.8	3.2	4.1	4.5	0.9	0.8	3.6
Germany	4.2	0.7	3.9	-0.2	0.8	1.0	1.5	2.6	4.5	5.2	5.8	6.2	1.9	1.5	5.4
Italy	0.4	-0.6	2.0	-0.3	-0.5	-1.1	-0.8	1.8	2.0	3.4	3.6	3.6	0.5	-0.2	3.2
Japan	5.3	-2.9	0.7	-8.6	-3.0	-1.9	-1.0	-0.4	0.4	1.9	2.7	3.3	-0.2	-1.6	2.1
United Kingdom	1.2	-1.8	0.7	-1.6	-3.2	-2.4	-1.6	0.0	0.0	1.6	3.6	4.5	0.2	-1.8	2.4
United States	8.5	2.8	3.8	2.0	1.0	1.5	2.0	3.0	4.0	4.5	5.5	5.5	6.3	1.9	4.9
Total OECD[2]	5.4	1.0	3.4	-0.3	0.1	0.7	1.3	2.4	3.6	4.3	5.2	5.5	3.1	1.1	4.7
Import of goods and services															
Canada	1.9	-2.6	0.9	-9.0	-3.0	-2.0	-1.0	0.0	1.0	2.0	2.8	3.0	-3.6	-1.5	2.2
France	1.9	-0.4	2.9	-1.4	-1.4	0.0	0.8	2.4	3.2	3.6	4.5	4.9	1.2	0.4	4.1
Germany	5.4	2.8	4.4	-0.6	0.7	1.8	2.5	3.4	4.7	5.4	6.2	6.7	6.2	2.1	5.7
Italy	-1.3	-0.7	2.5	-1.2	-1.2	-1.1	-0.6	1.8	2.6	4.1	4.9	5.0	-1.1	-0.3	4.1
Japan	0.9	1.2	3.5	-0.5	2.4	2.7	-1.2	1.3	4.2	5.4	5.9	6.5	0.3	1.3	5.5
United Kingdom	0.2	-3.4	1.1	-4.7	-3.9	-2.8	-2.4	-0.4	1.6	3.0	3.4	3.4	-3.2	-2.4	2.9
United States	-2.3	-2.1	1.6	-2.5	-2.5	-1.5	-0.5	0.5	1.5	3.0	4.0	4.5	-3.1	-1.0	3.2
Total OECD[2]	1.2	-0.2	2.9	-1.1	-0.8	0.0	0.2	1.5	3.1	4.2	5.0	5.5	-0.2	0.2	4.5
GDP															
Canada	0.5	-0.5	2.1	-1.6	-1.4	-0.3	0.8	1.9	2.3	2.7	3.0	3.6	-0.5	0.2	2.9
France	0.9	-0.4	1.5	-1.2	-0.9	-0.1	0.6	0.8	1.6	2.0	2.6	2.9	-0.1	0.1	2.3
Germany	1.4	-0.8	1.2	-1.0	-0.7	-0.4	0.2	0.8	1.4	1.7	1.9	2.3	0.2	-0.1	1.8
Italy	-0.4	-1.0	0.8	-1.2	-1.0	-0.9	-0.6	0.5	0.6	1.4	1.9	2.1	-0.7	-0.5	1.5
Japan	0.5	-0.1	0.6	-1.0	0.8	0.6	-0.3	0.2	0.7	0.9	1.0	1.0	-0.4	0.3	0.9
United Kingdom	0.8	-1.1	0.9	-2.1	-1.1	-0.9	-0.4	0.3	1.0	1.4	1.9	2.6	-0.7	-0.5	1.7
United States	1.4	-0.9	1.6	-2.8	-2.0	-0.8	0.6	1.2	1.7	2.1	2.7	2.9	0.1	-0.3	2.3
Euro area	1.0	-0.6	1.2	-1.0	-0.8	-0.4	0.1	0.7	1.3	1.7	2.2	2.5	0.0	-0.1	1.9
Total OECD	1.4	-0.4	1.5	-1.4	-0.8	-0.2	0.5	1.1	1.7	2.0	2.5	2.7	0.2	0.2	2.2

Note: The adoption of new national account systems, SNA93 or ESA95, has been proceeding at an uneven pace among OECD member countries, both with respect to variables and the time period covered. As a consequence, there are breaks in many national series. Moreover, some countries are using chain-weighted price indices to calculate real GDP and expenditures components. See Table "National Account Reporting Systems and Base-years" at the beginning of the Statistical Annex and *OECD Economic Outlook* Sources and Methods *(http://www.oecd.org/eco/sources-and-methods).*

1. Year-on -year growth rates in per cent.
2. Includes intra-regional trade.

Source: OECD Economic Outlook 84 database.

StatLink ᵃⁱˢᴾ *http://dx.doi.org/10.1787/505420435326*

Annex Table 56. **Quarterly price, cost and unemployment projections**

Percentage changes from previous period, seasonally adjusted at annual rates, volume

	2008	2009	2010	2008 Q4	2009 Q1	Q2	Q3	2010 Q4	Q1	Q2	Q3	Q4	Fourth quarter[1] 2008	2009	2010
Consumer price index[2]															
Canada	2.6	1.2	1.0	-3.0	1.3	1.4	1.2	1.1	1.0	0.9	0.9	1.0	2.7	1.2	0.9
France	3.3	1.0	0.8	0.0	0.8	1.0	0.9	0.8	0.8	0.7	0.6	0.6	2.5	0.9	0.7
Germany	2.9	1.1	1.3	-0.2	0.7	1.0	1.3	1.4	1.3	1.3	1.3	1.3	2.1	1.1	1.3
Italy	3.5	1.5	1.5	0.0	1.2	1.6	1.7	1.6	1.5	1.5	1.4	1.4	2.9	1.5	1.4
Japan	1.4	0.3	-0.1	-0.5	-0.3	-0.2	-0.1	-0.1	-0.1	-0.1	-0.1	-0.1	1.4	-0.2	-0.1
United Kingdom	3.7	2.7	1.9	1.6	2.2	2.0	2.0	2.0	2.0	1.8	1.7	1.6	4.2	2.1	1.8
United States	4.3	1.6	1.5	-1.7	0.8	1.6	1.5	1.5	1.4	1.4	1.4	1.4	3.6	1.3	1.4
Euro area	3.4	1.4	1.3	0.1	1.1	1.3	1.4	1.4	1.3	1.3	1.2	1.2	2.7	1.3	1.3
GDP deflator															
Canada	3.3	-1.0	1.0	-9.6	0.4	0.7	0.6	0.7	1.2	1.1	1.3	1.3	1.0	0.6	1.2
France	2.3	1.7	1.1	2.0	1.7	1.7	1.3	1.3	1.1	1.0	0.9	0.9	2.1	1.5	1.0
Germany	1.6	1.8	1.4	2.7	1.2	1.2	1.4	1.3	1.4	1.4	1.3	1.3	2.3	1.3	1.4
Italy	3.9	2.5	1.3	3.3	0.8	1.2	1.2	1.4	1.3	1.3	1.3	1.3	5.2	1.1	1.3
Japan	-1.0	1.3	-0.3	9.4	0.3	-0.4	-0.3	-0.3	-0.3	-0.3	-0.3	-0.3	1.0	-0.2	-0.3
United Kingdom	3.3	2.5	1.5	2.9	2.1	2.0	1.9	1.6	1.4	1.2	1.2	1.4	3.7	1.9	1.3
United States	2.2	1.8	1.5	1.2	1.5	1.7	1.6	1.6	1.5	1.5	1.4	1.4	2.3	1.6	1.5
Euro area	2.4	2.0	1.3	2.4	1.6	1.7	1.5	1.4	1.3	1.3	1.2	1.2	2.8	1.6	1.2
Total OECD	2.6	2.1	1.5	2.6	1.7	1.7	1.6	1.5	1.5	1.4	1.3	1.3	2.9	1.6	1.4
Unit labour cost (total economy)															
Canada	3.9	1.6	0.3	1.6	1.9	1.6	0.6	-0.2	0.3	0.0	0.5	1.2	3.5	1.0	0.5
France	2.5	2.0	0.8	3.3	2.0	1.1	0.9	1.1	0.9	0.7	0.3	0.4	2.9	1.3	0.6
Germany	2.4	2.6	0.4	4.1	1.4	1.0	0.4	0.1	0.5	0.5	0.6	0.2	4.2	0.7	0.4
Italy	5.6	2.7	1.1	3.9	1.9	1.6	2.0	1.1	1.3	0.8	0.9	0.0	4.7	1.6	0.7
Japan	0.8	0.0	-0.5	0.3	-0.8	-0.7	0.1	-0.2	-0.5	-0.6	-0.7	-0.8	1.5	-0.4	-0.7
United Kingdom	2.8	2.7	-0.8	4.0	2.5	1.7	0.8	-0.5	-2.0	-1.4	-0.7	-1.2	4.4	1.1	-1.3
United States	2.2	3.4	1.4	4.9	4.5	3.0	1.7	1.4	1.4	1.1	0.8	0.8	2.8	2.7	1.0
Euro area	3.4	2.7	1.1	3.7	2.4	1.9	1.6	1.2	1.1	0.8	0.7	0.4	3.7	1.8	0.7
Total OECD	3.0	2.8	1.1	4.0	2.8	2.1	1.5	1.2	1.1	0.9	0.8	0.6	3.5	1.9	0.8
Unemployment						Per cent of labour force									
Canada	6.1	7.0	7.5	6.4	6.7	6.9	7.1	7.3	7.4	7.5	7.5	7.4			
France	7.3	8.2	8.7	7.6	7.8	8.2	8.4	8.6	8.7	8.8	8.8	8.6			
Germany	7.4	8.1	8.6	7.4	7.7	8.0	8.2	8.4	8.5	8.6	8.6	8.6			
Italy	6.9	7.8	8.0	7.2	7.5	7.7	8.0	8.2	8.2	8.1	8.0	7.8			
Japan	4.1	4.4	4.4	4.3	4.4	4.4	4.4	4.4	4.4	4.4	4.4	4.4			
United Kingdom	5.5	6.8	8.2	6.0	6.4	6.7	7.0	7.3	7.9	8.2	8.3	8.3			
United States	5.7	7.3	7.5	6.5	6.9	7.2	7.4	7.5	7.6	7.6	7.5	7.4			
Euro area	7.4	8.6	9.0	7.8	8.2	8.5	8.8	9.0	9.1	9.1	9.0	9.0			
Total OECD	5.9	6.9	7.2	6.3	6.6	6.9	7.1	7.2	7.3	7.3	7.2	7.2			

Note: The adoption of new national account systems, SNA93 or ESA95, has been proceeding at an uneven pace among OECD member countries, both with respect to variables and the time period covered. As a consequence, there are breaks in many national series. Moreover, some countries are using chain-weighted price indices to calculate real GDP and expenditures components. See Table "National Account Reporting Systems and Base-years" at the beginning of the Statistical Annex and *OECD Economic Outlook* Sources and Methods *(http://www.oecd.org/eco/sources-and-methods).*

1. Year-on-year growth rates in per cent.
2. For the United Kingdom, the euro area countries and the euro area aggregate, the Harmonised Index of Consumer Prices (HICP) is used.

Source: OECD Economic Outlook 84 database.

StatLink ⬛🔗 http://dx.doi.org/10.1787/505456246623

Annex Table 57. **Contributions to changes in real GDP in OECD countries**

	2007	2008	2009	2010		2007	2008	2009	2010
Australia					**Germany**				
Final domestic demand	5.5	4.1	2.0	2.9	Final domestic demand	1.0	0.7	-0.3	1.2
Stockbuilding	0.7	-0.1	-0.1	0.0	Stockbuilding	0.1	0.9	0.4	0.0
Net exports	-1.9	-1.7	-0.2	-0.2	Net exports	1.4	-0.2	-0.9	0.0
GDP	4.4	2.5	1.7	2.7	GDP	2.6	1.4	-0.8	1.2
Austria					**Greece**				
Final domestic demand	1.7	1.2	-0.4	1.0	Final domestic demand	5.1	2.1	2.2	2.8
Stockbuilding	-0.2	-0.1	0.0	0.0	Stockbuilding	0.1	-0.3	0.4	0.0
Net exports	1.1	0.6	0.3	0.2	Net exports	-1.3	1.9	-0.7	-0.3
GDP	3.0	1.9	-0.1	1.2	GDP	4.0	3.2	1.9	2.5
Belgium					**Hungary**				
Final domestic demand	2.8	2.1	0.7	1.7	Final domestic demand	-1.1	0.3	-0.3	0.6
Stockbuilding	0.1	0.6	0.0	0.0	Stockbuilding	0.1	0.6	0.1	0.0
Net exports	-0.3	-1.4	-0.8	-0.5	Net exports	2.1	0.3	-0.3	0.5
GDP	2.6	1.5	-0.1	1.3	GDP	1.1	1.4	-0.5	1.0
Canada					**Iceland**				
Final domestic demand	4.3	3.1	-0.5	1.9	Final domestic demand	-1.0	-7.8	-16.6	-3.1
Stockbuilding	0.2	-0.3	0.1	0.0	Stockbuilding	-0.6	-0.2	0.3	0.0
Net exports	-1.5	-2.1	-0.1	0.4	Net exports	6.5	7.6	7.1	2.5
GDP	2.7	0.5	-0.5	2.1	GDP	4.9	1.5	-9.3	-0.7
Czech Republic					**Ireland**				
Final domestic demand	4.5	2.9	3.1	3.5	Final domestic demand	4.1	-5.5	-4.0	0.7
Stockbuilding	1.1	-1.4	-0.4	0.0	Stockbuilding	-0.8	0.7	0.1	0.0
Net exports	1.1	3.0	-0.2	0.9	Net exports	2.6	2.5	1.9	1.9
GDP	6.6	4.4	2.5	4.4	GDP	6.0	-1.8	-1.7	2.6
Denmark					**Italy**				
Final domestic demand	2.9	1.1	-0.5	0.2	Final domestic demand	1.3	-0.4	-1.1	0.9
Stockbuilding	-0.3	-0.3	-0.2	0.0	Stockbuilding	0.0	-0.5	0.0	0.0
Net exports	-0.9	-0.7	0.1	0.7	Net exports	0.1	0.5	0.0	-0.1
GDP	1.7	0.2	-0.5	0.9	GDP	1.4	-0.4	-1.0	0.8
Finland					**Japan**				
Final domestic demand	3.4	1.9	0.9	1.4	Final domestic demand	0.8	-0.1	0.6	1.0
Stockbuilding	0.3	-1.4	-0.1	0.0	Stockbuilding	0.1	-0.2	0.0	0.0
Net exports	1.4	1.8	0.0	0.5	Net exports	1.1	0.8	-0.7	-0.4
GDP	4.4	2.1	0.6	1.8	GDP	2.1	0.5	-0.1	0.6
France					**Korea**				
Final domestic demand	2.7	0.9	-0.4	1.6	Final domestic demand	4.1	1.5	0.0	0.9
Stockbuilding	0.2	0.0	0.0	0.0	Stockbuilding	-0.4	0.5	0.0	0.0
Net exports	-0.8	0.1	0.1	-0.1	Net exports	1.3	2.1	2.7	3.2
GDP	2.1	0.9	-0.4	1.5	GDP	5.0	4.2	2.7	4.2

Note: The adoption of new national account systems, SNA93 or ESA95, has been proceeding at an uneven pace among OECD member countries, both with respect to variables and the time period covered. As a consequence, there are breaks in many national series. Moreover, some countries are using chain-weighted price indices to calculate real GDP and expenditures components. See Table "National Account Reporting Systems and Base-years" at the beginning of the Statistical Annex and *OECD Economic Outlook* Sources and Methods *(http://www.oecd.org/eco/sources-and-methods)*. Totals may not add up due to rounding and/or statistical discrepancy.

1. Chain-linked calculations for stockbuilding and net exports except Australia, Finland, Greece and Korea.

Source: OECD Economic Outlook 84 database.

StatLink ⧉ http://dx.doi.org/10.1787/505480038832

Annex Table 57. **Contributions to changes in real GDP in OECD countries** *(cont'd)*

	2007	2008	2009	2010		2007	2008	2009	2010
Luxembourg					**Spain**				
Final domestic demand	3.2	0.4	1.0	1.4	Final domestic demand	4.6	0.7	-2.4	0.0
Stockbuilding	-0.4	-1.6	-0.7	0.0	Stockbuilding	-0.1	0.0	-0.1	0.0
Net exports	2.7	5.3	-0.5	0.5	Net exports	-0.8	0.6	1.5	0.7
GDP	5.2	2.4	-0.5	1.9	GDP	3.7	1.3	-0.9	0.8
Mexico					**Sweden**				
Final domestic demand	4.2	3.4	1.9	2.4	Final domestic demand	3.0	1.6	0.1	1.6
Stockbuilding	-0.6	-0.4	-0.2	0.0	Stockbuilding	0.7	0.3	0.2	0.0
Net exports	-0.4	-1.1	-1.3	-0.6	Net exports	-1.1	-0.2	0.0	0.5
GDP	3.2	1.9	0.4	1.8	GDP	2.9	0.8	0.0	2.2
Netherlands					**Switzerland**				
Final domestic demand	2.7	2.3	0.2	0.9	Final domestic demand	1.7	1.4	0.2	1.4
Stockbuilding	-0.2	0.3	0.0	0.0	Stockbuilding	-0.7	-1.2	-0.1	0.0
Net exports	1.0	-0.4	-0.2	-0.1	Net exports	2.3	1.7	-0.2	0.2
GDP	3.5	2.2	-0.2	0.8	GDP	3.3	1.9	-0.2	1.6
New Zealand					**Turkey**				
Final domestic demand	4.3	0.6	-2.7	2.0	Final domestic demand	4.9	3.5	1.7	4.6
Stockbuilding	0.2	0.3	0.0	0.0	Stockbuilding	0.9	-0.1	0.1	0.0
Net exports	-1.7	-1.7	2.1	0.0	Net exports	-1.3	0.1	-0.2	-0.3
GDP	3.0	-0.5	-0.4	1.9	GDP	4.6	3.3	1.6	4.2
Norway					**United Kingdom**				
Final domestic demand	5.3	2.5	1.0	1.6	Final domestic demand	3.5	0.7	-1.7	1.0
Stockbuilding	-0.3	1.1	0.3	0.0	Stockbuilding	0.2	-0.2	0.1	0.0
Net exports	-1.2	-0.9	0.1	0.0	Net exports	-0.7	0.3	0.6	-0.1
GDP	3.7	2.7	1.3	1.6	GDP	3.0	0.8	-1.1	0.9
Poland					**United States**				
Final domestic demand	7.3	6.0	3.7	3.7	Final domestic demand	1.8	0.2	-1.7	1.3
Stockbuilding	1.6	-0.1	-0.1	0.0	Stockbuilding	-0.4	-0.3	0.0	0.0
Net exports	-2.0	-0.3	-1.0	-0.1	Net exports	0.6	1.4	0.8	0.2
GDP	6.7	5.4	3.0	3.5	GDP	2.0	1.4	-0.9	1.6
Portugal					**Euro area**				
Final domestic demand	1.8	0.9	-0.4	0.6	Final domestic demand	2.3	0.7	-0.6	1.1
Stockbuilding	0.0	0.0	0.0	0.0	Stockbuilding	0.0	0.2	0.1	0.0
Net exports	0.1	-0.4	0.2	0.0	Net exports	0.3	0.2	0.0	0.1
GDP	1.9	0.5	-0.2	0.6	GDP	2.6	1.0	-0.6	1.2
Slovak Republic					**Total OECD**				
Final domestic demand	6.1	6.0	3.6	4.8	Final domestic demand	2.4	0.9	-0.6	1.4
Stockbuilding	-0.1	0.4	-0.1	0.0	Stockbuilding	-0.1	-0.1	0.0	0.0
Net exports	4.3	-1.5	0.0	0.7	Net exports	0.3	0.6	0.2	0.1
GDP	10.4	7.3	4.0	5.6	GDP	2.6	1.4	-0.4	1.5

Note: The adoption of new national account systems, SNA93 or ESA95, has been proceeding at an uneven pace among OECD member countries, both with respect to variables and the time period covered. As a consequence, there are breaks in many national series. Moreover, some countries are using chain-weighted price indices to calculate real GDP and expenditures components. See Table "National Account Reporting Systems and Base-years" at the beginning of the Statistical Annex and *OECD Economic Outlook* Sources and Methods *(http://www.oecd.org/eco/sources-and-methods)*.
Totals may not add up due to rounding and/or statistical discrepancy.

1. Chain-linked calculations for stockbuilding and net exports except Mexico, Portugal and the euro area.
Source: OECD Economic Outlook 84 database.

StatLink 🔗 http://dx.doi.org/10.1787/505480038832

Annex Table 58. **Household wealth and indebtedness**[1]

	1996	1997	1998	1999	2000	2001	2002	2003	2004	2005	2006	2007
Canada												
Net wealth	493.3	501.2	498.4	507.0	502.2	503.2	512.7	516.1	518.1	534.6	546.7	549.2
Net financial wealth	232.4	237.3	233.7	239.1	240.1	235.5	231.4	224.0	214.6	217.6	219.0	212.4
Non-financial assets	260.9	263.9	264.7	267.9	262.0	267.7	281.3	292.1	303.5	317.0	327.7	336.7
Financial assets	339.3	346.9	345.6	353.2	352.7	349.6	348.5	344.7	338.9	347.3	352.0	351.2
of which: Equities	66.8	74.1	79.5	81.1	84.3	84.2	83.6	81.0	79.4	84.6	91.6	91.9
Liabilities	106.8	109.6	112.0	114.1	112.6	114.1	117.1	120.6	124.3	129.7	133.0	138.7
of which: Mortgages	70.8	71.6	71.8	71.8	69.6	69.6	71.2	73.2	75.9	79.6	82.2	86.5
France												
Net wealth	478.9	487.3	494.9	545.8	552.5	552.3	571.4	621.1	682.0	748.2	787.7	791.1
Net financial wealth	168.3	180.5	185.5	211.8	205.7	188.4	183.2	189.6	194.9	200.5	206.0	199.8
Non-financial assets	310.5	306.8	309.4	334.1	346.8	363.9	388.3	431.6	487.2	547.7	581.8	591.3
Financial assets	234.6	247.9	258.1	287.2	282.5	266.4	258.8	269.2	278.6	291.5	302.9	298.6
of which: Equities	58.6	60.5	67.3	86.6	83.5	69.8	63.1	69.7	72.3	77.5	84.5	79.8
Liabilities	66.3	67.4	72.5	75.4	76.8	78.0	75.6	79.7	83.7	91.0	97.0	98.8
of which: Long-term loans	50.1	50.8	51.5	53.8	53.4	53.6	54.6	57.1	60.2	65.3	69.5	73.3
Germany												
Net wealth	508.3	523.6	538.0	549.9	547.7	543.2	546.6	561.2	576.0	587.8	614.9	..
Net financial wealth	132.7	143.0	151.3	161.1	158.4	158.0	153.3	165.4	175.0	186.9	198.7	..
Non-financial assets	375.6	380.6	386.7	388.7	389.3	385.2	393.2	395.8	401.0	400.8	416.2	..
Financial assets	234.4	248.1	260.7	275.3	272.9	269.7	265.4	276.3	284.7	294.1	303.7	..
of which: Equities	44.8	53.8	61.1	74.0	74.8	71.0	57.2	63.2	64.4	71.3	74.4	..
Liabilities	101.7	105.1	109.3	114.1	114.5	111.7	112.0	110.9	109.6	107.2	105.0	..
of which: Mortgages	62.4	65.2	67.1	71.0	71.7	71.2	72.3	72.2	71.8	70.9	70.9	..
Italy												
Net wealth	713.1	753.9	784.0	808.3	826.6	821.0	858.7	903.3	958.8	934.1	..	..
Net financial wealth	234.0	260.4	293.4	324.6	330.2	307.1	297.3	296.1	303.5	312.5	313.0	..
Non-financial assets	412.5	428.2	433.5	429.8	439.1	442.4	465.7	492.5	509.4	534.0	..	..
Financial assets	273.9	303.2	338.8	373.3	382.7	359.1	351.3	352.9	364.3	377.6	381.8	..
of which: Equities	36.2	48.6	63.0	94.0	98.0	82.0	75.1	70.7	74.3	84.3	86.5	..
Liabilities	39.9	42.9	45.5	48.8	52.5	52.0	53.9	56.8	60.7	65.1	68.8	..
of which: Medium and long-term loans	23.4	24.5	24.6	27.2	28.5	28.3	29.5	31.0	34.1	37.0	39.4	..
Japan												
Net wealth	745.7	732.6	726.9	750.1	747.7	744.0	722.4	731.0	722.3	740.4	745.1	..
Net financial wealth	291.2	289.4	296.5	327.4	335.7	341.7	340.8	361.2	369.5	397.2	403.7	..
Non-financial assets	454.6	443.2	430.4	422.7	411.9	402.3	381.5	369.8	352.8	343.2	341.4	..
Financial assets	423.9	421.5	429.1	460.9	470.3	477.6	474.5	494.9	500.9	529.1	534.8	..
of which: Equities	40.1	28.8	27.0	45.6	41.5	31.8	29.8	42.1	49.0	75.6	77.1	..
Liabilities	132.8	132.1	132.6	133.5	134.6	136.0	133.7	133.7	131.4	131.9	131.1	..
of which: Mortgages	53.7	55.4	56.0	58.9	61.1	63.2	62.8	63.9	63.5	64.1	65.1	..
United Kingdom												
Net wealth	597.3	648.8	686.4	769.1	768.1	714.3	715.6	748.1	801.1	823.4	861.3	910.0
Net financial wealth	300.2	348.2	359.6	410.3	380.3	323.5	260.8	265.9	271.6	303.6	309.1	315.3
Non-financial assets	297.1	300.6	326.8	358.8	387.8	390.8	454.9	482.3	529.5	519.8	552.2	594.6
Financial assets	407.4	455.3	469.0	524.0	497.4	445.0	394.7	410.9	432.4	465.1	484.0	501.4
of which: Equities	80.6	96.5	97.1	121.4	113.6	85.9	61.4	67.3	71.7	75.9	76.7	78.8
Liabilities	107.1	107.1	109.4	113.7	117.1	121.4	134.0	145.0	160.7	161.5	174.9	186.1
of which: Mortgages	79.3	78.2	79.4	82.7	85.4	88.5	97.1	106.8	119.6	120.6	129.2	138.7
United States												
Net wealth	534.3	569.0	585.7	633.4	580.9	544.9	500.8	542.1	556.0	573.2	580.3	571.1
Net financial wealth	327.6	362.4	376.3	416.4	361.7	318.9	266.7	298.4	302.5	304.3	311.3	309.8
Non-financial assets	206.7	206.6	209.4	216.9	219.2	226.0	234.1	243.8	253.5	268.9	269.0	261.3
Financial assets	422.8	458.6	473.5	517.9	464.5	426.2	379.5	419.2	429.7	438.9	451.1	451.4
of which: Equities	119.6	146.3	157.2	191.0	151.6	121.9	87.4	106.2	107.8	107.2	109.8	104.3
Liabilities	95.2	96.2	97.2	101.5	102.9	107.3	112.8	120.8	127.2	134.6	139.8	141.6
of which: Mortgages	63.9	64.3	65.1	67.9	68.8	73.1	79.3	86.3	92.4	100.2	104.8	106.2

1. Assets and liabilities are amounts outstanding at the end of the period, in per cent of nominal disposable income. Figures after the most recent breaks in the series are based on the UN System of National Accounts 1993 (SNA 93) and, more specifically, for European Union countries, on the corresponding European System of Accounts 1995 (ESA 95).
   Households include non-profit institutions serving households, except in the case of Italy. Net wealth is defined as non-financial and financial assets minus liabilities; net financial wealth is financial assets minus liabilities. Non-financial assets consist mainly of dwellings and land. For Canada, Germany, Italy and the United States, data also include durable goods. For all countries except Italy, data also include non-residential buildings and fixed assets of unincorporated enterprises and of non-profit institutions serving households, although coverage and valuation methods may differ. Financial assets comprise currency and deposits, securities other than shares, loans, shares and other equity, insurance technical reserves; and other accounts receivable/payable. Not included are assets with regard to social security pension insurance schemes. Equities comprise shares and other equity, including quoted, unquoted and mutual fund shares. See also OECD Economic Outlook Sources and Methods (http://www.oecd.org/eco/sources-and-methods).
2. Fiscal year data.
Sources: Canada: Statistics Canada; France: INSEE; Germany: Deutsche Bundesbank, Federal Statistical Office (Destatis); Italy: Banca d'Italia; Japan: Economic Planning Agency; United Kingdom: Office for National Statistics; United States: Federal Reserve.

StatLink http://dx.doi.org/10.1787/505554516165

Annex Table 59. **House prices**
Percentage change from previous year

	1991	1992	1993	1994	1995	1996	1997	1998	1999	2000	2001	2002	2003	2004	2005	2006	2007
Nominal																	
United States	1.6	2.6	2.1	2.3	2.9	3.7	3.5	5.1	4.8	6.5	7.7	6.4	6.3	9.6	11.6	7.8	2.5
Japan	4.3	-3.9	-4.3	-2.4	-1.6	-1.9	-1.4	-1.6	-3.2	-3.7	-4.1	-4.6	-5.4	-6.1	-4.8	-3.0	-1.0
Germany					1.0	-0.9	-1.8	-1.9	1.9	0.0	0.0	-2.8	-1.0	-1.9	-2.0	0.0	0.0
France					-0.6	0.1	1.9	7.1	8.8	7.9	8.3	11.7	15.2	15.3	12.1	6.6
Italy		6.2	0.2	-2.9	0.8	-3.3	-4.6	2.1	5.6	8.3	8.2	9.6	10.3	9.9	7.5	6.4	5.2
United Kingdom	-1.4	-4.0	-1.7	2.6	0.7	3.7	8.8	11.5	10.9	14.9	8.1	16.1	15.7	11.9	5.5	6.3	10.9
Canada	4.6	1.1	2.0	3.3	-4.5	0.1	2.5	-1.5	3.8	3.7	4.6	9.9	9.4	9.4	9.9	11.3	10.8
Australia	2.6	1.6	2.6	3.6	1.2	0.8	4.0	7.4	7.2	8.3	11.2	18.8	18.2	6.5	1.5	7.8	11.3
Denmark	1.3	-1.6	-1.0	12.2	7.6	10.7	11.5	9.0	6.7	6.5	5.8	3.6	3.2	8.9	17.6	21.6	4.6
Spain	13.9	-0.7	-0.3	1.5	3.5	2.6	4.2	4.9	7.0	7.5	9.5	16.9	20.0	18.3	14.6	10.0	5.5
Finland										5.8	-0.9	10.5	5.9	6.1	5.9	9.8	7.2
Ireland	2.8	1.9	2.0	4.8	6.3	15.0	20.0	31.0	21.7	16.5	8.2	10.7	15.8	11.6	11.8	13.5	1.0
Korea	10.3	-6.5	-3.4	-1.6	-0.1	0.7	3.0	-9.2	-1.3	1.8	3.9	16.7	9.0	1.1	0.8	6.2	9.0
Netherlands	2.6	8.4	8.2	12.3	6.9	10.8	12.0	10.9	16.3	18.2	11.1	6.5	3.6	4.3	3.8	4.6	4.2
Norway		-5.1	1.0	13.2	7.2	9.3	11.8	11.1	11.2	15.7	7.0	4.9	1.7	10.1	8.2	13.3	12.2
New Zealand	-2.3	0.7	4.1	13.7	9.3	10.3	6.1	-1.7	2.1	-0.4	1.8	9.5	19.4	17.8	14.5	10.5	10.9
Sweden	6.9	-9.4	-11.0	4.6	0.3	0.8	6.6	9.5	9.4	11.2	7.9	6.3	6.6	9.3	9.0	12.2	10.4
Switzerland	-1.7	-4.4	-5.2	-0.1	-3.9	-5.3	-3.5	-0.9	-0.1	0.9	1.9	4.6	3.0	2.4	1.1	2.5	2.1
Real																	
United States	-2.5	-0.5	-0.9	-0.3	0.1	0.7	1.2	3.5	2.6	3.1	4.7	4.8	3.9	6.7	7.9	4.4	-0.3
Japan	1.0	-5.5	-5.5	-3.0	-1.5	-1.9	-3.0	-2.3	-2.8	-3.2	-3.4	-3.8	-5.2	-6.1	-4.3	-3.3	-1.1
Germany					-0.7	-2.1	-3.3	-2.4	1.2	-1.4	-1.9	-4.1	-2.0	-3.6	-3.8	-1.8	-2.2
France					-2.6	-1.2	1.3	6.5	6.8	6.0	6.2	9.4	12.6	13.2	10.0	4.9
Italy		1.2	-4.1	-6.8	-4.4	-7.0	-6.4	0.1	3.8	5.5	5.7	6.8	7.3	7.5	5.2	4.1	3.1
United Kingdom	-8.3	-7.9	-4.2	0.7	-2.0	1.1	6.9	9.7	9.4	14.1	6.8	14.7	14.2	10.4	3.4	3.8	8.4
Canada	-1.0	-0.4	0.1	3.1	-6.6	-1.5	0.9	-2.4	2.0	1.0	2.0	7.4	6.5	7.4	7.6	9.1	8.4
Australia	-0.7	0.6	0.8	1.7	-3.3	-1.8	3.7	6.4	5.7	3.7	6.5	15.3	15.0	4.1	-1.1	4.1	8.8
Denmark	-0.9	-3.5	-1.9	10.3	5.4	8.4	9.4	7.6	4.6	3.7	3.5	1.2	1.2	8.0	15.6	19.4	2.9
Spain	7.5	-6.2	-4.9	-2.9	-1.0	-0.9	2.3	3.1	4.7	3.9	6.5	12.9	16.4	14.8	10.9	6.3	2.6
Finland										2.8	-3.5	8.3	4.5	5.9	5.1	8.4	5.5
Ireland	-0.3	-1.2	0.6	2.3	3.6	12.6	18.5	28.2	18.8	10.7	4.1	5.6	11.4	9.1	9.4	10.5	-1.8
Korea	1.0	-12.0	-7.8	-7.5	-4.4	-4.0	-1.4	-15.5	-2.1	-0.4	-0.2	13.6	5.2	-2.4	-1.9	3.8	6.3
Netherlands	-0.6	5.4	6.5	10.0	5.5	9.2	9.9	9.0	14.0	15.5	5.7	2.5	1.3	2.8	2.3	2.9	2.6
Norway		-7.3	-1.3	11.7	4.6	7.9	9.0	8.7	8.6	12.3	3.9	3.6	-0.7	9.6	6.6	10.7	11.5
New Zealand	-4.8	-0.3	2.8	11.7	5.4	7.8	4.9	-3.0	2.3	-2.9	-0.8	6.6	17.3	15.2	11.1	6.9	8.3
Sweden	-1.8	-10.6	-15.1	1.6	-2.3	0.0	4.7	8.4	8.8	9.8	5.1	4.3	4.2	8.2	8.1	10.6	8.6
Switzerland	-7.1	-8.1	-8.2	-0.9	-5.6	-6.1	-4.0	-0.9	-0.9	-0.6	0.9	4.0	2.3	1.5	-0.1	1.4	1.3

Source: Various national sources and Nomisma, see table A.1 in Girouard, N., M. Kennedy, P. van den Noord and C. André, "Recent house price developments: the role of fundamentals", *OECD Economics Department Working Papers,* No. 475, 2006.

StatLink http://dx.doi.org/10.1787/505558857864

Annex Table 60. House price ratios
Long-term average = 100

	1991	1992	1993	1994	1995	1996	1997	1998	1999	2000	2001	2002	2003	2004	2005	2006	2007
Price-to-rent ratio																	
United States	91.7	91.0	90.2	89.5	89.2	89.6	90.0	91.5	93.3	96.3	99.9	102.5	106.4	113.5	123.5	128.6	127.2
Japan	136.6	127.4	118.7	113.4	109.4	105.8	102.8	100.6	97.5	93.6	89.6	85.5	80.9	76.2	72.5	70.4	69.8
Germany					93.1	89.4	85.8	83.2	84.0	83.0	82.1	78.8	77.3	75.1	73.0	72.1	71.1
France						81.5	80.3	80.3	84.5	92.1	98.9	104.5	113.6	127.2	141.6	153.5	158.6
Italy						92.0	82.2	79.8	81.5	86.1	91.1	97.6	104.7	112.0	117.8	122.4	125.9
United Kingdom	93.9	85.6	82.4	80.8	78.4	78.7	84.1	92.7	100.5	114.0	120.5	136.5	154.9	167.2	166.0	161.5	170.6
Canada	97.8	99.8	103.9	109.6	102.1	102.5	107.3	106.7	109.9	110.8	113.0	124.2	134.6	146.3	159.4	174.5	186.8
Australia	89.1	89.8	91.7	94.3	93.9	91.8	92.8	96.6	100.9	106.1	114.3	132.6	153.8	159.9	158.7	165.6	174.8
Denmark	74.7	71.1	68.4	74.6	78.6	85.9	93.3	99.7	103.7	107.6	110.9	111.9	112.5	119.2	136.7	163.0	167.0
Spain	136.8	125.5	114.7	110.2	108.2	103.2	101.4	101.4	104.8	108.5	114.0	127.7	146.9	166.9	183.5	193.5	195.5
Finland										116.1	111.0	123.2	131.2	138.0	142.1	149.4	151.1
Ireland	64.0	60.6	65.4	72.8	73.4	84.6	96.9	123.3	171.2	181.9	168.9	188.3	225.6	244.7	255.3	246.1	198.4
Korea	131.3	114.3	104.3	98.3	94.0	91.3	91.0	80.8	82.8	84.4	84.5	93.7	98.6	97.5	98.1	103.2	110.3
Netherlands	70.0	72.0	73.9	79.1	80.5	85.6	92.4	98.9	111.7	128.4	138.6	143.4	144.1	145.8	147.6	150.7	153.6
Norway		67.5	66.3	74.1	77.6	83.4	91.0	98.7	106.3	118.2	121.5	122.0	119.6	128.8	136.3	151.0	165.3
New Zealand	86.0	86.8	87.1	92.6	95.0	100.0	102.9	98.8	101.5	99.2	101.7	107.9	122.3	135.3	146.9	154.4	162.9
Sweden	95.2	79.7	67.2	69.0	67.7	67.5	73.2	82.4	91.5	101.3	106.9	111.0	117.3	128.7	140.4	155.0	162.6
Switzerland	119.2	106.6	96.1	95.5	90.8	84.8	81.5	80.7	80.1	79.6	78.9	81.7	83.9	84.9	84.6	85.0	84.8
Price-to-income ratio																	
United States	92.0	89.9	90.0	88.9	88.2	87.9	87.5	87.1	88.3	88.5	92.6	95.2	98.0	101.7	109.4	111.6	109.2
Japan	117.1	109.4	103.2	98.9	97.2	96.3	93.5	92.0	90.0	88.4	87.7	83.9	80.7	75.2	71.0	68.2	66.9
Germany					91.4	89.0	86.1	83.1	82.6	80.4	77.5	74.9	72.7	70.2	67.5	66.2	65.2
France						84.4	82.8	81.8	85.7	88.5	91.3	94.9	103.9	114.9	128.6	138.0	140.0
Italy		104.8	103.2	96.0	91.2	83.3	77.9	79.1	81.3	85.0	87.2	92.1	98.7	104.9	109.7	113.1	115.0
United Kingdom	99.3	88.7	81.8	81.4	77.5	75.5	77.2	82.5	88.5	96.8	98.7	111.0	122.5	134.7	134.8	137.7	149.7
Canada	103.7	103.7	104.5	107.6	100.2	99.8	99.9	95.3	95.1	92.8	93.7	100.4	106.7	111.6	118.6	124.4	131.3
Australia	99.7	98.0	97.6	96.1	92.4	89.3	91.5	96.4	98.8	101.6	106.9	126.0	143.3	143.1	137.6	139.5	144.9
Denmark	77.2	73.8	73.1	79.5	79.1	85.5	93.8	98.3	106.4	110.1	110.3	111.1	111.1	116.2	132.8	156.3	153.5
Spain	120.8	112.3	105.8	104.7	96.8	94.5	94.9	95.3	97.5	98.8	102.6	114.8	131.5	145.5	154.7	159.1	158.8
Finland										98.6	91.7	96.7	97.3	98.4	102.5	109.0	111.2
Ireland	78.5	75.6	71.9	73.4	71.1	75.5	83.3	98.4	114.0	120.5	116.1	129.0	142.8	147.7	157.8	168.8	155.0
Korea	150.6	125.5	110.2	93.2	83.9	75.4	72.7	64.2	60.6	59.5	59.7	66.1	69.6	67.0	65.1	66.0	68.2
Netherlands	72.0	73.7	80.6	86.5	88.8	94.2	99.6	105.3	118.5	133.0	134.9	141.3	147.3	151.4	154.7	160.1	158.5
Norway		72.3	69.1	76.6	78.4	82.0	86.8	89.5	95.8	104.5	110.0	105.9	100.8	106.9	106.8	127.3	133.9
New Zealand	78.0	81.2	83.3	92.5	94.3	100.3	102.1	96.7	92.3	94.0	89.8	100.3	110.6	125.5	142.7	149.8	154.7
Sweden	94.4	81.7	71.6	73.8	72.4	73.0	77.1	82.4	86.7	91.4	91.2	92.4	95.8	102.8	109.5	118.9	124.3
Switzerland	110.5	102.6	96.0	95.5	89.4	85.1	80.7	78.1	76.0	73.8	73.2	77.5	80.7	80.5	79.2	77.4	75.1

Source: Various national sources and Nomisma, see table A.1 in Girouard, N., M. Kennedy, P. van den Noord and C. André, "Recent house price developments: the role of fundamentals", *OECD Economics Department Working Papers,* No. 475, 2006 and OECD estimates.

StatLink ⬛⬛⬛ http://dx.doi.org/10.1787/505601768334

Annex Table 61. Central government financial balances
Surplus (+) or deficit (-) as a percentage of nominal GDP

	1993	1994	1995	1996	1997	1998	1999	2000	2001	2002	2003	2004	2005	2006	2007
Canada	-5.5	-4.6	-3.9	-2.0	0.7	0.8	0.9	1.9	1.1	0.8	0.3	0.8	0.1	0.7	1.0
France	-5.2	-4.6	-4.5	-3.6	-3.1	-2.8	-2.4	-2.1	-2.1	-3.1	-3.6	-2.6	-2.6	-2.0	-2.2
Germany[1]	-2.1	-1.1	-7.9	-1.9	-1.6	-1.8	-1.5	1.4	-1.3	-1.7	-1.8	-2.4	-2.1	-1.5	-0.8
Italy	-10.0	-8.9	-7.5	-6.8	-2.6	-2.5	-1.5	-1.2	-3.1	-3.1	-3.0	-3.0	-4.0	-2.7	-2.4
Japan[2]	-3.5	-4.3	-4.4	-4.1	-3.5	-10.6	-7.3	-6.4	-5.9	-6.7	-6.7	-5.2	-6.2	-1.1	-2.9
United Kingdom[3]	-7.9	-6.6	-5.5	-4.1	-2.0	0.2	1.1	3.9	0.9	-1.8	-3.4	-3.1	-3.0	-2.6	-2.7
United States	-4.4	-3.1	-2.7	-1.9	-0.6	0.5	1.1	1.9	0.4	-2.6	-3.8	-3.6	-2.8	-1.9	-2.1
less social security	-5.1	-4.0	-3.5	-2.8	-1.6	-0.7	-0.4	0.4	-1.2	-4.2	-5.2	-4.9	-4.1	-3.3	-3.5
Total of above countries	-4.8	-3.9	-4.2	-2.9	-1.5	-1.9	-1.0	0.2	-1.1	-3.0	-3.8	-3.4	-3.2	-1.7	-2.1

Note: Central government financial balances include one-off revenues from the sale of mobile telephone licenses.
1. In 1995, the data includes the central government's assumption of the debt of the Inherited Debt Fund.
2. Data for central government financial balances are only available for fiscal years beginning April 1 of the year shown. The 1998 deficit includes the central government's assumption of the debt of the Japan Railway Settlement Corporation and the National Forest Special Account which represent some 5.3 percentage points of GDP. The data for 2007 is an estimation.
3. The data for 2000 and onwards reflect Eurostat's decision concerning the recording of one-off revenues from the sale of the mobile telephone licenses.
Source: OECD Economic Outlook 84 database.　　StatLink ⟶ http://dx.doi.org/10.1787/505620158080

Annex Table 62. Maastricht definition of general government gross public debt
As a percentage of nominal GDP

	1996	1997	1998	1999	2000	2001	2002	2003	2004	2005	2006	2007	2008	2009	2010
Austria	68.3	64.3	64.8	67.1	66.5	67.0	66.5	65.5	64.8	63.7	62.0	59.5	60.2	62.4	65.3
Belgium[1]	127.2	122.3	117.1	113.7	107.8	106.5	103.4	98.6	94.5	92.0	87.7	83.9	88.5	88.6	88.4
Czech Republic	12.5	13.1	15.0	16.4	18.5	25.1	28.5	30.1	30.4	29.8	29.6	28.7	26.5	25.6	25.2
Denmark	69.2	65.2	60.8	57.4	51.5	48.7	48.3	45.8	43.8	36.4	30.5	26.2	23.6	23.7	24.7
Finland	56.7	53.9	48.1	45.5	43.8	42.4	41.4	44.4	44.1	41.4	39.2	35.2	33.3	32.6	32.9
France	58.0	59.3	59.4	58.9	57.3	56.9	58.8	62.9	65.0	66.4	63.6	63.9	66.4	69.7	72.8
Germany	58.4	59.6	60.4	61.0	59.7	58.7	60.2	63.7	65.9	67.9	67.6	65.0	64.4	65.8	65.9
Greece	99.4	96.6	94.5	94.0	103.4	103.8	100.8	97.9	98.9	98.4	95.5	94.4	93.0	91.9	91.3
Hungary	71.7	62.3	60.4	59.5	54.2	52.1	55.8	58.1	59.4	61.7	65.6	65.8	65.6	67.5	69.2
Ireland	73.6	64.3	53.6	48.5	37.8	35.5	32.2	31.1	29.4	27.3	24.7	24.8	29.7	37.6	45.1
Italy	120.9	118.0	115.0	113.9	109.1	108.8	105.7	104.3	103.9	105.9	106.8	104.1	103.8	105.3	106.7
Luxembourg	7.5	7.4	7.0	6.4	6.2	6.3	6.3	6.1	6.3	6.0	6.6	7.0	15.2	14.4	17.3
Netherlands	74.1	68.2	65.7	61.1	53.8	50.7	50.5	52.0	52.4	51.8	47.4	45.7	48.6	48.3	48.7
Poland	43.4	42.9	38.9	39.6	36.8	37.6	42.2	47.1	45.7	47.1	47.7	44.9	43.6	44.1	45.3
Portugal	59.9	56.1	52.1	51.4	50.5	52.9	55.6	56.9	58.3	63.6	64.7	63.6	64.5	66.4	68.6
Slovak Republic	31.2	33.8	34.5	47.9	50.4	49.0	43.4	42.4	41.4	34.2	30.4	29.4	30.9	32.0	33.0
Spain	67.4	66.1	64.1	62.3	59.3	55.5	52.5	48.7	46.2	43.0	39.6	36.2	37.8	41.3	45.3
Sweden	73.0	71.0	69.1	64.8	53.6	54.4	52.6	52.3	51.2	50.9	45.9	40.4	38.1	34.9	34.0
United Kingdom	51.3	49.8	46.7	43.7	41.0	37.7	37.5	38.7	40.6	42.3	43.4	44.2	56.0	60.9	66.6
Euro area	75.4	73.6	72.9	72.1	69.4	68.4	68.2	69.3	69.8	70.4	68.6	66.5	67.4	69.4	71.1

Note: For the period before 2008, gross debt figures are provided by Eurostat, the Statistical Office of the European Communities, unless more recent data are available, while GDP figures are provided by National Authorities. This explains why these ratios can differ significantly from the ones published by Eurostat. The 2008 to 2010 debt ratios are in line with the OECD projections for general government gross financial liabilities and GDP. See *OECD Economic Outlook* Sources and Methods (*http://www.oecd.org/eco/sources-and-methods*).
1. Includes the debt of the Belgium National Railways Company (SNCB) from 2005 onwards.
Source: OECD Economic Outlook 84 database.　　StatLink ⟶ http://dx.doi.org/10.1787/505620231035

Annex Table 63. **Monetary and credit aggregates: recent trends**
Annualised percentage change, seasonally adjusted

		Annual change (to 4th quarter)					Latest twelve months	
		2003	2004	2005	2006	2007		
Canada	M2	5.8	5.9	5.6	8.9	6.5	8.8	(Sep 2008)
	BL[1]	4.6	8.2	8.3	7.5	10.2	8.2	(Aug 2008)
Japan	M2	1.5	2.0	1.9	0.6	2.0	2.2	(Sep 2008)
	BL[1]	-0.5	1.4	1.0	-0.2	-0.9	-0.3	(Sep 2008)
United Kingdom	M2	10.2	9.1	9.0	8.1	7.6	8.5	(Sep 2008)
	M4	6.4	9.3	11.8	13.5	11.9	11.8	(Sep 2008)
	BL[1]	8.0	10.5	8.8	12.6	12.5	13.1	(Sep 2008)
United States	M2	5.5	5.4	4.0	5.1	5.7	7.4	(Oct 2008)
	BL[1]	5.9	10.3	11.8	11.9	11.0	8.9	(Oct 2008)
Euro area	M2	6.8	6.3	8.8	8.7	11.2	9.3	(Oct 2008)
	M3	7.0	6.0	8.2	9.0	12.2	8.7	(Oct 2008)
	BL[1]	5.6	5.8	9.1	7.9	11.0	8.4	(Oct 2008)

1. Commercial bank lending.
Source: OECD Main Economic Indicators; US Federal Reserve Board; Bank of Japan; European Central Bank; Bank of England; Statistics Canada.

StatLink http://dx.doi.org/10.1787/505654182624

OECD ECONOMICS DEPARTMENT

A wide range of news and information about recent Economics Department studies and publications on a variety of topics is now regularly available via Internet on the OECD website at the following address: *www.oecd.org/eco*. This includes links to the *Economics Department Working Papers* series (*www.oecd.org/eco/Working_Papers*), which can be downloaded free of charge, as well as summaries of recent editions in the *OECD Economic Surveys* **(www.oecd.org/eco/surveys)** series, the Department's new innovative study *Economic Policy Reforms: Going for Growth* (*www.oecd.org/growth/GoingForGrowth2007*) and the *OECD Economic Outlook* (*www.oecd.org/OECDEconomicOutlook*).

OECD ECONOMIC OUTLOOK

The *OECD Economic Outlook* Flashfile, containing a summary of the *Economic Outlook* forecasts is available on Internet at the time of its preliminary publication (a month to six weeks before the final publication date) at **www.oecd.org/OECDEconomicOutlook** under extracts. This includes key macroeconomic variables for all OECD countries and regions in Excel format, which can be input directly into most statistical and analytical software. The *Economic Outlook* Flashfile is available free of charge.

Subscribers to the *OECD Economic Outlook*, in addition to the two print editions, also have access to an online (PDF) edition, published on internet six to eight weeks prior to the release of the print edition :

www.SourceOECD.org/periodical/OECDeconomicOutlook

The full set of historical time series data and projections underlying the *OECD Economic Outlook* is available online as a **statistical database** via SourceOECD and on CD-ROM. It contains approximately 4 000 macroeconomic time series for OECD countries and non-OECD zones, beginning in 1960 and extending to the end of the published forecast horizon. Subscriptions to the database editions can be combined in sets with the subscriptions to the Print and PDF editions and can be made at any time of the year.

For more information, visit the OECD bookshop at **www.OECDbookshop.org,** or contact your nearest OECD supplier : **www.oecd.org/publishing/distributors** .

OECD PUBLICATIONS, 2, rue André-Pascal, 75775 PARIS CEDEX 16
PRINTED IN FRANCE
(12 2008 03 1 P) ISBN 978-92-64-05469-1 – No. 56283 2008